Correctional Boot Camps

To Todd Armstrong
and
to the memory of David R. MacKenzie

Correctional Boot Camps

Military Basic Training or a Model for Corrections?

Editors

Doris Layton MacKenzie

University of Maryland at College Park

Gaylene Styve Armstrong

Arizona State University West

SAGE Publications
International Educational and Professional Publisher
Thousand Oaks ▪ London ▪ New Delhi

For information:

Sage Publications, Inc.
2455 Teller Road
Thousand Oaks, California 91320
E-mail: order@sagepub.com

Sage Publications Ltd.
1 Oliver's Yard
55 City Road
London EC1Y 1SP
United Kingdom

Sage Publications India Pvt. Ltd.
B-42, Panchsheel Enclave
Post Box 4109
New Delhi 110017 India

Printed in the United States of America

Library of Congress Cataloging-in-Publication Data

Correctional boot camps: Military basic training or a model for corrections?
Editors, Doris Layton MacKenzie, Gaylene Styve Armstrong.
    p. cm.
Includes bibliographical references and index.
ISBN 0-7619-2938-X (cloth)—ISBN 0-7619-2939-8 (pbk.)
   1. Shock incarceration. 2. Criminals—Rehabilitation. I. MacKenzie, Doris L. II. Armstrong, Gaylene Styve.
HV9278.5.C683 2004
365'.34—dc22

2003027810

04 05 06 10 9 8 7 6 5 4 3 2 1

Acquiring Editor:	Jerry Westby
Editorial Assistant:	Vonessa Vondera
Production Editor:	Diana E. Axelsen
Typesetter:	C&M Digitals (P) Ltd.
Indexer:	David Luljak
Cover Designer:	Edgar Abarca

CONTENTS

1

INTRODUCTION

DORIS LAYTON MACKENZIE

In 1987, Dr. Gary Pettigrew, a clinical psychologist who worked with the Louisiana Department of Corrections (LDOC), called me and said the LDOC was starting a new program that I might be interested in evaluating. The program would be modeled after military basic training. Participants would have to volunteer. Also, in order to be eligible, they had to be serving their first term of incarceration for a nonviolent crime. If they completed the program, they would be released earlier than their scheduled release date.

I was very skeptical about the program. I was worried about the possibility of abuse by staff. I did not think that a boot camp basic training model was a particularly good model for a prison treatment program. On the other hand, the project did present a good opportunity to evaluate a new program. I visited the prison, observed the program, and decided that it might be worth evaluating even if we found that the program was not successful. I applied for and was awarded a grant from the National Institute of Justice (NIJ) for funding to complete the evaluation. The LDOC was very supportive because they, too, were interested in evaluating the effectiveness of the program. I worked closely with staff and administrators to develop the evaluation.

At the time, in the 1980s, the country was conservative, incarceration rates were rapidly increasing in most states, and there was little interest in or money for rehabilitation programs.

Boot camp programs quickly became a popular correctional option. One of our first tasks in researching boot camps was to describe the programs. As we investigated, we found that there were many different models for the camps. Part I of this book describes the development of adult and juvenile boot camps and the different models and operating procedures.

As I began to explore the different boot camp models, I concluded that we would not be able to draw conclusions about the effectiveness of boot camps because one camp might have important components that were not part of the boot camps in other jurisdictions. For this reason, I proposed to the National Institute of Justice that we should initiate a multisite study of boot camps. This would permit us to study a variety of programs—all would have the basic military atmosphere, but they would differ in other important aspects. For example, some camps would devote a relatively large amount of time in the daily schedule to treatment, education, and rehabilitation, whereas other program schedules would keep inmates busy almost all day with hard physical labor and drill and ceremony. If we found differences in the effectiveness of the various programs, we could examine the components of the successful programs and hypothesize about why some programs were successful and some were not.

At the time I began talking with the NIJ about the possibility of a multisite study, they were looking for research scholars who would be willing to relocate toWashington, DC, to complete research on-site at NIJ. My proposal for a multisite study of adult boot camps seemed an ideal match to NIJ's search for a researcher. So, in 1989, I applied and was accepted for a position as a visiting NIJ research scholar, where I began the multisite study. I completed a survey of adult boot camp programs in operation at the time and asked programs in eight different states to participate in the research. The eight camps differed in aspects of the programs that I hypothesized would have an impact on outcomes. The states all agreed to participate and sent representatives to biannual meetings to plan and conduct the evaluation. These representatives conducted the evaluations within their own jurisdictions. We combined our data so that we could compare results across sites.

While developing the first evaluation in Louisiana, I worked closely with representatives from the prison. The multisite evaluation was based on this methodology. When we began, we had many questions about the boot camp model. What was or were the goals of the program—deterrence? retribution? treatment? In the beginning, there were many opinions about why the camps were being developed. Certainly, those working to develop innovative boot camp programs did not want to just punish these offenders. People like Marty Lensing from Louisiana, Cherie Clark from New York, Robert McWhorter from Maryland, and many others were working hard to see that sufficient programming was included in the daily activities so that the major problems of these offenders were addressed while they were in the camps. Part II of this book reports on the answers we found about the general goals of boot camps from the perspectives of different actors in the criminal justice system. As is evident in these chapters, from the beginning, there was a great deal of controversy about boot camps. This controversy continues. Chapters 5 and 6 give information about some of the important issues in the debate about boot camps.

In my role as the first researcher to complete evaluations of the correctional boot camps, I had the opportunity to visit a large number of boot camps to observe the activities, consult with staff and administrators, review evaluations, and collect data for our studies. I visited programs for males and females, for juveniles and adults, and in federal, state, and local jurisdictions. My initial, near-complete skepticism about these programs changed. It became very clear to me that there was something positive going on in many of the camps. In juvenile institutions, children seemed more mentally and physically active. In school classrooms, they seemed more interested and focused on their work. They appeared to spend less time "hanging out" and watching commercial TV. They seemed more physically fit. My impression was that inmates, staff, and administrators found the environment more positive than the environments of other institutions. Because of these impressions, it seemed worthwhile to collect data to examine whether these first impressions stood up to empirical scrutiny. Part III reviews our research examining the environments of boot camps from the view of inmate participants and staff. In a national study of juvenile correctional facilities, we compared the experiences of boot camp staff and participants to the experiences of inmates and staff in traditional institutions.

Past research on correctional adjustment has demonstrated the importance of attitudes in predicting recidivism. In particular, antisocial attitudes are strongly associated with future criminal activities and are one of the best predictors of performance after release from prison. Other research has examined the attitudes of inmates toward staff and programs. Inmates with negative attitudes toward both the institution and staff are expected to reject the programming, be uncooperative, and fail to fully engage in therapeutic programming even if it is offered. Part IV examines the adjustment of inmates to incarceration. We compare juvenile and adult inmates in boot camp facilities to similar inmates in other institutions. We compared how each group changed during its incarceration. If boot camp inmates make more positive changes, we hypothesized that this is an intermediate step demonstrating change that may be expected to have an impact on later recidivism.

To many laypeople and policymakers, the bottom line on effectiveness is whether a program such as boot camp will reduce later recidivism. Part V addresses our research on the future criminal activities of boot camp participants. We compare participants to groups of similar offenders who have served other types of sentences. As discussed in the final chapter of this part, my colleagues and I made an extensive and careful search for all quasi-experimental and experimental studies examining the impact of correctional boot camps on offending. We then submitted the results to a meta-analysis to examine whether this synthesis revealed any evidence that boot camps are effective in reducing future criminal activities. Disappointing to many, but also very consistent, is the evidence that these boot camps do not reduce the future criminal activities of participants in comparison to similar offenders who serve other sentences.

Many of the advocates of boot camps say that recidivism is not the only measure of success after incarceration. Those who developed and operated boot camps were particularly interested in examining whether the boot camp participants adjusted more positively after boot camp in comparison to others who did not go to boot camp. Section VI explores how boot camp participants adjusted to the community after release. We were interested in whether they attended drug treatment (if required), worked, supported their families, and so on. These data were very difficult to get, so we had to settle for some very basic data to answer our questions. We also studied what characteristics were associated with successful adjustment to community supervision and report on this in Chapter 16.

Another issue that arose in discussion of boot camps was whether the camps were appropriate for certain special offender populations such as women, substance abusers, or those with a history of abuse. Some people were concerned that boot camps were particularly inappropriate for women. Because relatively few women were in boot camps, we could not complete a quantitative investigation of their adjustment. Therefore, we completed a qualitative study of women offenders in boot camps. We interviewed participants, staff, and administrators in the camps, and Chapter 17 reports on our findings from this study. There are some major problems

for women in the boot camps, particularly the camps in which the women are mixed with men. Few boot camps have special visiting times for families, and many women who are mothers of young children may spend less time with their children than they would in another type of program. Additionally, other major needs of women were not addressed in the camps.

Some boot camps have been designed specifically for offenders convicted of drug-related crimes. Such camps provide substance abuse treatment for all inmates, whereas other camps identify inmates with substance abuse problems and provide treatment. We examined the impact of boot camps on offenders with substance abuse problems.

The critics of boot camps have been particularly concerned about the impact of the camps on men and women who have been in abusive relationships or who have been sexually or physically abused as children. Chapter 11 discusses how juveniles who have been victims of family violence adjust to boot camps. As predicted by critics of the boot camps, these youth do have more adjustment difficulties in the boot camps.

Originally, those who developed boot camps asserted that one of the goals of the camps was to reduce prison crowding. Dale Parent developed a simulation model for assessing the impact of the programs on the correctional system. We used data from the multisite study to examine whether the programs were successful in reducing prison crowding in these states. The simulation models we ran demonstrated that if a program held a large number of inmates, and if a large percentage of these inmates completed the program and were released sufficiently early, there was a possibility of saving prison bedspace. However, almost no camp fulfilled these requirements; therefore, few camps would be expected to have an impact on prison crowding.

In the final section of the book, we discuss the future of boot camps. Where do we go from here in the operation of and research on correctional boot camps?

Part I

THE BOOT CAMP MODEL

2

BOOT CAMPS AS A CORRECTIONAL OPTION

GAYLENE S. ARMSTRONG

INTRODUCTION

Boot camps are a correctional sanction based on programming that is modeled after military basic training camp. Earlier versions of boot camps were commonly known as "shock incarceration," but more recent programs have varied in name from the general "boot camp" terminology to variations such as "accountability programs" and "leadership camps." Boot camp programs typically exist as an alternative sanction that is meant to be a punishment less severe than a sentence to prison incarceration, yet more severe than a sentence of probation (Morris & Tonry, 1990). The underlying philosophy of early shock incarceration programs sought to "shock" offenders in their early stages of incarceration through tough, regimented treatment in an attempt to lay the groundwork for positive change in their behavior. Boot camp programs have experienced a metamorphosis from their early days, when they focused on the drill and ceremony program characteristics, into programs that now utilize primarily the military regimen to create a structured environment conducive to treatment delivery and educational programming.

Boot camps currently exist throughout the United States for males and females, youth and adult offenders. Programs grew exponentially for each of these populations during the late 1980s and early 1990s. In 1994, 30 states, 10 local jurisdictions, and the Federal Bureau of Prisons had boot camp programs serving adult populations (U.S. General Accounting Office, 1993). During 1995, citing the Census of State and Federal Adult Correctional Facilities, the Bureau of Justice Statistics reported the existence of 52 state-level and three federal boot camp programs (BJS, 1995). At this time, there were more than 8,000 beds dedicated to adult offenders. With the average offender spending 107 days in boot camp prisons, more than 27,000 offenders could complete the program in a 1-year time period. A more recent report on juvenile boot camps identified 56 juvenile correctional boot camp programs in 26 states that operated during 2000 (Koch Crime Institute, 2000).

HISTORY OF BOOT CAMPS

Boot camp programs have experienced a large amount of media and political attention since their rebirth in 1983 in Georgia and Oklahoma. This attention has continued into the 21st century, resulting in a proliferation of programs throughout the United States. Although their widespread existence and programming for female offenders and juvenile delinquents are recent trends, the roots of correctional boot camps can actually be traced to a program for male prisoners developed in the late 1800s. In 1888, New York's Elmira Reformatory was the first correctional program to incorporate the idea of boot camp programming into the prison environment ("Nation's First Reformatory," 1998). It was during this era that antilabor legislation known as the Yates law was passed, deeming the inmate labor system illegal. Prior to the formation of these laws, the majority of an inmate's day was spent in some form of trade or labor that resulted in marketable products used to support the prison operation. Because inmate labor was comparatively inexpensive, prison officials were able to market these products at a much lower cost to the consumer, thereby undercutting the prices of other manufacturers' goods. As a result, unions and manufacturers bonded together to fight for legislation that prevented competition from the inmate labor system. With the passage of the Yates law, inmate labor was halted.

One of the major indirect effects of this legislation was that the prison administrators were forced to occupy the inmates' time, which would have been previously spent manufacturing goods, in some other type of activity. Zebulon Brockway of the New York reformatory was the first documented administrator to suggest and implement military-style training as a useful substitute for the hard labor. As a result of this decision, military organizational aspects were incorporated into almost every facet of the correctional facility, including inmate schooling, supervision of inmates, physical training, and even parole practices. The militarization of the reformatory was expected to have a number of benefits in addition to occupying the inmates' time. The military-style training was also used as a tool to help inmates reform their behavior and learn various marketable, honest skills during their time in the Elmira Reformatory. Additionally, the military discipline helped to add obedience, attention, and organization to the prison environment. Many of the current-day programs reflect these same values and beliefs.

This militarization of correctional programming was not widely adopted despite the efforts within the Elmira program. One reason for the lack of proliferation during this era may be attributed to the dominant rehabilitation perspective that existed for much of the 20th century, and perhaps the beliefs regarding the causes of deviant behavior during that time. With the paradigmatic shift away from rehabilitation and correctional treatment in the later part of the 20th century, new doors were opened for the revitalization of military-style correctional programs termed "boot camps" or "shock incarceration." These programs were first reborn in Georgia and Oklahoma in 1983. The development of these programs was supported by some of the same rationales and philosophies that were suggested nearly 100 years earlier, in addition to new, economically based concerns with the costs of imprisonment and overcrowding.

Perspectives on Boot Camps

A myriad of factors supported the proliferation of boot camp programs from 1983 onward across the United States. The harsh physical nature of discipline and activity in boot camp programs was in tune with the emerging political climate of getting "tough on crime." Boot camps were often perceived as an alternative sanction with "teeth," an imperative in the developing political climate of the late 20th century (MacKenzie & Parent, 1992). This era's "individual responsibility" perspective (Walker, 2001) encouraged the criminal justice system to hold offenders accountable for their actions rather than allowing for the consideration of various social ills as explanations for the underlying causes of their criminal behavior. The nature of the programs allowed for the implementation of this desired accountability. Boot camp advocates took advantage of many related catchphrases from this perspective in order to garner funding and support for the development of their programs. For example, some boot camps were aptly named "accountability programs" and emphasized holding offenders responsible for their actions through military discipline and, when necessary, military-style punishment as part of their mission statement.

Another factor that played a large role in proliferating boot camp programs was media attention. Correctional innovations rarely attract more than minimal media attention, yet boot camps have received a great deal of coverage by both the local and national media. Why are boot camp programs attracting so much attention? In part, they are popular with the media because they have such a strong visual impact. Video footage and photographs of a drill sergeant yelling in the faces of boot camp participants present an evocative image for television viewers. As a result of this interest, journalists widely publicized these powerful visual images of "offenders paying for their crimes" through a variety of forms of media.

Finally, boot camps have received added interest because of the unique nature of the boot camp model itself. The model is part punitive and part rehabilitative. As such, it has wide appeal to a diverse audience. For those who are concerned that punishments should be appropriately punitive, boot camps are seen as a get-tough approach to crime and delinquency. For these advocates, individuals sentenced to boot camps receive their "just desserts." Boot camps are one of the few intermediate sanctions accepted as being tough on crime. The "tough" aspects of the programs can be thought of as achieving a sentencing goal of punishment or retribution. This makes the boot camp program acceptable in lieu of a longer sentence in a traditional facility. Thus, the short, intense program is a mechanism for offenders to earn their way back to society earlier than they would have if they had been sentenced to a traditional prison. In a sense, they have paid their debt to society by being punished in a short-term but strict boot camp.

Empirical evidence supports this perception of the boot camp's punitive nature. Wood and Grasmick (1999) surveyed male and female inmates serving time for nonviolent offenses and found that inmates viewed boot camps as significantly more punitive than traditional imprisonment and various forms of other alternative sanctions. Thus, participants and potential participants reaffirm the belief held by the public and correctional officials that boot camps are tough and punitive.

At the other end of the continuum are people who support boot camps because they believe that the educational, drug treatment, and counseling services that are part of many boot camp programs will rehabilitate offenders. By addressing the root causes of criminal behavior and delinquency, these therapeutic programs and services may effect positive changes in offenders. Furthermore, the potential cost savings from a reduction of time served adds to the appeal of the boot camp model for all supporters.

Support for boot camps as a rehabilitative tool is not universal. Critics of boot camps suggest that the confrontational nature of the program is antithetical to treatment. In fact, they argue that some aspects of the boot camps are diametrically opposed to the constructive, interpersonally supportive treatment environment necessary for positive change to occur (Andrews et al., 1990; Lipsey, 1992). Others argue that boot camps hold inconsistent philosophies and procedures (Marlowee, Marin, Schneider, Vaitkus, & Bartone, 1988), set the stage for abusive punishments (Morash & Rucker, 1990), and perpetuate an "us versus them" attitude that suggests inmates are deserving of degrading treatment (Raupp, 1978). Critics anticipate that inmates may fear staff and that the boot camps will have less individualized programming than traditional facilities. As a result, offenders will be less prepared for their return to the community.

Empirical evidence from a national evaluation of juvenile correctional facilities supports this argument to one extent, finding that juvenile delinquents do perceive some danger from correctional staff related to physical aggression and threats. However, this finding was not unique to boot camps. Styve, MacKenzie, Gover, and Mitchell (2000) found no statistically significant differences in the self-reported perceptions of fear of physical danger from correctional staff members between juvenile delinquents held in boot camps as compared to those in traditional facilities. Thus, according to the juvenile delinquents surveyed, critics who argue that the boot camp environment is antithetical to treatment should make their argument inclusive of other types of correctional environments as well.

Characteristics of Boot Camp Programs

Most boot camp programs operate under a constructive punishment philosophy. This philosophy assumes that if a person experiences or is placed within an environment of radical change, this environment will create a reasonable amount of stress. As a result of this stress, people will be particularly susceptible to external influences. In the case of boot camp, offenders who are forced to engage in a very different, regimented lifestyle that requires extensive physical exertion and mental discipline will become stressed and thus amenable to behavioral change. The behaviors that are targeted for change are criminal thoughts and actions.

Boot camp programs can be difficult to identify because of vast disagreement on the definition of a boot camp. According to 42 U.S.C. § 5667(f) (Zaehringer, 1998, as cited by Koch Crime Institute, 2000),

> the only criterion necessary for a juvenile program to be called a boot camp is that it must have a paramilitary style. This style should implement a highly regimented schedule of discipline, physical training, work, drill and ceremony characteristic of military basic training; provide regular, remedial, special and vocational education; and provide counseling and treatment for substance abuse and other health and mental problems. (p. 5)

Often, programs will be developed in the militaristic style of a boot camp but be referred to as some other program, such as an accountability camp, forestry camp, Outward Bound program, and so forth. Typically, boot camps, as well as many of these other programs, will incorporate similar basic characteristics such as program length and daily activities. Boot camp sentences often replace an offender's traditional prison sentence. In most cases, offenders spend 90 to 120 days in boot camp rather than serve their full sentence in traditional prison. However, alternative or hybrid boot camp models also exist in which the boot camp program is used only for a short time period prior to a more lengthy traditional prison sentence, or it is used in conjunction with a probation sentence.

The most distinguishing characteristic of a boot camp is the quasi-military atmosphere that resembles military basic training. This atmosphere may include military dress and titles, drill and ceremony, as well as the general organizational structure. Boot camp inmates are usually separated from the general prison population. Their entry into the boot camp program usually occurs in small groups, platoons, or squads of inmates. Boot camp inmates will remain with their entry group from intake to graduation, work together as a unit, and depend heavily on their fellow "cadets" throughout their stay in the program.

The underlying focus of boot camp programs lies within an earlier version of their name—shock incarceration. The program is intended to shock the offender into changing his or her behavior. This philosophy is put into practice upon the inmate's arrival at the facility. Males are required to have their heads shaved (females may be permitted short haircuts), and they are informed of the strict program rules. At all times, inmates are required to address staff as "sir" or "ma'am," or an associated military title such as "Captain"; request permission to speak; and refer to themselves in the third person as "this inmate" or "this cadet." The incoming group of inmates is called a "platoon." Platoons are kept together in all aspects of the program, including housing, meal times, physical training, and other activities. Additionally, the platoon is expected to complete the program at the same time.

Regardless of the program's overall structure and purpose, an inmate's day while in the boot camp component is typically 10 to 16 hours long beginning with a predawn reveille. Inmates dress quickly and march to an exercise area, where they participate in an hour or two of physical training followed by drill and ceremony. Then, they march to breakfast, where they are ordered to stand at parade rest while waiting in line and to exercise military movements when the line moves.

During meal period, inmates are required to stand in front of the table until commanded to sit and are not permitted to converse during the 10-minute eating period. After breakfast, they march to work sites, where they participate in hard physical labor that frequently involves community service, such as cleaning state parks or highways. When the 6- to 8-hour working day is over, inmates return to the compound, where they participate in additional exercises and drills.

Failure to comply with program rules results in additional punishment of the inmates.

Punishments for minor rule violations are summary and certain, frequently involving physical exercise such as push-ups or running. Major rule violations may result in dismissal from the program, typically resulting in a return to a more lengthy, traditional prison sentence. Depending on the facility, somewhere between 8% and 50% of the entrants will fail to complete the program.

In addition to the military style of daily routine, another characteristic that is common to boot camp programs is the military style of dress. Military-style fatigues are provided to inmates, who must maintain a neat appearance, including polished boots. Correctional staff members are also dressed in military-style uniforms indicative of rank. They, too, pay close attention to professional, military-style appearances. As part of some programs, inmates are gradually able to earn more privileges and responsibilities as their performance and time in the program warrants. The attainment of these privileges is often displayed in their uniforms as a different color hat or badge marking their new prestige.

Another interesting component of boot camp programs is the militaristic nature of the correctional officers. Frequently, correctional officers whom boot camp programs employ have a military background and experience, including former Marine Corps officers or officers who have served in special army units. One of the reasons boot camps employ a large number of staff with a military background is that the boot camp atmosphere can be a much more difficult work environment for correctional officers who do not have this type of military experience.

The philosophy of the correctional staff is to lead by example, and to act as role models who display physical and mental fortitude as a means to gain the inmate's respect. The staff members often perform the same exercises in the daily physical regime that inmates are asked to perform. Additionally, staff follow military codes of discipline, such as standing at attention and saluting superior officers; address superiors as "sir" or "ma'am"; and use military jargon, such as referring to floors as decks and windows as portholes.

For those inmates who successfully complete the boot camp program, an elaborate graduation ceremony occurs, to which visitors and family are invited. Frequently, awards are given for achievements made during the program. In addition, the inmates perform the drill and ceremony they have practiced throughout their time in the program.

Boot camp programs exhibiting these types of characteristics have continued through the 21st century; however, the more recently developed programs have tended toward an alternative perspective that maintains the military style while incorporating therapeutic components. Early boot camp programs emphasized the military atmosphere with drill and ceremony, physical training, and hard labor, as discussed above. Although these components remain central to boot camps today, rehabilitative, educational, and drug treatment services now take an increasingly large share of the participants' time in the program.

GOALS OF BOOT CAMP

The heterogeneity among boot camp programming and goals makes broad conclusions about the achievement of those goals and effectiveness of boot camps problematic. Often, program effectiveness must be examined at the state level or on a facility-by-facility basis. The determination of the success of a program will also depend greatly on the definition of success. Toby and Pearson (1992) surveyed juvenile boot camps and found that the goals rated most important by the staff were providing safe custody for the youth in their charge, providing academic education, attempting to rehabilitate, and lowering recidivism. Punishment was relatively deemphasized—only two states rated it as "somewhat important," and the rest of the boot camps did not believe that it was an important goal at all. More traditionally, program officials at boot camps have considered rehabilitation and a reduction of offender rates of recidivism as their top indicators of success (MacKenzie & Souryal, 1991). According to a survey of 26 boot camp programs (MacKenzie & Souryal, 1991), the priorities next in importance were reducing prison overcrowding and providing a safe environment. This section will consider the impact of boot camps on inmate attitudes, recidivism, community adjustment, prison crowding, and the prison environment.

Changing Inmates

As noted earlier, critics of the boot camp model have theorized that because of the military atmosphere, drill, and hard physical labor (i.e., the stress-producing aspects of the model) components of boot camp programs, offenders would leave these programs more hostile, aggressive, and antisocial than when they entered (Morash & Rucker, 1990). In response, through a multisite study of adult boot camps, researchers examined the impact of the boot camp programs on inmate attitudes. When researchers examined the attitudes of adult offenders in eight different boot camps, they found that despite the differences between programs, boot camp participants were more positive about their experience in the program than were control groups of offenders in traditional prisons (MacKenzie & Souryal, 1994). Boot camp participants generally agreed that their experience in the program had taught them to be more self-disciplined and mature. These results were true of boot camp programs that emphasized treatment as well as those in which the military components of the boot camp model dominated. Thus, contrary to the assertions made by boot camp critics, even in boot camp programs that emphasized strict discipline, drill, and hard physical labor, participants experienced positive attitudinal change. Furthermore, when boot camp participants and the conventional prisoner groups were compared on antisocial attitudes, both groups became less antisocial while incarcerated. Researchers concluded from these findings that there was no evidence that boot camps had a negative effect on the attitudes of participating inmates.

In a national evaluation, MacKenzie, Gover, Styve, and Mitchell (2000) found similar results in juvenile correctional populations. Researchers found that the boot camp juveniles became more social (less antisocial), less impulsive, and less risk-taking-oriented, whereas inmates in traditional facilities became significantly more antisocial, more impulsive, and more risk-taking-oriented over time.

Impact on Recidivism

As critics predict, offenders released from boot camps do not fare any better after they return to the community. Comparisons of juvenile (Bottcher, Isorena, & Belnas, 1996; Clawson, Coolbaugh, & Zamberlan, 1998; MacKenzie, 1997) or adult (MacKenzie, Brame, McDowall, & Souryal, 1995) boot camp inmates to inmates who have received a more traditional correctional option (prison, probation, training schools, detention centers) have shown no differences in recidivism rates or participation in constructive community activities such as work and school (MacKenzie & Brame, 1995). However, despite the empirical evidence, boot camps have remained a popular sentencing option for both juveniles and adults. Current recidivism data are based on programs developed from early boot camp models. As boot camps have continued to develop, so has the need for additional recidivism studies.

Impact on Community Supervision

Offenders exit boot camps through dismissal, voluntarily dropping out (in some programs), or through successful completion of the program. MacKenzie and Souryal (1994) found that some states had dismissal rates of 50% or more.

Offenders who successfully complete boot camp programs are placed on regular parole or intensive parole according to their assessed risk. The importance of supervision cannot be underestimated. Not surprisingly, it is very difficult for many inmates to maintain the change initiated in the boot camp once they are released back to their community. Success in many cases is linked to postrelease support. New York recognized the difficulty offenders were having returning to the community and established an innovative "after shock" program to help offenders during the community supervision phase of their sentence (MacKenzie, 1993). The program incorporates work programs, employment counseling, drug treatment, and a continuation of therapeutic community meetings.

Other state correctional jurisdictions are developing additional community release innovations. For example, in Maryland, officials are developing transitional housing for boot camp graduates who do not have acceptable housing in the community. While in the program, boot camp inmates are renovating the housing that will be used for the transitional housing program.

In Illinois, boot camp graduates are electronically monitored for their first 3 months in the community (MacKenzie, 1993). In California's boot camp program at San Quentin, participants spend 120 days in the boot camp, after which they live at a nearby naval air station for 60 days. Participants are allowed to leave the base if they have a job; unemployed participants work on the base while they look for employment. When participants do leave the base, they are intensively supervised in the community for an additional 4 months.

Reducing Prison Crowding

Many state correctional departments that developed boot camp prisons did so specifically as a means to reduce prison overcrowding. By reducing the time an offender spends in prison, boot camp prisons can potentially reduce the demand for bed space and alleviate overcrowding. However, to accomplish this goal, attention must be paid to program design (MacKenzie & Piquero, 1994).

Decisions regarding program entry have an impact on whether boot camps can reduce crowding. Risk-aversive criminal justice practitioners may potentially use alternatives to incarceration, such as boot camps, for offenders who would otherwise have been on probation or parole as opposed to incarcerated. This "net widening" makes cost savings and alleviation of overcrowding difficult to realize (Morris & Tonry, 1990).

Another factor that affects the ability of boot camp programs to reduce overcrowding is the eligibility requirement. When eligibility criteria are set too stringently, potential participants do not qualify for boot camp programs and are sent to conventional prisons, adding to the crowding problem. Furthermore, when eligibility criteria restrict participation to offenders with a limited criminal history who have been convicted of nonserious offenses that carry short sentences, there is no incentive for these offenders to participate in boot camps.

Finally, graduation or completion rates must be worked into the equation in order to determine the true impact of the boot camp program on prison crowding. Programs must graduate a sufficient number of offenders to take advantage of the reduction in time served. If offenders are dismissed (i.e., fail the program) at a high rate and are then sent to conventional prisons to serve their sentences, overcrowding will not be alleviated. An interaction between failure rates and net widening is demonstrated by Parent (1994), who estimated that for boot camps with a 40% failure rate, the probability that the offender would have been imprisoned has to be near 80% just to reach a break-even point. MacKenzie and Piquero (1994) estimated this break-even point to be 75%.

Positive Environment Conducive to Change

For the past several years, quality management has played an important role in the restructuring of private organizations and corporations. These concepts are now also being applied to public agencies (MacKenzie, Styve, & Gover, 1998). The development of performance-based standards for corrections involved the examination of relationships between the prison environment or conditions of confinement and the desired outcomes. Quantification of environmental perceptions of prison environments has allowed researchers to compare the environment of boot camps to the environment of traditional facilities as viewed by the inmates.

Critics of boot camps assert that the camps are expected to be perceived by the juveniles as less caring and less just; to have less individualized planning and fewer programs focusing on reintegration; and, overall, to focus less on therapeutic treatment. Furthermore, the yelling, direct commands, and summary punishments by drill instructors in the boot camps will result in the boot camp youth perceiving themselves to be in more danger from the staff as compared to the youth in the traditional facilities.

Contrary to critics, Styve et al. (2000) found that inmates in a national sample of juvenile boot camps perceived the boot camps as having more therapeutic programming, activity, structure, and control, as well as a more thorough process preparing them for release from the facility. Boot camp inmates also perceived that the facility posed fewer dangers from other inmates and the general environment, and had fewer risks to residents. In the majority of the boot camps, inmates perceived the environments as high in the characteristics expected in a boot camp environment (i.e., structure, control, safety from other inmates), but they also viewed the environments as more therapeutic (i.e., more programming and better preparation for release).

CONCLUSION

Boot camp programs are an alternative to traditional prison incarceration that has become very popular since its rebirth in 1983. The militarization of correctional programs through boot camp provides a structured environment requiring a strict physical regime that is followed by both inmates and correctional staff. Traditionally, these programs have focused on the military style of training and punishment. More recently, they have been subsumed by boot camps that contain the military components but also incorporate therapeutic elements. Although boot camp programs have not been very successful in reducing the recidivism level of offenders upon their graduation, on average, they have not been any less successful as compared to their traditional facility counterparts. It is expected that with the incorporation of treatment elements into boot camp programs, these new boot camps may be more effective than traditional boot camp programs in reducing recidivism.

The proliferation of boot camps from their redevelopment almost two decades ago has led to a diversity of programs for offender populations across the country. Boot camps now exist for adults and juveniles, men and women. Boot camps have been based in jails, prisons, and juvenile detention centers. Some programs have focused on special populations such as drug offenders or nonviolent offenders, whereas other boot camps accept a variety of offenders. Although there is some diversity between individual boot camp programs with respect to their programming, selection process, goals, and eligibility criteria, a number of basic components common to most can be used to describe a basic boot camp program.

Disagreement remains about the effectiveness, utility, and appropriateness of correctional boot camps. Researchers have found boot camps to be perceived as significantly more punitive than traditional imprisonment and various forms of alternative sanctions. They have been shown to be effective in changing inmates' attitudes to be less antisocial than comparison groups. Furthermore, boot camps hold the potential for reducing prison crowding if participants successfully complete the program and net widening is avoided. Although early studies on the recidivism rates of boot camps found that the camps are no more effective than comparison facilities, recent research finds that the environment in a boot camp is perceived as more positive and therapeutic than that in comparison facilities. These perceptions suggest that updated recidivism studies on newer boot camp models are needed to completely understand the impact of boot camps on offender populations.

REFERENCES

Andrews, D. A., Zinger, I., Hoge, R. D., Bonta, J., Gendreau, P., & Cullen, F. T. (1990). Does correctional treatment work? A clinically relevant and psychologically informed meta-analysis. *Criminology, 28*(3), 369–404.

Bottcher, J., Isorena, T., & Belnas, M. (1996). *LEAD: A boot camp and intensive parole program: An impact evaluation, second year findings.* Ion, CA: Department of the Youth Authority, Research Division.

Bureau of Justice Statistics. (1995). *Census of state and federal adult correctional facilities.* Washington, DC: U.S. Government Printing Office.

Clawson, H., Coolbaugh, K., & Zamberlan, C. (1998, November). *Further evaluation of Cleveland's juvenile boot camp: A summary report.* Paper presented at the annual meeting of the American Society of Criminology, Washington, DC.

Koch Crime Institute. (2000, March). *Juvenile boot camps and military structured youth programs.* New York: Author.

Lipsey, M. (1992). Juvenile delinquency treatment: A meta-analytic inquiry into the variability of effects. In T. Cook et al. (Eds.), *Meta-analysis for explanation: A casebook.* New York: Russell Sage Foundation.

MacKenzie, D. L. (1993, November). Boot camp prisons 1993. *National Institute of Justice Journal,* pp. 21-28.

MacKenzie, D. L. (1997). Criminal justice and crime prevention. In L. W. Sherman, D. Gottfredson, J. Eck, P. Reuter, & S. Bushway (Eds.), *Preventing crime: What works? What doesn't? What's promising?* Washington, DC: National Institute of Justice.

MacKenzie, D. L., & Brame, R. (1995). Shock incarceration and positive adjustment during community supervision. *Journal of Quantitative Criminology, 11,* 111–142.

MacKenzie, D. L., Brame, R., McDowall, D., & Souryal, C. (1995). Boot camp prisons and recidivism in eight states. *Criminology, 33*(3), 401-430.

MacKenzie, D. L., Gover, A. R., Styve, G. J., & Mitchell, O. (2000). *National Institute of Justice research in brief: A national study comparing boot camps with traditional facilities for juvenile offenders.* Washington, DC: National Institute of Justice.

MacKenzie, D. L., & Parent, D. (1992). Boot camp prisons for young offenders. In J. Byrne, A. Lurigio, & J. Petersilia (Eds.), *Smart sentencing: The emergence of intermediate sanctions* (pp. 103–122). Newbury Park, CA: Sage.

MacKenzie, D. L., & Piquero, A. (1994). The impact of shock incarceration programs on prison crowding. *Crime & Delinquency, 40*(2), 222–249.

MacKenzie D. L., & Souryal, C. C. (1991). States say rehabilitation and recidivism reduction outrank punishment as boot camp program goals. *Corrections Today, 53,* 90–96.

MacKenzie, D. L., & Souryal, C. (1994). *Multi-site evaluation of shock incarceration: Executive summary.* Report to the National Institute of Justice. Washington, DC: National Institute of Justice.

MacKenzie, D. L., Styve, G. J., & Gover, A. R. (1998). Performance based standards for juvenile corrections. *Corrections Management Quarterly, 2,* 28–35.

Marlowee, D. H., Marin, J. A., Schneider, L. I., Vaitkus, M. A., & Bartone, P. (1988). *A look at army training centers: The human dimensions of leadership and training.* Washington, DC: Department of Military Psychiatry, Walter Reed Army Institute of Research.

Morash, M., & Rucker, L. (1990). A critical look at the idea of boot camp as a correctional reform. *Crime & Delinquency, 36,* 204–222.

Morris, N., & Tonry, M. (1990). *Between prison and probation: Intermediate punishments in a rational sentencing system.* New York: Oxford University Press.

Nation's first reformatory: Elmira. (1998, October). *DOCS Today, 7.* Retrieved June 4, 2002, from http://www.correctionhistory.org/html/ichronicl/docs2day/elmira.html.

Parent, D. (1994). Boot camps failing to achieve goals. *Overcrowded Times, 5*(4), 8–11.

Raupp, E. (1978). *Toward positive leadership for initial entry training: A report to the Task Force on Initial Entry Training Leadership.* Fort Monroe, VA: United States Army Training and Doctrine Command.

Styve, G. J., MacKenzie, D. L., Gover, A. R., & Mitchell, O. J. (2000). Perceived conditions of confinement: A national evaluation of juvenile boot camps and traditional facilities. *Law and Human Behavior, 24*(3), 297–308.

Toby, J., & Pearson, F. S. (1992). Juvenile boot camps 1992. In *Boot camps for juvenile offenders: Constructive intervention and early support-implementation evaluation.* Final Report to the National Institute of Justice, U.S. Department of Justice.

U.S. General Accounting Office. (1993). *Prison boot camps: Short-term prison costs reduced, but long-term impact uncertain.* Washington, DC: U.S. Government Printing Office.

Walker, S. (2001). *Sense and nonsense about crime and drugs: A policy guide.* Belmont, CA: Wadsworth.

Wood, P. B., & Grasmick, H. G. (1999). Toward the development of punishment equivalencies: Male and female inmates rate the severity of alternative sanctions compared to prison. *Justice Quarterly, 16*(1), 19–50.

3

Boot Camp Prisons for Young Offenders

Doris Layton MacKenzie

Dale G. Parent

Shock incarceration, or "boot camp" prison, programs are a rapidly growing phenomenon in U.S. corrections. Correctional boot camps are patterned after military basic training. Offenders, usually young adults serving their first prison terms, spend 90 to 180 days in a boot camp atmosphere. There is a demanding daily schedule of activities characterized by strict rules and discipline. If offenders succeed in completing the program, they are released to community supervision. Those who leave the program, either as disciplinary cases or by voluntarily dropping out, must serve longer terms in traditional prisons or go before judges for resentencing.

On a typical day in a boot camp, participants arise before dawn, dress quickly and quietly, march in cadence to an exercise area, spend an hour or more doing calisthenics and running, and march back to their quarters. Following this, they march to breakfast, where they stand at parade rest when the serving line is not moving, and execute crisp military movements and turns when the line does move. Inmates are required to approach the table, stand at attention until commanded to sit, and eat without conversation. After breakfast, they practice drill and ceremony. They then march to (or are transported to) a work site, where they perform six to eight hours of labor selected specifically to exact maximum physical effort from them. Upon completing the workday, they return to their living compound, where they face more exercises, and drill and ceremony. After a quick evening meal, inmates may spend four to five hours in treatment or educational programs before lights out. During their stay in the boot camp, they have no direct contact with regular prison inmates, strict rules govern all facets of their comportment and behavior, and punishments for rule violations are summary, certain, and often physical in nature (push-ups, running, and so on).

Rapid Growth of Shock Incarceration Programs

The first shock incarceration programs began in 1983 in Georgia and Oklahoma (Parent, 1989).

Reprinted from MacKenzie, D. L., and Parent, D. G. (1992). In J. M. Byrne and A. Lurigio (Eds.), *Smart Sentencing: The Emergence of Intermediate Sanctions.* Newbury Park, CA: Sage. Used with permission from Sage Publications, Inc.

By early 1990, there were more than 21 programs for adults in 14 state correctional systems (MacKenzie, 1900; MacKenzie & Ballow, 1989) and 10 more states were considering opening programs. Several city and county jurisdictions had opened boot camp prisons for adults and a number were also considering boot camp prisons for juveniles.

Several factors account for this rapid growth. Boot camps clearly were in tune with the conservative political climate of the 1980s. Politicians who failed to appear tough on crime did so at extreme peril (remember Willie Horton?). Likewise, sanctions such as probation that seemed "soft" on criminals had trouble attracting political support and adequate funding. Boot camps appealed directly to the "gut instincts" of a public that wanted criminals punished swiftly and harshly, in austere, no-frills settings, where they learned to respect authority and to obey rules (see White House, 1989, p. 25).

Journalists publicized shock incarceration widely. Boot camps and electronic journalism, in particular, are a perfect match. Television needs powerful visual images, and boot camps provide them: young criminals snapping to attention when a staff member approaches; a swaggering street thug entering a boot camp whose bravado quickly cracks under a barrage of verbal abuse (delivered in high decibels at extremely close range) by a tough-as-nails drill sergeant; an inmate work crew digging ditches under the scorching sun. The electronic media also need to portray stories quickly; television news programs rarely have the time to give viewers lengthy explanations or detailed background. Millions of Americans have experienced military basic training, and those who have not usually know someone who has, or have seen a score of movies portraying basic training. Boot camps have a "face validity" (Gauthier & Reichel, 1989) that is absent in most corrections programs. Hence they make great 60-second features in the evening news. Americans' wide exposure to military basic training promotes immediate, widespread, and uncritical public and political support for boot camp prisons.

Boot camps are linked to strong traditions in American culture. The basic training model typifies police recruit training in the United States, and tends to reinforce law enforcement support for boot camp prisons. Middle- and upper-income families have long placed unruly male offspring whose behavior borders on the deviant in military boarding schools. In the past, courts sometimes gave these boys' older and less affluent counterparts the choice of going to jail or joining the army, which, it was believed, would "make a man" out of a troublesome boy.

Boot camps also have strong links to U.S. correctional history. Prisons have long been organized around a military-style command structure, even down to custodial job titles—captains, lieutenants, sergeants, and so on. Hard labor, strict rules, rigid discipline, and enforced silence existed in early penitentiaries. More than a hundred years ago, New York's Elmira Reformatory incorporated many elements of today's shock incarceration programs, including drill and ceremony (during which the inmates carried dummy rifles). Inmate movement in lockstep and use of chain gangs are features of prison life many current correctional employees recall. Until the 1960s, summary punishment, unencumbered by written charges and disciplinary hearings, was the rule. In a real sense, boot camps involve returning to familiar themes in American corrections.

Boot camps also are consistent with several current correctional needs and trends. Boot camps let prison officials use the media to spread "good news" about corrections for a change. Severe crowding during the 1980s led to a search for new sanctions that were both tough and affordable, and that plausibly could reduce commitments or inmate populations. Boot camps fit the bill. Crowding also heightened administrators' need to control prisoners via more stringent regulations and stricter discipline.

The Controversy

Opposition to boot camp prisons has been muted, especially from correctional practitioners, but opponents have cited varied reasons for their anti-boot camp positions (see, e.g., Meachum, 1990; Morash & Rucker, 1990). Some question the relevance of the military basic training model for corrections. Obviously, the ultimate mission of military training—teaching killing skills and eliminating soldiers' reluctance to employ them—is not relevant. Although real-world employment requires individuals to be able to exercise self-discipline and, to an extent, suppress their individuality to accommodate organizational needs, the military requires immediate obedience to command and unquestioning acceptance of authority.

More thoughtful critics have argued that basic training prepares soldiers for three to four years of military life, during which they are fed, clothed, sheltered, and given medical care, a job with chances of promotion and pay increases, and opportunities for continued education and training. If the experience changes soldiers' attitudes, behaviors, and postmilitary adjustment for the better, it probably is due more to the period of extended support and structure than to six or eight weeks of basic training. By contrast, under current practice, most prison boot camp graduates return from whence they came, usually no better off in terms of education, jobs, and living conditions or prospects for the future. They daily face the same problems and temptations that got them into trouble before. Critics argue that if a military model has correctional relevance, we must provide a parallel extended period of support, services, and opportunities. They maintain that when we expect 90 days of verbal abuse, push-ups, and marching to cure addiction and reduce recidivism, we not only deceive ourselves, we also sidetrack chances for really effective reforms in the vain search for cheap and quick panaceas.

Critics raise concerns that boot camp prisons expose inmates to increased likelihood of abuse by staff, and injury or even death during physical exercises or hard labor. (To date, two inmates have died during boot camp physical training sessions—both had serious preexisting medical problems that were not detected during routine prison medical examinations.) They argue that boot camp prisons tend to attract the wrong kind of staff—those who are on a "power trip," or who would use enhanced control and discipline to "get even" with inmates. They note that staff burnout and turnover rates are higher in boot camps than in regular prisons, making it especially difficult to recruit and retain qualified

staff. Finally, they note that many facets of boot camp prisons (summary punishment, humiliation of inmates, and the like) conflict with standards of accepted professional practice promulgated by the American Correctional Association.

Advocates respond that inmates are abused and injured in regular prisons as well, and that some die there. The key to preventing such incidents lies in effective program design and proper control of staff recruitment, training, and supervision. They argue that, by comparison with regular prisons, boot camps are remarkably free of inmate-on-inmate violence. Properly detailed medical assessments can screen out inmates whose health problems make their participation dangerous. Standards were promulgated before the concept of boot camp prisons appeared, and may need revision. In boot camps, summary physical punishments (push-ups, running, and the like) and verbal humiliation are not intended to degrade inmates (which is what standards try to prevent), but are part of a treatment model designed ultimately to improve inmates' self-esteem, self-control, and respect for authority.

Finally, opponents argue that, as most boot camps are currently used, they cannot help but "widen the net" of correctional control and increase prison populations. Supporters counter that if eligibility and selection are properly structured, boot camps can cut prison populations.

DIFFERENT MODELS OF SHOCK INCARCERATION

In all shock incarceration programs, offenders serve a short period of time in a military boot camp prison (MacKenzie, 1990). They are separated from other prison inmates and are required to participate in military drills, physical training, and hard labor. Beyond this core of similarities, shock incarceration programs differ in purposes, the numbers and sizes of programs provided, the locations of those programs, the types of offenders eligible to participate, selection and screening procedures, program content, release mechanisms, and types of postrelease community supervision. The following sections highlight these differences.

Number and Size of Programs

In January 1990, the number of participants in boot camp programs varied from a low of 42 offenders in the Tennessee program to more than 1,600 in New York's programs, with most states having between 100 and 250 boot camp participants (MacKenzie, 1990). Most states operate only one or two programs, although New York now operates five. Other than in New York, the participants make up a very small proportion of the total inmate population.

The size of a program is determined in part by the number of offenders who are eligible and the number who are permitted to drop out or are dismissed for disciplinary reasons. Programs differ in these respects. Some programs have high dropout rates. For example, in the early years of the shock program in Louisiana, 30–40% of the offenders left the program before completion, and in Florida 50% were dismissed. In contrast, almost all who begin the Oklahoma program complete the full program, in part because participants are sent to a "motivational squad" if they are not performing up to expectations. In eight programs the offender must volunteer in order to be eligible to enter the program, and in seven programs offenders can voluntarily drop out.

The average number of days offenders spend in a boot camp prison varies from 90 to 120 in all programs except the New York model, which lasts 180 days. Because program durations are relatively short, their annual capacity is substantially greater than the number of beds they provide. In a 90-day program, each boot camp bed turns over more than four times a year, when dropout and in-program failures are considered. Thus more than 800 inmates can be processed annually through a 200 bed, three-month boot camp program.

Program Location

Most correctional boot camps are housed in units at larger medium- or maximum-security prisons that serve general inmate populations.

This gives participants a more accurate (if distant) vision of what "real" prison is like. It also lets general-population inmates direct taunts and catcalls (often of a threatening sexual nature) at participants when they pass within earshot. Some advocates think locating boot camps at regular prisons improves deterrent effects. It also lets boot camps use resources and services (such as treatment, education, and vocational programs) that might not be available in a small separate institution, or that would be costly to provide separately. Staff recruitment and replacement also are easier when the boot camp is located within a larger general-population prison.

In early 1990, New York was the only state that operated "stand-alone" correctional boot camps. In New York, existing minimum-security forestry camps were converted to house only boot camp inmates. Many staff previously employed at the forestry camps continued to work at the facilities when they were converted to boot camps. The department of corrections developed an elaborate training program for all individuals (including teachers and kitchen staff) working at the shock facilities. Such training may be particularly important when programs are located at separate facilities and staff cannot be rotated in and out of the program.

Advocates of separate facilities note that boot camp inmates do not require expensive high-security facilities. Hence, even if enhanced support programs and services are needed, separate minimum-security boot camps may be a more economical use of existing bed space.

Eligibility

The majority of the offenders admitted to shock programs are young, convicted of nonviolent crimes, and have not served time in prison on previous felony convictions. There is some variance in programs regarding these characteristics. Of the 14 states with programs in January 1990, half permitted offenders convicted of violent crimes to enter the program. However, all states except Michigan report that most participants were convicted of nonviolent crimes.

Most programs are also designed for first offenders, but the definition of *first offender* varies among states. *First felony offender* means first state felony incarceration in five states, first state felony in one state, and first felony conviction ever in the remaining states. Participating offenders in many of the programs could have served time in jail for felonies or misdemeanors. Only Idaho and Michigan do not necessarily have first felony offenders (by any definition) in their programs.

Most programs were open to males only; however, Louisiana, Mississippi, and New York have programs that include males and females, and South Carolina has a separate program for females. There are also wide differences among programs in age limits for participants. The majority of the states limit participation to those under 25 years old, some have no age limits, and in a few states the offender must be less than 30 or 40. Although the maximum age limit varies, the majority of the participants are young.

Selection Processes

Of the 14 state jurisdictions that had programs operating in 1990, judges selected participants in 8, judges and corrections departments shared selection responsibility in 2, the parole commission selected participants in 1, and corrections departments selected participants in 3.

Program Content

Programs differ greatly in the number of hours devoted to physical training, work, and education or counseling. If the time allotted to rehabilitation-type activities (including such activities as counseling, any type of treatment, education, and vocational training activities) is compared with time spent working, the wide differences among programs become obvious. In some states, offenders spend an amount of time in rehabilitation activities equal to or greater than the amount of time they spend working (e.g., in Alabama, Arizona, Mississippi, New York). For example, Louisiana offenders spend approximately 4.5 hours each day in rehabilitation activities, 4.5 hours working, and 4.5 hours in physical training or drill.

In other states, offenders spend one-half to one-quarter less time in rehabilitation (e.g., in Michigan offenders spend approximately 6 hours

per day working, 2.5 hours in rehabilitation activities, and 1.5 hours in physical training and drill). In comparison with offenders in other programs, the Georgia participants spend the least time in rehabilitation activities. They spend less than half an hour per day in rehabilitation. Despite the fact that there is a wide variance in the amount of time devoted to rehabilitation in shock incarceration programs, it appears that most of these offenders spend more time in rehabilitation-type activities in shock programs than they might in traditional prisons.

Several programs are being designed to focus on treatment for drug offenders. Texas, New York, Oklahoma, and Illinois have received federal funding to develop innovative programs addressing the needs of these offenders.

Release and Supervision

Programs vary greatly in regard to release decision making, and this depends, in part, on the placement authority and the state release mechanism. There are also differences in release supervision. In some cases the offender returns to regular supervision, in eight states the supervision varies as a function of risk level, and in Louisiana, Michigan, and New York offenders are intensively supervised upon release from shock programs.

Only New York has developed an enhanced aftercare program for releasees. While intensive supervision increases the surveillance of offenders in the community, the aftercare program increases their opportunities. In New York City the shock releasees are given work, drug treatment, and counseling opportunities. They are also given the opportunity to meet with other shock offenders in a supervised setting in order to share their experiences and difficulties during transition from shock to the community.

DO BOOT CAMPS WORK?

In order to determine whether or not boot camps "work," officials must define, in clear, operational terms, what boot camps are supposed to achieve. The differences noted above in structure and design suggest differences among programs in goals and in what goals can be achieved.

Data are currently being collected from a study of seven different shock incarceration programs (MacKenzie, 1990). The sites were selected specifically because they varied in characteristics that are expected to have a major impact on whether specific goals can be achieved by the shock programs. Although the multisite study of shock incarceration is still in progress, some research has been completed examining specific programs.

Reducing Prison Crowding

Officials in virtually all shock incarceration programs say one of their major goals is to reduce prison crowding. That could occur in two ways. The first, or direct, way is to shorten the period of time offenders spend in prison. The second, or indirect, way is to change the postrelease behavior or boot camp graduates so that fewer return to prison for new convictions or violations of conditions of supervision. This section deals with the direct method; changing offenders' postrelease behavior is considered below.

Boot camps' impact on prison bed space will vary with five factors:

1. the size of the pool of eligible offenders
2. the probability that those offenders would be imprisoned if placement in the boot camp program were not available
3. the rate at which those admitted to boot camps complete the program
4. the difference between the offenders' regular prison terms and the duration of the boot camp program
5. the rate at which boot camp graduates return to prison, either for violations of release conditions or for new criminal convictions

Using these characteristics, a model was developed for one jurisdiction, Louisiana, to examine changes in bed space needs as a function of the shock program. The model indicated that a program such as shock incarceration could be used to reduce prison crowding (MacKenzie & Parent, 1991). However, the results of this analysis were dependent upon unique features of the Louisiana program that might differ from other jurisdictions.

One of the estimates necessary for a bed space model is the probability that an offender would have been imprisoned if the program had not been operational. That is, the effectiveness of the program in reducing crowding would depend upon the selection of offenders for the program who would, under other circumstances, be serving time in prison. A frequently encountered problem with intermediate punishments is that they actually *widen* the net of control. According to this thesis, as options are developed that are less restrictive, those who have been treated more leniently in the past will be placed in the program instead of those who previously have been treated more severely (Austin & Krisberg, 1982; Morris & Tonry, 1990).

It was hypothesized that an important distinguishing factor among programs in the degree of net widening would be whether the judge or the department of corrections selected offenders. If the judge made the decisions, net widening was expected to be more apt to occur. The rationale for this hypothesis was that judges appear to be searching for options for offenders who would normally be given probation, and this is why net widening occurs when intermediate punishments are introduced into the system. On the other hand, if selection decisions were made by the department of corrections, offenders would already be prison bound and, theoretically, their time in prison would be reduced if they completed the shock program. As noted above, the authority for selecting offenders differs among jurisdictions.

There are other differences among programs that would be expected to have an impact on prison crowding as well. For instance, there must be a sufficient number of offenders who are eligible and who complete the program. The voluntary nature of a program might limit the number of participants. Shock programs differ in this respect. In eight programs the offender must volunteer in order to be eligible to enter the program, and in seven programs the offenders can voluntarily drop out of the program.

Cost of Boot Camp Prisons

Many policymakers seem to accept, uncritically, a belief that boot camps are less costly than regular prison. However, studies show that prison boot camps cost as much as or more than regular prisons on a per inmate per day basis (Aziz, 1988; MacKenzie, Shaw, & Gowdy, 1990). Boot camps that offer minimal programming and focus mostly on the military regime, exercise, and hard work cost about the same as regular prison on a per inmate per day basis. Boot camps that offer an array of treatment programs and services cost more than regular prisons on a per inmate per day basis. Stand-alone boot camps cost somewhat more than those co-located in regular prisons, because administrative and support costs are not shared among several housing units (Parent, 1989).

Thus boot camps are less costly than regular prisons only if they shorten the duration of confinement for persons who otherwise would be imprisoned. Because boot camps cost much more than probation (even in its most intensive forms), if a large percentage of participants would have been on probation if boot camps had not been available, then boot camps increase total correctional costs. If prison durations are shortened only slightly, boot camps are unlikely to cost less.

Studies of shock incarceration programs in New York and Louisiana found that boot camps reduced correctional costs (Aziz, 1988; MacKenzie et al., 1990). In both of these states prison officials select participants from regular prison admissions.

Changing the Offender

Of course, not everyone expects a short-term program such as shock incarceration to reduce prison crowding. Some advocates of shock may support the programs as an option for those who would previously have served their sentences on probation. They might believe that offenders who complete these programs may be rehabilitated or deterred from future criminal activities. This might secondarily have an impact on prison crowding because these offenders would not return to prison.

Prison populations could be reduced if the criminal activities of shock offenders were reduced upon release. This would be an indirect effect on prison crowding, and would take some time to have an impact. The assumption is that offenders would be rehabilitated or deterred by

the experience of the shock incarceration program and would be less apt to be involved in crime in the future. As a result, there would be fewer criminals, fewer convictions, and, hence, fewer offenders sentenced to prison.

Some early research has examined the performance of offenders during community supervision after release from shock incarceration programs. Studies have been completed in Georgia (Georgia Department of Corrections, 1989), Florida (Florida Department of Corrections, 1989), New York (New York Department of Correctional Services, 1989; New York State Division of Parole, 1989), and Louisiana (MacKenzie, 1991) comparing the recidivism of shock offenders with similar offenders released on parole after spending a longer period of time in a traditional prison and, in Louisiana, with offenders entering a term of probation. No differences were found between the shock offenders and others in either rearrests or reincarcerations.

The groups in the studies cited above were not randomly assigned to treatment conditions. It is hoped that in the future true experimental designs will give more conclusive results. However, to date no research we have seen suggests that the offenders who complete shock programs will have lower recidivism rates in comparison with other offenders. Thus there is no support for the idea that prison crowding will be reduced by shock programs by decreasing the recidivism of offenders.

Deterrence and rehabilitation are two sentencing goals that would result in changing offenders; both methods would be expected to reduce criminal activities. The failure to find that offenders who complete shock programs have lower recidivism than others suggests that these programs may neither deter nor rehabilitate offenders.

It is possible that the measures of recidivism used are not sensitive enough to reflect differences among offender groups, or that the length of follow-up has not been sufficiently long to show the differences in behavior. The New York State Department of Correctional Services (1989) argues that the programs represent a cost savings and that, at the least, the offenders who complete the shock programs do no worse than offenders who spent longer periods in prison. In the end, however, the possibility that these programs do not have a rehabilitative effect cannot be ruled out.

Constructive Punishment

One question is whether the punishment aspect of boot camp prisons could have a constructive effect on offenders (MacKenzie, 1991). Physical training, drill, hard labor, and the difficult daily regime may have advantages that should be examined in the future. For example, the physical exercise may free offenders of drugs and make them physically fit. Offenders interviewed near the ends of their sentences in shock report that, in their view, these are benefits of the program (MacKenzie et al., 1990). Another advantage, in the opinion of inmates, is that they have learned to get up in the morning and be active all day.

There may also be an advantage in the fact that boot camp prisons create radical changes in the everyday living patterns of these offenders. Zamble and Porporino (1988) believe that a period of radical change that creates reasonable stress may be a time when people are particularly susceptible to outside influences. In their opinion this may be an excellent time to have an impact on offenders, making them reconsider their past choices. If the program makes an attempt to change the thinking of offenders, the boot camp prison atmosphere may help facilitate this change.

Programs that are not rigorous, that do not allow dropouts, or that do not kick offenders out may have problems with troublemakers in the program; also, such programs provide little test of an individual's commitment to change (MacKenzie & Shaw, 1990). Such programs would also lose some of their challenge; consequently, graduates may not feel that they have succeeded at accomplishing a difficult task. The importance of this aspect of programs is still unknown.

If shock programs were changed to focus on therapy but the boot camp atmosphere was eliminated, perhaps the most important change would be in the attitudes of the public and policymakers. If they are willing to trade a longer term in prison for a program such as this because the program involves hard work and strict discipline, it might be possible to combine the punishment aspects with other components that bring about constructive change in offenders.

Retribution

Few people mention retribution or punishment as a goal of shock incarceration programs. However, this may be one of the most desirable features of these programs from the perspective of the public and policymakers.

To some extent, shock incarceration programs may be a marketing ploy designed to sell today's policymakers treatment when what they really want to buy is retribution. Correctional administrators are more likely to receive support and funding for programs in which treatment interventions have a punitive aura, which, with some embellishment and clever packaging, enable a legislator to portray it to his or her constituents as punishment.

There are several questions related to the retributive aspects of shock programs that remain unanswered. Retribution has been a generally acknowledged sentencing goal. The degree of punishment of a sentence is usually measured by the sentence length: A longer prison sentence is considered to be more punishment than a shorter sentence; similarly, a longer term of probation is thought to be more punishment than a shorter sentence. The question that arises with regard to shock incarceration is whether the shorter but harsher shock programs are sufficiently retributive and can be exchanged for longer but possibly less harsh terms in traditional prisons. In a sense, this might be considered an issue of quality versus quantity of punishment—shock, with its more intense delivery of punishment, gives "quality" retribution, whereas a longer but less harsh sentence in prison gives "quantity" punishment.

From this perspective, shock programs involving hard work, strict rules, and discipline are punishing environments. Opponents of shock incarceration point out that this is a major change for corrections (Meachum, 1990). According to them, prisons (traditional corrections) have been used *for* punishment, not, as in the shock programs, *as* punishment.

Impact of Boot Camps on Staff

Prisons officials note that boot camps have immediate rejuvenating effects on staff who work in them, by giving them a renewed sense of mission (rehabilitation) and by letting them work with a population of inmates (young, never in prison before) who develop positive rather than negative attitudes toward staff.[1] However, these effects seem transitory. As shock programs mature, particularly intense staffing problems emerge. The programs are high-stress environments for both inmates and staff. Staff burnout rates reportedly are much higher than in regular prison assignments. Given the high potential for staff to abuse inmates physically, administrators must be especially vigilant, monitoring staff performance and intervening before it degrades seriously. One state routinely rotates boot camp staff back into regular prison assignments every six months in order to prevent burnout.

Because boot camps have higher staff turnover rates than do regular prisons, recruitment of suitable replacement staff is a continuing problem, particularly if the boot camp is attached to a small general-population prison located in a remote area. In states with small boot camp programs, training for new and replacement staff is minimal and generally done on the job. (With its large-scale boot camp operation, New York has the most elaborate training program for new and replacement boot camp staff.)

Legal Issues

Prison boot camps pose important legal issues. The potential for injury and staff abuse increases the risk of liability for both the state and individual employees. Appropriate shields against liability, including setting forth written policy and procedures, would minimize chances of inmate injury or death, and stringent program administration would ensure that those policies and procedures are, in fact, followed. For example, routine prison medical assessments may need to be supplemented with additional tests to discover conditions such as endocarditis, which could be life threatening to an inmate doing heavy physical exercise. During hard labor in hot weather, inmates' attire, water intake, and number of breaks must be clearly prescribed in regulations and rigorously observed in practice.

Summary punishments—those inflicted on the spot by officials who have observed infractions, without benefit of written charges or hearings—are the rule in many boot camp prisons. There is a need to develop written policy to guide the use of such punishments. They might be restricted to minor violations, while major violations—those that could adversely affect inmates' liberty interests—could continue to receive due-process guarantees.

There are also legal issues related to those who are not given the opportunity to shorten their sentences through participation in boot camp prisons. Equal-protection requirements imply that if young, physically able male inmates can shorten their prison terms by completing boot camp programs, female inmates and physically handicapped inmates should be eligible for the same reductions. Programs differ on whether or not participation by these groups is possible.

CONCLUSION

Shock incarceration as a correctional approach is relatively new, but there are precedents in U.S. society in general and in corrections in particular that make these programs not an entirely new method of handling young men. This fact, along with several trends (conservative philosophy, prison crowding), has probably led to the rapid growth of these programs in the United States.

This growth has not, however, been without controversy. Some people strongly oppose these programs and they have numerous reasons for their position. On the other hand, there are many who believe strongly in the worth of these programs. In this chapter we have tried to present both sides of this issue and to examine the available research to support or refute the two positions. Part of the difficulty in examining the research is the need to identify the goals of the programs. Two of the major goals of most programs appear to be to reduce prison crowding and to reduce recidivism. Debate continues about the role of the tough boot camp atmosphere and whether it is a framework for positive change or a method of punishment.

There are other aspects of shock incarceration programs that are of concern to opponents and advocates of the programs. Protecting inmates' rights, screening for medical problems, equal opportunities for women and handicapped offenders, and standards and guidelines are just a few of these issues.

NOTE

1. During interviews with one of the authors, a drill instructor emotionally described getting a "thank you" letter from a recent boot camp graduate—a first during his 15 years as a prison guard. Also, a probationer who graduated from boot camp two years earlier noted he frequently corresponded with his favorite drill instructor.

REFERENCES

Austin, J., & Krisberg, B. (1982). The unmet promise of alternatives to incarceration. *Crime and Delinquency, 28,* 374–409.

Aziz, D. (1988). *Shock incarceration evaluation: Preliminary data.* Unpublished report to the New York Department of Correctional Services, Shock Incarceration Legislative Report.

Florida Department of Corrections. (1989). *Boot camp evaluation and boot camp commitment rate.* Unpublished report by the Bureau of Planning, Research and Statistics.

Gauthier, A. K., & Reichel, P. L. (1989). *Boot camp corrections: A public reaction.* Paper presented at the annual meeting of the Academy of Criminal Justice Sciences, Washington, DC.

Georgia Department of Corrections. (1989). *Georgia's special alternative incarceration.* Unpublished report to the Shock Incarceration Conference, Washington DC.

MacKenzie, D. L. (1990). Boot camp prisons: Components, evaluations, and empirical issues. *Federal Probation, 54*(3), 44–52.

MacKenzie, D. L. (1991). The parole performance of offenders released from shock incarceration (boot camp prison): A survival analysis. *Journal of Quantitative Criminology, 7,* 213–236.

MacKenzie, D. L., & Ballow, D. B. (1989). Shock incarceration programs in state correctional jurisdictions: An update. *NIJ Reports, 214,* 9–10.

MacKenzie, D. L., & Parent, D. G. (1991). Shock incarceration and prison crowding in Louisiana. *Journal of Criminal Justice, 19,* 225–237.

MacKenzie, D. L., & Shaw, J. W. (1990). Inmate adjustment and change during shock incarceration: The impact of correctional boot camp programs. *Justice Quarterly 7*(1), 125–150.

MacKenzie, D. L., Shaw, J. W., & Gowdy, V. B. (1990). *An evaluation of shock incarceration in Louisiana.* Unpublished report to the Louisiana Department of Public Safety and Corrections.

Meachum, M. (1990). *Boot camp prisons: Pros and cons.* Paper presented at the annual meeting of the American Society of Criminology, Baltimore.

Morash, M., & Rucker, L. (1990). A critical look at the ideal of boot camp as a correctional reform. *Crime and Delinquency, 36,* 204–222.

Morris, N., & Tonry, M. (1990). *Between prison and probation: Intermediate punishments in a rational sentencing system.* New York: Oxford University Press.

New York State Department of Correctional Services. (1989). *Initial follow-up study of shock graduates.* Unpublished report by the New York State Department of Correctional Services, Division of Program Planning, Research and Evaluation.

New York State Division of Parole. (1989). *Shock incarceration: One year out.* Unpublished report.

Parent, D. (1989). *Shock incarceration: An overview of existing programs.* Washington, DC: National Institute of Justice.

White House. (1989). *National drug control strategy.* Washington, DC: Government Printing Office.

Zamble, E., & Porporino, F. J. (1988). *Coping, behavior, and adaptation in prison inmates.* New York: Springer-Verlag.

4

CORRECTIONAL BOOT CAMPS FOR JUVENILES

DORIS LAYTON MACKENZIE

ANDRE B. ROSAY

Burgeoning prison populations have led states to search for innovative alternatives to address correctional problems (Morris & Tonry, 1990). Many of the alternatives proposed, however, place the offender in the community and may be viewed by the public as being "soft" on crime. Not wanting to appear to be soft on criminals, politicians hesitate to support many of these alternatives. Boot camp prisons are one alternative that can be touted as tough on crime. Supporting this perspective are the media reports of boot camps, where drill instructors are shown yelling at young offenders. Perhaps this is what has most influenced the rapid growth of the boot camps. Since their beginning in Oklahoma and Georgia in adult prisons in 1983, more than thirty-two states, the Federal Bureau of Prisons, ten local jurisdictions, and an increasing number of juvenile detention centers have opened correctional boot camps (Cronin, 1994).

Originally, boot camps programs were distinguished from other correctional programs by their emphasis on physical labor, exercise, and a military-style atmosphere (Cronin, 1994; United States General Accounting Office, 1993; MacKenzie & Souryal, 1994; MacKenzie & Parent, 1992). Although most of the boot camp programs used military basic training to some extent, they differed considerably in other respects (Cronin, 1994; United States General Accounting Office, 1993; MacKenzie & Souryal, 1994; Clark & Aziz, 1996; Cowles & Castellano, 1995). More recently, the camps are referred to as second-, third- or even fourth-generation boot camps indicating a series of changes that placed an increased emphasis on rehabilitation, aftercare, or work skills and a diminished emphasis on the tough, confrontational, military components (Gransky, Castellano, & Cowles, 1995). These new camps take names such the Work Ethic Camp in Washington's Department of Corrections, or the Youth Leadership Academy in New York's Division for Youth. The new camps have moved away from the old-fashioned view of military boot camps with aggressive confrontation, tough physical training, and hard labor towards the newer view of boot camps as

Reprinted by permission from MacKenzie, D. L., & Rosay, A. (1996). *Boot Camps: What Works for Whom? A Practitioners' Guide.* Maryland: American Correctional Association.

leadership training opportunities. However, there are still a wide variety of correctional boot camps. Some continue to emphasize aspects of the old-style military boot camps while others emphasize individual programming, positive behavioral change, or work skills. Obviously, these differences among programs will result in wide variation in the effectiveness of the programs in achieving specific goals. While the boot camp programs originally developed in adult prisons, an increasing number of programs are currently being designed for local jails and juvenile populations. As the boot camps become popular for juveniles, new issues have arisen (Cronin, 1994; Austin et al., 1993). For example, while adult programs could target nonviolent offenders in prison, nonviolent juveniles were much less apt to be incarcerated. Thus, net widening and the associated cost have become critical issues for juvenile programs. This is particularly relevant given the history of concern with the destructive environment of detention centers for nonviolent juveniles or status offenders.

The deceptively seductive idea of providing discipline and structure for disruptive juveniles means there is a real threat that increasingly large numbers of juveniles will be placed in boot camps, whether or not it is a suitable alternative sanction. Furthermore, in contrast to adult boot camps, academic and therapeutic programming and aftercare are viewed as necessary components in juvenile programs. In fact, there are questions about how much the boot camp programs actually differ from other residential facilities for juveniles. Questions revolve around the specific conditions of confinement or the environment of the boot camps. How do the boot camp conditions differ from traditional detention or training centers? What are the impacts of these conditions on those involved? If they do indeed differ, there are questions about the effectiveness of the camps for certain types of juveniles (such as higher risk, older, those with more past detention experiences). Furthermore, some are fearful that aspects of the camps may be particularly damaging for some juveniles such as those who were physically or sexually abused in the past or those who are first-time offenders.

SURVEY OF JUVENILE BOOT CAMPS

Starting in June 1995, we surveyed state and local juvenile correctional administrators to identify all juvenile boot camps currently operating. In all, we located thirty-eight different boot camps (see Table 4.1). We obtained descriptive information on thirty-seven of the boot camps in twenty-two different states. One of these programs, The First Arizona Youth Academy in Arizona, will not begin operations until later this year. All administrators were asked to return a survey addressing key characteristics of their programs. The results are summarized below and shown in Tables 4.1 through 4.11.

The emergence of juvenile boot camps has indeed been a recent but explosive trend (see Table 4.2). Out of the thirty-eight boot camps we surveyed, we only found one boot camp, the Challenge Program in Texas, which started operating before the 1990s (one other boot camp, called About Face, near Memphis, Tennessee that existed in the 1980s has been closed). The next program to develop was the Los Angeles County Drug Treatment Program in 1990 in two different camps. Two programs were implemented in 1991 and an additional four in 1992. All others started operating during or after 1993. Currently, we estimate that about 10,500 juveniles participate in boot camps each year. In 1995, the Office of Justice Programs (OJP) in the United States Department of Justice with funding from the Crime Act provided funds to twelve jurisdictions to renovate or construct facilities for juvenile boot camps; another twelve jurisdictions were given funds for the purpose of planning juvenile boot camps. Given these numbers, juvenile boot camps most likely will continue to increase in the next few years.

The existing juvenile boot camps vary dramatically. For example, while the Challenge program in Texas has a capacity of twelve juveniles, the Tallulah Correctional Center for Youth in Louisiana has a capacity of 396 youth. The duration of the programs show as much variation as the capacity (see Table 4.2). One program, the specialized Treatment and Rehabilitation in Texas, can be a one-day program for juveniles whose parents and school

Table 4.1   Juvenile Boot Camps: Who Operates Them and Their Placement Authority

State	Name of Program	Who Operates	Placement Authority
AL	A.D.Y.S. Autauga Campus	Alabama Dept. of Juvenile Services	Dept. of Youth Services and Juvenile Court Judges
AL	A.D.Y.S. Chalkville HIT Program	Alabama Dept. of Juvenile Services	Dept. of Youth Services and Juvenile Court Judges
AL	A.D.Y.S. Thomasville campus	Alabama Dept. of Juvenile Services	Dept. of Youth Services and Juvenile Court Judges
AR	First Arizona Youth Academy[1]	First Corrections Corporation of America	Dept. Youth Treatment & Rehabilitation
CA	L.E.A.D.[2]	California Youth Authority	California Youth Authority
CA	LA County Drug Treatment[2]	LA County Probation Department	LA County Superior Juvenile Court
CA	Twin Pines Ranch	Riverside County Probation Dept.	Juvenile Court
CA	Rehabilitation Oriented Training Center	San Bernardino County Probation	Juvenile Court
CO	Camp Falcon	Rebound Corporation	Juvenile Court Judges[3]
DC	Thurgood Marshall Boot Camp	L.S.W.A.	Courts; OHYC Treatment Team Coordinators
FL	Martin County Sheriff's Office Juvenile Boot Camp	Martin County Sheriff's Office	Juvenile Court
FL	Pinellas County Boot Camp	Pinellas County Sheriff's Department	Juvenile Justice
FL	Leon County Sheriff's Off. Boot Camp	Leon County Sheriff's Department	Florida Department of Juvenile Justice
FL	Regimental Wilderness Program	North American Family Institute	State Department of Juvenile Justice
GA	Irwin Youth Development Campus	Bobby Ross Group	Juvenile Judges
IN	Camp Summit	Dept. of Corrections, Juvenile Division	Juvenile Division Intake
IA	Highly Structured Program for Juveniles	Clarinda Youth Corp./ Family Resources, Inc.	Juvenile Court
KY	Green River Boys' Camp	Dept. for Social Services, Div. of Youth Services	Department for Social Services
LA	Tallulah Correctional Center for Youth	Trans American Development Assoc., Inc.	State Diagnostic Center
MD	Juvenile Boot Camp at Doncaster	North American Family Institute	Juvenile Justice
MS	Columbia Training School	Division of Youth Services	Juvenile Courts
MS	Oakley Training School	Division of Youth Services	Juvenile Courts
NJ	Wharton Tract Juvenile Boot Camp	State of NJ; Dept. of Law and Public Safety	Juv. Reception Classification Committee
NY	Youth Leadership Academy	Division for Youth	Division for Youth
OH	Camp Roulston	North American Family Institute	Cuyahoga County
PA	Abraxas Leadership Development Prog.	Abraxas Foundation Inc.	Juvenile Courts
PA	Fort Charles Young Boot and Hat Camp	VisionQuest	Juvenile Courts
SC	Junior Reserve Officers Training Corps	Department of Juvenile Justice	None, voluntary placement
TX	Challenge Program	Juvenile Probation	Juvenile Judge
TX	Community Corrections Inc. (C.C.I.) Boot Camp	Community Corrections Inc.	Probation Department
TX	Specialized Treatment and Rehabilitation	Dept. of Community Supervision and Corrections	Juvenile Court and Probation
TX	S.T.A.R. Day Boot Camp	Juvenile Probation	Juvenile Judge
LIT	Genesis Youth Center	Division of Youth Corrections	Juv. Court Bench/Youth Parole Authority
VA	Camp Washington	Youth Services International, Inc.	Commonwealth of VA; City of Richmond
WA	Basic Training Boot Camp	Juvenile Rehabilitation Administration	Juvenile Rehabilitation Administration

[1]Scheduled to start July 1, 1996.

[2]Operates in two locations; data has been combined.

[3]Judges act on probation officer recommendations.

Table 4.2   Juvenile Boot Camps: Year Started, Capacity, and Length of Stay

State	Name of Program	Year Began	Capacity	Usual Stay in Days	Stay Can Be Extended (Length)
AL	Autauga	1994	78	28	Yes, for 7 days
AL	Chalkville	1991	24	28	Yes, for 17 days
AL	Thomasville	1992	37	28	Yes, for 17 days
AR	First Academy	1996	24	90	Yes, for 30 days
CA	L.E.A.D.	1992/1993	120	120	Yes, for 30 days
CA	Drug Treatment	1990	210	168	Yes, for 60 days
CA	Twin Pines	1993	70	180	Yes, for indefinite period
CA	R.O.T.C.	1995	40	150	Yes, for 30 days
CO	Camp Falcon	1994	80	60	No
DC	Thurgood Marshall	1991	30	540	Yes
FL	Martin County	1994	30	125-130	Yes, for 30 days
FL	Pinellas County	1993	30	120	Yes, for indefinite period
FL	Leon County	1994	60	240	Yes
FL	Regimental Wilderness	1994	30	120	Yes, for 30 days
GA	Irwin Youth	1995	316	90	No
IN	Camp Summit	1995	42	90	Yes
IA	Highly Structured	1995	50	90	No
KY	Green River	1994	40	90	No
LA	Tallulah	1994	396	90-180	Yes, for 90 days
MD	Doncaster	1994	30	84	Yes
MS	Columbia	1993	175	105	Yes, for indefinite period
MS	Oakley	1992	200	105	Yes, for indefinite period
NJ	Wharton Tract	1996	60-70	120	Yes
NY	Leadership Academy	1992	30	180	Yes, for 60 days
OH	Camp Roulston	1993	30	90	Yes, for 30 days
PA	Abraxas	1994	105	105	Yes, for 35 days
PA	Boot and Hat	1994	90	90	Yes, for 30 days
SC	J.R.O.T.C.	1993	150	240	No
TX	Challenge	1988	12	180	Yes, for 180 days
TX	C.C.I.	1995	54	180	Yes, for 30 days
TX	Treatment & Rehabilitation	1993		1-180	
TX	S.T.A.R.	1995	24	168	Yes
UT	Genesis	1994	72	54	Yes, for indeterminate period
VA	Washington	1996	45	150	Yes, for 30 days
WA	Basic Training	1996	48	120	No

believe a one-day participation in drill will be effective. The longest program we surveyed was the Thurgood Marshall Boot Camp in the District of Columbia, where juveniles stay for 540 days. The types of juveniles who participate in boot camp programs tend to be fairly similar (see Tables 4.3 and 4.4). However, unlike adult boot camps, juvenile programs are rarely limited to individuals convicted of or committed for their first serious offense, nor are juveniles apt to be required to volunteer. The typical juvenile in boot camp is a nonviolent male between the ages of fourteen and eighteen. These juveniles are placed in the boot camp by a juvenile judge. Only about 60 percent of the boot camps are limited to nonviolent offenders; the other 40 percent will accept offenders convicted of violent offenses.

Table 4.3   Age and Gender of Juvenile Boot Camp Enrollees

State	Name of Program	Age Limits	Gender
AL	Autauga	12-18	Males
AL	Chalkville	12-18	Females
AL	Thomasville	12-18	Males
AR	First Academy	14-17	Males
CA	L.E.A.D.	14-24	Males
CA	Drug Treatment	16-18	Males
CA	Twin Pines	15-19	Males
CA	R.O.T.C.	13-16	Males
CO	Camp Falcon	12-18	Males
DC	Thurgood Marshall	14-18	Males
FL	Martin County	14-18	Males
FL	Pinellas County	14-18	Males
FL	Leon County	14-18	Males
FL	Regimental Wilderness	14-17	Males
GA	Irwin Youth	11-17	Males
IN	Camp Summit	13-17	Males
IA	Highly Structured	14-17	Males
KY	Green River	14-17	Males
LA	Tallulah	13-20	Males
MD	Doncaster	15-18	Males
MS	Columbia	10-17	Both
MS	Oakley	10-17	Males
NJ	Wharton Tract	14-19	Males
NY	Leadership Academy	13-17	Males
OH	Camp Roulston	13-18	Males
PA	Abraxas	14-18	Males
PA	Boot and Hat	13-18	Males
SC	J.R.O.T.C.	9th–12th grade	Both
TX	Challenge	14-16	Males
TX	C.C.I.	11-16	Both
TX	Treatment & Rehabilitation	10-16	Both
TX	S.T.A.R.	10-14	Both
UT	Genesis	14-21	Males
VA	Washington	14-18	Males
WA	Basic Training	13-18	Both

Because of a heavy emphasis on education and counseling (see Table 4.6), it is no surprise that juvenile boot camp administrators rate rehabilitation as a very important goal of their programs (see Table 4.5). On a scale of 0 (not a goal) to 4 (a very important goal), administrators, on average, rated rehabilitation as a 3.7. Reducing recidivism also was rated as very important. The ratings for reducing crowding and costs, punishing, and deterring were varied. Nevertheless, it appears that reducing crowding and costs are more important goals than punishment. Note,

the ratings we received are very dependent upon the raters. Because different administrators have different goals and because goals tend to change over time, these results lack reliability. However, we can safely conclude that while rehabilitation and lowering recidivism are important goals, punishment is not.

Almost all of the boot camps that these juveniles go to emphasize a military atmosphere with military drill, platoon grouping, discipline, physical labor, military titles and uniforms (see Table 4.6). Only three of the boot camps

Table 4.4   Enrollment Limits for Juvenile Boot Camp Enrollees

State	Name of Program	Non-violent	First Offense	First Serious	First Commitment	Volunteers	Other Target Groups
AL	Autauga	No	No	No	No	No	Low risk
AL	Chalkville	No	No	No	No	No	Low risk
AL	Thomasville	No	No	No	No	No	Low risk
AR	First Academy	Yes	No	No	Yes	Yes	
CA	L.E.A.D.	Yes		No	Yes (to CYA)	Yes	
CA	Drug Treatment	No	No	No	No	No	Drug/Alcohol abuse history
CA	Twin Pines	Yes	No	No	No	No	Serious offenders
CA	R.O.T.C.	Yes	No	No	No	Yes	Failed in alternative programs
CO	Camp Falcon	No	No	No	No	No	
DC	Thurgood Marshall	No	Yes	Yes	Yes	Yes	Detained and committed youths
FL	Martin County	No	No	No	No	No	
FL	Pinellas County	No	No	No	No	No	Committed for life/capital/1st degree felony with 2+ prior felonies
FL	Leon County						
FL	Regimental Wilderness	No	No	No	No	No	
GA	Irwin Youth	No	No	No	No	No	
IN	Camp Summit	Yes	No	No	No	No	
IA	Highly Structured	Yes	No	No	No	Yes	Out-of-home placements
KY	Green River	No	Yes	No	No	No	
LA	Tallulah	Yes	Yes	Yes	Yes	No	Property crime offenders
MD	Doncaster	No	No	No	No	No	
MS	Columbia	Yes*	Yes	Yes	Yes	No	All training school youths
MS	Oakley	Yes*	Yes	Yes	Yes	No	All training school youths
NJ	Wharton Tract	Yes	No	No	No	Yes	Committed to NJ Training School
NY	Leadership academy	No	No	No	No	Yes	
OH	Camp Roulston	No	No	No	No	No	
PA	Abraxas	No	No	No	No	No	
PA	Boot and Hat	No	No	Yes	No	No	Probation violations
SC	J.R.O.T.C.	No	No	No	No	Yes	
TX	Challenge	Yes*	No	Yes	No	No	
TX	C.C.I.	No	No	No	No	No	
TX	Treatment & rehabilitation	No	No	No	No	No	Youths disruptive at school
TX	S.T.A.R.	Yes	Yes			Yes	Middle school
LIT	Genesis	No	No	No	No	No	
VA	Washington	Yes*	Yes	No	Yes	No	
WA	Basic Training	Yes	No	No	No	Yes	

*Also includes violent offenders.

Table 4.5   Goals of Juvenile Boot Camp Programs

		(Not a Goal = 0 to Very Important = 4)						
State	Name of Program	Reduce Crowding	Reduce Costs	Punishment	Protect Public	Deterrence	Rehabilitation	Lower Recidivism
AL	Autauga	3	2	2	4	2	4	4
AL	Chalkville	3	3	0	3	3	3	4
AL	Thomasville	3	2	0	4	3	4	4
AR	First Academy		3			4	4	
CA	L.E.A.D.	4	4	0	3	0	4	4
CA	Drug Treatment	1	1	1	4	4	4	4
CA	Twin Pines	4	4	3	4	4	4	4
CA	R.O.T.C.	4	2	0	4	1	4	4
CO	Camp Falcon	2	4	1	3	0	2	4
DC	Thurgood Marshall	2	1	3	3	3	4	3
FL	Martin County	3	3	2	4	4	4	4
FL	Pinellas County	0	0	1	4	4	4	3
FL	Leon County							
FL	Regimental Wilderness	4	1	3	3	2	2	3
GA	Irwin Youth	4	2	2	3	3	3	2
IN	Camp Summit	4	2	2	4	3	3	3
IA	Highly Structured	2	2	3	2	4	4	4
KY	Green River	0	2	0	1	4	3	4
LA	Tallulah	0	1	0	3	3	4	4
MD	Doncaster	2	2	0	4	4	4	4
MS	Columbia	4	4	N/A	4	4	4	4
MS	Oakley	4	4	N/A	4	4	4	4
NJ	Wharton Tract	4	4	3	3	3	4	4
NY	Leadership Academy	3	3	0	3	2	4	4
OH	Camp Roulston	4	4	0	3	1	4	4
PA	Abraxas	2	2	0	2	0	4	3
PA	Boot and Hat	3	4	0	4	2	4	4
SC	J.R.O.T.C.	0	0	0	0	4	4	4
TX	Challenge	3	3	3	4	4	4	4
TX	C.C.I.	0	0	0	3	3	4	4
TX	Treatment & Rehabilitation	1	3	1	2	4	4	4
TX	S.T.A.R.	4	4	4	4	4	4	4
UT	Genesis	4	3	3	3	2	2	2
VA	Washington	2	2	2	4	4	4	4
WA	Basic Training	4	3	1	4	1	3	3

surveyed do not use military drill (the Alabama Department of Youth Services Chalkville HIT Program, the Highly Structured Program for Juveniles in Iowa, and the Genesis Youth Center in Utah). The Chalkville HIT Program and the Genesis Youth Center were also two of the four that do not have platoon grouping. All surveyed programs use discipline. We were concerned because there has been some debate about whether either group punishments or summary punishments are appropriate for juveniles. Some group punishments entail punishing the whole group for the poor performance of one individual while summary punishments involve

Table 4.6   Activities and Hours of Juvenile Boot Camp Programs

State	Name of Program	Military Drill	Discipline	Physical Labor	Physical Fitness/Sports	Challenge Adventure	Drug & Alcohol Education	Education	Vocational Training	Platoon Grouping	Summary Punishment	Group Rewards/ Punishment	P.T/ Drill/Work	Education Counseling
													Hours/Day	
AL	Autauga	Yes	Yes	No	Yes	Yes	No	Yes	No	Yes	No	No	3	3.5
AL	Chalkville	No	Yes	No	Yes	Yes	Yes	Yes	No	No	No	No	2	6
AL	Thomasville	Yes	Yes	Yes	Yes	Yes	Yes	Yes	No	No	No	No	3	6.5
AR	First Academy	Yes	Yes	No	Yes	Yes	Yes	Yes	Yes	Yes	No	Yes	—	—
CA	L.E.A.D.	Yes	Yes	No	Yes	No	Yes	Yes	No	Yes	No	Yes	3	6
CA	Twin Pines	Yes	Yes	Yes	Yes	Yes	Yes	Yes	Yes	Yes	No	Yes	4.0	3.5
CA	Drug Treatment	Yes	Yes	Yes	Yes	No	Yes	Yes	Yes	Yes	Yes	Yes	2	8
CA	R.O.T.C.	Yes	Yes	Yes	Yes	No	Yes	Yes	Yes	Yes	Yes	Yes	—	—
CO	Camp Falcon	Yes	Yes	No	Yes	No	No	Yes	No	Yes	Yes	Yes	8	4
DC	Thurgood Marshall	Yes	Yes	No	Yes	Yes	Yes	Yes	Yes	Yes	Yes	Yes	2	5
FL	Martin County	Yes	Yes	Yes	Yes	Yes	Yes	Yes	Yes	Yes	Yes	No	10	6
FL	Pinellas County	Yes	Yes	Yes	Yes	Yes	Yes	Yes	No	Yes	Yes	Yes	2	8
FL	Leon County	Yes	Yes	No	Yes	No	Yes	Yes	Yes	Yes	No	No	3	12
FL	Regimental Wilderness	Yes	Yes	Yes	Yes	Yes	Yes	Yes	Yes	Yes	No	Group reward only	2-3	8-10
GA	Irwin Youth	Yes	Yes	Yes	Yes	No	Yes	Yes	No	Yes	No	Yes	6	5
IN	Camp Summit	Yes	Yes	No	Yes	—	Yes	Yes	—	Yes	Yes	Yes	5	4
IA	Highly Structured	No	Yes	Yes	Yes	No	Yes	Yes	Yes	Yes	No	Yes	2-3	—
KY	Green River	Yes	Yes	Yes	Yes	Yes	Yes	Yes	Yes	Yes	Yes	Group reward only	5	7.5

(Continued)

Table 4.6 (Continued)

State	Name of Program	Military Drill	Discipline	Physical Labor	Physical Fitness/Sports	Challenge Adventure	Drug & Alcohol Education	Education	Vocational Training	Platoon Grouping	Summary Punishment	Group Rewards/ Punishment	P.T./ Drill/Work	Education Counseling
													Hours/Day	Hours/Day
LA	Tallulah	Yes	Yes	Yes	Yes	No	Yes	Yes	No	Yes	No	No	3	6
MD	Doncaster	Yes	Yes	Yes	Yes	Yes	Yes	Yes	Yes	Yes	No	No	1	6
MS	Columbia	Yes	Yes	Yes	Yes	Yes	Yes	Yes	Yes	Yes	N/A	Group reward only	3	5
MS	Oakley	Yes	Yes	Yes	Yes	Yes	Yes	Yes	Yes	Yes	N/A	Group reward only	3	5
NJ	Wharton Tract	Yes	Yes	Yes	Yes	Yes	Yes	Yes	Yes	Yes	—	Yes	7.5	6.5
NY	Leadership Academy	Yes	Yes	Yes	Yes	Yes	Yes	Yes	Yes	Yes	No	No	1.5-4	6-6.5
OH	Camp Roulston	Yes	Yes	No	Yes	Yes	Yes	Yes	Yes	Yes	No	No	4	8
PA	Abraxas	Yes	Yes	Yes	Yes	Yes	Yes	Yes	No	Yes	No	No	1.5	8-9
PA	Boot and Hat	Yes	Yes	Yes	Yes	No	Yes	Yes	No	Yes	No	Yes	4	7
SC	J.R.O.T.C.	Yes	Yes	No	Yes	Yes	Yes	Yes	Yes	Yes	Yes	Yes	3	13
TX	Challenge Program	Yes	Yes	No	Yes	Yes	Yes	Yes	No	No.	No	No	3	6
TX	C.C.I.	Yes	Yes	Yes	Yes	Yes	Yes	Yes	No	Yes	No	No	3	8
TX	Treatment & Rehabilitation	Yes	Yes	Yes	No	No	No	Yes	No	Yes	No	No	3	9
TX	S.T.A.R.	Yes	Yes	Yes	Yes	Yes	Yes	Yes	No	Yes	Yes	Yes	4	8
UT	Genesis	No	Yes	Yes	Yes	No	Yes	Yes	No	No	No	Yes	5.5	4
VA	Washington	Yes	Yes	Yes	Yes	Yes	Yes	Yes	Yes	Yes	No	Yes	2	7
WA	Basic Training	Yes	Yes	Yes	Yes	Yes	Yes	Yes	Yes	Yes	No	Yes	5	7

Table 4.7   Degree of Military Involvement in Juvenile Boot Camp Programs

		Staff		Juvenile
State	Name of Program	Military Titles	Military Uniforms	Military Uniforms
AL	Autauga	No	No	No
AL	Chalkville	No	No	No
AL	Thomasville	No	No	No
AR	First Academy	Yes	Yes	No
CA	L.E.A.D.	Yes	Yes	Yes
CA	Drug Treatment	Yes	Yes	Yes
CA	Twin Pines	Yes	Yes	Yes
CA	R.O.T.C.	Yes	Yes	Yes
CO	Camp Falcon	Yes	Yes	Yes
DC	Thurgood Marshall	Yes	Yes	Yes
FL	Martin County	Yes	No, Police Uniforms	Yes
FL	Pinellas County	Yes	No	Yes
FL	Leon County	Yes	Yes	No
FL	Regimental Wilderness	Yes	Yes	Yes
GA	IrwinYouth	Yes	Yes	Yes
IN	Camp Summit	Yes	Yes	Yes
IA	Highly Structured	No	No	No
KY	Green River	No	No	No
LA	Tallulah	Yes	Yes	No
MD	Doncaster	Yes	Yes	Yes
MS	Columbia	Yes	Yes	Yes
MS	Oakley	Yes	Yes	Yes
NJ	Wharton Tract	Yes	Yes	Yes
NY	Leadership Academy	Yes	Yes	Yes
OH	Camp Roulston	Yes	Yes	Yes
PA	Abraxas	Yes	Yes	Yes
PA	Boot and Hat	Yes	Yes	Yes
SC	J.R.O.T.C.	No	Yes	Yes
TX	Challenge	No	No	No
TX	C.C.I.	Yes	Yes	Yes
TX	Treatment & Rehabilitation*	Yes	Yes	No
TX	S.T.A.R.*	Yes	Yes	Yes
UT	Genesis	No	No	No
VA	Washington	Yes	Yes	Yes
WA	Basic Training	Yes	Yes	Yes

*Do not live at facility.

immediate sanctions such as doing push-ups or running laps by the individual.

Nine of the boot camps use neither group rewards and punishments nor summary punishments. On the other hand, about fourteen of the programs use either group rewards and punishments or summary punishments and about twelve use both methods. The Green River Boys' Camp in Kentucky, the Columbia and Oakley Training Schools in Mississippi, and the Regimental Wilderness Program in Florida use both group rewards and summary punishments but do not use group punishments (see Table 4.6). About 75 percent use military titles and uniforms for staff and juveniles (see Table 4.7).

In addition to the military atmosphere, the majority of the programs include physical labor in the daily activities (see Table 4.6). All but one of the boot camps engage youth in physical fitness and sports activity, and the majority also

Table 4.8   Dropout and Expulsion from Juvenile Boot Camp Programs

State	Name of Program	Voluntary Dropout			Expulsion		
		Yes/No	%	Consequence	Yes/No	%	Consequence
AL	Autauga	No	0		Yes	10	Returned to court
AL	Chalkville	No	0		Yes	5	Returned to court
AL	Thomasville	No	0		Yes	14	Returned to court
AR	First Academy	Yes					
CA	L.E.A.D.	No	0		Yes	30	Returned to standard correctional programs
CA	Drug Treatment	No	0		Yes	5	Returned to court, placed in more secure camp
CA	Twin Pines	Yes	2	Returned to court	Yes	3	Returned to court
CA	R.O.T.C.	Yes		Returned to juvenile hall	Yes		Returned to juvenile hall
CO	Camp Falcon	No	0		Yes	3	Probation revocation and commitment
DC	Thurgood Marshall	Yes	2	Transferred to another unit	Yes	3	Transferred to another unit
FL	Martin County	No	0		No	0	
FL	Pinellas County	No	0		Yes	2	Transferred to other program
FL	Leon County	No	0		Yes[1]	5	
FL	Regimental Wilderness	No	0		Yes	<10	Transferred to other facility
GA	Irwin Youth	No	0			0	
IN	Camp Summit	No	0			0	
IA	Highly Structured	No	0				
KY	Green River	No	0		Yes	S	Transferred to other facility
LA	Tallulah	No	0		Yes	2	Transferred to more secure Facility
MD	Doncaster	No	0		No	0	
MS	Columbia	No	0		Yes	1	Referred back to court
MS	Oakley	No	0		Yes	1	Referred back to court
NJ	Wharton Tract	Yes					
NY	Leadership Academy	No	0		No	0	
OH	Camp Roulston	No	0		Yes	1	Returned to juvenile court
PA	Abraxas	No	0		Yes	0	Referred back to court
PA	Boot and Hat	No	0		Yes	10	Sent to court or to year long VisionQuest Impact Program
SC	J.R.O.T.C.	Yes	1	Returned to non-JROTC dorm	Yes	20	Returned to non-JROTC dorm
TX	Challenge Program	No	0		Yes	1	Returned to institution/court
TX	C.C.I.	No	0		No	0	
TX	Treatment & Rehabilitation	Yes		Returned to court	No	0	
TX	S.T.A.R.	No	0		Yes	0	Sent to youth commission or placement
UT	Genesis	No	0		Yes	3	Returned to detention
VA	Washington	No	0		No	0	
WA	Basic Training	Yes		Transferred to institution	Yes		Transferred to institution

[1]Released only for medical reasons.

have some type of challenge or adventure programming for the juveniles. Overall, juveniles spend between one-to-ten hours per day in physical training, military drill, and work. For example, while youth in the Boot Camp in Doncaster, Maryland only spend one hour per day in these activities, youth in the Martin County Sheriff's Office Juvenile Boot Camp in

Table 4.9   Graduation From Juvenile Boot Camp Programs

State	Name of Program	%	Public Ceremony
AL	Autauga	90	Yes
AL	Chalkville	95	No
AL	Thomasville	86	Yes
AR	First Academy		Yes
CA	L.E.A.D.	70	Yes
CA	Drug Treatment	95	No
CA	Twin Pines	95	No
CA	R.O.T.C.		Yes
CO	Camp Falcon	94	Yes
DC	Thurgood Marshall	95	Yes
FL	Martin County	95	Yes
FL	Pinellas County	98	Yes
FL	Leon County	95	No
FL	Regimental Wilderness	>90	Yes
GA	Irwin Youth	100	No
IN	Camp Summit	100	No
IA	Highly Structured		
KY	Green River	92	Yes
LA	Tallulah	98	No
MD	Doncaster	100	Yes
MS	Columbia	99	Yes
MS	Oakley	99	Yes
NJ	Wharton Tract		Yes
NY	Leadership Academy	100	No
OH	Camp Roulston	99	Yes
PA	Abraxas	100	Yes
PA	Boot and Hat	90	Yes
SC	J.R.O.T.C.	80	No
TX	Challenge Program	99	No
TX	C.C.I.	90	Yes
TX	Treatment & Rehabilitation	100	Yes
TX	S.T.A.R.	99	Yes
UT	Genesis	0[1]	NIA
VA	Washington	100	Yes
WA	Basic Training		Yes

[1]The Genesis Youth Center does not graduate youths.

Florida spend ten hours per day in these activities. On the average, juveniles spend about three and a half hours on physical training, military drill, and work, depending on the boot camp.

In comparison, they will spend, on average, about six and a half to seven hours in educational classes or counseling (see Table 4.6). No juvenile boot camp program spends less than three and a half hours per day on education and counseling. In some programs, such as the Junior Reserve Officer's Training Corps in South Carolina and the Leon County Sheriff's Office Boot Camp in Florida, youth respectively spend thirteen and twelve hours per day on these activities. More specifically, juvenile boot camp programs offer drug and alcohol counseling, education programs, and vocational training. Youth in all but three of the programs spend some time in drug and alcohol counseling. All programs surveyed had educational programs, and about half of the surveyed programs offered vocational training. The boot camps also vary in their dropout and expulsion policies and rates (see Table 4.8). Our survey reveals that most

Table 4.10   Supervision and Aftercare in Juvenile Boot Camp Programs

State	Name of Program	For Whom	Days	Capacity	Setting
AL	Autauga	Some	90		Home with family
AL	Chalkville	Some	90		Home with family
AL	Thomasville	Some	90		Home with family
AR	First Academy	All	180	96	Home with family; community transition center; crisis center
CA	L.E.A.D.	All	180	120	Home with family; halfway house; group home; other
CA	Drug Treatment	All	180	250	Home with family
CA	Twin Pines	Some	180	35	Home with family; halfway house; Conservation Corps.
CA	R.O.T.C.	All	240	60-80	Home with family
CO	Camp Falcon[1]				
DC	Thurgood Marshall	Some	180-360		Home with family; group home
FL	Martin County	All	240	90	Home with family
FL	Pinellas County	Some	120-240	30	Home with family
FL	Leon County	All	120	30	Home with family
FL	Regimental Wilderness[2]	All	90	25	Halfway house; day treatment
GA	Irwin Youth	Some	Varies		
IN	Camp Summit	All	180-270	100	Correctional facility
IA	Highly Structured	All	180	400+	Home with family
KY	Green River	All	90	Unlimited	Home with family; group/foster home; private child care facility
LA	Tallulah	Some	360-990		Home with family; group home
MD	Doncaster	All	270-360	105/yr	Home with family
MS	Columbia	All	360	Unlimited	Home with family; transitional living centers
MS	Oakley	All	360	Unlimited	Home with family; transitional living centers
NJ	Wharton Tract	All	240	100	Home with family; group home; residential program
NY	Leadership Academy	All	150	30	Home with family
OH	Camp Roulston	All	270	120/yr	Home with family
PA	Abraxas	All	Varies	24	Home with family; group home; residential placements
PA	Boot and Hat	Some	1 weekend per month for 3 months	Unlimited	Platoon
SC	J.R.O.T.C.	Some	180-360		Home with family; halfway house; group home
TX	Challenge	All	90	Unlimited	Home with family
TX	C.C.I.	Some	Remainder of probation	0	
TX	Treatment & Rehabilitation	All	Indefinite		Home with family
TX	S.T.A.R.	All	180-360		Home with family
UT	Genesis	Some	Varies		Home with family; group home; foster care
VA	Washington	All	180	100	Home with family
WA	Basic Training	All	Remainder of disposition		Home with family; group home; foster care

[1]Information on aftercare program has not yet been gathered.
[2]This is a day treatment program.

boot camp programs do not allow voluntary dropout. When voluntary dropout is permitted, very few juveniles actually decide to drop out of the program. Indeed, dropping out of the boot camp programs is very much discouraged. For example, while both the Twin Pines Ranch in California and the Junior Reserve Officers' Training Corps in South Carolina permit the

Table 4.11   Aftercare Components of Juvenile Boot Camp Programs

State	Name of Program	Treatment	Employment	Education	Vocational Training	Family Counseling	Intensive Supervision
AL	Autauga	No	No	No	No	No	Yes
AL	Chalkville	No	No	No	No	No	Yes
AL	Thomasville	No	No	No	No	No	Yes
AR	First Academy[1]	Yes	Yes	Yes	Yes	Yes	
CA	L.E.A.D.		Yes	Yes			Yes
CA	Drug Treatments	Yes	Yes	Yes	Yes	Yes	Yes
CA	Twin Pines[1]	Yes	Yes	Yes	No	Yes	Yes
CA	R.O.T.C[1]	Yes	Yes	Yes	Yes	Yes	Yes
CO	Camp Falcon						
DC	Thurgood Marshall	Yes	Yes	Yes	Yes	Yes	Yes
FL	Martin County	Yes	Yes	Yes	Yes	Yes	Yes
FL	Pinellas County	Yes	Yes	Yes	No	Yes	Yes
FL	Leon County	Yes	Yes	Yes	No	Yes	Yes
FL	Regimental Wilderness[1]	Yes	Yes	Yes	Yes	Yes	No
GA	Irwin Youth						
IN	Camp Summit	Yes	No	Yes	No	Yes	Yes
IA	Highly Structured	Yes	No	Yes	Yes	Yes	Yes
KY	Green River[1]	Yes	Yes	Yes	Yes	Yes	Yes
LA	Tallulah[1]	Yes	No	Yes	No	Yes	Yes
MD	Doncaster[1]	Yes	Yes	Yes	Yes	Yes	Yes
MS	Columbia[1]	Yes	Yes	Yes	Yes	Yes	Yes
MS	Oakleys	Yes	Yes	Yes	Yes	Yes	Yes
NJ	Wharton Tract	Yes	Yes	Yes	Yes	Yes	Yes
NY	Leadership Academy[1]	Yes	Yes	Yes	Yes	Yes	Yes
OH	Camp Roulston[1]	Yes	Yes	Yes	Yes	Yes	Yes
PA	Abraxas	Yes	Yes	Yes	No	Yes	Yes
PA	Boot and Hats	Yes	No	No	No	Yes	Yes
SC	J.R.O.T.C.[1]	Yes	Yes	Yes	Yes	Yes	Yes
TX	Challenge[1]	Yes		Yes		Yes	Yes
TX	C.C.I.[1]					Yes	
TX	Treatment & Rehabilitation	Yes	Yes	Yes	No	Yes	Yes
TX	S.T.A.R.	Yes		Yes		Yes	Yes
UT	Genesis[2]						
VA	Washington	Yes	Yes	Yes	Yes	Yes	Yes
WA	Basic Training[1]	Yes	Yes	Yes	Yes	Yes	Yes

[1]Other services also offered.
[2]Genesis offers a wide range of options. There is not a formal aftercare program.

youth to drop out, only 2 and 1 percent, respectively, do so. Almost all boot camps have a procedure to expel juveniles who have not met the program requirements. The percentages of those expelled are usually fairly low (about 10 percent). Some programs, such as L.E.A.D. in California tend to have higher expulsion rates. L.E.A.D. has an expulsion rate of about

30 percent. On the other hand, several boot camps report that although expulsions are possible, no juveniles are expelled (the Abraxas Leadership Development Program in Pennsylvania and the S.T.A.R. Day Boot Camp in Texas). Juveniles who drop out or who are expelled are usually returned to either juvenile court or to their institution of origin for longer sentences.

The boot camps surveyed also report high graduation rates (see Table 4.9). The majority of the boot camps report rates of above 90 percent, and several have graduation rates of 100 percent (the average rate is 95 percent). The Juvenile Boot Camp at Doncaster, Maryland, the Youth Leadership Academy in New York, and Camp Washington in Virginia allow neither dropouts nor expulsions; all participants must graduate from the program. Most of the programs have public graduation ceremonies for the graduates.

On release, boot camp graduates most often participate in aftercare programs with varying levels of supervision (see Table 4.10). While participating in aftercare, the graduates stay at home with their families. These aftercare programs vary as much as the boot camps themselves do. The capacity of the programs tends to be fairly large as many have over 100 juveniles. Several aftercare programs report an unlimited capacity. There are several, however, which are kept small. For example, the Abraxas Youth Leadership Development Program reports a capacity of twenty-four delinquents. On average, boot camp graduates stay in these aftercare programs for about a year, but again this varies greatly. The three boot camps in Alabama keep graduates in their aftercare programs for three months. On the other hand, graduates from the Tallulah Correctional Center for Youth in Louisiana can participate in their aftercare programs for up to three years.

While in the aftercare programs, boot camp graduates participate in a wide array of activities (see Table 4.11). Most programs include treatment, education, family counseling, and intensive supervision as components of the aftercare. About half of the programs also include employment and/or vocational training. Beyond these basic components, aftercare programs emphasize a variety of other elements such as, among others, anti-gang programs, community service projects, mentorships, independent living training, recreation programs, and financial resources and assistance. This short survey of the juvenile boot camps indicates substantial differences among the programs, both during the incarceration phase and the aftercare phase. While there are some consistencies (for example, a military atmosphere and physical training), there are many differences that we expect have varying impacts on the participating youth.

EXAMINING THE EFFECTIVENESS OF BOOT CAMP PROGRAMS

Most of the research examining correctional boot camps comes from studies of adult programs. Some research indicates that boot camps can reduce prison crowding if they are designed as early release mechanisms (MacKenzie & Piquero, 1994). While the programs may have the potential to reduce prison crowding, in actuality they seldom do. For example, in the multisite evaluation, two of the five boot camp programs appeared to save prison beds (MacKenzie & Piquero, 1994; MacKenzie & Souryal, 1994). In the remaining three states, the boot camp program appeared to cost the state jurisdiction prison beds. Thus, the evidence that boot camp prisons reduce crowding is not extremely persuasive to date. Given the rapid proliferation of boot camp prisons across the nation and the fact that reducing recidivism is one of the major objectives of many of the programs, it is somewhat surprising that there have been few empirical studies of the impact of these programs on recidivism. Much of the existing literature has been produced by state correctional officials themselves (Florida Department of Corrections, 1990; Flowers, Carr, & Ruback, 1991; State of Texas, 1989; New York State Department of Correctional Services, 1992). However, after reviewing some of these studies, Cullen, Wright and Applegate (1993) warned that the results should be viewed with caution due to methodological problems. A particularly important criticism centered on the failure of these efforts to rely on experimental designs in their group comparisons. Compounding this problem, argued Cullen and his colleagues, was the lack of statistical controls for potentially important variables (such as community supervision intensity) whose levels differ among comparison groups. Although not a random assignment study, MacKenzie et al. (1995) did control for differences among groups in a multisite study of boot camps in eight states. The analysis suggested that those who completed boot camp performed about the same as their comparison group counterparts. The researchers found some evidence that suggested a reduction in recidivism for boot camp participants in programs where participants received three or more hours of treatment or education, volunteered, and had follow-up aftercare. They ended with the question: "Does the military atmosphere add anything above and beyond a short-term, quality prison treatment program?" In another study, MacKenzie and Brame (1995) found that boot camp releasees adjusted more positively than comparison samples during community supervision in only one of five sites. Thus, both the recidivism studies and the positive adjustment studies suggest that there may be some programs that have positive impacts on participants. However, the specific components that lead to the positive effects are unclear. To date, research examining boot camps has shown very little negative impact from the programs. Offenders report being drug free and physically healthy when they leave the boot camps (MacKenzie & Souryal, 1992). They also believed the program helped them, and they were optimistic about the future. This was true of the "enhanced" boot camp programs that emphasized treatment as well as programs that focused predominantly on military training, hard labor, and discipline. However, when MacKenzie and Souryal (1995) examined changes in antisocial attitudes, they found that those in the boot camps as well as the comparison samples of prisoners became less antisocial. Again, results on the effectiveness of the boot camps are mixed, and we are left with questions about the specific components of the camps that led to positive change. In some exploratory analyses, MacKenzie and Souryal (1995) did find some evidence that participants became less antisocial in boot camps that devoted more time to rehabilitation, had higher dismissal rates, and were voluntary.

RESEARCH ON JUVENILE BOOT CAMP PROGRAMS

Few studies of juvenile boot camp programs have been completed. The Office of Juvenile Justice and Delinquency Prevention of the United States Department of Justice funded three juvenile boot camps in Cleveland, Ohio, Denver, Colorado, and Mobile, Alabama. The intention was to demonstrate and test juvenile boot camps for nonviolent offenders. The boot camps, opened in April 1992, combined military regimentation and conditioning with rehabilitation and aftercare services. The study used random assignment to the programs (versus comparison facilities) so that differences in recidivism rates could be compared within each state. Early analyses of the data indicate no difference between the boot camp graduates and comparison samples in two sites, and in the third, the boot camp graduates actually had higher recidivism rates than the control group. In all the sites, there were problems related to the development and implementation of the boot camps, and the researchers speculate that these difficulties are most likely the reason for the failure to see a positive impact of the boot camps. In 1992, the California Youth Authority (CYA) established a boot camp called L.E.A.D. (Leadership, Esteem, Ability, and Discipline) designed to serve the state's nonviolent and least serious offenders (Bottcher & Isorena, 1996). Its expressed goals were to reduce recidivism and to provide a cost effective sentencing option for these juveniles. The California Youth Authority research branch has initiated a study of the program including a random assignment comparing participants to controls. The researchers provide valuable yearly evaluation reports describing interim information on the implementation and impact of the program. While the full results of the recidivism portion of the study are not yet available, preliminary analysis comparing the boot camp juveniles with the comparison sample do not show any significant differences in recidivism during the first thirty days after release. However, the researchers caution that the data is very limited at this time. As was found with adults, the boot camp participants in L.E.A.D. report being physically healthy and safer in the boot camp in comparison to the control group. Also, similar to the adult programs, the data examining cost savings indicated that the program has the potential to reduce costs. However, the researchers cautioned that there are many factors at play that could rapidly decrease any savings realized by the program. For example, an examination of judicial recommendations indicated that some judges may be committing youth to detention for the boot camp; youth who would not otherwise be sent to a facility. Between 29 and 33 percent of the entrants do not complete the boot camp programs. Most of the time this is because of gang-related conflicts, general disciplinary problems related to lack of motivation, and/or assaultiveness.

Florida operates more juvenile boot camps than any other state in the nation (Cass & Kaltenecker, 1996). An unusual aspect of the programs is the partnership between local and state governments. The camps are run by the county sheriff's departments with oversight by the Florida Department of Juvenile Justice. General guidelines are established by statute and defined by administrative rules; otherwise, each locality has the flexibility to develop a program that makes use of local resources and involves the community. All of the camps are required to last at least six months and to provide intensive education, physical training, and rehabilitative programs appropriate for children. According to early reports, most of those who enter the programs eventually graduate (87 percent or more) and 75 percent do so in the expected four months.

Preliminary information on recidivism from one of the boot camps shows that 74 percent of the youths who finished the program in 1993 were arrested in 1994 (*Miami Tribune,* March 21, 1995), a number the program administrators found to be disappointingly large. In contrast to the adult programs, the Florida boot camps target juveniles committed for serious offenses or who have a record of past felony adjudications. Preliminary data from the programs indicates that juveniles placed in Florida's boot camps have extensive histories of delinquency.

This short review of the literature on boot camp programs for juveniles and adults demonstrates that most research has focused on individual programs and the impact of these programs on later criminal activities. The problem is that the programs differ dramatically in goals and components. Thus, knowledge about the effectiveness of one program may be dependent upon very atypical aspects of the program or even a charismatic leader, and not necessarily be related to boot-camp-type characteristics of the program. The research results may show us a program that works but not why it works. To understand why the program works, we need to know more about the relationship between the specific components of the program and the impacts on the individuals involved.

THE DEBATE ABOUT CORRECTIONAL BOOT CAMPS FOR JUVENILES

Boot camps are controversial for a variety of reasons (MacKenzie & Hebert, 1996; MacKenzie & Souryal, 1995a; MacKenzie & Parent, 1992; Meachum, 1990; Morash & Rucker, 1990). Much of it has to do with a kind of instinctive reaction toward the military atmosphere. It is important, however, to separate this instinctive reaction from the debates that occur among people who are knowledgeable about juvenile programming and corrections in general. Here, there is a much more interesting debate. One perspective exhibited by many knowledgeable correctional experts is what might be called a "Machiavellian point of view" (MacKenzie & Souryal, 1995). These individuals expect little direct benefit from the military atmosphere of the boot camp programs, but they are willing to use it to achieve two ends: early release for nonviolent offenders and additional funds for treatment programs (both within and outside prison). In their opinion, the popularity of the boot camps with policy makers and the public allows corrections to obtain early release, separate less serious offenders from others, and provide treatment that otherwise would not be available to these offenders.

From 1984 until 1990, the admission rate for juveniles in public facilities rose from just over 400,000 in 1984 to 570,000 in 1990 (Parent et al. 1994). A large percent of the juveniles in secure confinement are committed for nonviolent offenses (Krisberg & Austin, 1993). In these facilities, they are mixed with more serious violent offenders. The resulting crowding means that the time and resources devoted to rehabilitation, education, and other constructive activities become increasingly limited (Altschuler, 1994). Boot camps provide a method of separating the less serious juveniles from others and a way to develop a daily schedule of constructive and therapeutic activities appropriate for these juveniles. The "get tough" appearance of the camps answers the policy makers' need to emphasize punishment, public safety, and offender accountability. However, as was shown in the survey we did of juvenile programs, those responsible for developing the boot camps are interested in rehabilitation as well as recidivism reduction. They are much less interested in the punishment aspects of the camps.

In contrast with those who use the boot camps to surreptitiously achieve their correctional goals, others fear the dangers of boot camps. Despite the potential benefits, many psychologists with experience in both corrections and behavioral change strongly argue against the boot camp programs. They believe that the potential dangers of the military models are too great to compromise for early release or funds for treatment. Furthermore, they argue that boot camps cannot provide a mechanism for treatment because many of the characteristics of the programs (confrontation, punishment instead of reward) are antithetical to treatment. The confrontational interactions may be particularly damaging for some individuals such as those who have been abused in the past or others who have problems with dependency in relationships. Morash and Rucker (1990) contend that aspects of the boot camps actually may inflict damage on participants.

Additionally, the boot camp opponents fear that, even though some programs may be used as early-release mechanisms, most have a serious potential for widening the net. This point is particularly critical for the newly developing juvenile programs. The boot camps appear to be a deceptively simple way of managing the disruptive juvenile who is a status offender or who has been involved in relatively minor criminal activities. There is a real danger that after working so hard for the past twenty-five years to deinstitutionalize status offenders, the boot camps will increasingly be used for status offenders (Holden & Kapler, 1995). The fear is that the programs appear to many to be the perfect solution for unruly and undisciplined juveniles.

There are some additional concerns about using these programs for juveniles. Juveniles are in a different stage of development than adults. It may be difficult for juveniles to obey authority figures if they do not believe that such obedience is in their own best interest. They may rail against the injustice of group punishment. Some juveniles, such as those who have been victimized in the past, may have additional problems that make the boot camps a harmful experience for them. Furthermore, the programs may not address the risk factors that are important precursors of delinquency (Gottfredson, Sealock & Koper, 1996). For example, by removing the children from the community, the boot camps may not provide family counseling or help the youth develop new and positive social activities with nondelinquent peers.

Practitioners also express concern about the need for individualized programming and whether the boot camps with group punishments and rewards will be able to address the variety of needs of these youth. Lipsey's (1992) meta-analysis of treatment programs found that interventions of longer duration involving more structured and focused treatment that were behavioral and skill-oriented, as well as those incorporating multimodal treatments were more effective than less structured and unfocused approaches. While the boot camps may have the required structure, they may lack other principles of successful treatment programs such as emphasizing rewarding good behavior much more frequently than punishing bad behavior, individualized programming, and skill-oriented education.

Yet, a third perspective argues that the military atmosphere is an effective model for changing offenders. Persons who have worked in drug treatment programs—where strict rules, discipline, and confrontational interactions are common—seem to be more comfortable with the military model. Military personnel assert that the leadership model of basic training provides new and appropriate techniques for correctional programming. Of course, many of those responsible for the development and implementation of individual boot camp programs are committed to and believe in the viability of this approach. They argue that the stress created in boot camp may shake up the inmates and make them ready to change and take advantage of the treatment and aftercare programs offered. Further, the military atmosphere of boot camp actually may enhance the effect of this treatment by keeping the offenders physically and mentally healthy and enabling them to focus on their education, treatment, and therapy.

So, the debate continues. What is clear is that these boot camps are proliferating across the nation, yet we do not know much about them— their effects on the individuals involved nor the impact on correctional systems. The main point may be that we need to learn exactly what are the beneficial aspects of the camps and what are the negative aspects. Certainly, we can assume that the effect of the camps will differ depending on the needs of the individuals involved. We need detailed information on the specific components of the programs and how these components affect those involved. We need to learn what type of boot camp is (or is not) effective for specific types of offenders.

REFERENCES

Altschuler, D. M. (1994). Tough and Smart Juvenile Incarceration: Reintegrating Punishment, Deterrence and Rehabilitation. *St. Louis University Public Law Review 14*, 217–237.

Austin, J., Jones, M., & Bollard, M. (1993). *The Growing Use of Jail Boot Camps: The Current State of the Art.* Research in Brief. Washington, DC: National Institute of Justice.

Bottcher, J., Isorena, T., Lara, J., & Belnas, M. (1995). LEAD: A Boot Camp and Intensive Parole Program: An Impact Evaluation. Unpublished report to the Legislature of the State of California, Department of the Youth Authority, Research Division. Sacramento, CA.

Bottcher, J., & Isorena, T. (1996). First Year Evaluation of the California Youth. Authority's Boot Camp. In D. L. MacKenzie & E. Hebert (Eds.), *Boot Camp Prisons: A Tough Intermediate Sanction.* Washington, DC: National Institute of Justice.

Cass, E. S., & Kaltenecker, N. (1996). The Development and Operation of Juvenile Boot Camps in Florida. In D. L. MacKenzie & E. Hebert (Eds.), *Boot Camp Prisons: A Tough Intermediate Sanction.* Washington, DC: National Institute of Justice.

Clark, C. L., & Aziz, D. W. (1996). Shock Incarceration in New York State: Philosophy, Results, and Limitations. In D. L. MacKenzie & E. Hebert (Eds.), *Boot Camp Prisons: A Tough*

Intermediate Sanction. Washington, DC: National Institute of Justice.

Cowles, E. L., & Castellano, T. C. (1995). *Boot Camp Drug Treatment and Aftercare Intervention: An Evaluation Review.* A Final Summary Report to the National Institute of Justice. Washington, DC: National Institute of Justice.

Cronin, R. C. (1994). Boot Camps for Adult and Juvenile Offenders: Overview and Update. National Institute of Justice Research Report. Washington, DC: National Institute of Justice.

Cullen F. T., Wright, J. P., & Applegate, B. K. (1993). Control in the Community: The Limits of Reform? Paper presented at the International Association of Residential and Community Alternatives, Philadelphia.

Florida Department of Corrections, Bureau of Planning, Research, and Statistics. (1990). Research Report: Boot Camp Evaluation. Tallahassee, FL.

Flowers, G. T., Carr, T. S., & Ruback, R. B. (1991). *Special Alternative Incarceration Evaluation.* Atlanta: Georgia Department of Corrections.

Gottfredson, D. C., Sealock, M. D., & Koper, C. S. (1996). Delinquency. In R. J. DiClemente, W. B. Hansen, & L. E. Ponton. *Handbook of Adolescent Health Risk Behavior.* New York: Plenum.

Gransky, L., Castellano, T. C., & Cowles, E. L. (1995). Is There a "Next Generation" of Shock Incarceration Facilities? The Evolving Nature of Goals, Program Components and Drug Treatment Services. In J. Smykla & W. Selke (Eds.), *Intermediate Sanctions: Sentencing in the 90s.* Cincinnati: Anderson.

Holden, G. A., & Kapler, R. A. (1995). Deinstitutionalizing Status Offenders: A Record of Progress. *Juvenile Justice, II*(2), 3–10.

Jablonski, J. R. (1991). *Implementing Total Quality Management: An Overview.* San Diego: Pfeiffer.

Krisberg, B., & Austin, J. F. (1993). Reinventing *Juvenile Justice.* Newbury Park, CA: Sage.

Lipsey, M. W. (1992). Juvenile Delinquency Treatment: A Meta-analytic Inquiry into the Variability of Effects. In T. D. Cook, H. Cooper, D. S. Cordray, H. Hartmann, L. V. Hedges, R. J. Light, T. A. Louis, & F. Mosteller (Eds.), *Meta-analysis for Explanation.* New York: Russell Sage Foundation.

MacKenzie, D. L., & Parent, D. G. (1992). Boot Camp Prisons for Young Offenders. In J. M. Byrne, A. J. Lurigio, & J. Petersilia (Eds.), *Smart Sentencing: The Emergence of Intermediate Sanctions.* London: Sage.

MacKenzie, D. L., Shaw, J. W., & Souryal, C. (1992). Characteristics Associated with Successful

Adjustment to Supervision. *Criminal Justice and Behavior, 19*(4), 437–454.

MacKenzie, D. L., & Piquero, A. (1994). The Impact of Shock Incarceration Programs on Prison Crowding. *Crime and Delinquency, 40*(2), 222–249.

MacKenzie, D. L., & Souryal, C. (1994). *Multi-Site Study of Shock Incarceration.* Final Reports I-IV and Executive Summary to the National Institute of Justice. Washington, DC: National Institute of Justice.

MacKenzie, D. L., & Brame, R. (1995). Shock Incarceration and Positive Adjustment During Community Supervision. *Journal of Quantitative Criminology, 11*(2), 111–142.

MacKenzie, D. L., Brame, R., McDowall, D., & Souryal, C. (1995). Boot Camp Prisons and Recidivism in Eight States. *Criminology, 33*(3), 401–430.

MacKenzie, D. L., & Souryal, C. (1995a). A Machiavellian Perspective on the Development of Boot Camp Prison: A Debate. University of Chicago Roundtable. Chicago: University of Chicago Press.

MacKenzie, D. L., & Souryal, C. (1995b). Inmate Attitude Change During Incarceration: A Comparison of Boot Camp with Traditional Prison. *Justice Quarterly, 12*(2), 325–354.

MacKenzie, D. L., & Hebert, V. (1996). Preface to *Correctional Boot Camps: A Tough Intermediate Sanction.* Washington, DC: National Institute of Justice.

Meachum, L. M. (1990). Boot Camp Prisons: Pros and Cons. Paper presented at Annual Meeting of American Society of Criminology, Baltimore, MD.

Morash, M., & Rucker, L. (1990). A Critical Look at the Ideal of Boot Camp as a Correctional Reform. *Crime and Delinquency, 36,* 204–222.

Morris, N., & Tonry, M. (1990). *Between Prison and Probation: Intermediate Punishments in a Rational Sentencing System.* New York: Oxford University Press.

New York State Department of Correctional Services and New York State Division of Parole. (1992). The Fourth Annual Report to the Legislature: Shock Incarceration–Shock Parole Supervision. Albany, NY.

Parent, D. G., Leiter, V., Kennedy, S., Livens, L., Wentworth, D., & Wilcox, S. (1994). *Conditions of Confinement: Juvenile Detention and Corrections Facilities.* Washington, DC: Office of Juvenile Justice and Delinquency Prevention, U.S. Department of Justice.

Texas Department of Corrections, Texas Adult Probation Commission, and Texas Criminal Justice Policy Council. (1989). Special Alternative Incarceration Program: Enhanced Substance Abuse Component. Austin, TX.

United States General Accounting Office. (1993). *Prison Boot Camps: Short-term Prison Costs Reduced, but Long-term Impact Uncertain.* Washington, DC: U.S. Government Printing Office.

Part II

The Debate About Boot Camps

5

Shock Incarceration: Rehabilitation or Retribution?

Doris Layton MacKenzie

Larry A. Gould

Lisa M. Riechers

James W. Shaw

Shock incarceration is a relatively new type of alternative to standard prison incarceration. The specific components of shock incarceration programs vary. The similarity among all programs is the short period of imprisonment in a military "boot camp" type program involving participation in military drills, rigorous exercise and maintenance of living quarters. Programs differ, however, in whether activities such as work, community service, education or counseling are also incorporated in the schedule of activities. In addition, some jurisdictions stress the need for intensive supervision upon release if the behavioral changes brought about by the shock incarceration are to be continued on the outside.

The major incentive for developing shock incarceration programs appears to be the need for cost-effective methods of reducing over crowding in prisons (Parent, 1988). Many people also feel that the enhanced discipline addresses a common problem of offenders and will, therefore, have rehabilitative benefits. After a national survey of shock incarceration programs, Parent (1988) stated that these programs have strong face validity to the public and to criminal justice personnel.[1] In his opinion this may account for their ready acceptance. Proponents of these programs argue that the short-term, demanding and rigorous boot camp component of the programs will be rehabilitative and deter future criminal behavior.

In the past there have been programs, called shock probation, which required offenders to spend a short period of time in prison (Vito, 1984; Parent, 1988). The major difference between the earlier shock probation programs and shock incarceration is the required participation in the drills and physical training that are components of the recent programs.

Reprinted by permission of Haworth Press from MacKenzie, D. L., Gould, L. A., Riechers, L. M. & Shaw, J. W. (1989). *Journal of Offender Counseling Services and Rehabilitation,* 14, 25–40.

The earliest shock incarceration programs began in 1983 in Georgia and Oklahoma (Parent, 1988). Since then another five states have started shock incarceration programs, five are developing programs and nine are seriously considering initiating such programs. Thus it is probable that in the next few years over 40 percent of the state correctional jurisdictions will have some type of shock incarceration program.

Of the seven state jurisdictions which presently have programs, most are designed for the young, non-violent, first-time offender who has a short sentence. In most jurisdictions offenders must volunteer, and additionally, they must not have any physical or mental impairment which would prohibit full participation in the program. There are large differences in the programs in terms of who controls placement and release decisions (judge, department of corrections or parole board). Jurisdictions also vary in whether, upon release, the offender receives intensive parole supervision.

To our knowledge there have been few formal evaluations of the shock incarceration programs. There are some early results from Georgia's Special Alternative Incarceration Program (SAIP) and from Oklahoma's Regimented Inmate Discipline Program (RID). During 1984, 260 offenders entered Georgia's SAIP and 92 percent of them successfully completed the program (Flowers, 1986). Of those who completed the program, 21.3 percent returned to prison within one year of program completion. This return rate was lower than the rate for those released from diversion centers (23.4 percent), higher than the rate for those on intensive probation supervision (18.8 percent) and much higher than those on regular probation supervision (7.5 percent).

One thing that must be kept in mind in comparing Georgia's program with other shock incarceration programs is the fact that in Georgia the "fundamental program concept is that a brief period of incarceration under harsh physical conditions, strenuous manual labor and exercise within a secured environment will 'shock' the younger and less seriously criminally oriented offender out of a future life of crime" (Flowers, 1986, p. 3). Thus the emphasis may be directed more towards a punishment model than are other shock incarceration programs that involve counseling, problem-solving or other treatments. SAIP was designed based in part on the earlier shock probation models.

In contrast to Georgia's shock incarceration program, treatment and individualized rehabilitation plans are an important ingredient of Oklahoma's RID program. In fact the program is part of the Nonviolent Intermediate Offender (NIO) program which is designed to be a method of planning rehabilitation programs for youthful offenders convicted of nonviolent crimes.

A study of 403 males, who completed the RID program between March 1984 and March 1985, revealed that 63 (15.7 percent) had been reincarcerated before March 1986 (Oklahoma Department of Corrections, 1986). The authors report this reincarceration rate is lower than the rate (45 to 77 percent) for the general population. However, it is difficult to make a meaningful comparison because the RID offenders are a carefully selected group who are most likely very different from the general population offender.

COMPONENTS OF SUCCESSFUL REHABILITATION PROGRAMS

In recent reviews of the literature on correctional rehabilitation it has been argued, contrary to a commonly expressed opinion, that there is empirical evidence of successful rehabilitation in some programs (Gendreau & Ross, 1987; Sechrest, White & Brown, 1979; Cullen & Gendreau, in press). However, rather than broad generalizations about types of programs (e.g., shock incarceration, intensive supervision, education) these reviewers suggest that it is necessary to consider the principles and strategies which have been associated with successful programs. That is, a program which incorporates anti-criminal modeling or problem solving, two principles that appear to be associated with successful correctional programs, should be more successful than one which does not incorporate these elements.

Early shock probation programs were attempts at getting tough and were designed to inculcate fear in offenders so they would be deterred from future criminal behavior (Vito,

1984; Vito & Allen, 1981). Such negative reinforcement does not appear to have strong support as a successful method of rehabilitation (Gendreau & Ross, 1981). Although such programs may help by reducing overcrowding in the short run, there is little evidence of a reduction in recidivism. Thus the impact on overcrowding may be relatively short lived.

There is little evidence that the "getting tough" element of shock incarceration will, by itself, lead to behavioral change. This would just be another type of punishment; and there is little research support for the effectiveness of punishment alone (Gendreau & Ross, 1987). However, voluntary participation in a "tough" program may be a test of commitment to change and other components (e.g., self-confidence) that may be indicative of success. Some of the other elements which have been identified as components of successful correctional rehabilitation programs are: formal rules, anticriminal modeling and reinforcement, problem solving, use of community resources, quality of interpersonal relationships, relapse prevention and self-efficacy, and therapeutic integrity (Gendreau & Ross, 1987; Cullen & Gendreau, in press; Andrews & Kiessling, 1980; Gendreau & Ross, 1983). Within the military framework of shock incarceration any or all of these elements could be present, although it is extremely difficult to tell to what degree or intensity they exist.

The goal of this paper is to describe the development and implementation of shock incarceration in one jurisdiction, Louisiana. In particular the elements of the program will be examined in terms of the principles which have been found to exist in successful rehabilitation programs according to recent reviews of the literature. This is part of a comprehensive evaluation of shock incarceration in Louisiana. The data reported are from correctional records and interviews with correctional personnel.

LOUISIANA'S IMPACT PROGRAM

Shock incarceration programs differ so widely at this point in time that any evaluation of them must begin with a description of the specific components of the program. Louisiana's Intensive Motivational Program of Alternative Correctional Treatment (IMPACT) is a two-phase shock incarceration program begun in 1987 by the Louisiana Department of Public Safety and Corrections (LDPSC). In the first phase of IMPACT offenders are incarcerated for 90 to 180 days in a rigorous boot camp type atmosphere (LDPSC, 1987). Following this period of incarceration offenders are placed under intensive parole supervision for the second phase of the program.

At the system level, the IMPACT program was designed to be an alternative for youthful first offenders, to help alleviate overcrowding, to promote a positive image of corrections, and to improve public relations. In regard to the individual, LDPSC (1987) states that IMPACT was designed to teach the offender responsibility, respect for self and others, and self confidence. Other stated goals of the program are to reduce recidivism, improve skills in everyday living and to generally improve the lives of the participants.

Selecting Offenders for IMPACT

To be legally eligible for the program offenders must be parole eligible, this must be their first felony conviction, they must have a sentence of seven years or less and they must volunteer. Furthermore, they must be recommended by (1) the Division of Probation and Parole, (2) the sentencing court and (3) a classification committee at the LDPSC diagnostic center. To be admitted to IMPACT the offender must receive a positive recommendation from all three evaluators (e.g., probation and parole agent, judge, and classification committee).

The law also states that offenders who are selected for the program must be those who are "particularly likely to respond affirmatively to participation" (LDPSC, 1987). As a consequence of this requirement a list of characteristics or disqualifiers have been developed to be used by the three groups who are required to make recommendations about the program. During the first year of operation this list of disqualifiers was gradually lengthened. At the end of 1987 the following characteristics were considered viable reasons for excluding an offender from the program: pending charges; sex offense; felony DWI; mental or physical health problem;

over age 40; pattern of assaultive behavior; assaultive escape; overt homosexuality; no acceptable residence identified for the intensive supervision phase of the program.

An important rationale for the three-group recommendation process was to insure that offenders who were sent to IMPACT would be drawn from the population of offenders who would normally be sent to prison not from those who would normally be given probation. Therefore, if for some reason the offender is disqualified at the diagnostic center, he or she is sent to the general prison population to serve time until the date of parole eligibility.

By the fall of 1987 (approximately October) 327 offenders had arrived at the LDPSC diagnostic center with recommendations for IMPACT from the judge and from the Division of Probation and Parole. The classification committee at the diagnostic center recommended IMPACT for 230 (or 70.3 percent) of these offenders. The remaining 97 offenders (29.7 percent) were excluded from (never entered) the program and almost all went into the general population. Thirty two (33 percent) of the 97 offenders were excluded because they did not volunteer, 23 (23.7 percent) because of a medical or psychological condition, and 21(21.6 percent) because of an assaultive history. The reasons the remaining 21 (21.6 percent) were excluded varied widely (sexual conduct, pending charges, not first offense, etc.).

Graduation or Dismissal From IMPACT

Once an offender enters the program there are rigorous requirements which must be satisfactorily completed to move through stages of the boot camp. Along with military training, the incarceration phase of IMPACT involves treatment programs such as ventilation therapy, reeducative therapy, substance abuse education, and pre-release education.

Offenders may be returned to general population after they enter the IMPACT program if they fail to receive satisfactory evaluations within the 180 days, if they commit some serious rule infraction (assault, escape, etc.), if a medical or psychological condition is identified, or if a pending charge is uncovered. Furthermore, at any time inmates may decide that they no longer wish to participate. In all of the above cases the offender would be returned to general population to await the regular parole hearing.

The first class of IMPACT inmates entered the program on February 8, 1987. By the end of December 1987, there were approximately 15 classes of entrants with an average of 18.3 offenders in each, for a total of 274 IMPACT entrants. Of these entrants, 117 offenders had completed the incarceration phase of the program and were paroled. Parole had been revoked for technical violations for nine (7.7 percent) of the parolees. Fifty four offenders were still in the program at the end of the year. The remaining 103 offenders (37.6 percent) left the program before completing the incarceration phase. Those who were admitted to IMPACT and then left before completing the incarceration phase left for the following reasons: medical (n = 9), voluntary (n = 63), disciplinary (n = 17), other (n = 14).

Overall the average offender who entered IMPACT was a male 23.3 years old with a sentence of 3.7 years. Only 12 women entered. More blacks (58.4 percent) than whites (41.6 percent) entered. A little less than one half of the entrants entered as probation violators and the others entered with a new crime. Most of those who entered were convicted of burglary or theft (63.1 percent) or drugs (22.1 percent).

Once an offender has completed between 90 and 180 days in IMPACT with satisfactory performance evaluations, institutional staff prepare a final report describing adjustment and progress. The parole board is responsible for release decisions. Once paroled the offender graduates from IMPACT and is released to the intensive parole phase of the program. This is a three-stage program involving less restrictions as offenders earn their way out of each stage.

IMPACT to General Population

An examination of the percent of the entrants to IMPACT who left the program and the number of offenders who were rejected at the diagnostic center suggests that a high percentage of the offenders recommended for IMPACT by the judge went to general population. At the time of sentencing, the judge may have expected the offender to have an alternative to standard prison (e.g. IMPACT) but, for many, this is not what happened. Thirty percent of the offenders who arrived at the diagnostic center with recommendations from the sentencing judge never entered IMPACT. Another 35 percent of the inmates who entered IMPACT did not complete the program. Using the data from both the entrants to IMPACT and the recommended IMPACT candidates, estimates can be made about the number of dropouts. Of the offenders who arrive at the diagnostic center with the judge's recommendation approximately 30 percent are excluded prior to entry to IMPACT. Of the remaining, another 35 percent will leave IMPACT before completing the incarceration phase. This means 54 percent of the total offenders recommended for IMPACT by the judge will go into the general prison population instead of being released after 90 to 180 days in IMPACT. An estimated 46 percent of the offenders who leave IMPACT before completing the incarceration phase, will either refuse to volunteer for IMPACT or will voluntarily ask to leave the program. The other 54 percent will leave for other reasons.

Selection and Dismissal Issues

A large number of the inmates recommended for IMPACT do not enter the program and still others do not complete the program. Personnel in the Division of Probation and Parole report some frustration with the large number of inmates who are dropped at the diagnostic center before entering IMPACT. According to probation and parole staff some judges are frustrated because the offenders they recommend for IMPACT are rejected at the diagnostic center. Everyone seems to understand a medical or psychological condition may be a legitimate reason for denying an offender access to the program. Less agreed upon are the denials due to a past history of violence. However, the specific reasons for denial of an individual may not always be known by those outside the diagnostic center. Judges and probation and parole staff may believe an inmate has been denied entry to IMPACT when actually the offender failed to volunteer or asked to be dropped from the program.

Probation and parole staff believe that their experience in supervising offenders on the street makes them good judges of who will perform well on parole. Therefore, in their opinion, they should have a major role in deciding who should enter IMPACT. On the other hand, personnel at the diagnostic center believe that they must make decisions very carefully and conservatively, first because any serious offense by an IMPACT offender may destroy the program. And, second, offenders must see the reward of early release at the end of the incarceration phase of the program. It is assumed that early release must be assured for the offenders who take part in the program. If the offenders who enter IMPACT are not the type who will be released by the Parole Board then inmates will no longer feel assured that they will be released if they successfully complete the program. For this reason, the diagnostic staff try to anticipate the decisions of the parole board and omit offenders who are traditionally denied parole at the first hearing. This issue came to the forefront when one offender who satisfactorily completed IMPACT was denied parole (eventually after serving a short additional time he was paroled). Subsequent to this case, the disqualifier list was developed. The list was created and added to when various actors complained that they were uncertain about how and why decisions were made excluding some offenders from the program. There are a variety of opinions about whether the disqualifiers are valid reasons for disqualifying a person from the program. But in all cases someone in the decision making chain believes that such a characteristic is indicative of a person who is not "particularly likely to respond affirmatively to participation," a legal requirement for selecting offenders for the program.

A large proportion of those who do not enter the program or who drop out do so voluntarily. LDPSC staff feel strongly that the program should be voluntary and, therefore, offenders are permitted to voluntarily drop out at any time. In their opinion this shows that an offender who remains is sincerely committed to change. There is some concern, however, about the large number of voluntary dropouts early in the program. Once they are sent to the general population they are not permitted to return to IMPACT.

In summary, there is some debate about the offenders who are most apt to benefit from

IMPACT, how to identify these offenders and who can best identify them. The offenders who are selected appear to relatively low-risk offenders. The high number of voluntary dropouts suggests a relatively rigorous program.

Staff and Inmate Interaction

The attitude of the staff toward inmates was examined. In particular we were interested in whether the drill instructors (DIs) saw their task as one of instilling obedience and respect for authority, and maintaining control, or whether they attempted to influence the offenders in other ways. The question was whether staff viewed themselves also as models, counselors, and as agents of behavior change through positive reinforcement and support.

In general, the philosophy of the program seems to be that the drill instructors, who work most closely with the inmates, are supposed to be authority figures who are also models and provide a supportive environment conducive to growth and change. For example, offenders are rewarded for good behavior by moving to more advanced squads or to higher positions within squads. They also earn privileges such as time to watch TV, visits and use of the canteen.

The DIs work closely with the squads. They march, exercise or run with the participants. The program is arranged so that early during training the control and authority of the DIs is emphasized. During this period military bearing, courtesy, drills and ceremony, and physical training are the major focus.

"Even though its framework is military, institutional IMPACT is more than a boot camp for criminal offenders" (LDPSC, 1987, p. 6). This becomes particularly salient after the offender moves out of the beginners squad. The DIs hold courses for the more advanced squads in which concepts and information related to work and work behaviors are discussed. To emphasize the supportive role of the staff, the parole agents pick up the offenders when they leave the institutional phase and take them home.

In summary, those who are assigned the task of setting the rules do not appear to see their job as only authority and control. They also take steps to be supportive and helpful in other areas.

Authority and Abuse

The emphasis from the administration is on both the supportive and authoritative position of the drill instructors. As is obvious, in programs such as this the line between abuse and authority (and control) is hard to define. It was reported that some correctional officers had difficulty changing from their traditional role of control to a role incorporating both the control and supportive guidance which they are expected to assume in this program. The administration is well aware of the need to carefully watch for signs of abuse. Overzealous control-oriented DIs have been removed from the program.

Facility Location

The program is located within a larger mixed (medium/maximum) security facility surrounded by the general population. At first glance this appears to be a disadvantage. However several important advantages have been identified. One advantage in having the program located within a large facility is that the program has close scrutiny from various personnel within (various administrations) and outside of the Department (visitors, news media). This is helpful in guarding against abuse.

A second important advantage in the location is the fact that staff can be easily rotated into and out of the program. One reason this is needed is if a correctional officer has difficulty in making the change to the DI job and appears to be having trouble in the roles expected (counselor, model or teacher) or if a DI's performance appears to be crossing the line from control/authority to abuse. In such cases staff can quickly be reassigned to another area of the prison. A second advantage in being able to rotate staff into and out of the program is burnout. Because the program is located in a large facility, staff who burn out or who might be abusive can be easily rotated.

Burnout

There does appear to be a high burnout rate for DIs (one estimate was that DIs have, on the average, spent only 6 months in the program). Burnout might also be expected for the parole agents. They work in pairs and have a 50 per pair caseload. According to the administration, many of the "best" agents have volunteered to work with IMPACT offenders. A new title has been given to those taking this assignment. Newly hired agents in these positions receive higher pay. However, the type and amount of work is heavy—for example, agents are required to write narratives for every contact made with the offender and they are required to make at least four face-to-face contacts per week in the first phase of intensive incarceration.

Rehabilitative Components

This examination of the IMPACT program did not suggest that either negative reinforcement (punishment) nor just a busier program were the major goals or organizing principles of the program. IMPACT does appear to include many of the elements that have been associated with successful rehabilitation in the opinion of several authors who have reviewed the correctional rehabilitation literature (Gendreau & Ross, 1987; Cullen & Gendreau, in press). Based on these reviews, we examined possible rehabilitative elements: rules and authority; anticriminal modeling and reinforcement; problem solving; use of community resources; interpersonal relationship; and an overall therapeutic integrity.

The most outstanding aspect of IMPACT, of course, is the approach to formal rules and authority (e.g., enforced contingencies), one characteristic that has been found to be associated with rehabilitation. This is a highly visible component of the IMPACT program. The high number of those dropping out or being forced to drop the program attests to the enforcement and, also, the rigor of the rules. For those who are able to complete the program it would appear that their belief in their own ability to control events (or a sense of responsibility) would be increased because the program is difficult and they were able to complete it.

Other factors that have been associated with successful rehabilitation programs are anticriminal modeling and reinforcement. Again there is evidence that these are components of IMPACT. The DIs do participate in the drills and physical exercise that are required of the offenders. Time and activities are carefully

controlled in the program, for example, the first squad is only permitted to watch the evening news on TV (which could be considered a prosocial activity) during the early weeks of the program. Group support and working together is encouraged during military drill and also in group counseling sessions. Furthermore the DIs encourage "positive thinking."

Many of the aspects of successful behavior modification programs are incorporated in the design of IMPACT. Most of the target behaviors (drill, attention to detail, hygiene, attitude, communication and physical training) are clearly defined and prosocial (Gendreau & Ross, 1983). The offender's peer group is involved in a positive way and it is the offender's choice as to whether to become involved in the program.

Problem solving is another component that has been associated with rehabilitation. This component is less obvious in the IMPACT schedule. It may be somewhat addressed during the prerelease and group counseling sessions. During the intensive supervision phase offenders are required to work (or show evidence of an intensive job search), complete community service, go to school, and keep to an early evening curfew among other requirements. Many of these would require problem solving skills. For example how to schedule one's time to arrive at work at the required hour, how to get a job, etc. are problems that must be solved, and the parole agent is there to assist the offender. Thus, problem solving is done in an applied setting.

The two phase structure of the program does make maximum use of community resources with some obvious advantages. For one, the intensive supervision on the street enables the parole agent to advise the offender about the availability and use of resources in the community. The parolee who has an alcohol problem can join AA and work with other nonoffenders (possibly better models). The offender learns to compete for resources with the help of the parole agent. Since resources in the community can be made available to everyone, the IMPACT program is more "acceptable" than other prison programs which are frequently criticized on the basis of why "excellent, costly" programs should be made available to offenders rather than to nonoffenders on the outside. This attitude almost always limits what is available to offenders in prison. Thus, maximizing the parolees use of community programs means that better programs may be available to them outside the prison than would be possible within prison. Theoretically the offender has learned basic skills of living and how to follow rules while in the incarceration phase of IMPACT. Now, on the outside, with the help of the agent, the offender has the skills necessary to attend school or keep a job if he or she has the ability.

The quality of interpersonal relationships is another factor which has been associated with successful rehabilitation. This also seems to be an aspect of the IMPACT program. Offenders are encouraged to cooperate and work as a team with members of their squads. The DIs report that they often receive letters from graduates of the program thanking them for their help and support. The parole agents report that they now feel as if they are really doing something in assisting the IMPACT graduates on parole. However the depth and consistency of this is difficult to objectively evaluate. At the least the philosophy of the program leans towards encouraging quality interpersonal relationships.

Therapeutic integrity or "to what extent do treatment personnel actually adhere to the principles and employ the techniques of the therapy they purport to provide? To what extent are the treatment staff competent? How hard do they work? How much is treatment diluted in the correctional environment so that it becomes treatment in name only?" (Gendreau & Ross, 1979, p. 467) might be considered the underlying requirement of any successful program. There is some evidence that the program has therapeutic integrity. For example, the high burnout rate of staff suggests that they are committed to the program and work hard. The program is so all encompassing that it does not appear to be diluted in the prison environment. Neither does it appear to be treatment in name only; there is definitely something going on or so many offenders would not leave the program and choose to spend a longer period of time in general population in prison. The extensive narratives written about the parolees by the parole agents during the intensive incarceration phase suggests the treatment is not diluted during this phase either.

There are some specific aspects of the program which should be examined for therapeutic integrity. For example, how strong the problem solving training is in the program, the quality of interpersonal relationships, and anticriminal modeling may all be more or less strongly evident. If these are to be incorporated into the program as important therapeutic elements it may be advantageous to initiate more formal staff training in these areas. This might also help reduce staff burnout, and the ability of staff to successfully act as DTs without abusiveness. To this same end, extra duty pay for staff when they are involved with the program may be a reasonable method of getting staff to volunteer for the program.

In summary, this paper has reviewed Louisiana's shock incarceration program and examined the components of the program in regard to rehabilitative potential. One of the major goals of the program is to foster prosocial changes in participants. The findings suggest that the term "shock incarceration" alone does not give enough information about the elements of a program to determine whether it includes components which might be expected to result in prosocial changes in the inmates. The examination of Louisiana's program suggests that many elements associated with successful rehabilitation are incorporated in IMPACT. Particularly important may be the intensity of the program, its volunteer nature and the two-phase (incarceration and intensive parole supervision) structure. The danger is that the punishment and retribution aspects of shock incarceration are emphasized and the possible rehabilitative components go unrecognized. Such an occurrence might lead to a rejection of such programs before their potential has been explored.

NOTE

1. Comparisons with programs in other jurisdictions is taken from Parent's 1988 address to the American Correctional Association based on his National Institute of Justice, U.S. Department of Justice funded research project.

REFERENCES

Andrews, D. A. & Kiessling, J. J. (1980). Program structure and effective correctional practices:

A summary of the CAVIL research. In R. R. Ross & P. Gendreau (Eds.), *Effective Correctional Treatment*. Toronto: Butterworths.

Cullen, F. T., & Gendreau, P. (In Press). The effectiveness of correctional rehabilitation: Reconsidering the "Nothing Works" debate. In L. I. Goodstein & D. L. MacKenzie (eds.), *The American Prison: Issues in Research and Policy*. New York: Plenum.

Flowers, G. T. (1986). *An evaluation of the use and performance of special alternative incarceration in Georgia*. Georgia Department of Corrections. Atlanta, Georgia. Unpublished manuscript.

Gendreau, P., & Ross, R. R. (1987). Revivification of rehabilitation: Evidence from the 1980s. *Justice Quarterly, 4,* 349–407.

Gendreau, P., & Ross, R. R. (1983). Success in corrections: Program and principles. In R. Corrado, M. Leblanc & J. Trepanier (eds.), *Issues in Juvenile Justice*. Toronto: Butterworths.

Gendreau, P., & Ross, R. R. (1981). Correctional potency: Treatment and deterrence on trial. In R. Roesch & R. R. Corrado (eds.), *Evaluation in Criminal Justice Policy*. Beverly Hills: Sage.

Gendreau, P., & Ross, R. R. (1979). Effective correctional treatment: Bibliotheraphy for cynics. *Crime and Delinquency, 25,* 463–489.

Louisiana Department of Public Safety and Corrections. (1987). *IMPACT. Purposes, Policies and Procedures*. Baton Rouge, LA.

Oklahoma Department of Corrections. (1986). *Oklahoma's Nonviolent Intermediate Offender Program: Its First Year of Operation*. Unpublished manuscript.

Parent, D. (1988). *Shock Incarceration Programs*. Address to the American Correctional Association Winter Conference, Phoenix, AZ.

Sechrest, L., White, S. O., & Brown, G. D. (1979). *The Rehabilitation of Criminal Offenders*. Washington, DC: National Academy of Sciences.

Vito, G. F. (1984). Developments in shock probation: A review of research findings and policy implications. *Federal Probation, 48,* 22–27.

Vito, G. F., & Allen, H. E. (1981). Shock probation in Ohio: A comparison of outcomes. *International Journal of Offender Therapy and Comparative Criminology, 25,* 70-76.

6

A "Machiavellian" Perspective on the Development of Boot Camp Prisons

A Debate

Doris Layton MacKenzie

Claire Souryal

Background

Faced with burgeoning prison populations, states search for innovative alternatives to address correctional problems. Many of the proposed alternatives place the offender in the community and, as a result, these alternatives are viewed by the public as being "soft" on criminals. Politicians today are well aware of the danger of appearing to coddle criminals. In this atmosphere the boot camp prison has become a popular alternative that is touted as tough on crime. Supporting this perspective are the widely publicized media reports of boot camps, showing powerful visual images of drill instructors yelling at young criminals. Perhaps this is what has most influenced the rapid growth of boot camps. Since their beginning in Oklahoma and Georgia in 1983, more than thirty-two

states, the Federal Bureau of Prisons, ten local jurisdictions, and an increasing number of juvenile detention centers have opened correctional boot camps (Cronin, 1994). Further support for these programs comes from the federal government. This year Congress appropriated $24.5 million to be used for discretionary grants to the states for the construction of correctional boot camps (Violent Crime Control and Law Enforcement Act, 1994). This investment is expected to increase enormously the number and size of the boot camps currently in operation (Little Hoover Commission, 1995). But does the investment make sense given what is known about boot camps?

The public and policy-makers appear to expect boot camps to accomplish spectacular results (Nossiter, 1993; White House, 1989, p. 25). Boot camps provide a short term of incarceration

Reprinted by permission from MacKenzie, D. L. & Souryal, C. (1995). *University of Chicago Roundtable.* Chicago, IL: University of Chicago Press.

in a strict military environment with a rigid daily schedule of hard labor, drill and ceremony, and physical training. There is obviously a hope that this tough punishment will deter offenders from continuing their criminal activities.

However, the literature on deterrence does not suggest that a program like the boot camp will have either a general or specific deterrent effect. Past research has reported limited or no deterrent effect from incarceration in a training school or from "scared straight" programs (Finckenauer, 1982, pp. 111-170; Lotz, Regoli, & Raymond, 1978, pp. 542-546). It is unlikely that the boot camp experience will alter an offender's perceptions of either the certainty or severity of punishment, which would be required for a deterrent effect (Paternoster, 1987).

In contrast to those who want boot camps as deterrents to crime, others see boot camps as appropriate punishment or just desert for offenders (see von Hirsch, 1992). While in the past, length of prison term has been equated with severity of sentence, boot camps introduce an intensity dimension. Intermediate sanctions are assumed, at some level of intensity, to be as punitive as a prison sentence. A short but intense boot camp program may be equal, in the public's mind, with a longer but less intense term in prison.[1]

While deterrence and punishment appear to be the two primary reasons for public and political support for boot camps, there is also interest in the rehabilitative aspects of the program. Boot camps seem to reflect some commonly held beliefs about young offenders and how they might be changed. In the past in this country, it has been generally accepted that sending a young man to the military "will straighten him out and make a man of him" (Arkin & Dobrofsky, 1978). Offenders are thought to lack discipline and structure in their lives, which are the very things, in the opinion of many, that a boot camp can instill (Frank, 1991; Hengesh, 1991; White House, 1989, p. 25). The regimented lifestyle and discipline of the boot camp is expected to be transferred to life on the outside (Osler, 1991).

In comparison to what appears to be the public and policy-makers' focus on deterrence and retribution, rehabilitation is a major emphasis of correctional administrators. When asked to rank the importance of various objectives, they rate rehabilitating offenders, lowering recidivism rates, and reducing prison crowding as the key objectives of boot camps (MacKenzie & Souryal, 1993).

In fact, many correctional administrators appear to view boot camps as a way to address two major problems that they confront: how to obtain funding for therapeutic programming and how to reduce prison crowding. However, among people who are knowledgeable about therapeutic programs and corrections in general, there is still a great deal of controversy surrounding the boot camps. This article reviews what is known about correctional boot camps as alternative punishments. In response to the question of whether continued investment in boot camps makes sense, we present two opposing perspectives. One, the Machiavellian perspective is characteristic of many correctional administrators who are forced to deal with limited budgets and increasing populations of inmates. Although questioning the effectiveness of the boot camps, they are willing to support them in order to obtain funding and in hopes of reducing overcrowding. The opposing point of view, more representative of many academics, researchers, and correctional psychologists, cautions that acceptance of these programs will have detrimental effects on both individual offenders and on the nation's correctional systems.

Boot Camps in a Rational System

Alternative sanctions, also called intermediate sanctions, have been proposed as ways to manage the burgeoning numbers of offenders without sacrificing public safety. A rational system of intermediate punishments would provide sentencing options between traditional prison and probation. Rather than sentencing offenders to either prison or probation, as is most often done, alternatives would provide intermediate levels of control (see Morris & Tonry, 1990). The assumption is that many offenders now in traditional prison could be adequately managed in less intrusive (and less costly) settings

(Morris & Tonry, 1990, p. 10). Furthermore, many offenders placed on traditional probation have inadequate amounts of supervision; intermediate sanctions would increase the level of control for high risk probationers (Morris & Tonry, 1990, p. 14). By carefully matching offenders to the appropriate correctional control, the system would permit a reasonable allocation of resources (Morris & Tonry, 1990, p. 159).

Although the proposal for developing a system of sanctions was accepted by many as an entirely reasonable method of allocating resources, it has not been well developed. As yet only a relatively small number of offenders receive intermediate sanctions.[2] While many probationers are required to comply with numerous conditions of supervision, these are often added to the conditions of traditional probation and are not necessarily part of a planned system of sanctions (e.g., see Langan, 1994).

A frequent problem with intermediate sanctions is that they widen the net of control. As new alternatives are developed that are less restrictive, offenders who would have been treated more leniently in the past are placed in the programs instead of those who would have been incarcerated (Austin & Krisberg, 1982; Morris & Tonry, 1990, pp. 157-158). In other words, the sanctions are used to increase the control over probationers but not to decrease the time in prison for prisoners. As a result, intermediate sanctions become much more costly because the additional level of control requires more staff, equipment, and supplies (Palumbo, Clifford, & Snyder-Joy, 1990). Tight budgets limit the number and type of intermediate sanctions that the system can afford.

Furthermore, many intermediate sanctions target the same offenders. As new sanctions are developed, they are used for the offenders who would have been in a previously developed intermediate sanction, not for those who would have been in prison or on probation (Taxman, 1994, p. 36). Instead of drawing people from the prison population, the alternative programs begin to compete for the same type of offender (the high risk probationer), and the number of offenders in the alternatives remains the same.

One explanation for the hesitancy to punish prison-bound offenders with intermediate sanctions is that the sanctions are considered "soft" on crime. When Taxman examined how severely people viewed intermediate sanctions, she found that the majority of the sanctions clustered together in a mid-range of severity (Taxman, 1994, pp. 35-36). Residential incarceration was always considered more severe than the nonresidential alternative sanctions (Taxman, 1994, pp. 35-36). It is little wonder that when new sanctions are developed they are frequently used for offenders who would otherwise be on probation (Austin & Krisberg, 1982, pp. 393-396; Palumbo et al., 1990, p. 234).

So where do boot camps fit in terms of severity in a rational system of sanctions? Boot camps appear to be considered tougher than most other intermediate sanctions (Taxman, 1994, pp. 35-36). Quite possibly, boot camps could be used as a surrogate for a longer term in prison (Taxman, 1994, p. 36). There is some indication that the public would accept boot camps in exchange for a longer term in prison, but we need more empirical data before we can be certain.

Furthermore, research indicates that boot camps can reduce prison crowding if they are designed as early release mechanisms (MacKenzie & Piquero, 1994, p. 222). According to MacKenzie and Piquero, in order to reduce prison crowding, boot camps must be carefully designed to target offenders who would otherwise be in prison, and they must release a sufficient number of offenders prior to the time they would otherwise be released (MacKenzie & Piquero, 1994, pp. 244-245). In this way, boot camps could have an impact on prison crowding by shortening the prison terms of a sufficient number of offenders.

The use of boot camps as early release options requires that decision makers consent to this early release. The fact that boot camps are viewed as "tough" may mean that the public and policy-makers will agree to use boot camps in lieu of a longer term in prison. Thus, boot camps fit within a system of sanctions, fulfill a need (reduce the use of prison), and do so in a way that other intermediate sanctions have not.

BOOT CAMP AND OFFENDER TREATMENT

A major deficit in the correctional systems today is the lack of treatment for offenders despite the fact that there is strong evidence that treatment works (Andrews, Zinger, et al., 1990, p. 374). Many offenders with drug problems do not receive drug treatment while under correctional supervision (Hser, Longshore, & Anglin, 1994, p. 31; Turner, Petersilia, & Deschenes, 1994, p. 240). As noted by Gendreau et al., the new generation of alternative sanctions, such as intensive probation, focus on controlling offenders and frequently omit any emphasis on treatment (Gendreau, Paparozzi, Little, & Goddard, 1993, pp. 31-32).

A review of the treatment literature reveals that the core elements of boot camp programs (e.g., military drill and ceremony, physical training, hard labor) can be expected to have little value in and of themselves (Andrews, Zinger, et al., 1990, p. 373; MacKenzie & Parent, 1992, p. 114; MacKenzie & Souryal, 1994; Morash & Rucker, 1990, pp. 210-214). However, most boot camp prisons also incorporate therapy, counseling, or educational programs in the daily schedule, and this rehabilitative component has grown over the years (Gransky, Castellano, & Cowles, 1995, pp. 89-110). Programs that previously focused exclusively on the physical training and military drill aspects have now introduced therapeutic programming within boot camps and increased aftercare to help offenders make the transition from the boot camp to the community (Cronin, 1994, pp. 26-27; Gransky et al., 1995, p. 94). Most likely, offenders spend more time in treatment-type activities while they are in boot camp prisons than they would if they were in traditional prisons. Correctional administrators appear to use the programs to obtain additional funds for these treatment and educational activities (Gransky et al., 1995, p. 110).

Research examining boot camps has shown very little negative impact from the program (Cullen, 1993, pp. 24-28; MacKenzie & Souryal, 1994, pp. 40-43; U.S. General Accounting Office, 1993, pp. 33-34). Offenders report being drug free and physically healthy when they leave the boot camps (MacKenzie & Souryal, 1994, pp. 10-11). They also believe the program helped them and are optimistic about the future (MacKenzie & Shaw, 1990, pp. 138-139). In contrast, offenders in traditional prisons do not say prison was a beneficial experience (MacKenzie & Shaw, 1990, pp. 138-139). Boot camp prisoners and their families also appear to take pride in completing the program. Indeed, a boot camp is one of the few places where parents take pictures of offenders successfully completing prison.[3]

When examined, there are few differences between boot camp graduates and probationers and parolees in terms of antisocial attitudes (MacKenzie & Shaw, 1990, p. 125), positive activities during community supervision (MacKenzie & Brame, 1995), and recidivism (Cullen, 1993, pp. 25-27; Flowers, Carr, & Ruback, 1991, p. 41; MacKenzie & Shaw, 1993, p. 463; MacKenzie & Souryal, 1994, p. 41; New York State Department of Correctional Services, 1992, 1993). When there are differences, boot camp graduates do better than comparison offenders (Cullen, 1993, p. 28). In the few instances when differences occur, such differences may be related to the intensive therapeutic activities in boot camp combined with intensive supervision in the community (MacKenzie & Souryal, 1994, p. 42). Thus, the boot camps, to the extent they have been studied, do not appear to harm offenders and may actually be beneficial.

Obviously, the rigorous activity, summary punishments, and authoritarian atmosphere of boot camps hold the potential for abuse and injury of inmates. On the other hand, so do traditional prisons. But, the dangers of traditional prisons differ from the dangers of boot camps. For example, the strict control and continual oversight of offenders in boot camps means inmate-on-inmate violence, intimidation, and conflict may be less than in traditional prisons. On the other hand, the power and control that staff have over the inmates in boot camps increases the possibility of staff-on-inmate abuse. The degradation and verbal abuse shown in media accounts of the program is hardly conducive to the "interpersonally warm, flexible, and enthusiastic ways" that some advise is characteristic of effective treatment programs (Andrews, Zinger, et al., 1990, p. 376).

However, there may be some advantages to the military atmosphere in the boot camps that are not immediately obvious. In addition to being a vehicle for obtaining additional treatment for offenders, boot camps may provide some advantages for treatment delivery. The environment may coerce offenders into treatment, either during the in-prison phase or afterwards during community supervision—treatment that they would not otherwise voluntarily obtain (MacKenzie & Brame, 1995). Research in drug treatment suggests that coercion can keep substance abusers in treatment longer, and the longer they stay in treatment, the better the outcome (Anglin & Hser, 1990, p. 396).

Another advantage may be that the military atmosphere facilitates other changes in offenders. The camps may do so by creating stress and radical change in the inmates' lives, making them more susceptible to personal change. As Zamble and Porporino proposed in their study of inmate coping and change in prison, this may be a time when the inmates reevaluate their lives and become more willing to make changes (Zamble & Porporino, 1990, p. 64). The stressful and demanding nature of the boot camp may be valuable in initiating this process.

Boot camp prisons also introduce the possibility of using correctional officers who work in the boot camps as agents of behavioral change, a relatively new role for these officers. They may provide an environment that is supportive and that reinforces anti-criminal attitudes and behavior (Andrews, Zinger, et al., 1990, p. 376). If this is a role correctional officers can assume, they would provide more continual treatment than would be possible if only trained therapists provided an hour or two of treatment per week.

A Machiavellian Perspective

In *The Prince,* Machiavelli rejected the idealism of the medieval tradition and pressed instead a political realism about how princes should govern (Machiavelli, 1950, pp. 3-102). In later years it has come to represent the conflict between the ethical and the ruthlessly realistic— the use of any means to achieve the desired end. While this has not been explicitly articulated, many knowledgeable correctional administrators seem to accept a "Machiavellian" perspective in regard to boot camp prisons (Quinlan, 1993, pp. 59-63). From this perspective, although boot camps may be popular for reasons that are not necessarily well informed

about either corrections or rehabilitation, they may have the potential to be used to achieve some desired objectives. First, within a rational sentencing system, they may be "tough" enough to truly be used as an alternative to prison and thereby help to reduce prison populations. Second, public acceptance of the boot camps can be used to obtain increased funding for rehabilitation programs that would not otherwise be available to these offenders. These two topics relate to two of the major issues in corrections and the goals of most intermediate punishments: how to reduce prison crowding and how to change offenders (Morris & Tonry, 1990, p. 180).

Is the boot camp environment so antithetical to treatment that we should adamantly oppose its development, or can we use boot camps to deliver treatment that would not otherwise be available? There may be some advantages to the boot camps even though there can be little hope that they will have a deterrent effect or that the military component by itself will successfully change offenders. For example, the boot camps may incarcerate offenders for a shorter period of time. In addition, their development brings with it money for enhanced treatment and aftercare for the offenders.

From this Machiavellian perspective, boot camps may be a viable intermediate sanction. Using the public acceptance of the tough military environment, we can explore the solutions these programs provide for prison overcrowding and the treatment of offenders. While knowledgeable correctional experts realize the limitations of the military atmosphere, public acceptance of the program may permit some offenders to earn their way out of prison, thus potentially reducing crowding, and public acceptance may also bring increased resources for additional treatment. Are we willing to use these programs as a means to these ends?

The Machiavellian Perspective Reconsidered

The Machiavellian perspective posits that boot camp prisons have been enthusiastically embraced by the public and politicians because they are perceived as being "tough on crime."

Perceptions of "toughness" spring mainly from the program's strict military-like atmosphere that encompasses military drill and ceremony, physical training, and strict discipline. In addition to providing sufficient punishment by virtue of their toughness, the Machiavellian perspective asserts that the public also expects the *military component* of the program to advance utilitarian objectives—namely, deterrence and rehabilitation (for example, through external structure and discipline).

Are the utilitarian expectations of the public and politicians regarding the military component of the program realistic? Most commentators would answer "NO" (Mathlas & Mathews, 1991, p. 322; Morash & Rucker, 1990, p. 204; Sechrest, 1989, p. 15), and the Machiavellian perspective admits as much. In essence, the Machiavellian perspective argues that the primary benefit of the boot camp military atmosphere is to gain popular support. It then advocates capitalizing upon the public support that the military atmosphere engenders—regardless of whether it is misinformed—to develop a rational sentencing system that would save prison beds and provide treatment to offenders who might not otherwise receive it. Thus, the military component of boot camp prisons is viewed as a tolerable means of achieving a desirable and otherwise illusive end.

The "Myth of the Punitive Public"

In attributing the popularity of boot camp prisons to their reputation as a "tough" sanction, the Machiavellian perspective implicitly dismisses as "idealistic" the possibility of developing correctional options that are not perceived as punitive. In doing so, it falls prey to what some have called the "myth of the punitive public" (Cullen, Clark, & Wozniak, 1985, p. 22; Cullen, Cullen, & Wozniak, 1988, p. 303; Cullen, Skovron, Scott, & Burton, 1990, p. 7; Skovron, Scott, & Cullen, 1988, p. 154). This "myth" refers to the belief—particularly common among policy-makers—that the public favors strictly punitive criminal penalties and is intolerant of rehabilitative approaches (Cullen et al., 1988, p. 305). Research reveals, however, that while it is true that public attitudes have grown more punitive

since the early 1970s, they cannot be characterized as predominantly punitive (Cullen et al., 1988, p. 314; Roberts, 1992; Skovron et al., 1988, p. 163). Cullen et al. effectively dispel the "myth":

> Although citizens clearly believe that the state has the legitimate right to sanction offenders on the basis of just deserts, they also believe that criminal penalties should serve utilitarian goals. Further, the evidence indicates that among the utilitarian goals, rehabilitation is supported as much as and usually more than either deterrence or incapacitation. (p. 314)

Not only has research indicated that the public subscribes to multiple correctional goals including rehabilitation, it has also revealed that policy-makers have overestimated public punitiveness (Cullen et al., 1988, p. 315; Cullen & Gendreau, 1989, pp. 23, 38; Roberts, 1992, pp. 157-158; Skovron et al., 1988, p. 165). A study that compared the attitudes of policy-makers with members of the general public is illustrative. Researchers discovered that the attitudes of samples of policy-makers and members of the general public were both "rather liberal, nonpunitive, utilitarian, and reform-oriented" (Cullen et al., 1988, p. 315). Notably, however, the sample of policy-makers believed the reverse to be true of the general public (Cullen et al., 1988, p. 315). In similar fashion, another study revealed that although two-thirds of the public were found to support rehabilitation as a correctional objective, only twelve percent of a sample of policy-makers believed that the public would be so inclined (Roberts, 1992, p. 158).

Misperceptions of the public "will" have profound implications for public policy (Cullen et al., 1988, pp. 313-315). Such misperceptions, for example, likely limit the range of public policy alternatives deemed politically feasible (Cullen et al., 1988, p. 315). Policy-makers may reject sound policy alternatives based simply on the fact that they do not appear punitive enough to satisfy what they misperceive as the will of the public. Sherman and Hawkins affirm that in general "those who formulate correctional policy typically see their choices as dictated by pressures and circumstances beyond their control" (Cullen et al., 1988, p. 315). Clearly, policy-makers need to be better informed about the realities of the public "will."

A major problem with the Machiavellian perspective, then, is that it is founded in common assumptions about public opinion that may be misinformed. Recent research indicates that the public is not more punitive than policy-makers or the judiciary and that it exhibits strong support for rehabilitation relative to deterrence and incapacitation. Thus, critics may argue, it is not necessary to cloak rehabilitative elements of a program under the guise of punitiveness in order to gain public support. Moreover, in adopting such a strategy the Machiavellian perspective serves to perpetuate both public misunderstandings about the potential of boot camp programs to achieve correctional goals and politicians' misperceptions of public opinion.

Hence, the choice between "idealism" and "ruthless realism" advanced by the Machiavellian perspective may be a false one. Examination of Machiavelli's work suggests that there is a middle ground. As Lerner observes, "Machiavelli sought to distinguish the realm of what ought to be and the realm of what is. He rejected the first for the second. But there is a third realm: the realm of what can be" (Machiavelli, 1950, p. xlvi). Such a middle ground would seek to elevate the corrections debate above the more common "get tough" rhetoric by encouraging open dialogue between policy-makers and the public such that policy-makers both "educate and [are] educated by the public" (Cullen et al., 1985, p. 23). Accordingly, it might seem more prudent to be forthright about the inadequacies/limitations of the boot camp military model, concentrate on developing more effective programs, and then sell those programs on their merits.

BOOT CAMPS AS A SUCCESSFUL MEANS TO AN END?

If in fact the military component of boot camp prisons is accepted as a means to an end, the following subsection will explore whether boot camp prisons are likely to achieve those ends. That is, are boot camps likely to reduce prison crowding and provide adequate treatment to offenders? And if they are, what are the dangers associated with accepting such a compromise?

Offender Treatment

Many boot camp prisons have supplemented the military component of the program with rehabilitative programming such as academic education, group counseling, and drug education and treatment (MacKenzie & Souryal, 1994, p. 1; U.S. General Accounting Office, 1993, p. 18). Such programming lies at the heart of the Machiavellian perspective because it represents one of the primary benefits of boot camp programming. In addition to providing treatment opportunities such as these, a Machiavellian would contend that correctional officers may have therapeutic potential if they act as positive, anti-criminal role models.

The provision of treatment necessarily takes place within the larger military like milieu. The pertinent question then becomes whether the military environment is conducive to effective treatment. Although some would argue that the military component actually facilitates successful treatment outcomes, review of the extant literature on effective correctional treatment would appear to suggest otherwise.

In recent years, examination of correctional treatment programs has moved beyond the question of whether correctional treatment programs "work" to examination of the principles that characterize successful programs (Cullen & Gendreau, 1989, p. 23). Based on numerous meta-analyses of treatment programs, several guiding principles of effective treatment have been enumerated (Andrews, Bonta, & Hodge, 1990, p. 20; Andrews, Zinger, et al., 1990, pp. 372-377; Cullen & Gendreau, 1989, p. 33). Andrews et al. contend that these characteristics of effective treatment "are sufficiently strong to inform professionals in rehabilitation and to lead to policy statements that actively encourage rehabilitative effort and evaluation of that effort" (Andrews, Bonta, & Hodge, 1990, p. 36).

In brief, effective correctional treatment (i.e., treatment that reduces recidivism) involves: (1) matching high-risk offenders to the most intensive programs; (2) targeting the criminogenic needs of offenders; (3) developing programs consistent with the literature on effective service within general offender samples; and (4) matching the style and mode of a program to the learning styles and abilities of offenders (Andrews, Bonta, & Hodge, 1990, p. 20). Attention here will focus on the development of treatment programs that are informed by the literature on effective service because this principle applies to the boot camp concept in general. Whether boot camp programs target high-risk offenders or criminogenic needs, on the other hand, is likely to vary from program to program and is therefore beyond the scope of this analysis.

Review of the literature on characteristics of effective programs reveals that successful programs involve workers who are interpersonally warm, tolerant, and flexible, yet sensitive to conventional rules and procedures. These workers make use of the authority inherent in their position *without engaging in interpersonal domination (firm but fair);* demonstrate in vivid ways their own anticriminal/prosocial attitudes, values, and beliefs; and enthusiastically engage the offender in the process of increasing rewards for noncriminal activity (Andrews, Bonta, & Hodge, 1990, pp. 36-37, emphasis added).

Consideration of this line of research calls into question the treatment potential of boot camp programs. Certainly, interactions based on the military ideal would not be characterized as "interpersonally warm; tolerant, and flexible." On the contrary, military-style interactions typically involve the interpersonal dominance and conflict specifically proscribed as ineffective. Consider the way in which boot camp inmates were introduced to the boot camp concept in one program:

> You are nothing and nobody, fools, maggots, dummies, motherf*** s, and you have just walked into the worst nightmare you ever dreamed. I don't like you. I have no use for you, and I don't give a f*** who you are on the street. This is my acre, hell's half acre, and it matters not one damn to me whether you make it here or get tossed out into the general prison population, where, I promise you, you won't last three minutes before you're somebody's wife. Do you know what that means, tough guys? (Fay, 1988, p. 82)

Further, it is questionable whether correctional officers will be perceived as prosocial/anti-criminal role models as stipulated above. Correctional officers are responsible for enforcing the strict military-style discipline characteristic of the program. In many programs they have the power to impose summary punishments. Morash and Rucker (1990) note, "The very idea of using physically and verbally aggressive tactics in an effort to 'train' people to act in a prosocial manner is fraught with contradiction" (p. 214).

Why should inmates who have been punished unreasonably or have seen others being punished unreasonably, such as carrying oversized logs on their backs while running, or humiliated, such as being forced to wear ridiculous beanies, respond positively to correctional officers as persons worthy of imitation? As Morash and Rucker (1990) contend, "virtually no empirically supported criminological theories have suggested that aggressive and unpredictable reactions by authority figures encourage prosocial behavior" (p. 212).

Thus, the inmate/staff interactions characteristic of boot camp prisons are inconsistent with interactions associated with effective treatment. Further, given the punishment-oriented tactics used by correctional officers to instill discipline and maintain order, it is unlikely that they will be perceived as positive role models. In fact, as Morash and Rucker (1990) warn, they may have the opposite effect by encouraging aggressive behavior. In short, then, the boot camp environment may interact with treatment efforts in such a way as to impede successful treatment outcomes.

Reducing Prison Crowding

An overall goal of most boot camp prisons is the reduction of prison overcrowding. Boot camp prisons are expected to reduce prison crowding by targeting prison-bound offenders for participation and allowing them to serve less time in the boot camp prison than they would have otherwise served in a conventional prison. By reducing sentence length in this way, boot camp prisons are hypothesized to save prison beds and thereby reduce prison crowding.

Obviously, this process hinges entirely on the selection of prison-bound offenders. Selecting offenders for participation in the program who would have otherwise served a sentence of probation would serve only to "widen (or strengthen) the net" of social control and as a consequence may adversely affect prison crowding.[4] Net-widening is a problem common to all intermediate sanctions

(Austin & Krisberg, 1981, p. 165; Palumbo et al., 1990, p. 231).

The Machiavellian perspective suggests that boot camp prisons may be more successful than other intermediate sanctions in avoiding net-widening because, in contrast to other intermediate sanctions, they are considered "tough" on crime. It is argued that the public may be more likely to accept time served in a boot camp as a fair trade for serving a longer term in prison due to the intensity of the boot camp experience.

In spite of their reputation as a tough sanction, however, boot camp prisons are quite likely to widen the net as well (Parent, 1994, p. 8). As part of a multi-site evaluation of boot camp prisons, for example, the bed space savings of five boot camp programs were examined (MacKenzie & Piquero, 1994, p. 222). In two of the five states, boot camp prison appeared to save prison beds (MacKenzie & Piquero, 1994, pp. 242-243). In the remaining three states, the boot camp program appeared to cost the state jurisdiction prison beds (MacKenzie & Piquero, 1994, pp. 243-244). The authors concluded that program design was critical to bed space savings (MacKenzie & Piquero, 1994, p. 244). Boot camp prisons that empowered the department of corrections to select program participants, for example, were more likely to target prison-bound offenders and hence reduce crowding (MacKenzie & Piquero, 1994, p. 242).

Thus, the evidence to date has not been extremely persuasive. Boot camp programs seem just as likely not to reduce crowding. Clearly, their image as a tough sanction is not enough to preclude net-widening. In light of the evidence, it may be that it is not the presumed toughness of the intermediate sanction that most influences net-widening, but the design of the intermediate sanction instead. For example, intermediate sanctions that are designed in such a way as to allow department of corrections, as opposed to the sentencing judge, to assume primary decisionmaking authority may be most successful at reducing prison crowding regardless of their perceived severity.

There is also reason to be skeptical of the ability of intermediate sanctions in general to substantially reduce prison crowding. Prison crowding is driven by two factors: the number of new admissions to prison and sentence length. Based on a cross-national analysis of imprisonment rates, Young and Brown (1993) contend that reductions in prison crowding are most influenced by sentence length (p. 44). Austin and Krisberg (1985) also argue that sentence length is critical to changes in prison population size (p. 29).

As a consequence, intermediate sanctions will likely play a limited role in reducing prison crowding because intermediate sanctions target offenders who already have relatively short sentences. And while these short-sentence inmates may make up a large proportion of new prison admissions, they generally make up only a small proportion of the entire prison population (Young & Brown, 1993, p. 19). Thus, Young and Brown conclude:

> Although an expansion in the number of such community-based sanctions may have an effect on the number of people who are sent to prison, this may not have the expected impact on the prison population because it is not tackling the major factor driving that population. Accordingly, efforts to control prison population growth by developing and expanding alternatives to imprisonment may well be misplaced. (p. 21)

DANGER ASSOCIATED WITH THE MILITARY MODEL

While the military model may generate the public support necessary for the development of boot camp prisons, it is not an entirely benevolent element of the program. Given the authoritarian atmosphere and the use of summary punishments, one principal danger associated with the military model is the abuse of inmates by correctional officers. Frightful stories of inmate abuse appear from time to time in the media (Karlson, 1993, p. 1B; Mackeiq, 1992, p. 1A; Maier, 1992, p. A5). In Houston, for example, five drill instructors were indicted on felony charges after they "allegedly choked and beat the inmates with their fists, feet and broomsticks—sometimes as they stood at attention" (Mackeiq, 1992, p. 1A). Correctional officers in fact admit to the stress associated with working so closely with inmates and acknowledge that such stress increases the likelihood for abuse (MacKenzie & Souryal, 1994, p. 10).

While the Machiavellian perspective acknowledges the possibility of inmate abuse, it raises the point that the presumed alternative to incarceration in a boot camp—conventional prison—is potentially as destructive, if not more so. While inmates incarcerated in a boot camp may be vulnerable to staff-on-inmate abuse, inmates incarcerated in prison are vulnerable to inmate-on-inmate violence.

It should be noted, however, that many inmates sentenced to boot camp programs today would not have otherwise served time in prison (MacKenzie & Piquero, 1994, p. 244). Thus, they would not have been subject to the living conditions characteristic of prison. Moreover, the fact that prison life is bad does not justify poor treatment in boot camps—especially not at the hands of the state. The state has the responsibility to provide humane living conditions, which include safety. Given the extremely crowded institutions and limited resources, this is clearly difficult to achieve. But this does not excuse the deliberate design of institutions or programs that tacitly allow for staff-on-inmate abuse to occur.

It is also important to consider that approximately 70 percent of the boot camp programs operating at the state level today are relatively small with total capacities of no more than three hundred (Cronin, 1994, pp. 12-13). The dynamics of such programs may be very different from the dynamics of programs that are likely to result from the infusion of federal money. Boot camp programs will not only grow in number, but they will likely grow in size.

The balance of research on the efficacy of boot camp programs to date has been conducted on smaller programs. In smaller programs, it is easier to conceive of staff who genuinely strive to act as positive role models. Some correctional officers in these programs may find their tasks manageable and, indeed, rewarding. It may also be easier to control staff-on-inmate abuse. Supervisors have the capacity to be intimately involved in the day-to-day activities of the program, thereby minimizing the potential for harm. However, if program size increases dramatically and corrections officers are forced to become more and more concerned with custodial duties and less and less concerned with treatment the potential for abuse may be exacerbated.

SUMMARY OF THE MACHIAVELLIAN PERSPECTIVE RECONSIDERED

The Machiavellian perspective argues that the military component, characteristic of boot camp prisons may be a small price to pay for the potential benefits of such programs—namely, the provision of correctional treatment and the reduction of prison crowding. In choosing to endorse boot camp programs under such terms, it dismisses as idealistic the possibility of developing correctional programs, absent the military environment, that may be better suited to achieving important correctional goals. This is due largely to the (mis)perception that the public will only condone the development of predominantly punitive correctional sanctions. Furthermore, in forcing the choice between "idealism" and "ruthless realism" and accepting the latter, the Machiavellian perspective serves to perpetuate both public misunderstandings of the efficacy of boot camp programs as well as policy-makers' understandings of the popular "will." As a result, it diminishes the prospect of meaningful dialogue between the general public and policy-makers and seemingly precludes the development of more efficacious alternatives.

Irrespective of such considerations, the presumed benefits of boot camp programs may be illusive indeed. Although many boot camps have incorporated therapeutic programming, the effectiveness of such programming may be compromised by the military-style environment and interactions. The scant evidence that boot camp graduates have lower recidivism rates than comparison samples of prison releasees is illustrative since successful treatment should be evidenced by reduced recidivism rates (MacKenzie & Souryal, 1994, p. 41).

Further, although a few boot camp programs have been shown to save prison beds, others are in fact having the opposite effect. It is also important to consider that even the perfectly designed boot camp is unlikely to have a substantial impact on prison crowding because prison crowding is primarily driven by sentence length. Thus, while some boot camp programs may be used to successfully divert young offenders from serving time in a conventional prison, it is unlikely that their diversion will have a significant impact on prison crowding.

Lastly, the dangers associated with the military component of boot camp programs should not be easily dismissed. The potential for abuse is real, and it is likely to increase if programs expand in size. Further, such abuse cannot be justified on the basis of poor prison conditions, particularly when many boot camp inmates would not have otherwise served time in prison.

Conclusion

The two perspectives presented in this article make different assertions about the punitiveness of the public, the impact of the military component of boot camp programs, and the potential of boot camp programs to reduce prison crowding and change offenders. The Machiavellian perspective argues that these programs may be reasonable means of addressing prison crowding and providing treatment to offenders. From this perspective, there is nothing wrong with the military model, particularly if it provides other benefits. For generations, the United States has sent wealthy and middle class youth to military academies and into the military. Why then protect offenders from the very methods that have been used with other youth? The military helps to prepare these individuals for leadership positions. Although certainly some people have been injured during the rigorous basic training, boot camps for these noncriminal individuals have not been considered abusive. In fact, there may be components that are beneficial if combined with treatment and aftercare that address the criminogenic needs of the offenders.

The alternative view is that the Machiavellian perspective does not really take into account the fact that the public is not as punitive as policymakers think.[5] By choosing to endorse the development of boot camp prisons, the Machiavellian perspective dismisses as idealistic the possibility of more constructive dialogue between policymakers and the public and, as a result, diminishes the prospect of developing more effective correctional programs. Doubt has additionally been cast on the ability of boot camp programs to reduce either recidivism or prison crowding.

Many questions have been raised about boot camp programs. There is research to support each perspective. What is clear is that these are experimental correctional programs. We need more information about the impact of specific components of the boot camps and the expectations of the public and policymakers. Social science is capable of scrutinizing the impact on inmates and staff and examining public attitudes towards these programs, thereby providing empirical data to address the unanswered questions underlying some of the controversy surrounding boot camp prisons. Other fields of science would require such study before introducing a speculative innovation. Yet, these correctional programs are rapidly expanding without the necessary corresponding study of their objectives and their impact.

Notes

1. There is some research that examines how inmates and correctional staff compare intensive supervision to prison. For example, Petersilia and Deschenes (1994) found that these groups viewed one year in prison as approximately equivalent in severity to three years of intensive probation supervision. It would be interesting to introduce boot camp prisons into some of the severity rankings to understand where they would fall in comparison to a two- or three-year prison term.

2. For example, a recent investigation found that only 2 percent of the 4.4 million adults under correctional control were in some type of intermediate sanction: This count included all those who were in house arrest, boot camps, intensive supervision, day reporting, electronic monitoring, and work release (Taxman, 1994).

3. Personal observation of Doris Layton MacKenzie at the Wisconsin Department of Corrections, St. Croix Correctional Center, in New Richmond, Wisconsin, 1993.

4. Placing offenders who would have otherwise served a term of traditional probation in a boot camp prison may adversely affect prison crowding in two ways. First, if offenders who would have otherwise served a probation term fail to graduate from the program for disciplinary reasons or if they choose to drop out, they would likely serve the remainder of their sentence in a state facility (MacKenzie & Souryal, 1993, pp. 19, 29, 43, 60, 79, 111, 123). Second, if offenders who would have otherwise served a probation term graduate from the in-prison phase of the boot camp program but violate the conditions of release associated with the intensive supervision

phase of some boot camp programs, their community supervision status may be revoked, potentially resulting in incarceration (Petersilia & Turner, 1993, pp. 311-312). Note that in-prison boot camp failure rates ranged from roughly 9 percent to 52 percent in an evaluation of eight such programs (see MacKenzie & Souryal, 1993, Table 3.5).

5. The public is likely to be interested in increased safety at reasonable cost and will support any program that promises to achieve this goal.

REFERENCES

Andrews, D. A., Bonta, J., & Hodge, R. D. (1990). Classification for effective rehabilitation: Rediscovering psychology. *Criminal Justice & Behavior, 17,* 19-52.

Andrews, D. A., Zinger, I., Hoge, R. D., Bonta, J., Gendreau, P., & Cullen, F. T. (1990). Does correctional treatment work? A clinically relevant and psychologically informed meta-analysis. *Criminology, 28,* 369-404.

Anglin, M. D., & Hser, Y. (1990). Treatment of drug abuse. *Crime & Justice, 13,* 393-460.

Arkin, W., & Dobrofsky, L. R. (1978). Military socialization and masculinity. *Journal of Social Issues, 34,* 151–155.

Austin, J., & Krisberg, B. (1981). Wider, stronger, and different nets: The dialectics of criminal justice reform. *Journal of Research in Crime & Delinquency, 18,* 165-196.

Austin, J., & Krisberg, B. (1982). The unmet promise of alternatives to incarceration. *Crime & Delinquency, 28,* 374-409.

Austin, J., & Krisberg, B. (1985). Incarceration in the United States: The extent and future of the problem. *Annals of the American Academy of Political & Social Science, 478,* 15-30.

Cronin, R. C. (1994). *Boot camps for adult and juvenile offenders: Overview and update.* Final summary report presented to the National Institute of Justice.

Cullen, F. (1993, November). *Control in the community: The limits of reform?* Presentation to the International Association of Residential and Community Alternatives (on file with the *University of Chicago Law School Roundtable*).

Cullen, F. T., Clark, G. A., & Wozniak, J. F. (1985). Explaining the get tough movement: Can the public be blamed? *Federal Probation, 49,* 16-24.

Cullen, F. T., Cullen, J. B., & Wozniak, J. F. (1988). Is rehabilitation dead? The myth of the punitive public. *Journal of Criminal Justice, 16,* 303-317.

Cullen, F. T., & Gendreau, P. (1989). The effectiveness of correctional rehabilitation: Reconsidering the "nothing works" debate. In L. Goodstein & D. L. MacKenzie (Eds.), *The American prison: Issues in research and policy.* New York: Plenum.

Cullen, F. T., Skovron, S. E., Scott, J. E., & Burton, V. S. (1990). Public support for correctional treatment: The tenacity of rehabilitative ideology. *Criminal Justice & Behavior, 17,* 6-18.

Fay, M. (1988, July). "Squeeze you like a grape": In Georgia, a prison boot camp sets kids straight. *Life,* p. 82.

Finckenauer, J. O. (1982). *Scared straight! and the panacea phenomenon.* Upper Saddle River, NJ: Prentice Hall.

Flowers, G. T., Carr, T. S., & Ruback, R. B. (1991). *Special alternative incarceration evaluation.* Atlanta: Georgia Department of Corrections.

Frank, S. (1991). Oklahoma camp stresses structure and discipline. *Corrections Today, 53,* 102-105.

Gendreau, P., Paparozzi, M., Little, T., & Goddard, M. (1993). Does "punishing smarter" work? An assessment of the new generation of alternative sanctions in probation. *Forum, 5*(3), 31-34.

Gransky, L. A., Castellano, T. C., & Cowles, E. L. (1995). Is there a "next generation" of shock incarceration facilities? The evolving nature of goals, program components and drug treatment services. In J. Smykla & W. Selke (Eds.), *Intermediate sanctions: Sentencing in the 90s.* Cincinnati, OH: Anderson.

Hengesh, D. J. (1991). Think of boot camps as a foundation for change, not an instant cure. *Corrections Today, 53,* 106-108.

Hser, Y., Longshore, D., & Anglin, M. D. (1994). Prevalence of drug use among criminal offender populations: Implications for control, treatment, and policy. In D. L. MacKenzie & C. D. Uchida (Eds.), *Drugs and crime: Evaluating public policy initiatives.* Thousand Oaks, CA: Sage.

Karlson, K. J. (1993, November 14). Wisconsin boot camp abusive, inmates say. *Saint Paul Pioneer Press,* p. 1B.

Langan, P. A. (1994). Between prison and probation: Intermediate sanctions. *Science, 264,* 791.

Little Hoover Commission. (1995, January). *Boot camps: An evolving alternative to traditional prison* (Report #128). Sacramento, CA: Author.

Lotz, R., Regoli, R. M., & Raymond, P. (1978). Delinquency and special deterrence. *Criminology, 15,* 539-548.

Machiavelli, N. (1950). *The Prince and the discourses* (Max Lerner, Ed.). New York: Random House.

Mackeiq, J. (1992, June 7). Five deputies at boot camp indicted, fired, charged with inmate abuse. *Houston Chronicle*, p. 1A.

MacKenzie, D. L., & Brame, R. (1995). Shock incarceration and positive adjustment during community supervision. *Journal of Quantitative Criminology, 11*(2), 111-142.

MacKenzie, D. L., & Parent, D. G. (1994). Boot camp prisons for young offenders. In J. M. Byrne, A. J. Lurigio, & J. Petersilia (Eds.), *Smart sentencing: The emergence of intermediate sanctions.* Thousand Oaks, CA: Sage.

MacKenzie, D. L., & Piquero, A. (1994). The impact of shock incarceration programs on prison crowding. *Crime & Delinquency, 40,* 222-250.

MacKenzie, D. L., & Shaw, J. W. (1990). Inmate adjustment and change during shock incarceration: The impact of correctional boot camp programs. *Justice Quarterly, 7,* 125-150.

MacKenzie, D. L., & Shaw, J. W. (1993). The impact of shock incarceration on technical violations and new criminal activities. *Justice Quarterly, 10,* 463-486.

MacKenzie, D. L., & Souryal, C. (1993). *Multi-site study of shock incarceration: Process evaluation.* Part I of the Final Report to the National Institute of Justice.

MacKenzie, D. L., & Souryal, C. (1994). *Multi-site evaluation of shock incarceration.* Final summary report presented to the National Institute of Justice.

Maier, T. W. (1992, November 29). At boot camp prison, drill instructor cleared in complaint. *Laurel (MD) Leader,* p. A5.

Mathlas, R. E. S., & Mathews, J. W. (1991). The boot camp program for offenders: Does the shoe fit? *International Journal of Offender Therapy & Comparative Criminology, 35,* 322-327.

Morash, M., & Rucker, L. (1990). A critical look at the idea of boot camp as a correctional reform. *Crime & Delinquency, 36*(2), 209-220.

Morris, N., & Tonry, M. (1990). *Between prison and probation: Intermediate punishments in a rational sentencing system.* New York: Oxford University Press.

New York State Department of Correctional Services and New York State Division of Parole. (1992). *The fourth annual report to the legislature: Shock incarceration in New York State.* Unpublished manuscript, Division of Program Planning, Research and Evaluation and the Office of Policy Analysis and Information, Albany.

New York State Department of Correctional Services and New York State Division of Parole. (1993). *The fifth annual report to the legislature: Shock incarceration-shock parole supervision.* Unpublished manuscript, Division of Program Planning, Research and Evaluation and the Office of Policy Analysis and Information, Albany.

Nossiter, A. (1993, December 18). As boot camps for criminals multiply, skepticism grows. *New York Times,* pp. 1, 9.

Osler, M. W. (1991). Shock incarceration: Hard realities and real possibilities. *Federal Probation, 55,* 34-36.

Palumbo, D., Clifford, M., & Snyder-Joy, Z. (1990). From net widening to intermediate sanctions: The transformation of alternatives to incarceration from benevolence to malevolence. In J. M. Byrne, A. J. Lurigio, & J. Petersilia (Eds.), *Smart sentencing: The emergence of intermediate sanctions.* Thousand Oaks, CA: Sage.

Parent, D. G. (1994, August). Boot camp failing to achieve goals. *Overcrowded Times, 5,* 8.

Paternoster, R. (1987). The deterrent effect of the perceived certainty and severity of punishment: A review of the evidence and issues. *Justice Quarterly, 4,* 173-194.

Petersilia, J., & Deschenes, E. P. (1994). *Perceptions of punishment: Inmates and staff rank the severity of prison versus intermediate sanctions.* Unpublished manuscript on file with the *University of Chicago Law School Roundtable.*

Petersilia, J., & Turner, S. (1993). Intensive probation and parole. *Crime & Justice, 17,* 281-335.

Quinlan, J. M. (1993). News of the future: Carving out new territory for American corrections. *Federal Probation, 57*(4), 59-63.

Roberts, J. V. (1992). Public opinion, crime, and criminal justice. *Crime & Justice, 16,* 99-180.

Sechrest, D. K. (1989). Prison "boot camps" do not measure up. *Federal Probation, 53,* 15-20.

Skovron, S. E., Scott, J. E., & Cullen, F. T. (1988). Prison crowding: Public attitudes toward strategies of population control. *Journal of Research in Crime & Delinquency, 25,* 150-169.

Taxman, F. S. (1994, Winter). Correctional options and implementation issues: Results from a survey of correctional professionals. *Perspectives, 18,* 32.

Turner, S., Petersilia, J., & Deschenes, E. P. (1994) The implementation and effectiveness of drug testing in community supervision: Results of an experimental evaluation. In D. L. MacKenzie & C. D. Uchida (Eds.), *Drugs and crime: Evaluating public policy initiatives.* Thousand Oaks, CA: Sage.

U.S. General Accounting Office. (1993, April). *Prison boot camps: Short-term prison costs reduced, but long-term impact uncertain.* Washington, DC: Author.

Violent Crime Control and Law Enforcement Act of 1994, Pub L. No. 103-322.

von Hirsch, A. (1992). Scaling intermediate punishments: A comparison of two models. In J. M. Byrne, A. J. Lurigio, & J. Petersilia (Eds.), *Smart sentencing: The emergence of intermediate sanctions.* Thousand Oaks, CA: Sage.

The White House. (1989). *National drug control strategy.* Washington, DC: Office of National Drug Control Policy.

Young, W., & Brown, M. (1993). Cross-national comparisons of imprisonment. *Crime & Justice, 17,* 1-49.

Zamble, E., & Porporino, F. (1990). Coping, imprisonment, and rehabilitation: Some data and their implications. *Criminal Justice & Behavior, 17,* 53-70.

Part III

The Environment of Boot Camps

7

PERFORMANCE-BASED STANDARDS FOR JUVENILE CORRECTIONS

DORIS LAYTON MACKENZIE

GAYLENE J. STYVE

ANGELA R. GOVER

Recidivism rates have long served as the critical measure for evaluating the effectiveness of correctional programs. Yet, few corrections practitioners believe that recidivism rates depend mainly on factors they can control. Recently, there has been a recognition of this problem and some have called for a new paradigm for the justice system (Boone & Fulton, 1995; DiIulio, 1993). This new paradigm would continue to recognize the importance of the long-range measures of success but would also recognize the importance of intermediate measures of effectiveness that are more directly under the control of correctional personnel. An important component of this new paradigm is the need for clearly identified performance-based standards.

The move toward performance-based standards is based on total quality management (TQM)—a concept that has revolutionized business and some government agencies. Performance-based standards would give correctional personnel a barometer to use for gauging whether they are achieving the desired outcomes. Traditionally, standards in corrections have been based on expert consensus. These standards were determined by knowledgeable experts' views of "best practices" in corrections. In contrast, performance-based standards use empirical measures of outcomes to determine the effectiveness of correctional practices.

At first glance, performance-based standards appear threatening to many corrections practitioners because recidivism has been the traditional outcome measure of interest. Most correctional personnel recognize that there are numerous factors that influence recidivism, and many of these factors are beyond their ability to control. However, the call for new measures for evaluating effectiveness, combined with a focus on more short-term measures of success, makes performance-based standards more acceptable.

This article describes how some of the new developments in business, government, and corrections can be used to change our view of how standards for juvenile corrections might be developed in light of the new paradigm. A change toward quality management will require clearly identified short- and long-term goals for corrections and the development of methods for obtaining information about the achievement of these goals.

TOTAL QUALITY MANAGEMENT

Quality management has been a driving force in recent years in the redesign of private organizations and corporations; only recently have these concepts begun to be applied in the public domain (Jablonski, 1991). The concept of quality management was originated by W.E. Deming, a statistician who was asked to provide some advice to Japanese manufacturers to get the economy back on its feet after World War II (MacKenzie, 1996). At the time, U.S. consumers were reluctant to purchase anything labeled "Made in Japan" because the quality of the products was usually so poor.

Deming argued that quality is in the eye of the beholder; if you are making a product or delivering a service the quality is judged by the customer (MacKenzie, 1996). Total quality means quality in all aspects of the work quality of the product, quality of the service, quality information, quality objectives, quality organization, and a quality institution. Using this broad view of quality, Deming developed the concept of TQM, a comprehensive, client-focused strategy to improve the output of an organization. TQM is a way of managing an organization at all levels from management to line staff. The goal is to achieve client satisfaction by involving all employees in continuously improving the work process of the organization.

Developing TQM requires leadership by top management with long-term strategic planning and short-term strategic tactical planning to implement TQM throughout the organization. Clearly defined measures for tracking progress and identifying improvement opportunities must be developed. The systems conforming to TQM require adequate resources for employee training and education as well as methods for recognizing and reinforcing positive behavior. Workers are empowered to make decisions, and teamwork is encouraged. Perhaps most important is the need to develop a system to ensure that quality is built in at the beginning and continues throughout the production of a quality product or the offering of a quality service.

REENGINEERING CORRECTIONAL AGENCIES

When an institution's circumstances require a major change, the incremental improvements of TQM may not be enough (MacKenzie, 1996). At such times drastic action is required. The process, called reengineering, involves a radical change in the way an institution operates. The philosophy is that of starting over—"If we could begin again, how would we recreate ourselves?" Unlike TQM, which is a bottom-up, continuous improvement, incremental process, reengineering is top down and seeks continuous improvement in work processes. Reengineering starts with the desired outcome from work processes, designs the work processes that are most likely to lead to these outcomes, and then constructs the organization required to implement the processes.

Osborne and Gaebler's (1982) book *Reinventing Government* applied TQM to government. They emphasized that performance standards could be developed for public agencies. Their research on cities illustrated that government could be just as effective as private entities when it was forced to depart from a monopoly position and compete in the marketplace. The idea is that government agencies could bring quality into all functions of government. And, in 1993, the U.S. Congress passed the Government Performance and Results Act (GPRA) with the purpose of improving "the efficiency and effectiveness of federal programs by establishing a system to set goals for program performance and to measure results" (RAND, 1995). The law attempts to improve program management through the process of operationalizing strategic plans and specifying outcome measures and how they will be evaluated. Budget allocations can then be made using this performance information.

HOW CAN THESE CONCEPTS BE APPLIED TO CORRECTIONAL AGENCIES?

While the use of such performance standards in public agencies is relatively new, it has important implications for use in correctional agencies. In order to succeed, reengineering may be necessary, beginning with a reexamination of the philosophy and operation of corrections. This reengineering will require clarification of the objectives, identification of the clients, and improvement in the quality of information used for decision making. Short- and long-term strategic planning will be necessary (Wright, 1994). Perhaps one of the most important aspects of such quality planning will be the development of measures that permit clearly defined methods for tracking progress and identifying improvement opportunities.

In Deming's opinion, workers are blamed frequently for failure to produce a quality product or provide a quality service (MacKenzie, 1996). He demonstrated this concept by asking a volunteer from the audience to select from an urn a sample of red and white plastic balls using a specially designed ladle. He asked the volunteer to select only white balls, an impossible task given the number of each in the urn. Deming's point was that it is not the worker's fault if there is something wrong with the process.

This feeling is shared by many correctional workers regarding what they are being asked to do. They are held responsible for outcomes that are so far in the future and influenced by so many other factors that they see little relationship between what they do and what happens later. Workers need information about short-term performance as well as long-term outcomes. As the system now exists, workers seldom receive information on either short- or long-term outcomes. They are forced to work with anecdotal information about success. However, they can hardly be expected to work to improve the correctional process if they have little idea of the goals and whether the outcomes reach the goals.

CONDITIONS OF CONFINEMENT AND PERFORMANCE-BASED STANDARDS

Much attention in the corrections community has focused on the standards used for corrections. Traditionally, these standards have been based on the opinions of experts in the field. High rates of conformance with nationally recognized standards do not necessarily mean that all is well. Many of the existing standards specify procedures and processes to be followed, but not outcomes to be achieved (OJJDP, 1994). However, recently, there has been a push toward verifying the validity of these standards through the use of data on actual performance (performance-based standards). These performance-based standards would tie the standards to the performance or outcomes desired.

Rather than depending on reports of the success of some program, such performance standards would require clear evidence of impact. There are several lines of research that have begun to move in the direction of providing information for quality management for corrections (Gendreau & Andrews, 1996; Moos, 1974; Toch, 1977; Wright, 1985). These projects are attempts to quantify aspects of the environment that can be used as indices of the quality of the environment. The first step requires methods to measure aspects or conditions of confinement. The next step requires a clear definition and a way to measure the expected relationship between the aspects or conditions of confinement and the outcomes to be achieved.

A substantial body of literature has begun to recommend the need to specify the components of programs and their relationships with outcomes. For example, a recent Office of Juvenile Justice and Delinquency Prevention (OJJDP) publication examined the conditions of confinement of juvenile detention and correctional facilities (OJJDP, 1994). Using mailed surveys, the Children in Custody Census, and site visits, researchers measured conformance to national professional standards and other selected aspects of conditions. They recommended further study of why facilities vary so dramatically in such factors as exercise of control and safety. Furthermore, they proposed that more research be completed to examine the effects of these conditions on the juveniles both while they are in the facilities and upon release.

Similarly, after completing their evaluation of the juvenile VisionQuest Program, Greenwood and Turner (1987) also recommended that future evaluations describe and measure the "program inputs and processes" that can influence the effectiveness of a program. As the authors are arguing here, they propose that the general classification of a program as a boot camp or a wilderness program does not give a detailed enough description to enable identification of the components that will produce the desired impact. More detailed information about the conditions of confinement is needed as well as how these conditions are associated with measures of performance and effectiveness.

Another line of work that has sparked discussions within the criminal justice community focuses on reevaluating commonly used performance measures. This subject was the topic of a 1993 Bureau of Justice Statistics-Princeton University project (DiIulio, 1993). The project working group proposed that the use of traditional criminal justice performance measures should be rethought. In particular, DiIulio (1993) argued that while rates of crime and recidivism may represent basic goals of public safety, they are not the only, or necessarily the best, measures of what criminal justice institutions do. He advised criminal justice agencies to develop mission statements that include any activities that the agency can reasonably and realistically be expected to fulfill (DiIulio, 1991). In line with this advice is Logan's emphasis on evaluating prisons on the day-to-day operations, not on ultimate, utilitarian goals of rehabilitation or crime reduction (Logan, 1992). Logan further argues that if we "do not want to set [prisons] up for failure, we must assign them a function and a mission that we might reasonably expect them to fulfill" (DiIulio, 1993, p. 24). To paraphrase Logan's point of view, goals must be narrow and consistent in scope, and achievable and measurable within the prison itself with intrinsic and not just instrumental value.

Petersilia (1993) argued that along with their public safety functions, community corrections should be evaluated on other activities such as the accuracy, completeness, and timeliness of pre-sentence investigations, monitoring of court-ordered sanctions, and how well offenders are helped to change in positive ways. Thus, these researchers emphasize not only the need to investigate components or conditions of the environments being studied but also the need to use a wider range of measures to examine effectiveness.

Taken as a whole, the work by these researchers emphasizes the need for methods to measure the conditions or environments of correctional programs. Moreover, the research needs to examine the relationship between these conditions and intermediate and long-term outcomes.

National Study of Juvenile Boot Camps and Comparison Facilities

The authors are currently in the progress of studying juvenile facilities to determine the conditions of confinement of boot camps and comparison facilities. More than 50 sites have agreed to participate in the study. To date, data have been collected from 49 facilities and surveys have been conducted of over 2,400 juvenile inmates. The study focuses on identifying the differences among institutions and the intermediate impacts of the environments on the juveniles who spend time in the facilities.

Environment Quantification

Despite the benefits such information would provide, a limited number of researchers have tried to quantify the correctional environment in a manner that is conducive to assessment of the environment. Yet, reliable quantification of juvenile facilities would allow different types of programs within a jurisdiction as well as nationwide to be compared. For example, can we generalize all types of "juvenile boot camps" and speak of them as a whole or are there significant differences within the boot camps or between them and other types of programs?

Quantification would also allow examination of program impact on youth, change over time while in the program, youth outcomes and institutional change over time including recidivism, positive adjustment, and community reintegration outcome measures. Researchers frequently focus on offender change due to participation in a program. This method of research would also provide an avenue for examining the role of institutional change and progression in the correctional process.

Models for Measuring the Conditions of Confinement

There are several different models that may be appropriately adapted for measuring the environments of juvenile facilities: OJJDP's (1994) Conditions of Confinement Study, Quality of Confinement indices used by Logan (1992), the Correctional Program Inventory (CPI) developed by Gendreau and Andrews (1996), the Prison Environment Inventory (PEI) tested by Wright (1985), and the Prison Social Climate Survey used by the Federal Bureau of Prisons (1993). Each study includes quantitative indices to measure aspects of the environment.

OJJDP researchers assessed 46 criteria that reflected existing national professional standards (from ACA, The National Commission on Correctional Health Care, ABA) in 12 areas representing the advisors' perceptions of the most important needs of the confined juvenile. They focus on four broad areas (basic needs, order and safety, programming, juveniles' rights). The researchers examined the association between these conditions and such factors as escapes, suicides, and injuries.

In a similar manner, in his comparisons of private and public prisons, Logan developed indices to measure the quality of confinement based on his perception of the goals of corrections. He proposed that correctional institutions should not be asked to do what other social institutions are more responsible for doing and have failed to do. He argued that it is unfair to expect corrections officials to somehow "correct the incorrigible, rehabilitate the wretched, deter the determined, restrain the dangerous and punish the wicked" (Logan, 1993, p. 23). They should instead be responsible for what they can do—"keep prisoners—keep them in, keep them safe, keep them in line, keep them healthy, and keep them busy—and do it with fairness, without undue suffering, and as efficiently as possible" (Logan, 1993, p. 25). While the authors disagree with Logan's philosophy of ignoring rehabilitation, his work provides an excellent example of how we can measure components of the environments that can be used to develop standards. He used various measures of safety, health, activity, and so on to compare private and public facilities.

In direct contrast to Logan's proposal, Gendreau and Andrews (1996) propose that rehabilitation and the reduction of recidivism are the very essence of corrections. The Correctional Program Evaluation Inventory (CPEI) was developed by Gendreau and Andrews to measure aspects of the environment that are indicative of the quality of therapeutic programs. The authors agree with Gendreau and Andrews. Correctional facilities for juveniles are not only designed to keep them in and keep them active but also to rehabilitate. Particularly in regard to juveniles, a major goal of corrections should be rehabilitation. Thus, if standards are to be developed, it is important to design methods to measure the components of the environment that are important to rehabilitation.

Last, there is a body of research showing the importance of environmental influences on inmate behavior (Goodstein & Wright, 1989; Moos, 1968, 1974; Toch, 1977; Wright, 1985, 1991; Zamble & Porporino, 1990). The prison environment is defined as a set of conditions that is perceived by its members and is assumed to exert a major influence on behavior (Lutze, in press). The prison environment affects inmates in different ways. A common theme appearing in this research is that some environments are supportive of rehabilitation, others are not.

The Prison Climate Survey, another environmental survey developed by Saylor and colleagues at the Federal Bureau of Prisons, provides an excellent example of how surveys can be used for management decisions (Federal Bureau of Prisons, 1993). They developed methods for surveying staff and inmates in facilities. This information is processed and rapidly returned to the facilities so administrators can use it to compare their facilities with others or to examine how their facility has changed over time. In the latter situation, the information is valuable as a gauge to see the impact of some administrative decision or change.

In all of the above-cited research, the researchers developed quantitative indices or scales that could be used to measure aspects or components of the environment. While they differ in their view of some correctional goals, in general they agree on the basic components of quality correctional programs.

Surveys of Juvenile Institutions

As shown in Table 7.1, there are many similarities among the dimensions used to measure the components of the environment. They

Table 7.1   Comparison of Prison Environment Indices

Performance Measures	Prison Environment Inventory	Correctional Institutions Environmental Scale	Conditions of Confinement	Prison Social Climate Survey
1. Security	1. Privacy	1. Staff Control	1. Security arrangements	1. Security
2. Activity	2. Activity Social stimulation	2. Involvement		2. Services
3. Safety	3. Safety		3. Staffing Deaths Health care issues	3. Personal safety
4. Justice		4. Clarity		
5. Order	5. Structure	5. Order Organization		
6. Conditions				6. Quality of life Personal well-being
7. Care	7. Emotional feedback Support	7. Expressiveness Support Personal problem Orientation		
8. Management and problems				
		9. Freedom	9. Autonomy 10. Practical orientation	9. Community access

provide excellent models for developing measures of the conditions of confinement for juvenile facilities.

In the authors' study of environments they designed four types of surveys to capture both objective "hard record" data and subjective or "soft perceptual" measures of the correctional environment. Separate survey questions were developed for inmates and staff in order to obtain subjective reports on questions regarding the various aspects of their environment. A facility survey obtains objective information such as the number of injuries and escapes (e.g., safety) that parallels the environmental conditions rated by staff and inmates.

Similarly, an innovative videotape survey technique allows for objective quantification of the environment. The videotape survey also parallels the perceptual information collected. The videotape aims to capture the complex interactions expected between individual and environmental factors. Wright noted the desirability of conceptualizing some interrelated dimensions that may act as behavioral predictors (Wright, 1985).

In each survey, the authors attempted to capture important components of the environment including control, activity, safety, care, risks to residents, quality of life, structure, justice, freedom, perceived benefits of rehabilitation, and aftercare/individualized planning. For example, the authors assumed that a well-run facility would be safe for staff and inmates. Therefore, in the survey for the juveniles and staff they were asked whether they were safe in the facility. They were also asked if they were afraid of being hurt by staff or other inmates. The facility survey served as another method for determining the safety of the environment because information such as the number of injuries or accidents that had occurred in the facility in a specific time period was requested. As a pilot study, the authors also included a video survey of the institutions in order to examine whether information about the environment obtained from a video would supplement the information on safety issues obtained from the other surveys.

Another example of the type of information being obtained is that coming from the justice

Table 7.2   Measures: Conditions of the Environment Showing Intermediate and Long-Term Outcomes

Conditions of the environment	Intermediate outcomes	Long-term outcomes
Control	Depression	Recidivism
Activity	Anxiety	School
Safety	Accomplishments	Employment
Care	(education, skills, vocational training)	Ties to the community
		• family
Risks to residents	Antisocial attitudes	• school
Quality of life	Locus of control	• employment
Structure	Dysfunctional impulsivity	Commitment to conventional behavior
Justice	Ties to the community	Peer associates
Freedom	• family	
Rehabilitation focus	• school	
Aftercare/Individualized planning	• employment	
	Commitment to conventional behavior	

scales. The authors assumed that quality facilities should have methods for inmates and staff to file grievances and that each group should know how this process worked. They should not be afraid to complain if they have been treated unfairly, they should have someone to turn to when they need help, and they should not believe that they are unfairly punished.

The authors propose that such empirical measures of the environments may be indicative of the quality of an environment and can represent the basis for developing standards. The next step is to identify intermediate and long-term goals that can be measured. The ultimate goal is to understand the relationship between the conditions and the intermediate and long-term goals and to further recognize mediating factors.

Table 7.2 shows some of the measures the authors are using in their study of juvenile facilities to examine the intermediate outcomes. A study of the long-term outcomes is being postponed to a later phase of the study. In the study, the authors will investigate whether a safe institution will result in changes in the juveniles spending time in the facility. Will they be less anxious and depressed? Will their antisocial attitudes decline? Will more juveniles complete treatment or educational programs? Theoretically, juveniles in a safe, caring environment that focuses on rehabilitation should experience less depression, anxiety, and antisocial attitudes and their ties to family, school, and employment should increase.

CONCLUSION

Many ideas from total quality management and reengineering can be used to improve juvenile institutions. One particularly important aspect is the need for quality information about the environments of juvenile institutions and the impact of these environments on the staff and juveniles who must live and work there. Such information will be an invaluable tool for administrators to gauge their institutions against others. Furthermore, by increasing understanding of the relationship between the components of the environment and the intermediate and long-term outcomes, the goal of developing reasonable performance-based standards for juvenile corrections will be closer.

REFERENCES

Boone, H. N., Jr., & Fulton, B. (1995). *Results driven management: Implementing performance-based measures in community corrections.* Washington, DC: American Probation and Parole Association.

DiIulio, J. J., Jr. (1991). *No escape: The future of American corrections.* New York: Basic Books.

DiIulio, J. J., Jr. (1993). Rethinking the criminal justice system: Toward a new paradigm. In J. J. DiIulio, Jr., et al. (Eds.), *Performance measures for the criminal justice system.* Washington, DC: Bureau of Justice Statistics.

Federal Bureau of Prisons. (1993). *Prison Social Climate Survey: Staff version and resident version.* Washington, DC: Government Printing Office.

Gendreau, P., & Andrews, D. A. (1996). *Correctional Program Evaluation Inventory.* Unpublished manuscript.

Goodstein, L., & Wright, K. N. (1989). Inmate adjustment to prison. In D. L. MacKenzie & L. Goodstein (Eds.), *The American prison: Issues in research and policy.* New York: Plenum.

Greenwood, P., & Turner, S. (1987). *The VisionQuest program: An evaluation.* Santa Monica, CA: RAND.

Jablonski, J. R. (1991). *Implementing Total Quality Management: An overview.* San Diego, CA: Pfeiffer.

Logan, C. H. (1992). Well kept: Comparing quality of confinement in private and public prisons. *Journal of Criminal Law and Criminology, 83,* 577-613.

Logan, C. H. (1993). Criminal justice performance measures for prisons. In J. J. DiIulio, Jr., et al. (Eds.), *Performance measures for the criminal justice system.* Washington, DC: Bureau of Justice Statistics.

Lutze, F. E. (in press). Do boot camp prisons possess a more rehabilitative environment than traditional prisons? A survey of inmates. *Justice Quarterly.*

MacKenzie, D. R. (1996). *Principles of agricultural research management.* New York: University Press of America.

Moos, R. H. (1968). The assessment of social climates of correctional institutions. *Journal of Research in Crime and Delinquency, 5,* 174-188.

Moos, R. H. (1974). *Correctional Institutions Environment Scale manual.* Palo Alto, CA: Consulting Psychologists Press.

Office of Juvenile Justice and Delinquency Prevention (OJJDP). (1994). *Conditions of confinement: Juvenile detention and correctional facilities.* Washington, DC: Government Printing Office.

Osborne, D., & Gaebler, T. (1982). *Reinventing government.* New York: Praeger.

Petersilia, J. (1993). Measuring the performance of community corrections. In J. J. DiIulio, Jr., et al. (Eds.), *Performance measures for the criminal justice system.* Washington, DC: Bureau of Justice Statistics.

RAND Corporation. (1995). *Assessment of fundamental science programs in the context of the Government Performance and Results Act.* Prepared for the Office of Science and Technology Policy. Santa Monica, CA: Author.

Toch, H. (1977). *Living in prison: The ecology of survival.* New York: Macmillan.

Wright, K. N. (1985). Developing the prison environment inventory. *Journal of Research in Crime and Delinquency, 22,* 257-277.

Wright, K. N. (1991). Successful prison leadership. *Federal Prisons Journal, 2*(3), 5-15.

Wright, K. N. (1994). *Effective prison leadership.* Binghamton, NY: William Neil Publishing.

Wright, K. N., & Boudouris, J. (1982). An assessment of the Moos correctional institution's environment scale. *Journal of Research in Crime and Delinquency, 19,* 255-276.

Zamble, E., & Porporino, F. J. (1990). Coping, imprisonment and rehabilitation: Some data and their implications. *Criminal Justice & Behavior, 17*(1), 53-70.

8

PERCEIVED CONDITIONS OF CONFINEMENT

A National Evaluation of Juvenile Boot Camps and Traditional Facilities

GAYLENE J. STYVE

DORIS LAYTON MACKENZIE

ANGELA R. GOVER

OJMARRH MITCHELL

In a national study of juvenile correctional facilities, the perceived environment of 22 juvenile boot camps were compared to the perceived environment of 22 traditional facilities. Self-report surveys completed by 4,121 juveniles recorded information on demographics, risk factors and perceptions of the facility's environment. Compared to juveniles in traditional correctional facilities, boot camp residents consistently perceived the environment as

Reprinted by permission of Kluwer from Styve, G. J., MacKenzie, D. L., Gover, A. R., & Mitchell, O. (2000). *Law and Human Behavior, 24*(3), 297-308.

AUTHORS' NOTE: An earlier version of this paper was presented at the 1998 Annual American Society of Criminology meeting in Washington, D.C. This investigation was supported in part by grant #96-SC-LX-0001 from the National Institute of Justice, Office of Justice Programs, U.S. Department of Justice, to the University of Maryland. Points of view in this document are those of the authors and do not necessarily represent the official position of the Department of Justice. Thanks are expressed to administrators, staff and juveniles at the correctional facilities who participated in this research as well as the Center for Substance Abuse Research who provided some technical assistance.

significantly more controlled, active, structured, and as having less danger from other residents. Boot camp juveniles also perceived the environment as providing more therapeutic and transitional programming. Overall, from the perspective of the juveniles, boot camps appear to provide a more positive environment conducive to effective rehabilitation considering almost all of the conditions measured. A major concern is that in both types of facilities, juveniles perceived themselves to occasionally be in danger from staff (rated as rarely to sometimes).

Correctional boot camps for juveniles is a controversial subject (MacKenzie & Hebert, 1996; MacKenzie & Parent, 1992; Meachum, 1990; Morash & Rucker, 1990). There is disagreement about the appropriateness of boot camps as a correctional program and whether the camps are conducive to positive growth and change. In contrast to traditional correctional programs, boot camps incorporate basic elements of the military philosophy into their program. For example, most boot camps require juveniles to wear military style uniforms, march to and from activities, enter and exit the program in squads or platoons, participate in military style drill and ceremony and emphasize physical fitness activities.

Advocates argue the focus on strict control and military structure provides a safer environment which is more conducive to positive change (Steinhart, 1993; Zachariah, 1996). From this perspective, the intense physical activity and healthy atmosphere of the camps provide an advantageous backdrop for therapy, education and other treatment activities (Clark & Aziz, in MacKenzie & Hebert, 1996; Cowles & Castellano, 1995).

Critics of the camps suggest the confrontational nature of boot camps is antithetical to treatment. In fact, they argue some aspects of the boot camps are diametrically opposed to the constructive, interpersonally supportive treatment environment necessary for positive change to occur (Lipsey, 1992; Andrews, Zinger, Hoge, Bonta, Gendreau & Cullen, 1990a). It is argued that boot camps hold inconsistent philosophies and procedures (Marlowee, Marin, Schneider, Vaitkus & Bartone, 1988), set the stage for abusive punishments (Morash & Rucker, 1990), and perpetuate a "we versus they" attitude suggesting newer inmates are deserving of degrading treatment (Raupp, 1978). Critics expect the boot camp environment to be perceived as less caring, unfair or unjust, and less therapeutic as compared to traditional facilities. They anticipate that youth may fear staff and that the camps will have less individualized programming, as a result, youth will be less prepared for their return to the community.

Although treatment in most boot camps is minimal and physical activities are extensive, studies have found boot camp inmates report a more positive institutional experience than comparable inmates in traditional prisons. However, as a treatment perspective would predict, boot camp inmates do not fare better after they return to the community. Comparisons of juvenile (Clawson, Coolbaugh, & Zamberlan, 1998) or adult boot camp inmates (MacKenzie, Brame, McDowall & Souryal, 1995) to inmates who received more traditional correctional options (prison, probation, training schools, detention centers) show no differences in recidivism rates or participation in constructive community activities such as work and school (MacKenzie & Brame, 1995). However, despite the empirical evidence, boot camps have remained a popular sentencing option for juveniles.

IMPACT OF THE FACILITY ENVIRONMENT ON ADJUSTMENT AND CHANGE

The impact of the prison environment on inmate adjustment and behavior inside and outside the prison walls has been well established in the research literature (Ajdukovic, 1990; Goffman, 1961; Johnson & Toch, 1982; Moos, 1971; Wright, 1985, 1991; Wright & Goodstein, 1989; Zamble & Porporino, 1990). Facilities have been found to "possess unique and enduring characteristics that impinge upon and shape individual behavior" (Wright & Goodstein, 1989, p. 266). As such, an understanding of potential differences in the perception of environments of boot camps and traditional facilities are important.

To positively impact inmate adjustment, correctional environments at minimum must provide an environment that is perceived as safe, supportive, structured and controlled to allow inmates to focus on the treatment programs. Though boot camps may provide some of these basic components, they may not be sufficient for rehabilitation to occur. Successful rehabilitation and the reduction of recidivism requires more. Care, justice, therapeutic programming, preparation for the future, and individual attention are the sufficient conditions for rehabilitation programs to be effective. The lack of these sufficient conditions within the boot camp environment may explain why they are no more successful in reducing recidivism than traditional programs.

CONDITIONS OF CONFINEMENT

Several models were adapted for quantifying the environmental conditions of juvenile facilities (see Federal Bureau of Prisons, 1993; Gendreau & Andrews, 1994; Logan, 1993; Moos, 1974; OJJDP, 1994; Wright, 1985). Although these authors often varied in their categorizations of physical dimensions, a closer examination of the survey instruments suggested many similarities (MacKenzie, Styve & Gover, 1998). The environmental scales utilized in this study were consistent with a combination of the multitude of concepts measured by previous researchers in prison environments.

In this study, we build on previous research which has examined the prison environment to determine how inmates perceive the environment of two dramatically different programs. We expect inmates in boot camps and traditional facilities will perceive consistent differences in their environments. If consistent differences between the two environments are confirmed, it is suggested the lack of sufficient conditions for rehabilitation in the boot camp environment may explain the similarity in recidivism rates between the two types of institutions.

METHOD

Participants

Incarcerated juveniles ($n = 4,181$) from 24 boot camps ($n = 2,668$) were surveyed and compared to 22 traditional facilities ($n = 1,848$)[1].

Traditional facilities were selected as a comparison for each boot camp facility by identifying the state facility in which the juveniles would have been confined if the boot camp was not in operation. These matched facilities are referred to as state pairs or state paired facilities.

Survey Instrument

The survey included 266 questions consisting of 17 demographic questions, 13 environmental conditions scales, 17 risk factor scales (criminal history and attitudes) and 9 intermediate outcome scales. Thirteen questions were open-ended (primarily demographics) with the remaining questions based on 5-point Likert scales[2]. Surveys were administered in classroom-like settings in groups of 15 to 20 participants in accordance with prevailing ethical principles. A videotaped presentation of instructions and survey questions were provided on televisions to ensure uniform administration and provide assistance to juveniles with reading difficulties.

Scale Development

Conditions of Confinement Scales. Items were developed for thirteen conditions of confinement summated scales: (1) Control, the security measures exerted over the residents to keep them in the facility and monitor their activities; (2) Resident Danger, the resident's risk of being injured by other residents; (3) Danger from Staff, the resident's risk of being injured by staff members; (4) Environmental Danger, the resident's risk of being injured as a result of being institutionalized; (5) Activity, the level and variety of activities available to inmates; (6) Care, the quality of interactions between juveniles as well as between staff and juveniles; (7) Risks to Residents, the risks to the residents as a result of facility conditions; (8) Quality of Life, the general social environment including resident's ability to maintain some degree of individuality; (9) Structure, the formality of daily routines and interactions with staff and other residents; (10) Justice, the appropriateness and constructiveness of punishments given to the residents; (11) Freedom, the provision of choice of activities and movement to residents; (12) Therapeutic

Programming, the availability and utility of therapeutic opportunities; (13) Preparation for Release, activities with juveniles prior to release to assist the juvenile in the transition back to society.[3]

Factor Analysis

All scales were formed utilizing confirmatory factor analysis methods for each scale. Initially, both the Barlett's Test of Sphericity and Kaiser-Meyer-Olkin (KMO) measure of sampling adequacy were performed to determine whether factor analysis of the questions was warranted. Given acceptable KMO and Bartlett scores, Varimax factor analysis with pair-wise deletion of missing cases was performed.[4] Additionally, Cronbach's alpha reliability test (1951) tested the internal consistency of the items. If acceptable, scale scores were computed controlling for missing data.[5] All scales contained less than 10 percent missing data. The only scale that was not developed was for a measure of Individualized Planning. Items pertaining to this concept failed to factor analyze or demonstrate internal consistency.

Analytic Model

Individual differences between inmate characteristics in each type of facility was determined using t-tests for continuous variables and the Kolmogorov-Smirnov (K-S) test for categorical variables. Subsequently, Analysis of Covariance (ANCOVA) was performed to examine the inmates' perceptions of the environments in boot camps and traditional facilities. Separate analyses were completed for each of the thirteen environmental conditions. Variables in the model were type of facility (boot camp vs. traditional facility), the state pair (grouping of boot camp and comparable traditional facility within a state), individual differences (gender, race, age, sentence, age at first arrest, length of incarceration, prior commitments, family violence history, substance use, and alcohol abuse) and an interaction between boot camps and the state pairs.

This interaction term indicated whether environmental differences were consistent among all the state pairs or if differences existed in only some of the state pairs. If the interaction term was significant, contrast statements in the ANCOVA model compared the mean difference between each boot camp and traditional facility to the overall mean difference between the two types of facilities. The contrast statement implemented the equation:

$$(X_{\text{boot camp}} - X_{\text{traditional facility}}) - (\text{boot camp}_i - \text{traditional facility}_i)$$

for $i = 1, \ldots 22$ facilities.

If the contrast statement was significantly different from zero as determined by a t-test, it was necessary to determine whether differences between environments are due to direction or magnitude. To do so it was necessary to refer to the estimated marginal means of the significant state paired facilities to compare them with the overall means of boot camps and traditional facilities.

If each mean difference between the facilities was similar to the difference between the overall mean of boot camps and traditional facility, conclusions regarding a consistent difference in environments are warranted. For example, if a state's boot camps had a higher mean level on the environmental control scale in comparison to the traditional facility, we conclude there is a consistent difference in environmental control between boot camps and traditional facilities. However, if some state boot camps have higher control than traditional facilities, while others do not (a directional difference from the overall mean) a lack of consistency in perceived environmental control exists.

RESULTS

Demographics and Risk Factors

In examining the inmates within boot camps and traditional facilities, as shown in Table 8.1, t-tests and K-S tests demonstrated significant differences between groups in the mean age, sentence length, age at first arrest, length of incarceration, number of previous commitments, family violence, substance use, and alcohol abuse. The magnitude of these differences is

Table 8.1   Demographic Comparison of Boot Camp and Comparison Facility Populations

Characteristic		Boot Camp (n = 2668)	Comparison (n = 1848)
Gender (% male)		92.1	95.6
Race (%)	African American	35.3	32.0
	White	34.1	31.1
	Hispanic	18.5	19.2
	Native American	3.7	5.6
	Asian	1.2	1.9
	Other	6.7	9.3
Age, M (SD)*		16.1 (1.2)	16.3 (1.4)
Sentence Length, M (SD)*		9.46 (14.4)	16.2 (26.5)
Age at first arrest, M (SD)*		13.5 (1.9)	12.9 (.75)
Length of incarceration, M (SD)*		3.01 (3.4)	6.54 (8.1)
Number of Prior Commitments, M (SD)*		2.59 (2.3)	2.96 (2.6)
Family Violence Scale, M (SD)*		1.55 (.64)	1.66 (.75)
Substance Use Scale, M (SD)*		1.48 (.27)	1.46 (.28)
Alcohol Abuse Scale, M (SD)*		1.69 (.31)	1.64 (.31)

*$p < .05$.

small in most cases; however, these individual differences were subsequently controlled for in the ANCOVA model as covariates.

Environmental Conditions

In the ANCOVA model there were significant main effects for state and type of facility (boot camp and traditional facility). The state by boot camp interaction was significant for all thirteen environmental conditions. The magnitude of the differences between means in the two types of facilities is displayed in the fourth column of Table 8.2. A standardized coefficient, Cohen's d effect size (ES), was calculated for each of the environmental conditions (Cohen, 1977). The Cohen's d coefficient was defined as the boot camp group mean minus the comparison group mean, divided by the pooled groups' standard deviation. A positive ES indicated a higher level of the outcome in the boot camp whereas a negative ES indicated a higher level of the outcome in the comparison facility.

The last column of Table 8.2 displays the number of state pairs that coincide with the overall means adjusted for the covariates. Our investigation of the interactions revealed that in 17 or more of the 22 facilities (more than 75%), inmates in the boot camps perceived the boot camps as having more therapeutic programming, activity, structure, control, and a more thorough preparation process for release from the facility. Boot camp inmates also perceived the facility to pose less dangers from other inmates, the environment and have fewer general risks to residents. Thus, in the vast majority of the camps, the juveniles perceived the environments as high in the characteristics expected in a boot camp environment (structure, control, safety from other inmates) but they also view the environments as most positive in the more therapeutic components such as therapeutic programming and preparation for release. Additionally, although somewhat less consistently, boot camps are perceived by the inmates as being more just and more caring.

Due to a lack of consistency, it is unclear which type of environment (boot camp vs. traditional facility) is perceived as having greater danger from staff, a better quality of life and more freedom. It appears these variables may be more specific to the individual facility rather than the type of program. Thus our initial hypothesis that boot camps would be perceived as consistently different environments from traditional facilities is confirmed for eight of the thirteen conditions. Our hypothesis is disconfirmed for three of the environments and unclear in two of the conditions.

Table 8.2   Adjusted Mean Scale Scores of Boot Camps and Comparison Facilities

Scale	Adjusted Means (SD)		Effect Size	Facilities consistent with the adjusted overall mean N (max. 22 facilities)
	Boot Camp	Comparison		
Therapeutic Programs*	3.66 (.99)	3.25 (1.0)	.41	21
Activity*	3.97 (.82)	3.50 (.91)	.54	21
Structure*	3.83 (.69)	3.47 (.68)	.49	22
Preparation for Release*	3.88 (.69)	3.73 (.73)	.21	21
Control*	3.14 (.59)	2.73 (.56)	.71	21
Resident Danger*	1.96 (.78)	2.49 (.77)	−.68	21
Environmental Danger*	2.31 (.88)	2.85 (.79)	−.65	21
Risks to Residents*	2.29 (.81)	2.72 (.85)	−.52	20
Justice*	3.10 (.79)	3.08 (.74)	.03	18
Care*	3.36 (.75)	2.12 (.68)	1.73	17
Danger from Staff*	2.45 (1.0)	2.27 (1.0)	.18	15
Quality of Life*	3.02 (.66)	2.86 (.71)	.23	15
Freedom*	2.11 (.74)	2.61 (.73)	−.68	11

*Interaction significant at $p < .001$.

DISCUSSION

Perceptions of juveniles in facilities are only one type of measure that can be used to develop standards for conditions conducive to positive inmate adjustment. We believe it is an important perspective. There is little reason to believe the juveniles in the boot camps would say the boot camp is positive in all of these aspects if that was not their experience. Observers of boot camps frequently argue that the active, structured environment provides safety for the inmates. Although some psychologists and others researchers believe the militaristic style of boot camp programs holds more potential for harm than benefit, the results from this investigation provide evidence contrary to this argument. Even though there are many critics of boot camp style programs, these programs were rated by the juveniles incarcerated in them as providing a much more positive atmosphere.

In contrast to studies of adult offenders (Lutze, 1998), we found that juveniles perceived both the external environment (structure, control, etc.) and the therapeutic environment (care, justice, programming, etc.) as more conducive to treatment. In addition to perceiving the environment as controlled and safe, juveniles in the boot camp believed their experience provides more opportunities for programming and that they were provided with more intensive preparation for transition into the community. Furthermore, they suggested that boot camps better prepared them for their future, helped them to focus on their goals, understand themselves and assisted them in learning things in classes that were held (therapeutic programming and planning for release scales). Results were surprisingly consistent given the number of facilities holding the different types of offenders as well as the vast number of juveniles surveyed.

It appears that the boot camp environments are consistently perceived to have the necessary components and hold higher levels of the conditions required for effective rehabilitation to occur when compared to traditional facilities. Despite the environmental readiness of the boot camp environment for rehabilitation, recidivism rates indicate these facilities are no more successful in achieving reduced recidivism rates. One possible explanation is the low treatment dosage. Boot camp inmates typically receive only half the treatment dosage (5 hours vs. 10.5 hours per week) provided in traditional facilities and for a shorter period of time (3 to 4 months). Increased intensity and/or duration of treatment within the treatment conducive boot camp environment may lead to more effective recidivism reduction.

Further, one of the largest concerns in these findings is the perceptions of danger from staff.

It is not clear whether a perception of greater danger from staff exists in boot camps or traditional facilities. This has been a concern of the critics of boot camps. However, our results suggest that this should be of concern for both boot camps and traditional facilities. The scores on this scale suggest that in both boot camp and comparison facilities, on occasion (rarely or sometimes), staff say mean things to inmates, grab, push or shove them and even place residents in fear of being hit or punched by staff members. Certainly, one goal should be to decrease the frequency of such behaviors.

The presence of juvenile danger from staff may, in part, be attributed to the explosion of the juvenile offender population. This explosion has resulted in an influx of new facilities to handle the vast numbers in the criminal justice system. In turn, the opening of new facilities, both private and public, has required numerous new and enthusiastic although potentially inexperienced staff members. It may be that the enthusiasm and zeal of these new staff has manifested itself in a dangerous fashion in not just the boot camps but all juvenile facilities. Factors such as previous years of correctional experience, hours of staff training and demographics of the staff such as age need to be taken into consideration in the examination of this complex and important issue. It may be that the type of facility is less important in determining the perceptions of juvenile danger from staff and more importantly the profiles of the staff members who are controlling these environments.

Results on the effectiveness of boot camps are mixed and numerous questions remain unanswered. In essence, we are left with disentangling the program components and conditions of the boot camps to determine the manner in which conditions are related to short term behavioral change (e.g., antisocial attitudes, risk taking behavior) which may in turn impact long term behavioral change (e.g., recidivism, return to school). Research examining recidivism rates clearly demonstrates that the core elements of military-style boot camp programs do not reduce offender recidivism (Brame & MacKenzie in MacKenzie & Hebert, 1996; Gimbel & Clawson, 1998; MacKenzie, 1997; Peters, 1996a; 1996b; 1996c). However, other research has shown positive impacts from the programs.

Offenders report being drug free and physically healthy when they leave the boot camps and are optimistic about their futures (Souryal & MacKenzie, in MacKenzie & Hebert, 1996). Furthermore, MacKenzie and Souryal (1995) found some evidence that boot camps as well as comparisons were effective in decreasing offender antisocial attitudes. Our research indicates juveniles perceive the conditions of confinement in boot camps as more positive than conditions in traditional facilities. An increase in the treatment provided in these facilities should lead to a promising reduction in the recidivism rates of delinquents.

NOTES

1. For two pairs of boot camps, the same facility was identified as the most appropriate comparison facility. Given these two boot camps did not significantly differ, the data from the two boot camps were combined. Thus, 22 matched boot camp and comparison pairs were included for analysis.

2. It is interesting to note that juveniles found the last 105 questions in the survey most appealing as they were asked concrete questions about their experiences in the institution. Most likely, this resulted in the high completion rate of over 85% of the total population.

3. A listing of individual items and related descriptive statistics of each scale may be obtained from the authors.

4. Varimax rotation was used because it was assumed the most interpretable factor has numerous high and low loadings but few of intermediate value (Comrey & Lee, 1992). This occurs because the variance of the variables are maximally spread apart. In the majority of cases, items were dropped if they did not load on a factor as .30 or greater.

5. If an individual failed to answer more than 20% of the questions contained in the scale, the case was excluded from the overall analysis.

REFERENCES

Ajdukovic, D. (1990). Psychosocial climate in correctional institutions: Which attributes describe it? *Environment and Behavior, 22,* 420-432.

Andrews, D. A., Zinger, I., Hoge, R. D., Bonta, J., Gendreau, P., & Cullen, F. T. (1990a). Does correctional treatment work? A clinically relevant and psychologically informed meta analysis. *Criminology, 28,* 369-404.

Clawson, H., Coolbaugh, K., & Zamberlan, C. (1998). *Further Evaluation of Cleveland's Juvenile Boot Camp: A Summary Report.* Paper presented at the Annual Meeting of the American Society of Criminology in Washington, DC.

Cohen, J. (1977). *Statistical Power for the Behavioral Sciences* (revised edition). New York: Academic Press.

Comrey, A. L., & Lee, H. B. (1992). *A First Course in Factor Analysis* (2nd edition). Hillsdale, NJ: Lawrence Erlbaum.

Cowles, E., & Castellano, T. (1995). *"Boot camp" drug treatment and aftercare intervention: An evaluation review* (NCJ 153918). Washington, DC: National Institute of Justice.

Cronbach, L. J. (1951). Coefficient alpha and the internal structure of tests. *Psychometrika 16,* 397-334.

Gendreau, P., & Andrews, D. A. (1994). *The Correctional Program Evaluation Inventory.* Unpublished Manuscript, University of New Brunswick.

Gimbel, C., & Clawson, H. (1998). *Further Evaluation of Cleveland Juvenile Boot Camp.* Paper presented at the Annual Meeting for the American Society of Criminology in Washington, DC.

Goffman, E. (1961). *Asylums: Essays on the Social Situation of Mental Patients and Other Inmates.* Chicago: Aldine.

Johnson, R., & Toch, H. (1982). *The Pains of Imprisonment.* Beverly Hills, CA: Sage.

Lipsey, M. (1992). Juvenile delinquency treatment: A meta-analytic inquiry into the variability of effects. In T. Cook et al. (Eds.), *Meta-analysis for explanation: A casebook.* New York: Russell Sage Foundation.

Logan, C. H. (1993). Criminal justice performance measure for prisons. *In Performance Measures for the Criminal Justice System* (pp. 19-60). U.S. Department of Justice (NCJ-143505).

Lutze, F. (1998). Are shock incarceration programs more rehabilitative than traditional prisons? A survey of inmates. *Justice Quarterly, 15,* 547-556.

MacKenzie, D. L. (1997). Criminal Justice and Crime Prevention. In L. W. Sherman, D. Gottfredson, D. MacKenzie, J. Eck, P. Reuter, & S. Bushway (Eds.), *Preventing Crime: What Works? What Doesn't? What's Promising* (pp. 9-1-9-76). Washington, DC: National Institute of Justice.

MacKenzie, D. L., & Hebert, E. E. (1996). *Correctional Boot Camps: A Tough Intermediate Sanction.* Washington, DC: U.S. Department of Justice, Office of Justice Programs.

MacKenzie, D. L., & Brame, R. (1995). Shock incarceration and positive adjustment during community supervision. *Journal of Quantitative Criminology, 11,* 111-142.

MacKenzie, D. L., & Souryal, C. (1995). A "Machiavellian" perspective on the development of boot camp prisons: A debate. *University of Chicago Roundtable.* Chicago: University of Chicago Press.

MacKenzie, D. L., & Parent, D. (1992). Boot camp prisons for young offenders. In J. Byrne, A. Lurigio, & J. Petersilia (Eds.), *Smart Sentencing: The Emergence of Intermediate Sanctions* (pp. 103-122). Newbury Park, CA: Sage.

MacKenzie, D. L., Styve, G. J., & Gover, A. R. (1998). Performance based standards for juvenile corrections. *Corrections Management Quarterly, 2,* 28-35.

MacKenzie, D. L., Brame, R., McDowall, D., & Souryal, C. (1995). Boot camp prisons and recidivism in eight states. *Criminology, 33,* 327-357.

Marlowee, D. H., Marin, J. A., Schneider, L. I., Vaitkus, M. A., & Bartone, P. (1988). *A Look at Army Training Centers' The Human Dimensions of Leadership and Training.* Washington, DC.: Department of Military Psychiatry, Walter Reed Army Institute of Research.

Meachum, L. M. (1990). *Boot camp prisons: Pros and cons.* Paper presented at the Annual Meeting of American Society of Criminology, Baltimore, MD.

Moos, R. H. (1971). Differential effects of the social climates of correctional institutions. *Journal of Research in Crime and Delinquency, 7,* 71-82.

Moos, R. H. (1974). *Correctional Institutions Environment Scale Manual.* Palo Alto, CA: Consulting Psychological Press.

Morash, M., & Rucker, L. (1990). A critical look at the ideal of boot camp as a correctional reform. *Crime and Delinquency, 36,* 204-222.

Peters, M. (1996a). *Evaluation of the impact of boot camp for juvenile offenders: Cleveland interim report.* Washington, DC: U.S. Department of Justice, Office of Juvenile Justice and Delinquency Prevention.

Peters, M. (1996b). *Evaluation of the impact of boot camp for juvenile offenders: Denver interim report.* Washington, DC: U.S. Department of Justice, Office of Juvenile Justice and Delinquency Prevention.

Peters, M. (1996c). *Evaluation of the impact of boot camp for juvenile offenders: Mobile interim report.* Washington, DC: U.S. Department of Justice, Office of Juvenile Justice and Delinquency Prevention.

Raupp, E. (1978). *Toward Positive Leadership for Initial Entry Training. A Report to the Task Force on Initial Entry Training Leadership.* Fort Monroe, VA: United States Army Training and Doctrine Command.

Steinhart, D. (1993, January/February). Juvenile boot camps: Clinton may rev up an old drill. *Youth Today.*

Wright, K. N. (1985). Developing the Prison Environment Inventory. *Journal of Research in Crime and Delinquency, 22,* 257-277.

Wright, K. N. (1991). A study of individual, environmental, and interactive effects in explaining adjustment to prison. *Justice Quarterly, 8,* 217-242.

Wright, K. N., & Goodstein, L. (1989). Correctional environments. In L. Goodstein & D. L. MacKenzie (Eds.), *The American Prison: Issues in Research and Policy.* New York: Plenum.

U.S. Department of Justice, Office of Juvenile Justice and Delinquency Prevention. (1994). *Conditions of Confinement: Juvenile Detention and Correctional Facilities.* Washington, DC.: Government Printing Office.

U.S. Department of Justice, Federal Bureau of Prisons. (1993). *Prison Social Climate Survey: Staff Version and Resident Version.* Washington, DC: Government Printing Office.

Zachariah, J. K. (1996). An overview of boot camp goals, components and results. In D. MacKenzie & E. Hebert (Eds.), *Correctional Boot Camps: A Tough Intermediate Sanction.* Washington, DC: Government Printing Office.

Zamble, E., & Porporino, F. (1990). Coping, imprisonment and rehabilitation: Some data and their implications. *Criminal Justice and Behavior, 17,* 53-70.

9

Boot Camps and Traditional Correctional Facilities for Juveniles

A Comparison of the Participants, Daily Activities and Environments

Angela R. Gover

Doris Layton MacKenzie

Gaylene J. Styve

Introduction

Boot camps have been a controversial correctional option since they were first developed for adults in 1983 (MacKenzie and Souryal, 1995b: MacKenzie and Parent, 1992: Meachum, 1990: Morash and Rucker, 1990). Despite the controversy, boot camps have become a popular and rapidly growing option for delinquents. Even so, concerns have been raised regarding the boot camp environment as to its overall conduciveness to rehabilitation, the ability to provide individualized programming, the lack of aftercare, and the potential for net-widening (Morash and Rucker, 1990; MacKenzie and Parent, 1992; MacKenzie and Piquero, 1994; Castellano and Plant, 1996: Peters, Thomas, and Zamberlan, 1997). Most boot camp research describes individual programs or compares recidivism rates of adult boot camp

Reprinted from Gover, A. R., MacKenzie, D. L., & Styve, G. (1999). *Journal of Criminal Justice, 28*(1), 53–68.

This investigation was supported in part by Grant #96-SC-LX-0001 from the National Institute of Justice, Office of Justice Programs, U.S. Department of Justice, to the University of Maryland. Points of view in this document are those of the authors and do not necessarily represent the official position of the Department of Justice. Thanks are expressed to administrators, staff, and juveniles at the correctional facilities who participated in this research. An earlier version of this paper was presented at the 1998 Annual Meeting of the American Society of Criminology in Washington, D.C. Please address correspondence to: Angela R. Gover. Phone: (301) 405–4731. Fax: (301) 405–4733; E-mail: agover@bss2.umd.edu.

completers to comparison groups (MacKenzie and Shaw, 1993; MacKenzie and Souryal, 1995a; MacKenzie et al., 1995; MacKenzie and Hebert, 1996; MacKenzie, 1997). Little research is available to tell us how juveniles in the boot camps differ from those in traditional facilities, or how the environment and daily activities in the camps compare to those of more traditional facilities. This paper reviews the controversy surrounding boot camps, examines differences between twenty-seven boot camps and twenty-two comparison facilities, and identifies how the populations, selection process, environments, and daily activities differ within these two types of institutions.

CONTROVERSIAL ISSUES SURROUNDING BOOT CAMP PROGRAMS

Boot camps are controversial for a variety of reasons. First, there is concern that they focus on lower risk cases, thereby failing to address the needs of juvenile delinquents most apt to recidivate (Souryal and MacKenzie, 1994). Boot camps appear to be deceptively seductive alternatives for youths with behavior problems compared to serious juvenile offenders (MacKenzie and Souryal, 1995b; Austin and Krisberg, 1982; Morris and Tonry, 1990). Since low risk cases are less apt to recidivate with or without treatment, the impact may be negligible (MacKenzie, 1997). Furthermore, in cases where program staff determine who may enter the camps, they may select juveniles who are at the lowest risk for recidivism.

The focus on lower risk cases means that camps may also widen the net of control over juveniles (MacKenzie and Piquero, 1994; MacKenzie, 1995a; MacKenzie, 1995b). Judges are often faced with the choice of sending juveniles to either a traditional state detention center or training school or of letting them remain in the community on probation (Byrne, Lurigio, and Petersilia, 1992; Tonry and Lynch, 1996). Given these choices, judges may tend to give juveniles the benefit of the doubt and let them remain in the community. If a boot camp alternative, however, is available. then many of these youths may be sent there, resulting in an increase in the overall number of youth who are

institutionalized. Pressure from the public and policy makers who view the programs as appropriate options for undisciplined youth may also affect judicial decisions to send increasing numbers of juveniles to boot camps (MacKenzie and Parent, 1992; MacKenzie and Piquero, 1994; Tonry and Lynch, 1996; Byrne, Lurigio, and Petersilia, 1992).

Those interested in juvenile programming have emphasized the need for individualized programs (Acoca, 1995; Peters et al., 1997). The needs of juveniles vary greatly and effective programs must assess each individual's needs and develop appropriate programming to address these needs. The majority of boot camps, however, group juveniles into units or platoons (Parent, 1989; Caldas, 1990; MacKenzie, 1990; MacKenzie, 1995a; MacKenzie and Rosay, 1996; Gover, Styve, and MacKenzie, 1999; Gover, Styve, and MacKenzie, 1998; MacKenzie, Styve, and Gover, 1998). Youths enter the facility in a unit, attend classes and treatment programs together, are punished as a group for one individual's misbehavior, and finally graduate as a single unit. Boot camps also tend to have rigid rules and inflexible daily schedules (Lutze, 1998) which may not address the individual needs of the inmates. Critics argue, therefore, that the military philosophy and high level of structure within boot camps programs prohibit the flexibility needed to address individual problems of inmates.

"Total institutions," such as juvenile residential facilities, have also been described as rigid in regard to rules and daily schedules (Goffman, 1961). While correctional boot camps may appear to be more military-like and structured, this may only be a matter of degree. Traditional facilities may be just as structured but without some of the military aspects. If a high level of organizational structure necessarily limits individualization in programming, this may be a concern with both types of juvenile facilities.

Critics are also skeptical about the treatment provided to inmates in military style programs. These critics have not been particularly surprised by the results from recidivism studies which have found no differences in recidivism rates among boot camp and non-boot camp offenders (Morash and Rucker, 1990; Mathlas and Mathews, 1991; Henggeler and

Schoenwald, 1994). Critics argue that because the boot camp environment has many elements that are antithetical to successful treatment, there is no particular reason to expect boot camp releasees to recidivate at lower rates. For example, mainstream psychologists believe that treatment and therapy require positive and supportive interpersonal relationships, not the confrontational characteristics of the boot camp environment (Andrews et al., 1990; Andrews, Bonta, and Hodge, 1990; Gendreau and Ross, 1987). Based on the previous research showing that therapeutic juvenile programs can be effective an important issue of concern is how activities are scheduled in boot camp programs in comparison to traditional facilities (Andrews and Bonta, 1994; Andrews, Bonta, and Hodge, 1990; Andrews et al., 1990; Lipsey, 1992: Gendreau and Ross, 1987; Palmer, 1983). At the most basic level, a sufficient amount of time must be scheduled for therapeutic activities if change is to occur.

Boot camps may in fact create an environment to encourage short-term change, but if juveniles do not participate in post-camp activities that can help them succeed in the community, these programs may not have an affect on recidivism. Attention is now being paid to what happens to juveniles once they leave facilities and return to the community (Peters et al., 1997; Acoca, 1995; Altschuler and Armstrong, 1994). This issue is moving towards the forefront in juvenile corrections in part because the literature suggests that progress made by juveniles while they are confined to facilities quickly diminishes following their release (Altschuler and Armstrong, 1991; Catalano, Hawkins, and Jensen, 1988). Therefore, reintegration to the community must start while juveniles are still confined to the facility.

Since juveniles frequently return to live with family members, return to their local schools, and are reunited with their previous social networks, it is important for them to maintain contact with the community while they are incarcerated. The Intensive Aftercare Program Model (IAP) stresses that individualized case planning focus on the special needs of juveniles' and their relationships with their social networks (e.g., family, close friends, etc.) (Altschuler and Armstrong, 1994). To accomplish this, an aftercare

counselor should be advising the juvenile from the beginning of the residential period.

In addition, the involvement of offenders' family members in programming activities, while they are confined, may have more impact on their behavior once they are released than other official interventions (Zhang, 1988). This assertion is directly related to the extent to which facilities allow institutionalized juveniles to maintain contact with the community. Such contacts are assumed to facilitate successful reintegration into the community, and according to Altschuler, reintegration into the community is the key to boot camp success (Peters et al., 1997).

The new emphasis in corrections is on performance-based standards and institutional accountability (MacKenzie, Styve, and Gover, 1998; Logan, 1993; Dilulio, 1993; Boone and Fulton, 1995). In order to develop programs that will successfully prepare juveniles for their return to the community, facility staff and administrators need information about what happens to juveniles who leave their programs. In addition to recidivism rates, it is important to measure juveniles' positive activities. Zhang (1998) notes that most program evaluations do not include measures of inmates' prosocial activity once they are released from institutions, such as school enrollment, employment, involvement in drug treatment, or vocational training. If facilities are to be held accountable for what happens to juveniles after they are released, information about post-release activities must be made available.

NATIONAL EVALUATION OF JUVENILE CORRECTIONAL FACILITIES

The current research is part of a national study of juvenile correctional facilities which compared the environments/conditions of boot camp confinement to those of traditional facilities. Twenty-seven boot camps were compared to twenty-two traditional facilities using surveys of juveniles and staff, administrator interviews, institutional records, and video tapes. This paper focuses on the data collected from administrator interviews and institutional records and attempts to answer the following six questions:

- Are boot camps selecting juveniles who have less delinquent backgrounds in terms of offense histories than traditional facilities?
- Do the environments in boot camps differ in their levels of structure or security and custody from traditional facilities?
- To what extent do facilities incorporate a military philosophy into their environments and do boot camps differ from traditional facilities with regard to this philosophy?
- Do boot camps and traditional facilities differ in the emphasis placed on therapeutic programming?
- Does the level of contact juveniles have with the community while institutionalized differ by type of facility?
- Do facilities have access to information regarding post-incarceration behavior?

METHODOLOGY

Facilities

Juvenile correctional agencies throughout the U.S. were contacted to identify all boot camps operating for juvenile delinquents. In all, fifty programs in twenty-seven states were identified and contacted. Two programs were eliminated from the pool of potential participants because they were non-residential facilities. An additional two were eliminated because they were in the process of developing their program and they would not be operating in time to participate in the research. The remaining 46 eligible programs were invited to participate in the research and of these, twenty-seven programs in twenty states (or 59 percent of the eligible programs) participated. There were several reasons programs did not participate. For example, some states require outside researchers to obtain written consent from parents of juveniles in order for youths to participate in research. This is not logistically possible due to the time constraints of data collection during the site visits. Some facility administrators believed the research would be too time consuming for their already overburdened staff and refused to commit staff time to assist with data collection. A few sites did not participate due to a decision on the part of the State's Correctional Research Division.

Finally, some sites did not reveal the basis for their decision to not participate.

A matched comparison facility was identified for each boot camp participating in the study. This facility was selected in consultation with the agency responsible for the boot camp facility and/or administrators at the boot camps. The goal was to identify the facility where the juveniles in the boot camps would have most likely been sent had they not gone to the boot camp. All comparison sites were in the same state as the boot camp. At times, the comparison site was a large facility with specialized programming for different types of offenders (e.g., sex offender units). In such cases, a subset of the facility was identified where juveniles similar to the boot camp residents would reside. This subset or unit was compared to the boot camp. All questions in the surveys referred to the smaller unit and not the total facility.

The number of traditional institutions (N = 22) serving as comparison facilities for the boot camps is smaller than the number of boot camps (N = 27) because four of the participating states had two boot camps. In one state the two boot camps were the only facilities where delinquents were confined so there was no viable comparison site. The remaining three states had one comparison site where the juveniles would reside if the boot camps had not been operating. This site was used as the comparison for both of the boot camps in the state. Thus, the data include twenty-five boot camps with comparison sites (three sites were used as comparisons for two boot camps) and two boot camps did not have a comparison site.

Responsibility for the operation of the participating facilities varied. Seventeen were privately operated (eleven boot camps), five were operated by county agencies (four boot camps), and twenty-seven were operated by state or multi-government agencies (twelve boot camps). Most of the programs (N = 40) were located in a small city, town or rural area (twenty-three boot camps) while only nine were located in a suburb of or in an urban area (four boot camps).

Procedure

The forty-nine participating correctional facilities were visited between April 1997 and

August 1998. During the site visits juveniles and staff were surveyed, a survey was administered to the facility administrator, and a video survey and checklist was completed during a walk through of the institution. This research focuses on information obtained from the survey conducted with the facility administrator(s), as summarized in this paper.

The survey consisted of 244 structured questions and took approximately two hours to complete. Questions in the survey related to the facility's population, selection and admission procedures, programming components, daily schedule, facility characteristics, such as health and medical assistance policies, staff issues, release supervision and aftercare, grievance procedures, safety and security issues, and institutional impacts. Some questions required information to be obtained from institutional records. When appropriate, these data were collected as summary statistics for a specific time period (one year).

To ensure consistency in the survey administration process, questions were asked in a structured interview format by one of the project's three co-investigators so that questions could be clarified and responses recorded in the same fashion. All co-investigators participated in the development of the survey and were equally familiar with the survey format. The data from all forty-nine surveys were coded by one co-investigator to guarantee reliability.

The majority of the interviews were conducted with the facility's main administrator, such as the warden or director. This was an indication that it was very important to facilities that questions from this survey were answered accurately. At a few facilities more than one administrator sat in on the interviews, such as an assistant director or assistant warden. This usually occurred at facilities where the director or warden had not been employed by the facility for at least one year.

Indices

Four indices were developed to examine differences between boot camps and comparison facilities: (1) Population Seriousness; (2) Institutional Structure; (3) Institutional Security and Custody; and (4) Military Atmosphere (see appendix for a description of items in each index).

The *Population Seriousness Index* was developed in order to describe the population admitted to each facility in terms of offense seriousness. Administrators were asked whether juveniles with specific characteristics were admitted to the facility (convicted of violent crimes, past history of violent acts, arson, sex offenses, waived to adult criminal court, etc.). Responses were coded as "0" if they were legally or administratively excluded from the facility, "1" if they were admitted to the facility but in limited numbers, or "2" if admitted. Responses were summed and divided by 7 (the total number of items) which yielded a seriousness score for the population. Each facility received a score between 0 and 2. Scores close to zero indicate that the population of juveniles admitted to the facility do not have serious delinquent backgrounds when considering type of current offense and past history of offending. A score close to 2 indicates that the population admitted to the facility has serious delinquent histories. Scores ranged from .29 to 2.0 (coefficient alpha = .71).

The ten-item *Institutional Structure Index* gauges the degree of structure in the daily routine of the facility. A high structure program requires juveniles to adhere to various rules with a recommended schedule of activities. For example, they might be required to wear uniforms, enter the facility in groups, pass inspection, and have a set daily schedule of activities. Responses were coded as "1" for yes and "0" for no for each of the ten questions. These responses were summed and divided by 10 (the total number of items) to form an index ranging from 0 to 1. A score close to 1 indicates a high degree of structure in the facility. Index scores ranged from .40 to 1.0 (coefficient alpha = .75).

The eight-item *Institutional Security and Custody Index* measures the degree to which physical barriers and supervision are used to control juveniles. A program with a high level of security and custody has locked buildings, requires staff to search juveniles and visitors when they enter the facility, and keeps juveniles within eyesight of officials when they leave the facility. Administrators were asked to respond to these items on a live-point Likert scale from never (coded as "1") to always (coded as "5"). Responses were summed and divided by 8 (the total number of items) to form index scores ranging from 1 to 5. A score of 1 indicates a facility with a low level of security and custody and a score of 5 indicates a facility with a high level of security and custody. Scores ranged from 1.38 to 5.0 (coefficient alpha = .71).

The *Military Index* measures the degree to which military aspects are incorporated into the program. For example, whether juveniles have to march to class, call staff by military titles, wear military uniforms, and practice drill and ceremony. Responses choices were no (coded as "0") or yes (coded as "1") to nine items. Index scores were formed by summing the responses and dividing by 9 (total number of items) to form an index ranging from 0 and 1. A score of 0 indicates low militariness and 1 indicates high militariness. Military index scores ranged from 0 to 1 (coefficient alpha = .71).

Results

The twenty-seven boot camp programs were developed between 1988 and 1997. Most of the twenty-two comparison facilities were much older than the boot camps, being developed between 1985 and 1995. Boot camp program capacities ranged from twenty-four to 250 juveniles. The overall capacity range for comparison facilities were much wider, from twenty-eight to 500. Juveniles in boot camp programs were between ten and twenty-one years old. The age ranges were slightly lower for comparison facilities which had an overall age limit of eight to twenty-one years old. Most of the boot camp facilities served males only, but five of them served both males and females. All but two of the comparison facilities served male delinquents only. The average length of stay for juveniles in boot camps ranged from two to fourteen months, with an overall average length of stay of 4.5 months, while the range on average length of stay in comparison facilities was from three to twenty-six months, with the average length of stay being 8.3 months. At the time of the site visits, boot camp programs were operating at an average capacity level of 93 percent

and comparison facilities were operating at an average capacity level of 100 percent.

Selection and Characteristics of Juvenile Participants

The first issue of interest was the selection process for juvenile participants in the different facilities. The question was whether most boot camps limited their population to juveniles who had the least delinquent offense histories, that is, did they limit the type of juveniles who could enter the facilities? If so, boot camps would have been widening the net of control over juveniles who would have otherwise received sentences of probation.

In general, the answer is that boot camps were admitting offenders with less serious offense histories. Traditional correctional facilities scored significantly higher on the Population Seriousness Index, t (47) = −4.7, $p < .001$, compared to boot camps, indicating that they admitted more seriously delinquent juveniles (See Table 9.1). Also, comparison of the Seriousness Index using the Mann-Whitney nonparametric test indicated that traditional facilities ranked significantly higher in the seriousness of their populations (See Figure 9.1). The individual items in the index and additional items from the survey indicated that all of the facilities, boot camps and comparisons, admitted nonviolent offenders to their facilities (See Appendix). Additionally, almost all of them admitted only juveniles who had been adjudicated as delinquent, while only five facilities permitted juveniles who were diverted from further criminal processing (three boot camps). Approximately half of the boot camp programs (16 facilities) accepted status offenders while only six comparison facilities included status offenders. The only indication that boot camps tried to target more serious delinquents was in three programs where first time offenders were excluded from participating. None of the comparison sites had such restrictions.

Not only was the populations' delinquent history more serious in traditional facilities, but also as shown on Table 9.1, traditional facilities (in comparison to boot camps) were less apt to target a 'certain type' of juvenile. Also, juveniles

Table 9.1 Differences on Juvenile Populations Within Boot Camp Programs and Traditional Correctional Facilities

	Boot Camp Programs (N = 27)	Comparison Facilities (N = 22)
*Serious Population Index M (SD). α = .71	1.01 (.43)	1.55 (.38)
Facility targets a certain type of juvenile, % Yes (n)	41.7% (10)	18.2% (4)
Juveniles must volunteer to be considered for the Facility, % Yes (n)	25.9% (7)	0.0% (22)
The personnel at this facility determine who is assigned to this facility, % Yes (n)	44.4% (12)	22.7% (5)
The court determines who is assigned to this facility, % Yes (n)	48.1% (13)	50% (11)
A juvenile corrections agency determines who is assigned to this facility, % Yes (n)	63.0% (17)	77.3% (17)
Juveniles are interviewed by a facility staff member prior to admission to the facility. % Yes (n)	55.6% (15)	31.8% (7)
Juveniles must pass a physical evaluation prior to admission to the facility. % Yes (n)	81.5% (22)	45.5% (10)
Juveniles must pass a medical evaluation prior to admission to the facility. % Yes (n)	88.9% (24)	40.9% (9)
Juveniles must pass a psychological evaluation prior to admission to the facility. % Yes (n)	66.7% (18)	40.9% (9)
Facility admits juveniles evaluated as being suicide risks, % Yes (n)	66.7% (18)	90.9% (20)
Facility admits juveniles evaluated as having psychological problems, % Yes (n)	70.4% (19)	100% (22)
Facility admits juveniles with histories of abuse (either physical or sexual). % Yes (n)	100% (27)	100% (22)

Note: *$p < .00$.

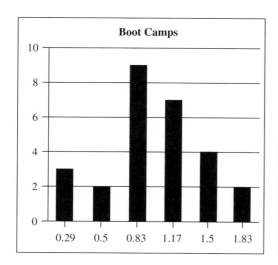 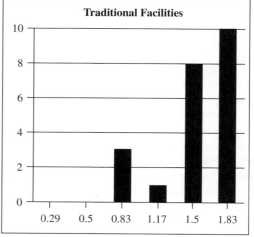

Figure 9.1 Distribution of Population Seriousness Index Scores for Boot Camps and Traditional Facilities

Boot Camps: Std. Dev = .43; Median = .86; N = 27. Traditional Facilities: Std. Dev = .38; *Median = 1.71; N = 22; *Significant Mann-Whitney U-Test: $p < .001$.

Table 9.2   Comparison of Boot Camps and Comparison Sites on Structure, Security & Custody, and Military Components

Indices	Boot Camp Programs (N = 27)	Comparison Facilities (N = 22)
*Institutional Structure Index *M* (SD), α = .75 (Range 0-1)	.94 (.08)	.63 (.14)
Security & Custody Index *M* (SD), α =.71 (Range 1-5)	3.33 (1.01)	3.43 (1.01)
*Military Index *M* (SD), α =.71 (Range 0-1)	.87 (.13)	.12 (.13)

Note: *$p < .001$.

who entered traditional facilities were never required to volunteer to participate, fewer were interviewed by facility staff before being admitted, and fewer were required to pass physical, medical, and psychological evaluations prior to being admitted. Furthermore, personnel at fewer of the comparison facilities were able to determine who would be assigned to the facility (44.4 percent of the boot camps versus 22.7 percent of the comparison sites). Thus, as well as having a less delinquent population, boot camps were able to be more selective about who entered the program.

The concern that more juveniles in the boot camps would be sent to the facility by the court instead of being sentenced to the jurisdiction of the juvenile correctional agency did not appear to be warranted since approximately the same percentage of the programs received juveniles who were court assigned (48.1 percent of boot camps compared to 50 percent of comparison facilities).

Little information was obtained that permitted conclusions about whether boot camp participants were juveniles who would, if the boot camps did not exist, be in the community or in a comparison facility. The data, however, suggest boot camps were able to be more selective in who they admitted to the facility and that the juveniles in boot camps were less serious delinquents in comparison to those in the traditional facilities.

Facility Environment

Of considerable interest was whether the environments in boot camps differed from the environments in traditional facilities, since environmental conditions might be expected to have a direct impact on inmate behavior. The boot camps were expected to have military basic training camp components, though traditional facilities might also be highly structured.

Table 9.2 shows that the environments of the boot camps were significantly more structured than those of the comparison facilities (t (32) = 9.5; $p < .001$), according to the institutional structure index. In addition, the Mann-Whitney nonparametric test indicated that boot camps rank significantly higher in terms of structure (Figure 9.2). It is important to note, however, that the individual index items suggested that several program characteristics were consistent across both types of facilities (see Appendices A–D). For example, nearly all facilities required juveniles to get up at the same time every day, make their beds, shower at specific times, and follow strict schedules every day. Major differences were found in how the juveniles entered the facilities (whether in groups or on an ongoing basis), how they were required to address the staff when speaking to them, and whether they were required to march to program activities.

There was no significant difference between boot camps and traditional facilities with regard to the security and custody index (t (46) = −.37; $p > .05$), indicating that the physical barriers and supervision of the juveniles was approximately the same in both types of facilities. Boot camps and traditional facilities did not really differ in the extent to which they maintain custodial control over the juveniles confined to their institutions. This finding was somewhat surprising because the juveniles in boot camps appeared to be less serious delinquents.

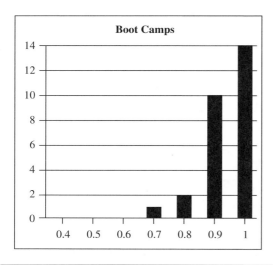
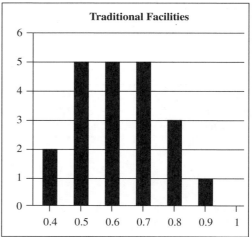

Figure 9.2 Distribution of Structure Index Scores for Boot Camps and Traditional Facilities

Boot Camps: Std. Dev = .08; *Median = 1.0; N = 27; Traditional Facilities: Std. Dev = .14; *Median = .60; N = 22; *Significant Mann-Whitney U-Test: $p < .001$.

Military Philosophy

A third question addressed the degree to which the military philosophy was incorporated into boot camps, compared to other facilities. According to the correctional literature, a military philosophy within a juvenile correctional environment is controversial. This research examined the incorporation of military components into facility environments for two main reasons. Although one expectation was to see if the military philosophy was incorporated to a higher degree within boot camps, it was important to see just how different facilities appeared on this aspect alone. On the other hand it might have been possible that military components created a therapeutic environment but on the other, this philosophy may have created a confrontational atmosphere that worked against treatment efforts. This question was also explored in order to determine how much variation existed in the incorporation of this philosophy within boot camps, since it is well documented that these programs differ in the extent to which the military model is emphasized.

As expected, boot camps incorporated significantly more military components than comparison facilities as measured by the Military Index, t (45) = 18.8; $p < .000$. The Mann-Whitney nonparametric test also confirmed that boot camps ranked significantly higher according to

the Military Index (See Figure 9.3). In short, boot camps were very different than traditional programs for juveniles.

Looking only at the boot camp facilities to examine the extent to which they involved this philosophy, it appeared that most of these programs incorporated the major, traditional military aspects. For example, all programs required juveniles to wear military uniforms, march to class, meals, and other activities, and to participate in drill and ceremony, and physical fitness training. The military philosophy was also incorporated in employee procedures at nearly all of the programs, such as requiring the staff to wear military uniforms and to use military titles. It is important to point out, however, that there was some variation in this regard. For example, approximately 75 percent of the programs used summary punishments and challenge courses. Also, juveniles in eleven boot camps entered the facility on an ongoing basis, instead of in platoons, squads, or groups. Thus, for the most part, most of the programs placed a heavy emphasis on military components, however, there were differences in some aspects.

Correctional Programming
Emphasis on Therapeutic Activities

Of additional interest was the differences between boot camps and traditional facilities in

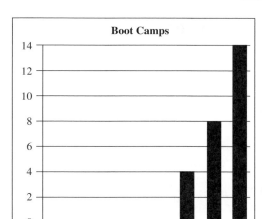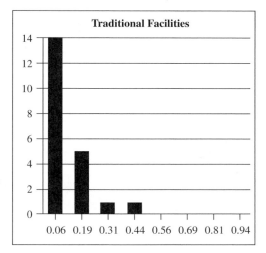

Figure 9.3   Distribution of Military Index Scores for Boot Camps and Traditional Facilities

Boot Camps: Std. Dev = .13; N = 21; *Median = .89; Traditional Facilities: Std. Dev = .13; *Median = .11; N = 26, *Significant Mann-Whitney U-Test: p < .001.

the priority they place on various programming components. There is a concern with juvenile residential facilities regarding what juveniles do during the day and whether they are kept occupied, and equally important is how they are kept occupied. Specifically, it was important to examine whether differences existed in the emphasis placed on therapeutic programming. Since previous research has established that therapeutic programming for juveniles can be effective, it was important to find out whether juveniles were participating in activities that would facilitate long term change.

Administrators were asked about the activities available for juveniles in the facilities and how many hours these activities were scheduled each week. Many facilities did not schedule programming components on a consistent basis each week and instead offered activities on an "as needed" basis or the activity was not available at all. Table 9.3 shows that the only activities consistently scheduled each week in both types of facilities were education, treatment services, physical fitness activities, and visitation.

While advocates argue that the atmosphere of boot camps is more therapeutic and critics argue that it is less conducive to treatment, significant differences were not found in the average amount of time scheduled by boot camps and traditional facilities each week for education, vocational training, and treatment services.

On average, however, comparison facilities scheduled 6.1 more hours each week for vocational training and 5.4 more hours for treatment services than boot camps. Treatment services includes the time juveniles spent in substance abuse treatment, psychological treatment, or individual one-on-one meetings between a juvenile and staff member.

All facilities scheduled time each week for juveniles' participation in physical fitness activities, which includes the time juveniles spent in adventure, challenge, or ropes courses, drill and ceremony, and sports. As expected, juveniles in boot camp programs spent significantly more time than those in comparison facilities participating in physical fitness activities. Juveniles in boot camps were scheduled to spend 22.7 hours each week in physical fitness activities whereas youngsters in comparison facilities spent 12.6 hours each week in such activities. While juveniles in boot camps had less free time, it appeared that most of the reduction was due to the increased time they spent in physical fitness activities. As mentioned earlier, one concern with the military philosophy within the correctional environment was that a higher priority would be placed on physical fitness activities rather than the type of therapeutic activities that have been found to have an impact on later behavior.

It is interesting to note that for four of the ten programming components examined there were

Table 9.3   Mean number of Hours Scheduled Each Week for Programming Components in Boot Camps and Traditional Facilities

Program Component	Boot Camps (N = 27)		Comparisons (N = 22)	
	% Schedules (N)	Mean Hours (SD)	% Schedules (N)	Mean Hours (SD)
Educational	100%	24.35	100%	25.74
Classes	(26)	(5.07)	(19)	(8.48)
Vocational	40.7%	7.25	54.6%	13.33
Training Classes	(10)	(7.35)	(6)	(9.25)
Treatment	100%	5.06	100%	10.49
Services	(23)	(3.93)	(16)	(12.25)
Physical Fitness	100%	22.67	100%	12.61
Activities*	(26)	(7.08)	(18)	(6.07)
Work	44.4%	10.58	59.1%	11.78
	(11)	(10.25)	(9)	(10.03)
Chores	88.9%	12.25	100%	11.50
	(22)	(8.99)	(19)	(8.98)
Visitation*	100%	4.29	100%	7.14
	(24)	(3.55)	(19)	(4.77)
Free-Time	63%	5.55	86.4%	9.57
During Week*	(15)	(3.08)	(15)	(6.27)
Free-Time on	81.5%	3.63	90.9%	10.88
Weekend*	(20)	(1.69)	(16)	(6.89)
Community	48.1%	5.66	54.6%	4.06
Service	(12)	(6.04)	(8)	(8.47)

Note: The N sizes for the cells in this table represent the programs who reported that they regularly schedule a specific number of hours for juveniles to participate in these activities each week. Some programs do not schedule each activity on a regular basis and instead use them as needed. Other programs may not use an activity at all. For boot camp programs, less than 10% of data are missing for all activities, except for the treatment category, where 15% of the programs did not respond to these questions. For comparison facilities, less than 20% of data are missing, except for the vocational training and treatment services category, where 27% of the programs failed to respond to these questions.
*$p < .05$.

significant differences in the number of hours scheduled by the two facility types. While boot camp programs scheduled significantly more time for physical fitness activities than traditional facilities, comparison facilities scheduled significantly more time for juveniles to engage in visitation, free-time during the week, and free-time on the weekend.

Table 9.4 shows that nearly all facilities conducted academic instruction inside the facility and held educational classes during the summer months. In addition, juveniles in over half of both types of facilities attended classes according to their appropriate grade levels instead of according to their squad, platoon, or housing unit. The remaining facilities which provided academic instruction according to groups have reduced flexibility in their ability to address

individual problems. It is interesting to note that of all the juveniles who entered all of the facilities last year, a higher proportion of juveniles at comparison facilities took a GED test (43 percent compared to 23 percent in boot camps). The two types of facilities, however, had approximately the same GED passing rate. About three-fourths of those who took a GED last year at both types of facilities passed the test.

One issue related to correctional programming has to do with the extent to which youth are provided with individualized attention while confined to an institution. Overall, boot camp programs had higher juvenile to staff ratios (see Table 9.4). The juvenile to teaching staff ratio was much higher for boot camps than for comparison facilities. In boot camp programs there

Table 9.4   Juvenile Correctional Facilities, Educational and Staffing Issues

Educational Programming	*Boot Camp Programs (N = 27)*	*Comparison Facilities (N = 22)*
Juveniles attend classes grouped according to their appropriate grade levels, % Yes (*n*)	59.3% (16)	59.1% (13)
Academic instruction is held inside the facility, % Yes (*n*)	100% (27)	95.5% (21)
Academic classes are held during the summer months, % Yes (*n*)	96.3% (26)	100% (22)
Proportion of juveniles who took a GED test last year, out of those who entered the facility last year, % (*n*)	23.3% (20)	42.9% (17)
Proportion of juveniles who passed a GED test last year, out of those who took a GED test last year, % (*n*)	74.0% (19)	75.2% (17)
Inmate to Teaching Staff Ratio	10.17 to 1	6.59 to 1
Inmate to Custody and Treatment Staff Ratio	3.46 to 1	1.62 to 1

were 10.2 juveniles for every one teaching staff member but in comparison facilities there were 6.6 juveniles for every one teaching staff member. This indicates that juveniles in comparison facilities have the opportunity for more individualized attention in school. In addition, for boot camps, there were 3.5 juveniles for every one custody and treatment staff member whereas in comparison facilities there were 1.6 juveniles for every one custody and treatment staff member. This study was unable to distinguish between staff members that are specifically assigned to custodial responsibilities versus treatment responsibilities. The majority of custody staff in juvenile institutions also had counseling and treatment responsibilities. These overall findings, however, indicate that there may be more opportunities for juveniles to receive individualized attention in traditional correctional facilities than in boot camp programs.

Juveniles' Contact With the Community

In addition to differences in programming, facilities were compared on the degree to which juveniles have community contact (See Table 9.5). Since most juveniles confined to institutions will return to the community after completing their sentence it is important for juveniles to maintain contact with their social networks. According to administrators, juveniles in boot camps returned to the community after an average of 4.5 months of confinement and juveniles in traditional facilities returned to the community

after an average of 8.3 months. One of the interests of this research was whether juveniles' contact with the community was different depending on the type of facility they are confined to.

Overall, policies and procedures in traditional facilities permitted juveniles to have more contact with the community while confined to the institutions than juveniles in boot camps. Boot camps had stricter policies for juveniles regarding visitation, phone calls, and letter writing (See Table 9.5). For example, juveniles in half of the boot camps were not allowed to receive visitors during the first to second months of confinement. Only three comparison facilities had this restriction on visitation. In addition, five boot camp programs did not allow juveniles to receive visitors during their entire confinement period. This was not a policy implemented at any of the comparison facilities.

Juveniles in comparison facilities had a significantly greater amount of time scheduled each week for visitation with family and friends. Comparison facilities scheduled an average of 7.1 hours each week for visitation, while boot camp programs scheduled only 4.3 hours. In addition to having a longer period of time for visitation, visitation was allowed more often in comparison facilities. On average, juveniles in boot camps were allowed to receive visitors about once each week (.92 times/week) while in comparison facilities juveniles were allowed to receive visitors one and a half times each week (1.5 times/week).

Table 9.5   Juvenile Correctional Facilities, Visiting, Letter Writing, and Phone Call Regulations

Program Regulations	Boot Camp Programs (N = 27)	Comparison Facilities (N = 22)
Program has a "no visit" policy during the first or second month juveniles are in the facility. % Yes (N)	51.9 (14)	13.6 (3)
Program has "no visit" policy during the entire time juveniles are in the facility. % Yes (N)	18.5 (5)	0 (0)
Visitors must schedule their visits in advance, % Yes (N)	59.3 (16)	36.4 (8)
Juveniles who have children are encouraged to have their children visit during visiting hours. % Yes (N)	77.8 (21)	81.8 (18)
Contact with family or friends through visits or phone calls can be limited as punishment. % Yes (N)	25.9 (7)	52.4 (11)
Facility permits juveniles to make a set number of phone calls each week, % Yes (N)	62.5 (15)	55.6 (10)
Juveniles are required to write letters to their relatives, % Yes (N)	37 (10)	22.7 (5)
Program limits the number of letters juveniles can write in one week. % Yes (N)	40.7 (11)	9.1 (2)
Average number of times per week juveniles are allowed to receive visits from family or friends. M (SD)	.921 (.52) ($n = 25$)	1.49 (.65) ($n = 21$)
Average number of hours per week open for visitation, M (SD)	4.29 (3.55) ($n = 27$)	7.14 (4.77) ($n = 21$)
Average number of phone calls juveniles are permitted per week (of those who have a set number), M (SD)	1.08 (.58) ($n = 15$)	1.60 (1.05) ($n = 10$)
Average number of minutes permitted per call, M (SD)	10.48 (6.97) ($n = 25$)	10.58 (7.83) ($n = 19$)

The same can be said for phone calls. Juveniles in boot camps were allowed to make an average of 1.1 calls each week while juveniles in comparison facilities were allowed to make an average of 1.6 calls each week. The length of the call permitted, however, by both types of facilities was approximately the same (about 10.5 minutes). In addition, boot camp programs were more likely than traditional facilities to limit the number of letters juveniles can write each week. Thus, boot camps' policies regarding visitation, phone calls, and letter writing were more restrictive than policies within traditional facilities.

Institutional Impacts

A final area of interest for this study involved the amount of access facilities have to information regarding institutional impacts. If facility staff and administrators plan to develop a program that will have an impact on juveniles once

they leave, it is necessary for the staff to know what happens to youth after they leave. Do facilities collect or receive any information at all about how the youth are doing once they are released from the facility? This is information that could be collected by the facility itself or by another agency who then provides it to the institution. If programs do not have access to this type of information (e.g., whether juveniles are attending school, working, participating in drug treatment, etc.), it is impossible for these programs to know whether their programming resources are appropriately focused and are having an impact on juveniles' behavior. In addition, this information could be used for the development of performance-based standards for the operation of the facility.

Table 9.6 shows that nearly all of the institutions who participated in this study were not provided with this type of impact information. In fact, answers to these questions were consistently missing from 20 percent of the facilities

Table 9.6   Facilities' Access to Measures of Institutional Impacts

Information collected on juveniles who were released from the facility last year regarding[1] . . .	*Information Unavailable % (N)*	*Information Available % (N)*	*Information Missing % (N)*
Juveniles who have returned to school	61.2% (30)	20.4% (10)	18.4% (9)
Juveniles who have since completed high school	63.3% (31)	12.2% (6)	24.5% (12)
Juveniles who have since obtained their GED	57.1% (28)	22.4% (11)	20.4% (10)
Juveniles who have since gained vocational training	65.3% (32)	14.3% (7)	20.4% (10)
Juveniles who have since gained employment	65.3% (32)	16.3% (8)	18.4% (9)
Juveniles who have continued in drug treatment	69.4% (34)	10.2% (5)	20.4% (10)
Juveniles who are receiving psychological counseling	71.4% (35)	6.1% (3)	22.4% (11)
Juveniles who have returned to live with their family.	59.2% (29)	18.4% (9)	22.4% (11)
Juveniles who have since been re-arrested in that year	65.3% (32)	10.2% (5)	24.5% (12)
Juveniles who have since returned to this facility	42.9% (21)	32.7% (16)	24.5% (12)
Juveniles who have since been sent to another facility	61.2% (30)	16.3% (8)	22.4% (11)
Juveniles who have died or been killed	57.1% (28)	24.5% (12)	18.4% (9)

[1]Administrator/s reported that they did not have access to this information (information unavailable), that they did have access to this type of information (information available), or did not respond to these questions (information missing).

while 43 percent to 69 percent of the facilities reported that this information was simply unavailable. Even sixteen facilities were unable to determine if juveniles who were released from their facilities last year had since been readmitted to their own facility.

DISCUSSION

Overall, these findings indicate that boot camps differed from traditional facilities in population, the level of structure in the environ- ment, and in the incorporation of the military model into the correctional atmosphere. Facilities did not differ significantly in their levels of security and custody. Traditional facilities, however, had visitation, phone call, and letter writing policies that enabled juveniles to have a greater amount of

contact with the community than juveniles in boot camps. In addition, traditional facilities scheduled more time each week for juveniles to participate in treatment services and vocational training. Traditional facilities also had more educators and custody/treatment staff for each juvenile. Thus, these juveniles potentially received more individualized attention than those in boot camps.

There are, however, limitations to these findings. For example, the data did not allow us to explicitly examine why the variation in boot camps and traditional facilities differed in terms of various factors, such as population serious-ness and structure. As a result, our conclusions are inferred from the answers to questions regarding the admission process, the facility environment, the military philosophy, the emphasis on therapeutic activities, and the level of contact with the outside community. Our findings indicate that there was substantial variation both between and within boot camps and traditional facilities. From these data, however, we cannot test how these differences across facilities affect actual post-release behavior. This presents an important limitation that should be addressed in future research.

Despite the limitations of these data, this research does provide some indication of why previous research comparing the recidivism rates of juveniles released from boot camps have not differed from those released from traditional facilities. Perhaps most important is the fact that while juveniles in the boot camps are kept busier and have less free-time, this increased activity was not in academic classes or therapeutic activities. As shown by previous researchers, the type of treatment provided to offenders must be carefully designed to address their "criminogenic needs" (Andrews and Bonta, 1994; Lipsey, 1992; Andrews et al., 1990). There is no reason to believe physical activity alone will be successful in reducing recidivism. Thus, from these results, boot camps would not be expected to be any more successful than traditional facilities in reducing recidivism.

In fact, many of these findings suggest that comparison facilities may be more successful than boot camps. In particular, they had more staff for each juvenile which presented the possibility for juveniles to have more individualized

attention. Traditional facilities were also less structured, again suggesting the possibility of more individual attention. More juveniles in traditional facilities took GED examinations. Furthermore, these juveniles had more access to outside contacts while they were in the facility. This may help them with the difficulties inherent in making the transition back to the community (Altschuler and Armstrong, 1991).

It is difficult to design a program that successfully changes juvenile delinquents without having some basic information about how the juveniles are adjusting once they return to the community. From the findings here, however, it is clear that institutional personnel do not have access to or are not provided with this type of information. As a result, we could not examine the potential impact of institutional differences on juveniles' post-release outcomes. This information is critical for determining what types of institutional programs or environmental settings are the most effective. Nearly all of this information could be collected by the agency responsible for juveniles' aftercare supervision and forwarded to the facility. Therefore, one recommendation from these results is that it is the responsibility of the correctional system to provide the resources and expertise so that institutions have access to this information. Certainly if performance-based standards are going to be developed, more outcome information will need to be documented.

Appendix

Table A.1 Serious Population Index Items

	Boot Camp Programs	Comparison Facilities
Juveniles waived to adult criminal court, M (SD)	.19 (.56)	.64 (.85)
Adjudicated juveniles convicted of violent crimes, M (SD)	1.44 (.80)	1.77 (.53)
Juveniles with a past history of engaging in violent acts, M (SD)	1.33 (.88)	1.91 (.29)
Juveniles convicted of arson, M (S D)	.81 (.88)	1.55 (.80)
Juveniles convicted of sex offenses, M (SD)	.67 (.88)	1.50 (.86)
Adjudicated juveniles previously convicted of serious offenses. M (SD)	1.48 (.75)	1.91 (.29)
*Status Offenders. M (SD)	1.11 (.93)	1.55 (.80)

Note: Items coded as: 0 = No; 1 = Limited; 2 = Yes; *Denotes Reversal.

Table A.2   Institutional Structure Index Items

	Boot Camp Programs (N = 27)	*Comparison facilities*[b]
Juveniles have to say "Sir" or "Ma'am" when addressing the staff, % Yes (N)	96.3% (26)	22.7 (5)
Juveniles are required to wear uniforms, % Yes (N)	100% (27)	59.1 (13)
Juveniles have to march to class, to meals, and to other activities. % Yes (N)	100% (27)	13.6 (3)
Juveniles enter the unit/facility in groups or platoons, % Yes (N)	59.3% (16)	0.0 (0)
*Juveniles have to make their beds everyday, % Yes (N)	100% (27)	100 (22)
Juveniles' beds are inspected to make sure it is made property. % Yes (N)	100% (27)	90.9 (20)
Juveniles in this unit/facility get up at the same time, % Yes (N)	96.3% (26)	86.4 (19)
*Every weekday, juveniles have a set schedule to follow, % Yes (N)	100% (27)	100 (22)
Juveniles have a set study time each weekday for homework. % Yes (N)	88.9% (24)	63.6 (14)
Juveniles have a set time each day when they must shower. % Yes (N)	96.3% (26)	90.9 (20)

Note: Items coded as 0 = No; 1 = Yes.
*These items were not included in the computation for the index reliability coefficient because there was no variation among facilities' responses to these items.

Table A.3   Institutional Security and Custody Index Items

	Boot Camp Programs	*Comparison Facilities*
Facility is operated to ensure that all entrances and exits are under the control of the staff of the facility. M (SD)	4.07 (1.54)	4.23 (1.45)
Facility relies on construction fixtures (locked rooms, buildings, and fences) to physically restrict free access into the community, M (SD)	3.37 (1.94)	3.55 (1.77)
Visitors are searched for weapons or contraband when entering the facility (Include pat down searches not just metal detectors), M (SD)	2.42 (1.72)	2.50 (1.82)
Visitors have to pass through a metal detector before entering the facility, M (SD)	2.41 (1.85)	2.82 (1.94)
Juveniles are searched for weapons or contraband when entering the facility (count pat down searches not just metal detector), M (SD)	4.59 (1.05)	4.82 (.85)
Juveniles have to pass through a metal detector before entering the facility, M (SD)	1.70 (1.46)	2.14 (1.70)
*Juveniles leave the facility routinely to work, attend activities, or utilize community resources, M (SD)	3.37 (1.55)	3.29 (1.52)
When outside of the facility, juveniles are within eyesight of direct care officials, M (SD)	4.67 (.55)	4.62 (.50)

Note: Items coded as 1 = Never; 2 = Rarely; 3 = Sometimes; 4 = Often; 5 = Always; *Denotes Reversal.

Table A.4   Military Index Items

	Boot Camp Programs (N = 27)	Comparison Facilities (N = 22)
Juveniles have to march to class, to meals, and to other activities. % Yes (N)	100% (27)	13.6% (3)
Facility has summary punishments that require physical exercise, % Yes (N)	74.1% (20)	9.1% (2)
Juveniles enter the unit/facility in groups or platoons, % Yes (N)	59.3% (16)	0.0% (0)
Facility staff in this unit have military titles, % Yes (N)	88.9% (24)	13.6% (3)
Facility staff in this unit wear military uniforms, % Yes (N)	96.3% (26)	9.1% (2)
Facility has challenge/adventure/ropes courses, %Yes (N)	76.9% (20)	35.0% (7)
Facility has drill and ceremony, % Yes (N)	100% (27)	9.5% (2)
Facility has a formal graduation ceremony, % Yes (N)	84.6% (22)	13.6% (3)
Juveniles are required to wear military uniforms, % Yes (N)	100% (27)	0.0% (0)

Note: Items coded as 0 = No; 1 = Yes.

REFERENCES

Acoca, L. (1995). Court as an effective consumer of substance abuse services. *Juvenile and Family Court Journal 46,* 33–35.

Altschuler, D. M., & Armstrong, T. L. (1991). Intensive aftercare for the high-risk juvenile parolee: Issues and approaches in reintegration and community supervision in probation and parole. In T. L. Armstrong (Ed.), *Intensive Interventions With High-Risk Youths: Promising Approaches in Juvenile Probation and Parole.* Monsey, NY: Criminal Justice Press.

Altschuler, D. M., & Armstrong, T. L. (1994). *Intensive aftercare for high-risk juveniles: A community care model.* Washington, D.C.: Office of Juvenile Justice and Delinquency Prevention.

Andrews, D. A., & Bonta, A. (1994). *The Psychology of Criminal Conduct.* Cincinnati: Anderson.

Andrews, D. A., Zinger, I., Hodge, R. D., Bonta, J., Gendreau, P., & Cullen, F. T. (1990). Does correctional treatment work? A clinically relevant and psychologically informed meta-analysis. *Criminology 28,* 375–404.

Andrews, D. A., Bonta, J., & Hodge, R. D. (1990). Classification for effective rehabilitation: rediscovering psychology. *Criminal Justice and Behavior 17,* 19–51.

Austin, J., & Krisberg, B. (1982). The unmet promise of alternatives to incarceration. *Crime and Delinquency 28,* 374–409.

Boone, H. N., & Fulton, B. (1995). *Results-Driven Management: Implementing Performance-Based Measures in Community Corrections.* Washington, D.C.: The American Probation and Parole Association.

Byrne, J. M., Lurigio, A. J., & Petersilia, J. (1992). Introduction: The emergence of intermediate sanctions. In J. M. Byrne, A. J. Lurigio, & J. Petersilia (Eds.), *Smart Sentencing: The Emergence of Intermediate Sanction.* Newbury Park, CA: Sage.

Caldas, S. J. (1990). Intensive incarceration programs offer hope of rehabilitation to a fortunate few: Orleans Paris prison does an "about face." *International Journal of Offender Therapy and Comparative Criminology 34,* 67–76.

Castellano, T., & Plant, S. (1996). Boot camp aftercare programming: Current limits and suggested remedies. In *Juvenile and Adult Boot Camps.* Laurel, MD: American Correctional Association.

Catalano, R. F., Hawkins, E. A., & Jensen, J. M. (1988). Transition and aftercare services for adjudicated youth. In L. Mixdorf, M. Goff, & P. Paugh (Eds.), *A Guide to Developing Substance Abuse Treatment Programs for Adjudicated Youth.* Laurel, MD: American Correctional Association.

Diluho, J. J. (1993). Rethinking the criminal justice system: Toward a new paradigm. In *Performance Measures for the Criminal Justice System.* Bureau of Justice Statistics and Princeton University: U.S. Department of Justice.

Federal Bureau of Prisons. (1993). *Prison Social Climate Survey: Staff Version and Resident Version.* Washington, D.C.: U.S. Government Printing Office.

Gendreau, P., & Andrews, D. A. (1996). Correctional program evaluation inventory. Unpublished manuscript.

Gendreau, P., & Ross, R. R. (1987). Revivacation of rehabilitation: Evidence from the 1980s. *Justice Quarterly 4,* 349–408.

Goffman, E. (1961). *Asylums: Essays on the Social Situation of Mental Patients and Other Inmates.* Garden City, NY: Doubleday.

Gover, A. R., Styve, G. J., & MacKenzie, D. L. (1998). Evaluating correctional boot camp programs: Issues and concerns. In K. C. Haas & G. P. Alpert (Eds.), *The Dilemmas of Corrections: Contemporary Readings.* Prospect Heights, IL: Waveland.

Gover, A. R., Styve, G. J., & MacKenzie, D. L. (1999). Boot camps. In P. M. Carlson & J. S. Garrett (Eds.), *Prison and Jail Administration.* Gaithersburg, MD: Aspen.

Henggeler, S. W., & Schoenwald, S. K. (1994). Boot camps for juvenile offenders: Just say no. *Journal of Child and Family Studies 3,* 243–248.

Lipsey, M. W. (1992). Juvenile delinquency treatment: A metal-analytic inquiry into the variability of effects. In T. D. Cook, H. Cooper, D. S. Corday, H. Hartman, L. V. Hedges, R. J. Light, T. A. Louis, & F. Mosteller (Eds.), *Metal-Analysis for Explanation: A Case Book.* New York: Russell Sage.

Logan, C. H. (1993). Criminal justice performance measures for prisons. In *Performance Measures for the Criminal Justice System.* Bureau of Justice Statistics and Princeton University: U.S. Department of Justice.

Lutze, F. E. (1998). Are shock incarceration programs more rehabilitative than traditional prisons? A survey of inmates. *Justice Quarterly 15,* 547–566.

MacKenzie, D. L. (1990). Boot camp prisons: Components, evaluations, and empirical issues. *Federal Probation 54,* 44–52.

MacKenzie, D. L. (1995a). Boot camp prisons. In Calhoun & Ritzer (Eds.), *Introduction to Social Problems.* New York: McGraw-Hill, Inc.

MacKenzie, D. L. (1995b). Boot camps – a national assessment. In Tonry & Hamilton (Eds.), *Intermediate Sanctions in Overcrowded Times.* Boston: Northeastern University Press.

MacKenzie, D. L. (1997). Criminal justice and crime prevention. In L. W. Sherman, D. C. Gottfredson, D. L. MacKenzie, J. Eck, P. Reuter, & S. Bushway (Eds.), *Preventing Crime: What Works. What Doesn't, What's Promising.* Washington, D.C.: National Institute of Justice.

MacKenzie, D. L., & Piquero, A. (1994). The impact of shock incarceration programs on prison crowding. *Crime & Delinquency 40,* 222–249.

MacKenzie, D. L., & Rosay, A. B. (1996). Correctional boot camps for juveniles. In *Juvenile and Adult Boot Camps.* Laurel, MD: American Correctional Association.

MacKenzie, D. L., & Souryal, C. (1995a). Inmates' attitude change during incarceration: A comparison of boot camp with traditional prison. *Justice Quarterly 12,* 325–353.

MacKenzie, D. L., & Souryal, C. (1995b). A Machiavellian perspective on the development of boot camp prisons: A debate. *University of Chicago Roundtable.* Chicago: University of Chicago Press.

MacKenzie, D. L., & Parent, D. (1992). Boot camp prisons for young offenders. In J. N. Byrne, A. J. Lurigio, & J. Petersilia (Eds.), *Smart Sentencing: The Emergence of Intermediate Sanction.* London: Sage.

MacKenzie, D. L., & Hebert, E. E. (1996). *Correctional Boot Camps: A Tough Intermediate Sanction.* Washington, D.C.: National Institute of Justice.

MacKenzie, D. L., Styve, G. J., & Gover, A. R. (1998). Performance-based standards for juvenile corrections. *Corrections Management Quarterly 2,* 28–35.

MacKenzie, D. L., & Shaw, J. W. (1993). The impact of shock incarceration on technical violations and new criminal activities. *Justice Quarterly 10,* 463–487.

MacKenzie, D. L., Brame, R., McDowall, D., & Souryal, C. (1995). Boot camp prisons and recidivism in eight states. *Criminology 33,* 326–356.

Mathlas, R. E. S., & Mathews, J. W. (1991). The boot camp program for offenders: Does the shoe fit? *International Journal of Offender Therapy and Comparative Criminology 35,* 322–6.

Meachum, L. M. (1990). Boot camp prisons: Pros and cons. Paper presented at Annual Meeting of American Society of Criminology, Baltimore, MD.

Morash, M., & Rucker, L. (1990). A critical look at the ideal of boot camp as a correctional reform. *Crime and Delinquency 36,* 204–222.

Morris, N., & Tonry, M. (1990). *Between Prison and Probation: Intermediate Punishments in a Rational Sentencing System.* New York: Oxford University Press.

Palmer, T. (1983). The effectiveness issue today: An overview. *Federal Probation 46,* 3–10.

Parent, D. (1989). *Shock Incarceration: An Overview of Existing Programs.* Washington, D.C.: U.S. Department of Justice.

Peters, M., Thomas, D., Zamberlan, C., & Caliber Associates. (1997). *Boot Camps for Juvenile Offenders.* Washington, D.C.: Office of Juvenile Justice and Delinquency Prevention.

Souryal, C., & MacKenzie, D. L. (1994). Shock incarceration and recidivism: An examination of boot camp programs in four states. In J. O. Smykla & W. L. Selke (Eds.), *Intermediate Sanctions: Sentencing in the 90s.* Cincinnati: Anderson.

Tonry, M., & Lynch, M. (1996). Intermediate sanctions. In M. Tonry & N. Morris (Eds.), *Crime and Justice: A Review of Research,* Vol. 20. Chicago: University of Chicago Press.

Zang, S. X. (1998). In search of hopeful glimpses: A critique of research strategies in current boot camp evaluations. *Crime and Delinquency 44,* 314–334.

10

THE ENVIRONMENT AND WORKING CONDITIONS IN JUVENILE BOOT CAMPS AND TRADITIONAL FACILITIES

OJMARRH MITCHELL

DORIS LAYTON MACKENZIE

ANGELA R. GOVER

GAYLENE J. STYVE

B oot camps have become increasingly popular as short-term residential sanctions for juvenile delinquents. Boot camps originated in adult corrections as a more punitive intermediate sanction for offenders of marginal seriousness, emphasizing drill and ceremony and physical activity similar to basic training in the military (Gowdy, 1996). Recently boot camps have been incorporated into juvenile corrections and have since proliferated. In 1996, MacKenzie and Rosay (1996) identified 36 juvenile boot camps; yet, only one of these juvenile boot camps had opened before 1990. The emergence of boot camps appears to have come primarily as a response to a shift in the prevailing juvenile justice philosophy and an increase in the number of juvenile offenders (Gowdy, 1996, p. 1). Policymakers appear to have moved away from the traditional juvenile justice philosophy of rehabilitation, and increasingly espouse protection of the public and deterrence of juvenile offenders as the most important goals of juvenile justice (Feld, 1999). Politicians and the public appear to expect boot camps to be sufficiently punitive to achieve both of these goals, and therein lies much of the appeal of boot camps.

The rapid spread of juvenile boot camps occurred in spite of many researchers' concerns that boot camps may not be appropriate for

Reprinted from Mitchell, O., MacKenzie, D. L. , Gover, A. R. & Styve, G. J. (1999). *Justice Research and Policy,* *1*(2), 1–22.

juvenile offenders. Advocates of boot camps argue that the structure and discipline of these programs result in a healthy and constructive environment that forces individuals to make changes in their lives (Clark & Aziz, 1996; MacKenzie & Hebert, 1996). Such environments are believed to be advantageous to therapy, education, and other treatment activities (Clark & Aziz, 1996; Cowles & Castellano, 1995). Conversely, many researchers knowledgeable about corrections and behavioral change assert that positive change occurs in an interpersonally supportive environment—an environment radically different from that of the confrontational, militaristic boot camp model. According to many psychological theorists, the boot camp environment is antithetical to effective treatment (Andrews, Zinger, Hoge, Bonta, Gendreau, & Cullen, 1990; Gendreau, Little, & Groggin, 1996; Lipsey, 1992; Morash & Rucker, 1990; Sechrest, 1989).

Further, the extant research assessing the treatment effectiveness of juvenile boot camp correctional programming consistently has found that boot camps are no more effective than more traditional facilities (Bottcher, Isorena, & Belnas, 1996; Peters, 1996a, 1996b, 1996c). However, all of this body of research has assessed juvenile boot camp program effectiveness through the problematic measure of post-incarceration official recidivism. While a number of commendable studies have compared recidivism rates of juveniles released from boot camps to those of juveniles released from traditional facilities (Bottcher et al., 1996; Peters, 1996a, 1996b, 1996c), such measures of the effectiveness of correctional programming are by themselves inadequate, as official measures of recidivism rely on numerous factors beyond the control of correctional practitioners (Boone & Fulton, 1995; Dilulio, 1993; Gottfredson, 1987). For example, Gottfredson (1987) asserts measures of criminal behavior such as recidivism, "may depend not only on the behavior of the persons . . . [but] also depend on the behavior of police, prosecutors, judges, or probation and parole officials" (p.14).

A number of practitioners and criminologists argue that measures more immediate to the control of correctional facilities may yield more equitable measures of correctional performance

(Logan, 1993). One set of measures assessing these facility characteristics are measures of the quality of correctional conditions, which quantify the extent to which correctional environments are conducive to rehabilitation and positive behavioral change. From this perspective, high-quality correctional environments should provide residents safety, structure, therapeutic programming, activity, and emotional support (Logan, 1993; DiIulio, 1993).

The impact of a facility's environment on inmates' adjustment and behavior has been well-documented in the research literature (Ajdukovic, 1990; Goffman, 1961; Johnson & Toch, 1982; Moos, 1971; Wright, 1985, 1991; Wright & Goodstein, 1989; Zamble & Porporino, 1990). Previous researchers have noted that facilities "possess unique and enduring characteristics that impinge upon and shape individual behavior" (Wright & Goodstein, 1989, p. 266), both in the facility and after they leave. Measures of correctional performance assessing the quality of the correctional environment instead of recidivism have the advantage of being independent of the actions of other criminal justice agencies.

As yet, little is known about the specific conditions of confinement in juvenile boot camps in comparison to more traditional juvenile correctional facilities. Most of the extant literature concerning components of boot camps have focused on adult inmates' perceptions of the environment (Lutze, 1998), or their attitudes towards the boot camp program and its impact on their future (MacKenzie & Shaw, 1990; MacKenzie & Souryal, 1995). In general, boot camp inmates have perceived the environment as having some components conducive to rehabilitation, such as safety and discipline; however, boot camps were not perceived to include more "internally" important components such as emotional feedback and support (Lutze, 1998). Adult inmates typically view boot camp programs as a positive experience that will assist them in the future (MacKenzie & Shaw, 1990; MacKenzie & Souryal, 1995).

While most previous studies of environmental conditions have used data from institutional records or inmate perceptions, we believe that a unique perspective can be gained by asking correctional facility staff for their perceptions of the environment for the inmates. The correctional staff perspective is expected to be insightful as staff spend a great deal of time in correctional facilities, and have a tremendous amount of interaction with inmates. The accumulation of these experiences qualifies correctional staff as discerning observers and evaluators of the correctional environment. Staff work from a theoretical perspective whether tacitly understood or openly acknowledged. The task, then, is to make these views explicit in order to understand what model drives their interactions with juveniles under their care (Gottfredson, 1984).

The present study attempts to address the issues of the appropriateness of boot camps for juveniles and offers an alternative, perhaps more equitable, measure of correctional effectiveness. The present authors do not attempt to measure correctional performance through recidivism; rather, the authors assess correctional performance through measuring staff perceptions of each facility's conditions of confinement and quality of correctional programming. With these research goals in mind, the conditions of confinement and the work climate in 47 juvenile correctional facilities were examined from the perspective of staff working in 25 boot camps and 22 traditional juvenile facilities. Interest focused on comparing how staff in the different types of facilities perceive the correctional environment and programming for juveniles, and the working conditions for themselves. The authors examined whether boot camps were viewed by staff as providing safe, supportive environments, conducive to positive growth and change, or whether boot camps were viewed by staff as focusing primarily on deterrence by creating a punitive, disagreeable environment.

This study is valuable to juvenile correctional policy as the continued proliferation and funding of juvenile boot camps may not be justifiable in the absence of answers to issues raised in the above. The present study is also a valuable addition to the correctional literature examining juvenile boot camps, as much conjecture has been written about the appropriateness of the boot camp model for juveniles, but no previous research has empirically assessed this question.

HYPOTHESES

From the previous research on adult inmate perceptions, recidivism, and description of boot camps, the authors expected to find that the staff in the boot camps perceive their correctional environments as having more activity, structure, and safety, while having less freedom for juvenile inmates. Furthermore, the authors expected staff in the traditional facilities to perceive the environments of their facilities as having more components important for positive behavioral change, such as care, therapeutic programming, planning for the future, and preparation for release. That is, boot camp staff would emphasize the structure, order, and active aspects of the facilities in order to force delinquents to obey rules, follow directions, and behave appropriately. In contrast, comparison facilities staff would be expected to perceive more treatment, individualized programming, fair and just procedures, and reintegration planning, reflecting the emphasis of their facilities.

METHODOLOGY

This research project began by identifying and locating all juvenile boot camps in operation at the commencement of the research project (April 1997). At that time, 50 privately and publicly funded secure residential boot camps were identified. These facilities were contacted and asked to participate in the research project. Twenty-seven of the 50 facilities agreed to participate in the research project and completed the evaluation process. Twenty-three programs did not participate for various reasons: parental consent issues, staffing and resource limitations, impending program closure, etc. Thus, the 27 boot camps agreeing to participate in this project represented 54% (27 out of 50) of the residential juvenile boot camps operating in 1997.[1] (Note two boot camps were later eliminated, as no comparison facility was available for these facilities).

In order to assess how the experiences of residents in boot camps differed from those in traditional facilities, a comparison facility for each boot camp was selected. Comparison facilities were selected for this research project by identifying those secure residential facilities where the juveniles would have been confined if the boot camp program were not in operation. This method of selection was chosen to ensure that the residents at the comparison facilities were as similar as possible to the boot camp residents. The chief administrator at each boot camp, with this definition of a comparison facility in mind, recommended the most appropriate comparison facility. Comparison facilities were then contacted and asked to join the research project. All of the 22 comparison facilities identified agreed to participate in the research project.

Note that there were only 22 comparison facilities for the 27 boot camps. The discrepancy between the two types of facilities was due to the fact that in three states, two different boot camp administrators identified the same non-boot camp facility as the most appropriate comparison facility. In these instances, one comparison facility served as the control facility for two boot camps; consequently, three comparison facilities served as control facilities for six boot camps.

Survey Administration

The staff survey was administered by a survey facilitator, who was an employee of each facility. The research investigators recommended that the survey facilitator distribute the survey packets to all staff members having direct contact with the residents. The investigators also recommended that staff be given time during their shift to complete the approximately 30-minute survey. The researchers stressed to staff that participation in the survey was voluntary and all responses would be kept strictly confidential. All data were collected between April 1997 and August 1998.

Scale Development

Numerous scales have been developed to measure the environments of correctional facilities: the Social Climate Scale (Moos, 1974), the Prison Environment Inventory (Wright, 1985), the Prison Social Climate Survey (BOP, 1993), the Conditions of Confinement Study (OJJDP,

1994), Quality of Confinement (Logan, 1993), and the Correctional Program Evaluation Inventory (Gendreau & Andrews, 1996). All of these measures assess correctional environments/climates using quantitative indices designed to evaluate components of the correctional atmosphere believed to be integral in promoting behavioral change.

An analysis of these scales reveals a considerable amount of consensus regarding which aspects of the correctional environment are viewed as important to achieving a high quality correctional environment. These scales measure similar constructs: activity/involvement, safety, support/care, order/structure, etc., and often ask similar questions. The current authors modeled the scales utilized in the current evaluation after the above-mentioned measures of correctional environments.

Staff Survey

The evaluation's 216-item staff survey contained 20 scales and 11 demographic questions. Fifteen of the scales concern staff perceptions of the environmental conditions in their facilities; these scales were designed to measure the staff's perceptions of residents quality of confinement at each facility. The environmental conditions scales comprised the following 15 scales: Structure, Activity, Control, Freedom, Resident Danger, Staff Danger, Environmental Danger, Risks to Residents, Care, Quality of Life, Justice, Therapeutic Programs, Preparation for Release, Planning, and Individual Emphasis.

The second component of the staff survey-the work experiences/attitudes scales-were designed to measure staff perceptions of the juvenile residents and how well each institution was run from an employee's point of view. The work experiences/attitudes scales were Staff Communication, Personal Stress, Job Satisfaction, Support of Staff, and Juvenile Culpability.

All of the above-mentioned scales used five-point Likert scales to measure the construct of interest, with the exception of the Planning and Preparation for Release scales, which use both five-point Likert scale items and yes-no-uncertain response options.

Scale Analysis

The scales utilized in the National Evaluation were not validated measures; therefore, all the scales were examined for internal reliability using an array of statistical devices. All of the scales were scrutinized by both Barlett's Test of Sphericity and the Kaiser-Meyer-Olkin test to measure the appropriateness of factor analysis. Using the above statistical devices, all the scales were deemed appropriate for factor analysis. Confirmatory factor analysis, using Principal Components and Varimax rotation with pair-wise deletion of missing data, was performed on all of the hypothesized scales. After the confirmatory factor analysis had been performed, Cronbach's alpha reliability test was performed to test the internal reliability of each scale. The Individual Emphasis scale did not meet the researchers' reliability coefficient criterion of .60; therefore, it was excluded from all analyses. Descriptions of each scale and scale reliabilities are reported in Table Al and A2, in the Appendix.

Demographic Information

Respondents were asked to describe themselves by a variety of demographic, background, and occupational characteristics, including age, race, education, experience working with juveniles, law enforcement experience, military experience, correctional training, job title, length of employment in current facility, frequency of contact with residents, and primary shift worked.

Analysis of Variance Model

Using an analysis of variance model (general linear model, [GLM]), we examined whether there were differences between boot camps and comparison facilities on the environmental and work experiences/attitudes scales, independent of demographic and regional variations. The environmental conditions and work experiences/attitudes scales were the dependent variables in the following analyses. The GLM model attempted to answer two questions: Were there significant differences between boot camps and comparison facilities in general on the scales after controlling for demographic and regional differences; and, if so, how consistent were these differences across regions?

The GLM model employs three categories of independent variables. First, in order to remove the possibility that the detected differences in staff perceptions are due to demographic dissimilarities, all of the models contain independent variables which control for the demographic differences. Second, the researchers expected to find regional differences between facilities, which were independent of type of facility. For example, perhaps the quality of juvenile correctional facilities differs from one state to the next, which would in turn produce regional differences between staff perceptions of quality of the correctional environment. The GLM contains a series of variables, which control for regional differences that may exist between facilities independent of the type of facility. To accomplish this task, all of the regional pairs of facilities, that is each boot camp and paired comparison facility in the same geographic area (usually the same state, but some larger states had more than one pair of facilities), were entered into the model. Stated another way, all of the facilities located in the same region were grouped into a separate variable for each region. These variables were then entered into the model to control for variations that are due strictly to regional differences.[2]

Finally, the GLM contains the two variables of interest: type of facility (boot camp or comparison facility) and an interaction term between type of facility and region. The type of facility variable determines whether there are general differences between the two types of facilities, while the interaction term determines whether the general difference between boot camps and comparison facilities was consistent across regions, i.e., the 22 pairs of facilities. If the interaction was significant in the analysis, we used contrast statements to compare the difference between each regional pair of facilities to the overall mean difference between boot camps and comparison facilities, in order to determine which pairs differed from the overall difference between boot camps and comparison facilities.

Stated differently, the type of facility variable determines whether there is a general (overall) difference between boot camps and comparison facilities. The interaction terms indicate whether the difference between a boot camp and its geographically similar paired comparison facility differs significantly from the overall difference between boot camps and comparison facilities. Thus, the type of facility variable indicates whether there are significant differences between the two types of facilities, and the interaction term measures how consistently the difference between each pair of boot camps and comparison facilities agrees with the overall (mean) difference between boot camps and comparison facilities.

RESULTS

Sample

A sample of 1,233 respondents was obtained.[3] These respondents came from 47 juvenile facilities (25 boot camps and 22 comparison facilities) in 19 states. The overall response rate for all 47 juvenile correctional facilities was 64%. The response rate of boot camps was 70% (N = 646), while the comparison facilities had a 58% response rate (N = 587).

Demographic Comparison

Table 10.1 shows the demographic characteristics of the boot camp staff and the comparison facility staff. The staff showed several significant differences on some of the variables. Most notably, the boot camp staff had less education, more law enforcement experience, more military experience, and had worked less time at the current facility, which was expected given the newness of most residential juvenile boot camps. The boot camp staff also were more racially diverse, with a higher proportion of minority staff members than the comparison facility staff.

Furthermore, there was a small, but statistically significant, difference in age between the two types of staff, with boot camp staff being slightly younger. More of the comparison sample identified their occupation as correctional officer, teacher, or counselor; more of the boot camp staff were drill instructors. The two groups of staff were demographically similar on all of the remaining characteristics.

Comparisons of Environmental Conditions and Staff Work Experiences

Boot camp and comparison facility staff means, adjusted for the control variables, on each of the environmental conditions and work experience/attitudes scales are shown in Tables 10.2 and 10.3. As shown in Table 10.2, even after controlling for regional and demographic differences, boot camps were perceived by their staff as having lower levels of freedom for residents, higher levels of structure, and more control over inmates than the levels reported by comparison facility staff on the same measures. Boot camps were also considered to be less dangerous for residents and staff, to have fewer environmental dangers, and less risks to residents. Boot camps were perceived to involve more activity, to be more caring and just, and to have a higher quality of life. Furthermore, they were viewed as providing significantly more effective therapeutic programming, taking more effective steps to prepare juveniles for release, and helping juveniles better plan for their futures.

Table 10.3 compares boot camp and comparison facility staff's perceptions of the work experiences/attitudes scales. Boot camp staff, in contrast to comparison facility staff, perceived significantly less personal stress and more job satisfaction. Boot camp staff also perceived more support from other staff in their facilities and more communication amongst staff. Moreover, boot camp staff in comparison to comparison facility staff rated the juveniles under their care as being significantly less culpable for their own misbehavior.

However, the interaction term was found to be significant in all of the scales, indicating that there was some variation in the difference between boot camps and comparison facilities by their geographic location. There were two major types of interactions - magnitudinal and directional (see Figure 10.1 and Figure 10.2 for

Table 10.1   Demographic Comparison of Boot Camp and Comparison Facility Staff

Characteristic	Boot Camp Staff (N = 646)	Comparison Facility Staff (N = 587)
Gender (% Male)	68.9	63.6
Race/Ethnicity (%)*		
African-American	21.4	19.0
White	63.8	70.4
Hispanic	9.2	5.6
Other	5.7	4.9
Age, *M* (SD)*	35.4 (9.37)	39.3 (10.8)
Highest Level of Education (%)*		
High School/Technical Training	16.5	13.7
Some College	35.3	22.7
College Degree	30.9	37.8
Graduate Study	17.3	25.7
Formal Training prior to work in this facility (% Yes)	70.4	65.1
Previous Law Enforcement Experience (% Yes)*	37.3	19.2
Military Experience (% Yes)*	51.8	24.9
Years in Current Facility, *M* (SD)*	1.9 (2.8)	6.4 (6.5)
Occupational Category (%)*		
Correctional officer	11.5	19.9
Medical staff	1.1	1.3
Psychologist	.5	.9
Administrative personnel	10.4	10.5
Teacher	14.0	22.2
Counselor	12.7	30.6
Caseworker	3.8	4.9
Drill instructor	39.3	.5
Other	6.7	9.1
Prior Experience in a Juvenile Facility (in Years), *M* (SD)	1.8 (4.2)	1.5 (3.4)
Frequency of Contact with Juveniles (%)		
Yearly	1.7	1.2
Monthly	2.1	1.6
Weekly	2.5	2.4
Every day	93.8	94.8
Predominant Shift (%)		
Day	55.0	57.0
Evening	18.2	23.1
Night	9.9	7.3
No predominant shift	16.8	12.5

*$p < .05$.

a graphical presentation of the interactions). When there were magnitudinal differences, the *magnitude* of the difference between a specific pair of facilities differed from the overall mean difference between all boot camps and comparison facilities; however, the direction of the difference was consistent with the overall difference. For example, the overall means for boot camps and comparison facilities on the Freedom scale were 2.15 and 2.66, respectively, a difference of .51, with the comparison facilities having the larger mean. The data analysis revealed that for the Freedom scale there was a significant interaction and the follow-up contrast

Table 10.2   Boot Camp and Traditional Facility Comparison on the Environmental Conditions Scales

Scale	Boot Camp Mean (SD)	Comparison Mean (SD)	Consistency of Finding (%)	Model Statistics	
				F	R^2
Activity	4.50 (.03)	4.02 (.03)*	95	9.32**	.35
Control	4.20 (.02)	2.79 (.03)*	91	13.63**	.44
Freedom	2.15 (.02)	2.66 (.03)*	86	18.24**	.51
Justice	4.31 (.02)	4.11 (.03)*	86	5.61**	.24
Structure	4.40 (.03)	4.03 (.03)*	86	7.06**	.29
Resident Danger	2.05 (.02)	2.61 (.03)*	100	22.57**	.56
Staff Danger	2.03 (.03)	2.56 (.03)*	95	15.51**	.47
Environmental Danger	1.76 (.03)	2.26 (.03)*	91	14.81**	.46
Risks to Residents	1.67 (.03)	2.00 (.03)*	91	7.18**	.29
Care	4.07 (.02)	3.70 (.03)*	91	10.03**	.36
Quality of Life	3.85 (.02)	3.62 (.03)*	77	8.60**	.33
Programs	4.01 (.03)	3.59 (.03)*	95	7.87**	.31
Preparation for Release	4.34 (.03)	4.06 (.04)*	77	7.38**	.30
Planning	4.40 (.03)	4.12 (.03)*	82	7.30**	.29

*Significant difference at the $p < .001$ level.
**Model significant at the $p < .001$ level.

Table 10.3   Boot Camp and Traditional Facility Comparison on the Work Experiences/Attitudes Scales

Scale	Boot Camp Mean (SD)	Comparison Mean (SD)	Consistency of Finding (%)	Model Statistics	
				F	R^2
Job Satisfaction	3.65 (.03)	3.47 (.03)*	86	3.75**	.18
Support of Staff	3.75 (.03)	3.46 (.04)*	82	5.17**	.23
Personal Stress	1.89 (.04)	2.13 (.04)*	91	3.24**	.16
Juvenile Culpability	2.63 (.03)	2.83 (.04)*	95	3.10**	.16
Staff Communication	3.74 (.04)	3.43 (.05)*	91	4.18**	.20

*Significant difference at the $p < .001$ level.
**Model significant at the $p < .001$ level.

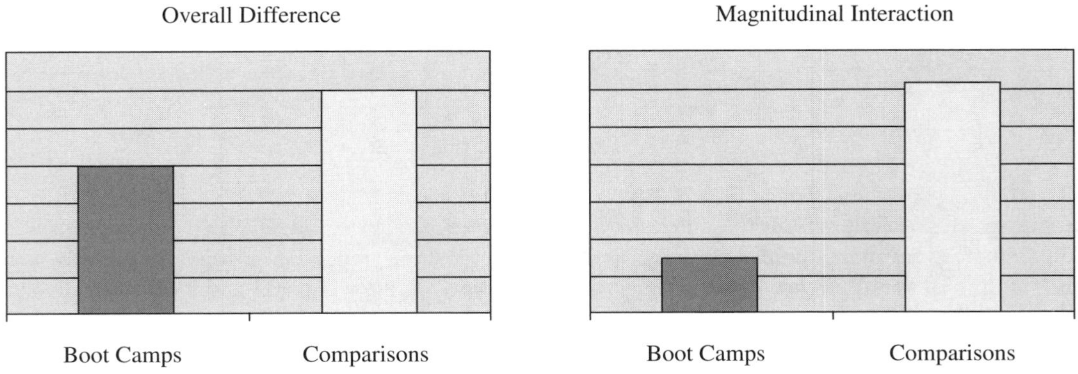

Figure 10.1   Illustration of Magnitudinal Interaction

Overall Difference

Directional Interaction

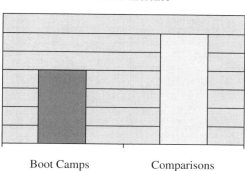
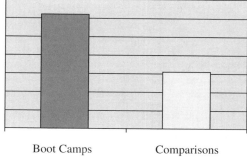

Boot Camps   Comparisons   Boot Camps   Comparisons

Figure 10.2   Illustration of Directional Interaction

comparison indicated that the comparison facility in Region 21 had a mean of 2.80 and the boot camp had a mean of 1.94, a difference of .86.[4] This is a magnitudinal difference because the direction of the difference between the means is in the same direction as the overall difference between all boot camps and comparison facilities (i.e., the comparison facility had more freedom than the boot camp), but the difference between facilities in Region 21 was significantly larger than the overall difference.

More interesting for our purposes were the directional interactions, because these directional interactions indicate that the difference between a boot camp and its paired comparison facility was inconsistent with the overall mean difference between boot camps and comparison facilities in the *direction* of the difference. For example, in the follow-up contrasts for the Freedom scale, Region 4 also was found to exhibit a directional interaction. The means were 2.96 and 2.86, respectively, for the boot camp and the comparison facility pair at this site. Thus, instead of perceiving less freedom than the comparison facility, the boot camp in this region perceived more freedom for juveniles, which was considered a directional interaction because it was *inconsistent* with the overall finding.

The consistency of the overall difference between boot camps and comparison facilities is reflected in the fourth column of Tables 10.2 and 10.3, with higher values indicating a more consistent finding. Consistency of finding is the quotient of the number of regions displaying

differences between boot camps and comparison facilities consistent with the overall findings to the total number of regions (22). Hence, the Activity scale had a consistency of 95%, as 21 of the 22 regions perceived the difference between boot camps and comparison facilities similarly. Twelve of the 14 environmental conditions scales-Control, Resident Danger, Staff Danger, Environmental Danger, Activity, Care, Risks to Residents, Structure, Justice, Freedom, Programming, and Planning-had four or fewer regions out of the twenty-two matched pairs of facilities display directional interactions, a consistency of finding at least 82% (18 of 22).

The interaction term was significant on all of the work experience/attitudes scales; however, none of the work experiences/attitudes scales had more than four directional interactions. The Support of Staff and Job Satisfaction scales had four and three directional interactions, an 82% and 86% consistent finding, respectively. Personal Stress, Juvenile Culpability, and Staff Communication each had two or fewer directional interactions, at least a 91% consistent finding.

Analysis of the follow-up contrasts revealed that the results were less consistent for the Quality of Life, and Preparation for Release scales. Both the Quality of Life and Preparation for Release scales exhibited five directional interactions. For these scales, the majority of boot camp staff in the 22 matched pairs of facilities (at least 17 of 22 regions, or 77%) perceived their environments more favorably on these scales than comparison facility staff, but the consistency of these findings was marginal.

Table 10.4   Number of Directional Interactions by Region

	Directional Interactions			
Scale	Environmental Conditions Scales	Consistency of Finding[5] (%)	Work Experiences Scales	Consistency of Finding (%)
Region 1	0	100	0	100
Region 2	3	79	3	40
Region 3	2	86	2	60
Region 4	1	93	0	100
Region 5	0	100	1	80
Region 6	0	100	0	100
Region 7	0	100	0	100
Region 8	0	100	0	100
Region 9	6	57	0	100
Region 10	0	100	0	100
Region 11	1	93	0	100
Region 12	0	100	0	100
Region 13	0	100	1	80
Region 14	3	79	0	100
Region 15	0	100	0	100
Region 16	0	100	0	100
Region 17	5	64	0	100
Region 18	0	100	1	80
Region 19	6	57	3	40
Region 20	1	93	0	100
Region 21	0	100	0	100
Region 22	6	57	1	80

[5]Consistency of finding is the number of consistent findings divided by the total number of scales: 14 for the environmental conditions, 5 for the work experiences/attitudes.

The authors also examined whether any region consistently demonstrated directional interactions (see Table 10.4). All but four of the matched pairs of facilities exhibited directional interactions on two or fewer of the environmental conditions scales (see columns 2 and 3 of Table 10.4). Thus, of the 22 regions, 82% (18/22) of these facilities perceived the differences between boot camps and comparison facilities on the environmental conditions scales similarly. The exceptions to these otherwise consistent findings were Regions 22, 19, and 9, which all displayed six directional interactions and Region 17 with five directional interactions on the 14 environmental conditions scales. These four regions did not appear to follow the overall difference between boot camps and comparison facilities as well as the other regions. That is, for these regions, the differences between boot camps and comparison facilities were not consistently similar to the overall differences between boot camps and comparison facilities.

The high number of directional interactions in Region 19 may be explained by the fact that the comparison facility in this region was not a truly *traditional* facility (i.e., training school or detention center). The comparison facility in this region was a residential forestry camp, which utilized a very treatment-oriented philosophy with a high level of therapeutic programming and vocational training. These qualitative observations are buttressed by the fact that this comparison facility was perceived by its staff to have high scores on those scales associated with a treatment-oriented philosophy (Care, Programs, Quality of Life, etc.).

Region 22 was dissimilar from the other regions in that the boot camp in this region was recently opened at the time of the survey, while the comparison facility was an older, well-established facility. The newness of the boot camp facility could account for some of the directional differences, as the boot camp staff may have not been fully accustomed to the boot camp philosophy at the time of the staff survey. This view is supported by the findings that the boot camp staff in this region perceived their environment as having lower scores on the scales that we expected boot camps to score strongest on, i.e., structure and activity.

We are unable to offer any explanations as to why Regions 9 and 17 displayed above average numbers of directional interactions on the environmental conditions scales. These sites do not appear to differ from the other regions in any apparent systematic manner.

DISCUSSION

Opponents of juvenile boot camps claim that these programs have harsh, punishment-oriented, and uncaring environments, which are antithetical to effective treatment (Morash & Rucker, 1990). The findings of the only previous study (Lutze, 1998) comparing the correctional environment of an adult boot camp to that of a traditional prison partially supports the conclusions of Morash and Rucker. Lutze concluded that the correctional environment of the adult boot camp she studied did not differ from a traditional prison in providing support for positive internal behavioral change. The present study's findings clearly were in opposition to both these previous studies.

As hypothesized and in concordance with the work comparing adult correctional environments (Lutze, 1998), perceptions of the environment revealed that boot camps were perceived to be significantly safer than comparison facilities on all of the measures of facility dangerousness. These findings are of utmost importance, as previous researchers have concluded that without a safe correctional environment, inmates are forced to focus on self-defense instead of internal change (Toch, 1977; Wright, 1985; Lutze, 1998). Also as expected, staff in boot camps perceived their facilities as having less freedom, but more control, structure, and activity, which is consistent with the discipline-oriented philosophy of boot camps. However, unexpectedly, boot camp staff perceived the environment of their programs as more caring, more just, more focused on individualized planning, incorporating more effective rehabilitative programming, having a higher quality of life, and better preparing residents for release.

Moreover, analysis of the work experiences/attitudes scales revealed consistent, significant differences between the two types of facility staff. Boot camp staff reported more job satisfaction, more support from other staff, more communication amongst staff, and less personal stress than did comparison facility staff. Boot camp staff also perceived that their residents were less culpable in their misbehavior than comparison facility staff.

These findings suggest that boot camp staff not only perceive the environment of boot camps as being more conducive to rehabilitation for juveniles, but also that the boot camp environment seems to produce more favorable work experiences for staff. In general, these findings were very consistent across sites, except in regard to quality of life and preparation for release; it should be noted, however, that even on these measures the majority of the paired sites (at least 77%) perceived the boot camp environment more favorably. Based upon these results, the authors conclude that while there was some variation across regions, in general there were consistent, significant differences between the quality of the correctional environment of boot camps and comparison facilities, with boot camps being overwhelming perceived more favorably. However, it is also possible that characteristics other than the military atmosphere, such as the newness of the boot camps or type of staff hired, may have led to some of these differences in perceptions.

The current study provides evidence of the efficacy of boot camp programming. Correctional policymakers deliberating the future of boot camp programs should take note of the present study's findings. While boot camps may not be a panacea against future criminality, our findings suggest that they are not the harmful, abusive environments some critics portray them to be.

This study has shown that valid measures of correctional programming effectiveness other than recidivism exist and should be the focus of future analyses. Evaluating correctional programs solely on the criterion of recidivism has limited value as many factors impact recidivism rates. It may prove productive in many instances to focus on the quality of inter-actions and programming within correctional facilities as intermediate indicators of correc-tional programming. Measures assessing how well correctional institutions and programs perform at those tasks directly within their control, such as providing safe, just, active, caring, controlled environments conducive to positive behavioral change are equally valid, necessary measures of correctional perfor-mance. Based upon these measures of program success, the environments of boot camps were clearly judged more favorably by the people who perhaps know correctional facilities best-their own staff.

APPENDIX

Table A.1 Description of Environmental Conditions Scales

Scale	Scale Description and Cronbach's Alpha
Control	This nine-item scale examined staff's perceptions of how much discipline the institution demands of its residents (coefficient alpha = .72).
Freedom	This seven-item scale assessed staff perceptions of the amount of choice present in the daily lives of residents (coefficient alpha = .70).
Justice	This 11-item scale examined perceptions of how fairly their institution is run (coefficient alpha = .77).
Care	This scale used 10 items to assess the amount of care and amicability staff members believe there is between the institution and the juveniles in their custody (coefficient alpha = .73).
Activity	This seven-item scale measured how busy residents typically are in their daily activities (coefficient alpha = .79).
Individual Emphasis	This four-item scale measured staff perceptions of how much individual attention the residents receive (coefficient alpha = .54). The alpha coefficient for this scale did not meet the standard for inclusion in the data analysis.
Environmental Danger	This scale, using eight items, measured staff perceptions of how much general institutional danger each facility poses to residents (coefficient alpha = .71).
Resident Danger	This scale measured perceptions of how much of a threat residents are to the safety of other residents (coefficient alpha = .85).
Staff Danger	This scale measured perceptions concerning how much danger staff believe residents pose toward the safety of staff members (coefficient alpha = .75).
Preparation for Release	This seven-item scale measured staff's perceptions of residents readiness to make a smooth transition back into society upon their release from custody (coefficient alpha = .68).
Risk to Residents	This scale contained seven items concerning the existence of hazardous conditions within each facility, which could potentially affect residents (coefficient alpha = .71).
Planning	This scale used 11 items to measure staff perceptions of the amount of planning residents have made toward their futures (coefficient alpha = .69).
Programs	This scale used 11 items to measure how beneficial staff members believe the residents' experiences in the institution have been (coefficient alpha = .90).
Quality of Life	This nine-item scale assessed perceptions of the quality of food, living spaces, and the amount of privacy, etc. residents received (coefficient alpha = .67).
Structure	This 10-item scale measured staff perceptions of the amount of regimentation residents are subject to in their daily activities (coefficient alpha = .80).

Table A.2   Description of Work Experiences/Attitudes Scales

Scale	Scale Description and Cronbach's Alpha
Support of Staff	This scale measured staff perceptions of the relationships between staff members and facility administrators, supervisors, and other staff members (coefficient alpha = .88).
Staff Communication	This scale used seven items to evaluate how effective lines of communication are between the various levels of staff (coefficient alpha = .93).
Personal Stress	This 14-item scale determined the amount of stress, depression, anxiety, and anger staff members have experienced in the past six months (coefficient alpha = .91).
Juvenile Culpability	This six-item scale measured staff's perceptions of how culpable the residents are in their behavior (coefficient alpha = .61); e.g., "Most of these kids are good kids, they have just had a tough life."
Job Satisfaction	This scale used 15 items to measure staff satisfaction with their jobs, coworkers, supervisors, facility administration, and training (coefficient alpha = .89).

NOTES

1. As a high percentage of all juvenile boot camps in operation at the time of study agreed to participate in the study, the researchers do not expect their sample of facilities to be meaningfully different from the population of all juvenile boot camps in operation at the time of the study.

2. Note that in order to protect the confidentiality of the facilities involved in the study all of the regions were assigned a random number. Also, some larger states had two pairs of boot camps and comparisons, thus there are more regions (22) than there are different states participating in the study (19).

3. These figures exclude the two boot camps that did not have comparison facilities.

4. Group pairs were given arbitrary numbers to protect the confidentiality of the sites.

REFERENCES

Ajdukovic, D. (1990). Psychosocial climate in correctional institutions: Which attributes describe it? *Environment and Behavior, 22,* 420–432.

Andrews, D. A., Zinger, I., Hoge, R. D., Bonta, J., Gendreau, P., & Cullen, F. T. (1990). Does correctional treatment work? A clinically relevant and psychologically informed meta-analysis. *Criminology, 28,* 369–404.

Boone, H. N., Jr., & Fulton, B. (1995). *Results-driven management: Implementing performance-based measures in community corrections.* Washington, D.C.: American Probation and Parole Association, 1995.

Bottcher, J., Isorena, T., & Belnas, M. (1996). *LEAD: A boot camp and intensive parole program. An impact evaluation: Second year findings.* Sacramento: State of California, Department of the Youth Authority, Research Division.

Clark, C. L., & Aziz, D. W. (1996). Shock incarceration in New York State: Philosophy, results, and limitations. In D. L. MacKenzie & E. E. Hebert (Eds.), *Correctional boot camps: A tough intermediate sanction.* Washington, D.C.: Government Printing Office.

Cowles, E., & Castellano, T. (1995). *"Boot camp" drug treatment and aftercare intervention: An evaluation review.* Washington, D.C.: National Institute of Justice.

DiIulio, J. J., Jr. (1993). Rethinking the criminal justice system: Toward a new paradigm. In *Performance measures for the criminal justice system.* Washington, D.C.: Bureau of Justice Statistics and Princeton University.

DiIulio, J. J., Jr. (1991). *No escape: The future of American corrections.* New York: Basic Books.

Federal Bureau of Prisons. (1993). *Prison social climate survey: Staff version and resident version.* Washington, D.C.: Government Printing Office.

Feld, B. C. (1999). Juvenile and criminal justice systems' responses to youth violence. In M. Tonry & M. Moore (Eds.), Youth violence. *Crime & Justice, 24,* 189–261. Chicago: University of Chicago Press.

Gendreau, P., & Andrews, D. A. (1996). *Correctional program evaluation inventory.* Unpublished manuscript.

Goffman, E. (1961). *Asylums: Essays on the social situation of mental patients and other inmates.* Chicago: Aldine.

Gottfredson, D. M. (1987). Prediction and classification in criminal justice decision making. In M. Tonry & D. M. Gottfredson (Eds.), *Crime & Justice: An Annual Review of Research,* 9, 1–19.

Gottfredson, G. D. (1984). A theory-ridden approach to program evaluation: A method for stimulating researcher implementer collaboration. *American Psychologist, 39*(10), 1101- 1112.

Gowdy, V. B. (1996). Historical perspective. In D. L. MacKenzie & E. E. Hebert (Eds.), *Correctional boot camps: A tough intermediate sanction.* Washington, D.C.: Government Printing Office.

Johnson, R., & Toch, H. (1982). *The pains of imprisonment.* Beverly Hills, CA: Sage.

Lipsey, M. (1992). Juvenile delinquency treatment: A meta-analytic inquiry into the variability of effects. In T. Cook et al. (Eds.), *Meta-analysis for explanation: A casebook.* New York: Russell Sage Foundation.

Logan, C. H. (1992). Well kept: Comparing quality of confinement in private and public prisons. *The Journal of Criminal Law and Criminology, 83,* 577–613.

Logan, C. H. (1993). Criminal justice performance measures for prisons. *In Performance measures for the criminal justice system.* Washington, D.C.: Bureau of Justice Statistics and Princeton University.

Lutze, F. E. (1998). Are shock incarceration programs more rehabilitative than traditional prisons?: A survey of inmates. *Justice Quarterly, 15,* 547–566.

MacKenzie, D. L. (1997). Criminal justice and crime prevention. In L. Sherman, D. Gottfredson, D. L. MacKenzie, J. Eck, P. Reuter, & S. Bushway, *Preventing crime: What works, what doesn't, what's promising.* A report to the U.S. Congress prepared for the National Institute of Justice.

MacKenzie, D. L., Brame, R., McDowall, D., & Souryal, C. (1995). Boot camps and recidivism in eight states. *Criminology, 33,* 327–357.

MacKenzie, D. L., & Herbert, E. E. (1996). *Correctional boot camps: A tough intermediate sanction.* Washington, D.C.: Office of Justice Programs.

MacKenzie, D. L., & Rosay, A. (1996). Correctional boot camps for juveniles. In *Juvenile and adult boot camps.* Laurel, MD: American Correctional Association.

MacKenzie, D. L., & Shaw, A. (1990). Inmate adjustment and change during shock incarceration: The impact of correctional boot camp programs. *Justice Quarterly, 7,* 125–150.

MacKenzie, D. L., & Shaw, A. (1993). Impact of shock incarceration on technical violations and new criminal activities. *Justice Quarterly, 10,* 463–487.

MacKenzie, D. L., & Souryal, C. (1995). A "Machiavellian" perspective on the development of boot camp prisons: A debate. *University of Chicago roundtable.* Chicago: University of Chicago Press.

MacKenzie, D. L., Styve, G. J., & Gover, A. R. (1998). Performance-based standards for juvenile corrections. *Corrections Management Quarterly, 2,* 28–35.

Moos, R. H. (1971). Differential effects of the social climates of correctional institutions. *Journal of Research in Crime and Delinquency, 7,* 71–82.

Moos, R. H. (1974). *Correctional institutions environment scale manual.* Palo Alto, CA: Consulting Psychological Press.

Morash, M., & Rucker, L. (1990). A critical look at the ideal of boot camps as a correctional reform. *Crime and Delinquency, 36,* 204–222.

Office of Juvenile Justice and Delinquency Prevention. (1994). *Conditions of confinement: Juvenile detention and correctional facilities.* Washington, D.C.: Government Printing Office.

Peters, M. (1996a). *Evaluation of the impact of boot camps for juvenile offenders: Denver interim report.* Washington, D.C.: Office of Juvenile Justice and Delinquency Prevention.

Peters, M. (1996b). *Evaluation of impact of boot camps for juvenile offenders: Cleveland interim report.* Washington, D.C.: Office of Juvenile Justice and Delinquency Prevention.

Peters, M. (1996c). *Evaluation of impact of boot camps for juvenile offenders: Mobile interim report.* Washington, D.C.: Office of Juvenile Justice and Delinquency Prevention.

Sechrest, D. (1989). Prison "boot camps" don't measure up. *Federal Probation, 53,* 15-20.

Toch, H. (1977). *Living in prison: The ecology of survival.* New York: Macmillan.

Wright, K. N. (1985). Developing the prison environment inventory. *Journal of Research in Crime and Delinquency, 22,* 257–277.

Wright, K. N. (1991). A study of individual, environmental, and interactive effects in explaining adjustment to prison. *Justice Quarterly, 8,* 217–242.

Wright, K. N., & Goodstein, L. (1989). Correctional environments. In L. Goodstein & D. L. MacKenzie (Eds.), *The American prison: Issues in research and policy.* New York: Plenum.

Zamble, E., & Porporino, F. (1990). Coping, imprisonment and rehabilitation: Some data and their implications. *Criminal Justice and Behavior, 17,* 53–70.

Part IV

Inmate Adjustment and Change During Incarceration

11

THE IMPACT OF BOOT CAMPS AND TRADITIONAL INSTITUTIONS ON JUVENILE RESIDENTS

Perceptions, Adjustment, and Change

DORIS LAYTON MACKENZIE

DAVID B. WILSON

GAYLENE STYVE ARMSTRONG

ANGELA R. GOVER

Despite their continuing popularity, correctional boot camps for juveniles remain controversial. The debate involves questions about the impact of the camps on the adjustment and behavior of juveniles while they are in residence and after they are released. According to advocates, the atmosphere of the camps is conducive to positive growth and change (Clark & Aziz, 1996; MacKenzie & Hebert, 1996). In contrast, critics argue many of the components of the camps are in direct opposition to the type of relationships and supportive conditions that are needed for quality therapeutic programming (Andrews, Zinger, Hoge, Bonta, Gendreau, & Cullen, 1990; Gendreau, Little & Groggin, 1996; Morash & Rucker, 1990; Sechrest, 1989). Research on the recidivism of releasees from

Reprinted by permission of the *Journal of Research in Crime and Delinquency,* from MacKenzie, D. L., Wilson, D. B., Armstrong, G. S., & Gover, A. R. (2001). *Journal of Research in Crime and Delinquency, 38,* 279-313.

Author's Note: This investigation was supported in part by grant #96-SC-LX-0001 from the National Institute of Justice, Office of Justice Programs, U.S. Department of Justice, to the University of Maryland. Points of view in this document are those of the authors and do not necessarily represent the official position of the Department of Justice. Thanks are expressed to administrators, staff and juveniles at the correctional facilities who participated in the research as well as the Center for Substance Abuse Research (CESAR) who provided some technical assistance.

correctional boot camps has not been particularly helpful in settling the controversy over the camps. Neither adult nor juvenile boot camps appear to be effective in reducing recidivism. In general, no differences are found in recidivism when boot camp releasees are compared to comparison samples who served other sentences or who had been confined in another type of juvenile facility (MacKenzie 1997; MacKenzie, Brame, McDowall & Souryal 1995).

This research examines the experiences of 2,668 juveniles confined in 26 boot camps and compares these experiences to those of 1,848 juveniles residing in 22 traditional facilities. We examine whether juveniles in the boot camps experience more anxiety and depression in comparison to those in traditional facilities and whether these experiences are related to perceptions of the environment. In addition, we compare the changes juveniles make during residency in the facilities. Specifically, we were interested in changes in stress (anxiety, depression), and impulsivity, social bonds, and antisocial attitudes. The latter characteristics have been found to be associated with criminal activity and are, therefore, reasonable targets for intermediate change during the time juveniles reside in the facilities. We also measured juveniles' perceptions of the environment in order to examine whether they perceived the environments of the two types of facilities differently and, if so, whether these perceptions were related to the type of changes they made while in the facilities.

Critics of boot camps propose that some juveniles will experience more difficulties than others in the boot camps due to the confrontational nature of the interactions between the juveniles and the staff (Morash & Rucker, 1990). In particular, the boot camps are proposed to be particularly stressful for girls and for juveniles who have experienced a past history of family violence. In order to examine this proposal, we compared the impact of the boot camps on girls and boys and whether there were differences in the impact of the boot camps on those who had experienced family violence.

For a subset of respondents, data were collected at two points in time, enabling us to examine change in anxiety and depression as well as social bonds, impulsivity and social attitudes during the time juveniles were in

the two different types of facilities. These characteristics are theoretically associated with criminal behavior. Increased social bonds and positive social attitudes and, conversely, decreased impulsivity are anticipated to be associated with reductions in later criminal activity. Thus, facilities that have an impact on these characteristics of juveniles may be successful in reducing recidivism.

We begin by reviewing the research literature establishing the importance of understanding the environments of facilities and the effects of different environments on the residents. Following this, we review the literature on juveniles' adjustment in facilities, the changes juveniles are hypothesized to make during their time in residential facilities, and the association of these changes with future criminal activities.

THE PERCEIVED ENVIRONMENT

The impact of the prison environment on inmates' adjustment and behavior both while they are in the facility and when they are released has been well established in the research literature (Ajdukovic, 1990; Goffman, 1961; Johnson & Toch, 1982; Moos, 1968; Wright, 1985, 1991; Wright & Goodstein, 1989; Zamble & Porporino, 1990). Facilities possess unique characteristics that "impinge upon and shape individual behavior" (Wright & Goodstein, 1989, p. 266).

Few people who have visited correctional boot camps doubt that the environments of these facilities are radically different from the environment of traditional facilities (MacKenzie & Hebert, 1996; MacKenzie & Parent, 1992; Styve, MacKenzie, Gover, Mitchell, in press; Lutz, 1998). Juveniles in these facilities are awakened early each day to follow a rigorous daily schedule of physical training, drill and ceremony, and school. They are required to follow the orders of the correctional staff. Orders are often presented in a confrontational manner, modeled after basic training in the military. Summary punishments such as push-ups are frequently used to sanction misbehavior. In comparison to traditional juvenile facilities, boot camps appear to be more physically and emotionally demanding for the residents. In fact, research on adult boot camps suggests that inmates in the boot camps will voluntarily drop out even if this means they will have to serve a longer term in the prison than they would if they completed the boot camp (MacKenzie & Souryal, 1995).

Perceptions of inmates in the different types of facilities would be expected to reflect the differences in environments. Continuing controversy exists about the appropriateness of the camps for managing and treating juvenile delinquents. Advocates of the boot camps argue that the focus on strict control and military structure provides a safer environment conducive to positive change (Steinhart, 1993; Zachariah, 1996). From their perspective, the intense physical activity and healthy atmosphere of the camps provides an advantageous backdrop for treatment and education (Clark & Aziz, 1996; Cowles & Castellano, 1996).

Critics disagree with this perspective (Morash & Rucker, 1990) and claim that the confrontational nature of the camps is diametrically opposed to the constructive, interpersonally supportive environment necessary for positive change to occur (Andrews, Zinger, Hoge, Bonta, Gendreau & Cullen, 1990). According to critics, juveniles in the boot camps, when compared to youth in traditional facilities, will perceive their facilities as less caring and less therapeutic, and, in general, preparing them less for reentry into the community. Furthermore, juveniles may be worried about their safety while they are in a boot camp facility. Given the hypothesized negative environmental characteristics, youth in boot camps would be expected to experience much more stress than youth in traditional facilities.

Morash and Rucker (1990) are particularly concerned that the boot camps will have a detrimental impact on girls and on both girls and boys who have experienced abuse. The confrontation nature of the interactions between staff and inmates is expected to be particularly problematic for these youth. For those who have a history of abuse and for girls who have dependency issues, these interactions will be reminiscent of the difficulties they faced in an abusive relationships; as a result, the environment will be particularly stressful for them and counter-therapeutic.

The environments of the facilities would also be expected to have an impact on the types of changes inmates make during their time in the different facilities. For example, research demonstrates that treatment programs with particular characteristics are effective in changing antisocial attitudes. An environment that emphasizes therapeutic programming instead of physical activity would be expected to have a greater impact on such attitudes (Andrews & Bonta, 1998; Goodstein & Wright, 1989).

In summary, we propose that juveniles in the boot camps and the traditional facilities will perceive the environment of their institutions differently and that the characteristics of the environments will have an impact on the level of stress experienced by the residents and on the changes they make in social bonds, antisocial attitudes and impulsivity.

STRESS

One concern regarding the boot camps is whether the environment creates dysfunctional stress for the participants. Some levels of stress may actually be beneficial. For example, critical life events may create stress, and this stress may result in changing the trajectories of the lives of those involved in criminal activities (Sampson & Laub, 1993). Instead of continuing in the previous path (e.g., criminal), youth may change and make a commitment to family, school or employment. The stress created by the critical life event in such cases has a functional and beneficial impact. In contrast, some stress is so severe that an individual's level of functioning is compromised. In such cases, the stress is considered dysfunctional.

The adjustment of inmates to the environments of correctional facilities has been the topic of numerous research studies (e.g., Goodstein & Wright, 1989). A concern has been that institutions such as prisons create a total environment that may severely limit inmates' development and create dysfunctional stress, particularly in youth (Goffman, 1961; Johnson & Toch, 1982; Moos, 1968; Wright, 1991). Critics of boot camps fear that the demanding nature of the boot camp environment will be beyond the coping ability of youth and, as a result, will be detrimental to them.

In contrast, advocates argue that it is a healthy environment that creates the type of stress that will lead youth to reevaluate their lives and make changes. Some level of stress may be effective in bringing about change. For example, Zamble and Porporino (1988) found adult inmates experienced stress when they first entered prison. This was also the time inmates were most willing to enter programs designed to help them make changes in their lives. Zamble and Porporino propose that the stress associated with entry to prison might be instrumental in getting inmates to reevaluate their lives and take steps toward positive change. This proposal is similar to the type of critical life event Sampson and Laub (1993) consider conducive to bringing about changes in life trajectories. That is, entering a new situation like a residential facility may be the type of life event that leads to changes in the trajectory of the lives of some juveniles. As a result of this event, the juveniles may become more pro-social and begin to build ties and bonds with conventional social institutions.

Frequently, boot camp staff refer to the early period in boot camps as a period when they "break-down" youth before they begin the "build-up period." The question is whether the breakdown period creates functional or dysfunctional stress. That is, do the youth in the boot camp experience the type of anxiety that will result in a reevaluation of their lives and a decision to make changes or is the stress so severe that they become depressed, anxious, and unable to adequately function in the new environment. Critics would suggest that the stress in boot camps is so severe as to be dysfunctional; advocates of the camps argue that it creates the type of stress that leads to positive changes.

CHANGING YOUTH

If institutional programs are going to have an impact on the future criminal activities and adjustment of youth, the programs must change the youth in some way. These intermediate changes can be thought to be signals of the impacts the facilities will have on the future criminal activities of the youth. This research examines adjustment and short-term change in boot camp facilities and compares these to the changes juveniles in traditional facilities make. Three correlates of criminal activity are: Social bonds, impulsivity and antisocial attitudes. These characteristics are theoretically and empirically associated with criminal activity and other antisocial behavior. We begin by reviewing evidence that these characteristics are associated with criminal behavior and that changes in the characteristics are associated with changes in criminal activity.

Increasing Social Bonds

Evidence exists that increases in social bonds are associated with declines in criminal activity. According to Sampson and Laub (1993) informal social controls form a structure of interpersonal bonds linking individuals to social institutions such as work, family and school. These ties or bonds are important in that they create obligations and restraints that impose significant costs for translating criminal propensities into action. While Sampson and Laub acknowledge that there is continuity in individual antisocial behavior, they argue, unlike the continuity theorists (e.g., Gottfredson & Hirschi, 1990), that such continuity does not preclude large changes in individuals' offending patterns. In a reanalysis of the Glueck and Glueck data, Sampson and Laub found support for the proposal that childhood antisocial behavior and deviance can be modified over the life course by adult social bonds (Sampson & Laub, 1993). Job stability and marital attachment were significant predictors of adult crime even when childhood delinquency and crime in young adulthood were statistically controlled.

Further evidence that criminal propensity can be modified comes from research by Horney and her colleagues which examined the self-reported criminal activities of offenders (Horney, Osgood & Marshall, 1995). They found that life circumstances indicative of changes in social bonds and commitment to conformity influenced offending behavior even over relatively short time periods.

Similar to the findings from research with adults, increased social bonds have been found to be associated with declines in the criminal activities of juveniles (Simons, Johnson, Conger & Elder, 1998; Jang, 1999). For example, Simons et al. (1998) found stronger ties to family and school and decreased affiliation with deviant peers lowered the probability that youth who had behavior problems during childhood would graduate to delinquency during adolescence.

In summary, the research on social bonds demonstrates that increased social bonds are associated with decreased criminal activity. The research does not demonstrate how or why bonds change. Sampson and Laub (1993) propose that bonds may change as a function of critical life events that lead individuals to reevaluate their life and begin to make positive changes. Theoretically, such a critical life event could occur for juveniles who enter a residential facility. If the experience of being in the facility or the programs provided in the facility increase the attitudes of commitment to conformity or ties the juveniles have to social institutions like family, work, and school then theoretically the future criminal activities of these youth may decrease. The major characteristics of boot camps do not suggest that these programs will incorporate elements that would increase ties or commitments to conventional activities outside the facility. Restrictions on visitation may limit contact with the outside and the environment of the camps is very different from the environment of work or school outside the camps. The traditional facilities may be much more likely to strengthen these ties or attitudes. Theoretically, a critical life event such as entering an institution could initiate changes in ties or attitudes. If either type of facility did have an impact on attitudes or times, we would anticipate that this would be a hopeful sign that such changes would be associated with a reduction in future criminal activities for the participants.

Impulsivity and Control

The connection between impulsivity and criminal activities is well established. According to Gottfredson and Hirschi's (1990) *General Theory of Crime,* antisocial acts are committed by people with low self-control. Impulsivity is one of the major characteristics of such individuals. Theorists interested in individual differences in temperament and personality have also emphasized the need to consider differences in impulsivity. For example, in her psychosocial

control theory, Mak (1990, 1991) emphasizes the importance for understanding criminal activity and delinquency of individual differences in thinking through consequences, a preference for immediate gratification, poor planning and a lack of patience. These impulsive characteristics are similar to the temperament and personality characteristics Glueck and Glueck (1950) linked to persistent and serious delinquent behavior.

Numerous key criminological studies have shown that impulsivity is a strong correlate of delinquent and criminal behavior (Glueck & Glueck, 1950; Farrington, 1998; Caspi, Moffitt, Silva, Stouthamer-Loeber, Krueger, & Schmutte, 1994; White, Moffitt, Caspi, Bartusch, Needles, & Stouthamer-Loeber, 1994; Loeber, Farrington, Stouthamer-Loeber, Moffitt, & Caspi, 1998). In comparison to non-delinquents, delinquents show markedly higher levels of impulsivity. These results held despite differences in whether impulsivity was measured by self-reports, teachers, independent raters, staff psychologists, or parents. Stronger impulsivity was related to increases in official measures of offending and delinquency, self-reported criminal activities, and childhood behavior problems as reported by teachers, mothers and peers. The association between impulsivity and crime is stronger than those of intelligence or socioeconomic status (White et al., 1994).

Controversy exists regarding whether an individual's impulsivity can be changed during the life course. Gottfredson and Hirschi (1990, p. 90) assert that "people who lack self-control will tend to be impulsive . . ." and that variation in self-control is a latent trait that provides the primary explanation for individual differences in involvement in antisocial behavior throughout the life-course (Hirschi & Gottfredson, 1994). In contrast, others believe that individuals can change during their life-course. For example, the life-course perspective views life-course trajectories as a sequence of events and transitions that either accentuate or redirect behavioral tendencies (Elder, 1992; Simons et al., 1998). From this perspective, characteristics such as antisocial behavior and impulsivity are associated with criminal activity but a trajectory may change as a result of life circumstances or critical life events. In their study,

Simons et al. (1998) found evidence that the correlation between childhood and adolescent deviant behavior reflects a developmental process as proposed by those with a life-course perspective rather than the latent antisocial trait proposed by Gottfredson and Hirschi (1990).

A critical life event that may change a juvenile's life trajectory is institutionalization in a juvenile facility. Impulsivity is a particular target for change in boot camps. The rigorous structure in the camps and the strict requirements for military bearing are designed, in part, to get youth to think before they act. We anticipate that this is one characteristic of juveniles that would change as a result of the boot camp experience. The traditional facilities are not expected to impact a youth's impulsivity.

Antisocial Attitudes

According to correctional theorists, treatment programs that are effective in reducing recidivism have certain clearly defined characteristics (Andrews, Bonta & Hoge, 1990; Andrews & Kiessling, 1980; Glaser, 1974; Gendreau & Ross, 1979, 1987; Palmer, 1974). These authors argue that "appropriate" treatment delivers services to higher-risk cases, uses styles and modes of treatment that are capable of influencing criminogenic "needs" and is matched to the learning styles of offenders. Criminogenic needs are defined as those that are dynamic or changeable as opposed to static (not changeable) and directly related to the criminal behavior of the offender. Meta-analyses examining the effectiveness of treatment programs have supported the proposed importance of these "appropriate" treatment characteristics (Lipsey, 1989; Andrews, Zinger, Hoge, Bonta, Gendreau & Cullen, 1990). Procriminal or antisocial attitudes have consistently shown significant associations with criminal behavior for adults (Andrews & Bonta, 1998, 1985; Bonta, 1990) and youthful offenders (Shields & Ball, 1990; Shields & Whitehall, 1994). The evidence showing the association between procriminal or antisocial attitudes and criminal behavior makes these prime criminogenic needs and, therefore, targets for change in correctional treatment.

SUMMARY

In summary, there is strong empirical evidence that social bonds, antisocial attitudes, and impulsivity are associated with criminal activity. Recent research supports the proposal that these characteristics do change during the life course. The question is how this change can be initiated. Life course theorists propose that critical life events may bring about change in adolescence or adulthood. One such critical life event, at least for some adolescents, may be incarceration in a juvenile correctional facility. Differences in the environments and programming in correctional boot camps and traditional facilities lead us to predict that the impacts of these facilities on the youth who spend time there will be different. Given the environment and programming in the boot camps, we anticipate that the camps may reduce the impulsivity of the youth who reside there. On the other hand, we anticipate that the traditional facilities may be more apt to change the social bonds and antisocial attitudes of the youth who reside there. For correctional facilities to have an impact on the future offending behavior of youth, these are the changes we would hope to observe during residency in a juvenile facility.

METHOD

Site Identification

In April of 1997, all juvenile boot camps in operation in the United States, excluding Hawaii and Alaska, were identified for inclusion in this study. At that time, 50 privately and publicly funded secure residential boot camps were identified. All facilities were contacted and asked to participate and 27 agreed. The 23 programs that did not participate did so for various reasons, including parental consent issues, staffing and resource limitations, and impending program closure. Thus, the 27 boot camps agreeing to participate in this project represented 54 percent (27 out of 50) of the residential juvenile boot camps operating in 1997 and unfortunately cannot be considered a random sample of the population of facilities.[1]

For each boot camp agreeing to participate, a comparison facility was sought to allow the contrast of youth's experiences in a boot camp with youth's experiences in traditional juvenile correctional facilities. Comparison facilities were selected by identifying those secure residential facilities where the juveniles would have been confined if the boot camp programs were not in operation. This method of selection ensured that the residents at the comparison facilities were as similar as possible to the boot camp residents. With this definition of a comparison facility in mind, the facility administrator at each boot camp or an individual from within the state's juvenile justice department recommended the most appropriate comparison facility. Comparison facilities were then contacted and asked to join the research project. All comparison facilities identified agreed to participate in the research project. Although there were 26 boot camp facilities included in the study, there were only 22 comparison facilities. There were two reasons for this discrepancy. First, two boot camps did not have a viable comparison facility within the state. Second, in two states, the same non-boot camp facility was identified as the most appropriate comparison for two different boot camps. In these instances, one facility served as the comparison for each of the two boot camps.

Participants

A full census of all juveniles at each facility on two occasions was sought. A total of 4,516 juveniles were surveyed, 2,668 from the boot camp facilities and 1,848 from the traditional facilities. The overall response rate for this survey was high and represented 85 percent of the juvenile population at the surveyed facilities. A common reason for nonparticipation was a juvenile's overriding need to be somewhere else at time of survey administration such as a court hearing or medical visit outside of the facility. A small number of youths started the surveys but chose to not complete it. A total of 2,473 were surveyed at the Time 1 administration and 2,030 at the Time 2 administration. The first administration of the survey was designed to include juveniles shortly after their entry into the boot camp program. The second administration of the survey was designed to include juveniles just prior to release from the boot camp.

The time interval between the two survey administrations in the comparison facilities was matched to the time interval between administrations for the corresponding boot camp. The interval between Time 1 and Time 2 administrations ranged from 3 months to 8 months with a median of 4 months. The Time 2 administration included 530 juveniles, 264 in boot camps and 266 in traditional facilities, who also were surveyed at Time 1. This subsample of the data is the major focus of this paper.

Juvenile Survey

The survey questionnaire for the youths included 266 questions. Thirteen questions were open-ended (primarily demographics items) with the remaining questions based either on a 4- or 5-point Likert response scale or a yes-no dichotomous response format. Overall, there was a high completion rate of over 85% of the population. Surveys were administered to groups of 15 to 20 youths in classroom-type settings in accordance with prevailing ethical principles. A videotaped presentation of the survey was shown on a large television providing instructions and the survey questions to ensure uniform administration and provide assistance to juveniles with reading difficulties.[2]

Administrator Interview and Institutional Records

A structured interview was conducted with the facility administrators or administrators to obtain information about the facilities where the juveniles resided. Some items in the interview survey required information from institutional records (e.g., hours of treatment per week) that were obtained by the administrator after the completion of the interview. Researchers placed follow up telephone calls within two weeks of the site visit to obtain outstanding information.

The interview included 264 items and provided information on a variety of factors including: the size of the facility (the average number of juveniles who usually reside in the facility), how selective the facility could be about who enters the facility (selectivity index), the seriousness of the delinquency history of the juveniles who were admitted to the facility (seriousness index), the number of hours the juveniles participated in treatment in a one week period, the contact juveniles had with the outside (contact with outside index), the staff to juvenile inmate ratio, the juveniles' average length of stay, and whether someone at the facility collected or obtained information on the juveniles who were released including re-arrest for delinquent or criminal activities, return to school, residence with family, and re-institutionalization.[3]

Measures

Individual-Level Measures

Five individual-level composite measures were the primary focus of the analyses below: depression, anxiety, commitment to conventional behavior (social bonds), dysfunctional impulsivity, and anti-social attitudes. Additional individual level variables included in this study were age, gender, ethnicity, the number of self-reported nonviolent arrests, the number of self-reported violent arrests, an indicator of history of family violence and child abuse, indicators of alcohol and drug abuse, peer criminality, criminal history, perceptions of the environment, and amount of time the youth had been in the facility at the time of the survey. The construction of these measures is discussed below. Items, factor scores and means for scales are shown in the Appendix.

Depression. Five Likert type items were taken from the Jesness Inventory (Jessness, 1962) to measure depression. These items were intended to measure state characteristics of depressed mood rather than trait characteristics of depression. The five items were summed and averaged. As such, the range for the depression index was from 1 to 5, with a mean of 3. The internal consistency of these items was high ($\alpha = .77$). High scores on this scale measured more depression. This scale was thought to indicate severe and, as previously described potentially, dysfunctional stress.

Anxiety. Six dichotomous (yes-no) items assessing state anxiety were combined to create the anxiety measure. The internal consistency was adequate ($\alpha = 0.71$). These six items were drawn from Spielberger et al. (1970). The goal of these items was to examine differences in the stress and anxiety levels of the youths. High scores on this scale indicated increased anxiety. In comparison to the depression scale this scale was designed to reflect low to moderate stress.

Dysfunctional Impulsivity. Four dichotomous (yes-no) questions comprised the dysfunctional impulsivity scale. The items of this scale focused on the cognitive aspects of impulsivity (i.e., thinking before acting or speaking). The internal consistency of this scale was adequate ($\alpha = 0.66$). High scores on this scale reflected high impulsivity.

Social Attitudes. The social attitude scale was a composite of 35 true-false items from the Antisocial Subscale of the Jesness Inventory (Jesness, 1962).[4] This scale measures attitudes of the juveniles towards conventional aspects of society such as authority figures. The internal consistency of this scale was adequate ($\alpha = 0.65$). Previous research with this scale has demonstrated that it measures short term change in confined youthful offenders and this change is associated with recidivism.

Commitment to Conventional Behavior. A measure of commitment to conventional behavior was constructed from three Likert type items assessing the importance of education, work, and spending time with family. The internal consistency for this scale was low ($\alpha = 0.56$). High scores on this scale indicate commitment to conventional behaviors or bonds. Originally, three separate scales had been developed to indicate commitments to family, school and work; however, factor analyses (eigenvalues, scree plot) indicated that the items formed one scale.

History of Family Violence. An index of the degree of physical and sexual abuse and neglect within the family of origin was constructed from nine Likert-type items. All but two of the items dealt with physical abuse directed either at the youth or at other family members. This scale had good reliability ($\alpha = 0.85$).

Alcohol and Drug Abuse Scales. Scales indicating alcohol and drug abuse were created from

10 dichotomous (yes-no) items. These items dealt with life-time substance use. For purposes of the present study, a composite alcohol and drug abuse scale was constructed from these items and showed good reliability ($\alpha = 0.77$). High scores indicated higher levels of substance abuse.

Peer Criminality. Peer criminality was measured using four five-point items asking the youth if their closest group of friends prior to arrest were in trouble with the law, incarcerated, involved with gangs, and users of drugs and alcohol. The internal reliability coefficient for this measure was adequate ($\alpha = 0.71$).

Criminal History. An index of criminal history was constructed as a composite of age at first arrest and the natural log of the number of previous commitments, number of prior nonviolent offenses, and number of prior violent offenses. The internal consistency of this scale was adequate ($\alpha = 0.69$).

Perception of Facility Environment. The youth were asked a series of 129 Likert type questions (with five response choices from strongly agree to strongly disagree) designed to measure their perception of the facility environment. These items were rationally constructed to represent 13 major dimensions of the juvenile facility: control, resident danger, danger from staff, environmental danger, activity, care, risks to residents, quality of life, structure, justice, freedom, programs, and emphasis on the individual. Scales were scored so that higher scores reflected higher perceptions in the direction of the name of the scale (e.g., more control, more danger, more activity, etc.). These facets have been previously identified in the literature as important elements of juvenile residential facilities (MacKenzie et al., 1998). At the individual level (e.g., $n = 2,473$ individuals at time 1), these 13 measures were correlated, with the absolute value of the correlations ranging from .05 to .63.

Facility-Level Measures

At the facility level (e.g., n = 48 facilities), the 13 facility level measures were, on average,

highly correlated, with a mean absolute correlation of .55 and a range from .05 to .90. Because of these high correlations and the limited degrees of freedom for facility level analyses ($df = 48$), we performed an exploratory factor analysis with the 129 items that made up the 13 measures. Examination of the eigenvalues suggested either a one or three-factor solution and both solutions produced interpretable results. The three factor solution produced factors we judged to measure the following aspects: (1) the therapeutic warmth of the environment (e.g., A counselor is available for me to talk to if I need one), (2) the general level of hostility (e.g., Residents have to defend themselves against other residents in this institution), and (3) the degree of freedom and choice available to the youths (e.g., Residents choose the type of work they do here).

In comparison to the three factor solution, the single factor solution appears to represent how positively, in general, the youth perceive the environment (staff care, staff are fair, learning useful skills, program is helpful, help in staying focused on future goals, etc.). When the individual level factor scores for the three-factor solution are aggregated up to the facility, the degree of facility level hostility is negatively correlated with the facility level therapeutic warmth ($r = -.88$). Thus, although these factors appear distinct based on the youths' perceptions, facilities that tend to be high on therapeutic warmth are, not surprisingly, low in perceived hostility and dangerousness.

The goal of this study was to assess the impact of the facility environment on the changes juveniles made while in the facilities using the five indicator variables (Depression, Anxiety, Dysfunctional Impulsivity, Social Attitudes, Commitment to Conventional Behavior) discussed above, not the impact of an individual's perception of the environment on his change while residing in the facility. Thus, we averaged the perception of the environment measures across individuals to create a facility level rating on each of the 3 dimensions using the three-factor solution for the environmental measures.

Other facility level measures, obtained from administrator interviews and institutional

Table 11.1   Demographics by Facility Type

Variable by Facility Type	Full Sample		Pre/Post Sample[a]	
	Percentage	N	Percentage	N
Gender (Percent Male)				
Boot Camps	92	2,390	93	264
Traditional Facilities	96	1,578	98	265
Race (Percent Caucasian)				
Boot Camps	33	2,382	43	264
Traditional Facilities	31	1,566	35	266
Race (Percent African American)				
Boot Camps	36	2,382	30	264
Traditional Facilities	33	1,566	24	266
Race (Percent Hispanic)				
Boot Camps	19	2,382	16	264
Traditional Facilities	20	1,566	17	266
Race (Percent Other)				
Boot Camps	12	2,382	11	264
Traditional Facilities	16	1,566	24	266

[a]Note: None of the above boot camps by traditional facility differences were statistically significant under a population averaged (facility) logistic regression model.

records, that were used in the analyses below included an index of the seriousness of the criminal histories of the youths admitted to the facilities, the admission selectivity of the facility, and the facility size. The index of seriousness was constructed as a composite score of dichotomous questions (yes-no) that determine whether the facility accepts specific categories of juvenile delinquents (e.g., juveniles with a history of violence or juvenile convicted of arson). The index of selectivity was constructed as a composite of dichotomous questions (yes-no) that demonstrate the stringency of admissions of the juveniles (did facility personnel interview juveniles prior to entry, did juveniles have to pass physical, mental and medical examinations in order to enter). The index demonstrates the extent of input by the individual facilities in choosing the juveniles that are admitted into their facilities. High scores on the seriousness and the selectivity indices indicated, respectively, that the facility accepted juveniles with more serious criminal histories and that facility personnel could be more selective about which juveniles were permitted to enter the facility. These variables provide a mechanism for examining the variability across and within the boot camps and traditional facilities.

RESULTS

Juvenile Characteristics

Comparisons of the boot camps and traditional facilities on the individual characteristics of the juveniles for the total sample and the pretest-posttest sample are shown in Tables 11.1-11.3. The demographic characteristics between these two facility types were comparable. The boot camps tended to have a higher percentage of girls, although boys dominated both facility types. The traditional facilities had a population that was more criminally involved, on average, than the boot camps, with a substantially higher mean number of prior nonviolent and violent arrests. Furthermore, at the time of the survey, the typical youth in the traditional facility had resided in the facility roughly twice as long as the typical boot camp youth. This reflects the generally longer lengths-of-stay in these facilities relative to the boot camps and the method of determining when to conduct the surveys at each facility.

Table 11.2   Individual Characteristics by Facility Type and Sample

Variable by Facility Type	Full Sample			Pre/Post Sample[a]		
	Mean	SD	N	Mean	SD	n
Age						
Boot Camps	16.0	1.2	2,383	15.9	1.2	264
Traditional Facilities	16.3	1.3	1,570	16.0	1.5	266
Number of Prior Nonviolent Arrests[b]						
Boot Camps	6.6*	8.3	1,407	6.1*	4.7	260
Traditional Facilities	9.3	10.0	982	10.5	11.8	261
Number of Prior Violent Arrests[b]						
Boot Camps	1.6*	2.7	1,409	1.6	2.0	260
Traditional Facilities	2.8	4.5	1,000	2.7	3.9	260
Number of Months Resided in Facility[b]						
Boot Camps	2.7*	3.3	2,310	1.6	3.0*	257
Traditional Facilities	6.0	7.9	1,500	5.3	7.1	260
Family Violence[b]						
Boot Camps	1.6*	.6	2,362	1.5	.6	262
Traditional Facilities	1.7	.7	1,545	1.7	.8	264
Alcohol Abuse Scale						
Boot Camps	1.3	.3	2,370	1.3	.3	262
Traditional Facilities	1.3	.3	1,556	1.4	.3	264
Drug Abuse Scale						
Boot Camps	1.4	.3	2,374	1.4	.3	262
Traditional Facilities	1.5	.3	1,553	1.5	.3	264
Peer Criminality						
Boot Camps	3.3	1.0	2,319	3.3	1.0	260
Traditional Facilities	3.4	1.0	1,516	3.4	1.0	262

[a]Values for the pre/post sample represent the first measurement for the 530 youths who were measured on two occasions.
[b]Analysis-of-variance performed on logged values.
*The difference between groups is statistically significant at $p < .05$.
Note: Mean difference tested using a nested analysis of variance, with facilities nested within facility type.

The two samples were highly similar on the psychosocial indices. A statistically significant but small difference was observed in the history of family violence, with higher levels of previous violence reported by the youths in the traditional facilities. A small difference was also observed on the commitment to conventional behavior index, with higher levels reported by the youth in the boot camps. Although the traditional facilities were selected because they were facilities to which the boot camp youths would have been sent in the absence of the boot camp, the general impression from these data is that the traditional facilities also serve youth who are more seriously delinquent, on average, than the youth admitted to the boot camps. It appears that whereas all of the boot camp youth may have been appropriate for the comparison facility, not all of the youth at the comparison facility may have been appropriate for the boot camp facilities.

Juveniles' Perception of the Facility Environment

The juveniles' perception of the environment differed between the two facility types (see Table 11.4). Surprisingly, the boot camps were perceived, on average, as more therapeutic and less hostile than the traditional facilities. Consistent with expectation, the youths perceived the boot camps as more restrictive of personal freedom and choice than the traditional facilities. These findings are consistent with the qualitative observations

Table 11.3 Psychosocial Measures by Facility Type and Sample

Variable by Facility Type	Full Sample			Pre/Post Sample[a]		
	Mean	SD	N	Mean	SD	n
Depression						
Boot Camps	3.0	1.0	2,355	3.2	1.0	260
Traditional Facilities	3.1	1.0	1,529	3.2	1.0	263
Anxiety						
Boot Camps	1.4	.3	2,338	1.5	.3	257
Traditional Facilities	1.4	.3	1,520	1.4	.3	261
Dysfunctional Impulsivity						
Boot Camps	1.6	.3	2,326	1.7	.3	261
Traditional Facilities	1.6	.3	1,506	1.6	.3	260
Antisocial Attitudes						
Boot Camps	1.5	.1	2,320	1.5	.1	261
Traditional Facilities	1.5	.1	1,490	1.5	.1	259
Commitment to Convention Behavior						
Boot Camps	4.4*	.7	2,332	4.3	.7	257
Traditional Facilities	4.2	.9	1,524	4.2	.9	259

[a]Values for the pre/post sample represent the first measurement for the 530 adolescents who were measured on two occasions.
*The difference between groups is statistically significant at $p < .05$.
Note: Mean difference tested using a nested analysis of variance, with facilities nested within facility type.

made within the facilities by the research staff. Within the typical juvenile boot camp, the increased structure does not appear to be associated with an increase in hostility or perceived danger from staff (an element of this factor). The greater selectivity of the boot camps in admissions criteria (see below) may also contribute to a safer overall environment if the more troubled and potentially violent youth are not allowed admission. These differences remained after statistically adjusting for measured characteristics of the youth, that is, the characteristics presented in Tables 11.1. 11.2, and 11.3. Thus, the evidence suggests that the observed differences represent actual differences in the environments and not just differential perceptions of comparable environments. We cannot determine from this data, however, whether the differences are produced by the structural, organizational, programmatic, and staffing aspects of a facility or by the juveniles themselves. That is, a facility with a higher proportion of violent offenders may genuinely be more dangerous, despite staffing and organization aspects. It is likely that both the characteristics of a program and the juveniles served contribute to the environmental conditions.

Facility Characteristics

On average, the boot camps were smaller and were more selective about the entrants than the traditional facilities (see Table 11.5). Traditional facilities permitted juveniles with more serious criminal histories to enter the program and were generally less selective about whom they admitted. The typical length of stay in the traditional facilities was nearly double that of the boot camps. Only 46 percent of the boot camps and 32 percent of the traditional facilities had any follow-up information on the releasees, including whether the youth were returned to the same facility sometime after being released (Gover, MacKenzie, & Styve 2000).

Initial Levels of Anxiety and Depression

The first hypothesis to be addressed was whether boot camp youths had higher initial levels of depression and anxiety. Although some individuals are generally more anxious or

Table 11.4   Perception of Facility Environment Measures by Facility Type and Sample

Variable by Facility Type	Full Sample			Pre/Post Sample[a]		
	Mean	SD	N	Mean	SD	n
Therapeutic Environment						
Boot Camps	3.8*	.7	2,341	3.7*	.7	263
Traditional Facilities	3.3	.7	1,508	3.5	.7	262
Hostile Environment						
Boot Camps	2.5*	.8	2,343	2.5*	.7	263
Traditional Facilities	2.8	.8	1,506	2.7	.8	262
Freedom and Choice						
Boot Camps	2.3*	.7	2,329	2.0	.7	263
Traditional Facilities	2.7	.8	1,486	2.7	.7	262
Positive Environment Composite						
Boot Camps	0.07*	.36	2,388			
Traditional Facilities	−0.12	.36	1,568			

[a]Values for the pre/post sample represent the first measurement for the 530 adolescents who were measured on two occasions.
*The difference between groups (boot camps versus traditional facilities) is statistically significant at $p < .05$.
Note: Mean difference tested using a nested analysis of variance, with facilities nested within facility type.

Table 11.5   Facility Level Descriptive Statistics

Variable by Facility Type	Mean	SD	n
Size*			
Boot Camps	70.9	64.4	25
Traditional Facilities	150.5	156.7	22
Selectivity Index*			
Boot Camps	.6	.2	26
Traditional Facilities	.3	.2	22
Seriousness Index*			
Boot Camps	1.0	0.4	26
Traditional Facilities	1.5	0.4	22
Level of Contact Permitted with the Outside			
Boot Camps	.7	.2	22
Traditional Facilities	.8	.1	21
Average Length of Stay*			
Boot Camps	4.5	2.3	25
Traditional Facilities	8.3	4.0	22
Follow-up Information on Youth			
Boot Camps	46%		25
Traditional Facilities	32%		22

*$p < .01$.

depressed than other individuals, depression and anxiety are not static and an individual's level of each will rise-and-fall depending on life stressors and environmental circumstances. The transition into an institutional setting, whether it is a traditional juvenile delinquency facility or a boot camp, is stressful and may lead to increased depression and anxiety for some youths. The boot camp, with its highly structured militaristic style and reputation, may be a more stressful environment, at least initially, for juveniles.

To examine this issue, we selected all survey respondents who completed the survey during their first month of residency (see Table 11.6). This resulted in a sample of 774 juveniles from boot camps and 274 juveniles from comparison facilities. The mean levels of both depression and anxiety were highly similar between the boot camp facilities and the traditional facilities for this sample (3.1 and 3.0 respectively for depression on a 5-point scale and 1.5 and 1.4 respectively for anxiety on a 1-point scale). Not surprisingly, a simple test of this difference using a nested analysis-of-variance (Kirk, 1982; Stata, 1999) showed that the slightly higher values for the boot camp facilities were not statistically significant.

A history of family violence is a risk factor for affective disorders, such as depression and anxiety. It was hypothesized that a history of family violence would be related not only to the initial level of anxiety and depression of the juveniles, but also that it would interact with facility type. We presumed that the more aggressive "in-your-face" atmosphere of the boot camps would be more traumatic for juveniles with a history of family violence and would therefore lead to a higher level of anxiety and depression. We tested this hypothesis for both anxiety and depression using a random-effects regression model estimated via maximum likelihood. Two regression analyses were estimated, one for depression and one for anxiety, each regressed on both individual level and facility level variables (see Table 11.7). These analyses were restricted to boys, since there were only four girls in traditional facilities for this subsample of the data set. Both analyses showed a statistically significant relationship between a history of family violence and level of anxiety and depression. As expected, facilities that were perceived, on average, as more hostile, had higher levels of both anxiety and depression. Contrary to expectation, however, the interactions of facility type and facility level hostility with history of family violence were not statistically significant. Based on these data, a history of family violence does not appear to interact with the type of facility (boot camp or traditional) or with the degree of perceived hostility. The regression analyses did show that youths

Table 11.6 Levels of Depression and Anxiety for Respondents Surveyed During First Month of Stay

Variable	Mean	SD	n
Depression			
Boot Camps	3.1	1.0	765
Traditional Facilities	3.0	1.0	267
Anxiety			
Boot Camps	1.5	.3	760
Traditional Facilities	1.4	.3	266

perceiving the facility as more hostile and having less freedom and choice relative to their peers in the same facility were more likely to be anxious and depressed. It may well be that anxious and depressed youths are more likely to perceive their environment negatively.

Changes in Anxiety, Depression, Social Bonds, Dysfunctional Impulsivity and Pro-Social Attitudes

A main question of this paper is whether the boot camp and traditional facilities produce positive changes in correlates of delinquency. That is, during youths' stay in a facility, do they become less impulsive, increase their bonds to conventional society, decrease their antisocial attitudes, and become less anxious and less depressed? To address this issue we examined a sub-sample of the study that was measured on two occasion, ranging from 1 to 6 months between occasions, 4 months on average. For this sample (264 boot camp respondents and 266 traditional facility respondents), a maximum likelihood estimated random effects regression model (Bryk & Raudenbush, 1992; Stata, 1999) was used to examine change in the five outcome variables.

Shown in Table 11.8 are the mean time 1, time 2, and difference scores for the five outcome variables by type of facility for the pretest-posttest sample. The boot camps observed larger average changes in the desired direction for all five outcomes. In standardized mean difference effect size units, this difference was largest for pro-social attitudes, depression, and dysfunctional impulsivity. The observed effect sizes for the traditional facilities were all less than 0.10 in absolute values; these are small

Table 11.7 Random Effects Regression Analyses (HLM) of Initial Levels of Anxiety and Depression for All Juveniles Completing a Survey During Their First Month, Excluding Girls

Variable	Anxiety[a]	Depression[a]
Individual level		
Age	.00	.01
Race (White)	.03*	.00
Drug/alcohol abuse	.01	.05*
Criminal history	−.00	−.05
History of family violence	.05***	.25***
By facility type	−.00	−.03
By hostile environment	.01	−.02
Perceived as therapeutic	−.02	−.15***
Perceived as hostile	.09***	.18***
Perception of freedom/choice	−.04***	−.10**
Facility level		
Facility type[b]	.02	−.00
Therapeutic environment	.04	−.08
Hostile environment	.06*	.02
Freedom/choice	−.06***	−.07
Selectivity	−.08	−.32*
Seriousness	−.02	−.09
Facility capacity	−.00*	−.00**
Intercept	1.39***	2.78***

Note: Sample sizes were (individuals/facilities) the following: anxiety 1,432/48; depression 1,432/48.
[a]Regression model significant ($p < .01$).
[b]Facility type coded as 1 for boot camp and 2 for traditional facility.
*$p < .10$.
**$p < .05$.
***$p < .01$.

effects by most standards. The magnitude of change for the boot camp facilities range from a small effect for bonds to conventional behavior to a modest effect for pro-social attitudes.

For purposes of analysis, residualized change scores were used, as is common practice in the analysis of change (see Campbell & Kenny, 1999). Table 11.9 presents the regression coefficients for four regression models applied to each of the five outcomes. Model 1 simply tests whether the boot camp facilities differ in the amount of change from the traditional facilities. For depression and social attitudes, boot camps observed greater change in the desired direction. Model 2 tests whether there is a relationship between the overall facility rating and amount of change. As with facility type, this effect was significant for the depression and social attitudes regression models. This is not surprising, for facility type and the overall facility rating are correlated. Model 1 and 2 do not control for known individual differences between the boot

camp and traditional facilities. It is not surprising that the regression effects for anxiety, social bonds, and dysfunctional impulsivity were statistically nonsignificant, since the amount of change observed on these variables was small.

Model 3 incorporated individual-level covariates, including age, race, history of alcohol and drug abuse, criminal history, and history of family violence and child abuse, and provides a more realistic test of the relationship between facility characteristics and individual change. The coefficients for these individual characteristics were assumed to be fixed, that is, constant across facilities. From Table 11.2 we know that the pretest-posttest sample differed across facility type in the average months in the facility. Therefore, this variable was also included in the analysis to control for any linear relationship between amount of change and time in facility at first measurement. At the facility level, coefficients were estimated for the facility type, the composite indicator of the facility

Table 11.8   Change in Anxiety, Depression, Bonds to Conventional Behavior, Dysfunctional Impulsivity, and Social Attitudes for the Pre/Post Sample

Variable	Time 1		Time 2		Difference			Effect size
	Mean	SD	Mean	SD	Mean	SD	n	
Anxiety								
Boot Camps	1.49	0.34	1.42	0.30	−0.06	0.36	254	−0.16
Traditional Facilities	1.42	0.32	1.40	0.30	−0.02	0.32	255	−0.05
Depression								
Boot Camps	3.17	0.99	2.86	1.05	−0.30	1.16	256	−0.25
Traditional Facilities	3.34	0.98	3.16	0.99	−0.09	1.06	258	−0.07
Bonds to Conventional Behavior								
Boot Camps	4.34	0.71	4.35	0.79	0.02	0.84	253	0.02
Traditional Facilities	4.20	0.87	4.12	0.83	−0.09	0.87	251	−0.08
Dysfunctional Impulsivity								
Boot Camps	1.66	0.35	1.61	0.35	−0.05	0.38	255	−0.12
Traditional Facilities	1.64	0.34	1.65	0.33	0.02	0.35	249	0.05
Pro-social Attitudes								
Boot Camps	1.49	0.13	1.53	0.15	0.05	0.14	252	0.36
Traditional Facilities	1.48	0.14	1.49	0.15	0.01	0.14	248	0.07

Note: None of the mean gain score differences between facility types were statistically significant ($p \leq .01$) using a nested ANOVA model. Effect size computed as the difference score divided by the pooled within facility standard deviation at Time 1.

environment (facility mean across the individual perceptions by the youths), the selectivity of the facility, and the seriousness of the juveniles admitted. Several interaction effects were also tested. We theorized that the facility environment may moderate the relationship between race, criminal history, and history of family violence, and amount of change on the outcome variables. We also theorized that the facility type might moderate the relationship between history of family violence and amount of change.

Facility type was statistically nonsignificant across all models with the full complement of covariates. For both change in depression and change in social attitudes (a predictor of delinquency), however, the overall rating of the facility environment was related to change in the desired direction. It appears that the boot camp versus traditional facilities distinction is far less relevant than how positively the youth perceive an environment to be. Recall that in these models, it is the facility means of the youths' perceptions that is used. Presumably, the composite of all of the youths' perceptions of the environment produced an index of the facility environment that is relatively independent of each individual youth's perceptions, although it might

be affected by the composition of youths completing the survey.

A hypothesis of these analyses was that facility type would interact with history of family violence. As expected, youths with histories of family violence changed less in social attitudes, on average, than youth without histories of family violence. Also, as expected, this relationship interacted with facility type, and was stronger for boot camp facilities. That is, there is only a slight relationship between history of family violence and change in social attitudes for the traditional facilities. The boot camp environment appears detrimental (or at least less therapeutic), based on these data, for youths with a history of family violence. This pattern of effect, albeit statistically nonsignificant, was consistent across all five regression models. Thus, youths with a history of family violence exhibit less positive change overall, yet fare better relative to their peers in traditional facilities.

An unexpected finding was the relationship between race and change in social attitudes and the interaction of this effect with the overall rating of the facility environment. On average, African Americans exhibited less positive change in social attitudes. Furthermore, a plot of

Table 11.9 Random Effects Regression Analyses (HLM) of Residualized Change for the Five Outcome Variables on the Pre/Post Sample, Excluding Girls[a]

Variable	Anxiety	Depression[1]	Social Bonds	Dysfunctional Impulsivity	Social Attitudes[b]
Model 1					
Facility Type[a]	0.027	0.313*	−0.093	0.060*	−0.044**
Model 2					
Positive Environment	−0.038	−0.358*	0.060	−0.037	0.043*
Model 3					
Individual Level					
Age	0.005	−0.040	−0.005	0.003	−0.007
Race (African Am.)	−0.056*	0.150	−0.041	−0.002	−0.025*
by + Environment	0.048	0.290	0.126	0.051	−0.059*
Drug/Alcohol Abuse	0.023	0.064	−0.046	0.008	−0.002
Criminal History	0.001	−0.058	0.022	0.010	−0.001
by + Environment	0.062*	0.060	−0.089	0.000	−0.016
History fam. violence	0.164	0.899*	−0.510	0.095	−0.163**
by Facility Type	−0.098	−0.326	0.228	−0.034	0.089**
by + Environment	−0.077	−0.311	0.263	−0.038	0.052
Time in Facility	0.002	0.013	−0.012*	−0.001	0.003**
Facility Level					
Facility Type[b]	0.004	0.157	−0.062	−0.061	−0.008
+ Environment	−0.044	−0.261**	−0.080	−0.048	0.048**
Seriousness	0.043*	−0.226	0.072	0.069	−0.037
Selectivity	0.117	−0.236*	0.151	−0.131	0.006
Intercept	−0.258	0.381	0.279	−0.020	0.221**

*$p < .10$; **$p < .05$; ***$p < .01$.
[1]regression model statistically significant, $p < .05$.
[a]Sample sizes were (individuals/facilities): anxiety (446/41), depression (450/41), social bonds (444/41), dysfunctional impulsivity (443/41), social attitudes (453/41).
[b]Facility type coded as 1 for boot camp and 2 for traditional facility.

the regression function shows that the relationship between the overall rating of the facility environment and change in social attitudes is not evident for African Americans. The average amount of change in social attitudes is roughly equal across facilities rated differentially on overall rating. These two regression coefficients are statistically significant at the rather liberal level of $p < .10$ and were not hypothesized effects. Therefore, these findings need replication for any confidence to be placed in them.

A final finding in this regression model worth noting is the positive relationship between the time in facility at first measurement and the amount of positive change in social attitudes. This coefficient suggests that larger changes in social attitudes tend to occur in later periods of a youth's stay in these facilities.

The amount of reduction in depressed mood was related, as expected, to a history of family violence. The higher the level of prior family violence, the less decrease in depressed mood between administrations of the survey instrument. Also as expected, the youths in environments judged positively were more likely to have decreased in depressed mood between survey administrations, as were youths in facilities that were highly selective of the youth admitted.

The regression models for anxiety, social bonds, and dysfunctional impulsivity were statistically nonsignificant. This may be due in part to the small amount of change observed on these three outcomes (see Table 11.7). In particular, a ceiling effect was observed for the measure of social bonds at time one, leaving little room for improvement in the scores of the youths.

Although there were a few significant regression coefficients across these models, little confidence can be placed in these findings given a nonsignificant overall regression model.

DISCUSSION

Boot camps for delinquent juveniles are a modern alternative to traditional detention and treatment facilities, although the notion that strict discipline and physical exercise will "straighten-out" wayward youth has a long history. The debate surrounding boot camps has focused on the potential stressfulness of the environment and the plausibility that the confrontation and militaristic style will be harmful to the juveniles, particularly those with a history of abuse. This study contributes to the debate by examining the environment of boot camps relative to traditional facilities as perceived by the youths in the facilities, the initial stress levels of the youths in the two facility types, and the intermediate changes of the youths on variables associated with future offending behavior.

Contrary to the expectation of the critics of boot camps, the juveniles perceived the boot camp environments more favorably relative to the traditional facilities. These differences in perceptions remained after accounting for measured differences in the characteristics of the youths across the two facility types. Not only did the youths in the boot camps generally feel safer, they also perceived the environment to be more therapeutic or helpful. Thus, the fears that the boot camps, in general, would be hostile, negative environments appear not to have been realized. While the boot camps were more structured and placed more constraints on the freedom of the juveniles, the implementation of the boot camp model for juveniles does not appear to produce environments that are perceived by juveniles as negative, relative to existing alternatives. Based on observational information gained through site visits to all of the surveyed facilities, it is our opinion that this finding reflects the positive atmosphere of many but not all of the boot camps. Most boot camps have strict rules and discipline for disobedience; however, despite this, or because of this, close and caring relationships seem to form between youth and staff.

A concern regarding boot camps is that the militaristic environment may contrast so sharply with the past home and community experiences of the juveniles that the camps will produce harmfully high levels of stress, resulting in high levels of depression and anxiety. It was not possible with the available data to determine if the observed levels of anxiety and depression among the youths in this study were at dysfunctional levels. A contrast between the initial levels of anxiety and depression between traditional and boot camp facilities, however, showed that youths in boot camps do not appear to have higher levels of anxiety and depression than comparable youths in traditional facilities. Considering the positive perception of the boot camp environment, this finding is not surprising, although it is counter to the expectation of many. Initial levels of depression and anxiety were related, however, to a history of family violence or abuse. Contrary to expectation, this relationship was not mediated by the facility type.

We hypothesized that the structured, disciplined nature of boot camps would increase the effectiveness of these facilities at reducing impulsivity among juveniles relative to traditional facilities. Furthermore, we anticipated that traditional facilities would be more effective at modifying a youth's social bonds and antisocial attitudes. These predictions were not confirmed. The raw differences in the mean change from pretest to posttest favored the boot camps for all three of these intermediate outcomes. These differences were substantially attenuated, and statistically nonsignificant, once the facility environment variable was included in the model, as well as characteristics of the individuals and other facility features. Thus, it appears that any differences in the effects of boot camps relative to traditional facilities on these variables can be explained by how positive the youths perceived the environment.

There is concern that the boot camp environment may be detrimental to youth with abuse histories (e.g., Morash & Rucker, 1990). This study provides some support for this view. For the anti-social attitude measure, youth with abuse histories exhibited substantially less change in the desired direction. Furthermore, this effect was twice as large for boot camps as for traditional facilities. That is, there was a statistically significant interaction between facility type and abuse history for anti-social attitudes, suggesting that boot camps may be ineffective and potentially detrimental to persons with a history of family violence.

An unexpected finding that deserves additional research was an interaction between the perceptions of the facility environment and race/ethnicity (African American versus other). For African Americans there was virtually no relationship between the characteristics of the facility environment, as measured by our single factor, and change in social attitudes, whereas non-African Americans exhibited greater change in the desired direction as the environment became more positive. As the result of an exploratory analysis, the finding may represent sampling error. However, if it is confirmed by additional research, it points to the need to examine the effect of environmental conditions on juvenile adjustment and change separately for African Americans relative to Caucasians and other racial/ethnic groups.

Almost anyone who visits a juvenile correctional boot camp recognizes the large difference between the environment of the camps and the environment of more traditional juvenile facilities. The question is whether this is a positive atmosphere conducive to positive growth and change or whether it is detrimental to juveniles and is in opposition to a high quality therapeutic environment. Our findings suggest that, at least from the perspective of the juveniles residing in the facilities, the boot camps are a more positive environment than traditional facilities. Boot camp residents perceive their environments as less hostile and more therapeutic than juveniles in traditional facilities. Furthermore, according to their self-reports, they are no more (or less) anxious or depressed even during the early period in boot camps when adjustment is hypothesized to be the most difficult. The boot camps also appear to have a more positive impact on the juveniles in regard to antisocial attitudes and depression; however, this effect appears to be related to the more positive atmosphere not whether a facility is a boot camp or not. The only problematic impact of the boot camps was for juveniles with a history of abuse and family violence. These youth did not do as well in the boot camps as they did in the more traditional facilities.

Several selection bias effects are obvious in our data. First, juveniles sent to boot camps may differ from those sent to traditional facilities. Juveniles sent to boot camps may be those who would not otherwise be incarcerated or they may be adjudicated for less serious crimes and sent to the boot camp because it requires a shorter period of confinement. When we compared the characteristics of the two samples and given our knowledge of these facilities, it appears that the boot camp youth were appropriate for the traditional facilities but not all those in the traditional facilities would be appropriate for the boot camps. To control for this in our multivariate analysis we included measured characteristics of the youth. Our analyses are unlikely to completely control for all selection bias. While we cannot rule out all selection bias, our examination of the data led us to believe this is not a major threat to our conclusions.

Prior research examining boot camp facilities has not demonstrated any differences in recidivism when those released from boot camps are compared to those released from traditional facilities (MacKenzie, 1997). One possible reason for this finding is that the two types of facilities being compared in the prior studies were similar in environmental characteristics. Our results suggest that whether a facility is called a boot camp or not is less important than the characteristics of the environment of the facilities. Facilities perceived as having more positive environments will be more apt to have an impact on social attitudes, and, in past research these attitudes have been found to be associated with recidivism. Despite a generally more positive assessment of the boot camp environment by the youth, both boot camp and traditional facilities varied greatly on these measures.

Overall, we found only small changes during their time in the facilities in the characteristics of these juveniles that are related to delinquent behavior. This is disappointing. This finding may reflect deficiencies in the scales or the short period of time between the pre and post measures of change. However, if this change truly reflects the very limited change these juveniles make during their time in the facilities it is worrisome because the characteristics we measured have been linked to criminal behavior. This suggests to us that these facilities will have a very limited impact on the future delinquent and criminal activities of these youth. Disappointingly, few of these facilities had any information about the juveniles who left their care. Few even knew if the juveniles returned to the same facility and fewer still had any information about whether the juveniles had recidivated, returned to a community school, or found employment. We wonder how staff and administrators who view their mission as the rehabilitation of juveniles can plan and improve programs if they do not know what happens to the youth once they leave the facility.

APPENDIX

Table A.1

Therapeutic Environment Scale – 35 items (range 1-5)	Factor Score	Mean (SD)
Residents do what the staff here tell them to do.	.445	3.78 (1.2)
Staff members check up on the residents regularly.	.437	4.04 (1.2)
If a resident believes he will be hurt by another resident, the staff will protect him.	.449	3.39 (1.5)
Staff have caught and punished the real troublemakers among residents.	.414	3.13 (1.4)
There are enough staff to keep residents safe here.	.507	3.41 (1.5)
Staff prevent violence among residents.	.427	3.42 (1.5)
Residents know what to do in case of a fire.	.450	3.93 (1.5)
Most of the jobs we have to do are safe.	.406	3.66 (1.3)
A counselor is available for me to talk to if I need one.	.543	3.55 (1.4)
I have things to do that keep me busy here.	.612	3.92 (1.2)
I spend time on school work.	.549	3.46 (1.4)
I can find something to do here at night.	.476	3.54 (1.4)
I am encouraged to plan for what I will be doing when I leave here.	.598	4.01 (1.3)
I get exercise here.	.571	4.37 (1.2)
There are things to do here when I am not in school.	.596	4.07 (1.2)
The staff encourage me to try new activities.	.576	3.56 (1.4)
Additional help with school work outside of classroom hours is available to me.	.467	2.99 (1.5)
The health care here is good.	.484	3.33 (1.4)
Staff care about residents here.	.491	3.23 (1.4)
I have a set schedule to follow each day here.	.511	4.20 (1.3)
I am required to study at certain times here.	.492	3.59 (1.5)
I know what will happen if I break a rule here.	.585	4.34 (1.1)
Staff here let me know what is expected of me.	.606	4.11 (1.2)
Problems between staff and residents can be worked out easily.	.404	2.97 (1.4)
I have a certain time that I must go to bed.	.428	4.57 (1.1)
My experiences here will help me find a job when I get out.	.608	3.48 (1.4)
The things I do here help keep me focused on my goals for the future.	.662	3.65 (1.3)
Being here helps me understand myself.	.606	3.37 (1.4)
I learn things in the educational courses given here.	.636	3.73 (1.3)
By trying new activities I am learning skills I can use when I leave.	.659	3.76 (1.3)
Things I learn here will help me with future school work.	.636	3.67 (1.3)
Substance abuse treatment services here help many residents.	.469	3.07 (1.5)
The opportunities for religious services here help me become a better person.	.429	3.16 (1.5)
I feel healthier since coming here.	.510	3.18 (1.6)
The individual attention here has helped me.	.479	2.73 (1.5)
Total Scale:		3.61 (.71)
Cronbach's alpha .926		

Hostile Environment – 29 items (range 1-5)	Factor Score	Mean (SD)
Staff members ignore conflicts among residents.	.473	2.10 (1.3)
Residents can get weapons at this facility.	.410	2.26 (1.5)
Residents say mean things to other residents at this institution.	.469	3.11 (1.5)
Residents use weapons when they fight.	.462	1.63 (1.1)
Residents fight with other residents here.	.591	2.61 (1.4)
Residents are extremely dangerous here.	.548	1.91 (1.2)
Residents have to defend themselves against other residents in this institution.	.617	2.46 (1.5)
Staff say mean things to residents.	.534	3.05 (1.5)
Residents are in danger of being hit or punched by staff here.	.608	2.06 (1.4)
Residents say they have been hurt by staff here.	.614	2.28 (1.4)
Staff grab, push or shove residents at this institution.	.560	2.83 (1.5)
There are gangs here.	.418	2.66 (1.7)
Insects, rodents and dirt are a problem here.	.562	2.71 (1.5)
There is a bad odor or poor air circulation.	.565	2.62 (1.5)
There are things lying around that could help a fire spread.	.467	2.59 (1.5)
People could get hurt because the place is so dirty.	.573	2.12 (1.4)
Many accidents happen here.	.623	2.38 (1.3)
Staff tease depressed residents.	.511	2.59 (1.4)
Residents give other residents with personal problems a hard time.	.500	2.72 (1.4)
Other residents are unfriendly.	.452	2.78 (1.3)
One thing bad about this place is that it's so noisy.	.408	3.03 (1.5)
It is hard to talk with visitors because the noise is too loud here.	.408	2.41 (1.4)
Many residents look messy here.	.532	2.43 (1.4)
Staff are always changing their minds about the rules here.	.531	3.05 (1.5)
Different staff members here have different rules so you never know what you are supposed to do.	.490	3.39 (1.4)
Residents are punished even when they don't do anything wrong.	.494	3.16 (1.4)
Staff use force when they don't really need to.	.603	2.93 (1.5)
Something bad might happen to me if I file a grievance.	.468	2.53 (1.5)
Staff treat residents fairly.*	−.407	3.09 (1.4)
Total Scale:		2.60 (.75)
Cronbach's alpha .915		

Freedom and Choice – 10 items (range 1-5)	Factor Score	Mean (SD)
Staff say mean things to residents.	−.438	2.95 (1.5)
I watch a lot of television here.	.499	1.96 (1.3)
I can talk to my friends and family on the telephone here.	.482	2.71 (1.5)
I can be alone when I want to here.	.508	1.71 (1.2)
Staff treat residents fairly.	.415	2.91 (1.4)
I can talk to my lawyer when I want.	.455	2.40 (1.5)
Residents choose the type of work they do here.	.460	2.10 (1.4)
I can read whenever I want.	.572	2.61 (1.5)
I can listen to music when I want.	.504	1.60 (1.1)
The individual attention here has helped me.	.402	2.73 (1.5)
Total Scale:		2.37 (.80)
Cronbach's alpha: .78		

(Continued)

Depression – 5 items (range 1-5)	*Factor Score*	*Mean (SD)*
At times I worry too much about things that don't really matter.	.573	2.74 (1.3)
Sometimes, recently, I have worried about losing my mind.	.726	3.27 (1.5)
I often feel angry these days.	.743	2.51 (1.3)
In the past few weeks, I have felt depressed and very unhappy.	.739	2.63 (1.4)
These days I can't help wondering if anything is worthwhile anymore.	.758	3.25 (1.4)

Total Scale: Scale Mean (SD): 3.12 (.98)
Cronbach's alpha: .7564

Anxiety – 6 items (range 1-2)	*Factor Score*	*Mean (SD)*
I feel calm.	.618	1.27 (.45)
I feel upset.	.710	1.39 (.49)
I feel anxious.	.378	1.56 (.50)
I feel nervous.	.688	1.37 (.48)
I am relaxed.	.728	1.37 (.48)
I am worried.	.697	1.51 (.50)

Total Scale: Scale Mean (SD): 1.41(.31)
Cronbach's alpha: .7121

Dysfunctional Impulsivity – 4 items (range 1-2)	*Factor Score*	*Mean (SD)*
I will say whatever comes into my head without thinking first.	.663	1.55 (.50)
I don't spend enough time thinking over a situation before I act.	.668	1.38 (.49)
I get into trouble because I don't think before I act.	.748	1.29 (.45)
I say and do things without considering the consequences.	.767	1.31 (1.5)

Total Scale: Scale Mean (SD): 1.62 (.34)
Cronbach's alpha: .6731

Social Bonds – 17 items (range 1-5)	*Factor Score*	*Mean (SD)*
I would like to be like my parents.	.651	3.22 (1.5)
I feel comfortable talking to my parents if I have a problem.	.679	3.39 (1.4)
I feel bad when I do something my parents wouldn't like.	.715	3.54 (1.3)
I can count on my parents to stick by me.	.688	4.34 (1.1)
I want my children to respect me.	.567	4.78 (.71)
It is important for people to spend time with their families.	.714	4.56 (.87)
I like school.	.757	3.16 (1.2)
Finishing my homework is important to me.	.797	2.89 (1.4)
I respect my teachers.	.720	3.52 (1.3)
Getting good grades is important.	.818	3.74 (1.3)
It would make me feel bad if my teachers criticized me.	.446	2.33 (1.5)
I get into trouble at school like being suspended or expelled.	.469	2.79 (1.3)
A good education is important to me.	.664	4.39 (1.1)
The most important things that happen to me involve my job.	.524	2.33 (1.4)
I enjoy thinking about where I will work in the future.	.772	3.86 (1.3)
Doing well at work is important to me.	.851	3.97 (1.3)
I feel good when I do my job well.	.802	4.35 (1.2)

Total Scale: Scale Mean (SD): 3.60 (.67)
Cronbach's alpha: .8125

NOTES

1. While 27 boot camps agreed to participate, one of the sites was very distinct from all other programs due to its 3-year length and transitory nature from a boot camp into a detention program. As a result of these anomalies, this program was excluded from analyses herein.

2. A copy of this survey is available from the first author.

3. A copy of this survey is available from the first author.

4. We label this scale social attitudes because a high score on the scale reflects more positive social attitudes, or conversely less antisocial attitudes.

REFERENCES

Ajdukovic, D. (1990). Psychosocial climate in correctional institutions: Which attributes describe it? *Environment and Behavior, 22,* 420-432.

Altschuler, D. M., Armstrong, T. L., & MacKenzie, D. L. (1999). *Reintegration, Supervised Release, and Intensive Aftercare. Bulletin.* Washington, D.C.: U.S. Department of Justice, Office of Justice Programs, Office of Juvenile Justice and Delinquency Prevention.

Andrews, D. A., & Bonta, J. (1998). *The Psychology of Criminal Conduct.* Cincinnati: Anderson Publishing Co.

Andrews, D. A., Bonta, J., & Hoge, R. D. (1990). Classification for effective rehabilitation: Rediscovering psychology. *Criminal Justice and Behavior, 17,* 19-52.

Andrews, D. A., & Kiessling, J. J. (1980). Program structure and effective correctional practices: A summary of the CAVIC research. In R. R. Ross & P. Gendreau (Eds.), *Effective Correctional Treatment* (pp. 439-463). Toronto: Butterworth.

Andrews, D. A., Zinger, I., Hoge, R. D., Bonta, J., Gendreau, P., & Cullen, F. T. (1990). Does correctional treatment work? A clinically relevant and psychologically informed meta-analysis. *Criminology, 28*(3), 369-404.

Bonta, J. (1990). Antisocial attitudes and recidivism. Paper presented at the Annual convention of the Canadian Psychological Association, Ottawa, Ontario.

Bryk, A. S., & Raudenbush, S.W. (1992). *Hierarchical Linear Models: Applications and Data Analysis Methods.* Newbury Park, NJ: Sage Publications.

Campbell, D. T., & Kenny, D. A. (1990). *A Primer on Regression Artifacts.* New York: The Guilford Press.

Caspi, A., Moffitt, T. E., Silav, P. A., Stouthamer-Loeber, M., Krueger, R. F., & Schmutte, P. S. (1994). Are some people crime-prone? Replications of the personality-crime relationships across countries, genders, races and methods. *Criminology, 32,* 163-195.

Clark, C. L., & Aziz, D. W. (1996). Shock incarceration in New York state: Philosophy, results, and limitations. In D. L. MacKenzie & E. E. Hebert (Eds.), *Correctional Boot Camps: A Tough Intermediate Sanction* (pp. 39-68). Washington, D.C.: National Institute of Justice, U.S. Department of Justice.

Cowles, E. L., & Castellano, T. C. (1996). Substance abuse programming in adult correctional boot camps: A national overview. In D. L. MacKenzie & E. E. Hebert (Eds.), *Correctional Boot Camps: A Tough Intermediate Sanction* (pp. 207-232). Washington, D.C.: National Institute of Justice, U.S. Department of Justice.

Elder, G. H., Jr. (1992). The life course. In E. F. Borgatta & M. L. Borgatta (Eds.), *The Encyclopedia of Sociology* (pp. 1120-1130). New York: Macmillan.

Farrington, D. P. (1998). Individual differences and offending. In M. Tonry (Ed.), *The Handbook of Crime & Punishment* (pp. 241-268). New York: Oxford University Press.

Gendreau, P., Little, T., & Goggin, C. (1996). A meta-analysis of the predictors of adult offender recidivism: What works! *Criminology, 34,* 575-607.

Gendreau, P., & Ross, R. R. (1979). Effective correctional treatment: Bibliotherapy for cynics. *Crime and Delinquency, 25,* 463-489.

Gendreau, P., & Ross, R. R. (1987). Revivication of rehabilitation: Evidence from the 1980s. *Justice Quarterly, 4,* 349-408.

Glaser, D. (1974). Remedies for the key deficiency in criminal justice evaluation research. *Journal of Research in Crime and Delinquency, 10,* 144-154.

Glueck, S., & Glueck, E. T. (1950). *Unraveling Juvenile Delinquency.* Cambridge, MA: Harvard University Press.

Goffman, E. (1961). *Asylums: Essays On The Social Situation of Mental Patients and Other Inmates.* Garden City, NY: Anchor Books.

Goodstein, L., & Wright, K. (1989). Adjustment to prison. In L. Goodstein & D. L. MacKenzie (Eds.), *The American Prison* (pp. 253-270). New York: Plenum Press.

Gottfredson, M. R., & Hirschi, T. (1990). *A General Theory of Crime.* Stanford, CA: Stanford University Press.

Gover, A. R., MacKenzie, D. L., & Styve, G. J. (2000). Boot camps and traditional correctional facilities for juveniles: A comparison of the participants, daily activities, and environments. *Journal of Criminal Justice, 28,* 53-68.

Horney, J. D., Osgood, W., & Marshall, I. H. (1995). Criminal careers in the short-term: Intra-individual variability in crime and its relationship to local life circumstances. *American Sociological Review, 60,* 655-673.

Jang, S. J. (1999). Age-varying effects of family, school, and peers on delinquency: A multilevel modeling test of interactional theory. *Criminology, 37*(3), 643-686.

Jesness, C. F. (1962). *Jessness Inventory.* North Tonawanda, NY: MultiHealth Systems Incorporated.

Johnson, R., & Toch, H. (Eds.). (1982). *The Pains of Imprisonment.* Beverly Hills, CA: Sage Publications, Inc.

Kirk, R. E. (1982). *Experimental Design* (2nd edition). Belmont, CA: Wadsworth, Inc.

Lipsey, M. (1992). Juvenile delinquency treatment: a meta-analytic inquiry into the variability of effects. In T. Cook et al. (Eds.), *Meta-analysis for explanation: A casebook* (pp. 83-127). New York: Russell Sage Foundation.

Loeber, R., Farrington, D. P., Stouthamer-Loeber, M., Moffitt, T. E., & Caspi, A. (1998). The development of male offending: Key findings from the first decade of the Pittsburgh Youth Study. *Studies on Crime & Crime Prevention, 7,* 141-171.

Lutze, F. (1998). Do boot camp prisons possess a more rehabilitative environment than traditional prison? A survey of inmates. *Justice Quarterly, 15,* 547-563.

MacKenzie, D. L. (1997). Criminal Justice And Crime Prevention. In L. W. Sherman, D. C. Gottfredson, D. MacKenzie, J. Eck, P. Reuter, & S. Bushway (Eds.), *Preventing Crime: What Works, What Doesn't, What's Promising* (pp. 9.1-9.76). Washington, D.C.: Office of Juvenile Justice and Delinquency Prevention.

MacKenzie, D. L., Brame, R., McDowall, D., & Souryal, C. (1995). Boot camp prisons and recidivism in eight states. *Criminology, 33*(3), 401-430.

MacKenzie, D. L., & Hebert, E. E. (Eds.). (1996). *Correctional Boot Camps: A Tough Intermediate Sanction.* Washington, D.C.: National Institute of Justice, U.S. Department of Justice.

MacKenzie, D. L., & Parent, D. (1992). Boot camp prisons for young offenders. In J. M. Byrne, A. J. Lurigio, & J. Petersilia (Eds.), *Smart Sentencing: The Emergence of Intermediate Sanctions* (pp. 103-119). Newbury Park, CA: Sage Publications.

MacKenzie, D. L., & Souryal, C. (1995). Inmate attitude change during incarceration: A comparison of boot camp with traditional prison. *Justice Quarterly, 12* (2), 325-354.

MacKenzie, D. L., Styve, G. J., & Gover, A. R. (1998). Performance-based standards for juvenile corrections. *Corrections Management Quarterly, 2,* 28-35.

Mak, A. S. (1990). Testing a psychological control theory of delinquency. *Criminal Justice and Behavior, 17,* 215-230.

Mak, A. S. (1991). Psychosocial control characteristics of delinquents and nondelinquents. *Criminal Justice and Behavior, 18,* 287-303.

Mitchell, O., MacKenzie, D. L, Gover, A. R., & Styve, G. J. (1999). Staff perceptions of the environment and work conditions in juvenile boot camps and traditional facilities. *Justice Research and Policy, 1,* 1-22.

Moos, R. H. (1968). The assessment of the social climates of correctional institutions. *Journal of Research in Crime and Delinquency, 5,* 173-188.

Morash, M., & Rucker, L. (1990). A critical look at the idea of boot camp as a correctional reform. *Crime and Delinquency, 36,* 204-222.

Palmer, T. (1974). The Youth Authority's community treatment project. *Federal Probation (March),* 3-14.

Sampson, R. J., & Laub, J. H. (1993). *Crime In The Making.* Cambridge, MA: Harvard. University Press.

Sechrest, D. D. (1989). Prison "boot camps" do not measure up. *Federal Probation, 53,* 15-20.

Shields, I. W., & Ball, M. (1990). *Neutralization in a population of incarcerated young offenders.* Paper presented at the Annual Meeting of the Canadian Psychological Association, Ottawa, Ontario.

Shields, I. W., & Whitehall, G. C. (1994). Neutralizations and delinquency among teenagers. *Criminal Justice and Behavior, 21,* 223-235.

Simons, R. L., Johnson, C., Conger, R. D., & Elder, G., Jr. (1998). A test of latent trait versus life-course perspectives on the stability of adolescent antisocial behavior. *Criminology, 36*(2), 217-244.

Spielberger, C. D., Gorsuch, R. L., & Lushene, R. E. (1970). *Manual for the State-Trait Anxiety Inventory.* Palo Alto, CA: Consulting Psychologists Press.

Steinhart, D. (1993, January/February). Juvenile boot camps: Clinton may rev up an old drill. *Youth Today, 2,* 15-16.

Styve, G. J., MacKenzie, D. L., Gover, A. R., & Mitchell, O. (2000). Perceived conditions of confinement: A national evaluation of juvenile boot camps and traditional facilities. *Law and Human Behavior, 24*(3), 297-308.

White, J. L., Moffitt, T. E., Caspi, A., Bartusch, D. J., Needles, D. J., & Stouthamer-Loeber, M. (1994). Measuring impulsivity and examining its relationship to delinquency. *Journal of Abnormal Psychology, 103,* 192-205.

Wright, K. N. (1985). Developing the prison environment inventory. *Journal of Research in Crime and Delinquency, 22,* 257-277.

Wright, K. N. (1991). A study of individual, environmental, and interactive effects in explaining adjustment to prison. *Justice Quarterly, 8,* 217-242.

Wright, K., & Goodstein, L. (1989). Correctional environments. In L. Goodstein & D. L. MacKenzie (Eds.), *The American Prison* (pp. 253-270). New York: Plenum Press.

Zachariah, J. K. (1996). An overview of boot camp goals, components, and results. In D. L. MacKenzie & E. E. Hebert (Eds.), *Correctional Boot Camps: A Tough Intermediate Sanction* (pp. 17-38). Washington, D.C.: National Institute of Justice, U.S. Department of Justice.

Zamble, E., & Porporino, F. J. (1988). *Coping, Behavior, and Adaptation in Prison Inmates.* New York: Springer-Verlag.

12

Inmates' Attitude Change During Incarceration: A Comparison of Boot Camp With Traditional Prison

CLAIRE SOURYAL

Boot camp prison programs, also known as shock incarceration programs, have become an increasingly common correctional option. Since such programs were begun in 1983, they have grown phenomenally. A mere decade later, 29 state jurisdictions were operating more than 45 programs for adults, totaling more than 7,500 beds.[1]

The programs are called boot camp prisons because they are modeled after military basic training. Offenders are required to participate in military drill and ceremony, physical training, and hard labor (U.S. General Accounting Office 1993). In addition, the day-to-day routine is characterized by strict rules and military-style discipline. Correctional guards, called drill instructors, keep close watch over boot camp inmates. Minor misbehavior is punished immediately, typically with some form of physical activity such as pushups. Serious misconduct leads to dismissal from the program.

Reprinted from MacKenzie, D. L., and Souryal, C. (1995). *Justice Quarterly, 12*(2), 325-354 by permission of the Academy of Criminal Justice Sciences. An earlier version of this paper was presented at the annual meeting of the American Society of Criminology, held in New Orleans in November 1992. This investigation was supported in part by Grant 90-DD-CX-0061 from the National Institute of Justice, Office of Justice Programs, U.S. Department of Justice to the University of Maryland. Points of view in this document are those of the authors and do not necessarily represent the official position of the U.S. Department of Justice. Researchers from states participating in the study collaborated in all phases of the research. Thanks are extended to Robert Kreigner and Kenneth Baugh Jr., Florida Department of Corrections; Judy Schiff, Judith Hadley, Charlotte Beard, and Gerald Flowers, Georgia Department of Corrections; Jean S. Wall, Louisiana Department of Public Safety and Corrections; Cheryl Clark and David Aziz, New York State Department of Correctional Services; Thomas J. Herzog, New York State Division of Parole; Robert McManus, South Carolina Department of Probation, Parole, and Pardon Services; Sammie Brown, South Carolina Department of Corrections; Anthony Fabelo, Nancy Arrigona, and Lisa Riechers, Texas Criminal Justice Policy Council.

Beyond the basic components of the military atmosphere, boot camp programs vary greatly. One important distinguishing characteristic is time devoted to rehabilitative or therapeutic programs. Some programs, for example, require offenders to participate in three or more hours per day of group counseling, drug abuse treatment, or academic education; other programs allot very little time to such activities. Other major differences among programs include the method by which offenders are selected for participation (e.g., court selection versus department of corrections), whether the program is voluntary, the percentage of dropouts, and the demographic and offense-related characteristics of participating offenders (MacKenzie 1990; U.S. Government Accounting Office 1993).

In this paper we examine the impact of the military-type regime on inmates' attitudes in six state-level boot camp programs. Specifically we assess whether boot camp inmates develop oppositional attitudes toward the program and staff and/or more antisocial attitudes, as skeptics of correctional boot camp would predict, or whether, over the course of the program, they develop positive attitudes toward correctional staff members and programs and less antisocial attitudes. In addition, because boot camp programs vary considerably from one jurisdiction to another, we examine whether attitudinal change is tempered by program-level characteristics such as time devoted to rehabilitative activities. Finally, we assess whether attitudinal change varies as a function of the participating inmates' demographic and offense-related characteristics. First, however, we briefly review the function of basic training in the military and present some of the arguments for and against its use in correctional settings as those arguments relate to the expected effects of such training on boot camp inmate attitudes.

MILITARY BASIC TRAINING AND CORRECTIONAL BOOT CAMPS

Proponents of correctional boot camp programs assert that military basic training builds character, instills personal discipline and responsibility, and increases self-esteem and self-worth (Hengesh 1991). Furthermore, they argue that

the discipline and the structure required of boot camp inmates inside prison will carry over to life in the community, thereby enabling graduates to cope more effectively upon release (Osler 1991). The attractiveness of military basic training within corrections seems to spring in part from the promise of the military to "make men out of boys." As Arkin and Dobrofsky (1978:154) assert, "In general, the military has been defined as an opportunity to grow up, a belief that youth leaving home will return as men."

Military basic training in fact may engender some of the positive changes that correctional boot camp proponents predict *among military recruits*. On the basis of in-depth interviews with 115 first-term Army enlistees, for example, Gottlieb (1980) concludes that although military enlistees complained about the "severe discipline, physical demands, and dehumanizing treatment" *during* basic training, they developed much more positive views after they completed the process. He writes, for example,

> [For] many of the enlistees survival of basic training represents, perhaps, the first clearly successful encounter with externally imposed physical, social and psychological challenges. There is a sense of pride in the completion of what is considered to have been a long and demanding test of personal strength, conviction, and endurance. Finally, with the completion of basic training comes a feeling of belonging—of no longer being a novice, but rather a qualified soldier of the U.S. Army (Gottlieb 1980:48).

Importantly the positive feelings toward basic training are associated not simply with completing basic training but also with what basic training has come to represent, namely membership in the armed services. As Gottlieb (1980:167) explains, "Basic training is perceived as the first step in an increasingly difficult and demanding progression of learning and achieving goals. . . . It is viewed then as the foundation for preparation for the unique role of soldier."

The function of basic training within the military certainly raises questions about its efficacy when applied to correctional settings. At the most fundamental level, after all, military basic training is combat training (Arkin and Dobrofsky 1978). Basic training is intended to indoctrinate new recruits into military life and to teach basic combat skills. Notably, military basic training also socializes new recruits into the military subculture. As Arkin and Dobrofsky write,

> Military discipline refers to and thus encompasses the total individual's conformity to a prescribed role, including one's behavior, attitudes, beliefs, values, and definitions. Conformity to the prescribed rules of conduct is the focal point for change within the military processes of indoctrination. . . . The objective of basic training is to shape the total person into being a disciplined cog within the military machine (1978:158).

Critics of correctional boot camp programs consequently have challenged the relation of military basic training to the correctional goals of either rehabilitation or deterrence (Hahn undated; Morash and Rucker 1990). Morash and Rucker (1990:206) ask, for example, "Why would a method that has been developed to prepare people to go into war, and as a tool for legal violence, be considered as having such potential in deterring or rehabilitating offenders?"

Further, critics argue that the military itself has questioned the efficacy of traditional military basic training. Morash and Rucker (1990:210) contend that such training "has been examined and rejected as unsatisfactory by many experts and scholars and by the military establishment itself." As an example of this growing trend among military institutions (Wamsley 1972), the Air Force discontinued its Aviation Cadet Pre-Flight Training School (ACPFTS) in 1964 and replaced it with the Officers Training School (OTS). The OTS uses "low-key techniques to presocialize managerial values" instead of using "harsh techniques to inculcate heroic values and eliminate the 'unfit,'" as was the practice of the ACPFTS. Wamsley critically compared the two models of training and concluded that there was a "lack of clear utility for Pre-Flight's intense socialization" and that "[the] socialization process was brutally expensive in human terms and produced exaggerated forms of behavior which were not clearly related to effective task accomplishment" (1972:416).

Negative consequences associated with traditional military basic training programs such as the ACPFTS include the following: 1) anger and disrespect stemming from inconsistent policies and procedures, the arbitrary imposition of power, and leadership by virtue of power alone; 2) dysfunctional stress resulting from irrelevant work assignments or contrived stressful situations; 3) a "we-versus-they" attitude evident between military trainees and other personnel; and 4) a tendency to develop, for example, slightly more aggressive, impulsive, and callous attitudes as measured by the Minnesota Multiphasic Personality Inventory (MMPI) (Morash and Rucker 1990).

In summary, proponents of the use of military basic training as a correctional technique argue that the completion of a difficult task such as military basic training engenders increases in self-esteem and self-discipline, and generates a new respect for discipline and authority. Indeed, interviews with military recruits suggest that this may be true within the military.

On the other hand, critics have raised questions about using military basic training as a correctional tool. Theoretically they question the relevance of basic training to correctional goals such as rehabilitation and deterrence. They note that boot camp programs seek to emulate a mode of military basic training that the military itself has found lacking and in some instances has revised. Furthermore, in view of the experience of military institutions, they warn that if military basic training in correctional boot camps is characterized by phenomena such as inconsistent policies and procedures, dysfunctional stress, or a "we-versus-they" attitude, the experience could prove detrimental to boot camp inmates.

EFFECTS ON INMATES' ATTITUDES

As mentioned earlier, this paper focuses on the effects of military basic training on boot camp inmates' attitudes. We test whether military basic training facilitates the formation of oppositional attitudes toward the program (reminiscent of "prisonization" research) and/or antisocial attitudes. We examine changes in boot camp (and prison) inmates' attitudes using two measures: program attitudes and antisocial attitudes. Below we present the rationale for examining these attitudes.

Program attitudes. Adjustment to prison is commonly examined in terms of "prisonization." This term refers to a socialization process in which prison inmates are assimilated into the prison inmate system or counterculture (Akers, Hayner, and Grunniger 1977; Clemmer 1940; Goodstein and Wright 1989; Thomas 1970; Thomas and Foster 1972; Wellford 1967; Wheeler 1961). This counterculture is characterized by rejection of "conventional" norms of conduct typically embodied by prison staff members and by the adoption of oppositional norms prescribed by the inmate subculture. Attitudes reflecting opposition to the larger prison (here called *oppositional attitudes*) are one of the by-products of prisonization (Thomas and Foster 1972).

Prizonization, however, assumes the existence of an identifiable inmate subculture (Akers et al. 1977). Because of brevity of the typical boot camp program (e.g., three months), the constant turnover, and the extremely restricted nature of inmates' interactions, it is unlikely that an enduring oppositional subculture would have the opportunity to form. Nevertheless, it is plausible that oppositional *attitudes* might develop independent of an existing inmate counterculture.

The boot camp environment, after all, is characterized by the "pains of imprisonment" hypothesized to contribute to the formation of the inmate subculture (Sykes 1958; Sykes and Messinger 1960). Furthermore, oppositional attitudes (e.g., antistaff or antiprogram) may be expected to spring from the inconsistent policy and procedures, the arbitrary imposition of power, the dysfunctional stress, and the "we-versus-they" attitude that Morash and Rucker (1990) characterize as typical of military basic training. In short, we hypothesize that the boot camp experience may engender oppositional attitudes independent of the prisonization process. The Program Attitudes scale is intended to measure such attitudes.

Antisocial attitudes. A frequent assumption about the prisonization literature is that the "pains of imprisonment" will be accompanied by the "harms of imprisonment." That is, the pains of imprisonment will lead to more strongly prisonized attitudes and prison has a negative effect on offenders either as a result of these attitudes or because of the pains. Even if certain types of facilities promote prisonization, the development of prisonized attitudes will not necessarily have a long-term negative effect on inmates. Most research in this tradition has focused fairly directly on attitudes toward the prison, the staff, and prison programs with the concern that such attitudes will decrease program participation and cooperation with prison authorities.

A more destructive consequence of military basic training may be the development (or exacerbation) of general antisocial attitudes. Antisocial attitudes have been associated with criminal activity and poor adjustment upon release from prison. Reviews of the evaluation literature, for example, indicate a positive association between antisocial attitudes and criminal activity (Andrews, Bonta, and Hoge 1990; Jesness 1983; Jesness and Wedge 1985). Theories of criminal behavior also implicate the criminogenic significance of attitudes, values, or thinking styles that are favorable to violating the law (Andrews et al. 1990).

Hypothesized impact. Prisonization research reveals that custodial institutions tend to engender higher levels of prisonization than do treatment-oriented institutions (Akers et al. 1977; Feld 1981). Institutions characterized by a degrading and punitive environment are generally defined as custodial. Treatment-oriented institutions, on the other hand, do not impose excessive deprivations and are considered less punitive.

Because of the harsh nature of military basic training, correctional boot camps could be classified as custodial institutions. Although factors unique to boot camp prisons may preclude the formation of a distinct inmate counterculture (and hence of prisonization), such research nevertheless would imply that the boot camp environment may facilitate the formation of oppositional attitudes. Oppositional attitudes are considered problematic because they interfere with progress in correctional programs. Insofar as these attitudes form as a result of military basic training, such training then may inhibit genuine cooperation and participation in programs such as drug abuse treatment or academic education.

In spite of the use of military basic training, however, correctional boot camps may not be perceived as predominantly custodial. Rather, many programs devote substantial time each day to therapeutic activities; some are staffed by caring individuals who are committed to making a difference in boot camp inmates' lives. From this perspective, the boot camp may not promote the development of oppositional and/or anti-social attitudes. On the contrary, according to advocates of the programs, the unique nature of the boot camp would be expected to increase individuals' self-esteem, promote positive relationships with staff members as role models, produce positive feelings toward the boot camp program in general, and perhaps as a consequence decrease antisocial attitudes.

Because boot camp programs vary considerably on characteristics relating to perceived levels of custody (versus treatment), we hypothesize here that the development of oppositional and/or anti-social attitudes probably varies across programs. Although all programs have incorporated military basic training, the intensity of such training is likely to vary from one program to the next. Some programs may be more apt to rely on punishment procedures that are perceived as unnecessarily harsh or arbitrary. High dismissal rates may be symptomatic of programs that emphasize punishment techniques, for example. Such programs may be more likely to promote the development of oppositional and/or antisocial attitudes.

On the other hand, programs that incorporate a substantial amount of rehabilitative activity are more likely to be perceived as treatment-oriented. Such programs may mediate the potentially harsh effects of military basic training. Further, programs in which participation is voluntary may increase inmates' sense of control over external events, thereby enhancing their positive attitudes towards the program (Goodstein, MacKenzie, and Shorland 1984).

Thus we expect that the direction and magnitude of attitudinal change will vary across programs primarily as a function of the way in which military basic training has been implemented and the extent to which rehabilitative programs have been incorporated into the daily routine. The greater the investment of the program in treatment, then, the less likely that oppositional and/or antisocial attitudes will form.

OVERVIEW OF THE STUDY

The present study is part of a larger multisite evaluation examining the impact of boot camp programs at both the individual and the system level. Six state programs participated in this portion of the study: Florida, Georgia, Louisiana, New York, South Carolina, and Texas. Each of the six programs was organized to revolve around military basic training. As we will describe shortly, however, the programs differed considerably on other dimensions. We chose these programs to participate in the study because we anticipated that the impact of the programs on inmates' attitudes would differ depending on how the boot camp model was implemented.

The Six Boot Camp Programs

As mentioned at the outset, offenders incarcerated in each of the six boot camp programs involved in the study were separated from general-population inmates in a military-type atmosphere characterized by strict rules, discipline, and mandatory participation in drill and physical training. Beyond this common core, however, differences among programs were substantial (see Table 12.1).[2]

The number of hours devoted to rehabilitative programs, for example, varied widely. Some programs emphasized treatment such as education, counseling, or vocational training during incarceration. In the programs developed in New York and Louisiana, for example, inmates spent a great deal of time in rehabilitative activities such as counseling or education. In contrast, inmates in Georgia and Texas (pre-enhanced) spent only a very short period each day in such activities. Table 12.1 shows the proportions of the day devoted to rehabilitative activities and to work and drill or ceremony.[3]

Programs also differed in decisions about entry (see Table 12.1). In Georgia and Texas, for example, the responsibility for this decision rested with the judiciary: offenders who were evaluated as unsuitable or who dropped out of

Table 12.1   Program Characteristics of Six Boot Camp Programs at the Time of Data Collection

	Florida	Georgia	Louisiana	New York	S. Carolina	Texas "Pre"	Texas "Enhanced"
Year of Data Collection	1990	1989	1987	1990	1989	1989	1990
Capacity	100	200	120	1500	120[a]	200	400
Date Program Began	1987	1983	1986	1987	1986	1989	1990
Placement Decisions	DOC	Judge	DOC	DOC	Judge	Judge	Judge
% Entrants Dismissed[b]	51.1	2.8	43.3	31.3	16.0	10.1	—
Time Served (Months)	3.3	3.0	4.0	6.0	3.0	2.1	2.1
Voluntary							
Entrance	No	Yes	Yes	Yes	No	No	No
Exit	No	No	Yes	Yes	No	No	No
Daily Activities (hrs/day)							
Work/drill/p.t.	8.0	8.0	6.5	9.0	9.0	9.0	9.0
Rehabilitation[c]	1.8	0.3	3.5	5.6	1.9	0.6	0.8
Ratio of Rehabilitation to Work	0.23	0.04	0.54	0.62	0.21	0.07	0.09

[a]The total capacity in South Carolina includes 24 beds for female inmates.

[b]Dismissal rates were collected during the following years: Florida: October 1987–January 1991; Georgia: 1984–1989; Louisiana: February 1987–1989; New York: calendar year 1988; Oklahoma: calendar year 1989; South Carolina: July 1989–June 1990; Texas "Pre": October 1989–October 1990.

[c]Rehabilitative activities include formal education, counseling, and drug treatment/education.

the program were returned to the court for resentencing. In contrast, in Florida, Louisiana, and New York, offenders first were sentenced to prison and then were selected for participation in the program by the Department of Corrections (DOC). If inmates in these states were dismissed from the program or if they dropped out voluntarily, they served the remainder of their sentence in prison.

Another important distinguishing characteristic was the voluntary nature of programs (see Table 12.1). In three states (Florida, South Carolina, and Texas) participation was mandatory; participants were not permitted to drop out voluntarily. In these states, dismissals from the program for disciplinary or medical reasons ranged from 10.1 percent in Texas to 51.1 percent in Florida. In the remaining states (Georgia, Louisiana, and New York) participation was voluntary. Inmates in these states (except for Georgia) were permitted to drop out of the program at any time. Dropout rates in Louisiana and New York were 43.3 percent and 31.3 percent respectively. Although such a large percentage of dismissals may attest to the challenging or arduous nature of the program, dismissal rates more probably were related to the

identity of the decision maker (judge or DOC). For example, in the states where the judge possessed the greatest control over placement of offenders (Georgia, South Carolina, and Texas), dismissal rates changed from 2.8 percent to 16 percent. In contrast, in the states in which the DOC made placement decisions, dismissal rates changed from 31.3 percent to 51.1 percent.

The basic criteria governing eligibility were similar across the six programs. Physical and mental fitness was a prerequisite in each program, for example. The programs also established age limits. The upper age limit in Florida, Georgia, and Texas was 25; in New York, 29; in Louisiana, 39; in South Carolina, 24.

METHODOLOGY

The antisocial and program (or oppositional) attitudes of offenders incarcerated in six state boot camp programs were measured and compared with the attitudes of demographically similar inmates serving time in prison. We assessed differences in attitudes among samples as well as changes in attitudes over time using a quasi-experimental pre- and posttest design with nonequivalent control groups. Such a design—sometimes considered a compromise between internal and external validity—is particularly strong in that it controls for the main effects of history, maturation, testing, instrumentation, selection, and mortality (Campbell and Stanley 1963).

Subjects

We compared a sample of prison inmates with a sample of boot camp inmates in each of the six states except Texas (see below). The states selected prison inmates to be as similar as possible to boot camp inmates in individual demographic characteristics, criminal history, and offense-related characteristics. All states required that the prison comparison sample meet the legal eligibility criteria of the boot camp program. Legal eligibility criteria typically limit participation in boot camp programs to young, nonviolent offenders without an extensive criminal history.

Although the original research design stipulated that samples of both boot camp and prison inmates include at least 100 subjects, the final sample sizes varied (see Table 12.2). Sample sizes varied mainly because some states found it difficult to identify prison offenders for the comparison sample who were eligible for the boot camp program within the time frame of the study. Louisiana and New York, however, were able to select boot camp samples larger than 100, and did so because of potentially high dropout rates.

The comparison samples selected varied slightly in New York and in Texas. New York selected two samples of prison inmates: 1) legally eligible offenders who refused to enter the boot camp and 2) legally eligible offenders who were deemed unacceptable at the reception center. Texas did not designate a prison comparison sample but instead selected two boot camp samples: 1) a sample selected before the implementation of enhanced substance abuse treatment and 2) a sample selected after the implementation of the treatment program. Researchers in Texas were particularly interested in examining the effect of the enhanced program by comparing it with the earlier boot camp program, which did not provide

much treatment. In each of the remaining states (Florida, Georgia, Louisiana, and South Carolina) one sample of prison inmates was selected as the comparison group.

Procedure

We collected institutional records and inmate self-report data. The self-report questionnaire was administered to both samples, each at two points in time; at the beginning of the prison term and again approximately 90 days later. Whenever possible, boot camp participants completed the Time 1 questionnaire in the DOC diagnostic center immediately before entering the boot camp program. If not completed at the diagnostic center, this questionnaire was completed within the first two weeks of the program. The comparison sample also completed the Time 1 questionnaire in a DOC diagnostic center or as soon as possible thereafter in prison.

Time 2 testing took place just before graduation from the boot camp program (approximately 90 days later) or after serving 90 days in prison. Because the New York program is 180 days long, boot camp participants and prison inmates in that state were tested at Time 2 after serving between 140 and 180 days in prison.

Instruments

We collected demographic and offense-related data from prison records (e.g., age, race, offense, sentence length). In addition, inmates were asked to report whether they had been arrested as a juvenile and to state their age at first arrest. The Inmate Self Report Attitude questionnaire was completed at each time. It consisted of two summated scales: a scale of 30 true-false items called Antisocial Attitudes (Jesness 1983; Jesness and Wedge 1985) and the Program Attitudes Scale.

The Antisocial Attitudes Scale was developed as part of the Jesness Inventory. The Jesness Inventory is a personality-attitude test originally intended to distinguish between delinquents and nondelinquents (Jesness 1969). The Antisocial Attitudes Scale, one of 11 scales that make up the entire Jesness Inventory, was designed to measure "the generalized

Table 12.2 Demographic Comparison of Boot Camp Offenders with Prison Comparison Samples in Each State

	Florida		Georgia		Louisiana		Texas	
	Boot Camp (N=102)	Prison (N=109)	Boot Camp (N=101)	Prison (N=62)	Boot Camp (N=207)	Prison (N=98)	Pre (N=296)	Post (N=191)
Race n (% white)	43 (42.2)	40 (36.7)	39 (39.4)	19 (27.1)	71 (39.7)	37 (37.8)	146 (49.7)	88 (46.3)
Mean Age (SD)	18.9 (1.7)	18.7 (1.8)	20.2 (2.3)	20.8 (2.4)	23.1 (4.5)	25.6 (5.3)[a]	21.5 (2.2)	21.1 (2.1)[a]
Mean Sentence Length (SD)	45.2 (12.0)	43.5 (14.7)	3.1 (0.9)	55.1 (32.8)[a,b]	46.3 (17.7)	43.6 (18.1)	7.8 (2.5)	8.1 (2.3)
Offense Type N (%):								
Robbery/other viol.	31 (30.4)	52 (47.7)[a]	10 (10.1)	26 (37.1)[a]	10 (6.0)	5 (5.2)	33 (11.1)	26 (15.4)
Burglary/theft/other	47 (46.1)	37 (33.9)	56 (56.6)	29 (41.4)	114 (68.3)	71 (74.0)	190 (65.5)	97 (57.7)
Drugs	24 (23.5)	20 (18.4)	33 (33.3)	15 (21.4)	43 (25.8)	20 (20.8)	72 (24.4)	45 (26.8)
Juvenile Arrest n (%)	80 (79.2)	75 (68.8)	45 (45.0)	32 (46.4)	149 (85.1)	72 (75.8)[c]	108 (36.5)	72 (37.9)
Mean Age at First Arrest (SD)	15.4 (2.7)	15.4 (2.8)	17.6 (2.5)	17.7 (2.3)	—	—	16.8 (2.3)	16.9 (2.3)

	New York			South Carolina	
	Boot Camp (N=299)	Ineligibles (N=101)	Refusals (N=61)	Boot Camp (N=94)	Prison (N=95)
Race n (% white)	38 (12.7)	19 (18.8)[a]	10 (16.4)	50 (53.2)	29 (30.5)[a]
Mean Age (SD)	22.7 (3.2)	23.1 (3.8)[b]	23.3 (3.5)	19.8 (1.6)	20.9 (2.1)[a]
Mean Sentence Length (SD)	20.2 (7.6)	21.2 (9.3)[b]	21.0 (8.3)	44.0 (18.2)	53.9 (33.9)[a]
Offense Type N (%):					
Robbery/other viol.	17 (5.7)	12 (11.9)	3 (4.9)	11 (11.7)	15 (15.8)
Burglary/theft/other	63 (21.1)	25 (6.3)	18 (29.5)	64 (68.1)	56 (59.0)
Drugs	219 (73.2)	64 (63.4)	40 (65.6)	19 (20.2)	24 (25.3)
Juvenile Arrest n (%)	126 (43.8)	47 (47.0)	25 (41.7)	40 (42.6)	47 (49.5)
Mean Age at First Arrest (SD)	18.2 (3.4)	18.3 (4.3)[b]	18.5 (3.9)	16.9 (2.3)[b]	17.1 (2.7)

[a] Significantly different from boot camp sample, $p < .05$.
[b] The approximate t-statistic was computed because of unequal variances.
[c] In Louisiana, juvenile arrest information was unavailable; therefore criminal history N (%) was substituted for juvenile arrest.

disposition to resolve problems of social and personal adjustment in ways ordinarily regarded as showing a disregard for social customs or rules" (Jesness 1969:45). This scale has been found to be associated with recidivism and short-term change (Jesness 1983; Jesness and Wedge 1985).

The Program Attitudes Scale, developed for use in Louisiana (MacKenzie and Shaw 1990; MacKenzie, Shaw, and Gowdy 1990), consists of 12 Likert-type items ("strongly agree" to "strongly disagree"). (See appendix.) The items in the scale measure attitudes toward the program (or oppositional attitudes) expressed as negative feelings toward the staff and the correctional programs (e.g., "The guards put on a big show, but that is all it is"; "The programs in this place will never help me in any way"). The scale also measures the degree to which offenders expect to benefit from their period of incarceration (e.g., "I am becoming more mature here;" "This place will help me learn self-discipline"). The questions were written to apply to either boot camp or prison inmates.[4]

Factor Analyses of Scales

We conducted factor analyses of the Program Attitude Scale in each state. The scree plots and eigenvalues indicated one major factor in most states.[5] Cronbach's alpha coefficients were .86 (Florida), .74 (Georgia), .85 (Louisiana), .84 (New York), .76 (South Carolina), and .43 (Texas).

Because the antisocial attitudes scale had been developed previously by Jesness and colleagues, we did not factor analyze it. Results of the validity and reliability analyses are reported in Jesness (1983) and Jesness and Wedge (1985). Cronbach's alpha coefficients were .77 (Florida), .80 (Georgia), .79 (Louisiana), .80 (New York), .73 (South Carolina), and .75 (Texas).

Comparisons of Samples

We compared boot camp samples with prison samples in each state on the following demographic and offense-related variables; age, race, sentence length, offense type, self-reported juvenile arrest, and self-reported age at first arrest. The results are shown in Table 12.2. In the states in which dropout rates were low (Georgia, South Carolina, and Texas), we compared boot camp *graduates* with the prison sample. In the states in which dropout rates were high (Florida, New York, and Louisiana), we first compared boot camp *entrants* (graduates and dropouts combined) with the prison sample (shown in Table 12.2). We then compared boot camp graduates with boot camp dropouts to identify characteristics of dropouts that might be consistent across states.

In general, the comparison samples were quite similar to the boot camp samples. In the following sections, we describe only the significant differences among samples in each state.

Florida. As shown in Table 12.2, the boot camp and the prison samples differed significantly only on offense type. Prison inmates were more likely to have been convicted of robbery and other violent crimes; boot camp entrants were more likely to have been convicted of burglary/theft and drug offenses; chi-square $(5) = 6.64$, $p = .036$.

Approximately 39 percent of the boot camp entrants failed to complete the program. Comparison of boot camp graduates with boot camp dropouts revealed one statistically significant difference: graduates were significantly older than dropouts; $t(100) = 2.0$, $p < .04$.

Georgia. On average, the prison sample had substantially longer sentences than boot camp graduates, 55.1 months and 3.1 months respectively; $t(69) = 13.24$, $p < .0001$. The sentence lengths differed because the boot camp program is considered a condition of probation, and time on probation is not counted as part of the total sentence. The two samples also differed significantly in offense type; chi-square $(3) = 17.99$, $p < .0001$. Although offenders in both samples were most commonly convicted of burglary/theft or drug offenses, a greater percentage of the prison sample was incarcerated for offenses classified as robbery or "other violent".

Five offenders dropped out of the boot camp program for medical reasons. Therefore statistical comparisons between boot camp graduates and boot camp dropouts were precluded.

Louisiana. Boot camp entrants and prison inmates differed significantly only in age: prison inmates were significantly older than boot camp inmates; $t(243) = 3.78$, $p < .0002$. The major difference between boot camp graduates ($n = 115$) and boot camp dropouts ($n = 92$) was in sentence length: on average, boot camp graduates had significantly longer sentences; chi-square $(170) = 2.8$, $p < .006$.

New York. Boot camp entrants in New York were more likely to be Hispanic than boot camp-ineligible inmates and less likely to be black or white; chi-square $(2) = 6.26$, $p < .04$. We found no other significant differences between boot camp graduates ($n = 200$) and boot camp dropouts ($n = 99$).

South Carolina. We found significant differences in age, race, and sentence length. Prisoners were older than boot camp offenders, had been sentenced to longer terms in prison, and were more likely to be nonwhite (see Table 12.2). Because only nine men dropped out of the program, statistical analyses comparing boot camp dropouts with boot camp graduates were precluded.

Texas. The pre-enhanced and enhanced boot camp samples did not differ significantly on any variable except age. The pre-enhanced sample was older than the enhanced sample; $t(419) = 2.02$, $p < .04$ (Table 12.2).

RESULTS

First, we compared the program and antisocial attitudes of all boot camp entrants (completers and dropouts combined) to prisoners in repeated-measures analyses to examine attitude change during incarceration. Second, we compared the attitudes of the two samples at Time 1 to examine whether their attitudes differed when they entered prison. Third, we separated boot camp entrants into subsamples of graduates and dropouts to examine whether graduates' and dropouts' attitudes differed. Finally, we pooled the data from five states to assess whether attitude change varied as a function of either individual demographic and

offense-related characteristics or of program-level characteristics.

Comparison of Boot Camp Entrants and Prison Inmate Samples

Using separate repeated-measures multivariate analyses of variance (MANOVA), we compared the program and antisocial attitudes of boot camp entrants (graduates and dropouts combined) with those of prison comparison samples.[6] We examined attitudes as a function of sample, time, and the sample × time interaction. The analyses focused on the interaction term, or the difference in attitudes of the boot camp sample, from Time 1 to Time 2, in comparison with the differences in attitudes of the prison sample from Time 1 to Time 2. A significant interaction shows that samples differ in attitude change from Time 1 to Time 2. The results of the analyses are illustrated in Figures 12.1 and 12.2.

Comparison of the mean Program Attitude scores of boot camp and prison inmates revealed significant sample x time interactions in Florida, Georgia, Louisiana, New York (ineligible comparison), and South Carolina. The sample x time interaction was not significant in either the New York refusal comparison or the Texas comparison (see Table 12.3). As shown in Figure 12.1, when the interaction term was significant, boot camp offenders developed more positive attitudes about the program from Time 1 to Time 2. In contrast, the prison samples either did not change (Florida, Georgia) or developed less positive (or more oppositional) attitudes toward prison (Louisiana, New York, South Carolina). The direction of the difference was the same for the New York refusal sample; the magnitude of the difference was small, however, and therefore the interaction was not significant. In Texas, both samples of boot camp inmates developed more positive attitudes toward the program from Time 1 to Time 2, as boot camp participants in other states.

In summary, the analysis of the Program Attitudes Scale shows that boot camp inmates developed more positive (less oppositional) attitudes toward the program over the course of the boot camp. In comparison, inmates incarcerated in traditional prisons either did not change or

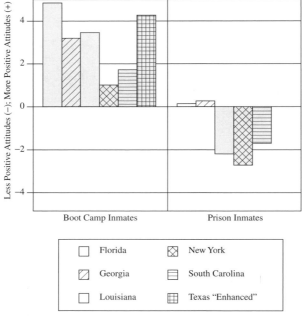

Figure 12.1   Change in Program Attitude Scale Scores From Time 1 to Time 2

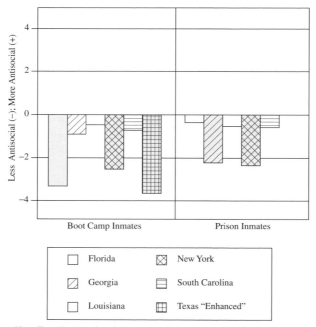

Figure 12.2   Change in Antisocial Attitude Scale Scores From Time 1 to Time 2

Table 12.3   Results of Separate Repeated-Measures MANOVA Analyses With Sample, Time, and Sample × Time Interaction for the Program Attitude Scale (Boot Camp Inmates vs. Prisoners and Boot Camp Graduates vs. Boot Camp Dropouts)

State Program	Boot Camp Sample and Prison Sample[a] F (df)	Boot Camp Graduates and Boot Camp Dropouts F (df)
Florida		
Sample	14.17 (1, 200), $p < .0002$	17.79 (1, 95), $p < .0001$
Time	24.83 (1, 200), $p < .0001$	24.77 (1, 95), $p < .0001$
Sample × time	24.08 (1, 200), $p < .0001$	16.45 (1, 95), $p < .0001$
Georgia		
Sample	04.25 (1, 161), $p < .0408$	N/A
Time	11.69 (1, 161), $p < .0008$	
Sample × time	9.93 (1, 161), $p < .0019$	
Louisiana		
Sample	58.52 (1, 168), $p < .0001$	$t = 0.68$ (125), $p < .4998$
Time	01.45 (1, 168), $p < .2308$	
Sample × time	26.17 (1, 168), $p < .0001$	
New York Ineligible		
Sample	11.03 (1, 269), $p < .0010$	33.97 (1, 195), $p < .0001$
Time	02.32 (1, 269), $p < .1293$	0.57 (1, 195), $p < .4512$
Sample × time	12.70 (1, 269), $p < .0004$	12.33 (1, 195), $p < .0006$
New York Refused		
Sample	16.20 (1, 242), $p < .0001$	
Time	00.52 (1, 242), $p < .4714$	
Sample × time	00.79 (1, 242), $p < .3747$	
South Carolina		
Sample	29.01 (1, 178), $p < .0001$	
Time	00.00 (1, 178), $p < .9899$	
Sample × time	08.13 (1, 178), $p < .0049$	
Texas	Pre-Enhanced vs. Enhanced	
Sample	04.99 (1, 396), $p < .026$	
Time	88.98 (1, 396), $p < .001$	
Sample × time	00.30 (1, 396) $p < .585$	

[a]In states where a substantial percentage of boot camp entrants dropped out of the program (Florida and New York), boot camp *entrants* were compared with the prison sample. Boot camp graduates were also compared with boot camp dropouts. In Louisiana, boot camp graduates were compared with the prison sample and also with boot camp dropouts at Time 1. Time 2 dropout scores were unavailable in Louisiana; thus repeated-measures analyses were precluded.

developed less positive (or more oppositional) attitudes during the same period.

In regard to the Antisocial Attitudes Scale, both samples (boot camp inmates and prisoners) became significantly less antisocial from Time 1 to Time 2, as shown in Figure 12.2. Repeated-measures analyses comparing boot camp offenders with prisoners on antisocial attitudes revealed that the main effect of time was significant in all analyses. We found one significant sample x time interaction, and borderline interactions in Georgia and Texas (Table 12.4). The main effect of sample was significant only in Louisiana. When the interaction term was

significant, the difference was due to the magnitude of the difference, not to the direction of change. Thus both boot camp entrants and prisoners became less antisocial during the period covered by the study.

Attitudes at Time 1

One danger associated with the quasi-experimental research design employed in this study is that of an interaction between selection and maturation effects. That is, if offenders selected for the program differed in attitudes at the beginning of the study, such differences may

Table 12.4   Results of Separate Repeated-Measures MANOVA Analyses with Sample, Time, and Sample × Time Interaction for the Antisocial Attitudes Scale (Boot Camp Inmates vs. Prisoners and Boot Camp Graduates vs. Boot Camp Dropouts)

State Program	Boot Camp Sample and Prison Sample[1] F (df)	Boot Camp Graduates and Boot Camp Dropouts F (df)
Florida		
Sample	01.36 (1, 204), $p < .2454$	20.33 (1, 95), $p < .0001$
Time	51.45 (1, 204), $p < .0001$	57.67 (1, 95), $p < .0001$
Sample × time	26.23 (1, 204), $p < .0001$	03.82 (1, 95), $p < .0535$
Georgia		
Sample	00.23 (1, 162), $p < .6350$	N/A
Time	21.70 (1, 162), $p < .0001$	
Sample × time	02.86 (1, 162), $p < .0927$	
Louisiana		
Sample	14.24 (1, 207), $p < .0002$	$t = 3.24$ (196), $p < .0014$
Time	08.13 (1, 207), $p < .0048$	
Sample × time	00.01 (1, 207), $p < .9116$	
New York Ineligible		
Sample	00.18 (1, 280), $p < .6739$	09.60 (1, 205), $p < .0022$
Time	47.23 (1, 280), $p < .0001$	35.75 (1, 205), $p < .0001$
Sample × time	00.38 (1, 280), $p < .5373$	20.48 (1, 205), $p < .0001$
New York Refused		
Sample	00.96 (1, 252), $p < .3280$	
Time	27.46 (1, 252), $p < .0001$	
Sample × time	01.54 (1, 252), $p < .2162$	
South Carolina		
Sample	00.90 (1, 185), $p < .3431$	
Time	06.73 (1, 185), $p < .0102$	
Sample × time	00.00 (1, 185), $p < .9889$	
Texas	Pre-Enhanced vs. Enhanced	
Sample	00.42 (1, 390), $p < .516$	
Time	191.6 (1, 390), $p < .001$	
Sample × time	03.76 (1, 390), $p < .053$	

[1]In states where a substantial percentage of boot camp entrants dropped out of the program (Florida and New York), boot camp *entrants* were compared with the prison sample. Boot camp graduates were also compared with boot camp dropouts. In Louisiana, boot camp graduates were compared with the prison sample and also with boot camp dropouts at Time 1. Time 2 dropout scores were unavailable in Louisiana; thus repeated-measures analyses were precluded.

indicate that the offenders who were selected as the experimental group had already begun to change and would continue to change regardless of the intervention.

To address this possibility, we compared the attitudes of boot camp offenders and prison inmates at Time 1. The comparison revealed no significant differences in Program Attitude Scale scores at Time 1 in Florida, Georgia, and New York (ineligible comparison). We found significant differences, however, between boot camp and prison samples in Program Attitude Scale scores in Louisiana ($t'(150) = 4.96$, $p < .001$), New York (refusal comparison)

($t'(180) = 2.13$, $p = 0365$), South Carolina ($t'(180) = 2.83$, $p = .0052$), and Texas ($t'(344) = 1.99$, $p = .0457$). In each state, boot camp entrants were more positive (less oppositional) about the program at Time 1 than were the prison comparison samples. The Texas enhanced boot camp sample also was more positive toward the program than the nonenhanced boot camp sample. Therefore we have evidence that some of the samples differed in program attitudes at Time 1 in the study.

We found no differences in antisocial attitudes between boot camp inmates and prisoners at Time 1, with one exception. In Louisiana, the prison sample was significantly more antisocial than the boot camp sample; $t'(335) = 4.09$, $p < .0001$.

It is possible that the boot camp offenders had more positive attitudes (or were less oppositional) about the program than were prisoners at the beginning of their prison term because they had heard positive things about the program. The pertinent question is whether they would have continued to become more positive absent any intervention or program. We cannot answer this question with the available data; yet because the items are fairly straightforward, we would expect that the boot camp offenders' attitudes would not necessarily have changed positively if they had been severely disappointed by the program.

Differences in antisocial attitudes at Time 1 would have been the cause of more concern because this scale measured general anti-social attitudes. In all states except Louisiana, however, prisoners and boot camp offenders showed no differences in antisocial attitudes at the start of their prison term.

Comparisons of Boot Camp Graduates With Dropouts

Three of the boot camp programs (Florida, Louisiana, and New York) had high dismissal rates. Data from offenders who were dismissed at Time 1 were available in each state; data at both Time 1 and Time 2 were available in Florida and New York. We examined the Time 1 scores of boot camp graduates and dropouts to assess whether their attitudes differed when they entered the program. We also conducted repeated-measures analyses to examine whether changes in attitudes from Time 1 to Time 2 were similar for both groups.

Comparisons of mean scores showed that boot camp graduates in New York had more positive attitudes toward the program at Time 1 than did dropouts; $t'(142) = 2.91$, $p = .0023$. Boot camp graduates and dropouts in Florida and Louisiana did not differ at Time 1.

Repeated-measures analyses comparing program graduates with dropouts in two states with high dismissal rates—Florida and New York—revealed a significant sample × time interaction. Boot camp graduates became more positive

about the program from Time 1 to Time 2. As in the prison comparison samples in this study, boot camp dropouts either did not change or developed less positive attitudes from Time 1 to Time 2. In both states, offenders who were dismissed from the program were required to spend the remaining portion of their sentence in prison.

Examination of boot camp graduates' and dropouts' antisocial attitudes revealed significant differences at Time 1 in Florida ($t(99) = 3.17$, $p = .002$) and Louisiana ($t(196) = 3.24$, $p = .0014$): the dropouts' attitudes in both states were more antisocial. We found no differences between program graduates and dropouts at Time 1 in New York.

The repeated-measures comparison of program graduates with dropouts in Florida and New York revealed significant interactions due to the magnitude of the change: both groups became significantly less antisocial. Proportionally, however, the change in antisocial attitudes was greater for the boot camp graduate samples.

In summary, the comparison of boot camp graduates' with dropouts' attitudes in each state shows that the dropouts' change in attitude was similar to that of prison inmates. Unlike boot camp graduates, the dropouts either did not change in attitude during incarceration or became less positive (or more oppositional). Like both boot camp graduates and prison inmates, however, they became less antisocial.

Participants' Characteristics and Change in Attitude

The repeated-measures analyses suggest that offenders who complete boot camp programs generally develop more positive attitudes toward the program (unlike similar offenders in the general prison population) and less antisocial attitudes (like other prisoners) during the course of the boot camp program. This appears to be true of all boot camp programs despite large differences in characteristics of the programs and of participating offenders.

It is obvious from Figures 12.1 and 12.2 that the magnitude of attitudinal change differs across boot camp participants in different states. For example, the change in attitudes toward the

Table 12.5   Program Attitude Difference Scores and Antisocial Attitude Difference Scores
of Boot Camp Offenders

	Florida	Georgia	Louisiana	New York	S. Carolina
Mean Program Difference Score (SD)[a]	7.29 (7.46)[1]	3.25 (5.75)[2]	3.35 (5.90)[2]	2.27 (6.14)[2]	1.67 (6.51)[2]
Mean Antisocial Attitude Difference Score (SD)[b]	4.06 (4.11)[1]	1.06 (3.48)[2]	0.79 (4.45)[2]	4.06 (5.84)[1]	0.90 (4.49)[2]

[a] A positive program difference score indicates more positive attitudes toward the program.
[b] A positive antisocial attitude difference score indicates less antisocial attitudes.
[1,2] Numbers not the same are different at $p < .05$.

program from Time 1 to Time 2 is much more dramatic for offenders graduating from Florida's program than for offenders graduating from South Carolina's program. Such differences may spring from differences in the participating inmates' characteristics.

To explore this hypothesis, we calculated difference scores for each inmate who completed the boot camp program by subtracting the Time 1 score from the Time 2 score for both attitude scales (see Table 12.5). We pooled data from five states[7] and examined the effects of race, age, offense type, juvenile arrest, and age at first arrest, controlling for the state in separate least squares regression models for each attitude scale.

The analyses did not reveal significant relationships between change in attitude toward program and age, race, offense type, juvenile arrests or age at first arrest. In all states, we found significant and positive changes in program attitudes; that is, the change was significantly different from 0. In addition, we found significant differences between boot camp programs in the degree of change; $F(4,447) = 7.59$, $p < .0001$. The magnitude of the change in attitudes was significantly greater in Florida than in any of the other programs (see Table 12.5). We observed no differences among offenders in the other programs.

Identical analyses examining the difference score for the Antisocial Attitude Scale failed to reveal significant relationships between offenders' characteristics and attitude change. Boot camp offenders in Florida, Georgia, and New York became significantly less antisocial over time. Offenders in Louisiana and South Carolina did not change; that is, change scores were not significantly different from 0. We

found significant differences among boot camp programs in the mean difference scores; $F(4,462) = 12.88$, $p < .0001$. Boot camp offenders in Florida and New York became significantly less antisocial than did boot camp offenders in Georgia, Louisiana, and South Carolina (see Table 12.5).

In short, then, we saw no evidence that the boot camp offenders' individual characteristics were associated significantly with attitudinal change.

Program Characteristics and Change in Attitude

Changes in attitudes also may be related to characteristics of the program, such as the amount of time devoted to rehabilitation versus work and physical training, the number of offenders dismissed from the program, and the voluntary nature of the program. Multivariate analysis was prohibited by the small number of programs available for this analysis and by the correlation among characteristics (e.g., programs that permitted voluntary exit also devoted a large proportion of time to rehabilitation activities). Therefore we estimated three separate regression equations to examine the effect of the following three program characteristics on the difference scores for the pooled data from five sites: 1) proportion of time in the daily schedule devoted to rehabilitation in comparison with work (see Table 12.1), 2) dismissal rates, and 3) voluntary exit.

Neither time devoted to rehabilitation nor voluntary exit was related significantly to difference scores for program attitudes. Higher dismissal rates were associated with a larger change in attitude (more positive);

$F(1,476) = 9.6, p < .003$. This effect disappeared, however, if Florida was omitted from the model. Thus the effect of dismissal rates was determined by the Florida program and by the magnitude of inmates' change in attitude there (see Table 12.5). It is quite possible that other differences in Florida's program account for this effect.

The analyses also showed that offenders became significantly less antisocial in programs that devoted more time to rehabilitation, $F(1,493) = 9.2, p < .003$; had higher dismissal rates, $F(1,493) = 8.7, p < .005$; and were voluntary (borderline significance), $F(1,493) = 3.6, p < .06$.

DISCUSSION

Despite the large differences in the characteristics of boot camp programs and participants, the results of these analyses were surprisingly consistent. To summarize, all boot camp inmates developed more positive (or less oppositional) attitudes during the course of the boot camp program. In comparison, the attitudes of prison inmates toward their prison experience either remained the same or became less positive (or more oppositional). With the exception of New York, this finding was supported by the statistical analyses in all states in which boot camp samples were compared with prison samples and boot camp graduates were compared with dropouts. Even in New York the direction of the difference was similar, although the comparison of boot camp entrants with those who refused to participate was not significant.

Furthermore, offenders in all states became less antisocial during incarceration both in a boot camp and in prison, although the change frequently was not so large for prison inmates. This finding was significant in all comparisons of boot camp offenders with prison inmates and (when available) of graduates with dropouts. We found no indication that the samples differed in the way in which they changed over time except in Florida and in one analysis in New York. These differences, however, were only a matter of degree, not of direction.

Initially we wished to learn whether boot camp prisons had a negative effect on participating offenders. For example, did boot camp inmates develop negative or oppositional attitudes toward the program and staff because of the harsh nature of military basic training? Or did these inmates leave the boot camp more alienated and more antisocial than before they entered? The results show that the reverse was true: rather than more alienated and antisocial, these offenders became less. We found no evidence that they developed negative (or oppositional) attitudes toward the program and/or the staff. In fact, over time inmates developed more positive attitudes towards the program, as measured by the Program Attitude Scale. Surprisingly, this was true whether the programs were voluntary, focused on rehabilitation, or had high dropout rates.

These boot camp prisons varied greatly; yet the consistency of the results indicates that the boot camp offenders feel more positive about the program than do offenders serving time in prison. The results suggest that something in the boot camp atmosphere produces more positive attitudes toward the program and the staff than does the traditional prison. Perhaps the environment enhances the effects of therapeutic programs because offenders are less oppositional and more cooperative.

Both the boot camp inmates and the prison comparison samples became less antisocial during incarceration. This finding supports previous research suggesting that prisons may have some positive influence on some inmates (Bonta and Gendreau 1987; Bukstel and Kilman 1980; Goodstein and Wright 1989). The analyses examining differences in the magnitude of change in antisocial attitudes suggested that program characteristics may affect the reduction in such attitudes. Although the small number of programs makes this analysis only exploratory, it is interesting that programs which were voluntary, offered more rehabilitation, and had higher dismissal rates seemed to have a greater effect in reducing antisocial attitudes.

In drawing conclusions from these results, one must remember that these offenders (in both samples) are different from the general prison population. On the whole, they are more likely to have been convicted of less serious crimes. In fact, in some states it is likely that many of the offenders would have received probation rather than prison if the boot camp had not been available. In addition, they probably had less extensive criminal histories and were somewhat younger. We point out these differences because these offenders' experiences in prison and changes in attitudes may not be characteristic of prisoners in the general population. As relatively low-risk inmates, they may have had opportunities in prison such as movement to minimum-security prisons or halfway houses or access to jobs or treatment programs that would have been unavailable to other offenders. These experiences may have led them to become less antisocial, even if they did not believe their experiences had been positive. (We do not have information on how these offenders spent their time in prison.)

Not unexpectedly, none of the offenders we talked to thought the boot camp was easy because of the living conditions, the daily schedule of activities, the early rising, the hard work, and the strict rules. Why, then, did offenders develop more positive attitudes toward the staff and the program? We suggest several possible answers. One possibility is a Hawthorne effect; these programs were highly visible, and participants knew they were being studied. Although this may explain positive changes in attitudes toward the program, as shown in the Program Attitudes Scale, it does not explain why these prisoners also became less antisocial.

Another possibility is that the boot camp programs employed committed staff members who worked hard to have a positive influence on participants, and that the inmates recognized this. Our interviews with staff members and inmates suggest that this factor may influence inmates' attitudes toward the program. Inmates often view staff members as helpful and caring; staff members appear to be seriously concerned about inmates. At the time of data collection, the programs were highly visible and the staff members were committed to making the program successful. One wonders what will happen when these programs become larger and more institutionalized. The largest program in this study was the one developed in New York. This program also has made a major investment in staff training and treatment programs. Therefore it is hard to generalize about the outcomes in a program with very different characteristics.

Both prisoners and boot camp participants became less antisocial during incarceration. Thus it appears that the short but the intense boot camp program will reduce antisocial attitudes as well as a similar term in a traditional prison. If these attitudes affect criminal behavior, as proposed by Andrews et al. (1990), we might hypothesize that boot camp graduates' and prison parolees' recidivism will be similar and that this will tend to be true of all boot camps. Such a hypothesis may explain why we do not see significant differences in time to recidivism when boot camp graduates are compared with prison parolees (MacKenzie 1991; MacKenzie and Shaw 1993). That is, both experiences may affect the antisocial attitudes of these types of offenders.

Such a conclusion, however, is probably dangerous because it assumes that antisocial attitudes are a major factor in producing criminal behavior. This perspective, without further analysis, might lead one to question why we should provide therapy, education, and treatment in boot camp prisons if all programs are effective in changing attitudes. We would be making a mistake if we left readers with this view. Among boot camp programs we found some evidence (although exploratory) that program characteristics such as time devoted to rehabilitation, rigor of the program, and voluntariness may lead to greater reductions in antisocial attitudes. Antisocial attitudes may be important in predicting antisocial behavior; this possibility should be the subject of research.

An exclusive focus on antisocial attitudes, however, may neglect the importance of other "criminogenic needs" (Andrews et al. 1990). Such factors may be associated much more directly with involvement in criminal activities. For example, drug addicts may develop less antisocial attitudes in the boot camp, but until their dependence on drugs is reduced they may continue to use and distribute illegal drugs and to engage in criminal activities to support the habit. Thus, although in general they will be less antisocial, this change in attitude alone will not enable them to overcome the problems that face them upon release from prison.

To conclude, the present research suggests that offenders in boot camp prisons do not become more alienated or more antisocial during the course of the program. On the contrary, they become less antisocial. They also feel more positive about their experience than do offenders serving time in a traditional prison. Future research should examine the association between these attitudes and future criminal behavior. Also valuable would be studies examining the effectiveness of program components such as drug treatment or academic education, which are designed to address specific needs of these offenders.

APPENDIX: PROGRAM ATTITUDES SCALE

*1. There is nothing in this place that will help me.

*2. This place will not help me get a job.

*3 I am tough enough to handle this place.

*4. This experience will not change me.

*5. This place will help me learn self-discipline.

*6. The guards put on a big show, but that is all it is.

*7. This place will never help me in any way.

*8. I will learn things about myself here.

*9. I am becoming a better person here.

*10. The programs in this place will never help me in any way.

*11. I am becoming more mature here.

*12. Because of my experience here, I will probably not get in trouble again.

NOTES

1. This figure does not include boot camp prisons developed for juveniles or those operating at the county level.

2. For a more complete description of these programs see MacKenzie and Souryal (1993). The data were collected in 1990; program descriptions contained herein describe the programs as implemented at that time. Since then, many of the programs have undergone significant changes. In particular, Georgia has added an extensive array of

treatment and educational programs. South Carolina has made a major change in program supervision and selection of participants.

3. Work in these programs consisted of physical labor, not of training in work skills for postrelease employment.

4. To compute total scale scores for subjects with missing data, we assigned the average value of the nonmissing items to the missing items for each case and then calculated the total scale score. If a subject did not answer 80 percent or more of the items in a scale, data for the subject were considered to be missing and were not included in the analyses. Subjects who answered 80 to 100 percent of the items were included in the analyses.

5. In some states two factors were indicated, but results of analyses using the separate factors were so similar to analyses using the total scale that reporting of separate results did not seem warranted.

6. In Florida and New York (states in which a large number of offenders dropped out of the program), we combined boot camp dropouts and boot camp graduates in the "boot camp entrants" sample. In the remaining states, we compared boot camp *graduates* with prison inmates because the number of boot camp dropouts was small.

7. Data from Texas were not available for this portion of the study.

REFERENCES

Akers, R. L., N. S. Hayner, and W. Grunniger (1977) "Prisonization in Five Countries: Type of Prison and Inmate Characteristics." *Criminology* 14:527–54.

Andrews, D. A., J. Bonta, and R. D. Hoge (1990) "Classification for Effective Rehabilitation: Rediscovering Psychology." *Criminal Justice and Behavior* 17:19–52.

Arkin, W. and L. R. Dobrofsky (1978) "Military Socialization and Masculinity." *Journal of Social Issues* 34:151–68.

Bonta, J. and P. Gendreau (1987) "Reexamining the Cruel and Unusual Punishment of Prison Life." Unpublished manuscript.

Bukstel, L. H. and P. R. Kilman (1980) "Psychological Effects of Imprisonment on Confined Individuals." *Psychological Bulletin* 88:469–83.

Campbell, D. T. and J. C. Stanley (1963) *Experimental and Quasi-Experimental Designs for Research.* Chicago: Rand McNally.

Clemmer, D. (1940) *The Prison Community.* Boston: Christopher.

*Reverse coded.

Feld, B. C. (1981) "A Comparative Analysis of Organizational Structure and Inmate Subcultures in Institutions for Juvenile Offenders." *Crime and Delinquency* 27:336–63.

Goodstein, L., D. L. MacKenzie and R. L. Shotland (1984) "Personal Control and Inmate Adjustment to Prison." *Criminology* 22:343–69.

Goodstein, L. and K. N. Wright (1989) "Inmate Adjustment to Prison." In L. Goodstein and D. L. MacKenzie (eds.), *The American Prison: Issues in Research and Policy*, pp. 299–251. New York: Plenum.

Gottlieb, D. (1980) *Babes in Arms: Youth in the Army.* Beverly Hills: Sage.

Hahn, P. Undated. "Are Boot Camps Really the Answer?" Unpublished manuscript, Department of Criminal Justice, Xavier University, Cincinnati.

Hengesh, D. J. (1991) "The Real Concept behind Boot Camps." *Corrections Today* 53(6): 106–108.

Jesness, C. F. (1969) "The Preston Typology Study: Final Report." Unpublished manuscript, California Youth Authority and American Justice Institute.

—— (1983) *The Jesness Inventory* (Rev. ed.). Palo Alto: Consulting Psychologists Press.

Jesness, C. F. and R. F. Wedge (1985) *Jesness Inventory Classification System.* Palo Alto: Consulting Psychologists Press.

MacKenzie, D. L. (1990) "Boot Camp Prisons: Components, Evaluations, and Empirical Issues." *Federal Probation* 54(September): 44–52.

—— (1991) "The Parole Performance of Offenders Released from Shock Incarceration (Boot Camp Prisons): A Survival Time Analysis." *Journal of Quantitative Criminology* 7:213–36.

MacKenzie, D. L. and J. W. Shaw (1990) "Inmate Adjustment and Change during Shock Incarceration: The Impact of Correctional Boot Camp Programs." *Justice Quarterly* 2:125–50.

—— (1993) "The Impact of Shock Incarceration on Technical Violations and New Criminal Activities." *Justice Quarterly* 10:463–87.

MacKenzie, D. L., J. W. Shaw, and V. B. Gowdy (1990) "An Evaluation of Shock Incarceration in Louisiana." Unpublished manuscript, Louisiana State University, Baton Rouge.

MacKenzie, D. L. and C. Souryal (1993) "Multi-Site Study of Shock Incarceration Process Evaluation: Final Report to the National Institute of Justice." Unpublished manuscript.

Morash, M. and L. Rucker (1990) "A Critical Look at the Ideal of Boot Camp as Correctional Reform." *Crime and Delinquency* 36:204–22.

Osler, M. (1991) "Shock Incarceration: Hard Realities and Real Possibilities." *Federal Probation* 55 (March):34–36.

Sykes, G.M. (1958) *The Society of Captives.* Princeton: Princeton University Press.

Sykes, G. M. and S. L. Messinger (1960) "The Inmate Social System." In R. Cloward (ed.), *Theoretical Studies in Social Organization of the Prison*, pp. 5–19. New York: Social Science Research Council.

Thomas, C. W. (1970) "Towards a More Inclusive Model of the Inmate Contraculture." *Criminology* 8:251–62.

Thomas, C. W. and S. C. Foster (1972) "Prisonization in the Inmate Contraculture." *Social Problems* 20:229–39.

U.S. General Accounting Office. (1993) *Prison Boot Camps: Short-Term Prison Costs Reduced, but Long-Term Impact Uncertain.* Washington, DC: U.S. General Accounting Office.

Wamsley, G. L. (1972) "Contrasting Institutions of Air Force Socialization: Happenstance or Bellwether?" *American Journal of Sociology* 78:399–417.

Wellford, C. (1967) "Factors Associated with Adoption of the Inmate Code: A Study of Normative Socialization." *Journal of Criminal Law, Criminology, and Police Science* 58: 197–203.

Wheeler, S. (1961) "Socialization in Correctional Communities." *American Sociological Review* 24:697–712.

Part V

Impact on Future Criminal Activities

13

BOOT CAMP PRISONS AND RECIDIVISM IN EIGHT STATES

DORIS LAYTON MACKENZIE

ROBERT BRAME

DAVID MCDOWALL

CLAIRE SOURYAL

BACKGROUND

Since their inception in 1983, boot camp prisons (also known as shock incarceration programs) have enjoyed considerable popular support. The programs have been enthusiastically embraced because they are designed to save scarce correctional dollars by reducing time served in institutions while simultaneously providing adequate punishment by virtue of the quasi-military environment, strict schedule, and daily work assignments (Cronin, 1994; General Accounting Office, 1993; MacKenzie & Parent, 1992). In contrast to other intermediate sanctions, they are perceived as alternative sanctions with "teeth"—an imperative in the current political climate (MacKenzie & Parent, 1992).

Boot camp prisons are distinguished from other correctional programs by their emphasis on physical labor, exercise, and a military-style atmosphere (MacKenzie & Souryal, 1993a, 1993b). Most are designed for young offenders convicted of nonviolent crimes who do not have a prior history of imprisonment (General Accounting Office, 1993; MacKenzie, 1994). Those who complete the programs are congratulated for their accomplishment, and many programs hold formal graduation ceremonies to mark the event.

Many boot camp prisons also offer greater access to rehabilitative programming, such as

Reprinted from MacKenzie, D. L., Brame, B., McDowall, D., & Souryal, C. (1995). *Criminology, 33*(3), 401–430. Copyright © 1995 by the American Society of Criminology; reprinted with permission.

This investigation was supported in part by Grant #90-DD-CX-0061 from the National Institute of Justice, Office of Justice Programs, U.S. Department of Justice, to the University of Maryland. Points of view in this chapter are those of the authors and do not necessarily represent the official position of the U.S. Department of Justice.

drug treatment/education or academic education, than would be available in a traditional prison (Clark et al., 1994). In large part, however, the appeal of such programs stems from their promise of providing an attractive intermediate sanction within severely overcrowded correctional systems. Whether policymakers place a premium on tougher sentencing, treatment and rehabilitation, or locating viable alternatives to conventional incarceration, boot camp prisons have the potential to meet a variety of demands imposed by policymakers.

But not everyone is convinced of the utility of such programs. Boot camps are controversial for a variety of reasons (MacKenzie & Parent, 1992; Meachum, 1990). Some worry that it is naive to expect a short term in a boot camp prison to be effective at changing offenders, while others argue that such institutions represent a return to earlier militaristic prisons. Morash and Rucker (1990) contend that aspects of the boot camps may actually inflict damage on participants.

Despite the controversy, boot camp prisons continue to grow in number and size. A recent survey revealed that 29 states, the Federal Bureau of Prisons, 9 juvenile systems, and 10 local jurisdictions were operating a total of at least 79 boot camp programs (Cronin, 1994). Further, boot camp prison capacity has increased dramatically among states where programs have been in existence for longer periods of time. For example, Georgia's program capacity of 250 in 1989 stands in marked contrast to its capacity of approximately 3,000 in 1994. Moreover, New York state prisons now devote 1,500 beds to their boot camp facilities (MacKenzie & Souryal, 1993b).

Although all of the boot camp prisons use military basic training as a model, they differ considerably in other respects. For example, some programs select participants from a pool of prisoners sentenced to a traditional sentence of incarceration. Other programs receive inmates directly from the sentencing court. Programs also differ in the proportion of inmates who are dismissed prior to graduation, whether offenders volunteer for the program, and whether offenders can voluntarily drop out (Cronin, 1994; General Accounting Office, 1993; MacKenzie & Souryal, 1993a). One of

the largest differences among programs is the amount of time in the daily schedule that is devoted to work, drill, and physical training versus such treatment-type activities as counseling, drug treatment, or academic education. Some programs, such as New York's, devote over five hours of the daily schedule to rehabilitative programming, while other boot camps devote little or no time to therapeutic activities. Another large difference among programs is in the type of community supervision provided for program graduates. Some graduates are released to traditional probation supervision, while others receive intensive supervision, aftercare, or electronic monitoring. With this in mind, one might well expect the impact of the programs on inmates to differ as a function of heterogeneity in type of offenders selected, program rigor, daily schedule of activities, and community supervision intensity.

One of the most commonly used criteria for evaluating the impact of correctional programs is recidivism (Hepburn & Albonetti, 1994; Lattimore et al., 1990; Maguire et al., 1988; Maltz, 1984; MacKenzie, 1991; Petersilia & Turner, 1993; Visher & Linster, 1990). Given the rapid proliferation of boot camp prisons across the nation and the fact that reducing recidivism is one of the major objectives of many of the programs, it is somewhat surprising that there have been few empirical studies of the impact of these programs on recidivism (MacKenzie & Souryal, 1993a). Much of the existing literature has been produced by state correctional officials themselves. Research in Texas, Georgia, and Florida indicates that boot camp graduates had lower reincarceration rates than some comparison samples while comparisons with other samples revealed similar reincarceration rates (Florida Department of Corrections, 1990; Flowers et al., 1991; State of Texas, 1990). Research examining New York's boot camp prisons found that the reincarceration rate of the boot camp graduates was lower when compared with offenders who either dropped out or refused to participate in the program (New York State Department of Correctional Services, 1992).

However, after reviewing some of these studies, Cullen et al. (1993) warned that the results should be viewed with caution due to methodological problems. A particularly important criticism centered on the failure of these efforts to rely on experimental designs in their group comparisons. Compounding this problem, argued Cullen and his colleagues, was the lack of statistical controls for potentially important variables (such as community supervision intensity) whose levels differ between comparison groups.

Although not a random assignment study, MacKenzie and Shaw (1993) did control for differences among groups in a study of the Louisiana boot camp program. Three important conclusions emerged from this analysis. First, the investigators found that the recidivism rates of boot camp graduates and boot camp dropouts did not differ from each other. Second, the analysis suggested that there were potential recidivism differences between boot camp graduates and comparison groups (prison releasees and probationers). The results leading to this second finding, however, varied by recidivism mode. New crime revocation rates were lower for boot camp graduates than for comparison groups but technical violation revocation rates were higher. Third, MacKenzie and Shaw (1993) suggested that differences in community supervision levels between the groups could have accounted for these differences in revocation rates, although a model designed to partially control this difference did not alter the above patterns.

Since boot camp programming content differs substantially from state to state (MacKenzie, 1994), it is problematic to generalize results in one state to other contexts. The current study is designed to examine the recidivism of boot camp releasees from eight state programs: Florida, Georgia, Illinois, Louisiana, New York, Oklahoma, South Carolina, and Texas. The performance of the releasees is compared with the performance of comparison groups (after controlling for between-group differences). All of the boot camp programs were selected because they had the basic core components of the boot camp prisons-military drill and ceremony, hard labor, physical training, and strict rules and discipline. Yet they differed in many other elements that might be expected to have an impact on recidivism (see Table 13.1 for short description of programs[1]). For example, programs differed in length of confinement (from 90 to 180 days). With the exception of

New York, most were small, holding only 100 to 200 inmates. However, they differed dramatically in the number of offenders dismissed prior to graduation (3% to 51%) and the amount of time in the daily schedule devoted to therapeutic activities. In some programs participation was voluntary, in others it was not.

If quasi-military and hard labor aspects of boot camp programs affect recidivism, then recidivism comparisons should be similar across all states. That is, under this hypothesis boot camp participants would have lower recidivism rates when compared with comparison samples within each state. On the other hand, if the results of such comparisons differed from state to state, it would be more difficult to conclude that the military nature of the program was what led to group differences within a particular state. Such an outcome would require more detailed examination of boot camp programming content to identify other factors capable of explaining group differences. This is the focus of our research.

METHODOLOGY

Subjects

In general, states impose strict eligibility criteria limiting the types of offenders who can enter their boot camp programs. Although eligibility criteria differed somewhat from state to state, most states limited participation to young males who were convicted of nonviolent crimes and had no history of felony convictions or incarceration. Physical or mental disorders that would limit participation also represent barriers to program entry in many states.

The recidivism rates of boot camp graduate samples (hereafter "camp completers") were compared with samples of prison parolees, probationers, and camp dropouts. In general, comparison samples were legally eligible for participation in boot camp programs. They were usually also judged to be "suitable" for the boot camps in terms of demographic, offense-related, and criminal history variables. All of the subjects in the current analysis were males. As described below, the number and types of comparison samples differed from state to state.

Table 13.1 Program Characteristics, by State

Characteristic	Florida	Georgia	Illinois	Louisiana	New York	Oklahoma	South Carolina	Texas
Inmate Capacity	100	200	230	120	1,500	150	96	200–400
Average Sentence Length (in days)	105	90	120	135	180	135	90	83
Supervision Intensity in Community	Regular	Varies based on risk	Intensive for Minimum of 6 months	Intensive for Minimum of 6 months	Intensive for Minimum of 6 months	Varies based on sentence	Varies based on risk	Varies based on location
Voluntary Entrance	No	Yes	Yes	Yes	Yes	No	No	No
Voluntary Exit	No	No	Yes	Yes	Yes	No	No	No
Program Dismissal/Dropout Rate	51.1%	2.8%	41%	43%	31%	10%	16%	29%
Officials Responsible for Placement Decisions (Court/Dept. of Corrections)	DOC	Court	Court & DOC	DOC	DOC	Court & DOC	Court (Old) & Court DOC (New)	Court
Daily Activities (Hours per Day)								
Work/Drill/Physical Training	8	8	11	6.5	9	12	9	9
Rehabilitation	1.8	0.3	3.0	3.5	5.6	3.0	1.9	<1.0
Percentage of Time in Rehabilitation Activities (Daily)*	18.4%	3.6%	21.4%	35%	38.4%	20%	17.4%	<10%

*Rehabilitative activities include formal education, counseling, and drug treatment/education.

In seven states (Texas excluded) performances of camp completers were compared with those of parolees. Additionally, performances of camp completers were compared with those of probationers in Louisiana, South Carolina, and Texas. The comparison group of probationers in Texas had been sentenced to shock probation; they, therefore, spent a short period of time in prison in the general prison population before beginning community supervision.

Five states (Florida, Illinois, Louisiana, New York, and Oklahoma) had sufficiently large dropout rates to facilitate a comparison between offenders who began but failed to complete the boot camp program (hereafter "camp dropouts") and the other groups.

In some cases, programming varied within the same state over time. In particular, data were collected twice in South Carolina and Texas to assess whether these states' programming modifications affect conclusions about the effects of the boot camp program. Offenders from the older of the two programs in these states are hereafter described as "old" camp completers while offenders from the newer of the two programs are hereafter described as "new" camp completers.

The South Carolina program change does not reflect programming modifications. Rather, it raises the possibility of a difference in the type of offender participating in the state's boot camp. Formerly, the Department of Probation, Parole, and Pardon Services (DPPPS) selected offenders for the program from those sentenced to probation and supervised them upon release. After the modification, the Department of Corrections (DOC) selected offenders from those who had been sentenced to prison. From the beginning the program was operated and staffed by the DOC so programming within the boot camp did not change during this time. But there was a strong possibility that the two selection processes would result in substantially different types of offender participants. For this reason, we examined the two groups separately. The "old" camp completers refer to those selected by DPPPS; the "new" camp completers were selected by the DOC.

During the course of the study, the Texas program developed an enhanced drug treatment component for the program. Thus, in addition to the shock probation comparison group in Texas, data were collected for two samples of camp program completers. The "old" group completed the boot camp before implementation of enhanced treatment. The "new" group received additional drug treatment but this was still of short duration (less than one hour per day).

Sample Comparisons

Although comparison samples were selected to be legally eligible for the boot camp programs, they were not randomly assigned to experimental (boot camp) and control conditions (probation, parole). Therefore, differences in recidivism could potentially occur because of differences in demographic and criminal history characteristics rather than as a result of the boot camp. For this reason we examined the groups on a number of characteristics (these tables are available on request). The comparisons revealed significant differences in several of the states on such variables as age, racial composition, offense classification, prior arrests or convictions, and intensity of community supervision. It is plausible that these variables are also related to recidivism during community supervision. Preliminary analysis indicated that offender age (in years) and race, the presence or absence of a prior offending record, current offense, and supervision intensity (where available) had the most important effects on our recidivism measures.

The following items were used as control variables: Race/ethnicity was coded 1 if the offender was nonwhite (0 otherwise); prior offending was coded 1 if there was evidence of any kind of prior offending history (either arrests or convictions) and 0 otherwise; and current offenses were classified as violent, drug related, youthful offenders (a classification used only in New York), property (burglary, larceny, arson, and other), and unknown (a small number in Louisiana and Oklahoma) based on the most serious offense of conviction. Offenses were dummy coded using property offenses as the reference category in the analyses. The level of detail in prior and current offense information varied considerably from state to state. The coding of these variables in the current analysis maintains as much consistency as possible in coding across states.

In four of the eight states (Florida, Georgia, Louisiana, and South Carolina), a variable measuring offenders' supervision intensity levels in the community was available. Supervision intensity, a time-varying covariate, was measured by the number of monthly contacts between the supervising officer and the offender in Florida, Georgia, and South Carolina. In Georgia, monthly contact information was collected for the first 12 months of a maximum 24 month follow-up period. Beyond the 12th month, we assume that community supervision levels are equivalent to their 12th-month level. In Louisiana, a one-time indicator of supervision intensity is available in the data but is missing for approximately half of the cases. For analysis purposes, we normalized the supervision intensity indicators for each time period within each state to zero mean and unit variance. To counteract the effect of extensive missing data on the indicator in Louisiana, we set all missing cases to the group mean (before normalizing) and created a dummy variable indicating whether a particular case possessed valid supervision intensity information. In states where supervision intensity data were not available for analysis, values on the normalized supervision intensity variable were set to zero.

Recidivism Measures

Recidivism data were collected for offenders completing boot camp programs and the comparison samples. Recidivism can legitimately be defined in a number of different ways, which yield quite different recidivism rates in any given population; yet each has a certain amount of content validity (Maltz, 1984; Schmidt & Witte, 1988). Rather than arguing for one particular measure over another, our study examines multiple indicators of recidivism: arrests, revocations in general (no distinction for different types), and revocations for either new crimes or technical violations.

The window within which recidivism patterns are studied has much to do with the rates that are observed (Allison, 1984; Maltz, 1984; Schmidt & Witte, 1988, 1989). The data for our study were collected for 12 months in Florida, Illinois, New York, and South Carolina and for 24 months in Georgia, Louisiana, Oklahoma,

and Texas. The time to recidivism for individuals who did not recidivate during the observation window was treated as censored. Durations (e.g., time between beginning community supervision and first arrest) were calculated by taking the difference in days between the date on which community supervision began and the date an event occurred. Dates were recorded for legal releases (in Georgia, Louisiana, New York, Oklahoma, and Texas), absconding (in Florida, Georgia, Louisiana, New York, and South Carolina), and recidivism incidents. Neither legal release nor absconding information was available in Illinois. Offenders were considered at risk as long as they were being supervised in the community by probation or parole agents. They were removed from the at-risk group (censored) if they were legally released, absconded, or recidivated. A more detailed description of the outcome measures follows.

Arrests

Offenders could have been arrested during community supervision for the commission of either a new crime or a technical violation of community supervision terms. Arrests were neither a necessary nor a sufficient condition for revocation. Offenders were, therefore, considered to be at risk for an arrest until they (1) absconded, (2) were legally released, (3) were revoked, or (4) the follow-up period ended. Such cases were treated as censored. Arrest data were available for analysis in five of the eight states in our study: Florida, Louisiana, New York, South Carolina, and Texas.

Revocations

Offenders could have been revoked for a variety of reasons. As noted above, an arrest is neither necessary nor sufficient for revocation. In some cases, therefore, arrests lead to revocations while in other cases they do not. As such, an arrest is not sufficient to remove an offender from the pool of those at risk for revocation. Thus, individuals who either completed the follow-up period without incident, absconded, or were legally released were censored in the analyses. Revocation data were available for analysis in all eight states.

Revocations for New Crimes or Technical Violations

Although revocations are significant events regardless of whether they are based on new crimes or technical violations, it is important to recognize the possibility of differences in the factors that are associated with one or the other type of violation. In six of the eight states (Oklahoma and Texas excluded), information was available to distinguish whether a revocation was for a new crime or a technical violation. As such, there are three possible outcomes for individuals at risk for revocation: (1) censored (i.e., legal release, absconded, or completed the follow-up period); (2) failure due to revocation for a new crime; and (3) failure due to revocation for a technical violation. These two failures modes are considered to be mutually exclusive and independent of one another. As a practical matter, the events in question are said to "compete" with each other, and therefore, models to analyze these data are often described as competing events models (Allison, 1984; Chung et al., 1991; Kalbfleisch & Prentice, 1980; Rhodes, 1986).

DATA ANALYSIS

As described above, our analysis examines recidivism rates between comparison groups in each of the participating states. The data are analyzed with discrete-time failure models (Allison, 1982, 1984) because of our reliance on time-dependent covariates (such as community supervision intensity) and the heterogeneity of observed hazard rates across states.

Our discrete-time models are based on data combined across all participating states. The analysis time unit is one month. For an individual who is observed for five months, for example, five records are contributed to the log-likelihood function. For the ith subject, at each time period, a dummy variable, δ is defined as 0 if the subject does not fail and 1 if the subject does fail. Within this framework, the log-likelihood is given by

$$\log L = \sum_i \sum_t \delta_{it} \log[\pi_{it}/(1-\pi_{it})] + \sum_i \sum_t \log(1-\pi_{it}), \quad (1)$$

where π_{it}, is the estimated probability that the subject fails at time t. Since a subject's presence in the data set at time t is conditional on his not having failed before time t, it follows that π_{it}, is a conditional rather than an unconditional probability. As such, π_{it} is also the discrete-time hazard rate, which is usually denoted as $\lambda(t_i; x_{it})$, where x_{it} is a vector of covariates for the ith subject at time t. The cumulative distribution function (the probability of failure through time t) for the ith subject is, therefore, given by

$$F(t_i; x_{it}) = 1 - \exp\left[-\int_o^t \lambda(u; x_{it})du\right], \quad (2)$$

where t is constant length of one month for all subjects over their entire observation window (see Petersen, 1991, p. 302). In the case of a model with a single transition (say, from no failure by arrest to failure by arrest), the hazard is given by

$$\lambda(t_i; x_{it}) = \exp(x_{it}'\Theta)/[1 - \exp(x_{it}'\Theta)] \quad (3)$$

where Θ is a vector of regression coefficients estimated by the method of maximum likelihood. In the case of a model with competing events (say, from no failure to either failure by new crime or failure by technical violation), the hazard for the first event is given by

$$\lambda_1(t_i; x_{it}) = \exp(x_{it}'\Theta_1)/[1 - \exp(x_{it}'\Theta_1) - \exp(x_{it}'\Theta_2)] \quad (4a)$$

and the hazard for the second event is simply

$$\lambda_2(t_i; x_{it}) = \exp(x_{it}'\Theta_2)/[1 + \exp(x_{it}'\Theta_2) + \exp(x_{it}'\Theta_2)] \quad (4b)$$

The probabilities in Equations 4a and 4b are then entered into a generalized log-likelihood function in which there are $J = 2$ failure outcomes:

$$\log L = \sum_i \sum_t \sum_j \delta_{itj} \log(\pi_{itj}) \sum_i \sum_t [(1-(\delta_{it1}+\delta_{it2})) \log(1-\pi_{it1}-\pi_{it2})] \quad (5)$$

and j is the index for the J failure outcomes (Maddala, 1983). The results are based on models estimated with SAS software (SAS Institute, 1990, p. 446) and interactions are assessed using the methods outlined by Friedrich (1982, pp. 828-831).

RESULTS

Covariates available for analysis included age, race, prior record, current offense (either property or drug-using violent offenses as the reference category), and supervision intensity levels (in Florida, Georgia, Louisiana, and South Carolina). Table 13.2 presents descriptive statistics for the arrest, revocation, and competing events studies. Expanding these data into discrete-time data sets in which the unit of analysis is the person-month yields 21,588 observations for the arrest analysis, 43,747 observations for the general revocation analysis, and 23,941 observations for the competing events analysis. Since each of these analyses stands largely on its own, we devote our attention to each one in turn.

Arrest

Our first objective is to derive a reasonable specification of the failure process with arrest data pooled across the states. We began by estimating separate failure models for each state. The sum of the log-likelihood values from these separate models is −3601.51 with 52 degrees of freedom. An examination of the hazard rates in each state suggested that a linear specification for time was most appropriate since arrest hazards tended to decline monotonically. A model with data pooled across states that imposes the constraint of constant effects (across state) on time, age, race, prior record, and current offense yields a log-likelihood value of −3616.57 with 29 degrees of freedom. A test of whether this pooled model is as consistent with the data as the completely state-restricted model is given by twice the difference in the two log-likelihoods, which is distributed asymptotically as χ^2 with degrees of freedom equal to the number of constraints imposed. In this case, we have $\chi^2_{23} = 30.12$, and the hypothesis of consistency is not rejected at the p < .05 level. The imposition of further restrictions results in a statistically significant drop in the log-likelihood. With arrest, it appears reasonable to conclude that a pooled specification that restricts sample effects to be the same across states is inconsistent with the data.

Our specification of the pooled arrest model with state restrictions on group effects is detailed in Table 13.3. The analysis reveals that offenders who were younger, nonwhite, and had prior offending records were most likely to be arrested. Coefficients for the offense categories suggested that drug-related offenses were associated with the lowest levels of arrest. The time effect indicates that the hazard rate for arrest declines monotonically over time. The supervision intensity coefficients reveal that higher levels of supervision intensity are associated with a lower probability of arrest in Florida and a higher probability of arrest in Louisiana. In South Carolina, supervision intensity is not significantly associated with arrests.

Evaluation of the comparison group effects indicates differences between camp completers and comparison groups in four states (boot camp program completers are the reference category in all states except South Carolina and Texas, where the "old" completer samples are used as the reference category). The camp completers in Louisiana had significantly fewer arrests than any of the three comparison groups. In Florida, the camp completers had a lower arrest rate than the parolees, but they did not differ from the shock camp dropouts. The New York contrast suggests that camp completers were more likely to be arrested than shock dropouts, but the results were not significant, and there was no difference between camp completers and parolees. In South Carolina, the old camp completer sample had a higher arrest rate than the parolees and the new camp completer samples, but it did not differ significantly from the probation sample. The new camp completer sample, however, did not differ from either the parolees or the probationers.[2] There were no differences between the groups in Texas.

In sum, the results from the five states for which we had arrest data showed little or no state-to-state consistency in the direction of sample differences. Out of the seven intrastate comparisons in Florida, Louisiana, and New York, four showed that camp completers had fewer arrests. The other three contrasts revealed no differences between camp completers and comparison groups. In South Carolina, where there were five possible contrasts, exactly the opposite occurred. Two of the three contrasts comparing old camp completers (to prison and new camp completers) indicated that the old camp

Table 13.2   Descriptive Statistics

Variable	Arrest Evaluation (N = 1,932)		Revocation Evaluation (N = 2,819)		Competing Events (N = 1,907)	
	Mean (S.D.)	Range	Mean (S.D.)	Range	Mean (S.D.)	Range
State = Florida	.143 (.350)	0-1	.098 (.297)	0-1	.145 (.352)	0-1
State = Georgia			.084 (.278)	0-1	.124 (.330)	0-1
State = Illinois			.100 (.301)	0-1	.148 (.356)	0-1
State = Louisiana	.269 (.444)	0-1	.184 (.388)	0-1	.273 (.445)	0-1
State = New York	.148 (.355)	0-1	.101 (.302)	0-1	.150 (.357)	0-1
State = Oklahoma	.116 (.320)	0-1				
State = South Carolina	.158 (.365)	0-1	.108 (.311)	0-1	.160 (.367)	0-1
State Texas	.282 (.450)	0-1	.208 (.406)	0-1		
Group = Boot Camp Completers	.392 (.488)	0-1	.407 (.491)	0-1	.346 (.476)	0-1
Group = New Boot Camp Completers	.137 (.344)	0-1	.099 (.299)	0-1	.040 (.197)	0-1
Group = Prison Parolees	.209 (.406)	0-1	.243 (.429)	0-1	.306 (.461)	0-1
Group = Probationers	.148 (.355)	0-1	.128 (.334)	0-1	.141 (.348)	0-1
Group = Boot Camp Dropouts	.115 (.319)	0-1	.123 (.329)	0-1	.167 (.373)	0-1
Age (in Years)	21.94 (3.80)	16 to 47	22.03 (3.58)	16 to 47	22.32 (3.89)	16 to 47
Race = Nonwhite	.631 (.483)	0-1	.564 (.496)	0-1	.663 (.473)	0-1
Prior Offending Record = Yes	.743 (.437)	0-1	.686 (.484)	0-1	.595 (.491)	0-1
Current Offense = Violent	.131 (.338)	0-1	.127 (.333)	0-1	.137 (.344)	0-1
Current Offense = Drug Related	.286 (.452)	0-1	.277 (.448)	0-1	.314 (464)	0-1
Current Offense = Youthful Offender	.025 (.156)	0-1	.017 (.129)	0-1	.025 (.157)	0-1
Current Offense/Property = Miscellaneous	.544 (.498)	0-1	.535 (.499)	0-1	.510 (500)	0-1
Current Offense = Missing	.013 (.115)	0-1	.044 (.205)	0-1	.014 (.116)	0-1
Supervision Intensity Level	.025 (.732)	−2.03 to 6.71	.013 (.678)	−2.11 to 6.80	.019 (.824)	−2.11 to 6.80
Missing Supervision Intensity Level = Yes	.117 (.322)	0-1	.081 (.272)	0-1	.119 (.324)	0-1

Note: Dummy variables, such as "Group = Boot Camp Completers," are coded 1 in the presence of the indicated attribute and 0 otherwise. In South Carolina and Texas, the "Boot Camp Completer" group is the older of the two boot camp programs and the "New Boot Camp Completer" group is only present in those states. The "Property/Miscellaneous" offense category is used as the reference offense group in all analyses.

Table 13.3   Arrest Model

Variable	Coefficient	Standard Error	$|t|$ ratio
Main Effects			
Time	−.035	.007	5.00*
Age	−.087	.013	6.69*
Nonwhite	.495	.077	6.43*
Prior Record	.353	.098	3.60*
Violent Offense	−.141	.111	1.27
Drug-Related Offense	−.228	.086	2.65*
Youthful Offender	−.267	.240	1.11
Missing Offense Information	.093	.311	0.30
Missing Supervision Intensity	.214	.162	1.32
State-Specific Effects			
Florida Intercept	−1.312	.298	4.40*
Supervision Intensity	−.270	.119	2.26*
Prison Parolee Sample	.480	.212	2.27*
Boot Camp Dropout Sample	−.119	.251	0.47
Louisiana Intercept	−1.932	.343	5.64*
Supervision Intensity	.403	.122	3.31
Prison Parolee Sample	.800	.213	3.75*
Probation Sample	.504	.249	2.02*
Boot Camp Dropout Sample	.547	.247	2.22*
New York Intercept	−1.209	.335	3.61
Prison Parolee Sample	.293	.219	1.34
Boot Camp Dropout Sample	.364	.216	1.69
South Carolina Intercept	−.847	.310	2.73*
Supervision Intensity	.024	.080	0.30
New Boot Camp v. Old Boot Camp	−.660	.246	2.68*
Prison Parolee v. Old Boot Camp	−.510	.255	2.00*
Probation v. Old Boot Camp	−.387	.234	1.65
Prison Parolee v. New Boot Camp	.151	.269	0.56
Probation v. New Boot Camp	.273	.244	1.12
Texas Intercept	−1.835	.290	6.33*
New Boot Camp v. Old Boot Camp	−.081	.140	0.58
Probation v. Old Boot Camp	−.054	.180	0.30
Probation v. New Boot Camp	.028	.191	0.15
Log-Likelihood (w/29 df)	−3616.57		

*$p < .05$.

completers had higher arrest recidivism rates. The contrast between probationers and old camp completers was not statistically significant. The other two contrasts (against new camp completers) were not statistically significant. There were no significant differences among samples in Texas.

Revocation

All eight of the participating states provided revocation data for analysis. As with the arrest analysis above, our first objective here is to derive a reasonable specification of the failure process with data pooled across states. Examination of the failure-time distributions in each of the states suggested considerable between-state variability in the trend and shape, of the hazard rate. Because the hazard rate displayed a prominent turning point in several states, it was evident that it would have to be modeled as a polynomial in time (this is achieved by squaring the time variable).

Estimating separate models within each of the states yields a log-likelihood value of

−2433.74 with 87 degrees of freedom. A pooled model with between-state constraints placed on age, race, and current offense but not on time (time × time; i.e., the quadratic effect), prior record, supervision intensity, and group membership yielded a log-likelihood value of −2449.39 with 61 degrees of freedom. A test for whether these log-likelihood values are different provided evidence for retaining the null hypothesis: $\chi^2_{26} = 31.31$ ($p > .05$). Any relaxation of constraints on supervision intensity, prior criminal record, time, or group membership led to a statistically significant decrease in the log-likelihood. On the basis of this evidence, it seems reasonable to conclude that comparison group, supervision intensity, prior behavior, and time effects are not the same across the eight states. As Table 13.4 suggests, the effects of age, race, and current offense are consistent across states. They indicate that younger, nonwhite, property offenders (compared with drug-related offenders) were most likely to be revoked.

Unlike the arrest model, the effect of time (or unmeasured correlates of time) on the hazard rate varies considerably across states. This is evident from an examination of the p values associated with the time × state interaction terms in Table 13.4. Diagnostic plots of the hazard led to similar conclusions. As a whole, this evidence suggests that the hazard rates for revocation differ considerably in trend and shape.

Prior criminal record was a significant predictor of revocation only in Georgia and South Carolina, where offenders with prior records were more likely to be revoked than offenders without prior records. Only in Louisiana was supervision intensity related to the probability of revocation; offenders in Louisiana who were supervised more intensively were more likely to be revoked.

Comparison group effects, also presented in Table 13.4, provide evidence of several group differences. In Florida, prison parolees were somewhat more likely to be revoked, but the results were not significant. In Georgia, camp completers were more likely to be revoked than offenders in the comparison groups. In Louisiana, camp completers were less likely to be revoked than camp dropouts and parolees, although differences between the camp completers and the probationers were not statistically

significant. In New York camp completers were less likely to be revoked than camp dropouts but camp completers and parolees did not differ from each other. In South Carolina, the analysis revealed that while new camp completers were less likely than probationers to be revoked, the new camp group appeared to fail at about the same level as the parolees. There were no differences among comparison groups in Texas, Oklahoma, and Illinois.

As in our arrest analysis, study results varied considerably from state to state. Of the 21 contrasts across states, 14 did not reveal differences between boot camp and comparison groups. One of the significant contrasts, in South Carolina, involved a comparison of old and new boot camp completers. Two of the remaining contrasts (in Georgia) indicated that camp completers failed at higher rates than comparison groups. The other four contrasts indicated that camp completer groups failed at lower rates than comparison groups.

Competing Events: New Crimes and Technical Violations

In Florida, Georgia, Illinois, Louisiana, New York, and South Carolina revocations could be identified as resulting from either new crimes or technical violations. Our specification of the competing events models in each of the separate states resulted in a log-likelihood of −2018.59 with 136 degrees of freedom. Shown in Table 13.5 is the model that imposed between state constraints on comparison group membership, prior record, supervision intensity, and time effects. The model yielded a log-likelihood value of −2044.11 with 98 degrees of freedom.[3] The difference between these log-likelihoods is not statistically significant ($\chi^2_{38} = 51.03$; $p > .05$). The imposition of additional constraints, however, did result in statistically significant differences.

As Table 13.5 indicates, the existence of a prior criminal record was positively related to the probability of a new crime revocation in Georgia and in South Carolina. In the other states, however, prior criminal record had no impact on new crime revocations. Prior criminal record was unrelated to the probability of revocation for a technical violation across states.

Table 13.4 Revocation Model

Variable	Coefficient	Standard Error	|t| ratio
Main Effects			
Age	−.069	.017	4.06*
Nonwhite	.614	.112	5.48*
Violent Offense	−.288	.149	1.93
Drug-Related Offense	−.484	.123	3.93*
Youthful Offender	−.001	.362	0.00
Missing Offense Information	−1.090	.507	2.15*
Missing Supervision Intensity	.506	.234	2.16*
State-Specific Effects			
Florida Intercept	−5.438	.876	6.21*
Time	.892	.260	3.43*
Time × Time	−.071	.020	3.50*
Prior Record	.129	.358	0.37
Supervision Intensity	−.102	.172	0.58
Prison Parolee Sample	.600	.355	1.69
Boot Camp Dropout Sample	−.081	.450	0.18
Georgia Intercept	−3.502	.545	6.43*
Time	.083	.068	1.21
Time × Time	−.001	.001	1.53
Prior Record	1.410	.255	5.53*
Supervision Intensity	−.114	.141	0.82
Prison Parolee Sample	−.648	.264	2.45*
Probation Sample	−.968	.326	2.97*
Illinois Intercept	−3.252	.744	4.37*
Time	.195	.206	0.94
Time × Time	−.014	.015	0.94
Prior Record	−.181	.319	0.58
Prison Parolee Sample	−.109	.375	0.29
Boot Camp Dropout Sample	−.339	.384	0.88
Louisiana Intercept	−4.886	.604	8.09*
Time	.249	.067	3.70*
Time × Time	−.009	.001	12.90*
Prior Record	.057	.245	0.23
Supervision Intensity	.603	.195	3.09*
Prison Parolee Sample	.680	.338	2.01*
Probation Sample	.514	.392	1.31
Boot Camp Dropout Sample	1.044	.352	2.96*
New York Intercept	−6.745	1.176	5.74*
Time	.843	.277	3.05*
Time × Time	−.044	.018	2.48*
Prior Record	.153	.462	0.33
Prison Parolee Sample	.386	.413	0.94
Boot Camp Dropout Sample	.944	.384	2.46*
Oklahoma Intercept	−4.518	1.000	4.52*
Time	.321	.128	2.52*
Time × Time	−.012	.004	2.97*
Prior Record	−.590	.580	1.02
Prison Parolee Sample	−.021	.403	0.07
Boot Camp Dropout Sample	.024	.547	0.04
South Carolina Intercept	−3.763	.714	5.27*

Table 13.4 (Continued)

Variable	Coefficient	Standard Error	|t| ratio
Time	.289	.189	1.53
Time × Time	−.023	.014	1.61
Prior Record	.754	.339	2.22*
Supervision Intensity	.045	.129	0.35
New Boot Camp v. Old Boot Camp	−1.571	.531	2.96*
Prison Parolee v. Old Boot Camp	−.946	.487	1.94
Probation v. Old Boot Camp	.264	.340	0.78
Prison Parolee v. New Boot Camp	.626	.612	1.02
Probation v. New Boot Camp	1.835	.497	3.69*
Texas Intercept	−6.025	1.157	5.21*
Time	.075	.080	0.94
Time × Time	−.003	.002	1.21
Prior Record	1.294	1.012	1.28
New Boot Camp v. Old Boot Camp	.320	.284	1.13
Probation v. Old Boot Camp	.541	.345	1.57
Probation v. New Boot Camp	.220	.346	0.64
Log-Likelihood (w/61 df)	−2449.39		

*$p < .05$.

Table 13.5 Competing Events Model

Variable	New Crime Revocation			Technical Violation Revocation		
	Coefficient	Std. Error	|t| ratio	Coefficient	Std. Error	|t| ratio
Main Effects						
Age	−.090	.025	3.60*	−.039	.028	1.39
Nonwhite	.848	.170	4.99*	.596	.185	3.22*
Violent Offense	−.753	.239	3.15*	−.015	.242	0.06
Drug-Related Offense	−.297	.163	1.82	−.917	.231	3.97*
Youthful Offender	−.468	.648	0.72	.145	.455	0.32
Missing Offense Information	−1.030	1.022	1.01	.317	.539	0.59
Missing Supervision Intensity	.599	.315	1.90	.345	.372	0.93
State-Specific Effects						
Florida Intercept	−6.233	1.254	4.97*	−6.361	1.269	5.01*
Time	1.121	.375	2.99*	.652	.364	1.79
Time × Time	−.092	.030	3.04*	−.050	.028	1.79
Prior Record	−.030	.475	0.06	.360	.543	0.66
Supervision Intensity	−.309	.291	1.06	.103	.208	0.49
Prison Parolee Sample	.871	.457	1.91	.258	.556	0.46
Boot Camp Dropout Sample	−.110	.619	0.18	−.044	.654	0.07
Georgia Intercept	−3.720	.697	5.34*	−4.443	1.036	4.29*
Time	.130	.076	1.72	−.146	.163	0.90
Time × Time	−.003	.002	1.12	.007	.006	1.14
Prior Record	1.478	.277	5.33*	.853	.687	1.24
Supervision Intensity	−.288	.198	1.45	.204	.184	1.11

(Continued)

Table 13.5 (Continued)

Variable	New Crime Revocation			Technical Violation Revocation		
	Coefficient	Std. Error	|t| ratio	Coefficient	Std. Error	|t| ratio
Prison Parolee Sample	−.493	.285	1.73	−1.682	.847	1.99*
Probation Sample	−1.044	.366	2.85*	−.944	.712	1.33
Illinois Intercept	−6.344	1.393	4.56*	−2.699	.945	2.86*
Time	.639	.334	1.92	−.308	.288	1.07
Time × Time	−.036	.023	1.60	.016	.023	0.70
Prior Record	−.533	.406	1.31	.264	.499	0.53
Prison Parolee Sample	1.318	.655	2.01 *	−1.499	.649	2.31
Boot Camp Dropout						
Sample	1.305	.646	2.02*	−2.037	.768	2.65*
Louisiana Intercept	−5.271	.856	6.16*	−6.541	.933	7.01*
Time	.241	.095	2.54*	.265	.095	2.79*
Time × Time	−.008	.004	2.40*	−.011	.004	2.48*
Prior Record	.003	.328	0.01	.135	.369	0.37
Supervision Intensity	.267	.234	1.15	1.130	.356	3.18*
Prison Parolee Sample	.860	.433	1.99*	.666	.568	1.17
Probation Sample	.513	.507	1.01	.517	.420	0.81
Boot Camp Dropout						
Sample	.864	.495	1.75	1.406	.535	2.63*
New York Intercept	−7.695	1.829	4.21*	−7.952	1.659	4.79*
Time	.693	.388	1.79	.979	.391	2.50*
Time × Time	−.034	.025	1.35	−.053	.026	2.09*
Prior Record	1.064	1.045	1.02	−.281	.535	0.53
Prison Parolee Sample	.452	.579	0.78	.287	.581	0.49
Boot Camp Dropout						
Sample	.684	.564	1.21	1.132	.526	2.15*
South Carolina						
Intercept	−4.629	1.113	4.16*	−4.818	.993	4.85*
Time	.272	.287	0.95	.313	.251	1.25
Time × Time	−.025	.023	1.09	−.023	.019	1.19
Prior Record	1.410	.631	2.24*	.381	.411	0.93
Supervision Intensity	.122	.179	0.68	−.024	.183	0.13
New Boot Camp v. Old						
Boot Camp	−1.822	.828	2.20*	−1.396	.690	2.02*
Prison Parolee v. Old						
Boot Camp	−.865	.705	1.23	−1.053	.674	1.56
Probation v. Old						
Boot Camp	.121	.527	0.23	.333	.442	0.75
Prison Parolee v. New						
Boot Camp	.957	.918	1.04	.344	.824	0.42
Probation v. New						
Boot Camp	1.943	.780	2.49*	1.729	.642	2.69*
Log-Likelihood (w/98 df)	−2044.11					

*p < .05.

The effect of supervision intensity was positive and statistically significant for technical violations in Louisiana, but it was not statistically significant in any of the other analyses. As in the arrest and revocation analyses discussed above, the effects of age, race, and offense type were statistically significant predictors for both failure modes in the competing events model. Younger offenders were more likely than older offenders to fail by new crimes but not technical violations. Nonwhites were more likely than whites to fail by both failure modes. Property offenders were more likely to fail by a new crime compared with violent offenders and to fail by technical violations when compared with those convicted of drug-related offenses.

Group comparisons, also presented in Table 13.5, suggest that there is considerable variability in group differences across the states. In Florida, camp completers were somewhat less likely to fail via a new crime than parolees, but the results were not significant, and camp completers and camp dropouts did not differ from each other. New crime failure rates were higher for camp completers than for probationers in Georgia. Parolees were also somewhat less likely than camp completers to fail by a new crime but the results were not significant. For technical violations, camp completers were more likely than parolees to fail, but there was no difference between camp completers and probationers. In Illinois, the camp completers were less likely than the comparison groups to fail via a new crime but more likely to fail by a technical violation.

Camp completers were less likely to fail by a new crime than parolees in Louisiana, but there was no difference in new crimes between the camp completers and either the probationers or the dropouts. For technical violations in Louisiana, only the difference between the camp completers and the camp dropouts was statistically significant. New York camp completers were less likely to fail by a technical violation than camp dropouts, but camp completers did not differ significantly from parolees. There were no group differences for new crime failures.

Probationers in South Carolina were significantly more likely to fail by both a technical violation and new crime than the new camp completers although all other contrasts between camp completers and comparison groups were statistically nonsignificant. As in the combined revocation analysis noted earlier, there is evidence that the new boot camp completers (those selected by the DOC from prison-bound offenders) tended to behave like parolees, while releasees from the old boot camp program

(selected by probation and parole officials) tended to behave like probationers.

In sum, an examination of differences among groups across states indicates little consistency. Of the 16 comparisons on revocations for new crimes, 6 were statistically significant. In South Carolina the old boot camp sample was more likely to fail than the new sample. In the remaining five tests, one revealed that boot camp completers were more likely to fail in one contrast, while the boot camp samples were less likely to fail in the other four.

Similar results were discovered in the technical revocation analysis. As with new crime revocations there were 16 comparisons. Seven of these comparisons were statistically significant. One of these is a comparison between new and old camp completers in South Carolina. Among the remaining six comparisons, three revealed that the boot camp completers were more likely to fail, while three suggested that they were less likely to fail. As with the arrest and revocation analyses, the results suggest that comparisons from one state cannot be generalized to other states.

MODEL OUTCOMES

The interpretation of regression coefficients in the above models almost inevitably leads one to question the actual group effects on failure probabilities implied by those models. A useful way to approach this problem involves the evaluation of the hazard and the cumulative distribution function for various sets of case characteristics. The cumulative distribution function, $F(t)$, returns the estimated probability of failure through time t (as implied by Equation 2).

The hazard rate $\lambda(t)$, which (as a practical matter) represents the probability of failure in a particular interval given no prior failure, also relies on time as a key argument. It is potentially useful to examine these distributions over time. To facilitate this, we randomly selected three cases from the data set and, using their case attributes, plotted the hazard and cumulative distribution function through time for an arrest (Figure 13.1) and a revocation (Figure 13.2) outcome.

For the arrest outcome (Figure 13.1), our earlier finding of a relatively stable hazard across

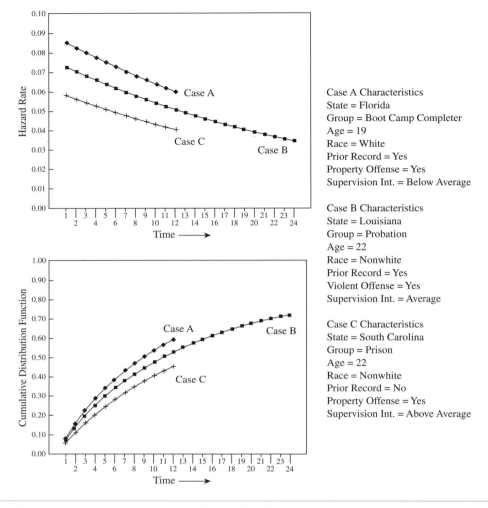

Figure 13.1   Individual-Level Evaluation of Arrest Model

states is evident. The conditional probabilities of failure are highest immediately after beginning community supervision and they decrease significantly thereafter. The revocation graph (Figure 13.2), however, tells a different story. Here, there is considerable variability in the hazard and, consequently, in the cumulative distribution function. The difficulty of placing an equal hazard constraint on the data across states is strongly in evidence here and consistent with our earlier results.

In practice, there is no difficulty in using these kinds of methods to generate estimated cumulative failure probabilities for our comparison groups in each state. To do this, we constrained all predictor variables in each of the regression models to their means. We then

allowed time, state, and group membership to vary. By evaluating the cumulative distribution function from zero to the upper limit of time (see Equation 2), we arrived at estimates of the cumulative failure probabilities for each of the comparison groups within each state at the end of the observation period. The results of this effort are presented in Table 13.6.

The estimated cumulative arrest failure probability for the boot camp completer group in Florida is 47%. That is, 47% of the boot camp completers are estimated to have failed by arrest at the end of one year. Since the contrast between the parolee group and the camp completer group is statistically significant, we should expect to see a somewhat lower cumulative arrest failure probability for the camp completer sample. The

Table 13.6 Estimated Percent Recidivating at End of Observation Period (12 or 24 Months) for Samples in Eight States, from the Analyses Controlling for Sample Differences

State and Group	Arrest %	Any Revocation %	New Crime %	Technical Violation %
		Failure Mode		
Florida (12 Months)				
Boot Camp Completers	46.6	12.2	6.6	6.2
Prison Parolees	63.1*	20.9	14.9	7.9
Boot Camp Dropouts	42.8	11.3	5.9	6.0
Georgia (24 Months)				
Boot Camp Completers		68.7	57.7	15.6
Prison Parolees		46.0*	41.3	3.1*
Probationers		36.2*	26.5*	6.5
Illinois (12 Months)				
Boot Camp Completers'		16.1	3.2	14.7
Prison Parolees		14.5	11.6*	3.5*
Boot Camp Dropouts		11.8	11.5*	—
Louisiana (24 Months)				
Boot Camp Completers	43.9	16.4	9.4	6.1
Prison Parolees	71.8*	29.7*	20.7*	11.5
Probationers	61.2*	25.8	15.2	10.0
Boot Camp Dropouts	62.8*	39.6*	20.7	22.5*
New York (12 Months)				
Boot Camp Completers	50.2	11.9	4.3	8.0
Prison Parolees	60.4	16.9	6.6	10.4
Boot Camp Dropouts	62.9	27.5*	8.1	22.4*
Oklahoma (24 Months)				
Boot Camp Completers		20.6		
Prison Parolees		20.1		
Boot Camp Dropouts		21.0		
South Carolina (12 Months)				
Old Boot Camp Completers	62.8**	20.8**	8.2**	12.5**
New Boot Camp Completers	40.6*	4.8*	1.4*	3.3*
Prison Parolees	45.4*	8.7	3.5	4.6
Probationers	49.4	26.1**	9.2**	16.9**
Texas (24 Months)				
Old Boot Camp Completers	46.7	5.4		
New Boot Camp Completers	44.1	7.3		
Probationers	45.0	9.1		

*Significantly different from old completers at $p < .05$.
**Significantly different from new completers at $p < .05$.

model's estimate for the prison releasee group's failure probability after 12 months is 63%. In each case, the failure probabilities lead to conclusions that follow directly from the model estimates discussed earlier.

The most striking pattern in Table 13.6 is the absence of a clear pattern. Although there is

some suggestion that camp completer samples have slightly lower failure rates, these differences are too weak and erratic to be of much consequence. For example, there appears to be strong evidence for a positive boot camp effect in Louisiana. But this evidence is immediately contradicted by strong evidence for a negative

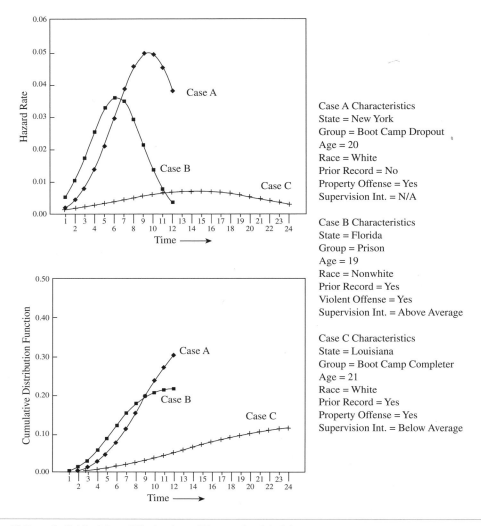

Case A Characteristics
State = New York
Group = Boot Camp Dropout
Age = 20
Race = White
Prior Record = No
Property Offense = Yes
Supervision Int. = N/A

Case B Characteristics
State = Florida
Group = Prison
Age = 19
Race = Nonwhite
Prior Record = Yes
Violent Offense = Yes
Supervision Int. = Above Average

Case C Characteristics
State = Louisiana
Group = Boot Camp Completer
Age = 21
Race = White
Prior Record = Yes
Property Offense = Yes
Supervision Int. = Below Average

Figure 13.2 Individual-Level Evaluation of Revocation Model

boot camp effect in Georgia. In other states, while the boot camp completers fail at lower rates than some groups, there is almost always at least one comparison group that does about as well as the camp completer group. Nevertheless, the table suggests that camp completers do as well as or better than their counterparts from other programs except in Georgia and in some contrasts in South Carolina. In Georgia there was a fairly consistent pattern showing lower recidivism for parolees and probationers than for camp program completers. In South Carolina, the new camp completers failed at lower rates than the old camp completers. Across most failure

modes, the South Carolina new camp completers also failed at a lower rate than the probationers.

DISCUSSION

All of the programs studied had military drill and ceremony, hard labor, physical training, and strict rules and discipline. These constitute the core components of boot camp prisons. If these components effectively reduce the recidivism of offenders, we would likely have observed a consistent pattern across states. That pattern would be one of lower recidivism rates for boot camp graduates in contrast to those of the comparison groups. This did not occur. As a result, we conclude that these components in and of themselves do not reduce the recidivism of participating offenders. We are then left to examine the results within each individual state.

After examining the characteristics of the programs, the samples, and the results of our analyses, we drew several conclusions. First, there was no evidence that the boot camps had an impact on those who completed the programs in four of the states. For two of these programs, Texas and Oklahoma, this conclusion is based on the fact that we found no significant differences in the recidivism analyses.

The other two programs that we believe do not show evidence of any impact on recidivism are those in Florida and South Carolina. In both of these states, we speculate that between-group differences can largely be explained by sample selection effects. We suspect that the offenders selected for the boot camp program in Florida differed in some unmeasured way from those sent to traditional prisons prior to selection for the program. We drew this conclusion because, although there were differences in recidivism between the completers and the parolees, there were no differences between the boot camp completers and the dropouts. Upon dismissal, those who dropped out of the boot camp program were treated like prison parolees. That is, they spent the remaining portion of their sentence in a traditional prison. Moreover, like the parolees they received more intensive supervision than the boot camp completers after release from prison. If the boot camp prison had the expected effect on participants, it would be reasonable to hypothesize that recidivism patterns between prison parolees and boot camp dropouts would be more similar than recidivism patterns between boot camp completers and boot camp dropouts. Although the boot camp completers had lower recidivism rates than the parolees, the recidivism patterns of boot camp completers did not differ from those of the boot camp dropouts.

We also speculate that the results from South Carolina reveal a possible sample selection effect. In the earlier program, boot camp offenders were selected by the probation department, and they would be expected to behave more like

probationers. Conversely, the new boot camp completers, selected from offenders sentenced to prison, might be expected to act like the parolees. Indeed, in most of the analyses these expectations were consistent with the evidence. In general the old boot camp completer sample selected by the probation department behaved like the probationers, and the new boot camp sample of prison-bound offenders acted like the parolees. If the boot camp prison had an impact on recidivism, we would have expected to see a consistent difference between these groups (old boot camp versus probationers and new boot camp versus prisoners).

There were some significant differences in recidivism between samples in the remaining four states. We believe these differences are important to examine in detail. First, Georgia is noteworthy because it is the only state where boot camp offenders did worse than the comparison sample. Our process evaluation (MacKenzie & Souryal, 1993a) reveals that the Georgia program stands out as the one program that has little treatment in the daily schedule of activities. In addition, offenders in this program are sentenced to the program by the court, few offenders drop out or terminate early, the daily schedule involves only a little over eight hours of activity (much less than other programs), and most are released to traditional probation. This research design does not enable us to separate the effects of these aspects of the program to identify what specific characteristics may have this negative impact on offenders. We suspect that the emphasis on the military basic training without any therapeutic emphasis is a key contributor to this negative impact, and future research should carefully address this issue.

Our analyses indicated that the boot camp offenders in the remaining three programs, Illinois, Louisiana, and New York, had lower estimated recidivism rates on some but not all measures of recidivism. Specifically, the Illinois boot camp completers had fewer new crime revocations; conversely, they had significantly more technical revocations. The boot camp program was designed to give the graduates more intensive supervision than the parolees and the dropouts. However, supervision intensity information was not available in the Illinois data and, therefore, we could not control for this in the analyses. Possibly, the boot camp completers were caught for technical violations and revoked before they became involved in new criminal activities.

The recidivism analysis revealed that the Louisiana boot camp completers had fewer arrests than any of the comparison groups, fewer revocations than the parolees and dropouts, fewer new crimes than parolees, and fewer technical revocations than the dropouts. New York completers had fewer revocations and technical revocations than the dropouts. There were no significant differences between them and the parolees.

There are several possible explanations for these results. First, our examination of these three programs clearly revealed that they differed from the other programs in several key characteristics. Primarily, in the daily schedule of activities the Illinois, Louisiana, and New York programs devoted a comparatively large amount of time (three or more hours) to therapeutic activities. The other programs had less than two hours of required therapeutic activity or treatment was voluntary. In addition, offenders completing these three programs were intensively supervised in the community upon release from the boot camp. Other similarities among these three programs were that participants were prison bound, a fairly high percentage were dismissed before completing the program, participation was voluntary, and the programs were longer (120-180 days) than many other programs. Although some of the other programs have some of these characteristics, they do not have all the similarities that exist among Illinois, Louisiana, and New York.

This research does not permit us to investigate separately the specific components of the programs that are responsible for decreased recidivism. We speculate that some combination of the characteristics of these programs may be responsible. Even this conclusion is somewhat difficult to sustain because in Illinois and New York we were not able to control for offenders' community supervision intensity. We know from program records that offenders who completed boot camp programs in these states were intensively supervised in the community. Finally, in New York, the only differences in estimated recidivism rates were between the

boot camp completers and the boot camp dropouts. One possible explanation for this result is that the boot camp program acted as a selection mechanism by identifying offenders who were at lower risk for recidivism in the first place. That is, the boot camp completers may be at lower risk than the dropouts for some unmeasured reason at the start of the program, and the boot camp program merely separates those who are low risks (the completers) from those who are higher risks (the dropouts).

More important is the issue of whether programs that incorporate the characteristics of the Illinois, Louisiana, and New York boot camps but without the military atmosphere would do as well or better than these programs in reducing recidivism. Past research examining correctional programs and drug treatment suggests that intensive treatment and quality aftercare are components of interventions that effectively lower recidivism (Andrews & Bonta, 1994; Andrews et al., 1990; Anglin & Hser, 1990). On the other hand, programs designed to promote fear and [to] shock offenders have not been found to be particularly successful (Gendreau & Ross, 1987; Vito, 1984). Thus, it is hardly surprising in our research that offenders were positively affected by their experience in the boot camps that had components characteristic of effective treatment programs but that the recidivism of boot camp releasees was actually higher than for the comparison groups in the camp that emphasized physical activity and military department without any therapeutic programming. Certainly, there is little past research to suggest that the physical exercise, military atmosphere, and hard labor aspects of these programs would successfully change the behavior of the offenders if, at the same time, the criminogenic needs of the offenders are not being addressed. The question that needs to be addressed in future research is whether programs similar to the boot camps but without the basic training model would reduce recidivism more or less than the boot camps. Quite possibly, other voluntary programs that include intensive therapy and enhanced aftercare would be at least as successful. The question then becomes: Does the military atmosphere add anything above and beyond a short-term, quality prison treatment program?

NOTES

1.   These descriptions refer to the programs as they were at the time of data collection (1989 to 1991). Many aspects of these programs have changed since that time. Updated information can be obtained from state correctional officials.

2.   To conduct these tests in South Carolina and Texas (where there was more than one shock completer sample), we manually calculated effects and significance tests. We begin by letting Δb be the difference between coefficients for the two groups being compared. Next, we calculate the variance of Δb by taking var(b1) + var(b1) − 2*cov(b1,b2). The square root of the variance is the standard error (se) of Äb. The significance test statistic is Δb /se (Δb) and is distributed as a random normal variable z (when N is large).

3.   Since there were no dropouts in Illinois who failed via a technical violation, we randomly assigned two Illinois dropout cases to fail by a technical violation at the 12th month. The results of this modified Illinois model do not change any of our conclusions regarding other effects.

REFERENCES

Allison, P. D. (1982). Discrete-time methods for the analysis of event histories. *Sociological Methodology, 12,* 61-98.

Allison, P. D. (1984). *Event History Analysis.* Beverly Hills, CA: Sage.

Andrews, D. A., & Bonta, J. (1994). *The Psychology of Criminal Conduct.* Cincinnati: Anderson.

Andrews, D. A., Zinger, I., Hoge, R. D., Bonta, J., Gendreau, P., & Cullen, F. T. (1990). Does correctional treatment work? A clinically relevant and psychologically informed meta-analysis. *Criminology, 28,* 369-404.

Anglin, M. D., & Hser, Y. (1990). Treatment of drug abuse. In M. Tonry & J. Q. Wilson (Eds.), *Drugs and Crime. Crime and Justice, Vol. 13.* Chicago: University of Chicago Press.

Chung, C., Schmidt, P., & Witte, A. D. (1991). Survival analysis: A survey. *Journal of Quantitative Criminology, 7,* 59-98.

Clark, C. L., Aziz, D. W., & MacKenzie, D. L. (1994). *Shock Incarceration in New York: Focus on Treatment.* Washington, D.C.: National Institute of Justice.

Cronin, R. C. (1994). *Boot Camps for Adult and Juvenile Offenders: Overview and Update.* Washington, D.C.: National Institute of Justice.

Cullen, F. T., Wright, J. P., & Applegate, B. K. (1993). *Control in the community: The limits of reform?* Paper presented at the International Association of Residential and Community Alternatives, Philadelphia.

Florida Department of Corrections. (1990). *Florida Executive Summary: Boot Camp: A 25 Month Review.* Tallahassee: Florida Department of Corrections.

Flowers, G. T., Carr, T. S., & Ruback, R. B. (1991). *Special Alternative Incarceration Evaluation.* Atlanta: Georgia Department of Corrections.

Friedrich, R. J. (1982). In defense of multiplicative terms in multiple regression equations. *American Journal of Political Science, 26,* 797-833.

General Accounting Office. (1993). *Short-Term Prison Costs Reduced But Long-Term Impact Uncertain.* Washington, D.C.: U.S. Government Printing Office.

Gendreau, P., & Ross, R. R. (1987). Revivication of rehabilitation: Evidence from the 1980s. *Justice Quarterly, 4,* 349-408.

Hepburn, J. R., & Albonetti, C. A. (1994). Recidivism among drug offenders: A survival analysis of the effects of offender characteristics, type of offense, and two types of intervention. *Journal of Quantitative Criminology, 10,* 159-179.

Kalbfleisch, J. D., & Prentice, R. L. (1980). *The Statistical Analysis of Failure Time Data.* New York: John Wiley & Sons.

Lattimore, P. K., Witte, A. D., & Baker, J. R. (1990). Experimental assessment of the effect of vocational training on youthful property-offenders. *Evaluation Review, 14,* 115-133.

MacKenzie, D. L. (1991). The parole performance of offenders released from shock incarceration (boot camp prisons): A survival time analysis. *Journal of Quantitative Criminology, 7,* 213-236.

MacKenzie, D. L. (1994). Results of a multisite study of boot-camp prisons. *Federal Probation, 58,* 60-67.

MacKenzie, D. L., & Parent, D. (1992). Boot camp prisons for young offenders. In J. M. Byrne, A. J. Lurigio, & J. Petersilia (Eds.), *Smart Sentencing: The Emergence of Intermediate Sanctions.* Newbury Park, CA: Sage.

MacKenzie, D. L., & Shaw, J. W. (1993). The impact of shock incarceration on technical violations and new criminal activities. *Justice Quarterly, 10,* 463-487.

MacKenzie, D. L., & Souryal, C. C. (1993a). *Multi-Site Study of Shock Incarceration: Process Evaluation. Final Report to the National Institute of Justice.* University of Maryland, College Park.

MacKenzie, D. L., & Souryal, C. C. (1993b). *Shock Incarceration and Recidivism: A Multi-Site*

Evaluation. Final Report to the National Institute of Justice. University of Maryland, College Park.

Maddala, G. S. (1983). *Limited-Dependent and Qualitative Variables in Econometrics.* New York: Cambridge University Press.

Maguire, K. E., Flanagan, T. J., & Thornberry, T. P. (1988). Prison labor and recidivism. *Journal of Quantitative Criminology, 4,* 3-18.

Maltz, M. D. (1984). *Recidivism.* New York: Academic Press.

Meachum, L. M. (1990). *Boot camp prisons: Pros and cons.* Paper presented at Annual Meeting of American Society of Criminology, Baltimore, MD.

Morash, M., & Rucker, L. (1990). A critical look at the ideal of boot camp as correctional reform. *Crime and Delinquency, 36,* 204-222.

New York State Department of Correctional Services. (1992). *Fourth Annual Report to the Legislature: Shock Incarceration-Shock Parole Supervision.* Albany: New York State Department of Correctional Services.

Petersen, T. (1991). The statistical analysis of event histories. *Sociological Methods and Research, 19,* 270-323.

Petersilia, J., & Turner, S. (1993). Intensive probation and parole. In M. Tonry & N. Morris (Eds.), *Crime and Justice: A Review of Research. Vol. 19.* Chicago: University of Chicago Press.

Rhodes, W. (1986). A survival model with dependent competing events and right-hand censoring: Probation and parole as an illustration. *Journal of Quantitative Criminology, 2,* 113-137.

SAS Institute. (1990). *SAS/STAT User's Guide. Vol. 1.* Cary, NC: SAS Institute, Inc.

Schmidt, P., & Witte, A. D. (1988). *Predicting Recidivism Using Survival Models.* New York: Springer-Verlag.

Schmidt, P., & Witte, A. D. (1989). Predicting criminal recidivism using "split-population" survival time models. *Journal of Econometrics, 40,* 141-159.

State of Texas. (1990). *Special Alternative Incarceration Program Enhanced Substance Abuse Component.* Austin: Texas Criminal Justice Policy Council.

Visher, C. A., & Linster, R. L. (1990). A survival model of pretrial failure. *Journal of Quantitative Criminology, 6,* 153-184.

Vito, G. F. (1984). Developments in shock probation: A review of research findings and policy implications. *Federal Probation, 48,* 21-34.

Wheeler, G. R., & Hissong, R. V. (1988). A survival time analysis of criminal sanctions for misdemeanor offenders. *Evaluation Review, 12,* 510-527.

14

Effects of Correctional Boot Camps on Offending

Doris Layton MacKenzie

David B. Wilson

Suzanne B. Kider

Correctional boot camps, also called shock or intensive incarceration, are short-term incarceration programs modeled after basic training in the military (MacKenzie & Parent, 1992; MacKenzie & Hebert, 1996). Participants are required to follow a rigorous daily schedule of activities including drill and ceremony and physical training. They rise early each morning and are kept busy most of the day. Correctional officers are given military titles, and participants are required to use these titles when addressing staff. Staff and inmates are required to wear uniforms. Punishment for misbehavior is immediate and swift and usually involves some type of physical activity like push-ups. Frequently, groups of inmates enter the boot camps as squads or platoons. There is often an elaborate intake ceremony where inmates are immediately required to follow the rules, respond to staff in an appropriate way, stand at attention, and have their heads shaved. Many programs have graduation ceremonies for those who successfully complete the program. Frequently, family members and others from the outside public attend the graduation ceremonies.

While there are some basic similarities among the correctional boot camps, the programs differ greatly in other aspects (MacKenzie & Hebert, 1996). For example, the camps differ in the amount of focus given to the physical training and hard labor aspects of the program versus therapeutic programming such as academic education, drug treatment, or cognitive skills. Some camps emphasize the therapeutic programming, while others focus on discipline and rigorous physical training. Programs also differ in whether they are designed to be alternatives to probation or to prison. In some jurisdictions judges sentence participants to the camps; in others, participants are identified by department of corrections personnel from those serving terms of incarceration. Another difference among programs is whether the residential

Reprinted from MacKenzie, D. L., Wilson, D. B., & Kider, S. B. (2001). *Annals of the American Academy of Political and Social Sciences.* Reprinted by permission from the American Academy of Political and Social Sciences.

phase is followed by an aftercare or reentry program designed to assist the participants with adjustment to the community.

Correctional boot camps were first opened in adult correctional systems in the United States in 1983, in Georgia and Oklahoma. Since that time they have rapidly grown, first within adult correctional systems and later in juvenile corrections. Today, correctional boot camps exist in federal, state, and local juvenile and adult jurisdictions in the United States. Juvenile boot camps developed later than the adult camps. However, during the 1990s camps for juveniles rapidly developed, and by 2000, 70 juvenile camps had been opened in the United States (see the Koch Crime Institute Web site at www.kci.org). The camps for adjudicated juveniles differ somewhat from the adult camps. In juvenile camps, less emphasis is placed on hard labor, and as required by law, the camps offer academic education. Juvenile camps are also apt to provide more therapeutic components. However, in many other aspects the juvenile camps are similar to adult camps with rigorous intake procedures, shaved heads, drill and ceremony, physical training, immediate physical punishment for misbehavior (for example, push-ups), and graduation ceremonies.

Despite their continuing popularity, correctional boot camps remain controversial. Primarily, the debate involves questions about the impact of the camps on the adjustment and behavior of participants while they are in residence and after they are released. According to advocates, the atmosphere of the camps is conducive to positive growth and change (Clark & Aziz, 1996; MacKenzie & Hebert, 1996). In contrast, critics argue that many of the components of the camps are in direct opposition to the type of relationships and supportive conditions that are needed for quality therapeutic programming (Andrews et al., 1990; Gendreau, Little, & Goggin, 1996; Morash & Rucker, 1990; Sechrest, 1989).

Research examining the effectiveness of the correctional boot camps has focused on various potential impacts of the camps. Some have examined whether the camps change participants' attitudes, attachments to the community, or impulsivity (MacKenzie et al., 2001; MacKenzie & Shaw, 1990; MacKenzie & Souryal, 1995). Others have examined the impact of the camps on the need for prison bed space (MacKenzie & Piquero, 1994; MacKenzie & Parent, 1991). However, the research receiving the most interest appears to be that examining the impact of the camps on recidivism (MacKenzie, 1997).

According to a survey of state correctional officials, the major goals of the camps are to deter future crime, protect the public, rehabilitate the offenders, reduce costs, and lower recidivism (Gowdy, 1996). Thus, except for reducing the costs of corrections, all of the major goals are associated in some way with reducing the criminal activities of participants. Sufficient time has now elapsed since the beginning of these camps so that a body of research examining the impact of the camps on the recidivism of participants has been produced. This systematic review is designed to examine this research in order to draw conclusions regarding what is currently known about the effectiveness of correctional boot camps in reducing recidivism.

METHOD

Search Strategy and Eligibility Criteria

The scope of this review was experimental and quasi-experimental evaluations that examined boot camp and boot camp-like programs for juvenile and adult offenders. To be eligible to be included in the review a study had to (1) examine a residential program that incorporated a militaristic environment (the programs were called by various names such as boot camp, shock incarceration, and intensive incarceration); (2) include a comparison group that received either community supervision (for example, probation) or incarceration in an alternative facility such as jail, prison, or juvenile residential facility; (3) include participants who were convicted or adjudicated; and (4) report a postprogram measure of criminal behavior, such as arrest or conviction (the measure may be based on official records or self-report and may be reported on a dichotomous or continuous scale). The comparison group in a quasi-experimental design had to be selected to be reasonably similar to the experimental group; thus any study that compared the experimental group to a general national or state sample was eliminated from the study. Furthermore the study eligibility criteria eliminated quasi-experimental designs that only compared program dropouts to program completers.

The strategies used to identify all studies, published or otherwise, that met these criteria included a keyword search of computerized databases and contact with authors working in this area. The following databases were searched: Criminal Justice Periodical Index, Dissertation Abstracts Online, Government Publications Office Monthly Catalog, Government Publications Reference File, National Criminal Justice Reference Service, PsycINFO, Sociological Abstracts, Social SciSearch, and U.S. Political Science Documents. The keywords used were "boot camp(s)," "intensive incarceration," and "shock incarceration." Several of the searched databases indexed unpublished works. This identified 771 unique documents. Review of the titles and abstracts suggested that 152 might meet the above criteria or were relevant review articles that might contain additional references. Of these, 152,144 were obtained and evaluated for eligibility, resulting in 29 eligible studies reported in 37 documents (see references). The majority of these studies were state or federal technical reports ($n = 22$). Only 9 of these studies were published in peer-reviewed journals. One study was conducted in Canada, and another study was conducted in England. The remaining studies evaluated boot camp programs in the United States.

Data Collection and Analysis

The coding protocol developed for the synthesis allowed for the coding of multiple samples from a single study (distinct evaluations reported in a single report, different cohorts or data reported for males and females separately). This resulted in 44 distinct samples, and these samples represent the primary unit of analysis for this systematic review. The coding protocol also allowed for the coding of multiple indicators of criminal involvement, such as arrest, conviction, and technical violation, measured at multiple time points following release from the program. A copy of the coding protocol can be obtained from the authors. All studies were double coded, and any discrepancies in the coding between the two coders were resolved.

The protocol captured aspects of the research design, including methodological quality, characteristics of the boot camp program, comparison group condition, study participants, outcome measures, and direction and magnitude of the observed effects. The primary effect of interest was recidivism or a return to criminal activity on the part of the offender after leaving the program. Recidivism data were reported dichotomously across all studies and were based on official records, generally reflected as arrest, reconviction, or reinstitutionalization. As such, the natural index of effectiveness is the odds ratio (see Fleiss, 1994) and was the index of effect (see below). The mean odds ratio and homogeneity of effects across studies was computed using the inverse variance weight method. A random-effects model was assumed, and the random-effects variance component was estimated using the methods outlined by Dersimonian and Laird (1986) and Raudenbush (1994). The computations were performed using macros written by the second author that are available for use with SAS, SPSS, and Stata (Lipsey & Wilson, 2001).

A total of 155 recidivism effect sizes were extracted from the studies. Recidivism effects that reflected technical violations only were excluded from the analyses reported below, reducing the set of effect sizes to 142. The recidivism effects were examined in two ways. First, multiple recidivism effects from a single study and sample were averaged prior to analysis, producing a set of 44 recidivism effect sizes for the analysis. The second set of analyses used arrest as the measure of recidivism if it was available; if not, reconvictions were used as the measure, and if neither of these was available, reinstitutionalizations were used. The results from the two methods of measuring recidivism were compared and did not yield any substantive differences in the results. Therefore, results based on the second method of measuring recidivism are reported in the following analyses.

RESULTS

The distribution of recidivism effects across the 44 boot camp versus comparison group samples is shown in Figure 14.1. Each row of this forest plot represents a distinct sample, identified by the label in the left column. The recidivism odds ratio (effect size) is represented by the small diamonds, and the line spans the 95 percent confidence interval around the odds ratio. The samples are sorted with the largest positive effect at the top and the smallest negative effect (odds ratios between 1 and 0) on the bottom. At the very bottom of the plot is the overall random-effects mean odds ratio.

The effects across these studies ranged from large reductions to large increases in the risk of recidivating for the boot camp participants relative to the comparison groups. The overall mean odds ratio was 1.02 (95 percent confidence interval of 0.90 to 1.17), indicating an almost equal odds of recidivating between the boot camp and comparison groups, on average. Thus there appears to be no relationship between program participation (boot camp or comparison) and recidivism. The equivalent recidivism rates

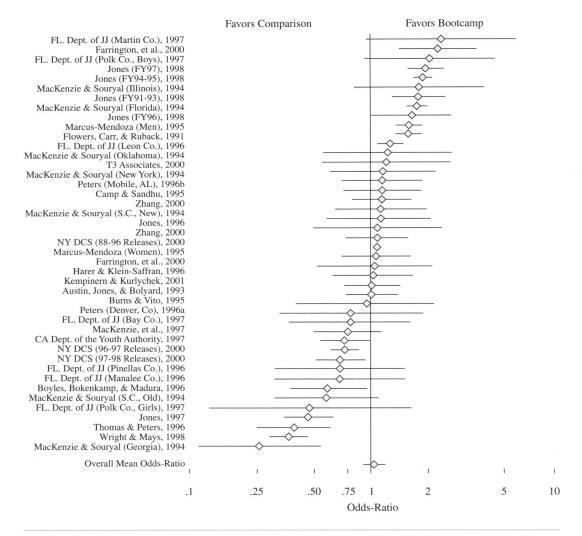

Figure 14.1   A Forest Plot Showing the Recidivism Odds Ratios and 95 Percent Confidence Interval for Each Study and Sample and the Overall Mean Odds Ratio

Table 14.1 Cross-Tabulation of Qualitative Methodological Quality Score and Other Method Descriptors (*N* = 44)

Method Variable	Qualitative Methodological Quality Scale		
	4 (n = 19)	*3 (n = 17)*	*2 (n = 8)*
Randomly assigned participants to conditions			
Yes	4 (21)	1 (6)	0 (0)
No	15 (79)	16 (94)	8 (100)
Used group level matching**			
Yes	14 (74)	5 (29)	1 (13)
No	5 (26)	12 (71)	7 (87)
Prospective research design**			
Yes	17 (89)	9 (53)	6 (75)
No	2 (11)	8 (47)	2 (25)
Used statistical controls in analyses**			
Yes	13 (68)	3 (18)	1 (13)
No	6 (32)	14 (82)	7 (87)
Boot camp dropouts in analysis**			
Yes	9 (47)	9 (53)	0 (0)
No	10 (53)	8 (47)	8 (100)
Overall attrition apparent			
Yes	3 (16)	2 (12)	1 (12)
No	16 (84)	15 (88)	7 (88)
Differential attrition apparent			
Yes	3 (16)	3 (18)	2 (25)
No	16 (84)	14 (82)	6 (75)

Note: Percentages are in parentheses.
**$p < .05$, based on a chi-square test.

for the average boot camp and comparison group, given this overall odds ratio, would be 49.4 percent for the boot camp and 50 percent for the comparison condition. This is a small difference by most any standard. Thus, overall, the evidence suggests that boot camps do not reduce the risk of recidivism relative to other existing criminal justice system forms of punishment and rehabilitation. From the forest plot, it is also evident that 9 studies observed a statistically significant positive benefit of boot camps, whereas 8 studies observed a statistically significant positive benefit of the comparison condition. The remaining 27 studies found no significant differences between the boot camp samples and the comparisons.

The distribution of odds ratios was highly heterogeneous, $Q = 464.6$, $df = 43$, $p < .0001$, suggesting the presence of moderators of the effects, either methodological or substantive,

such as the nature of the boot camp program and comparison conditions and the types of offenders served. Possible moderating effects are explored below.

Methodological Characteristics of the Studies

Any conclusion regarding the effectiveness (or ineffectiveness, as the data suggest) of boot camps relative to more traditional correctional approaches in reducing the risk of recidivism is valid only if the methodological quality of this collection of studies is sufficiently high. Table 14.1 displays the frequency of studies with various methodological characteristics by our qualitative methodological rating scale. This scale was developed by Sherman and colleagues (1997) and has five levels of methodological rigor. The lowest level of methodological quality was excluded from this synthesis and reflects studies without a comparison group. The highest level of methodological rigor (level 5) represents randomized designs that are not compromised through attrition or other common problems in carrying out a randomized evaluation study.

As can be seen in Table 14.1, none of the five randomized evaluations included in this synthesis were granted a method quality score of 5. This was generally because the studies had high attrition or excluded program dropouts from the recidivism analysis, creating a potential threat from selection bias. Thus there were no evaluations of the effectiveness of boot camps that were free from methodological blemishes. That said, however, many of the studies (19 of 44, or 43 percent) were judged to be methodologically

solid (method score of 4). These studies were generally the higher-quality quasi-experimental designs that either carefully selected the comparison group so as to maximize similarity with the boot camp group (for example, selecting boot camp eligible offenders and matching the groups on demographic characteristics) or used statistical controls in the analysis of recidivism effects. Only 8 of the 44 evaluations (18 percent) were judged to be of poor methodological quality.

To assess the robustness of the general finding of no effect, a separate mean odds ratio was computed for each category of the different methodological variables (see Table 14.2). The mean effect size was slightly lower for the studies judged to be of overall higher methodological

Table 14.2 Mean Odds Ratio and 95 Percent Confidence Interval by Method Variables ($N = 44$)

Method Variable	Mean Odds Ratio	95 Percent Confidence Interval		k^a
		Lower	Upper	
Qualitative methodological quality score				
Random assignment, not degraded				0
High-quality quasi-experiment	0.92	0.73	1.15	19
Standard quasi-experiment	1.07	0.85	1.34	17
Poor-quality quasi-experiment	1.15	0.84	1.59	8
Randomly assigned participants to conditions				
Yes	0.75	0.48	1.17	5
No	1.06	0.91	1.24	39
Used group-level matching				
Yes	1.11	0.88	1.40	20
No	0.97	0.80	1.17	24
Prospective research design**				
Yes	1.13	0.95	1.34	32
No	0.83	0.65	1.06	12
Used statistical controls in analyses**				
Yes	0.85	0.68	1.07	17
No	1.14	0.96	1.37	27
Boot camp dropouts in analysis				
Yes	1.03	0.82	1.28	18
No	1.02	0.83	1.24	26
No overall attrition apparent				
Yes	1.06	0.91	1.24	39
No	0.72	0.46	1.14	5
No differential attrition apparent				
Yes	1.03	0.87	1.21	36
No	0.96	0.67	1.41	8

$^a k$ = number of samples included in analysis.
**$p < .05$.

Table 14.3   Mean Odds Ratio And 95 Percent Confidence Interval By Offender Characteristics (*N* = 44)

Offender Characteristic	Mean Odds Ratio	95 Percent Confidence Interval		k^a
		Lower	*Upper*	
Age group of offender				
Juvenile	0.88	0.68	1.14	16
Adult	1.09	0.92	1.30	28
Offender type				
Juveniles				
Nonviolent/nonperson crimes	0.92	0.61	1.38	4
Mixed (violent and nonviolent)	0.85	0.65	1.11	12
Adults				
Nonviolent/nonperson crimes	1.17	0.92	1.50	13
Mixed (violent and nonviolent)	1.01	0.79	1.31	15

$^a k$ = number of samples included in analysis.

quality, although the trend was statistically nonsignificant. Studies that used a prospective research design had observed larger positive effects (although not significantly different from a null odds ratio of 1) than did retrospective designs. That is, while the mean odds ratio of prospective and retrospective designs are significantly different from each other, neither design produces an odds ratio that suggests that the experimental and control samples are significantly different from each other (for example, confidence interval includes 1). In contrast to studies that did not use statistical controls in the analysis of recidivism outcomes, studies that used controls observed smaller effects that were negative in direction. Once again, neither category differed significantly from the null hypothesis. All other methodological variables were unrelated to the observed odds ratios.

Offender Characteristics Across Studies

There was generally little information regarding the characteristics of the offenders in the studies. For 11 of the 44 samples, the authors did not indicate the gender, although it is reasonable to assume that in these cases the samples were all male. Only 3 of the 44 samples were all female, and the mean odds ratio for these samples was, 1.06 and statistically nonsignificant. This mean odds ratio is roughly the same as that for the overall sample. Four samples were mixed gender, although they were

predominantly male (equal to or greater than 80 percent). Thus there are insufficient data to adequately explore whether boot camps are differentially effective for males and females, as some theorists have hypothesized (Morash & Rucker, 1990).

All samples were successfully classified as either juvenile or adult. The adult samples were typically young adults and in some cases included at least a small percentage of juveniles who were adjudicated as adults. As shown in Table 14.3, the mean odds ratio for the studies evaluating the effectiveness of juvenile boot camps was lower than that of the studies evaluating adult (often young adult) boot camps, although this difference was not statistically significant. This difference may reflect a difference in the typical comparison group for juveniles relative to adults. Traditional juvenile detention facilities are qualitatively different from adult prison or adult probation, the common comparison groups for the studies of adult boot camps. Juvenile detention facilities are more likely, although not guaranteed, to have a greater emphasis on rehabilitation than their adult counterparts. Unfortunately, the availability of rehabilitative treatment within the comparison facilities was not reported by the primary studies.

The racial/ethnic makeup of the offender populations and the offender risk level were often unreported, with no information available for 9 of the 44 samples (20 percent). For an additional 8 samples, only the percentage of

Table 14.4   Mean Odds Ratio and 95 Percent Confidence Interval by Program Characteristics
(Juveniles $n = 16$, Adults $n = 28$)

Program Characteristic	Mean Odds Ratio	95 Percent Confidence Interval		k^a
		Lower	Upper	
Aftercare treatment component				
Juveniles				
Yes	0.88	0.70	1.12	14
No	0.79	0.44	1.43	2
Adults***				
Yes	1.46***	1.14	1.87	11
No	0.89	0.72	1.10	17
Academic education				
Juveniles				
Yes	0.88	0.68	1.14	16
No				0
Adults				
Yes	1.13	0.93	1.38	24
No	0.86	0.51	1.43	4
Vocational education				
Juveniles				
Yes	0.98	0.62	1.55	3
No	0.84	0.66	1.08	13
Adults*				
Yes	0.82	0.56	1.20	6
No	1.17*	0.97	1.43	22

$*p \le .10$; $***p \le .01$.
^{a}k = number of samples included in analysis.

African Americans was reported. Thus roughly half of the samples had complete racial/ethnic makeup information. In general, African Americans were the predominant racial group, representing roughly 52 percent of the samples reporting this information. Caucasians represented 23 percent of the 24 samples, and Hispanics represented roughly 9 percent of the 21 samples reporting these data. The data did not lend themselves to an analysis of the relationship between racial/ethnic makeup of the samples and the observed odds ratios.

Programmatic Differences Across Studies

Boot camps vary in the emphasis placed on rehabilitative treatment relative to physical exercise and military drill and ceremony. It has been speculated that the greater the emphasis on treatments, such as drug abuse counseling, vocational education, and aftercare transition

assistance, the greater the likelihood that boot camps will have positive benefits relative to alternative correctional approaches, such as prison and probation. To assess this issue, we coded whether the evaluation report described the boot camp program as providing various rehabilitative programs listed in Table 14.4. Mean odd ratios were computed separately for juvenile and adult programs.

The only program characteristic that showed a strong relationship to the effectiveness of the boot camp programs was the presence of an aftercare treatment component for the adult programs. The 11 odds ratios for boot camps with an aftercare component versus comparison group contrasts had a mean of 1.46 with a 95 percent confidence interval that did not include 1, indicating a statistically significant positive effect. This evidence suggests that aftercare may be important in reducing the risk of recidivism, at least for adult samples.

Program Characteristic	Mean Odds Ratio	95 Percent Confidence Interval		k^a
		Lower	*Upper*	
Drug treatment				
Juveniles				
Yes	0.90	0.70	1.15	12
No	0.78	0.49	1.24	4
Adults				
Yes	1.08	0.88	1.33	22
No	1.12	0.73	1.72	6
Counseling (group and individual)				
Juveniles				
Yes	0.91	0.70	1.17	10
No	0.79	0.52	1.18	6
Adults				
Yes	1.17	0.95	1.44	21
No	0.85	0.58	1.26	7
Manual labor				
Juveniles				
Yes	1.03	0.73	1.44	7
No*	0.79	0.61	1.02	9
Adults				
Yes	1.07	0.88	1.31	24
No	1.22	0.73	2.04	4

[a]k = number of samples included in analysis.
*$p \le .10$.
***$p \le .01$.

A counterintuitive finding is the negative relationship between vocational education and odds ratio for the adult samples. Study samples with vocational education had a lower mean odds ratio than did those without. The number of boot camp programs with vocational education was small, however, raising the possibility that this relationship is confounded with other study differences.

Multivariate Analysis of Effect Size and Study Characteristics

The simple univariate analyses of the relationships between odds ratios and study characteristics do not take into account the possible confounding of study features. To assess this possibility, a mixed effects regression model (see Lipsey & Wilson, 2001; Raudenbush, 1994) was estimated, regressing the logged odds ratios onto study features. The basic model included the major methodological features, accounting for significant variability in odds ratios across studies, $R^2 = .28$, $Q = 16.19$, $df = 7$, $p = .02$. Significant variability remained, however, after accounting for methodological differences. Building on this basic methods model, separate regression analyses were run for each major program characteristic shown in Table 14.4. Because of the possibility of an interaction between program characteristics and offender age, these models were run separately for juveniles and adults. The finding of a positive benefit from aftercare for the adult offenders remained statistically significant after adjusting for methods features.

The counterintuitive finding regarding vocational education was not robust to method difference; that is, it was statistically nonsignificant once conditioned on method features. This reinforces our hunch that this finding was the result of a confounding of study features and not due to any negative effects of vocational education. No new significant study characteristics emerged in the multivariate analyses.

DISCUSSION AND CONCLUSION

In our overall meta-analysis of recidivism, we found no differences between the boot camp and comparison samples. Our analysis predicts that if the comparison sample's recidivism is estimated to be 50 percent, the boot camp sample's recidivism would be estimated to be 49.4 percent, or only 0.6 percent lower. When the individual studies were examined, no significant differences were found between the boot camp samples and the comparisons in the majority of the studies. In only 17 samples out of the total of 44, a significant difference between the experimental and control samples was found; approximately half favored the boot camp while the remaining favored the comparisons. Thus, by whatever criteria are used, there is no evidence that the boot camps reduce recidivism.

The results of this systematic review and meta-analysis will be disappointing for many people. Advocates of the programs expect them to successfully reduce the future criminal activities of adults and juveniles. Critics argue that the programs are poorly conceived as therapeutic interventions, they will not reduce recidivism, and they may actually have the opposite effect by increasing criminal activities. Our results do not support either side of this argument because we found no differences in recidivism between the 44 boot camp samples and the comparisons. Correctional boot camps are neither as good as the advocates assert nor as bad as the critics hypothesize.

An examination of the forest plot of the individual studies (see Figure 14.1) and our analysis of the data demonstrated large differences in the studies in terms of the effect of boot camps. Some studies found boot camp participants did better than the comparisons, and others found comparison samples did better. For this reason, we explored whether the differences among studies could be attributed to the methods or design of the studies or to characteristics of the programs or individual participants. In our examination of the methodological variables,

we did not find any evidence that differences in the results of studies could be explained by the study methodology.

Our examination of the offender characteristics was disappointing because very few studies reported sufficient information to enable us to code and analyze the possible impact of these characteristics on study outcomes. Few studies even reported on the gender of the samples. The only variables we could examine were (1) whether the studies focused on adult offenders or adjudicated juveniles, and (2) whether the participants were limited to those convicted or adjudicated for nonviolent/nonperson crimes or mixed violent and nonviolent crimes. Again we found no evidence that differences in these characteristics explained the differences in the results.

We were able to code and analyze the possible impact of six program characteristics, including whether the boot camps had aftercare, academic education, vocational education, drug treatment, counseling, or manual labor components. It is important to note that this information was limited to general information about the characteristics of the programs. We assume the quality and intensity of the programs differed greatly. From our knowledge of the boot camps we know that some programs consider Narcotics Anonymous or Alcoholics Anonymous meetings drug treatment, whereas others provide a more intensive drug treatment experience using a Therapeutic Community-type model. We did not have enough information to code such differences. Almost no information was given about what happened to the comparison samples. The potential impact of these differences on recidivism cannot be overlooked.

When we examined the impact of program characteristics, the only differences we found were for adult studies and, after controlling for methodological differences, the only difference was for boot camps that included an aftercare component. In other words, whereas the odds ratios differed for boot camps with and without aftercare, in neither case did the boot camp samples differ significantly from the comparisons. While the recidivism of releasees from boot camps with aftercare differed from the recidivism of releasees from boot camps without aftercare, there were no significant differences in recidivism between boot camp releasees and comparisons for either type of boot camp (for example, with or without aftercare). Thus we were unable to identify any characteristic of the methods, offenders, or programs that would explain differences in results of the studies.

Why don't boot camps reduce recidivism when compared to other correctional alternatives? In our opinion, one possible reason boot camps are not any more or less effective than other alternatives is because they may offer no more therapy or treatment than the alternatives. That is, boot camps by themselves have little to offer as far as moving offenders away from criminal activities. Sufficient research currently exists to demonstrate that appropriate correctional treatment with particular characteristics can be effective in changing offenders (Andrews & Bonta, 1998; Gendreau & Ross, 1987; Lipsey, 1992). Some boot camps incorporate this type of treatment and therapy into the regime of the camps, while others do not. Similarly, some comparison facilities or programs provide such treatment. Almost all studies compared offenders or juveniles in boot camps to others in correctional programs within the same jurisdictions. We hypothesize that there are similarities within jurisdictions such that boot camps with therapy and treatment will be located in jurisdictions that also provide such treatment to those in the comparison programs within the jurisdiction. Thus, in terms of the type of treatment or therapy that has been shown to be effective, correctional programs within the same jurisdictions will be similar. The boot camps may only differ from other correctional programs in the same jurisdiction in the military aspects and not in therapy and treatment. It seems likely that the therapy and treatment are the important components in reducing recidivism. Therefore, since boot camps and other correctional programs provide similar therapy and treatment, the impact on recidivism will be similar.

The research demonstrates that there are no differences in recidivism when boot camp samples are compared to those who receive other correctional sanctions. In our opinion, this can be interpreted to show that a military atmosphere in a correctional setting is not effective in reducing recidivism. However, many questions remain. It would be particularly valuable to have more information about the characteristics of the participants, and the components of the programs, both for the boot camps and for the comparisons. From these studies, we were able to code very little of this information. We anticipate that programs with more treatment and therapy will be more successful in reducing recidivism. The question is whether this would explain some of the differences in results across studies. Future research would greatly benefit by increasing the amount of detailed information about the programs and the participants.

APPENDIX: SECONDARY SOURCES USED IN THE META-ANALYSIS*

1. Burns & Vito (1995)
   Burns, J. C. (1994). *A Comparative Analysis of the Alabama Department of Corrections Boot Camp Program.* Unpublished Ph.D. diss., University of Alabama, Tuscaloosa.

2. State of New York Department of Correctional Services (2000)
   Courtright, K. E. (1991). *An Overview and Evaluation of Shock Incarceration in New York State.* Unpublished master's thesis, Mercyhurst College, Erie, PA.

3. Marcus-Mendoza (1995)
   Holley, P. D. & Wright, D. E. (1995). Oklahoma's Regimented Inmate Discipline Program for Males: Its Impact on Recidivism. *Journal of the Oklahoma Criminal Justice Research Consortium, 2,* 58-70.

4. Kempinem & Kurlychek (2001)
   Kempinem, C. & Motivans, M. (1998). *Who Goes to Pennsylvania's Boot Camp?* Paper presented at the meeting of the American Society of Criminology, Washington, DC.

---

*Secondary sources are shown after the primary sources included in the reference list.

5. Harer & Klein-Saffran (1996)

Klein-Saffran, J. (1991). Shock Incarceration, Bureau of Prisons Style. *Research Forum, 1,* 1-9.

6. MacKenzie & Souryal (1994)

MacKenzie, D. L., Brame, R., McDowall, D., & Souryal, C. (1995). Boot Camp Prisons and Recidivism in Eight States. *Criminology, 33,* 327-57.

MacKenzie, D. L., Shaw, J. W., & Gowdy, V. B. (1990). *Evaluation of Shock Incarceration in Louisiana, Executive Summary.* Washington, DC: U.S. Department of Justice, National Institute of Justice.

7. Peters (1996a), Peters (1996b), and Thomas & Peters (1996)

Peters, M., Thomas, D., & Zamberlan, C. (1997). *Boot Camps for Juvenile Offenders: Program Summary.* Rockville, MD: U.S. Department of Justice, National Institute of Justice.

REFERENCES

Andrews, D. A., & Bonta, J. (1998). *The Psychology of Criminal Conduct.* Cincinnati: Anderson.

Andrews, D. A., Zinger, I., Hoge, R. D., Bonta, J., Gendreau, P., & Cullen, F. T. (1990). Does Correctional Treatment Work? A Clinically Relevant and Psychologically Informed Meta-Analysis. *Criminology, 28,* 369-404.

Austin, J., Jones, M., & Bolyard, M. (1993). *Assessing the Impact of a County Operated Boot Camp: Evaluation of the Los Angeles County Regimented Inmate Diversion Program* (NCJRS document reproduction service no., 154401). San Francisco: National Council on Crime and Delinquency.

Boyles, C. E., Bokenkamp, E., & Madura, W. (1996). *Evaluation of the Colorado Juvenile Regimented Training Program.* Golden: Colorado Department of Human Services, Division of Youth Corrections.

Burns, J. C., & Vito, G. C. (1995). An Impact Analysis of the Alabama Boot Camp Program. *Federal Probation, 59,* 63-67.

California Department of the Youth Authority. (1997). *LEAD: A Boot Camp and Intensive Parole Program, the Final Impact Evaluation* (Report to the California Legislature). Sacramento: Author.

Camp, D. A., & Sandhu, H. S. (1995). Evaluation of Female Offender Regimented Treatment Program (FORT). *Journal of the Oklahoma Criminal Justice Research Consortium, 2,* 50-57.

Clark, C. L., & Aziz, D. W. (1996). Shock Incarceration in New York State: Philosophy, Results, and Limitations. In D. L. MacKenzie & E. E. Hebert (Eds.),*Correctional Boot Camps: A Tough Intermediate Sanction.*Washington, D.C.: U.S. Department of Justice, National Institute of Justice.

Dersimonian, R., & Laird, N. (1986). Meta-Analysis in Clinical Trials. *Controlled Clinical Trials 7,* 177-88.

Farrington, D. P., Hancock, G., Livingston, M., Painter, K., & Towl, G. (2000). *Evaluation of Intensive Regimes for Young Offenders* (Home Office research findings). London: Home Office Research, Development and Statistics Directorate.

Fleiss, J. L. (1994). Measures of Effect Size for Categorical Data. In H. Cooper & L. V. Hedges (Eds.), *The Handbook of Research Synthesis* New York: Russell Sage.

Florida Department of Juvenile Justice. (1996a). *Leon County Sheriffs Department Boot Camp: A Follow-Up Study of the First Five Platoons.* Tallahassee: Florida Department of Juvenile Justice, Bureau of Data and Research.

Florida Department of Juvenile Justice. (1996b). *Manatee County Sheriffs Boot Camp. A Follow-Up Study of the First Four Platoons.* Tallahassee: Florida Department of Juvenile Justice, Bureau of Data and Research.

Florida Department of Juvenile Justice. (1996c). *Pinellas County Boot Camp: A Follow-Up Study of the First Five Platoons* (research rep. no. 33). Tallahassee: Florida Department of Juvenile Justice, Bureau of Data and Research.

Florida Department of Juvenile Justice. (1997a). *Bay County Sheriffs Office Boot Camp: A Follow-Up Study of the First Seven Platoons* (research rep. no. 44). Bay County: Florida Department of Juvenile Justice, Bureau of Data and Research.

Florida Department of Juvenile Justice. (1997b). *Martin County Sheriffs Office Boot Camp: A Follow-Up of the First Four Platoons* (research rep. no. 43). Martin County: Florida Department of Juvenile Justice, Bureau of Data and Research.

Florida Department of Juvenile Justice. (1997c). *Polk County Juvenile Boot Camp: A Follow-Up Study of the First Four Platoons.* Tallahassee: Florida Department of Juvenile Justice, Bureau of Data and Research.

Florida Department of Juvenile Justice. (1997d). *Polk County Juvenile Boot Camp-Female Program: A Follow-Up Study of the First Seven Platoons.* Polk County: Florida Department of Juvenile Justice, Bureau of Data and Research.

Flowers, G. T., Carr, T. S., & Ruback, R. B. (1991). *Special Alternative Incarceration Evaluation.* Atlanta: Georgia Department of Corrections.

Gendreau, P., Little, T., & Goggin, C. E. (1996). A Meta-Analysis of the Predictors of Adult Offender Recidivism: What Works! *Criminology, 34,* 575-607.

Gendreau, P., & Ross, R. R. (1987). Revivication of Rehabilitation: Evidence from the 1980s. *Justice Quarterly, 4,* 349-408.

Gowdy, V. B. (1996). Historical Perspective. In D. L. MacKenzie & E. E. Hebert (Eds.), *Correctional Boot Camps: A Tough Intermediate Sanction.* Washington, D.C.: U.S. Department of Justice, National Institute of Justice.

Harer, M. D., & Klein-Saffran, J. (1996). An Evaluation of the Federal Bureau of Prisons Lewisburg Intensive Confinement Center. Unpublished manuscript, Federal Bureau of Prisons, Research and Evaluation, Washington, D.C.

Jones, M. (1996). Do Boot Camp Graduates Make Better Probationers? *Journal of Crime and Justice, 19, 1*-14.

Jones, M. (1997). Is Less Better? Boot Camp, Regular Probation and Rearrest in North Carolina. *American Journal of Criminal Justice, 21,* 147-61.

Jones, R. J. (1998). *Annual Report to the Governor and the General Assembly: Impact Incarceration Program.* Springfield: Illinois Department of Corrections.

Kempinem, C. A., & Kurlychek, M. C. (2001). *Pennsylvania's Motivational Boot Camp (2000 Report to the Legislature).* Quehanna: Pennsylvania Commission on Sentencing.

Lipsey, M. (1992). Juvenile Delinquency Treatment: A Meta-Analytic Inquiry into the Variability of Effects. In T. Cook, H. Cooper, D. S. Cordray, H. Hartmann, L. V. Hedges, R. J. Light, T. A. Louis, & F. Mosteller (Eds.), *Meta-Analysis for Explanation: A Casebook.* New York: Russell Sage.

Lipsey, M. W., & Wilson, D. B. (2001). *Practical Meta-Analysis.* Thousand Oaks, CA: Sage.

MacKenzie, D. L. (1997). Criminal Justice and Crime Prevention. In L. W. Sherman, D. C. Gottfredson, D. L. MacKenzie, J. Eck, P. Reuter, & S. Bushway (Eds.), *Preventing Crime: What Works, What Doesn't, What's Promising.* Washington, D.C.: U.S. Department of Justice, National Institute of Justice.

MacKenzie, D. L., & E. E. Hebert, Eds. (1996). *Correctional Boot Camps: A Tough Intermediate Sanction.* Washington, D.C.: U.S. Department of Justice, National Institute of Justice.

MacKenzie, D. L., & Parent, D. G. (1991). Shock Incarceration and Prison Crowding in Louisiana. *Journal of Criminal Justice, 19,* 225-37.

MacKenzie, D. L., & Parent, D. G. (1992). Boot Camp Prisons for Young Offenders. In J. M. Byrne, A. J. Lurigio, & J. Petersilia (Eds.), *Smart Sentencing: The Emergence of Intermediate Sanctions.* Newbury Park, CA: Sage.

MacKenzie, D. L., & Piquero, A. (1994). The Impact of Shock Incarceration Programs on Prison Crowding. *Crime & Delinquency, 40,* 222-49.

MacKenzie, D. L., & Shaw, J. W. (1990). Inmate Adjustment and Change During Shock Incarceration. *Justice Quarterly, 7, 1*25-50.

MacKenzie, D. L., & Souryal, C. (1994). *Multi-Site Evaluation of Shock Incarceration: Executive Summary.* Washington, D.C.: U.S. Department of Justice, National Institute of Justice.

MacKenzie, D. L., & Souryal, C. (1995). Inmate Attitude Change During Incarceration: A Comparison of Boot Camp with Traditional Prison. *Justice Quarterly, 12,* 325-54.

MacKenzie, D. L., Souryal, C., Sealock, M., & Bin Kashem, M. (1997). *Outcome Study of the Sergeant Henry Johnson Youth Leadership Academy (YLA).* Washington, D.C.: University of Maryland, U.S. Department of Justice, National Institute of Justice.

MacKenzie, D. L., Wilson, D. B., Armstrong, G. S., & Gover, A. R. (2001). The Impact of Boot Camps and Traditional Institutions on Juvenile Residents: Perception, Adjustment, and Change. *Journal of Research in Crime and Delinquency, 38,* 279-313.

Marcus-Mendoza, S. T. (1995). Preliminary Investigation of Oklahoma's Shock Incarceration Program. *Journal of the Oklahoma Criminal Justice Research Consortium, 2,* 44-49.

Morash, M., & Rucker, L. (1990). A Critical Look at the Idea of Boot Camp as a Correctional Reform. *Crime & Delinquency, 36,* 204-22.

Peters, M. (1996a). *Evaluation of the Impact of Boot Camps for Juvenile Offenders: Denver Interim Report.* Fairfax, VA: U.S. Department of Justice, Office of Juvenile Justice and Delinquency Prevention.

Peters, M. (1996b). *Evaluation of the Impact of Boot Camps for Juvenile Offenders: Mobile Interim Report.* Fairfax, VA: U.S. Department of Justice,

Office of Juvenile Justice and Delinquency Prevention.

Raudenbush, S. W. (1994). Random Effects Models. In H. Cooper & L. V. Hedges (Eds.), *The Handbook* of *Research Synthesis*. New York: Russell Sage.

Sechrest, D. D. (1989). Prison "Boot Camps" Do Not Measure Up. *Federal Probation, 53, 15*-20.

Sherman, L. W., Gottfredson, D. C., MacKenzie, D. L., Eck, J., Reuter, P., & Bushway, S. (1997). *Preventing Crime: What Works, What Doesn't, What's Promising.* Washington, DC: U.S. Department of Justice, National Institute of Justice.

State of New York Department of Correctional Services, Division of Parole. (2000). *The Twelfth Annual Shock Legislative Report (Shock Incarceration and Shock Parole Supervision).* Albany, NY: Division of Parole.

Thomas, D., & Peters, M. (1996). *Evaluation of the Impact of Boot Camps for Juvenile Offenders: Cleveland Interim Report.* Fairfax, VA: U.S. Department of Justice, Office of Juvenile Justice and Delinquency Prevention.

T3 Associates Training and Consulting. (2000). *Project Turnaround Outcome Evaluation. Final Report.* Ottawa, Canada: Author.

Wright, D. T., & Mays, G. L. (1998). Correctional Boot Camps, Attitudes, and Recidivism: The Oklahoma Experience. Journal of Offender Rehabilitation, 28, 71-87.

Zhang, S. X. (2000). *An Evaluation of the Los Angeles County Juvenile Drug Treatment Boot Camp (Final Report).* Washington, D.C.: U.S. Department of Justice, National Institute of Justice.

Part VI

ADJUSTMENT IN THE COMMUNITY

15

SHOCK INCARCERATION AND POSITIVE ADJUSTMENT DURING COMMUNITY SUPERVISION

DORIS LAYTON MACKENZIE

ROBERT BRAME

INTRODUCTION

Shock incarceration programs ("boot-camp prisons") have been at the forefront of correctional developments in recent years. Along with programs ranging from shock probation, where offenders are incarcerated for short periods of time and then placed on probation (MacKenzie et al., 1992; Latessa & Vito, 1988), to intensive community supervision (Petersilia & Turner, 1993) to house arrest, electronic monitoring, and work release (Gowdy, 1993), policy makers have looked to shock incarceration programs with a diverse set of hopes and expectations (Souryal & MacKenzie, 1994).

Shock incarceration programs have been advocated as a means to deter novice offenders from the continued pursuit of crime. The rigor and highly structured shock program environment is expected to expose the offender to the hard reality of prison life. Simultaneously, the shock program is viewed as a method for providing offenders with a sense of discipline, purpose, and motivation to work hard and engage in positive activities.

For others, the unique atmosphere that the shock program provides holds the potential for being a powerful rehabilitative agent. The military drill, physical labor, and highly structured daily regimen of the boot camp may include some rehabilitative components. But many advocates of the rehabilitative position contend that the traditional "boot-camp" atmosphere is, in and of itself, insufficient for rehabilitation. From this perspective, treatment, education, and counseling are crucial components of any attempt to change offenders. Rehabilitation proponents are, therefore, not necessarily impressed with the shock experience *per se*. Still, they often view the shock program as a reasonable environment in which to pursue more traditional rehabilitative objectives.

Although these two positions differ on the importance of different programming tactics,

Reprinted with permission of Kluwer, from MacKenzie, D. L., & Brame, R. (1995). *Journal of Quantitative Criminology, 11*, 111-142. The authors thank David McDowall for his advice on the application of multilevel models in panel data.

they do share a common predicted outcome: Offenders will experience positive change. Some of the popularity of shock incarceration is undoubtedly attributable to its potential compatibility with a wide range of underlying correctional strategies. Consequently, there is considerable variability in the structure and content of shock incarceration programs around the United States. Some states offer very little programming beyond the core military and physical components, while others integrate these components with intensive treatment for substance abuse and psychological problems, counseling, education, and vocational training as described above (MacKenzie & Souryal, 1991). In some states, the decision to place an offender in shock incarceration resides with the sentencing judge. In other states, correctional officials have the discretion to decide who enters the shock program. Still other states use some combination of these decision making processes. Clearly, all shock incarceration programs are not the same.

The empirical literature provides some basis for expecting that increased treatment and supervision intensity can have a positive impact on offenders (Gendreau & Ross, 1987; Petersilia & Turner, 1993). The empirical literature does not, however, provide much understanding of the effect of shock incarceration programs on community adjustment (MacKenzie et al., 1992). Part of the problem is that it is difficult to make general statements about phenomena that are as variable as the content of shock incarceration programs. Additionally, there have been little data available until recently for answering questions about the effectiveness of shock incarceration. While there is some evidence that the shock experience is associated with improved offender attitudes (MacKenzie & Shaw, 1990; MacKenzie & Souryal, 1992), other evidence suggests that shock offenders recidivate at about the same rates as offenders in other correctional programs (Souryal & MacKenzie, 1994).

There is also evidence that shock participants do not adjust more positively to life in the community than their prison parolee and probationer counterparts. In a study of offenders released from a shock incarceration program in Louisiana, MacKenzie et al. (1992) found that those offenders adjusted more positively

(i.e., participated in larger numbers of positive activities) in the community than comparison groups of prison parolees and probationers. However, when supervision intensity was held constant, these differences largely disappeared. Differences between the positive adjustment of shock program completers and comparison groups were attributed to differences in levels of community supervision.

Other studies have explicitly examined the role of intensive supervision. Latessa and Vito (1988) discovered that intensively supervised shock probationers were more likely to find employment than shock probationers who received regular supervision. They also found that intensive supervision of shock probationers did not significantly reduce recidivism. Similarly, Petersilia and Turner's (1993) recent experimental study of the effectiveness of intensive supervision programs (ISPs) found that greater supervision intensity was associated with a higher probability that offenders would secure employment and attend drug treatment and counseling programs. Anglin and Hser's (1990) research showed that offenders who are compelled to be in drug treatment programs benefit from those programs as much as "volunteer clients." Coerced participation in such programs, say Anglin and Hser, may be a useful device for establishing a pattern of involvement in positive activities.

On more traditional outcome measures such as the incidence of technical violations and recidivism, speculation about whether intensive supervision programs are effective depends to some extent on how one reads the evidence. Petersilia and Turner's (1993) work clearly indicates that offenders participating in ISPs were more likely than offenders in control groups to be detected for technically violating conditions of community supervision. They attribute this higher technical violation rate directly to the "more stringent conditions and closer supervision" that is part and parcel of the intensive supervision programs (p. 319). Thus, offenders in intensive supervision programs are more likely to be detected for technical violations simply because they are observed more closely.

Not unlike the findings associated with studies of shock incarceration, there is little evidence that intensive supervision has much impact on recidivism (Petersilia & Turner, 1990,

1993). Although Petersilia and Turner speculate that such a finding could be construed as a positive result since offenders in intensive supervision are observed more closely, they suggest that the only conclusive resolution of the impact of intensive supervision on new crime recidivism is through the use of self-report surveys of criminal activities. The more conservative conclusion is that intensive supervision programs simply do not provide an "evident payoff in deterrence or incapacitation" (Petersilia & Turner, 1993, p. 321).

One important limitation of relying exclusively upon recidivism as an outcome is that it only captures a single dimension of an offender's behavior in the community (Petersilia & Turner, 1993; MacKenzie et al., 1992; Latessa & Vito, 1988). Although recidivism is clearly an important dimension of behavior, behavioral change is a process rather than an event. Consequently, improvements in other life areas may actually precede or lead to changes in criminal behavior.

Despite the generally lackluster findings associated with research on shock incarceration programs, anecdotal reports of dramatic changes in the behavior of individuals emerging from shock programs have become commonplace. Correctional officials, policy makers, and participating offenders alike have commented widely on their positive perception of what the shock experience represents for the offender who completes the program. Such commentary is useful because it recognizes the broader question of whether offenders are, in fact, experiencing positive change.

One possible criterion for assessing the validity of statements such as these is the level of participation in positive activities among offenders completing shock programs. Such a construct would include but not be limited to recidivism. It would also be comprised of items that capture employment, vocational training, substance abuse treatment, meeting financial obligations, achieving and maintaining residential stability, and the like.

In the current five-state study, we seek to examine the impact of shock incarceration programs on a broad index of positive behavior. Although this index includes a measure of recidivism, it is also sensitive to a broad array of positive activities. The behavior of those who complete the shock programs is compared to that of other offenders serving different sentences. The comparison groups were all eligible for the shock programs but groups were not randomly assigned to treatment conditions. Therefore, differences among groups in intensity of supervision and offender characteristics were used as controls in the analyses.

METHODS

Study Sites

The data for this study were collected as part of the National Institute of Justice multisite study of shock incarceration (MacKenzie, 1990). Shock programs participating in the study were selected to represent different program characteristics, and varying program eligibility/suitability criteria. The five states participating in this portion of the study included: Florida, Georgia, Louisiana, New York, and South Carolina. Table 15.1 presents a descriptive profile of the shock incarceration programs in each of the five states.

These data reveal that the five programs examined in this analysis do, in fact, represent a broad range of programming emphases.[1] New York's shock incarceration program has a comparatively large inmate capacity, with a 6-month sentence followed by a minimum of 6 months of intensive community supervision. The programs in the other states (at the time of data collection) were much smaller (100-200 inmates) and generally imposed shorter confinement terms (3 to 6 months). While Louisiana's program required a minimum of 6 months intensive supervision in the community, the programs in Florida, Georgia, and South Carolina were not tied to mandatory intensive community supervision upon release.

Military drill and physical exercise are core components of all shock incarceration programs (MacKenzie & Souryal, 1991). Counseling, treatment, and educational activities are important components of some programs and are virtually nonexistent in others. The states in our study reflect considerable variability in the prevalence of "rehabilitative/treatment" activities. At the time of data collection, the programs in Georgia, South Carolina, and Florida

Table 15.1   Profile of Shock Incarceration Programs in Participating States

Characteristics	Florida	Georgia	Louisiana	New York	S. Carolina
Time of data collection	1989-1991	1989-1991	1987-1988	1988-1990	1988-1990
Inmate capacity	100	200	120	1500	96
Average sentence (mo)	3.3	3.0	4.0	6.0	3.0
Supervision intensity in Community[a]	Regular	Varies based on risk	Intensive for 6-mo minimum	Intensive for 6-mo minimum	Varies based on risk
Voluntary entrance	No	Yes	Yes	Yes	No
Voluntary exit	No	No	Yes	Yes	No
Program dismissal dropout rates (%)[b]	51.1	2.8	43.3	31.3	16.0
Officials responsible for placement decisions [court/dept. of corrections (DOC)]	DOC	Court	DOC	DOC	Court
Daily activities (hr day)					
Work/drill physical training	8.0	8.0	6.5	9.0	9.0
Rehabilitation[c]	1.8	0.3	3.5	5.6	1.9
Percentage of time in rehabilitative activities (daily)[c]	18.4	3.6	35.0	38.4	17.4

[a]In Georgia and South Carolina, community supervision intensity levels are decided on a case-by-case basis after reviewing relevant criteria.

[b]Dismissal/dropout rates were collected during the following years: (1) Florida, October 1987-January 1991; (2) Georgia, 1984-1989; (3) Louisiana, February 1987-1989; (4) New York, calendar year 1989; (6) South Carolina, July 1989-June 1990.

[c]Rehabilitative activities include formal education, counseling, and drug treatment/education.

devoted little time to treatment, counseling, and educational activities. In Louisiana and New York, officials reported allocating a larger proportion of time to these therapeutic activities.

Instruments

Data were collected from two sources. Demographic information, current offense characteristics,[2] and prior criminal history variables (i.e., prior arrest and/or conviction) were available from offenders' official records. An instrument was also used for compiling supervision intensity and positive adjustment information during community supervision. These data were collected from offenders' supervising officers at predetermined intervals over a 1-year follow-up period. The positive adjustment index used in Florida, Georgia, New York, and South Carolina was first used by Latessa and Vito (1988). A different positive adjustment instrument, first

discussed by MacKenzie et al. (1992), was used in Louisiana.

The positive adjustment index (calculated at the end of each interval) scores the number of positive activities in which offenders are involved during the preceding time interval. Examples of positive activities include employment, education, residential and financial stability, fulfillment of family responsibilities, participation in treatment programs for substance abuse and psychological problems, compliance with community supervision requirements, and avoiding illegal activities. Thus, the measure of positive adjustment considered here is somewhat broader in scope than measures of successful adjustment that focus only on, recidivism.

The index used in Florida, Georgia, New York, and South Carolina is comprised of 10 items (Latessa & Vito, 1988). The index used in Louisiana is the same as the 17-item measure used by MacKenzie et al. (1992) but for the addition of an item that indicates whether the offender was arrested for any offense during the current time interval.[3]

To simplify interpretation we standardized the positive adjustment scores in each of the five states by taking the ratio of the number of positive activities indicated to the number of positive activities listed on the instrument. The result is a proportion that indicates less positive adjustment as the score approaches 0.0 and more positive adjustment as the score approaches 1.0 (mean scores ranged from 0.38 to 0.51 and standard deviations ranged from 0.15 to 0.30). Substantive interpretation of the results does not depend upon whether the scores are standardized.

We conducted a reliability analysis on the positive adjustment scale in each of the states at each of the intervals. Item-to-total correlations (ranging from 0.38 to 0.59) and coefficient alpha reliability measures (ranging from 0.81 to 0.89) were averaged over all intervals. In each of the five states, we conclude that items comprising the index are positively correlated with each other and that the index achieves reasonable levels of internal consistency.

Supervision intensity was operationally defined as the number of monthly telephone and face-to-face contacts between supervising officers and subjects in Florida, Georgia, and South Carolina (supervision intensity data were not collected in New York). In Louisiana, supervision intensity was measured with three indexes that relate to different dimensions of the offender's contact experience with community supervision officials (MacKenzie, 1991; MacKenzie et al., 1992). A "lack of knowledge" index measures the extent to which the community supervision officer is not aware of the offender's activities (higher scores imply lower levels of knowledge). Surveillance intensity and requirements indexes were also compiled; higher scores on these measures imply greater levels of surveillance and more stringent sets of requirements, respectively.

Subjects

A sample of male shock program completers was selected within each of the five states. Each state also selected at least two offender samples from other correctional programs to which the shock program completers could be compared. Samples examined varied by state, although each of the states collected data from a group of prison parolees for comparison to the shock completer sample. Florida, Louisiana, and New York provided data for groups of offenders who entered the shock program but terminated before completing it. We refer to this group as the "shock dropout" sample. Georgia, Louisiana, and South Carolina collected information on samples of probationers. Subjects in each of the samples met the formal eligibility criteria for their state's shock incarceration program but subjects were not randomly assigned to their respective samples. The comparison groups in the current study do share important similarities with the shock incarcerated samples. Offenders in all groups typically occupy the less serious end of the offense seriousness continuum. Moreover, these offenders are typically eligible for probation or short terms of incarceration. Because of the nonrandom assignment procedure, sample differences were evident (we return to this issue below).

Procedure

The research design relied on the evaluations of community supervision (probation or parole) officers. At each of the measurement intervals for a particular subject, officers indicated the positive activities in which the offender had participated during the preceding interval. A count of these activities represents the level of positive activity for a particular subject within the preceding interval.

Subjects were evaluated for positive adjustment at three-month intervals in Florida, Georgia, New York, and South Carolina. Louisiana subjects were evaluated at one-month intervals. In all states subjects were not necessarily evaluated at all intervals. As with many panel analytic studies, there is considerable attrition in the sample size as follow-up time increases (see Appendix, Table A-1).

The data reveal that attrition rates are relatively high in Florida and Georgia while these rates are more modest in the other states. The most frequent cause of attrition in each state is recidivism or revocation for a violation of probation or parole conditions (MacKenzie & Brame, 1993). Given that the preponderance of cases drop out of the study for reasons that tend to be inconsistent with successful adjustment, we expected that individuals dropping out of the study sooner rather than later would not be adjusting as successfully as offenders who managed to continue. Thus, we explicitly enter the timing of exit from the study as a predictor variable in our analyses. Supervision intensity levels were also collected over time in 3-month intervals in Florida, Georgia, and South Carolina. The supervision intensity indexes are calculated at 1-month intervals in Louisiana.

Analytic Method

The analysis of panel data entails a number of important statistical considerations (Greene, 1993; Littell et al., 1991; Hsiao, 1986). The most important issue is that there are multiple measurements per subject. The multiple disturbances associated with the same subject are often not independent of one another. Mixed model methods are useful for analyzing panel data, such as those encountered here, where there are systematic patterns of error rather than simple random error.

For such an analysis, several avenues of flexibility are desirable. First, we wish to make an explicit distinction between time-varying variables (within subject) and variables whose levels are established at the beginning of the study and do not change thereafter (between subjects) (Allison, 1990). Second, we want to test for interactions between time-varying variables and effects that are established at the beginning of the study. Since these interactions occur across two levels of analysis (between subject and within subject), they are usually described as "cross-level" interactions (Bryk & Raudenbush, 1992). As a practical matter, they amount to adjustments of the within-subject effects across levels of between-subject effects (Horney et al., 1993; Raudenbush & Chan, 1992). Finally, we desire a more parsimonious assessment of the data in the face of panel mortality than what is provided by conventional repeated measures analysis techniques.

The statistical theory of hierarchical linear and multilevel models described by Bryk and Raudenbush (1987, 1992) and Mason et al. (1983), respectively, is responsive to each of the above considerations. In this class of models, there is an explicit distinction between processes that occur within subjects and those that occur between subjects. The simple within-subject process assumes the form

$$y_{it} = a_i + \delta_{it} + e_{it} \qquad (1)$$

where t is indexed over measurement intervals and i is indexed over subjects. If t is set to zero at the first interval, then a_i is equal to the expected value of y_i at the first interval. Next, δ_i is an estimate of the expected growth or decay (i.e., a trend coefficient) in the expectation of y_{it} associated with a unit change in time. Note that a and δ are indexed by i, which means simply that they vary from individual to individual. Finally, e_{it} is a mixed disturbance (which we discuss later) due to subjects and time-specific observations within subjects.

If T_{max} is the maximum number of measurements and T_i is the number of measurements for the ith case, Bryk and Raudenbush (1987) note that all of the e_{it} can be collected into a covariance matrix Σ of dimension $T_i \times T_i$. While Σ can assume different forms, it is conventional with short time series (as we have here) to impose the constraint that $cov(e_{it-1}, e_{jt}) = 0$ (where $i \neq j$) and assume that there is no serial correlation (Bryk & Raudenbush, 1987, 1992; Horney et al., 1993). There is nothing in the theory underlying the use of the mixed model requiring that $T_i = T_{max}$, for all subjects. This is a particularly useful characteristic since our data demonstrate considerable attrition over time.

Provided that the elements of the disturbance term from Eq. (1) are independent over all N subjects, no problems are introduced by estimating the coefficients in Eq. (1) by the method of ordinary least squares. This assumption is unlikely to be consistent with data such as those encountered here and the possibility of a mixed (more complex) disturbance term must be explicitly acknowledged. The key to this is to complete the specification of the within-subject process by estimating the between-subjects model via generalized least squares. In this model, the coefficients in Eq. (1) which vary over the N subjects are regressed on between-subjects characteristics. In the simple within-subjects process, there are no between-subject covariates and the within-subjects parameters are a function of a between-subjects intercept term such that

$$\alpha_i = \eta - u_i \qquad (2a)$$

$$\delta_i = \gamma + \upsilon_i \qquad (2b)$$

where η and γ are intercept terms estimated for the N subjects as a group, while u_i and v_i are disturbances (Bryk & Raudenbush, 1987; Berk, 1991; Horney et al., 1993).

The within-subjects terms can be estimated, in the terminology of Bryk and Raudenbush (1992), as fixed, randomly varying (variance components), or nonrandomly varying. In the fixed effects model, an assumption that the effects are constant across observations is imposed on the data and any observation-to-observation variability is thrown into the error term in Eq. (1). As a practical matter, treating an effect as fixed constrains the corresponding disturbance vector element for that effect to be zero in Eq. (2).

In the random effects model, the effects are not assumed to be constant across subjects. The model assumes that the effects are drawn from a probability distribution with mean and variance estimated from the data. Finally, the nonrandomly varying effects are assumed to vary systematically between subjects. But for the systematic variability in these coefficients, the effects are assumed fixed and remaining variability is thrown into the error term in Eq. (1). As is clear from the above discussion, the prediction equation for y_i, in the simple within-subject process takes the form

$$y_{it} = \eta - \gamma t - e_{it} \qquad (3)$$

where

$$e_{it} = u_i - v_i + \varepsilon_{it} \qquad (4)$$

and ε_{it} is a purely random disturbance. Generalizations to more complex processes are straightforward. The most useful generalizations include the addition of time-varying

covariates (e.g., supervision intensity) and between subject effects such as sample membership, demographic characteristics, and current and prior offending behavior. To make this explicit, we expand Eq. (1) to include an additional term

$$y_{it} = \alpha_i + \delta_i t + \Theta_i x_{it} + \varepsilon_{it} \qquad (5)$$

where x_i is a vector of covariates whose values can change over time and Θ is a conformable vector of coefficients specifying the effects of time-varying covariates on y_{it}. The link to the between-subjects model is also straightforward

$$\alpha_i = \eta \, z_{0i} + u_i \qquad (6a)$$

$$\delta_i = \gamma_1 \, z_{1i} + v_i \qquad (6b)$$

$$\Theta_i = \gamma_2 \, z_{2i} + w_i \qquad (6c)$$

where η is a vector of coefficients that estimate the effect of between-subject covariates (such as race or sample membership) in z_0 on the intercept term (a_i) in Eq. (5). These effects constitute adjustments to the within-subject intercept term. Similarly, γ_1 and γ_2 are conformable with z_1, and z_2 (both of which include an intercept term and, when warranted, one or more between subject covariates), respectively, and can have different dimensions and elements. Thus, we do not impose the constraint that $z_0 = z_1 = z_2$.

The estimates in γ_1 tell us whether the between-subject covariates have an effect on the time trend. Moreover, the estimates in γ_2 help us discern whether between-subject variables such as sample membership have implications for the effects of supervision intensity on positive adjustment. As mentioned above, the coefficients in γ_1 and γ_2 are often described as "cross-level" interaction effects. They can also be thought of as adjustments to the within-subjects factors that depend on between-subjects characteristics. Finally, u_i, v_i, and w_i in Eq. (6) are disturbance vectors which can have elements that are constrained to zero or free to vary, depending upon the specification of the within-subject effects as fixed, nonrandomly varying, or randomly varying.

In sum, the hierarchical or mixed linear model approach facilitates the construction of a composite error term that allows us to partition between and within-subject variation in an efficient manner. Moreover, the number of follow-up periods is not required to be the same for each subject. Finally, the model provides us with the flexibility to regress within subject coefficients on between-subject effects and the ability to accommodate time-varying covariates.

RESULTS

Descriptive Statistics and Sample Differences

Group assignment was not random, and not surprisingly, there were differences between the samples within each state (see Table 15.2). Considering these differences among samples in demographic and offending characteristics, we concluded that it was necessary to control for their confounding effects in the analysis of positive adjustment.

Descriptive statistics for supervision intensity indicators in Florida, Georgia, Louisiana, and South Carolina (supervision intensity data were not collected in New York) were summarized by averaging scores for all subjects over the duration of their respective follow-up periods. Positive skewness was apparent in each of these indicators of supervision intensity (see Appendix, Table A-l).

Close inspection of the distributions revealed small groups of cases in each state that were supervised at extremely high levels. For example, in Florida, Georgia, and South Carolina, some subjects were contacted at rates exceeding 20 to 30 contacts per month. A natural log transformation of these indicators reduces the skewness considerably. We concluded that contact data could be most usefully summarized by working with the natural log of the number of contacts instead of the raw number of contacts. For similar reasons, we decided to work with the log transform of the knowledge and surveillance indexes in Louisiana as well.

We next examined the relationship among supervision intensity, time, and sample membership. The objective of this analysis was to see whether supervision intensity levels differed between samples. Because we expect that supervision intensity is related to positive adjustment,

the question of sample differences in supervision intensity is particularly important. Table 15.3 presents the results of this assessment.[4] Column 2 in each state, from Eqs. (3) and (4), reveals that supervision intensity levels declined over time. In Florida, for example, Column 2 indicates that the mean number of logged contacts per month during the first 3 months (i.e., the first interval) of the follow-up period was 1.552. This corresponds to the estimate of η in Eq. (3). When the model is specified this way, the within-subject intercept term is simply the mean initial level. The trend coefficient indicates that each increase of 1 time unit (i.e., $t = 0, 1, \ldots, T_i$) was accompanied by an expected decrease of 0.140 log monthly contact. This parameter estimate corresponds to the y coefficient in Eq. (3). Both the within-subject intercept term and the trend coefficient(s) for supervision intensity are statistically significant in each state. Thus, the intensity of supervision declines over time.

Column 3 in Table 15.3, based on estimates for Eqs. (5) and (6), introduces between-subject effects for sample membership and cross-level interactions for time and sample membership. In Florida and Georgia, the crosslevel interactions were not statistically significant. Between-sample differences were statistically significant, however. In both these states, prison parolees were supervised more intensively than shock completers. The nonsignificant, cross-level interaction terms suggest that these differences were time-stable. Things are slightly more complicated in South Carolina. Shock completers experienced a greater decline in supervision intensity over time than did the prison parolees or the probationers. Both the shock completers and the prison parolees were supervised more intensively than probationers at the beginning of the study but the interaction between sample and time suggests that the shock completers' levels approached those of the probationers as the study progressed.

Table 15.3 presents similar findings for the analysis of supervision intensity sample membership in Louisiana. The data reveal that shock completers were supervised more intensively than subjects in other groups and that the shock completer supervision levels approach those of the other samples with the passage of time. This is not surprising since the Louisiana program

Table 15.2   Descriptive Statistics[a]

	Shock completers	Shock dropouts	Prison parolees	Probationers
Florida (*N* = 273)	105	63	105	N/A
Nonwhite (%)	58.1	46.0	61.0	
Age at comm. supv., M (SD)*	19.7(1.9)	19.4(1.6)	19.0(1.9)	
Type of offense*				
Violent (%)	24.8	31.8	41.9	
Drug (%)	22.9	4.8	12.4	
Property/other (%)	52.4	63.5	45.7	
New crime (%)	78.1	82.5	89.5	
Prior arrests/convictions (%)	30.4	29.4	23.9	
Georgia (*N* = 237)	73	N/A	88	76
Nonwhite (%)	56.2		67.1	59.2
Age at comm. supv., M (SD)*	20.4 (1.9)		23.5 (2.7)	20.9 (2.5)
Type of offense*				
Violent (%)	15.1		20.5	6.6
Drug (%)	19.0		29.6	31.8
Property/other (%)	63.3		50.0	61.2
New crime (%)*	82.3		62.2	98.8
Prior arrests/convictions (%)*	39.2		75.5	10.6
Louisiana (*N* = 248)	69	14	71	94
Nonwhite (%)	59.4	50.0	70.4	66.0
Age at comm. supv., M (SD)*	23.7 (4.7)	25.1 (4.8)	23.5 (5.6)	20.9 (5.4)
Type of offense				
Violent (%)	5.8	0.0	16.9	7.5
Drug (%)	63.8	78.6	60.6	57.5
Property/other	30.4	21.4	22.5	35.1
Prior arrests/convictions (%)	81.2	92.9	67.6	69.2
New York (*N* = 237)	85	75	77	N/A
Nonwhite (%)	81.2	81.3	77.9	
Age at first arrest, M (SD)*	19.1 (2.7)	17.5 (1.7)	17.5 (1.8)	
Type of offense*				
Drug (%)	69.4	53.3	41.6	
Property (%)	15.3	20.0	26.0	
Youthful offender (%)	15.3	26.7	32.5	
Prior arrests/convictions (%)*	81.2	94.7	93.5	
South Carolina (*N* = 206)	81	N/A	61	64
Nonwhite (%)	48.2		60.7	57.8
Age at comm. supv., M (SD)	20.6 (2.1)		21.0 (1.9)	21.1 (2.2)
Type of offense				
Violent (%)	12.4		19.7	12.5
Drug (%)	24.7		18.0	21.9
Property/other (%)	63.0		62.3	65.6
New crime (%)*	87.7		80.3	98.4
Prior arrests/convictions (%)	51.9		60.7	62.5

[a]A chi-square test of independence is used to test differences in percentages and a single-factor analysis of variance test is used to test differences between means.

*Differences between samples are significant beyond the $p < 0.05$ level.

Table 15.3   Random Effects Models of Supervision Intensity by State[a]

	Simple W/S model	W/S model augmented with sample effects
Florida[b]		
Within-subject effects		
Intercept	1.552* (0.059)	1.720* (0.093)
Time trend	−0.140* (0.028)	−0.113* (0.042)
W/S intercept adjustments		
Shock completers		−0.383* (0.133)
Shock dropouts		−0.090 (0.155)
Cross-level interactions with time		
Shock completers		−0.059 (0.062)
Shock dropouts		−0.010 (0.085)
Variance components		
W/S intercept	0.725*	0.701*
W/S time trend	0.048*	0.049*
Georgia[c]		
Within-subject effects		
Intercept	1.163* (0.042)	0.976* (0.072)
Time trend	−0.132* (0.024)	−0.104* (0.043)
W/S intercept adjustments		
Shock completers		0.128 (0.102)
Prison parolees		0.402* (0.099)
Cross-level interactions with time		
Shock completers		0.018 (0.061)
Prison parolees		−0.093 (0.059)
Variance components		
W/S intercept	0.256*	0.225*
W/S time trend	0.056*	0.053*
Louisiana[c]		
Model 1: Knowledge index		
Within-subject effects		
Intercept	0.593* (0.031)	0.781* (0.045)
Time trend	0.003 (0.004)	−0.001 (0.007)
W/S intercept adjustments		
Shock completers		−0.495* (0.070)
Shock dropouts		−0.098 (0.127)
Prison parolees		−0.154* (0.069)
Cross-level interactions with time		
Shock completers		0.021* (0.011)
Shock dropouts		0.002 (0.021)
Prison parolees		−0.007 (0.011)
Variance components		
W/S intercept	0.178*	0.140*
W/S time trend	0.003*	0.003*
Model 2: Surveillance index		
Within-subject effects		
Intercept	0.506* (0.037)	0.156* (0.037)
Time trend	−0.026* (0.004)	0.005 (0.005)
W/S intercept adjustments		
Shock completers		1.065* (0.058)
Shock dropouts		0.174 (0.105)
Prison parolees		0.162* (0.057)

Table 15.3 (Continued)

	Simple W/S model	W/S model augmented with sample effects
Cross-level interactions with time		
Shock completers		−0.094* (0.008)
Shock dropouts		−0.026 (0.015)
Prison parolees		−0.016* (0.008)
Variance components		
W/S intercept	0.295*	0.097*
W/S time trend	0.003*	0.001*
Model 3: Requirements index		
Within-subject effects		
Intercept	2.991* (0.089)	2.363* (0.108)
Time trend	−0.052* (0.010)	0.003 (0.014)
W/S intercept adjustments		
Shock completers		2.121* (0.166)
Shock dropouts		0.581 (0.303)
Prison parolees		0.048 (0.165)
Cross-level interactions with time		
Shock completers		−0.159* (0.022)
Shock dropouts		−0.070 (0.042)
Prison parolees		−0.038 (0.022)
Variance components		
W/S intercept	1.737*	0.877*
W/S time trend	0.015*	0.010*
South Carolina[c]		
Within-subject effects		
Intercept	1.069* (0.041)	0.844* (0.071)
Time trend	−0.116* (0.016)	−0.060* (0.028)
W/S intercept adjustments		
Shock completers		0.349* (0.094)
Prison parolees		0.299* (0.101)
Cross-level interactions with time		
Shock completers		−0.092* (0.037)
Prison parolees		−0.068 (0.040)
Variance components		
W/S intercept	0.274*	0.253*
W/S time trend	0.027*	0.026*

[a]Entries are regression coefficients and their standard errors are in parentheses. Supervision intensity is measured by the natural log of the number of monthly contacts in all states except New York (where supervision intensity data were not available) and Louisiana (where three indexes described in text were used).

[b]Prison parolees are the reference category.

[c]Probationers are the reference category.

*$p < 0.05$.

requires shock completers to be intensively supervised for at least the first 6 months they are in the community. The differences here however, are striking. They place the shock completer group at a very high level of supervision intensity compared to what was observed in other groups. Given the magnitude of this difference, our attempt to adjust for supervision intensity when we make sample comparisons on positive adjustment may not yield the desired results. Such adjustments impose the assumption that all variables are equal on the group comparisons. But if this assumption is purely hypothetical it may be of questionable value (Cook & Campbell, 1979). Although it appears that some adjustment in this context is better than no adjustment, the results in Louisiana must be interpreted cautiously since the scores on these variables are clearly confounded.

In sum, as with several of the demographic and offender characteristics identified above, there is sufficient evidence in the data to conclude that supervision intensity and sample membership are not independent of one another. Our analysis of the relationship between sample membership and positive adjustment scores should, therefore, be based on comparisons that are adjusted for the differences that have been identified in Tables 15.2 and 15.3.

Simple Within-Subjects Analysis of Positive Adjustment

In Column 2 of Table 15.4, we present the results of a pure within subjects analysis of positive adjustment scores. These results are based on the model implied by Eqs. (3) and (4). The initial levels of positive adjustment range from 0.427 in Florida to 0.546 in New York. Both the intercept and a negative trend coefficient are statistically significant in all states except Georgia. In Georgia, the intercept is significantly different from zero but the trend coefficient is not (although the negative direction of this coefficient is consistent with what we see in the other states). Thus, in each state we find evidence (stronger in some that in others) that positive adjustment declines over time.

Multivariate Model of Positive Adjustment

Recall that within-subject effects include the passage of time and supervision intensity (in all states except New York). Early investigation of patterns in the data revealed that positive adjustment declined over time (Table 15.4). Diagnostics suggested that it was not unreasonable to impose a linear trend on this decline.

Our early analysis of the relationship between supervision intensity and positive adjustment was not so simple. Although a linear effect seems plausible for each of the three

indexes in Louisiana, there appears to be a more complex relationship when supervision intensity is operationally defined as the number of monthly contacts (as it is in Florida, Georgia, and South Carolina).

Specifically, in each of these states, we sorted supervision intensity scores in descending order and created 10 equal-n deciles with class marks defined at every tenth percentile of monthly contacts. We then calculated the mean positive adjustment score within each of the 10 groups. A graph of these means indicated that the pattern might well be summarized by a third order polynomial. The pattern was evident in all three states. Despite the generally positive relationship between the two variables (i.e., positive adjustment increased with increasing supervision intensity), there was also an unmistakable pattern of nonlinearity. We, therefore, included linear, quadratic, and cubic monthly contacts effects in the models in Florida, Georgia, and South Carolina.[5]

An attempt was made to specify multivariate hierarchical linear models letting all within-subject effects vary randomly. The analyses revealed significant subject to subject variability in the within-subject intercept term and in the time trend coefficients in each state. In all states except Louisiana, the coefficients for supervision intensity indicators did not demonstrate statistically significant random variability. This was true both in models with between-subject effects and in simpler models that included only within-subject effects. We concluded that the absence of random variability in the supervision intensity effects is robust under a variety of model specifications. As a result, the effects for supervision intensity were treated as fixed in these states. In Louisiana, random variability was observed in the supervision intensity coefficients and variance components were estimated for all within-subject effects. These variance components were statistically significant. As a result, we conclude that a mixed model with random effects for the within-subject intercept and time trend coefficients is appropriate for the data considered here.

Finally, we tested the plausibility of several sets of interactions. In none of the states except Louisiana did we find evidence that sample membership interacted with supervision

Table 15.4   Random Effects Models of Positive Adjustment by State[a]

	Simple within-subjects model
Florida	
Within-subject effects	
Intercept	0.427* (0.017)
Time trend	−0.042* (0.010)
Variance components	
W/S intercept	0.056*
W/S time trend	0.071*
Georgia	
Within-subjects effects	
Intercept	0.441* (0.018)
Time trend	−0.019 (0.012)
Variance components	
W/S intercept	0.036*
W/S time trend	0.011*
Louisiana	
Within-subject effects	
Intercept	0.503* (0.011)
Time trend	−0.013* (0.001)
Variance components	
W/S intercept	0.024*
W/S time trend	0.0003*
New York	
Within-subject effects	
Intercept	0.546* (0.020)
Time trend	−0.032* (0.009)
Variance components	
W/S intercept	0.082*
W/S time trend	0.009*
South Carolina	
Within-subject effects	
Intercept	0.513* (0.020)
Time trend	−0.024* (0.008)
Variance components	
W/S intercept	0.055*
W/S time trend	0.004*

[a]Entries are regression coefficients and their standard errors are in parentheses.
*$p < 0.05$.

intensity. These results suggest that supervision intensity impacts positive adjustment in much the same way in different samples. Since this interaction was significant in Louisiana we included this term in the full model for Louisiana.

An assessment of the interaction between supervision intensity and time indicated that the effect of supervision intensity on positive adjustment was stable over time in all states except Georgia. A graph of the interaction in Georgia suggested that the over-time variation

in the effect of supervision intensity, while statistically significant, was substantively trivial.[6]

In order to see if samples adjusted differently over time, we examined the time x sample interaction. This interaction was statistically significant in New York and Louisiana and was, therefore, included in the models.

Multivariate Hierarchical Linear Models

Table 15.5 presents the multivariate hierarchical linear models of positive adjustment for

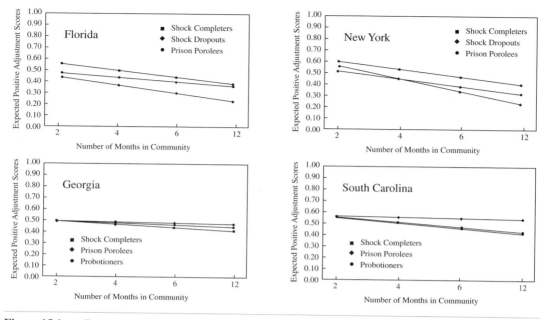

Figure 15.1   Expected positive adjustment scores distributed over time by sample category

each of the states except Louisiana. The model in Louisiana is considerably more complicated and is treated separately (Table 15.6). These analyses continue to provide evidence of a significant decline in positive adjustment scores over the year of the study in four of the five states: Florida, Louisiana, New York, and South Carolina. In Georgia, the trend coefficient is also negative but it is not statistically significant.

Substantively, the models provide evidence of important effects for supervision intensity, demographic and offense-related characteristics, and sample membership. In general, nonwhites adjusted less positively than whites. Older offenders (in New York, offenders who were older at the time of their first arrest) adjusted more positively than younger offenders. Subjects with no prior arrests or convictions tended to do better than subjects with prior records. Additionally, in Florida, offenders serving a sentence for a new crime adjusted more positively than offenders serving a sentence for a technical violation. The data also suggest that property offenders did not adjust as positively as offenders in other groups although the magnitude of this difference varied considerably from state to state.

As expected, early attrition was negatively related to positive adjustment. Offenders who were supervised for shorter periods of time in

the community had lower positive adjustment scores (in all states except Georgia where persistence made no difference). Most likely, many of those who were not supervised as long had been arrested or revoked. Moreover, the positive adjustment scores of offenders with longer follow-up periods did not decline as much over time as those of short-time participants.

Figure 15.1 presents a graphic depiction of the effects of sample membership as implied by Table 15.5. To produce these graphs, all variables except time and sample membership were constrained to their means. We then allowed both time and sample membership to vary over their respective ranges. Under these constraints, we calculated the expectation from the model at each level.

The most striking similarity in the plots in Figure 15.1 is the downward trajectory in positive adjustment scores over time. There are no consistent themes regarding the effect of sample membership. In Georgia and South Carolina, there is virtually no evidence that the samples differ in their positive adjustment scores either in initial levels or over time. In Florida and New York, however, there is evidence of important group differences in successful adjustment.

In Florida, the shock completer group adjusted more positively than both the shock dropouts and the prison parolees, and the

Table 15.5   Hierarchical Linear Model of Positive Adjustment in Four States[a]

	Florida	*Georgia*	*New York*	*South Carolina*
Within-subject effects				
Intercept	−0.683* (0.173)	0.474* (0.145)	0.061 (0.170)	0.230 (0.128)
Time trend	−0.115* (0.045)	−0.010 (0.049)	−0.250* (0.056)	−0.259* (0.072)
Supervision	0.069* (0.019)	0.030 (0.032)	N/A	0.057 (0.034)
Supervision squared	−0.041* (0.014)	−0.189* (0.029)	N/A	−0.131* (0.036)
Supervision cubed	0.014 (0.008)	0.104* (0.019)	N/A	0.069* (0.031)
Adjustments to				
W/S intercept				
Shock completers	0.115* (0.034)	−0.013 (0.047)	0.033 (0.046)	−0.014 (0.047)
Shock dropouts	0.035 (0.040)	N/A	−0.039 (0.045)	N/A
Prison paroless	Reference	−0.012 (0.054)	Reference	−0.000 (0.050)
Probationers	N/A	Reference	N/A	Reference
Nonwhite	−0.116* (0.030)	−0.110* (0.029)	−0.077 (0.046)	−0.145* (0.034)
Age	0.035* (0.008)	0.001 (0.006)	0.015 (0.008)	0.017* (0.008)
Type of offense				
Violent	0.096* (0.034)	0.084* (0.040)	N/A	−0.001 (0.049)
Drug	0.070 (0.040)	0.111* (0.034)	−0.050 (0.044)	0.044 (0.042)
Property/other	Reference	Reference	−0.099 (0.053)	Reference
Youthful offender	N/A	N/A	Reference	N/A
Prior arrest/convictions	0.006 (0.041)	−0.071* (0.032)	0.033 (0.058)	−0.072* (0.034)
New crime				
(vs. technical)	0.126* (0.050)	−0.022 (0.036)	N/A	0.070 (0.055)
Periods followed	0.087* (0.015)	0.013 (0.021)	0.101* (0.015)	−0.010 (0.028)
Cross-level interactions				
with time				
Shock completers	0.012 (0.020)	−0.008 (0.029)	0.044* (0.021)	−0.000 (0.019)
Shock dropouts	0.032 (0.028)	N/A	0.040 (0.022)	N/A
Prison parolees	Reference	0.012 (0.028)	Reference	0.038 (0.021)
Probationers	N/A	Reference	N/A	Reference
Periods followed	0.020 (0.013)	−0.002 (0.015)	0.049* (0.014)	0.060* (0.018)
Variance components				
W/S intercept	0.029*	0.036*	0.063*	0.043*
W/S time trend	0.004*	0.011*	0.009*	0.003*

[a]Entries are regression coefficients accompanied by standard errors in parentheses.
*$p < 0.05$.

nonsignificant interaction suggests that this is true at all time periods. Moreover, the shock dropouts and the prison parolees did not differ in adjustment. Although there is some evidence in Figure 15.1 that the shock completers and the shock dropouts approach each other over the course of the 1-year follow-up period, the interaction between sample and time is not statistically significant.

In New York, the data suggest an initial difference between the shock completers and the shock dropouts but not parolees. The interaction indicates that over time the positive adjustment scores of the shock completer sample decline at

a significantly lower rate than those of the prison parolee sample. The rate of decline for the shock dropout sample is not significantly different from that of the prison parolee sample or the shock completer sample. Because of these differences in the rates of decline, what seems to be a trivial difference between samples at the beginning of the study appears somewhat more important by the end of the twelve month follow-up period. At the end of 12 months, the shock completers were adjusting significantly more positively than the prison parolees, although their performance no longer differed from that of the shock dropouts.

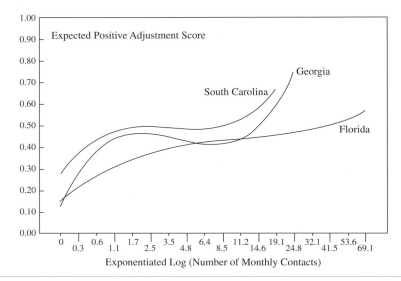

Figure 15.2   Expected positive adjustment scores by varying numbers of monthly contracts in Florida, Georgia, and South Carolina

An important limitation of the New York model is the absence of sample adjustments for supervision intensity. Since New York's shock incarceration program requires intensive supervision for at least 6 months following program completion, it seems reasonable to expect that sample membership and supervision intensity are not independent. However, the evidence in the other states indicates that the relationship between supervision intensity and successful adjustment is positive and statistically significant. If this same or a similar set of conditions holds in New York, our model suffers from specification bias due to an omitted variable (supervision intensity). Under such a scenario, we would expect the bias to create the appearance that the shock completer group performs better than the comparison groups. In general, the sample difference depicted in Figure 15.1 provides little compelling evidence for a general positive effect of shock incarceration.

The data do support the hypothesis that supervision intensity is an important correlate of positive adjustment. In every state, we see evidence of a strong and generally positive impact of supervision intensity on successful adjustment. Figure 15.2 presents the effects of supervision intensity implied by the effects in Table 15.3 for Florida, Georgia, and South Carolina. In this analysis, the sample membership dummy variables were constrained to their means. The

results are relatively straightforward. In general, the relationship between supervision intensity as measured by the log of the number of monthly contacts is positive and statistically significant.

In all three states, there was evidence of nonlinearity in the relationship (significant quadratic and cubic terms). Increases in positive adjustment scores were not the same at all levels of contact. The shape of the curves seem to imply that increases in contacts were accompanied by increases in positive adjustment up to a point of about two contacts per month. After this the relationship levels off (additional contacts have little effect on adjustment) until very high levels of contact are reached. At these extremely high levels of contact the relationship between adjustment and intensity again becomes positive. Thus, the incremental change in positive adjustment is not as great at moderate to high levels of contact as it is at low or extremely high levels of contact.[7] On the basis of this evidence, we conclude that the relationship between supervision intensity and successful adjustment is positive but not necessarily linear.

The Louisiana model was more complicated than the models constructed in the other states. The results in Table 15.6 indicate that the shock completers did not adjust as well as either the probationers or the prison parolees, although the shock completers and the shock dropouts did not differ. The rate of decline in positive

Table 15.6   Hierarchical Linear Model of Positive Adjustment in Louisiana[a]

Within-subject effects			
Intercept	0.225* (0.057)		
Time trend	−0.070* (0.006)		
Knowledge index	−0.053 (0.028)		
Surveillance index	0.100* (0.038)		
Requirement index	0.061* (0.015)		
Adjustments to W/S intercept			
Shock completers	−0.078* (0.034)		
Shock dropouts	−0.092 (0.054)		
Prison parolees	0.021 (0.031)		
Probationers	Reference		
Nonwhite	−0.045* (0.012)		
Age	0.003* (0.001)		
Type of offense			
Violent	−0.005 (0.020)		
Drug	0.009 (0.013)		
Property/other	Reference		
Prior arrest/convictions	−0.013 (0.013)		
New crime (vs. technical)	N/A		
Periods followed	0.016* (0.004)		
Cross-level interactions with time			
Shock completers	0.005 (0.003)		
Shock dropouts	0.004 (0.005)		
Prison paroless	−0.002 (0.003)		
Probationers	Reference		
Periods followed	0.006* (0.001)		
Cross-level interactions with supervision intensity	*Knowledge*	*Surveillance*	*Requirements*
Shock completers	−0.006 (0.016)	0.033 (0.020)	0.010 (0.009)
Shock dropouts	0.070* (0.029)	0.011 (0.040)	0.028* (0.015)
Prison parolees	0.028 (0.016)	0.006 (0.021)	0.001 (0.009)
Probationers	Reference	Reference	Reference
Periods followed	−0.003 (0.002)	0.002 (0.003)	−0.004*(0.001)
Variance components			
W/S intercept	0.020*		
W/S time trend	0.0001*		
W/S knowledge	0.004*		
W/S surveillance	0.005*		
W/S requirements	0.001*		

[a]Entries are regression coefficients accompanied by standard errors in parentheses.
*$p < 0.05$.

adjustment over time, however, was not as strong for the shock completers as it was for the other groups. Although the decay coefficient fails to achieve statistical significance at 95% confidence level ($t = 1.902$, $p < 0.057$). A graph of this effect is presented in the upper left-hand panel in Figure 15.3. The model predicts that differences between the groups, which are substantively important at the study's outset, are reduced to nonsignificant levels by the end of 1 year. This result replicates the finding of MacKenzie et al. (1992) and suggests that supervision intensity rather than sample membership plays the more important role in explaining successful adjustment in Louisiana.

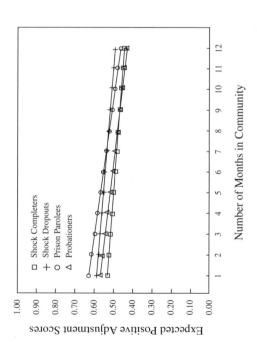

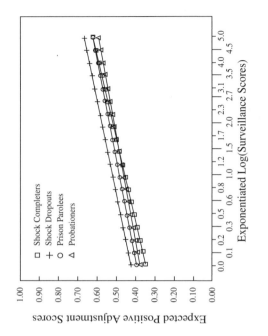

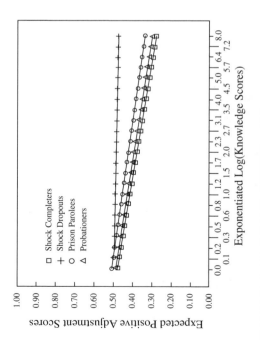

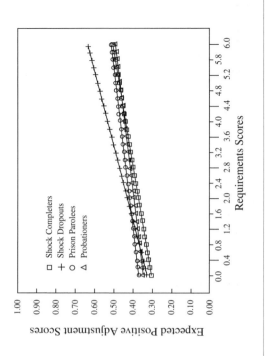

Figure 15.3 Expected positive adjustment scores by sample, time, and varying supervision intensity levels in Louisiana

The remaining panels in Figure 15.3 clearly depict the positive relationship between supervision intensity and positive adjustment.[8] Although there are potentially meaningful interactions between the degree of this effect and sample membership the only aberrant group is the shock dropout sample, which is comprised of only 14 subjects. Thus, we hesitate to place much importance on it. We see more similarities than differences in the supervision intensity results in Louisiana and the other states. In sum, the relationship between the two variables is positive and statistically significant in all states. This suggests, once again, that supervision intensity may play an especially important role in the explanation of positive adjustment.

DISCUSSION AND CONCLUSIONS

The results of our analysis indicate that shock incarceration had limited impact on successful adjustment. Despite the programming differences detailed in Table 15.1, this finding was relatively consistent across states. By comparison, the effect of supervision intensity was positive and much more consistently observed across states.

The analysis revealed that demographic and offender characteristics also played an important role. Nonwhite and younger offenders tended to adjust less positively than their counterparts who did not share those characteristics. Property offenders did not adjust as well as violent and drug offenders. Finally, offenders with prior records or evidence of prior technical violations did not adjust as well as offenders with no prior criminal history.

In two states (Georgia and South Carolina), we found no evidence that shock incarceration improved offender adjustment in the community. In New York, there is evidence that shock completers adjusted more positively than shock dropouts at the beginning of community supervision and prison parolees at the end of community supervision. But the New York data also provide cause for restraint. First, the shock completers and the shock dropouts were adjusting at similar levels by the end of the 1-year follow-up period. This suggests that factors related to shock program entrance might be operative instead of factors related to completing the shock program. Second, we were unable to control for supervision intensity in New York. This introduces considerable uncertainty into our conclusions surrounding the New York data since the shock program completers were required to undergo at least 6 months of intensive supervision in the community. In Louisiana, we find evidence that the shock completers did not adjust as positively as the other groups at the outset of the follow-up period. The data also indicate, however, that adjustment levels for the shock completers actually approached those of the other groups as the follow-up period progressed. By the end of the one year follow-up period, the differences between the groups were trivial.

The notable exception to the prevailing pattern occurred in Florida. Although demographic and offender characteristics as well as supervision intensity were important in Florida, the state's shock completer sample adjusted significantly more positively than either the shock dropout sample or the prison parolees.

Our analysis raises important questions about potential distinguishing characteristics of the Florida shock program. We speculate that there are several plausible explanations. The Florida shock program may, in fact, be responsible for changing offenders so that they perform better during community supervision.

It may be that the therapeutic programs in the Florida shock program had a positive impact on the offenders. Offenders in the Florida program did not spend as much time in treatment and counseling as some programs (e.g., Louisiana and New York). However, it could be that the quality or type of therapeutic programming in Florida was more effective in initiating positive changes in the offenders.

A comparison of the characteristics of offenders in Florida with those in other states shows that Florida offenders had, on the whole, lower rates of prior convictions and arrests. Moreover, the Florida offenders tended to be younger than offenders in other states. It is at least conceivable, then, that shock incarceration has more potential to induce better adjustment in younger offenders who have not previously been involved with the adult criminal justice system. Future research should explore this issue with samples where there is more variability on these measures to assess whether the effects of shock incarceration are conditional on these factors.

A prominent feature of our analysis of the effect of offender-officer contacts was its non-linear quality. Nevertheless, positive adjustment increased in the presence of greater levels of supervision intensity and this broader pattern was evident in all four states where supervision intensity data were collected.

In sum, the positive adjustment construct taps an offender's choice to participate in positive activities. Not all offenders are equally capable of participating in such activities. They may face internal restrictions (e.g., ability or motivation) or external restrictions (e.g., high unemployment rates or limited access to treatment and educational opportunities). The strong association between supervision intensity and positive adjustment suggests that offenders might be coerced to participate in positive activities. Although there may be some limits on the efficacy of supervision intensity (the observed "leveling-off" effect), the consistent result among the states we studied is that greater supervision intensity is associated with more successful adjustment during community supervision.

The relatively weak association between shock incarceration and positive adjustment should give policy makers reason for pause. While efforts to identify circumstances where shock incarceration is effective might be useful, it seems that the evidence weighs against concluding that shock incarceration programs are broadly effective at enhancing the ability of offenders to adjust more successfully in the community. This research has evaluated the impact of these programs on offenders' adjustment to the community. As long as these programs remain a part of correctional strategy, such evaluations will continue to be important. The content of such programs should receive special scrutiny so that the effective components can be identified along with those offenders who stand to benefit most.

APPENDIX

Table A.1   Attrition Profiles by State

	Number completing follow-up period	Cumulative attrition rate (%)
Florida		
Interval 1	273	—
Interval 2	207	24.2
Interval 3	130	52.4
Interval 4	51	81.3
Mean (SD) periods followed*		
Shock completers	2.5 (1.0)	
Shock dropouts	1.9 (1.0)	
Prison parolees	2.6 (1.1)	
Georgia		
Interval 1	237	—
Interval 2	216	8.9
Interval 3	148	37.6
Interval 4	56	76.4
Mean (SD) periods followed		
Shock completers	2.8 (1.0)	
Prison parolees	2.8 (0.9)	
Probationers	2.6 (0.8)	
Louisiana		
Interval 1	248	—
Interval 2	242	2.4
Interval 3	237	4.4
Interval 4	231	6.9
Interval 5	223	10.1
Interval 6	209	15.7

	Number completing follow-up period	Cumulative attrition rate (%)
Interval 7	190	23.4
Interval 8	176	29.0
Interval 9	164	33.9
Interval 10	155	37.5
Interval 11	144	41.9
Interval 12	134	46.0
Mean (SD) periods followed*		
Shock completers	9.1 (3.2)	
Shock dropouts	8.6 (3.8)	
Prison parolees	8.7 (3.7)	
Probationers	10.5 (2.8)	
New York		
Interval 1	237	—
Interval 2	188	20.7
Interval 3	153	35.4
Interval 4	133	43.9
Mean (SD) periods followed		
Shock completers	3.1 (1.2)	
Shock dropouts	2.8 (1.3)	
Prison parolees	3.1 (1.2)	
South Carolina		
Interval 1	206	—
Interval 2	204	1.0
Interval 3	183	11.2
Interval 4	144	30.1
Mean (SD) periods followed		
Shock completers	3.6 (0.7)	
Prison parolees	3.5 (0.7)	
Probationers	3.6 (0.7)	

*$p < 0.05$.

Table A.2 Supervision Intensity Indicators by State[a]

	Median	Mean	SD	Skewness
Florida				
Monthly Contacts	2.25	6.63	9.53	+2.25
Log Transform	1.18	1.50	0.94	<1.0
Georgia				
Monthly Contacts	1.82	2.55	3.07	+4.60
Log Transform	1.04	1.08	0.56	<1.0
Louisiana				
Knowledge Index	1.00	1.24	1.13	+1.65
Log Transform	0.69	0.70	0.46	<1.0
Surveillance Index	0.39	0.71	0.84	+1.35
Log Transform	0.33	0.43	0.43	<1.0
Requirement Index	2.61	2.72	1.11	<1.0
South Carolina				
Monthly contacts	1.50	1.73	1.40	+2.95
Log Transform	0.92	0.90	0.43	<1.0

[a]Descriptive statistics were calculated by averaging scores for all subjects over their entire set of follow-up periods.

NOTES

1. Program characteristics described here were accurate at the time of data collection but may have changed since that time. Particularly significant changes have occurred in the Georgia and South Carolina programs since the time these data were collected.

2. Offense classifications include (1) violent crimes, (2) drug offenses, and (3) property and "other" offenses in all states except New York, where classifications include (1) drug offenses, (2) property offenses, and (3) crimes by youthful offenders. In all states except Louisiana and New York, offenders were classified as serving their current sentence for either (1) a new crime or (2) a technical violation.

3. Data used in the current study were analyzed in the previous MacKenzie et al. (1992) study.

4. The models in Table 15.6 and throughout the remainder of the paper allow for random subject to subject variability in both the within-subject intercept and the effect of time. The statistical significance of the variance components observed in each of these models provides empirical support for specifying the model in this fashion.

5. The quadratic and cubic terms in these models were mean centered to reduce inflation of the variance associated with the parameter estimates (Neter et al., 1989, p. 317).

6. The results in Georgia suggested slight variability in the second and third degrees of the polynomial but the general shape of the function was time stable.

7. Note that the third-degree polynomial in each state corresponds to approximately the 90th percentile of the contact distribution in each state, and therefore these results are based on very few cases.

8. Recall that increasing values of the knowledge index are associated with less knowledge of offender activities. Thus, the graph for the effect of knowledge implies a positive relationship between supervision intensity and positive adjustment.

REFERENCES

Allison, P. D. (1990). Change scores as dependent variables in regression analysis. *Sociological Methodology, 20,* 93-114.

Anglin, M. D., & Hser, Y. (1990). Treatment of drug abuse. In M. Tonry & J. Q. Wilson (Eds.), *Crime and Justice: A Review* of *Research, Vol. 13 (Drugs and Crime)* (pp. 393-460). Chicago: University of Chicago Press.

Berk, R. A. (1991). *An Introduction to Multilevel Analysis for Cross-Site Program Evaluations.* Unpublished discussion paper.

Bryk, A. S., & Raudenbush, S. W. (1987). Application of hierarchical linear models to assessing change. *Psychological Bulletin, 101*(1), 147-158.

Bryk, A. S., & Raudenbush, S. W. (1992). *Hierarchical Linear Models: Applications and Data Analysis Methods.* Newbury Park, CA: Sage.

Cook, T. D., & Campbell, D. T. (1979). *Quasi-Experimentation: Design and Analysis Issues for Field Settings.* Chicago: Rand-McNally.

Gendreau, P., & Ross, R. (1987). Revivification of rehabilitation: Evidence from the 1980s. *Justice Quarterly, 4,* 349-407.

Gowdy, V. B. (1993). *Intermediate Sanctions* (Research in Brief). Washington, D.C.: National Institute of Justice.

Greene, W. H. (1993). *Econometrics* (2nd ed.), New York: Macmillan.

Horney, J., Osgood, D. W., & Marshall, I. H. (1993). *Criminal careers in the short-term: Month-to-month variation in crime and its relation to local life circumstances.* Paper presented at the meetings of the American Society of Criminology in Phoenix, AZ.

Hsiao, C. (1986). *The Analysis of Panel Data.* Cambridge, MA: Cambridge University Press.

Latessa, E. J., & Vito, G. F. (1988). The effects of intensive supervision on shock probationers. *Journal of Criminal Justice, 16,* 319-330.

Littell, R. C., Freund, R. J., & Spector, P. C. (1991). *SAS System for Linear Models* (3rd ed.). Cary, NC: SAS Institute, Inc.

MacKenzie, D. L. (1990). Boot camp prisons: Components, evaluations and empirical issues. *Federal Probation, 54*(3), 44-52.

MacKenzie, D. L. (1991). The parole performance of offenders released from shock incarceration (boot camp prisons): A survival time analysis. *Journal of Quantitative Criminology, 7,* 213-236.

MacKenzie, D. L., & Brame, R. (1993). *Shock Incarceration and Positive Adjustment During Community Supervision: A Multi-Site Evaluation.* Unpublished Final Report to the National Institute of Justice, University of Maryland, College Park.

MacKenzie, D. L., & Shaw, J. W. (1990). Inmate adjustment and change during shock incarceration: The impact of correctional boot camp programs. *Justice Quarterly, 7,* 125-150.

MacKenzie, D. L., & Shaw, J. W. (1993). The impact of shock incarceration on technical violations and new criminal activities. *Justice Quarterly, 10*(3), 463-487.

MacKenzie, D. L., & Souryal, C. (1991). States say rehabilitation, recidivism reduction outrank punishment a main goals. *Corrections Today, 53*, 90-96.

MacKenzie, D. L., & Souryal, C. (1992). *Inmate Attitude Change During Incarceration. A Comparison of Boot Camp and Traditional Prison.* Unpublished Final Report to the National Institute of Justice, University of Maryland, College Park.

MacKenzie, D. L., & Souryal, C. (1993). *Multi-Site Study' of Shock Incarceration: Process Evaluation,* Unpublished Final Report to the National Institute of Justice, University of Maryland, College Park.

MacKenzie, D. L., & Souryal, C. (1995). Inmate attitude change during incarceration: A comparison of boot camp and traditional prison. *Justice Quarterly, 12*(2), 325-354.

MacKenzie, D. L., Shaw, J. W., & Souryal, C. (1992). Characteristics associated with successful adjustment to supervision: A comparison of parolees, probationers, shock participants, and shock dropouts. *Criminal Justice and Behavior, 19*(4), 437-453.

Mason, W. M., Wong, G. M., & Entwistle, B. (1983). Contextual analysis through the multilevel linear model. *Sociological Methodology, 13,* 72-101.

Neter, J., Wasserman, W., & Kutner, M. H. (1989). *Applied Linear Regression Models* (2nd ed.), Homewood, IL: Irwin.

Petersilia, J., & Turner, S. (1990). *Intensive Supervision for High-Risk Probationers: Findings from Three California Experiments,* Santa Monica, CA: RAND.

Petersilia, J., & Turner, S. (1993). Intensive probation and parole. In *Crime and Justice: A Review of Research, Vol. 19* (pp. 281-335). Chicago: University of Chicago Press.

Raudenbush, S. W., & Chan, W. (1992). Growth curve analysis in accelerated longitudinal designs. *Journal of Research in Crime and Delinquency, 29*(4), 387-411.

Souryal, C., & MacKenzie, D. L. (1994). Shock incarceration and recidivism: An examination of boot camp programs in four states. In J. O. Smykla & W. L. Selke (Eds.), *Intermediate Sanctions: Sentencing in the 90s.* Cincinnati: Anderson.

16

CHARACTERISTICS ASSOCIATED WITH SUCCESSFUL ADJUSTMENT TO SUPERVISION

A Comparison of Parolees, Probationers, Shock Participants, and Shock Dropouts

DORIS LAYTON MACKENZIE

JAMES W. SHAW

CLAIRE SOURYAL

The new "boot camp" prisons have attracted the attention of the media and the public. These programs, also called shock incarceration programs, are modeled after military boot camps (MacKenzie, 1990; Parent, 1989). Offenders spend a short period, usually 120 days, in the program and then are supervised in the community. The similarity among various shock incarceration programs is the short period served in prison in an environment that emphasizes discipline, military drills, and physical training. Although programs differ

substantially in other ways, most incorporate some type of daily rehabilitation activities in addition to work.

Shock incarceration is similar to shock probation, shock parole, or split-sentences. Offenders in these programs spend a short time in prison. Shock incarceration differs from such programs because offenders are separated from other offenders during the incarceration phase and spend time in the boot camp-like atmosphere.

The study reported here is part of a larger evaluation examining the effectiveness of Louisiana's

Reprinted with permission from MacKenzie, D. L., Shaw, J. W., & Souryal, C. (1992). *Criminal Justice and Behavior, 19*(4), 437–454. An earlier version of this article was presented at the 1989 Annual Meeting of the American Society of Criminology, Reno, Nevada. This investigation was supported in part by Grant 87-IJ-CX-0020 from the National Institute of Justice, U.S. Department of Justice to the Louisiana State University. Opinions expressed in this article are those of the authors and not necessarily those of the U.S. Department of Justice. Thanks are expressed to the Louisiana Department of Public Safety and Corrections staff and the Project Advisory Board, who have given their time, interest, and talent to this project.

shock incarceration program in reaching its goals. An earlier qualitative and descriptive analysis of the program, using record data and intensive interviews with staff and inmates revealed that a major focus of the program was on rehabilitation (MacKenzie, Gould, Riechers, & Shaw, 1989). Offenders spend a considerable portion of their time in counseling and treatment during the incarceration phase of the Louisiana program. On release, offenders begin a three-stage intensive parole supervision program. Staff working with offenders throughout the process view themselves as agents of behavior change and models for the offenders.

A primary goal of most shock incarceration programs is to change offenders while incarcerated so they will engage in more socially positive activities and fewer criminal activities. Before any such changes in behavior, changes in attitudes and expectations might first be expected to occur (Cullen & Gendreau, 1990). To examine this hypothesis, MacKenzie and Shaw (1990) compared the prison adjustment, expectations, and attitudes of offenders participating in the shock program in Louisiana to offenders who dropped out of the program and to a comparable group of offenders serving their sentences in a regular prison. In comparison to regularly incarcerated offenders, shock offenders were more positive about the program and the staff when they first entered prison (MacKenzie & Shaw, 1990). They were also more positive about the future and, in general, had more positive social attitudes. After 3 months in the shock program, offenders became even more positive about the program, staff and their future, and they developed more positive social attitudes. During the same period a comparison group of offenders in a traditional prison did not change in these attitudes. Those who completed the shock program had more positive social attitudes than those who dropped out of the program.

Another study compared the performance of shock offenders during community supervision to samples of offenders serving time on parole and probation (MacKenzie, 1991). There were no significant differences in recidivism between the shock parolees and either parolees from traditional prisons or probationers. Approximately 30% of the offenders were returned to prison during the first year of community supervision.

In summary, previous research examining the Louisiana shock incarceration has indicated that the program emphasizes rehabilitation within a strict and demanding boot camp-like regime. Those who complete the program appear to have more positive social attitudes in comparison to those who drop out or who serve time in a regular prison. Such attitudes may be expected to be positively associated with successful adjustment in the community. However, the percentages of shock parolees, regular parolees, and probationers who were involved in criminal activities did not differ in the MacKenzie (1991) study. These results suggest that although offenders who complete the shock program may change in a positive manner, such changes may not be enough to enable them to overcome the difficulties they face in returning to the home environment.

This article examines the adjustment of offenders during the community supervision phase of the shock program. The performance of shock graduates is compared to those serving other sentences. The first study examined the positive social activities of shock parolees, regular parolees, probationers, and dropouts from the shock program. The second study assessed the characteristics of offenders who completed the two phases of the shock incarceration program in an attempt to identify factors associated with successful program completion.

STUDY 1

The social adjustment of offenders paroled after successfully completing the shock incarceration program was compared to that of regular prison parolees, shock dropout parolees, and probationers. An adjustment index was developed using monthly reports from the community supervision agents to reflect positive adjustment in various areas of offenders' lives.

Method

Subjects

The performance during community supervision of the following four samples of males, each of whom received different correctional experiences, was assessed: (a) graduates of the shock incarceration program ($n = 74$), (b) probationers ($n = 108$), (c) parolees who had served time in a regular prison ($n = 74$) and (d) dropouts from the shock incarceration program ($n = 17$).[1] The subjects were those studied in the MacKenzie (1991) study of recidivism.

As a comparison group study, subjects were not randomly assigned to sentence type. All subjects, however, met the legal eligibility requirements of the shock program, as well as the suitability and acceptability criteria developed for the program by the Department of Corrections. These criteria required that the offender: (a) be less than 40 years of age, (b) have no known medical or psychological problems that could interfere with participation, (c) have no record of felony DWI, (d) have no record of sexual offenses, (e) have no assault escapes, (f) demonstrate no overt homosexuality, and (g) have no history of assaultive behavior.[2] The dropout sample included those offenders who voluntarily dropped out of the shock program or were asked to leave for disciplinary reasons prior to graduation. They had served the remainder of their sentence in a traditional prison.

The shock participants' mean age was 24.0 years ($SD = 4.7$), with a mean of 10.6 ($SD = 1.6$) years of education. Forty percent were White. Thirty-one percent had entered as probation violators. Most were convicted of burglary (42.7%), theft (17.7%), and drug offenses (30.9%), with average maximum sentence lengths of 50.4 months ($SD = 19.4$). They had first been arrested at 19.5 years of age. Seventy-six percent had some prior adult criminal history, and 16.7% had previously served time in a prison or jail.

In comparison to the parole sample, the shock offenders were significantly younger, had longer sentences, and were also younger at first arrest. (On average the parolees were 26.8 years old, serving a sentence of 35 months, and had first been arrested at age 21.8.)[3] In comparison to the probationers, as might be expected, more of the shock sample had entered as probation violators. (Only 8.4% of the probationers were violators.) The shock sample also had longer sentences and were more likely to have spent time in a prison or jail than probationers (who

had average sentences of 30.8 months, and 3.7% of whom had spent time in a prison or jail). In comparison to dropouts, the shock sample had more education and had longer sentences. Fewer of the shock sample had spent time in prison or jail. Dropouts had 9.3 years of education and sentences of 30.4 months, and 46.7% had spent time in prison or jail. Overall, the results depict the shock sample as having slightly more of the characteristics associated with higher levels of recidivism and poorer behavior during community supervision—namely, criminal history, youth, and young at first arrest.

Procedure

Data collection began in Spring, 1988, and was either completed in Spring, 1989, or when the number in a sample reached approximately 100 (whichever came first). The differences in sample sizes reflect the fact that there were fewer offenders released from prison and from the shock program in comparison to the number of probationers who met the criteria for the study.

Data were collected from (a) Department of Corrections records and (b) monthly performance evaluations. Basic demographic and criminal history data were collected from Department of Corrections records. The parole or probation agent responsible for each case completed the standardized monthly performance evaluations describing the performance of each subject during each month the offender was being supervised in the community. The forms were returned by mail to the researchers. Month 1 for each offender was the first month of community supervision after release for parolees (shock, regular parolees, and dropouts) and on probation for the probationers.

Instruments

The researchers developed the performance evaluation form after reviewing extensive narratives of inmate contacts written by agents supervising shock-program graduates on intensive supervision. The evaluation form included 27 questions in six domains of offenders' lives: (a) alcohol and drug abuse, (b) education,

(c) employment, (d) interpersonal, (e) legal, (f) program requirements (e.g., curfews, restitution) and other.[4]

Agents were asked to respond to a series of questions designed to elicit information about offenders' performance during the previous month. For example, under employment, questions asked whether offenders were employed during the month and, if so, whether they were working full- or part-time. Under substance abuse, questions asked whether offenders had been required to attend a substance abuse program and, if so, whether they were making satisfactory progress. In addition, the instrument included three general questions and one final open-ended question asking for further comments or information about the subject.

For this study, 17 of the questions were used to create the Adjustment to Prosocial Living Index, an index indicating adjustment to parole supervision (see Appendix). Each item is scored 0 or 1, for total index scores ranging from 0 to 17. A high score indicates positive adjustment.

The samples received different types of supervision. All shock offenders were intensively supervised. The level of supervision of the parolees, dropouts, and probationers differed, depending on their risk level as assessed by a probation/parole agent. There was thus a danger that sample differences in Adjustment to Prosocial Living Index scores could be dependent on the intensity of supervision. An examination of the percentage of subjects in each sample who received a positive score for individual items showed that a larger percentage of the shock group received points for items that were associated with supervision requirements, such as a negative drug screen or alcohol sensor. Thus the differences between samples could, in part, be a function of the number of offenders who were tested for drugs and alcohol, not just whether they tested positive.

Therefore, three indices were used that had been developed previously from items in the monthly performance evaluations and used in MacKenzie (1991) to examine offenders' performance during community supervision. These Level of Supervision Indices are summated scales designed to reflect the level of intensity of supervision: (a) knowledge, (b) requirements, and (c) surveillance.

The knowledge supervision index measures the degree to which the agent had knowledge of the daily life of the offender. The requirements index measures the number of restrictions placed on the offender during community supervision, and the third index measures surveillance activities. High scores on the requirements or surveillance indices mean that the offender had more requirements (e.g., compulsory substance abuse treatment, curfew, appointments, restitution) and that his activities were checked regularly during the month (e.g., contacts with employers, teachers, or supervisors and drug or alcohol tests). A high score on the knowledge index means the agent did not know much about the offender's activities (employment, school, family, or health problems). More intense supervision should mean that the agent has more knowledge about an offender, that the offender has more restrictions and requirements on supervision, and that the agent oversees the activities of the offender more aggressively. Unlike the Adjustment to Prosocial Index, which measures how well the offender does during community supervision, these indices measure only supervision intensity.

Results and Discussion

Adjustment to Prosocial Living

Scores for the four samples were calculated for months 1, 3, 6 and 12. Separate repeated measures multivariate analysis of variance (MANOVA), with Sample, Time and the Sample × Time interaction, measured adjustment for all offenders who (a) completed 3 months ($n = 261$), (b) a subset who completed 6 months ($n = 229$), and (c) a subset of these who completed all 12 months ($n = 145$) of community supervision. The effect of sample was significant ($p < .001$) in all analyses. There was also a significant effect ($p < .001$) for time in the 6 and 12 months analyses. The Sample × Time interaction was not significant in the either the 3- or 6-month analyses but was significant ($p < .001$) in the 12-month analysis.[5]

Post hoc comparisons indicated that the shock parolees adjusted significantly more positively than the other three groups in the 3-, 6-, and 12-month analyses. The parolees had more positive adjustment scores than the probationers. The dropouts from shock incarceration did not differ in adjustment from regular prison parolees, but adjusted more positively than the probationers. Over the 6- and 12-month periods, the performance of all groups declined. The Sample × Time interaction at 12 months indicated that although there was some general decline in the scores of the parolees, dropouts, and probationers during the 12 months, the decline for the shock releasees was more dramatic.

Level of Supervision Indices

The three supervision indices were entered as control variables in regression analyses with positive adjustment as the dependent variable. For the group who had completed 12 months of supervision, the knowledge index, $F(df) = 83.5_{(1,271)}$, the requirements index, $F(df) = 17.0_{(1,271)}$, and the surveillance index, $F(df) = 13.6_{(1,271)}$, were significant in predicting the offenders' adjustment to community supervision. The samples differed significantly in adjustment when examined without the control variables in the analysis. When the three indices were entered as control variables, there were no differences among samples in positive social adjustment. The separate analyses examining the adjustment of those who had completed 3 months and 6 months were similar to the results for the 12-month group; the three intensity of supervision scales were significant, and when they were entered as control variables the sample differences in adjustment were eliminated.

Thus it appeared that the more intense the supervision, the more positive the adjustment to community supervision. That is, the more knowledge the agent had about the offender, the greater the requirements of supervision, and the more surveillance, the better the offender scored on the positive adjustment index. These results suggest that the significant differences in positive adjustment among the samples were a byproduct of the intensity of supervision. In other words, although the shock parolees adjusted more positively during community supervision in comparison to parolees and probationers, the higher level of positive adjustment appears to have been a function of the intensity of supervision, not self-directed choice of activities.

Criminal History and Individual Characteristics

Also examined was the relationship of three sets of independent variables (personal characteristics, criminal history variables, and current sentence characteristics) to positive social adjustment during community supervision. Analyses were based on the average positive adjustment score for the months during which the offender was in the community under supervision (offenders differed in the number of months they had been on community supervision).

There were three personal characteristic variables: (a) age at release, (b) race, and (c) years of education completed. The analyses also examined three criminal history variables: (a) previous criminal history, (b) prior incarceration, and (c) age at first arrest. Lastly, the two current sentence characteristics variables examined were maximum possible sentence (only for those who had been incarcerated) and whether the person entered prison or probation as a probation violator. The relationship between each set of variables (personal characteristics, criminal history, current sentence) and the offender's positive adjustment during community supervision was examined in separate regression analyses.

The shock parolees did not differ from the three other samples when the intensity of supervision variables were included in each analysis. However, when the analyses were completed *without* the intensity of supervision variables as control variables but with only the personal characteristics, criminal history, and sentence characteristics variables as control variables, shock parolees continued to outperform the other samples. In addition, for each of the four samples, offenders who were older, older at first arrest, White, and had longer sentences adjusted more positively during community supervision.[6]

In summary, shock parolees adjusted more positively during community supervision in comparison to traditional parolees, probationers, and dropouts. Differences in performance among groups of offenders disappeared when the intensity of supervision was controlled. The performance of all groups declined over time but the decline in performance was greatest for the shock parolees. Although the shock parolees adjusted more positively, this appeared to be a result of the intensity of supervision, not self-directed choice. This significant deterioration in performance of shock parolees over time was most likely the result of a reduction in the intensity of their supervision. Thus it appears that shock parolees and similar offenders on community supervision will be involved in positive activities and perform satisfactorily if this is required of them as a condition of community supervision.

The same appears not to be true for offenders who are younger, younger at first arrest, non-White, and have shorter sentences. These characteristics predicted poor adjustment regardless of level of supervision. When level of supervision was controlled, differences in these characteristics remained significantly associated with adjustment. Thus, if offenders are supervised at a similar level of intensity, offenders who are older, were older when first involved in criminal activities, are White, and have longer sentences will perform better during supervision. Although refraining from drug use, finding employment, attending counseling, and similar positive activities may be influenced by whether an agent checks on offenders' activities or requires certain behavior, they are also, in part, a function of such variables as age and race. Thus positive adjustment is apparently more than simply a question of supervision level.

Study 2

Study 2 focused only on offenders who entered the shock program. The characteristics of those who succeeded in completing both the in-prison phase and the community supervision phase of the program were examined. A substantial percentage (44.2% during the first year of the program) of the offenders who begin the shock program in Louisiana drop out before completing the in-prison phase program (MacKenzie, Shaw, & Gowdy, 1990). These offenders must serve their original court-imposed sentence in a traditional prison until they are eligible for parole.

Those who successfully complete the in-prison phase are paroled and are intensively supervised in the community. Approximately 31.1% of these releasees from shock fail during the community supervision phase of the shock

program (MacKenzie, 1991). As can be seen, a relatively small percentage of the initial shock entrants can be considered a "success." In this study we focused on these offenders in an attempt to identify the characteristics associated with successful completion of the shock-incarceration program's two phases.

Method

Subjects

Data were collected from 208 offenders who entered the shock-incarceration program in Louisiana from Fall, 1987, through Spring, 1988. One hundred and sixteen of the 208 offenders (55.8%) completed the program. During the period of data collection, 74 of the 116 offenders who completed at least 90 days of the shock program were released to community supervision.

During 1 year of community supervision, 28 (37.8%) of the 74 offenders were arrested at least once, 13 (17.6%) legally exited supervision, and 38 (51.4%) were still being supervised at the end of the 12 months. A total of 23 failed during this time: 16 (21.6%) were in jail at the end of the 12-month supervision period; 5 (6.8%) were revoked, and 2 (2.7%) had absconded.[7]

Instruments

Data from records were collected for age, race, maximum sentence length, probation violation, IQ, education, and criminal history.

Attitudes were measured using three Jesness scales (Social Maladjustment, Alienation, Manifest Aggression), two prisonization scales (Positive Future, Staff and Program), and a Locus of Control (LOC) Scale. The three Jesness scales have been found to be associated with criminal behavior in previous work by Jesness and his colleagues (Jesness, 1983; Jesness & Wedge, 1985). The two prisonization scales were developed for use in the Louisiana evaluation (MacKenzie & Shaw, 1990). The LOC scale is an abbreviated version of Rotter's locus of control scale developed by Valecha and Ostrom (1974). It measures the extent to which an individual believes that it is possible to control events in one's environment. Individuals who score low in LOC believe that they cannot control events.

Monthly performance evaluations completed by the parole agent were used to determine activities during community supervision (e.g., employment, drug and alcohol treatment, school), overall adjustment (one item asking agent the overall adjustment of the offender to community supervision), and positive adjustment (using the Adjustment to Prosocial Living Index described in Study 1).

Results and Discussion

In-Prison Phase

Logistic regression analyses were completed separately for (a) demographic characteristics, (b) criminal history variables, and (c) attitudes and expectations. Success or failure in completing the in-prison phase of the shock program was the dependent variable.

Variables contributing significantly to success were sentence length, IQ, and LOC. Those who completed the program's in-prison phase had longer sentences, higher IQs, and believed that they had more control of events in their lives.

The reason offenders with longer sentences complete the program appears to be because leaving before completion results in transfer to a traditional prison, where they will serve the remainder of their court-imposed sentence until they are granted parole. Those who are returned to a traditional prison will most likely serve a longer time in prison than the 90 to 180 days required for completion of the shock program. Thus those with longer sentences may reduce their time in prison proportionately more than those with shorter sentences by successfully completing the shock program.

The association of IQ and control of events (LOC) with completion of the shock program is more difficult to explain. The program emphasizes accountability for one's actions; there are daily performance evaluations, and punishment for misbehavior is immediate. Possibly, this direct relationship between behavior and rewards and punishment in the program may be compatible with the belief that one is in control of events in one's life. Thus it might be easier

for those who believe they can control events to respond to the demands of the program. We speculate that individuals with higher IQs may be better able to more easily identify what is necessary to succeed in the program. It may also be easier for them to understand the delayed rewards to be gained from completing the program (e.g., a shorter period in prison).

Community Supervision Phase

Separate logistic regression analyses examined the relationships of the following sets of variables to failures and arrests during community supervision: (a) demographic characteristics, (b) criminal history variables, (c) attitudes and expectations, (d) activities during community supervision, and (e) adjustment during community supervision. Significant contributions in the failure analyses were age, race, probation violations, age at first arrest, prior incarcerations, working during the first month of supervision, and positive social adjustment. Shock-program completers who succeeded on community supervision were more likely to be older, be older at age of first arrest, be White, enter with a new crime versus a probation violation, be employed during the first month of community supervision, and score higher on the positive social adjustment index.

In the logistic regression models examining arrests, only (a) working during the first month of community supervision and (b) the positive adjustment index were significant. Those who completed the first year without an arrest were more likely to have been working during the first month and to score higher on the positive adjustment index.

SUMMARY AND GENERAL DISCUSSION

The present research first examined the adjustment to community supervision of four samples—shock parolees, regular parolees, probationers, and shock drop-outs. The shock-program graduates adjusted in the community, at least initially, significantly better than all other samples. Although performance declined for all samples over time, the shock-program sample maintained the highest mean score (see Figure 16.1).

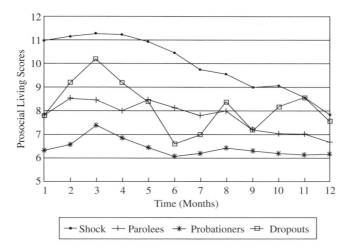

Figure 16.1   Monthly Prosocial Adjustment Scores for Four Samples Over 12 Months

When the intensity of supervision was controlled, sample differences in positive social adjustment disappeared. Apparently the more intense the supervision, the better these offenders adjusted during community supervision. Thus the shock offenders' better adjustment appears to have been a function of the requirements of the supervision and not only self-directed choice.

These results are consistent with research examining the effectiveness of substance-abuse treatment for offenders (Anglin & Hser, 1990). Offenders stay in treatment longer if they are coerced to attend as a condition of probation or parole. Length of time in treatment is consistently associated with better outcomes. Those who are legally coerced into treatment in this way do as well as others who are not. Therefore, legal coercion appears to be an effective method of reducing drug use and other illegal behavior of drug-involved offenders.

The present results suggest that offenders may be coerced to participate in positive social activities. The offenders sentenced to shock programs adjusted more positively than others in general, but they did not differ from the parolees and probationers supervised at the same level of intensity. The shock parolees' performance declined over 6 months of community supervision, as the intensity of supervision was reduced. In general, the more intense the supervision the better the offenders performed, probably

because this was required of them. There was a threat of revocation if they did not comply.

As reported in Study 2, those who adjusted more positively to community supervision were less apt to fail or be arrested. Thus we speculate that it might be possible to force such offenders, through legal coercion, to participate in positive activities, with this participation reducing their criminal activities during community supervision. We emphasize that there is no evidence that coercing positive activities would be more effective for shock parolees than for similar offenders on probation or parole.

Above and beyond the effects of supervision level, differences in age, age at first arrest, race, and sentence length were associated with adjustment during community supervision. Specifically, offenders supervised at similar levels of intensity who were younger, younger at first arrest, non-White, and had shorter sentences performed worse during supervision. Note that these are the same risk factors (except possibly for race) that have been associated with higher recidivism rates (Schmidt & Witte, 1988). Regardless of supervision levels, such high-risk individuals seem to be involved in fewer activities resulting in positive adjustment.

Interestingly, these were not the characteristics that predicted failure during the shock program. That is, age and criminal history were not associated with failure in the in-prison phase of the shock program. Offenders with a sufficiently high IQ who believed they could control events in their lives were more apt to complete the program. A longer prison term was also associated with program completion, with the threat of a long term in a traditional prison appearing to motivate offenders to complete the shock program.

There is no evidence from this research that shock incarceration will reduce recidivism or improve positive adjustment. Offenders at high risk for recidivism can successfully complete the shock program and do no worse than other offenders while in the program. On release, their performance during community supervision appears similar to offenders receiving other types of sentences. Thus the shock incarceration program in Louisiana does not appear to solve the problems faced by offenders as they return to their community. Such problems as unemployment, drug use, and lack of social support may be so strong that it is hard for offenders to make radical changes in their lives even if they have some desire to change.

If reducing recidivism and improving adjustment are goals of shock-incarceration programs, changes in the programs may have to be made to achieve them, with enhanced aftercare perhaps being necessary to help these offenders successfully avoid the problems confronted in the community. It is noteworthy that New York's shock program has made this a target for improving its program (New York State Division of Parole, 1989).

A multisite study of shock incarceration comparing programs that differ in components, types of offenders, and aftercare is currently in progress (MacKenzie, 1990). Offenders' performance during community supervision will be examined and compared. The results should provide further information about the design and characteristics of programs, if any, having an impact on postincarceration performance.

APPENDIX: ITEMS IN THE ADJUSTMENT TO PROSOCIAL LIVING INDEX

*1. At the end of this month was the subject working?

*reversed for scoring

*2. When contacted by the parole/probation officer, was the employer's evaluation of the subject favorable?

*3. If the subject is required to attend AA, is his progress with the SA counseling satisfactory?

*4. If the subject is required to attend a drug treatment program, is his progress with the counseling satisfactory?

*5. Has the subject had a positive alcohol sensor this month?

*6. Has the subject had a positive drug screen this month?

*7. Is the subject pursuing Vo Tec training or attending school and if so, do teachers describe the subject's progress as satisfactory?

*8. Is the subject experiencing difficulties in family relationships?

*9. Is the subject spending time with a delinquent type group or clique?

*10. When visited by the parole/probation officer, was subject's attitude and appearance satisfactory?

*11. When visited by the parole/probation officer, does the subject cooperate and comply with the officer's decisions?

*12. Has the subject violated his curfew, failed to make known his whereabouts, missed appointments with the officer, or lied to the officer?

*13. When corrected for probation/parole violations, does the subject shift blame, make excuses, or complain of unfairness?

*14. When contacted by the parole/probationer officer, is the Community Service supervisor's evaluation of the subject satisfactory?

*15. In the parole/probation officer's assessment, is the subject emotionally stable?

*16. Is the subject making a successful/somewhat successful adaption/adjustment?

*17. In the officer's opinion, is the subject performing better than/much better than indicated by the foregoing answers?

NOTES

1. Although females are admitted to the boot camp prison and participated in the study, there were too few to include in the analysis.

2. The Louisiana Department of Corrections has since revised the eligibility criteria.

3. Results of significance tests and a detailed comparison of the samples was given in MacKenzie (1991).

4. These categories were taken from Clements' (1986) system of classifying inmate needs (Clements, 1986).

5. Tables summarizing these analyses are available from the first author.

6. Tables summarizing all regression analyses for Studies 1 and 2 are available from the first author.

7. "Failures" were defined as those offenders who were not making progress during community supervision and had therefore been removed from parole caseloads.

REFERENCES

Anglin, M. D., & Hser, Y. (1990). Treatment of drug abuse. In M. Tonry & J. Q. Wilson (Eds.), *Drugs and crime* (Vol. 3, pp. 393–460). Chicago: University of Chicago Press.

Clements, C. B. (1986). *Offender needs assessment.* College Park, MD: American Correctional Association.

Cullen, F. T., & Gendreau, P. (1990). The effectiveness of correctional rehabilitation: Reconsidering the "nothing works" debate. In L. I. Goodstein & D. L. MacKenzie (Eds.), *The American prison: Issues in research and policy* (pp. 23–44). New York: Plenum.

Jesness, C. F. (1983). *The Jesness Inventory* (rev. ed.). Palo Alto, CA: Consulting Psychologist Press.

Jesness, C. F., & Wedge, R. F. (1985). *Jesness Inventory classification system.* Palo Alto, CA: Consulting Psychologists Press.

MacKenzie, D. L. (1990). Boot camp prisons: Components, evaluations, and empirical issues. *Federal Probation, 54,* 44–52.

MacKenzie, D. L. (1991). The parole performance of offenders released from shock incarceration (boot camp prisons): A survival time analysis. *Journal of Quantitative Criminology, 7,* 213–236.

MacKenzie, D. L., Gould, L. A., Riechers, L. M., & Shaw, J. W. (1989). Shock incarceration: Rehabilitation or retribution? *Journal of Offender Counseling, Services & Rehabilitation, 14,* 25–40.

MacKenzie, D. L., & Shaw, J. W. (1990). Inmate adjustment and change during shock incarceration: The impact of correctional boot camp programs. *Justice Quarterly, 7,* 125–150.

MacKenzie, D. L., Shaw, J. W., & Gowdy, V. B. (1990). *An evaluation of shock incarceration in Louisiana.* Unpublished manuscript, Louisiana State University, Baton Rouge.

New York State Division of Parole. (1989). *Preliminary supervision assessment of the first six shock incarceration platoons.* Unpublished Shock Incarceration Legislative Report.

Parent, D. (1989). Shock incarceration: An overview of existing programs. *NIJ Issues and Practices.* Washington, DC: National Institute of Justice.

Schmidt, P., & Witte, A. (1988). *Predicting recidivism using survival models.* New York: Springer-Verlag.

Valecha, G. K., & Ostrom, T. M. (1974). An abbreviated measure of internal-external locus of control. *Journal of Personality Assessment, 38,* 369–376.

Part VII

SPECIAL OFFENDER POPULATIONS IN BOOT CAMPS

17

Boot Camp Prisons for Women Offenders

Doris Layton MacKenzie

Heidi Donaldson

Shock incarceration programs, commonly referred to as boot camp prisons, are modeled after military basic training. Similar to military boot camps, the shock programs emphasize strict discipline and respect for and obedience to authority. Offenders are required to participate in a full day of activities beginning at 5 or 6 in the morning. In most boot camp prisons, the daily schedule includes military drill and ceremony, physical training, and physically demanding job assignments.

Although the early boot camp programs focused on the military atmosphere and hard labor, increasingly an array of treatments and therapy have been added to the daily schedule of activities (MacKenzie, 1993; U.S. General Accounting Office). Many programs include academic education, drug education or treatment, and life skills courses for the participants. The time devoted to these oriented activities is frequently more than the offenders would receive if they were in a traditional prison.

Furthermore, some boot camp prisons are developing an intensive aftercare component to aid offenders in the transition from prison to the community.

Although many boot camp prisons appear to widen the net of control by admitting offenders who would otherwise be on probation, some boot camps offer offenders the opportunity to get out of prison earlier than would otherwise be the case. Such boot camps are designed to be mechanisms for early release from prison (MacKenzie & Piquero, 1994). Offenders earn their way out of prison by successfully completing the three- to six-month boot camp program. Their prison sentence can be reduced by as much as five years.

Generally, the boot camps are designed for young, nonviolent, first-time offenders. The participants have been overwhelmingly male. However, as the number of shock incarceration programs has increased, some states have opened programs admitting women. Given the

Reprinted with permission from MacKenzie, D. L. & Donaldson, H. (1996). *Criminal Justice Review, 21*(1), 21–43. An earlier version of this paper was presented at the annual meeting of the American Society of Criminology in Phoenix, Arizona, October 1993, and a summary was submitted as a final report to the National Institute of Justice. This investigation was supported in part by Grant #90-DD-CX-0061 from the National Office of Justice Programs, U.S. Department of Justice, to the University of Maryland. Points of view in this document are those of the authors and do not necessarily represent the official position of the Department of Justice.

public support of the programs, there is every reason to believe that more money will be funneled into them in the future. If shock incarceration provides benefits for participants, such as therapeutic programming or early release, these benefits should be available equally to men and women offenders. Legally, incarcerated women have a right to the same level of programming and benefits that is available to men (Van Ochten, 1993). However, the prison boot camps were developed for men, and often women were admitted as an afterthought or in the interest of equality. The programs may be inappropriate or may have unintended consequences that are destructive for the female inmates (Rafter, 1989, 1990). On the other hand, if women are excluded from participation they may not have an equal opportunity for early release or access to comparable programming.

This paper examines the adequacy of boot camp prisons for women. State correctional systems were surveyed to identify the number of state programs with women participants, and 50 percent of the camps with women participants were selected for a more in-depth descriptive study of women in boot camps. Prior to initiation of the study, a focus group of feminist scholars, correctional experts, and criminologists was convened. This group identified an extensive list of issues important to consider in examining the appropriateness of boot camps for females. Of particular concern were whether female offenders had equal opportunities to participate, whether the programs addressed the needs of female offenders, whether there were potential harmful effects for women offenders, whether alternative correctional programs might be more appropriate for women, and whether the potential advantages of boot camps outweighed the disadvantages.

PRIOR RESEARCH EXAMINING BOOT CAMP PRISONS

Most of the research examining shock incarceration programs has focused on male inmates (MacKenzie & Shaw, 1990; MacKenzie & Souryal, 1994). In a recent eight-site study of boot camp prisons, MacKenzie and Souryal (1994) found that the two major goals of the

programs were to change offenders and to reduce prison crowding. Their study focused on male offenders because there were too few women in the programs to provide reasonable numbers for statistical analyses. In examining the impact of the programs on offenders, they found that inmates reported positive experiences in the boot camps and claimed that they had changed for the better. Comparison samples of inmates incarcerated in traditional prisons did not believe that their experiences had been positive. However, inmates in the boot camps and also those in traditional prisons became less antisocial during the time they were incarcerated.

MacKenzie and Souryal (1994) also compared the recidivism rates of those who had successfully completed the boot camp programs with those of comparable offenders who had spent a longer term in prison and those who had been sentenced to probation. In general, the recidivism rates of the boot camp graduates were similar to those of the other offenders. However, graduates from three of the state boot camp programs had lower recidivism rates on some but not all measures of recidivism. The programs in these three states had components that were similar: During the time they were in the boot camp, inmates received three or more hours of rehabilitative programming, and, furthermore, all graduates were intensively supervised during the first six months of community supervision. It was not possible for these researchers to separate the effect of the military atmosphere from the effect of the intensive supervision and treatment in order to identify which particular components had an effect on recidivism. Any of these components alone or in combination could have had the positive impact.

MacKenzie and her colleagues also examined the impact of boot camps on the need for prison beds. They found that boot camps could potentially lead to a reduction in prison crowding (MacKenzie & Piquero, 1994; MacKenzie & Souryal, 1994). Using data from five sites, they investigated the impact of the program if the percentage of prison-bound (versus probation-bound) offenders varied. If the programs admitted offenders who would have been in prison and therefore did not widen the net of control to include those who would otherwise have been on probation, the programs had the potential to reduce prison crowding. This reduction would come about because the boot camps function as early release mechanisms permitting some offenders to earn their way out of prison earlier than they would otherwise be released. However, if the camps are to have an appreciable effect on prison crowding, they must be large enough to release a sufficient number of inmates (i.e., they must complete the program) early enough that it will have an effect on the total inmate population.

Thus, there seems to be evidence that some of the boot camps have positive impacts on the attitudes and behavior of male offenders. Furthermore, some of the boot camps do provide offenders with a method of getting out of prison earlier. On the other hand, some boot camps are widening the net of control over offenders by admitting those who would otherwise be on probation.

A few studies have examined the use of shock incarceration for women. Parent (1989) interviewed women in boot camp prisons and found that they reported favorable experiences in the boot camps. They actually reported more positive feelings about the program than male inmates.

MacKenzie and Souryal (1993), in their study of attitude change, included one female boot camp. The results for the females were identical to findings regarding attitude change in male inmates. While in the boot camp female offenders became more positive in their attitudes both toward the program and toward their own future, and they became less antisocial. The comparison group of female offenders in prison did not become more positive in their attitudes about their experiences in the traditional prison; they did, however, become less antisocial.

A one-year study of recidivism rates for female offenders in New York (New York Department of Correctional Services, 1992) found that only seven percent of the 398 female shock incarceration graduates had returned to prison. Five percent of the women had returned for new crimes, and the remaining two percent had returned as a result of technical violations. Although these figures are low, they are not significantly different from comparison groups of women sentenced to prison and women who had been removed from the shock incarceration

program. This is consistent with the finding of few differences in recidivism rates when male boot camp graduates are compared with male comparison groups, although the recidivism rates for women are much lower than the rates for men (MacKenzie & Souryal, 1993).

METHODOLOGY

In March 1992, there were 39 boot camp programs in 25 states.[1] Of these 25 states, 13 had women in their programs. In all, women made up 6.1 percent ($n = 378$) of the offenders in the boot camps. One major difference among the boot camp programs was that some integrated the females into the program with the male inmates, while others had completely separate female programs. In the combined programs, the female inmates were housed either at the male boot camp or at a nearby female prison. They participated with the males in most of the daily activities. Nine of the states with boot camp programs for women combined the women offenders and the male offenders in the same program.

In the separate female programs, the female boot camp was completely separate from the male program. Male and female inmates did not come into contact with one another. Separate boot camp prisons for women were much less common than combined programs, as only four states had separate female programs. The authors were interested in studying both types of programs (combined and separate) because of some of the additional issues that arise in co-correctional prisons (Ruback, 1980).

Site Selection

The six boot camp sites included in this research were randomly selected from 12 female correctional boot camp programs in operation in March 1992.[2] Selection was stratified by type of program: (a) combined and (b) separate. Fifty percent of each type of program were selected for site visits. That is, of the eight combined programs four were selected for participation in the study (sites 1 to 4), and of the four separate programs two were selected (sites 5 and 6). The rationale for stratification by program type was based on the perception that the policies, procedures, activities, and effectiveness would differ between the integrated and the separate boot camps. Because of the small number of women participants in the six randomly selected sites, a seventh site was added to the study (see below). Sites were contacted and all of those selected agreed to participate in the research.

Data Collection

Data were collected through administrator interviews, a facility/security checklist, inmate questionnaires, and inmate interviews. All of the female inmates in the boot camps were asked to voluntarily complete a questionnaire soliciting information concerning family, demographic characteristics, history of physical abuse, and prior drug and alcohol use. In addition, an attempt was made to obtain interviews with 15 randomly selected inmates during the site visit. In sites with fewer then 15 inmates, all female inmates in the program who volunteered were interviewed.

RESULTS

Small Number of Women Participants

The most conspicuous problem that was identified with the randomly selected sites was the small number of women in the boot camps. Of the six sites that were visited, two did not currently have any women in the program. It appears that few women enter the program or that those who do enter are apt to drop out. It is particularly a problem where women and men are combined in the same program.

At the time of the site visits, the boot camp programs included a total of 69 participants ($n = 1, 0, 8, 0, 55, 5$ in sites 1 to 6, respectively). Prior to the visit most boot camps reported more women participants than were found when the researchers actually arrived at the site. Sites that did not have women inmates at the time of the visit were not eliminated, because the authors were interested in what was occurring nationally with females in boot camp prisons; the random assignment procedure permits generalizations to be made from these boot camps to others throughout the nation.

In five of the six sites the number of beds available for women in the program was much larger than the actual number of offenders participating in the program. For example, the four integrated programs had from 8 to 24 beds, yet there were only 0 to 8 women in those camps. The 9 women in these boot camps were occupying only 14 percent of the total number of 64 beds that were available for women in the camps. In comparison, of the 646 beds available for males, 68.4 percent were being used. Women made up only 0 to 3 percent of the total participants in the integrated boot camps.

The total number of beds available for the two separate female boot camps was 79. At the time of the site visits, 60 females (75.9 percent of capacity) were in those camps: 55 (93.2 percent of capacity) were in site 5 (with 59 available beds), and 5 (25 percent of capacity) were in site 6 (with 20 available beds). Women in the separate programs made up 13 percent (site 5) and 2 percent (site 6) of the total number of people in boot camp programs in these states.

Thus, in general, with the exception of one camp, the beds in boot camps for women were empty, particularly in the combined programs. From the six randomly selected sites, it was concluded that boot camps around the country have very few female participants entering or staying in the programs. The sites did not have any data on how many women had been recommended or on the number who were legally eligible but had been judged unsuitable for the program. However, administrators in five of the six sites reported that they seldom had many women in the program. In fact, administrators at the site that had only one woman were reevaluating the program and its appropriateness for women; so few women were sent to the boot camp that the program officials felt they should reconsider the coed nature of the program. Another site had originally had 80 beds for women but, because of the low numbers of women participants, the capacity had been reduced to 24. The problem was particularly acute in the combined programs, where only 14 percent of the beds for females were being used, and females made up less than 3 percent of the boot camp participants. The fact that many of the beds were not occupied suggests that there may be some problems in designing or operating the programs for women, and these factors were investigated further in the interviews.

Additional Site

Because the authors were also interested in the experiences of women in the boot camps, another site (site 7) was added to the original six because of the small numbers of women who were participating in the originally selected sites. The selected boot camp had the largest number of women in any state boot camp prison at the time of the study. This site was selected because the authors wanted to obtain additional information about the experiences of women in boot camps; an adequate sample of women was therefore needed. It is important to note that this site was not randomly selected.

At the time of the visit to site 7, approximately 60 percent of the 180 beds at the boot camp were occupied. The program was located at the same facility as a male boot camp. The females were housed in separate buildings from the male inmates. The women did not mix with men during work assignments and, although they were mixed with the male inmates at meals, they were required to eat at separate tables. Male and female inmates participated together in education, physical training, drill and ceremony, and drug education and counseling. Although this program was considered to be a combined program, according to the authors' classification of programs it was actually somewhere in between—offenders were at the same facility but in some activities they were separated.

Program Characteristics

There were some differences among the programs in eligibility requirements and program length. Most sites targeted nonviolent offenders who did not have an extensive past history of criminal activity. Although the programs focused on nonviolent offenders, only two sites specifically prohibited the participation of violent offenders. Two sites limited participants to those convicted of their first felony; the other four did not. All but one program limited participation to those who had not previously been sentenced to a term in an adult prison. Most

sites targeted young offenders, although one site had no age restrictions, and another site had no age restrictions for those who entered as prisoners (if they entered directly from the court there were age restrictions). The other sites limited participation to adults, from ages 16 to 18 up to the age of 25 to 35. Two sites reported that the program was designed specifically for substance abusers. Three of the programs lasted 120 days, two lasted 90 days, and two lasted six months. In one site a small number of offenders were "recycled" through the program and were required to spend an additional month or two in the camp.

There were several differences between the sites with separate programs and those with male-female combined programs. In both of the separate programs people were sent to the program by a judge and participation was not voluntary. In the combined sites the process for deciding who entered the boot camps differed: In some, either the judge or the Department of Corrections could send offenders to the program. At four of the combined program sites, offenders had to volunteer for entry.

In all of the combined programs males and females were integrated during physical training. Identical standards for physical training were used for males and females, except in one site where females were permitted to keep their knees on the ground when doing push-ups.[3]

Inmate Characteristics

Data were summarized from the questionnaires from the four sites (including site 7) that had two or more women at the camp at the time of the site visit. The majority of the women in the boot camps had children whom they anticipated living with upon release, most were the sole financial support for themselves and their children, they were serving time for nonviolent crimes, and a large percentage of them had previous contact with the criminal justice system. Thus, these women were very similar to the average female offender entering prison (American Correctional Association, 1993; Baunach, 1985; Morris, 1987). Also, as suggested by a review of the literature, a large number of these women had substance abuse problems, and they had a history of past abusive relationships (Bureau of Justice Statistics, 1994; Robinson, 1992).

In their examination of the characteristics of the women who were participating in the boot camps, the authors were particularly interested in examining two factors. First, they were interested in any characteristics that might limit the participation of the women in the boot camps, either because they would not be eligible to be admitted or because they would find the experience more difficult or stressful. Second, they were interested in identifying characteristics that might reveal the particular type of therapeutic programming these women needed.

The women, on average, were between 23 and 29 years of age and had two or three children. Before being sentenced to prison most of them had lived with their children, and almost all expected to live with their children after release. The majority of their children were staying with grandparents or with another family relative, but not with the father or stepfather. While in the boot camp, fewer than 50 percent of the women had visits with their children. Those who did see their children saw them only two or three times.

On average, the women were employed when they were arrested, but the average amount of money that they reported earning per week varied greatly. Approximately 50 percent to 60 percent of the women had been the sole economic support for themselves and their children. Most reported that they had completed 11 or 12 grades in school.

The majority of the women were serving time for a drug, fraud, or theft offense. Many of them had previously been arrested and convicted.

The women inmates were asked to respond to six "yes or no" questions designed to indicate significant problems with alcohol or drug use (higher scores indicated more problems). The questions dealt with serious issues such as whether police, doctors, or family members had urged them to stop drinking or using drugs and whether drugs or alcohol had altered eating habits and daily routine. Only a small percentage of the women reported serious problems due to alcohol. A large proportion, however, reported at least one serious problem associated with their drug use.

The women were queried regarding their most recent relationship and were asked whether it involved relatively mild physical abuse (threatening to hit, throwing something, pushing, grabbing, or shoving) or more serious physical abuse (threatening or using a knife or gun). Eight questions (four each for mild and for serious abuse), derived from a scale developed by Straus (1979), were used to determine the extent of the abuse. On average, in their most recent relationship these women had experienced mild abuse less than once a month. They reported much less serious abuse. Respondents were also queried regarding the number of previous relationships in which they had been physically abused. On average, the women had been in one or two past relationships in which their partner had threatened to hit, push, or slap them. They also reported being involved in an average of one relationship with a partner who had beaten them. Thus, although the most recent relationship had not involved serious abuse, a fairly large number of these women had been in relationships in the past that had involved mild or serious physical abuse.

The characteristics of the women in the boot camps were very similar to those of the typical incarcerated female (American Correctional Association, 1990). If these women are compared to the men in another study of boot camps (MacKenzie & Souryal, 1994), they are found to be similar in type of crime charged and in percentage employed. However, the women were older (23 to 29 years) than the men in the boot camps (19 to 24 years).

Age restrictions for eligibility may be one reason that there were few women in the boot camps. Four of the sites had an upper age limit of 25 for participants in the programs. These programs had less than 34 percent of their capacity filled at the time of the site visit. The two programs that had the majority of the beds for women filled had either no upper age limit or an upper age limit of 35. Thus, if women offenders are, on the average, older than men when they enter prison, they may be excluded from the camps because they are too old to fit within the age requirements. However, other difficulties were found to be experienced by the women that may be more important in explaining the limited participation of women in boot camps.

Adjustment in the Boot Camp

Physical and Emotional Stress

There are some other obvious problems that may account for the small number of women in the boot camps. The programs appear to be designed for male participants, and the physical demands are difficult for the women to meet. In the interviews, participants frequently discussed health problems, and those who were in the process of dropping out of the program were often doing so because of some type of physical problem.

Research has shown that women enter the correctional system with more chronic physical health problems and more mental health needs than men (American Correctional Association, 1993; Bershad, 1985; Pollock-Byrne, 1990). Such differences may limit the participation of women in the boot camps if the standards for participation are based on the characteristics of male offenders (Chesney-Lind & Pollock-Byrne, 1993). In the interviews, the women in the combined programs almost always emphasized the emotionally and physically stressful nature of the program. They did not feel that the drill instructors were harder on them than on males, but they felt that the demands of the program were more difficult for them. They frequently mentioned physical problems, such as the difficulties they had with the physical exercise (running) or the physically demanding work. Many reported that they had spent time out of the program because of medical problems.

Another problem reported by the women was the emotionally stressful nature of the program. Both males and females report that these programs are stressful (see for instance, MacKenzie & Souryal, 1994). However, without doubt, being alone or being one of only a few women in a program that is mostly male creates additional stress for female inmates. There were differences between the combined boot camp programs and the separate programs in regard to physical and emotional stress. The women in the separate programs reported much less emotional stress experienced during the program, fewer physical problems, and less need for female drill instructors.

Although the programs were stressful for the women, most of the program administrators attributed the small number of women participants to the small number who entered, not the percentage who entered but were dismissed for disciplinary reasons or voluntarily dropped out. They had no hard data to support their viewpoint, but they did not believe that more women than men left the programs after they entered. Thus, they rejected the idea that the low number of female participants was a result of physical or mental stress experienced in the boot camp. They gave various explanations for why the number of female entrants was so small. One attributed the low numbers to judges who did not believe that the strenuous activities in the camps were appropriate for women and therefore did not sentence women to boot camp. Another believed that women who dropped out went back to the female prison and scared the other inmates with horror stories about the program; as a result, few would volunteer.

Interactions Between Male and Female Inmates

There appeared to be some misunderstandings between the male and female inmates. In the interviews the women frequently mentioned how the male inmates were like brothers and were careful to help them or to take care of them. Although there were some males who made unpleasant comments, the women reported that most were helpful and considerate. However, the administrators said that some of the males complained that the females could not pull their share during hard physical labor and that, for that reason, the male inmates did not want too many of the women in their work squads. Thus, although the women reported generally positive relationships with the male participants, there were some underlying tensions of which the women may have been unaware. Site 7 solved this problem by separating the genders during work assignments.

Gender Differences

According to the administrators in the combined programs, female and male inmates in the programs were treated identically even in regard to toilet and shower supervision, physical training, and work. The administrators emphasized the equality of treatment, but few mentioned or seemed aware of the concept of equitable treatment. Several did mention the importance of having female staff and the benefits of having a separate program for the women. They also noted that the yelling and physical activity appeared to be more difficult for the women to handle.

When asked to compare the female and male inmates, most of the administrators commented in some way on the emotionality of the females (e.g., "they are more emotional," "they cry more"). The administrator in one program asserted that in his experience the women inmates adjusted faster to the boot camp. He attributed this to the fact that they were often older and better educated. He further argued that the women made more drastic (positive) changes during the program. Another administrator noted that the women who dropped out did so immediately but that those who stayed usually did well and successfully completed the program.

There may be additional difficulties for women because they have different standards of modesty, privacy, or aesthetics in comparison to men. Many of the boot camps' bathroom facilities permitted little privacy and there was cross-gender supervision. Furthermore, dormitories were barren; the women were not permitted to display personal items such as photographs. These rules and procedures may make the environment more difficult for women. Reminders of home and children, if permitted, may actually act as incentives for women to work harder to succeed in the program.

One woman in a combined program did complain about having to wear male uniforms. She did not mind the underwear and socks, but in her opinion the uniforms were ugly. Several women at this site also said that they had problems because the men did the laundry. The men would not do the women's underpants carefully, and they were often returned dirty. Women also complained that they were forced to have their hair cut when they entered the boot camp and that they did not have sufficient time to fix their hair in the morning. In one program in which the women were required to have their hair cut extremely short, a number of the female participants complained that they felt as if they looked like men. A few mentioned that this made them feel unattractive, resulting in a loss of self-esteem. Overall, however, although some of the women did comment on uniforms, haircuts, and cleanliness, these factors did not seem to be critically important to them. Nor did the administrators or staff seem concerned with these issues. Any impact or adjustment difficulties were probably very subtle.

What seemed more important to the women was having female staff at the boot camp. Both of the combined programs that had women in the program at the time of the site visit had female drill instructors. The women inmates felt that this was very important. They said they frequently needed to talk to the female instructor for support, for personal items (tampons), or to criticize the inappropriate behavior of the male drill instructors.

Sexual Abuse and Harassment

Problems related to sexual activities or harassment were frequently mentioned in the interviews with both staff and inmates. For example, in one boot camp program a male drill instructor had required the women to exercise in their nightgowns first thing in the morning. The women felt that some of the exercises were too revealing because the male drill instructor walked through the dormitory while the women were exercising. They complained to a female DI, and the male DI was no longer assigned to the women's dormitory. In one of the separate programs a woman said that one of the DIs had made inappropriate comments to her and that she had complained to another inmate who said that she would report it if it continued.

One of the administrators in a separate program reported that at one time the program had been coed, but several pregnancies had occurred and one woman had been murdered by a male inmate. This contributed to the decision to separate the male and female boot camp programs.

Another example of the type of sexual problems that occurred involved a male drill instructor who had sexual relations with a female boot camp inmate. Although there was some question about whether the woman had agreed, in the opinion of the administrator, given the power the DI had over the inmate, it could not be considered consensual sexual relations. This boot camp had gone to great lengths to protect the female participants from the male inmates. A DI had to be with the women at all times. For example, in the interest of equality and to protect the females from the male inmates, a DI (either male or female, depending upon who was on duty) had to stay in the bathroom while the females showered. The inmate was required to strip down to her underwear in front of the DI before moving into a shower stall (partially concealed from view) to shower. The DI who told the authors about this procedure said that he was very careful to observe the female inmate—there was only one in the program at the time—because he wanted to be sure that he acted just as he would with the males. This close supervision by DIs protected the women from the male inmates, but it increased the opportunity for abuse by drill instructors.

This is another example of the emphasis on equal treatment despite the fact that equality in this case was questionable given that there was only one female inmate in the program.

Although some women mentioned that they had been pushed or shoved by correctional officers, none said that they had been touched sexually. In the combined program they frequently said that the men were pushed more often than the women.

Women in two of the facilities had filed formal sexual harassment complaints against a guard, and in one site a complaint had been filed against a male inmate. Female inmates had also filed a criminal complaint against a guard for physical assault in one of the sites, and in one site female inmates had filed other criminal complaints against male inmates.

Notwithstanding the fact that women may have been placed in the boot camps in the interest of equality, mixing the women into a program that was designed for men did not create an equal situation. Rather, such programs appeared to be unequal and unfair for women because they did not take into consideration the average woman's physical stamina. Furthermore, women in the programs had to cope with the additional stress created by having so few women in an environment where the majority of participants and staff were men. To protect them from abuse and harassment their activities were often severely restricted; yet, as the above incidents demonstrate, there were many instances of problems. Protecting the inmates from sexual activity or harassment was a major concern of administrators in the programs that combined males and females.

Physical Abuse

Most of the women's complaints about physical abuse related to what staff did to male inmates. In one of the boot camps, for instance, several women said that they were unhappy with the fact that the staff kicked and hit the males. Typical was the comment by one woman who said, "I've seen officers hit, smack people in the face." Frequently they reported that women got easier treatment and that they could complain about female problems if they wanted to get out of work. One reported, "The female inmates get away with a lot more than the male inmates. Males have to PT [physically train] harder and have to work harder on the work crews; females are let off the hook by all of the DIs." She went on to say that if the females complained about cramps or not feeling well the DIs let them off and they did not have to work as hard.

Verbal Abuse

Frequently in the interviews, the inmates mentioned name-calling and offensive comments by the drill instructors. They reported being told, "you are nothing but a convict" and "you're always gonna be a loser." Several reported being called "bitch." Perhaps the most offensive comments were those about the women's abilities as parents or about their children. One woman who told a DI about having a stillborn child believed that the DI was out of place to say, "Good, you didn't bring another slimeball into the world." Another reported that being told "your child is a coke baby" made her "feel hurt." They reported about being "dogged" and about how the DIs attempted to "tear them down." There were many comments about how, after being torn down, they were supposed to be built up—but there were few comments about how this building up was done. According to these inmate reports, the DIs in the combined programs were the source of the harshest verbal abuse.

Some of the comments about abuse may have related to what was considered legitimate confrontation (using a "command voice not yelling"), strict rules, and disciplinary consequences for misbehavior. This was evident at times from comments that the women made about how their attitudes toward the staff had changed since they first entered the boot camp. One woman said, "Right away I had a negative attitude towards the program and I didn't want to join because I didn't like the fact that you would have DIs yelling in your face and low grading you and pushing your buttons and stuff like that." However, once she had been in the program for a while her attitude changed: "As long as you do what you have to do, you don't have to worry about the drill instructors yelling at you and making you feel ashamed because you're not doing something right. . . . The DIs only yell at the inmates who 'screw-up.' . . . There are a lot of DIs who really care. . . . They help you get through the program."

Staff Training

Some of the staff behavior described by the inmates, such as requiring women to exercise in flimsy nightgowns, slapping and hitting inmates, and name-calling, was obviously inappropriate, unprofessional, and abusive. It was clear that only some staff were involved in these activities and that the behavior was not condoned by the administration. Administrators were well aware of the dangers of the boot camp atmosphere. Many reported that they had to watch new staff carefully to be sure they did not abuse their power. Only three of the camps had training programs specifically for staff working in the boot camp. And, although all programs permitted cross-gender supervision, only one combined program reported that it included gender sensitivity in the boot camp training course. Three of the others had some gender sensitivity training within a general training curriculum, and the remaining two programs did not have any gender sensitivity training for correctional officers or drill instructors. Given the fact that administrators recognized the potential for abuse and were concerned about the women, it was disappointing that more programs did not have formal training sessions for staff working in the boot camps.

The administrators were also concerned about staff burnout. They voiced the opinion that the boot camp programs were more demanding than traditional assignments in correctional institutions, both mentally and physically. It was seldom possible to rotate staff in and out of the boot camps. The administrators noted that even experienced staff would become short-tempered and show signs of stress, characteristics that would be associated with abusive behavior. Nevertheless, there were no formal counseling programs for them, nor was it easy to move them temporarily to other assignments.

Impact on Those With a History of Abuse

Even if the atmosphere were not abusive, it is possible that the confrontational nature of military-style interaction and the required obedience to authority could have a detrimental impact on the inmates. This may be particularly detrimental for women who have been battered or abused in the past. Several inmates made comments such as this from a woman who had just made the decision to leave the boot camp: "I was physically and mentally abused and just being here reminds me of it." She went on to say, "I have bruises on my arms. They grab you and they push you around. . . . They shouldn't be that harsh on you. They get in your face and make you feel like dirt. For someone like me that's been physically and mentally abused that's all it reminds me of, being abused."

A woman in a different program, who had been in the program only a week, said, "You can't talk to the DIs like they are people because you are not allowed to even look at them." She could not get used to this, and "when you look at them, they scream at you 'don't look at me.'" She said that this scares people like her who have been abused in the past.

Another inmate recalled, "When I first got here and I had people screaming at me in my ears . . . I thought I was gonna just come apart, have a nervous breakdown. . . . For the two months I was here I cried because it triggered all that stuff from my childhood that I just started remembering when I came here."

On the other hand, some of the women who had been in the boot camps longer felt that the camp had taught them to stand up for themselves. One inmate reported, "The program teaches you how to stand up for yourself and that you don't have to take anybody's crap. . . . The DIs are in your face all the time and you get to express your feelings, you can explain to them how you feel."

Thus there was a real difference of opinion about the impact of the program on women who had a history of abuse. Some staff as well as some of the inmates believed that the boot camp could teach women to stand up for themselves and to realize that they were capable of doing things they did not think they could. On the other hand, one cannot eliminate the concern that the program might have a detrimental impact on those who have a history of abuse or, at the very least, that it can be a particularly difficult experience for them and that they might benefit more from a different type of program.

Addressing the Unique Needs of Women

Programming

The review of the literature on women offenders and the focus group meeting suggested that some of the most important needs of these women include vocational or employment training to raise their ability to support themselves and their children, substance abuse treatment, programming that considers the family obligations of these women (parenting classes, life skills training, transition to the community, etc.), and counseling for victims of domestic violence and sexual assault (American Correctional Association, 1993; Baunach, 1985; Bureau of Justice Statistics, 1994; Morris, 1987; Rafter, 1990; Smart, 1989). In addition, the self-reported characteristics of the women in the boot camps suggest that their needs are consistent with those of the female inmates described in the literature.

Almost all of the boot camp personnel reported that financial planning, stress and anger management, nutrition, GED preparation, and drug education were included in the program schedule. About half of the programs included courses in parenting, balancing family and work, sex education, and drug treatment. None of the programs offered vocational education. Only one, the largest, which was a separate

women's boot camp, included formal counseling programs for family issues, surviving sexual assault, and battered women (site 7 did this as well). Only one of the boot camps had a formal program for facilitating the transition to the community.

There was a great deal of inconsistency between the responses of program officials and those of the women inmates regarding the availability of programs at the boot camps. Program officials often said that they did offer a particular program while the inmates said that it was not available in the camp. This difference could be due in part to the fact that some programs were not offered until the end of the boot camp. Inasmuch as all of the female inmates were interviewed at one point in time, many may not yet have had the opportunity to attend a particular program. In the boot camps that included drug education and treatment and academic education, a high proportion of the inmates did report that these programs were available. More alarming is the fact that few of the women in the one randomly selected site that had sexual assault survivor and battered women counseling (18 percent and 16 percent, respectively) actually knew that it was available. This was true of programs in several of the other sites as well.

There were some conspicuous omissions in the treatment programs that were offered. According to the Bureau of Justice Statistics (1994), most of the 75 percent increase in the number of females in state prisons from 1986 to 1991 was due to drug offenses. Despite the fact that many of the women who enter boot camp programs may be drug-involved and have serious problems involving drug use, only half of the boot camps had drug treatment programs available to the participants.

Few of the boot camps offered therapeutic programs for the problems that many of these women face (e.g., surviving sexual assault, battered women, transition to the community, vocational training). Many of the boot camps also failed to address some of the critical family obligations of women inmates (Baunach, 1985; Glick & Neto, 1982; Morris, 1987; Rafter, 1990).

During the interviews, many of the offenders suggested that the boot camps could be improved by adding specific types of programs. In their opinion the programming aspect of the boot camp was very important. Many said that something should be done to help inmates obtain job skills, and they believed that they would benefit from parenting classes and sexual abuse counseling. The women in one boot camp were upset because the men took part in vocational training classes that were not open to women. One female inmate said that they had been excluded because some women had gone to the classes and tried to talk with the men.

Most of the comments about programming depended upon the focus of the boot camp. Many participants complained that the focus was on a particular type of treatment, such as drug treatment, and that this was not their specific problem. When asked whether they would recommend the boot camp to others, the most important factor in determining whether they would recommend it or not was the type of programming available in the boot camp and the question of whether it matched the problems of the offender. For example, if the boot camp emphasized drug treatment, offenders would recommend the program to others with drug treatment needs.

Interestingly, many of the women in the separate programs said that they would not recommend the program to men because men had "attitudes" that would make it particularly hard for them to complete the program successfully. They seemed to be referring to the difficulty that men would have in obeying the orders given to them by the drill instructors. On the other hand, in the combined programs the women were less apt to recommend the program to other women because of the difficulties and stress that they experienced in the program. This again draws attention to the substantial differences between the programs that combine men and women and those that separate the women. The women who were in boot camps that emphasized programming focused on the various programs offered (drug treatment, education, decision-making) and the positive impact of the programs (improved self-esteem, learned responsibility) for them.

Parenting and Visitation Programs

Because most of the women had children with whom they anticipated being reunited upon release, visitation programs were particularly important for them. However, the strict rules and rigid schedule of the boot camps limited the length and type of visitation, and women in boot camps were often less likely to see their children than inmates in prison facilities (Weisheit, 1985). The time in boot camp could be used to improve women's parenting skills and to strengthen the mother-child bond, but there was little evidence that this was occurring. Interaction with children could act as a positive influence on the female offender. Both mother and child could benefit from programs designed to give aftercare support and help in making the difficult transition to the community at the end of the program (Rafter, 1990). It appears that the boot camps fail to take into consideration that the majority of these women will have children to look after upon release and that these children are very important to them.

Again, differences were found between the separate and combined programs in the regulations for visiting. The two separate women's programs permitted visitors on weekends throughout the woman's term in the boot camp. Three of the combined programs restricted visits during the early period in the boot camp, and the other did not allow visitors to the camp at any time until graduation. However, in neither type of camp were there programs for such things as innovative child visitation, helping parents reunite with their children, or helping the inmates establish a relationship with their child's caretaker. Yet such activities might be expected in correctional programs that were specifically designed with women offenders' needs in mind.

Discipline and Physical Conditioning

Many of the women inmates mentioned that one benefit of the program was discipline: that they would learn discipline, that having discipline would help them in the outside world, or that the discipline would help them have self control. Several said that they had entered the program, in part, so that they would learn discipline. They also said that the program would make them stop and think before they said something. Furthermore, they would recommend the program to others who needed discipline; it is "better than general population because general population has no structure." Several reported that a benefit of the program was that they were now in good physical condition; they were exercising and getting in shape and losing weight.

The importance of the discipline and structure of the military atmosphere was also emphasized by the staff and administrators as an important part of the program. In their opinion it was particularly important for women: "The women learn to do things they never thought they could," "they realize they can rely on themselves and don't have to rely on some jerk," "the military discipline instills pride in them, even those who had been abused." One administrator felt that it was particularly important to combine drug treatment with the military atmosphere if the treatment was going to work.

Opportunity for Early Release

The two primary aspects of the boot camp prison that can be considered advantages are the chance for early release and the increased opportunity for therapeutic programming. In the interviews the most frequently mentioned benefit of the program was the fact that participants would get out of prison earlier than might otherwise be the case. This would allow them to return to their families; women who had children mentioned how important it was to them to get home to their children.

Another difference that stands out when this research is compared with the research examining males' experiences in boot camps is the emphasis that women place on children. In the authors' review of previous studies examining men in boot camp prisons, no information could be found about the number of men who had children whom they planned to be reunited with. Researchers who intensively interviewed men in boot camps have reported that many entered the boot camps because this would shorten their time in prison. However, the men did not say that this shorter imprisonment was important because they wanted to return to their children. In comparison, the women in this study also wanted to get out early but they almost always emphasized that this was because they wanted to be reunited with their children.

Some of the participants also mentioned that if they completed the program they would not have a record of conviction. In one program the women were upset because they had had to wait a long time in prison or jail from the time they signed the papers to enter the boot camp until the time they were actually admitted, and the result was that they had had to spend a longer time in prison. They had not had a choice between this program and other programs offering early release-it was this program or no early release. When asked what was the best thing about the boot camp prison many said that it was the possibility for early release.

The program with the largest number of female offenders was one of the separate programs. The procedure for entry to this boot camp differed from that of many of the other programs in that offenders were sentenced directly to the camp. Therefore, the possibility of early release was mentioned much less frequently by offenders in this program, most likely because they were not as sure what their sentences would have been if they had not gone to the boot camp. Some had been given a choice of either the boot camp, a longer sentence to prison, or a delayed sentence. They did not know how long they would have had to serve in prison if they had not chosen the boot camp.

Although the majority of the women in site 7 said that they had originally entered the boot camp because they would serve less time in prison, most of them emphasized the therapeutic programs and what they had learned while in the boot camp as the best thing about their experience.

SUMMARY

In conclusion, there were serious problems in the boot camp programs that combined women and men; the drill instructors were harsher, the stress was greater, there were few women participants, their activities were restricted, and there were problems with sexual behavior. These programs did not offer women an equal opportunity for early release and appropriate programming. Few women entered and stayed in these programs, their experiences in the programs were not the same as the experiences of men, nor did the therapeutic programming address some of their major needs. Women may have been admitted to the programs in the interest of equality, but the situation was not equitable for them.

The fact that two of the boot camps had a reasonable number of women inmates indicates that it is possible to design a boot camp program so that a number of the women who are sent to the program will remain if there are enough women incarcerated in the jurisdiction. In comparison to the randomly selected combined programs, women in the separate programs reported less physical and emotional stress. Although many of the inmates were not aware of the therapeutic programs, there were more programs in the separate boot camps that were designed to address the specific needs of these women (e.g., surviving sexual assault). Visitation policies were less restrictive, and more of the women had seen their children while they had been in the boot camp. In the interviews, these inmates did not focus on the importance of female drill instructors. Surprisingly, some of them said that they would not recommend the boot camps to males because men would have "attitude" problems that would make it difficult for them to complete the program.

In general, the separate or semi-separate programs seemed to have fewer problems than the combined programs. However, there were some serious concerns that arose in regard to both types of programs. One was the impact of the programs on inmates with a history of abusive relationships. The women often related how, when DIs confronted them, it reminded them of earlier abusive situations. Only a few said that they had learned to stand up for themselves. Many female inmates suffer from a sense of powerlessness to control events in their lives (Pollock-Byrne, 1990; Rafter, 1990; Robinson, 1992). Drill instructors confronting inmates and the lack of choice in the boot camps may actually exacerbate these feelings of powerlessness. Unquestioned obedience to authority and discipline can reinforce feelings learned as children or adults in abusive situations. The drill instructors' ability to punish inmates who do not respond to their unquestioned authority can be very detrimental to an inmate who is attempting to cope with a violent background (Robinson,

1992). Along with the potential for sexual, physical, and verbal abuse, this seems to be one of the most dangerous aspects. The experience may damage already fragile egos. Furthermore, in some of the programs the drill instructors said things that would be considered abusive. The participants were hurt most by the comments about their ability as mothers. The authors are concerned that many, particularly those who drop out of the program, carry with them additional attacks on their self-confidence and strength.

Many of the issues of concern for women in boot camps are similar to those for men. The military atmosphere carries with it some dangers (e.g., staff-on inmate abuse, injury, accidents). There is little evidence that the military atmosphere alone will change offenders so that they will not be involved in crime in the future. If we are going to be successful in changing these offenders, therapeutic programs that address the precise problems they have will need to be available for them while they are in the boot camps. One advantage of the boot camps may be that they permit offenders to earn their way out of prison earlier than they would otherwise be released. This may save prison beds, but only if the programs are carefully designed not to widen the net of control (MacKenzie & Piquero, 1994). Also, the boot camps may provide intense therapy for offenders while they are in the program, and this would be better than no therapy.

The question, then, is whether this is the best way to provide therapy to female offenders. Although some of the dangers of the boot camps are the same for women and men, others are particularly important for women. Morash and Rucker (1990) believe that boot camps may be inappropriate for female offenders. There is serious doubt about the efficacy of placing women in a militaristic environment that emphasizes masculinity and aggressiveness and that in some cases rejects essentially prosocial images and related patterns of interaction associated with the stereotype of femininity. The boot camp environment emphasizes unquestioned authority and a regimented schedule. The confrontation and requirements for this absolute obedience may be particularly bad for women who have been dependent on male criminal associates, or for women who have been in abusive relationships. These issues arose many times in the interviews with the women participants.

In conclusion, this research has uncovered serious problems for women offenders who are placed in boot camps with men. These programs are designed for men, and they do not provide true equality for women. The separate boot camps for women have fewer problems. Many of the advantages and disadvantages for females in all-female boot camps are the same as those for male participants. However, there may be some additional difficulties for many women who have past histories of abuse or dependency. Furthermore, the boot camps may not maximize some factors that could be used as positive incentives for women. For example, developing positive social interactions with others (e.g., positive peer cultures) or more interaction with their children may furnish experiences that are strong reinforcers for these women. Nor do many of the boot camps address the needs of the women for vocational training, drug treatment, or transition to the community. On the other hand, if the boot camp is the only way that these women can obtain treatment and early release from prison, it might be possible to design programs that are more responsive to the needs of women offenders. At this point, these boot camps should be considered experimental. They should be carefully monitored and studied so that future programs can be designed to successfully achieve the correctional objectives and not harm offender participants.

NOTES

1. This does not include local or juvenile boot camp programs (Cronin, 1994).

2. Data collection instruments were pretested at the boot camp program in Louisiana. Therefore, that site was excluded from the random selection process.

3. Frequently the standards were the same because the sites emphasized setting individual goals and did not have any overall required standards.

REFERENCES

American Correctional Association. (1990). *The female offender: What does the future hold?* Washington, D.C.: St. Mary's Press.

American Correctional Association. (1993). *Female offenders: Meeting needs of a neglected population.* Laurel, MD: Author.

Baunach, P. J. (1985). *Mothers in prison.* New Brunswick, NJ: Transaction Books.

Bershad, L. (1985). Discriminatory treatment of the female offender in the criminal justice system. *Boston College Law Review, 26,* 389-438.

Bureau of Justice Statistics. (1994). *Survey of state prison inmates 1991: Women in prison.* Washington, D.C.: U.S. Department of Justice.

Chesney-Lind, M., & Pollock-Byrne, J. (1993). Women's prisons. Equality with a vengeance. Unpublished manuscript. University of Hawaii at Manoa.

Cronin, R. C. (1994). Boot camps for adult and juvenile offenders: Overview and update. Report to the National Institute of Justice. Washington, D.C.: National Institute of Justice.

Glick, R. M., & Neto, V. (1982). National study of women's correctional programs. In B. R. Price & N. J. Sokoloff (Eds.), *The criminal justice system and women* (pp. 141-154). New York: Clark Boardman Company.

MacKenzie, D. L. (1993). Boot camp prisons 1993. *National Institute of Justice Journal, 217,* 21-28.

MacKenzie, D. L., & Piquero, A. (1994). The impact of shock incarceration programs on prison crowding. *Crime and Delinquency, 40,* 222-249.

MacKenzie, D. L., & Shaw, J. (1990). Inmate adjustment and change during shock incarceration: The impact of correctional boot camp programs. *Justice Quarterly, 7,* 125-150.

MacKenzie, D. L., & Souryal, C. (1992). Inmate attitude change during incarceration: A comparison of boot camp and traditional prison. Final report to the National Institute of Justice. Washington, D.C.: National Institute of Justice.

MacKenzie, D. L., & Souryal, C. (1993). Multi-site study of shock incarceration: Process evaluation. Unpublished final report to the National Institute of Justice. College Park, MD: University of Maryland.

MacKenzie, D. L., & Souryal, C. (1994). Multi-site evaluation of shock incarceration: Executive summary. Report to the National Institute of Justice. Washington, D.C.: National Institute of Justice.

Morash, M., & Rucker, L. (1990). A critical look at the idea of boot camp as a correctional reform. *Crime and Delinquency, 36,* 204-222.

Morris, A. (1987). *Women, crime and criminal justice.* London: Basil Blackwell.

New York Department of Correctional Services. (1992). Report to the Legislature on shock incarceration in New York. Unpublished report.

Parent, D. (1989). *Shock incarceration: An overview of existing programs*. NIJ Issues and Practices. Washington, D.C.: National Institute of Justice.

Pollock-Byrne, J. (1990). *Women, prison and crime*. Pacific Grove, CA: Brooks/Cole Publishing Company.

Rafter, N. H. (1989). Gender and justice: The equal protection issue. In L. Goodstein & D. L. MacKenzie (Eds.), *The American prison: Issues in research and policy* (pp. 89-109). New York: Plenum Press.

Rafter, N. H. (1990). *Partial justice: Women, prisons and social control*. New Brunswick, NJ: Transaction Publishers.

Robinson, R. (1992). Intermediate sanctions and the female offender. In J. Byrne, A. Lurigio, & J. Petersilia (Eds.), Smart sentencing. *The emergence of intermediate sanctions* (pp. 245-260). Newbury Park, CA: Sage Publications.

Ruback, B. (1980). The sexually integrated prison: A legal and policy evaluation. In J. O. Smykla (Ed.), *Coed prison* (pp. 33-60). New York: Human Sciences Press.

Smart, C. (1989). *Feminism and the power of law*. London: Routledge.

Straus, M. A. (1979). Measuring intrafamily conflict and violence: The conflict tactics (CT) scales. *Journal of Marriage and the Family*, 41, 75.

U.S. General Accounting Office. (1993). *Prison boot camps: Short-term costs reduced, but long-term impact uncertain*. Washington, D.C.: U.S. Government Printing Office.

Van Ochten, M. (1993). Legal issues and the female offender. In *Female offenders: Meeting needs of a neglected population* (pp. 31-36). Laurel, MD: American Correctional Association.

Weisheit, R. (1985). Trends in programs for female offenders: The use of private agencies as service providers. *International Journal of Offender Therapy and Comparative Criminology*, 29, 35-42.

18

SHOCK INCARCERATION AND ITS IMPACT ON THE LIVES OF PROBLEM DRINKERS

JAMES W. SHAW

DORIS LAYTON MACKENZIE

INTRODUCTION

Shock incarceration is a relatively new type of sanction in which young adult offenders spend a short time in prison in a regimented military "boot-camp" style program. Specific components of these programs, such as length of stay, counseling and educational programs, release decision-making, and follow-up supervision vary among states (Parent 1989; MacKenzie, Gould, Riechers, & Shaw, 1989); however, shock incarceration programs are attracting considerable public and political attention for their potential as (1) an effective means for dealing with prison crowding and (2) a viable alternative to long-term incarceration.

Since the inception of the first program in November 1983 in Oklahoma (and only a month later in Georgia) 11 states have developed shock programs, and another 11 states are developing them (MacKenzie & Bellow, 1989). Recently different states have expressed interest in shock programs as a potential environment for treating drug and alcohol abusers. Currently the Bureau of Justice Assistance is working with New York and Texas to develop model shock incarceration programs that will focus on substance abusers and their specific problems. Also, the White House National Drug Control Strategy (September, 1989) mentions shock programs as a potentially "efficient and less expensive way" for dealing with certain drug offenders (p. 25). This paper focuses on shock incarceration and one specific type of substance abuser, individuals having problems with alcohol.

Voluminous research has implicated the use of alcohol in large percentages (ranging from 24 to 64 percent) of crimes such as murder and

Reprinted with permission from Shaw, J. W., & MacKenzie, D. L. (1991). *American Journal of Criminal Justice, XVI*(1), 63-93. An earlier version of this paper was presented at the Annual Meeting of the American Society of Criminology, Reno, 1989. This study was supported in part by Grant *87-U-CX-0020 from the National Institute of Justice, U.S. Department of Justice to the Louisiana State University for a cooperative project with the Louisiana State Department of Public Safety and Corrections. Opinions expressed in this paper are those of the authors and not necessarily those of the U.S. Department of Justice.

rape down to simply "hurting someone" (e.g., Wolfgang, 1958; Voss & Hepburn, 1968; Amir, 1967; Peterson & Braiker, 1980). The magnitude of alcohol-related deviant or criminal behavior can be seen in the fact that, as Young and Lawson (1984) report, alcohol related arrests outnumber arrests for any other type of crime including those for property crimes.

Findings such as these suggest that alcohol use may be extensive in incarcerated offender populations, and this has indeed been found. For example, the Bureau of Justice Statistics (1983) survey of state prisoners found that nearly a third of all inmates admitted to consuming large amounts of alcohol just prior to their current offense. In another study Miller and Welte (1986) found that 60 percent of the sampled inmates reported alcohol or drug use prior to their current offense; thirty percent reported having used alcohol only.

PROBLEM DRINKING

Most social science research, cautious of attempting to make a medical diagnosis such as alcoholism, has instead focused on problem drinking. There is an extensive literature on problem drinking and there are numerous definitions of the term. Most definitions, however, have some commonalities. Usually problems are identified as such because their operationalization denotes something that is either injurious to the individual or his/her associates (Polich, 1979). Plaut (1967) states that "problem drinking is a repetitive use of beverage alcohol causing physical, psychological, or social harm to the drinker or to others" (pp. 37-38). Keller (1982a) identifies problem drinking as "heavy, deviant or implicative drinking that causes private or public harm—that is seen to cause problems for the drinker or for others" (p. 129).

A potential problem with definitions such as these is the difficulty of proving causality (Cahalan, 1970). Unable to establish that drinking is either a sufficient or necessary cause of some problems, Knupfer's definition (1967) may be more appropriate. "A problem—any problem—connected fairly closely with drinking constitutes a drinking problem" (p. 974). A major advantage of focusing on problems

related to drinking (and problem drinkers) is that such an approach will undoubtedly include cases of alcoholism, but it is not limited to those more difficult to establish cases.

Measuring problem drinking varies to some extent, as does its definition, but it generally includes several key elements. The following categories discussed by Collins (1986) are fairly representative: (1) an excessive use of alcohol, determined by a measure of quantity and/or frequency of intake; (2) adverse consequences such as family and work (social), or health problems due to drinking; and (3) perceptions by the drinker or others that the he/she has a drinking problem, i.e., psychological involvement (Room, 1977; Cahalan, 1982; Clark & Midanik, 1982).

Identifying Characteristics of Problem Drinkers

Shortly after Prohibition conceptualizations of alcoholism began to change in favor of the disease model (Keller, 1982b). Consistent with this position and due in part to the inception of Alcoholics Anonymous in 1935, studies on alcoholism began to emphasize research on the "alcoholic personality" (Cox, 1987).

Although findings have sometimes varied, researchers have identified personality characteristics distinguishing alcoholics and problem drinkers from "normals." Manson (1949) found that alcoholics differed from normals in areas dealing with social maladjustment, poor interpersonal relationships, feelings of inadequacy and insecurity, and believing they received a raw deal from life. MacAndrew and Geertsma (1963) found that two scales they called Social Deviance and Remorseful Intrapunitiveness differentiated alcoholics from a non-alcoholic sample. Since then findings of elevated social maladjustment scores have consistently been found in alcoholic samples. In an extensive review of the literature Barnes (1979) reports that one conclusion which can be drawn from the sometimes conflicting literature on the alcoholic personality is that psychopathic deviate scores are higher than for normals.

Barnes (1979) also reports that scales measuring neuroticism arc higher for alcoholics, but that this fording is less consistent in the literature. One reason for this inconsistency is that some research may actually be studying pre-alcoholics. Hoffman, Loper, and Kammeier (1974) report that young pre-alcoholics are more impulsive, conforming, and gregarious but are not otherwise "grossly maladjusted compared with their peers" (p. 491). McCord (1981) also reports that, as children, future alcoholic criminals were more aggressive and resentful of authority, but that they were least likely to be lacking in self-confidence and exhibit symptoms of anxiety, depression and low self-esteem.

Once these individuals develop problems due to alcohol, or by the time they enter treatment, Cox (1987) reports that alcoholics then also measure higher in neuroticism, e.g., depression and anxiety. Cox suggests this change may be a consequence of the accumulative stresses in alcoholics lives due to their drinking problems. Similarly Barnes (1979) suggests that drinking may have positive rewards for the pre-alcoholic, such as reducing anxiety; however, in later stages of alcoholism, as the drinker becomes apprehensive about his/her condition, drinking tends to produce anxiety and depression.

Treatment of Problem Drinkers

Most alcohol treatment personnel believe that proper motivation is essential for successful treatment; however, the psychotherapeutic community has traditionally considered the coerced "patient" to be unmotivated and thus a poor treatment risk (Fagan & Fagan, 1982). There is nonetheless some evidence that alcoholics can improve with mandatory treatment. Gallant et al. (1968) showed that a coerced group improved significantly in a number of problem areas compared to a voluntary group. Similarly, Dunham and Mauss (1982) found that treatment of problem drinkers coerced into treatment by the court "did not subvert the goals of the therapeutic model; indeed, it rendered successful treatment outcome considerably more likely than with strictly voluntary self-referral" (p. 18).

Gendreau and Ross (1987) contend that, in general, treatment programs for alcohol abusers in offender populations have been casually disregarded in the literature. However they discuss several studies which demonstrate that alcohol programs can be effective for offenders. Assuming the similarity of alcohol problems to

drug problems, they conclude that "the pertinent question is not whether drug abuse programs work but rather what types of programs work for what types of addicts at different points in their addictive career" (p. 386).

Two general categories of personality correlates characteristic of problem drinkers have been identified, social maladjustment and neuroticism. Regarding the latter, programs which enhance an individual's sense of self-confidence and self-esteem have been successful in dealing with depression and anxiety (Cox, 1987; Barnes, 1979). Efforts to build self-confidence and self-esteem are seen to be important for successful treatment of problem drinkers in Alcoholics Anonymous, as such efforts can counteract their sense of failure and hopelessness (Young & Lawson, 1984).

Another component of treatment which has been beneficial for problem drinkers is stress management, along with social skills training and behavior self control (Gendreau & Ross, 1987). Paredes, Hood, Seymour, and Gollob (1977) state that role expectations ascribed according to age, sex, kinship, education, and training are often considered trivial; however, they contend that such demands involve considerable psychological and psychophysiological stress. Consequently, many alcoholics use alcohol, whether consciously or subconsciously, to avoid coping with those pressures. They have found in their experience and work that helping alcoholics formulate more adaptive methods of coping with life stressors has been beneficial.

Social maladjustment characteristics on the other hand have been found to be more resistant to change (Barnes, 1979). One critical characteristic Boyatzis (1975) argues must be addressed is learning social responsibility. Much of the research on the alcohol-crime relationship (e.g., expectancy theory: Goldman, Brown, & Christiansen, 1987; drunken comportment: MacAndrew & Edgerton, 1969) appears to minimize the significance of the pharmacological effects of alcohol. Boyatzis contends though that if the individual does not feel integrated into society as a "responsible citizen" he may be especially susceptible to physiological disinhibiting effects of alcohol which may, for example, increase aggressive behaviors.

Although social maladjustment characteristics may be more resistant to change, there is evidence which demonstrates such change is possible. A study of drug abusers over a three-month period by Zuckerman, Sola, Masterson, and Angelone (1975) found that psychopathic (ie., antisocial and aggressive) scores decreased significantly in each of three different programs. A particularly interesting finding was that the psychopathic types did fairly well in the program, e.g., 75 percent in contrast to 43 percent of all other types stayed in the program. Although Cox (1987) reports that psychopathic types generally do not work as hard as others to achieve difficult to obtain goals, Zuckerman et al. contend that these individuals can learn that it is in their best interest to be honest and give up their self-defeating antisocial behaviors.

LOUISIANA'S SHOCK INCARCERATION PROGRAM

This research was part of a larger evaluation of the Louisiana Department of Public Safety and Correction's (LDPSC) shock incarceration program which began in 1987 (LDPSC, 1987). A primary objective of this program is to increase participants' skills and abilities to live law-abiding, creative, and fulfilling lives once they are released. Efforts to achieve this goal are evident throughout the two-phase program. The first phase is a 90 to 180 day program in a medium-security correctional institution modeled after military basic training. This is an extremely rigorous period during which inmates are instructed in military bearing, courtesy, drills and ceremony, physical training, and personal skills, such as good grooming, personal hygiene, and maintenance of their living quarters. The intent of such training is to instill discipline in offenders' lives and encourage them to take responsibility for their actions.

The drill instructors also spend several hours each week working informally with the inmates in an attempt to develop insights into how their training and instruction relates to real life situations and how inmates can profit thereby. Concepts related to work are explored, such as how to look for employment, how to present oneself to a potential employer, and the

importance of responsibility and self-discipline when employed. Recreation periods are also structured and managed in such a way as to reinforce concepts related to successful living. Organized sports are developed which emphasize leadership ability, goal-oriented behavior, and particularly the benefits of teamwork. Finally, formal treatment programs include ventilation therapy, reeducative therapy, substance abuse group, and a pre-release group (LDPSC, 1987).

Advancement through the shock program is itself designed to instill a sense of self-confidence and responsibility for one's actions. Inmates start in a beginners squad and (on the basis of daily evaluations regarding their performance and conduct) have the opportunity to move into an intermediate squad and finally into the advanced squad every 30 days. Once inmates successfully complete 30 days in the advanced squad they are eligible for parole and may formally graduate from the institutional phase of the program.

In the second phase of the program shock graduates are assigned to an intensive supervision parole team, who guide and monitor the inmates' progress in the community. In addition to regular parole requirements parolees are required to have multiple unscheduled weekly contacts with their parole officers, comply with a strictly enforced curfew (8:00 p.m.), and perform 100 hours of unpaid community service (LDPSC, 1987). After three months if parolees demonstrate prosocial and responsible living they may graduate to a less restrictive phase of parole supervision. Depending on the length of their original sentence they may later graduate to the third phase of supervision, after which they may finally be transferred to regular parole supervision. The gradational method of advancement through parole may also contribute to a sense of responsibility, self-confidence, and accomplishment as parolees progress through the program.

There is some evidence that shock incarceration programs may produce changes in self-concept, self-esteem, and respect for authority. Parent (1988) reviews several studies of regimented Challenge programs, stressing physical training and stimulating mental challenges, which have demonstrated positive changes. Not only were increases in self-esteem and respect for authority found, but rates of recidivism were significantly lower for participants than controls in several of the studies. On the other hand several studies of actual military basic training have found recruits to become more callous, impulsive, and indifferent to the needs of others (Parent, 1988). Thus it is possible that changes could be negative. However, although shock incarceration "borrows" from the discipline and regimen enforced in basic training, the goals of programs such as Louisiana's are clearly different, and aspects of treatment are stressed which promote prosocial behaviors and attitudes.

It may be argued that the rigorous shock program which attempts to instill self-esteem, self-confidence, self-respect, individual and social responsibility, and respect for others and their values, can contribute considerably to a goal of rehabilitating problem drinkers. Efforts to build self-confidence and self-esteem are seen as essential for successful treatment of problem drinkers in Alcoholics Anonymous, since such efforts can counteract their sense of failure and hopelessness (Young & Lawson, 1984). Also, developing a sense of self-esteem and self-confidence may decrease problem drinkers "need" to use alcohol in order to feel masculine, powerful, or simply confident in themselves, as postulated by the power (McClelland, Davis, Kalin, & Wanner, 1972) or dependency (McCord & McCord, 1962) theories.

Boyatzis (1975) argued that an individual who does not feel a sense of social responsibility may be more susceptible to the physiologically disinhibiting effects of alcohol. Thus, learning individual and social responsibility may decrease this effect. Further, learning that aggression and other forms of antisocial behavior are not acceptable may help strengthen the cultural norms which MacAndrew and Edgerton (1969) argue govern drunken comportment, as well as possibly lessen individual's expectancy (Goldman et al., 1987; Pihl, 1983; Lang, Goecknor, Adesso, & Marian, 1975) of aggression under the influence of alcohol.

In view of this literature, it was hypothesized first that problem drinkers would score higher than non-problem drinkers on scales measuring social maladjustment and, to the extent they had experienced adverse consequences from their drinking, also higher on scales measuring neuroticism. A second research hypothesis was that problem drinkers in the shock program would become more prosocial than would regularly incarcerated problem drinkers. Finally, problem drinkers were expected to have more difficulty adjusting to prosocial lives on parole than would nonproblem drinkers.

METHODS

Subjects

The subjects for this study consist of (1) a group of male offenders who participated in Louisiana's shock program and (2) a comparison group of regularly incarcerated male inmates selected to be similar to the shock sample. To be eligible for the Louisiana shock program, candidates must not have a previous felony incarceration, be sentenced to seven years or less and eligible for parole, and have three recommendations by: (1) the Division of Probation and Parole, (2) the sentencing judge, and (3) the Adult Reception and Diagnostic Center of the DOC (MacKenzie & Shaw, 1990). Candidates must volunteer to participate, and they may drop out of the program at any time. They may also be removed by program staff for inadequate progress or inappropriate behavior. Once inmates are "dropped on request," for whatever reason, they must serve their regular prison sentence.

Shock Sample. All male offenders who participated in the shock incarceration program from October 1987 to October 1988 volunteered to participate in the study for a total sample of 192. Of the total shock sample, 80 (42%) dropped from the shock program, resulting in 112 who completed this study.[1]

Incarcerated Sample. The comparison group consists of male offenders who were selected for their legal eligibility for the shock program but who were not recommended by either the Division of Probation and Parole, the sentencing judge, or the DOC diagnostic center. Ninety-eight inmates who volunteered and who were available for the entire evaluation were examined this study.

Procedure

A quasi-experimental, non-equivalent control group design (Cook & Campbell, 1979) was employed to examine any changes occurring in offenders during the evaluation. For this study all offenders (shock participants and regularly incarcerated) were administered questions containing several Jesness (1983) personality scales and self report demographic questions at Time 1 (just prior to entering either the shock program or regular prison) at the diagnostic center. Both samples were then tested again at Time 2 (approximately 90 days later) nearing possible completion of the shock program for participants. At this time shock inmates were tested in an area regularly used for shock education and treatment classes. Inmates in the incarcerated sample were brought to several centralized location by DOC personnel throughout the state for this testing.

In order to assess offenders' performance while on parole, a standardized parole evaluation form was distributed to intensive supervision and regular parole officers. The forms were completed by the officers each month for all shock and regularly incarcerated offenders who were paroled during the time frame for this study (i.e., those released to parole from the study samples between January, 1988 and April, 1989; N = 109).

Finally, demographic and criminal justice system data were collected from DOC records for both the shock and regularly incarcerated samples. Relevant demographic data include age, race, and education. Criminal justice data included information on offenders' present sentence and prior involvement with the criminal justice system.

Instruments

Problem Drinking Index. A number of potential problems inmates might have in relation to drinking were identified in the data that was collected. Items were selected for the index which have face validity for problem drinking and which were consistent with items found in the literature on problem drinking. One of the first indications of problem drinking is heavy consumption of alcohol; in fact Polich (1979) argues that this can be considered a problem in itself. As such the first item in the index deals with the frequency of drinking beer, wine, or liquor. Cahalan and Room (1974) found that problems with the law and loss of control both precede heavy intake. By making the remaining items contingent upon respondents first answering that they drank daily or almost daily, problems identified should be more serious.

An exact measure of quantity was not available to determine excessive intake. However, if the respondent said he drank daily or almost daily and said he was very drunk or pretty drunk by the time he would usually stop drinking, this would indicate that he drank to intoxication more or less regularly, consistent with Clark's (1966) description of excessive intake. Of the various possible adverse consequences related to drinking, a number of authors (eg., Cahalan & Cisin, 1976; Room, 1977; Cahalan, 1982) state that having problems with the law indicates a serious problem. Thus five items deal with arrests, convictions, and self-reports of driving while intoxicated and other alcohol-defined crimes. The last two items indicate a possible loss of control, whether actual or subjective; e.g., I can stop drinking before I get drunk or I could go without drinking.

On the basis of the items in this index, 58 (20%) inmates were identified as problem drinkers and 232 as nonproblem drinkers out of a total of 290 inmates. It may be noted that identification of 20 percent of the inmates as problem drinkers appears to be a conservative estimate in comparison to other prison surveys. However, considering that these are primarily young, first felony, non-violent offenders, these results are reasonable estimates.

Social Maladjustment. Although a number of scales were administered to the inmates, several scales from the Jesness Inventory were used in this research (Jesness, 1983). The scales were initially developed by Jesness for classification and treatment of disturbed adolescents; however, they have been subsequently used in a variety of settings and modified for use with adults. The scales have been shown to successfully distinguish between identified-delinquent and nondelinquent groups and to be especially good in measuring short-term changes.

Previous reviews of the literature (Barnes, 1979; Cox, 1987) have found that problem drinkers are characterized by general social maladjustment. The specific Jesness scales that were used to identify this characteristic are Social Maladjustment, Alienation, and Manifest Aggression. The Social Maladjustment scale identifies attitudes associated with disturbed socialization; the resulting behavior generally involves failing to meet environmental demands in socially accepted ways (Jesness, 1983). Items in the Alienation scale refer to distrust and estrangement towards others and particularly towards those in authority. The Manifest Aggression scale reflects an awareness of anger and frustration, a tendency to act out in such a manner, and discomfort in controlling anger and frustration.

Neuroticism. The second category of personality correlates characteristic of problem drinkers as identified in the literature is neuroticism. Two of Jesness' scales were used for this category. The Withdrawal scale identifies individuals who are depressed, are dissatisfied with themselves, are sad, and feel misunderstood by others. The items in the Social Anxiety scale refer to general discomfort in interpersonal relations. Individuals scoring high in social anxiety tend to feel nervous, self-conscious, and intropunitive, a characteristic MacAndrew and Geertsma (1963) found to distinguish alcoholics from normals.

Parole Performance Index. The parole performance evaluation included items regarding the parolees' performance at work, in school, substance abuse counseling, interpersonal relations, intensive supervision program requirements, and contacts with the criminal justice system. In order to examine whether shock incarceration helped problem drinkers adjust to law-abiding, prosocial lives, several items from each of the above categories were chosen for inclusion in the Adjustment to Prosocial Living Index. This index is similar to the Positive Adjustment Scale used by Latessa and Vito (1988) in that it is intended to assess parolees' overall adjustment to law-abiding, prosocial living, rather than focusing only on,

e.g., whether the offender had been rearrested. The 20 items included in the index were scored by assigning a value of +1 for an item if the parolee was doing well (or not doing poorly) and a value of 0 if otherwise.

RESULTS

Demographic Comparisons

Initial demographic comparisons of problem drinkers (PD), nonproblem drinkers (NPD), inmates sent to the shock program, and (prison) inmates who were regularly incarcerated indicated that they were fairly similar. Two-way Analysis of Variance (ANOVA) and tests of Chi Square showed no difference in education (M = 10.4, SD = 1.8) on either factor, and race in type prison sample (39.3% white ($n = 103$) and 60.7% nonwhite ($n = 159$)); there was however a significant difference in race for drinker type. Twenty-eight (27.2%) white inmates compared to only 25 (15.7%) nonwhite inmates were problem drinkers ($\chi^2(1) = 5.1$, $p < 0.02$). Finally there was a significant difference ($F(1,226) = 7.8$, $p < 0.006$) in age entering the diagnostic center, with prison inmates being two and a half years older (M = 25.7, SD = 5.3) than the shock inmates (M = 23.1, SD = 4.6).

Both shock and prison inmates were also similar on all characteristics related to their current sentence. The average sentence length was 45.4 months (SD = 18.0), a majority ($n = 186$, 71.5%) had been convicted of a new crime versus probation violation, and most had been convicted of property crimes ($n = 167$, 69.9%) compared to 60 (25.1%) for crimes that could be described as vice (e.g., prostitution, gambling, and drug offenses) and only 12 (5.0%) for violent type crimes. One difference in this category was with type of drinker. Only 25.1 percent ($n = 52$) of NPD inmates had entered prison due to a probation violation compared to 41.5 percent ($n = 22$) of PD inmates who entered on a probation violation ($\chi^2(1) = 5.6$, $p < 0.02$).

The criminal justice histories of both samples were also similar. There was a slightly higher percentage of shock inmates (84.5% ($n = 136$)) who had an adult criminal history compared to 71 (75.5%) prison inmates ($\chi^2(1) = 3.1$, $p < 0.08$).

Table 18.1   Mean Scores[1] and F Values[2] for Sample (Shock versus Prison) and Drinker Type (Nonproblem Versus Problem) at Time 1 for Social Maladjustment, Alienation, Manifest Aggression, Withdrawal, and Social Anxiety

	Mean Scores			Main Effects		
	Sample	Drinker type	Overall Model	Sample	Drinker	Age
	SHOCK n = 192	NONPROBLEM n = 232	F (df)	F (df)	F (df)	F (df)
	PRISON n = 98	PROBLEM n = 58	Prob < F	Prob < F	Prob < F	Prob < F
Social Mal-	100.9	100.5	10.37 (3,225)	11.26 (1,225)	5.66 (1,225)	17.97 (1,225)
adjustment	96.5	96.9	$p < 0.0001$	$p < 0.0009$	$p < 0.02$	$p < 0.0001$
Alienation	40.7	40.2	3.83 (3,225)	4.60 (1,225)	0.31 (1,225)	7.06 (1,225)
	39.3	39.8	$p < 0.02$	$p < 0.03$	NS	$p < 0.008$
Manifest	49.4	49.2	6.05 (3,226)	6.88 (1,226)	3.15 (1,226)	10.40 (1,226)
Aggression	47.3	47.6	$p < 0.0006$	$p < 0.009$	$p < 0.08$	$p < 0.001$
Withdrawal	34.9	35.2	1.60 (3,226)	0.26 (1,226)	2.06 (1,226)	2.88 (1,226)
	34.6	34.3	$p < 0.19$	NS	$p < 0.15$	$p < 0.09$
Social	35.7	36.7	2.65 (1,226)	1.79 (1,226)	4.49 (1,226)	2.58 (1,226)
Anxiety	36.4	35.4	$p < 0.05$	$p < 0.18$	$p < 0.04$	$p < 0.11$

[1]Mean scores are adjusted for age.
[2]Tests of sample by drinker type interactions were first conducted; all were insignificant.

However there were no differences in percentages having a prior incarceration, 39 (15.2%) had at least spent some time in a jail; and there were no differences in age at first arrest (M = 19.9, SD = 4.0) for either sample or drinker type.

It was mentioned earlier that a large percentage (42%) of shock inmates dropped out of the program, presumably because they did not like the rigorous nature of the program. This raises the important question as to whether shock dropouts were different in some important way from shock completers in this study. However, of all the demographic, present sentence, and criminal history variables examined above, dropouts differed only in sentence length. The average sentence length for dropouts was 42.0 months (SD = 15.5) compared to 49.0 months (SD = 18.7) for completers (F(1,161) = 6.0, $p < 0.02$). Although only marginally significant, it is interesting that a larger percentage of shock completers (18.896 ($n = 21$)) than shock dropouts (10.096 (N = 8)) were problem drinkers (χ^2 (1) = 2.79, $p < 0.10$).

Preprogram Attitudes

Social Maladjustment Scales. Three scales were used to examine prosocial attitudes:

Social Maladjustment, Alienation, and Manifest Aggression. As mentioned, the large number of shock dropouts raises the concern that they might be different from shock completers. Also, in a quasi-experimental design such as this, it is possible that the comparison group (prison inmates) could be different in some significant way.

To examine these concerns a two-way ANOVA for sample (shock versus prison) and type of drinker (PD versus NPD) controlling for age was conducted. The decision to control for age was made since shock inmates were significantly younger than the prison inmates; moreover it is reasonable to expect that offenders' age should influence their attitudes. Overall tests of significance and interaction were first conducted before examining main effects (main effects and interactions are not discussed unless the overall model is significant at $\alpha = 0.05$). There were no interactions between drinker type and sample for these scales.

There were however main effects for sample and drinker type; prison inmates were less prosocial than shock inmates (see Table 18.1) in social maladjustment, alienation, and in manifest aggression. Similarly, PD inmates were also less prosocial than NPD inmates in social

Table 18.2   Mean Scores[1] and F Values[2] for Shock (Completers Versus Dropouts) and Drinker Type (Nonproblem versus Problem) at Time 1 for Social Maladjustment, Alienation, Manifest Aggression, Withdrawal, and Social Anxiety

| | Mean Scores | | Main Effects | | | |
	Sample	Drinker type	Overall Model	Sample	Drinker	Age
	COMPLETERS n = 112	NONPROBLEM n = 163	F (df)	F (df)	F (df)	F (df)
	DORS n = 80	PROBLEM n = 29	Prob < F	Prob < F	Prob < F	Prob < F
Social Mal-	101.1	102.1	6.67 (3,158)	3.69 (1,158)	6.08 (1,158)	12.21 (1,158)
adjustment	98.5	97.5	p < 0.0003	p < 0.06	p < 0.01	p < 0.0006
Alienation	40.6	40.8	4.06 (3,158)	3.65 (1,158)	2.95 (1,158)	6.64 (1,158)
	39.4	39.3	p < 0.008	p < 0.06	p < 0.09	p < 0.01
Manifest	49.7	49.9	4.28 (3,159)	5.78 (1,159)	4.38 (1,159)	3.98 (1,159)
Aggression	47.7	47.6	p < 0.006	p < 0.02	p < 0.04	p < 0.05
Withdrawal	35.3	35.1	1.87 (3,159)	4.36 (1,159)	0.68 (1,159)	0.86 (1,159)
	34.2	34.4	p < 0.14	p < 0.04	NS	NS
Social	35.9	36.3	2.26 (1,159)	1.17 (1,159)	2.85 (1,159)	2.59 (1,159)
Anxiety	35.3	35.0	p < 0.08	NS	p < 0.09	p < 0.11

[1]Mean scores are adjusted for age.
[2]Tests of sample by drinker type interactions were first conducted; all were insignificant.

maladjustment and marginally in manifest aggression. There were no differences for drinker type in alienation.

Although shock dropouts were fairly similar to completers in demographic and criminal justice data, there were significant differences in prosocial attitudes. Dropouts were less prosocial than completers (see Table 18.2) in social maladjustment, in alienation, and in manifest aggression. Problem drinkers were also less prosocial than NPD inmates in these comparisons. As there was no problem by dropout interaction it would at least not appear that being a problem or nonproblem drinker affected the dropout rate.

Neuroticism Scales. Two scales, Withdrawal and Social Anxiety, were used to examine neuroticism. In contrast to the social maladjustment scales, there were no differences between shock and prison inmates in withdrawal or social anxiety at Time 1. While not significant, problem drinkers were, as hypothesized, more withdrawn than NPD inmates; and they were significantly more anxious than NPD inmates (see Table 18.1). Although shock dropouts did not differ from completers in anxiety, dropouts were more withdrawn than completers (Table 18.2).

Program Comparisons

These analyses examine the changes between Time 1 and Time 2 for shock completers and prison inmates. Ideally the shock dropouts would also be examined for change over time either as part of the shock sample (the most appropriate method if this were a true experimental design) or possibly as a third group. However, a majority of the shock dropouts left the program within one week (and almost all by two weeks) and so were not available for testing at Time 2.[4] Since the shock dropouts do appear to be different from shock completers, any program effects must be interpreted with this in mind. A repeated-measures analysis examining two factors (sample and drinker type) and controlling for age, with two levels of time as the repeated-measure, was conducted separately for each scale.

Social Maladjustment Scales. As with the tests at Time 1 the prison inmates remained less prosocial (see Table 18.3) in social maladjustment, in alienation, and in manifest aggression. There was also a main effect for drinker type with PD inmates being less prosocial than NPD inmates in social maladjustment and in manifest aggression.

Table 18.3 Mean Scores[1] and F Statistics for Social Maladjustment (SM), Alienation (AL), and Manifest Aggression by Time (1 & 2), Type of Drinker (Nonproblem and Problem), and Sample (Shock and Prison)

Type of Drinker	Sample	N	SM Time1	SM Time2	AL Time1	AL Time2	MA Time1	MA Time2
Nonproblem	Shock	86	104.0	104.7	41.7	43.1	51.1	50.6
Nonproblem	Prison	45	98.4	100.6	39.1	40.5	48.1	49.0
Problem	Shock	18	99.1	102.6	39.3	42.8	48.8	48.7
Problem	Prison	21	95.6	95.3	40.0	39.3	47.2	46.2
Within Subjects Effects								
Time*Sample*Drinker		F(df)	4.91 (1,165)		8.11 (1,166)		2.24 (1,165)	
		Prob	*p* < 0.04		*p* < 0.005		*p* < 0.13	
Time*Sample		F(df)	0.79 (1,165)		8.26 (1,166)		0.16 (1,165)	
		Prob	NS		*p* < 0.005		NS	
Time*Drinker		F(df)	0.02 (1,165)		0.00 (1,166)		0.86 (1,165)	
		Prob	NS		NS		NS	
Time		F(df)	0.81 (1,165)		2.17 (1,166)		0.03 (1,165)	
		Prob	NS		*p* < 0.14		NS	
Between Subjects Effects								
Drinker*Sample		F(df)	0.03 (1,165)		0.65 (1,166)		0.01 (1,165)	
		Prob	NS		NS		NS	
Drinker		F(df)	6.20 (1,165)		0.86 (1,166)		5.38 (1,165)	
		Prob	*p* < 0.01		NS		*p* < 0.02	
Sample		F(df)	11.30 (1,165)		6.68 (1,166)		6.06(1,165)	
		Prob	*p* < 0.001		*p* < 0.01		*p* < 0.01	
Age		F(df)	13.65 (1,165)		4.42 (1,166)		8.08(1,165)	
		Prob	*p* < 0.0003		*p* < 0.04		*p* < 0.005	

[1]Mean Scores are adjusted for age.

In support of the second research hypothesis there were several interactions with time. There was first a three-way interaction of drinker type by sample with time for social maladjustment. It can be seen in Table 18.3 that PD inmates in the shock sample became more prosocial over the three month period, whereas there was no change in the anti-social attitudes of PD prison inmates.

Two interactions were significant with alienation. First there was a time by sample interaction. Examination of scale means shows that the shock sample became less alienated while the prison sample made no change. Perhaps explaining some of this two-way interaction is the highly significant drinker type by sample with time interaction. Of particular interest is the fact that PD inmates in the shock sample became less alienated (see Table 18.4) while PD prison inmates became more alienated than when they entered. While not significant the slight three-way interaction for manifest aggression is also interesting. Although problem drinkers did not change in the shock sample, PD inmates became more aggressive in the prison sample.

Neuroticism Scales. There were no differences between shock and prison inmates over this time in withdrawal or social anxiety; however it may be noted that NPD inmates were significantly both less anxious and less withdrawn than PD inmates. There were no interactions for drinker types or sample with time on either of these two scales.

Positive Adjustment on Parole. A two-way repeated-measures ANOVA was performed for sample and drinker type, again controlling for age, with positive adjustment as the dependent variable and six levels of time (i.e., parolees first

Table 18.4   Mean Scores[1] and F Statistics for Withdrawal (WD) and Social Anxiety (SA) by Time (1 & 2), Type of Drinker (Nonproblem and Problem), and Sample (Shock and Prison)

Type of Drinker	Sample	N	WD Time1	WD Time2	SA Time1	SA Time2
Nonproblem	Shock	86	35.8	35.4	36.5	35.9
Nonproblem	Prison	45	35.3	35.5	37.1	37.0
Problem	Shock	18	34.8	34.9	35.0	34.9
Problem	Prison	21	33.9	34.0	35.7	35.8

Within Subjects Effects

Time*Sample*Drinker		F(df)		0.12 (1,165)		0.06 (1,166)
		Prob		NS		NS
Time*Sample		F(df)		0.21 (1,165)		0.26 (1,166)
		Prob		NS		NS
Time*Drinker		F(df)		0.15 (1,165)		0.35 (1,166)
		Prob		NS		NS
Time		F(df)		0.43 (1,165)		11.09 (1,166)
		Prob		NS		$p < 0.001$

Between Subjects Effects

Drinker*Sample		F(df)		0.37 (1,165)		0.00 (1,166)
		Prob		NS		NS
Drinker		F(df)		0.43 (1,165)		4.02 (1,166)
		Prob		$p < 0.04$		$p < 0.05$
Sample		F(df)		0.92 (1,165)		1.43 (1,166)
		Prob		NS		NS
Age		F(df)		1.48 (1,165)		0.17 (1,166)
		Prob		NS		NS

[1]Mean Scores are adjusted for age.

six months on parole). The reduction in N size which can be seen in Table 18.5 is a result of two factors. First, this is the extent of the sample which had been released onto parole by April 1989 (a logistic limitation to this data), and second, the repeated measures analysis excludes any observations having missing data from the six month period.

In the analysis there was no interaction between sample and drinker type. Although there was no difference between the performance of PD and NPD inmates on parole, there was a significant main effect for sample. Examination of mean scores in Table 18.5 shows that the shock sample's behavioral performance was as a whole better than that of prison parolees.

As expected there was a significant interaction between drinker type and time. It can he seen in Figure 18.1 that the performance of PD parolees was more sporadic than that of the

NPD parolees. Although the main effect for time was marginally significant, this could probably be explained by the highly significant drinker type by time interaction.

DISCUSSION AND CONCLUSIONS

The regularly incarcerated (prison) sample was chosen to be similar to the shock incarceration shock inmates studied in this research. Basically in support of this selection process, prison inmates were not significantly different on the selection variables (i.e., in demographic, present sentence, and criminal history records) except in age. This however is an important difference because, as prison inmates were on the average 2.5 years older than shock inmates, they might be expected to improve more than the younger shock inmates in tests of prosocial attitudes. On the other hand they might be expected to be more

Table 18.5   Mean Adjustment to Prosocial Living Scores[1] and F Statistics for Parolees' First Six Months on Community Supervision by Sample (Shock and Prison) and Drinker Type (Nonproblem and Problem)

	Sample		Type Drinker	
	Shock (44)	Prison (13)	Nonproblem (47)	Problem (10)
Month 1	11.8	9.1	10.0	11.0
Month 2	11.5	9.6	11.3	9.7
Month 3	13.4	9.2	10.8	11.8
Month 4	10.7	7.9	10.1	8.6
Month 5	12.1	8.0	9.2	11.0
Month 6	11.3	8.5	8.8	11.0

Within Subjects Effects

Time*Sample*Problem		F(df)		1.19 (5,260)
		Prob		NS
Time*Sample		F(df)		0.72 (5,260)
		Prob		NS
TIme*Problem		F(df)		2.40 (5,260)
		Prob		NS
Time		F(df)		1.21 (5,260)
		Prob		NS

Between Subjects Effects

Drinker*Sample		F(df)		0.05 (1,52)
		Prob		NS
Drinker		F(df)		0.24 (1,52)
		Prob		NS
Sample		F(df)		8.89 (1,52)
		Prob		$p < 0.004$
Age		F(df)		6.48(1,52)
		Prob		$p < 0.01$

[1]Mean Scores are adjusted for age.

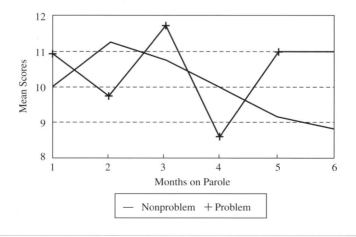

Figure 18.1

neurotic (anxious, depressed) due to being older, and possibly having had more problems related to the use of alcohol. It was for these reasons that age was entered as a concomitant variable.

Two other differences found stress the need to consider in particular two threats to internal invalidity when discussing the findings of this study. First, due to the quasi-experimental design of this study, it is possible that the comparison sample of regular prison inmates differs significantly in some unmeasured way. The fact that shock inmates, even before entering the shock program, are more prosocial than prison inmates indicates a possible pattern of selection. It has been suggested that decision makers who selected inmates for the shock program may have detected subtle attitudinal differences in offenders and gave preference for the program to those who were more prosocial (MacKenzie & Shaw, 1990).

While this suggestion is plausible, it must be noted that "antisocial" offenders are recommended to the shock program. This is evidenced by shock dropouts who score significantly lower than shock completers in each of the three social maladjustment scales, even before entering the shock program. This second difference indicates the possible threat of mortality interacting with self-selection. Their being less prosocial undoubtedly contributes to their decision to leave the program; however the fact that dropouts' sentences are significantly shorter (an average of seven months) than completers must also reduce their motivation to stay with such a difficult program.

While self-selection creates problems for evaluation purposes, it should be noted that self-selection may be an important component of shock incarceration/boot-camp programs. Future research should address whether offenders who self-select themselves out of the program are worse offenders or are individuals who would do more poorly on parole.

Of particular interest for this study is the potential the Jesness scales demonstrated in differentiating problem and non-problem drinkers.[5] In support of the literature (e.g., Barnes, 1979; Cox, 1987) problem drinkers were found to be more socially maladjusted and aggressive than non-problem drinkers. This is particularly significant due to the fact that the sample is an offender population, which as a whole would be expected to be more socially maladjusted than the general population.

Although comparisons at Time 1 showed no difference in neuroticism it is important that the more powerful repeated-measures analysis did detect a significant difference between problem and non-problem drinkers in both withdrawal and social anxiety. The reason that this difference was more difficult to detect may simply be that there are some problems with this construct, as evidenced by the fact that this finding is less consistent in the literature (Barnes, 1979). One problem which certainly applies to this data is that this construct is most likely correlated with age. And, since the inmates are all fairly young (an average of 23.8 years of age) in this study, it may be that a majority of these inmates have not experienced serious adverse consequences to the point they would begin to have much greater feelings of depression and anxiety.

Although it was hypothesized that attempts in shock incarceration to develop offenders' self-confidence and self-esteem should reduce feelings of neuroticism, a lack of interaction for drinker type with time on these scales did not support this. Perhaps the lack of any change in these scales also reflects their young age and lack of serious problems in neuroticism at this time.

On the other hand the significant three-way interactions (with PD inmates in the shock program becoming more prosocial and PD inmates in the prison sample making no change or changing in a negative direction) found with social maladjustment and alienation are encouraging. Perhaps the more prosocial problem drinkers will be less affected by the physiologically disinhibiting effects of alcohol (e.g., Boyatzis, 1975), because the attainment of more prosocial attitudes should help to develop and strengthen norms which may govern problem drinkers' "drunken comportment" (e.g., MacAndrew & Edgerton, 1969).

A second reason that change such as was found with alienation warrants encouragement is that such change is atypical of offenders' experience in prison. The fact that PD inmates in the shock sample (and the shock sample as a whole) became less alienated during this period of 90 days is in direct contrast to findings of previous studies of prisonization, where inmates become more prisonized and negative toward staff with increased time in prison (Goodstein & Wright, 1989). A possible reason for this difference may be the fact that drill instructors are a significant part of shock inmates' lives in contrast to guards in regular prison. While much of the drill instructors' interaction with inmates is disciplinary in nature and regimented, there are opportunities for them to be more socially involved with the inmates, e.g., when coaching the inmates in sports, the informal classes they hold with the inmates, as well as the constant formal training they are involved in.

It should be noted that while positive changes were observed for problem drinkers in the shock sample compared to the regular prison sample, the exact cause of such changes cannot be specifically known. Shock incarceration as implemented in Louisiana is a variety of interventions, ranging from various types and amounts of counseling to intense discipline and group sports. What can be said is that something about the bootcamp/shock incarceration program appears to have some beneficial value for offenders identified as problem drinkers.

Finally, the performance of shock inmates on parole suggests that the program did benefit the offenders. It was found that shock parolee scores on the whole were significantly higher than prison parolee scores. This suggests that shock parolees at least appear to be making a more successful adaptation to prosocial living than are prison parolees.

It is interesting that PD Adjustment to Prosocial Living scores fluctuate considerably more than those of NPD parolees. Based on this it would appear that problem drinkers are indeed having more difficulty making a stable adjustment to life on parole. In any case the fact that shock PD scores are on the average higher than prison inmates as a whole suggests that shock incarceration was beneficial for problem drinkers. The fact that shock problem drinkers have a more difficult time adjusting to prosocial lives demonstrates the importance of future programs emphasizing additional support for problem drinkers not only in prison (or in special programs such as shock incarceration) but also when these individuals are on the outside on parole.

In other words it is not enough to simply put problem drinkers (or most likely other substance abusers for that matter) into a shock program and expect their problems to somehow disappear. While this program did appear to have some success with problem drinkers, this is undoubtedly due to the intensive counseling the offenders receive in the Louisiana program. As such it is possible that these programs, if combined with the proper amount of counseling and treatment as well as after-care, may prove to be a viable setting or environment for treating problem drinkers. In the future it will be interesting to see how successful these programs are with other types of substance abusers.

Notes

1. Only two inmates refused to participate, and an additional 39 were not available because of medical, disciplinary, or work reasons.
2. These were recorded on tape, courtesy of professional radio broadcaster Dave Prince at WJBO in Baton Rouge, LA, to ensure uniformity in administration.
3. Scales were scored so that high scores are more prosocial, e.g., low scores indicate more alienation.
4. When dropouts leave the program they are required to serve their regular sentence. Due to their being sent to different institutions around the state we were unable to test them at Time 2.
5. This is a new application, to the authors' knowledge, for the use of the Jesness scales.

References

Amir, M. (1967). Alcohol and forcible rape. *British Journal of Addiction, 62,* 219-232.

Barnes, G. E. (1979). The alcoholic personality. A reanalysis of the literature. *Journal of Studies on Alcohol, 40,* 571-634.

Boyatzis, R. E. (1975). The predisposition toward alcohol-related interpersonal aggression in men. *Journal of Studies on Alcohol, 36,* 1196-1207.

Bureau of Justice Statistics. (1983). Prisoners and Alcohol. *Bulletin,* January.

Cahalan, D. (1982). Epidemiology: Alcohol use in American society. In L. Gomberg, H. R. White, & J. A. Carpenter (Eds.), *Alcohol. Science and Society Revisited* (pp. 96-118). Ann Arbor: The University of Michigan Press.

Cahalan, D. (1970). *Problem Drinkers.* San Francisco: Jossey-Bass Inc.

Cahalan, D., & Cisin, I. H. (1976). Drinking behavior and drinking problems in the United States. In B. Kissin & H. Begleiter (Eds.), *Social Aspects of Alcoholism: Vol. 4* (pp. 77-115). New York: Plenum Press.

Cahalan, D., & Room, R. (1974*). Problem Drinking American Men*. New Haven, CT: College & University Press.

Clark, W. (1966). Operational definitions of drinking problems and associated prevalence rates. *Quarterly Journal of Studies on Alcohol, 27*, 648-668.

Clark, W., & Midanik, L. (1982). Alcohol Use and Alcohol Problems Among U.S. Adults: Results of the 1979 Survey. *Alcohol Consumption and Related Problems* (pp. 3-52). Alcohol and Health Monograph No. 1, DHHS Publication No. ADM 82-1190. Washington, D.C.: U.S. Government Printing Office.

Collins, J. J. (1986). The relationship of problem drinking to individual offending sequences. In A. Blumstein, J. Cohen, J. A. Roth, & C. A. Vishet (Eds.), *Criminal Careers and "Career Criminals"* (pp. 89-120). Washington, D.C.: National Academy Press.

Cook, T. D., & Campbell, D. T. (1979). *Quasi-Experimentation: Design & Analysis Issues for Field Settings*. Boston: Houghton Mifflin Company.

Cox, W. M. (1987). Personality theory and research. In H. T. Blane & K. E. Leonard (Eds.), *Psychological Theories of Drinking and Alcoholism* (pp. 55-89). New York: The Guilford Press.

Dunham, R. G., & Mauss, A. L. (1982). Reluctant referrals: The effectiveness of legal coercion in outpatient treatment for problem drinkers. *Journal of Drug Issues, 12,* 5-20.

Fagan, R.W., & Fagan, N. M. (1982). The impact of legal coercion on the treatment of alcoholism. *Journal of Drug Issues, 12,* 103-114.

Gallant, D. M., Bishop, M. P., Faulkner, M. U., Simpson, L., Cooper, A., & Lathrop, D. (1968). A comparative evaluation of compulsory (group therapy and/or antabuse) and voluntary treatment of the chronic alcoholic municipal court offender. *Psychosomatics, 9,* 306-310.

Gendreau, P., & Ross, R. (1987). Revivification of rehabilitation: Evidence from the 1980's. *Justice Quarterly, 4,* 349-408.

Goldman, M. S., Brown, S. A., & Christiansen, B. A. (1987). Expectancy theory: Thinking about drinking. In H. T. Blane & K. E. Leonard (Eds.), *Psychological Theories of Drinking, and Alcoholism* (pp. 181-226). New York: The Guilford Press.

Goodstein, L. I., & Wright, K. (1989). Inmate adjustment to prison. In L. I. Goodstein & D. L. MacKenzie (Eds.), *The American Prison: Issues in Research and Policy*. New York: Plenum.

Hoffman, H., Loper, R. G., & Kammeier, M. L. (1974). Identifying future alcoholics with MMPI alcoholic scales. *Quarterly Journal of Studies on Alcohol, 35,* 490-498.

Jesness, C. F. (1983). *The Jesness Inventory*. Palo Alto, CA: Consulting Psychologists Press.

Keller, M. (1982a). On defining alcoholism: With comment on some other relevant words. In L. Gomberg, H. R.White, & J. A. Carpenter (Eds.), *Alcohol. Science and Society Revisited* (pp. 119-133). Ann Arbor: The University of Michigan Press.

Keller, M. (1982b). Alcohol, science and society: Hindsight and forecast. In L. Gomberg, H. R. White, & J. A. Carpenter (Eds.), *Alcohol, Science and Society Revisited* (pp. 1-16). Ann Arbor: The University of Michigan Press.

Knupfer, G. (1967). The epidemiology of problem drinking. *American Journal of Public Health, 57,* 973-986.

Lang, A. R., Goeckner, D. J., Adesso, V. J., & Marlatt, G. A. (1975). Effects of alcohol on aggression in male social drinkers. *Journal of Abnormal Psychology, 84,* 508-518.

Latessa, E. J., & Vito, G. F. (1988). The effects of intensive supervision on shock probationers. *Journal of Criminal Justice, 16,* 319-330.

Louisiana Department of Public Safety and Corrections. (1987). *IMPACT: Purposes, Policies and Procedures*. Unpublished manuscript. Baton Rouge, LA.

MacAndrew, C., & Edgerton, R. B. (1969). *Drunken Comportment*. Chicago: Aldine Publishing Company.

MacAndrew, C., & Geertsma, R. H. (1963). An analysis of responses of alcoholics to scale 4 of the MMPI. *Quarterly Journal of Studies on Alcohol, 24,* 23-38.

MacKenzie, D. L., & Ballow, D. (1989). Shock incarceration programs instate correctional jurisdictions: An update. *NIJ Reports* No. 214, 9-10.

MacKenzie, D. L., Gould, L. A., Riechers, L. M., & Shaw, J. W. (1989). Shock incarceration in Louisiana: Retribution or rehabilitation? *Journal of Offender Counseling, Services and Rehabilitation, 14,* 25-40.

MacKenzie, D. L., & Shaw, J. W. (1990). Inmate adjustment and change during shock incarceration: The impact of correctional boot camp programs. *Justice Quarterly, 7,* 125-150.

Manson, M. P. (1949). A psychometric analysis of psychopathic characteristics of alcoholics. *Journal of Consulting Psychology, 13,* 111-118.

McClelland, D. C., Davis, W. N., Kalin, R., & Wanner, E. (1972). *The Drinking Man: A Theory of Human Motivation.* New York: Free Press.

McCord, J. (1981). Alcoholism and criminality: Confounding and differentiating factors. *Journal of Studies on Alcohol, 42,* 739-748.

McCord, W., & McCord, J. (1962). A longitudinal study of the personality of alcoholics. In D. J. Pittman & C. R. Snyder (Eds.), *Society, Culture, and Crime Patterns* (pp. 413-430). New York: John Wiley & Sons, Inc.

Miller, B. A., & Welte, J. W. (1986). Comparisons of incarcerated offenders according to use of alcohol and/or drugs prior to offense. *Criminal Justice and Behavior, 13,* 366-392.

Paredes, A., Hood, W. R., Seymour, H., & Gollob, M. (1977). In E. M. Pattison, M. B. Sobell, & L. C. Sobell (Eds.), *Emerging Concepts of Alcohol Dependence* (pp. 96-119). New York: Springer Publishing Company.

Parent, D. (1989). *Shock Incarceration: An Overview of Existing Programs.* National Institute of Justice Report.

Parent, D. (1988). *Shock Incarceration and the Attainment of Sentencing and Corrections Goals.* Paper presented at the annual meeting of the American Society of Criminology, Chicago.

Peterson, M. A., & Braiker, H. B. (1980). *Doing Crime: A Survey of California Prison Inmates* (with S.M. Polich). Santa Monica, CA: Rand Corporation Report.

Pihl, R. O. (1983). Alcohol and aggression: A psychological perspective. In E. Gottheil, K. A. Druley, T. E. Skoloda, & H. M. Waxman (Eds.), *Alcohol. Drug Abuse and Aggression* (pp. 292-313). Springfield, IL: Thomas.

Plaut, T. F. (1967). *Alcohol Problems: A Report to the Nation by the Cooperative Commission on the Study of Alcoholism.* New York: Oxford University Press.

Polich, J. M. (1979). Alcohol problems among civilian youth and military personnel. In H. T. Blase & M. E. Chafetz (Eds.). *Youth, Alcohol, and Social Policy* (pp. 59-86). New York: Plenum Press.

Room, R. (1977). The measurement and distribution of drinking patterns and problems in general populations. In G. Edwards, M. M. Gross, M. Keller, J. Moser, & R. Room (Eds.). *Alcohol-Related Disabilities* (pp. 61-87). Geneva: World Health Organization.

Voss, H. L., & J. R. Hepburn. (1968). Patterns in criminal homicide in Chicago. *Journal of Criminal Law, Criminology, and Police Science, 59,* 499-508.

Wolfgang, M. E. (1958). *Patterns in Criminal Homicide.* Philadelphia: University of Pennsylvania Press.

Young, T. J., & Lawson, G. W. (1984). A.A. referrals for alcohol related crimes: The advantages and limitations. *International Journal of Offender Therapy and Comparative Criminology, 28,* 131-140.

Zuckerman, M., Sola, S., Masterson, J., & Angelone, J. V. (1975). MMPI patterns in drug abusers before and after treatment in therapeutic communities. *Journal of Consulting and Clinical Psychology, 43,* 286-296.

19

THE ONE-YEAR COMMUNITY SUPERVISION PERFORMANCE OF DRUG OFFENDERS AND LOUISIANA DOC-IDENTIFIED SUBSTANCE ABUSERS GRADUATING FROM SHOCK INCARCERATION

JAMES W. SHAW

DORIS LAYTON MACKENZIE

INTRODUCTION

Since approximately 1980 the correctional system in the United States has been required to expand in order to accommodate the ever-increasing influx of offenders (e.g., in the six-year period prior to 1986, expenditures in corrections increased by 116 percent; National Institute of Justice, 1990). This has forced criminal justice administrators and public officials to search for alternative punishments and methods for processing offenders through the system.

At the same time, a growing body of empirical evidence has implicated drugs as an influential factor in burgeoning crime rates. Illustrative is research that appears to demonstrate a significant relationship between drugs and offending (e.g., Wish & Johnson, 1986). In 1986 the Bureau of Justice Statistics (1988) found that 35 percent of inmates surveyed reportedly had been under the influence of drugs when they committed their current offense and 43 percent reportedly had been using illegal drugs on a near-daily basis during

Reprinted by permission of Elsevier Science, from Shaw, J. W., & MacKenzie, D. L. (1992). *Journal of Criminal Justice, 20*, 501-516. An earlier version of this article was presented at the annual meeting of the American Society of Criminology, Baltimore, 1990. This research was supported in part by Grant 87-U-CX-0020 from the National Institute of Justice, U.S. Department of Justice. Opinions expressed are those of the authors and not necessarily those of the U.S. Department of Justice.

the month prior to their arrest. Estimates of drug usage obtained through urinalysis by the Drug Use Forecasting (DUF) have indicated that over half of all male arrestees in 1989 had been using drugs prior to arrest. The percentages of men testing positive for drugs at arrest ranged from 53 percent in San Antonio to 84 percent in New York (National Institute of Justice, 1990). Research also has demonstrated a more direct relationship between hard drug use and crime. For example, different studies have found that high and low rates of involvement in criminal activity by addicts correspond to periods of heavy and lesser narcotics use (e.g., McGlothlin, Anglin, & Wilson, 1977; Ball, Shafer, & Nurco, 1983). More generally, in a review of the literature Wish and Johnson (1986) reported that as illicit drug use increases so does criminal activity.

The fact that large percentages of incarcerated offenders appear to have problems with drugs has been the impetus behind considerable attention and research directed toward programs and alternatives for drug offenders. One intermediate sanction that has received widespread support since its initial development in the early 1980s is the shock incarceration (SI) or prison "boot camp" program (Parent, 1989; MacKenzie & Shaw, 1990). Although SI was not originally developed for drug offenders, it has received considerable attention since the late 1980s as a viable option for dealing with youthful drug offenders (National Institute of Justice, 1990). In September 1989 the White House National Drug Control Strategy suggested that SI programs may be a potentially "efficient and less expensive way" for dealing with certain drug offenders (25). Currently the Bureau of Justice Assistance is funding four state SI programs (Texas, New York, Illinois, and Oklahoma) to develop model shock programs specifically designed for substance abusers. The purpose of the present study was two fold: first, it examined the effect of one SI program in Louisiana on drug-involved offenders. A second objective was to compare the performance of two types of drug involvement. Specifically, the performance of offenders with a legal drug history, that is, prior drug arrests and convictions, was compared to that of offenders identified by the Louisiana Department of Public Safety and Corrections (LDPSC) as being in need of community counseling for substance abuse.

TREATMENT OF SUBSTANCE ABUSERS

Although the U.S. criminal justice system recently has experienced a period in which the goal of rehabilitating or treating offenders in correctional settings has been in general disrepute (e.g., Lipton, Martinson, & Wilks, 1975; Sechrest, White, & Brown, 1979), a number of researchers have continued to develop and evaluate service programs. Summarizing a voluminous literature, Cullen and Gendreau (1989) contended that a number of programs, including substance abuse programs, have been found to reduce offender involvement in criminal activity.

Significantly, researchers have been able to identify specific therapeutic strategies which have been shown to "work" with substance abusers. In particular, Andrews and Kiessling (1980) stated: (1) program staff must provide anti-criminal modeling that inmates can regard as behavior worth imitating; (2) staff should develop quality interpersonal relationships with inmates, demonstrating their care and concern for the inmates, while at the same time (3) strictly enforcing program contingencies; (4) community resources must be utilized to provide services relevant to inmates' needs, and (5) particularly important for substance abusers, coping skills must be taught that may enable inmates to deal with high-risk situations that are likely to precipitate their return to or involvement in illegal activity upon their release. In general, successful programs have been based on a social learning theory of behavior (e.g., Bandura, 1979; Gendreau & Ross, 1987) on the assumption that prosocial behaviors must be learned in order to replace deviant behaviors. Equally important as the content of service is the process of service delivery, or what Gendreau and Ross (1987) have designated as therapeutic integrity the extent to which staff truly provide a treatment service rather than treatment in name only.

Another important consideration regarding the treatment of drug-involved offenders is that their lifestyle puts them at greater risk for violence and other social and health problems such as AIDS and tuberculosis (Wexler, Lipton, & Johnson, 1988). Consequently, if treatment is to be effective, it must bring about long-term changes in their lifestyle. And, as Anglin and Hser (1990) duly noted, it is not unreasonable to assume that such a process may take years. That time, however, simply is not available, especially in a program such as SI, in which reducing the length of sentences is a primary goal (MacKenzie, 1990). Nonetheless, as a minimum, Simpson (1979) found that the benefit of treatments lasting less than 90 days was very limited, regardless of the type of treatment involved. This is consistent with a number of other studies reviewed by Anglin and Hser.

SHOCK INCARCERATION IN LOUISIANA

This research was part of a larger evaluation of the LDPSC's SI program, which began in 1987 (MacKenzie, Gould, Riechers, & Shaw, 1989; MacKenzie & Shaw, 1990; MacKenzie, Shaw, & Gowdy, 1990). The program began in February of that year, and the evaluation began in October. A primary objective of this program is to increase participants' skills and abilities to live law-abiding and fulfilling lives when they are released (Louisiana Department of Public Safety and Corrections, 1987). Efforts to achieve this objective are evident in every aspect of the two-phase program. The first phase is a 90 to 180-day regimen, modeled after military basic training, in a medium-security correctional institution. This is an extremely rigorous curriculum, in which inmates are instructed in military bearing, courtesy, drills and ceremony, physical training, and personal skills. In general, program developers and staff anticipate that this training will instill discipline in offenders' lives and encourage them to take responsibility for their actions.

In addition to the time spent in formal drill, instructors also spend several hours each week working informally with the inmates. The objective here is to develop insights into how their formal training and instruction relate to real-life situations and how inmates can profit from them. Issues related to work are explored, for example, how to look for employment, how to present oneself to a potential employer,

and the importance of responsibility and self-discipline when employed. Additionally, sports are organized to emphasize goal-oriented behavior as well as the necessity and benefits of teamwork. Finally, formal treatment programs include ventilation therapy, reeducative therapy, a substance abuse group, and a prerelease group (Louisiana Department of Public Safety and Corrections, 1987).

The structure of advancement through the shock program is designed to instill a strong sense of responsibility for actions and feelings of self-confidence. Inmates enter in a beginners' squad and (based on daily evaluations regarding their performance and conduct) progress through three levels into an advanced squad. When inmates successfully complete 30 days in the advanced squad, they are eligible for parole and may graduate formally from the institutional phase of the program.

The second phase of the program is a period of intensive parole supervision. In addition to regular parole requirements, the shock parole program includes: (1) multiple unscheduled weekly contacts with parole officers, (2) random urinalysis tests at the parolee's expense, (3) a strictly enforced curfew (8:00 P.M.), and (4) completion of 100 hours of unpaid community service (Louisiana Department of Public Safety and Corrections, 1987).

As in the first phase of the program, parolees progress through three phases of intensive supervision, with each phase being less restrictive. Depending on the length of their original sentences, they may be transferred eventually to regular parole supervision. This gradational method of advancement through parole also may contribute to a sense of responsibility, self-confidence, and accomplishment.

Drug-Involved Offenders in Shock Incarceration

One important finding in the meager research that has been done to date on shock incarceration is the considerable diversity among the goals and elements of SI programs in different states (Parent, 1989; MacKenzie, 1990). Consequently, the findings from any one study, such as this one, may be generalized only with caution. Although Louisiana's program was not designed specifically for drug-involved offenders, a number of aspects of the program are consistent with the drug treatment approaches described in the literature discussed above. Specifically, the entire program focuses on learning prosocial behaviors; program components range from instruction in military bearing and courtesy to organized sports. The strict discipline and emphasis on accepting responsibility for actions form the basis of the program strategy of enforced contingencies. In addition, during the informal training sessions, inmates learn that staff are concerned about their welfare and future, while they also learn new coping skills to deal with future problems. Further, it is evident from the "staff and program attitudes" scale (see MacKenzie & Shaw, 1990) that shock inmates believe staff are people worth imitating.

A condition conducive to effective treatment is the minimum program enrollment time of 90 days. During the first year of operation, offenders who completed Louisiana's SI program spent an average of 125 days in the program (MacKenzie, Shaw, & Gowdy, 1990). Finally, the second phase maximizes the use of community resources, for example, it involves community supervision, performing community service, and attending community treatment.

Past research has found that substance abuse sets are often resistant to treatment. For example, Chaiken (1989b) has reported that drug-involved offenders are particularly resistant to change and program participation and Steer (1980) found that polydrug abusers were more likely to drop out of treatment than others. Thus, one question examined in this study was whether drug-involved offenders are more likely to drop out of the SI program. The rationale for asking this question was that MacKenzie et al. (1989) identified several characteristics of the Louisiana SI program that suggest it may have "therapeutic integrity." The extent to which the program does have therapeutic integrity could impact the types of inmates who complete the program.

A final point that should be noted is that treatment within the SI program is essentially the same drug "treatment," that is, NA and AA, that is provided for offenders in general prison populations, albeit very few offenders in traditional prisons participate.[1] Thus, the Louisiana SI program as a whole, at least for purposes of this

evaluation, must be considered the treatment. Any differences or similarities between shock offenders and others cannot be attributed to anything other than the SI program as a whole.

Methods

Samples

Three offender samples were examined in this study: shock participants, regular population parolees, and probationers. Although no claim is made that there were no preexisting differences among these groups, the two nonshock samples were selected to be similar to the shock sample. Specifically, they were legally eligible for the shock program, and they also met the basic LDPSC suitability criteria for program entry (see MacKenzie et al., 1989). Probation and parole samples were selected from geographical areas that would balance urban/rural composition, religion, and ethnicity (MacKenzie, Shaw, & Gowdy, 1990).

To be eligible for the Louisiana SI program, candidates must have no previous felony incarceration, they must be sentenced to seven years or less and be eligible for parole, and they must be recommended by each of the following: the division of probation and parole, the sentencing judge, and the adult reception and diagnostic center of the LDPSC. Candidates also must volunteer to participate, and they may drop out of the program at any time. Once in the program, inmates may be removed by staff for inadequate progress or inappropriate behavior. If inmates leave the program prior to graduation, regardless of the reason, they must serve their regular prison sentences.[2]

All male offenders who participated in the SI program between October 1987 and October 1988 volunteered to participate in the study, for a total sample of 208. Of the total shock sample, 92 (44.2 percent) inmates dropped out of the shock program before they had been in it for 90 days. A majority of the dropouts left the program within two weeks.

Shock offenders who were paroled between March 1988 and April 1989 ($N = 74$) were followed on community supervision and compared to the probation and parole samples.

Both the probation sample ($N = 108$) and the parole sample ($N = 74$) were legally eligible for the shock program but had not been recommended by one of the following: the division of probation and parole, the sentencing judge, or the LDPSC diagnostic center.

Procedure

Once offenders have been selected for the shock program, they wait in the diagnostic center, separated from other prison offenders, until a group of 15 to 25 offenders can enter the shock program together as a platoon. Approximately three days before each group of offenders in the sample was to enter the shock program, its members were asked to respond confidentially to a number of psychological tests and answer questions regarding past criminal activity and substance abuse.

In order to assess offenders' performance while on probation or parole, standardized community supervision evaluation forms were distributed to intensive supervision and regular probation and parole officers. The forms were completed by the officers each month for all offenders. These forms provided information on community substance abuse treatment and parole requirements and legal information such as arrests, convictions, and revocations.

Also, demographic and criminal justice system data were collected from Department of Corrections records for each of the three samples. Relevant demographic data included age, race, and education. Criminal justice data included information on offenders' present sentences and prior involvement with the criminal justice system.

Data Operationalization

Offenders were classified first according to whether (yes/no) they had a legal drug history (LEGAL). A legal history was defined as one or more drug arrests or convictions, including the current conviction. Of shock graduates, regular parolees, and probationers for whom such information was available, 97 (38 percent) offenders were identified as having a legal drug history.

The second classification was according to whether (yes/no) offenders had been identified

by the division of probation and parole as being in need of and required to attend community substance abuse counseling, forming the variable TREAT. It was assumed that the pre- or post-sentence investigation had revealed a drug abuse problem; hence these offenders were required to attend a community treatment program. Of the parolees and probationers for whom this information was available, 72 (23 percent) were required to attend community substance abuse counseling and were classified on this basis as drug-involved.

In a previous study MacKenzie (1991) developed three indices (knowledge, requirements, surveillance) to reflect the intensity of supervision. These indices do not measure the offender's performance (e.g., good or bad behavior) but rather suggest (1) how much KNOWLEDGE about the offender the agent has, (2) the REQUIREMENTS placed on the offender as part of community supervision, and (3) how closely the agent scrutinizes the offender's activities (SURVEILLANCE). She found that the shock sample was supervised more intensely than the other two samples, as evidenced by the three indices. Because of this known difference, the three supervision indices were included as control variables in the analyses.

Two additional control variables also were included in the analyses: (1) whether the parole officer believed the parolee was making satisfactory progress in the community drug treatment, SSAC, and (2) whether the officer believed the parolee was progressing unsatisfactorily in treatment, USSAC. The reference category for these comparisons was offenders not required to attend treatment. Four measures of failure were utilized to assess community performance: positive drug screens, drug arrests, any arrest, and jailed/revoked. Since the purpose of this study was to examine the performance of drug-involved offenders, the two categories identified above were used as predictor variables.

RESULTS

Comparisons of Drug Involvement

Several points are worth noting in regard to the demographic comparisons between the two

Table 19.1   Comparisons Between Drug Involvement on Demographics and Criminal History

Demographic or History Variable	Drug Involvement Categories			
	Legal History		Treatment Required	
	No (N = 158)	Yes (N = 97)	No (N = 181)	Yes (N = 72)
% Treatment required	17.5	47.7[c]		
Demographics				
%White	30.5	43.3[a]	31.0	44.6[a]
Age (mean)	24.3	26.7	24.7	26.5[a]
Education (mean)	10.6	10.5	10.5	10.6
Criminal history				
% With adult history	57.6	87.6[c]	63.5	84.4[b]
% With prior incarceration	6.6	12.6	5.1	17.5[b]
Age at 1st arrest (mean)	20.8	21.0	21.0	20.3
Current offense				
Entering with probation violation	27.0	19.1	21.5	26.2
Sentence length in months (mean)	37.7	44.5[a]	36.1	45.9[b]

Numbers are percentages unless identified as means.
[a] $p < 0.05$.
[b] $p < 0.01$.
[c] $p < 0.001$.

categories of drug-involved offenders (Table 19.1). First, offenders with a legal drug history were more likely to be required by probation and parole to attend treatment (47.7 percent) than those without a legal drug history (17.5 percent). Although the relationship was significant, it should be noted that about 52 percent of the offenders with a legal drug history were not required to attend treatment. Thus, these two classification schemes appear to have identified some different offenders as drug-involved, which lends some initial support for examining the two groups separately rather than together.

A more general finding, which is consistent with other research (e.g., Bureau of Justice Statistics, 1988) is that nonwhites were less likely to be drug-involved offenders. Specifically, both offenders with a legal drug history and those required to attend treatment were almost half-again as likely to be white, compared to all others. Legal drug offenders were, on the average, 2.4 years older than other offenders; likewise, offenders required to attend treatment were, on average, 1.8 years older than the others. Drug-involved offenders also were more likely to have a criminal history, and they had significantly longer sentences-an average

difference of almost seven months for those with a legal drug history and almost 10 months for those required to attend treatment.

Sample Comparisons

Presented in Table 19.2 are basic demographic comparisons among the SI graduate, regular parole, and probation samples. First, of primary interest for this article, no one sample was more likely than another to have a legal drug history. However, both the SI graduate and the regular parole samples were much more likely than probationers to be identified as drug abusers and to be required to attend treatment, with shock offenders having by far the highest probability of any sample. Possible reasons for this finding of potential discrimination are discussed in a later section.

Another noteworthy result of these comparisons was that the SI offenders appeared to have had a slightly higher risk for reoffending in comparison to the other samples. Specifically, although the difference in percentages having a criminal history was not significant, SI offenders were at the time of release onto parole slightly younger, they were slightly younger at

Table 19.2   Sample Comparisons on Drug Involvement, Demographics, and Criminal History

| Demographic or History Variable | Offender Samples | | | | |
	Shock (N = 74)	Regular parole (N = 74)	Probation (N = 108)	Total (N = 256)	Test
Drug involvement					
% LEGAL[c]	40.0	37.5	38.5	38.6	$X^2_{(2)} = 0.10^{ns}$
TREAT[d]	55.9	15.6	2.1	22.0	$X^2_{(2)} = 26.7^{***}$
Demographics					
% White	40.0	30.6	35.8	35.5	$X^2_{(2)} = 1.4^{ns}$
Age (mean)	24.0[a]	27.3[b]	24.7[a]	25.34	$F_{(2, 244)} = 7.8^{***}$
Education (mean)	10.6	10.3	10.7	10.5	$F_{(2, 239)} = 1.1^{ns}$
Criminal history					
% With adult history	76.1	65.3	67.9	69.4	$X^2_{(2)} = 2.1^{ns}$
%With prior incarceration	16.7	9.7	3.7	8.9	$X^2_{(2)} = 8.6^{**}$
Age at 1st arrest (mean)	19.4[a]	22.4[b]	20.8[a]	20.9	$F_{(2, 231)} = 6.9^{***}$
Current offense					
% Entering with probation violation	31.4	38.0	8.3	24.1	$X^2_{(2)} = 22.7^{***}$
Sentence length in months (mean)	50.0[a]	35.0[b]	30.9[b]	40.6	$F_{(2, 163)} = 18.3^{***}$

Note: Mean comparisons with letters a and b are significant at $\alpha = 0.05$.
* = $p < 0.05$.
** = $p < 0.01$.
*** = $p < 0.001$.
Numbers are percentages unless identified as means.
[c]Legal drug history (past/current drug arrests/convictions).
[d]Identified by Probation and Parole as drug abusers and required to attend community drug treatment.

the time of their first arrest, they were more likely to have had a prior jail incarceration and they were sentenced to much longer sentences for their current offense. These are characteristics that have been identified in prior studies as being associated with increased risk levels.

Performance in Shock

The first major question addressed in this study pertains to the performance of drug-involved offenders in the shock program. As noted earlier, previous research has found that substance abusers were resistant to change and program participation and also were more likely to drop out of treatment than other offenders. Thus, although it is admittedly a gross measure of performance, a reasonable question is whether drug-involved offenders are more likely than others to drop out of the difficult shock program. This question is more salient in light of the fact that a very large percentage (about

44 percent) of inmates do drop out, presumably because of the rigorous nature of the program (MacKenzie et al., 1989; MacKenzie & Shaw, 1990).

Surprisingly, there was no evidence that drug-involved offenders were more likely to drop out of the shock program. Only 38.6 percent ($N = 27$) of the offenders who dropped out of the shock program had a legal drug history, compared to 41.8 percent ($N = 46$) of those who completed the program. The number of shock dropouts who were released onto parole was too small for any meaningful comparisons to be made; thus, for the second category, offenders identified by probation and parole as drug abusers, comparisons were not possible.

For the shock offenders, information was obtained regarding self-reported drug use (commission of multiple drug offenses, daily drug use, drug use before the current crime, or poly-drug use). This information was not available for the prison parolees or probationers, and thus

Table 19.3 Percentages of Offenders Having One or More Positive Drug Screens, Drug Arrests, Any Arrest, and Revoked/Jailed by Drug Involvement Category During 12 Months of Community Supervision

| | Drug Involvement Categories | | | |
| | Legal History | | Treatment Required | |
Measure of Failure	No (N = 158)	Yes (N = 97)	No (N = 181)	Yes (N = 72)
% Positive drug screens	5.2	11.3[a]	0.6	25.0[d]
% Drug arrests	5.7	7.2	3.9	12.5[b]
% Any arrest	32.5	25.7	24.3	43.1[c]
% Jailed/revoked	24.7	16.5	16.6	31.9[c]

[a] $p < 0.10$.
[b] $p < 0.05$.
[c] $p < 0.01$.
[d] $p = 0.001$.

Table 19.4 Percentages of Offenders Having One or More Positive Drug Screens, Drug Arrests, Any Arrest, and Jailed/Revoked by Offender Samples During 12 Months of Community Supervision

| | Offender Samples | | |
Measure of Failure	Shock (N = 74)	Regular Parole (N = 74)	Probation (N = 108)
% Positive drug screens[a]	13.5	4.2	5.5
% Drug arrests	9.5	5.4	4.5
% Any arrest	37.8	24.7	27.9
% Jailed/revoked	28.4	20.3	18.0

[a] $p < 0.10$.

these behaviors were not used as an overall classification variable. However, an examination of dropout behavior for the shock program as a function of self-reported drug-involvement produced findings similar to those from the comparison of offenders with and without legal drug histories, that is, self-reported drug abuse was unrelated to performance in the program. Of shock dropouts, only 32.1 percent ($N = 25$) reported drug use, compared to 40.2 percent ($N = 45$) of shock graduates.

Performance During Community Supervision

The second major question addressed is this study was how drug-involved offenders from the SI, regular parole, and probation samples performed during one year of community supervision. Examination of the percentages for the four measures of failure reported in Table 19.3 shows different effects for the two categories of drug involvement. Specifically, it appears that both legal drug offenders and offenders required to attend treatment were much more likely than other offenders to have a positive drug screen, whereas only offenders required to attend treatment were more likely to have a drug arrest. On the other hand, while offenders required to attend treatment were more likely than others to have an arrest of any type and to be jailed or revoked, it appears that legal drug offenders were somewhat less likely to have any type of arrest or to be jailed or revoked.

Table 19.4 presents some initial evidence that offenders who graduated from the SI program were no less likely to fail than either the prison parolees or probationers. In fact, they were somewhat more likely to fail in every instance,

Table 19.5 Log-Logistic Regression Models Examining Drug Involvement Classification and Treatment Progress for Offenders Having Positive Drug Screens During 12 Months of Community Supervision

	Dependent Variable: Positive Drug Screens					
Independent Variable	*Model 1[c] Beta (X[2])*		*Model 2[c] Beta (X[2])*		*Model 3[c] Beta (X[2])*	
LEGAL	1.05	$(3.78)^a$	0.03	(0.00)	–0.00	(0.00)
TREAT			3.91	$(12.17)^c$	3.20	$(5.90)^b$
Prison	0.26	(0.09)	–0.25	(0.08)	–0.30	(0.11)
Probation	1.27	(1.81)	1.60	(2.30)	1.32	(1.47)
Requirements	–0.02	(0.00)	–0.22	(0.35)	–0.26	(0.51)
Surveillance	1.44	$(14.80)^c$	1.01	$(5.76)^b$	0.85	$(3.56)^a$
Knowledge	0.14	(0.35)	–0.06	(0.04)	–0.12	(0.14)
SSAC[d]					0.65	(0.50)
USSAC[e]					1.16	(1.67)
Slope	–5.26	(12.61)	–6.16	(11.86)	–5.70	(10.07)
Mean of dependent variable (N)	0.08	(19)	0.08	(19)	0.08	(19)

[a]$p < 0.10$.
[b]$p < 0.05$.
[c]$p < 0.01$.
[d]Report by parole /probation agent that offender was making satisfactory progress in substance abuse counseling.
[e]Report by parole/probation agent that offender was making unsatisfactory progress in substance abuse counseling.

although not significantly. These preliminary findings were supported by the more sophisticated analyses described below. Several possible explanations are discussed in the final section of this article.

Although there is some difference in opinion regarding the most appropriate method for analyzing recidivism data and the appropriate assumptions (see, e.g., Schmidt & Witte, 1988), the question of interest in this study was simply whether the parolee or probationer "failed" during a one-year period. In such a situation, in which the dependent variable is binary, a logistic regression analysis is an appropriate method for analyzing the data (Greene, 1990; Neter, Wasserman, & Kutner, 1989). The Statistical Analysis Systems (SAS Institute Inc., 1986) logistic regression procedure was utilized to analyze these data.

The following sections describe the effects of offender sample and drug involvement on each of the four measures of failure. For each outcome measure, three models were run. The first two models evaluate the differential effect of the two measures of drug involvement. The final model then controls for the type of progress offenders were making in community substance abuse treatment.

Positive Drug Screens and Drug Arrests. The first set of analyses assessed the likelihood of parolees and probationers to have one or more positive drug screens during one year of community supervision. The first two models in Table 19.5 are identical except that the variable TREAT was excluded from the first model. With the different levels of supervision held constant, it can be seen that offenders with a legal drug history were somewhat more likely than others to have a positive drug screen. However, in the second model, when TREAT, or an estimate of drug abuse, was entered into the model, the effect of having a legal history dropped to zero. Hence, in a model of causality it appears that the variable TREAT mediated the effect on positive drug screens of having a legal drug history.

In the third model, how offenders were progressing in substance abuse counseling was entered. Offenders who were doing poorly in their substance abuse counseling were somewhat more likely to have a positive drug screen ($p < 0.10$). As would be expected, the amount of surveillance was significantly related to positive drug screens.

Table 19.6 presents the results of similar analyses examining the probability of having

Table 19.6   Log-Logistic Regression Models Examining Drug Involvement Classification and Treatment Progress for Offenders Having Positive Drug Arrests During 12 Months of Community Supervision

Independent Variable	Dependent Variable: Drug Arrests					
	Model 1^{ns} Beta (X^2)		Model 2^{ns} Beta (X^2)		Model 3^{ns} Beta (X^2)	
LEGAL	0.23	(0.18)	−0.21	(0.13)	−0.08	(0.02)
TREAT			1.39	$(4.42)^a$	1.88	$(4.37)^a$
Prison	−0.64	(0.53)	−0.78	(0.78)	−1.16	(1.42)
Probation	−0.87	(0.94)	−0.89	(0.97)	−1.00	(1.08)
Requirements	0.03	(0.01)	−0.05	(0.03)	−0.21	(0.34)
Surveillance	0.02	(0.00)	−0.31	(0.49)	−0.15	(0.11)
Knowledge	0.10	(0.18)	0.05	(0.05)	−0.05	(0.03)
$SSAC^b$					−1.05	(1.23)
$USSAC^c$					0.26	(0.08)
Slope	−2.52	(4.17)	−2.29	(3.38)	−1.88	(2.05)
Mean of dependent variable (N)	0.06	(16)	0.06	(16)	0.06	(15)

Note: No full model was significant at $\alpha = 0.05$.
[a] $p < 0.05$.
[b] Report by parole/probation agent that offender was making satisfactory progress in substance abuse counseling.
[c] Report by parole/probation agent that offender was making unsatisfactory progress in substance abuse counseling.

one or more drug arrests during the one-year period. The only substantive finding in this table is that inclusion of the different variables in any of the three models did not enhance the capacity to predict who would have one or more drug arrests, beyond the overall likelihood of approximately 6 percent.

In terms of individual effects, it can be seen that only substance abusers identified by probation and parole were more likely to have an arrest. It is interesting that LEGAL drug offenders were no more or less likely to have a drug-related arrest than others. A final point, which is illustrated in Tables 19.5 and 19.6, is that the parole and probation samples were not performing significantly differently from the reference group, the SI sample. Thus, SI as a treatment appeared not to impact the drug-related outcomes of offenders.

Any Arrest. The next set of analyses, presented in Table 19.7, examined the effect of drug involvement on having one or more arrests of any type during a one-year period. From the first model it can be seen that with the level of supervision held constant, those offenders with a legal drug history were somewhat less likely to have any arrest, although the difference was not significant. In the second model, however, when the effect of required treatment was controlled, offenders with a legal drug history were significantly less likely to have any arrest. In contrast, offenders required to attend treatment were significantly more likely to have an arrest. Although TREAT represents an important factor in explaining any arrest, the type of progress offenders were making in substance abuse counseling contributed nothing to the capacity to predict or explain this outcome.

Jailed/Revoked. Results of the final set of analyses, which examined the most serious measure of failure, being jailed or revoked, were similar to the findings for any type of arrest. Specifically, offenders with a legal drug history again were less likely to fail; in contrast, those required to attend treatment were significantly more likely to fail. One difference, however, appeared in the final model, which examined the effects of progress in treatment. When type of progress was entered, the overall effect of required treatment dropped. It can be seen from Table 19.8 that the effect of offenders doing poorly in substance abuse counseling was highly significant and appeared to mediate the effect of treatment or drug abuse.

Table 19.7 Log-Logistic Regression Models Examining Drug Involvement Classification and Treatment Progress for Offenders Having Any Arrests During 12 Months of Community Supervision

	Dependent Variable: Any Arrest					
Independent Variable	*Model 1[b] Beta (X^2)*		*Model 2[c] Beta (X^2)*		*Model 3[d] Beta (X^2)*	
LEGAL	−0.41	(1.88)	−0.71	(4.51)[b]	−0.67	(3.88)[b]
TREAT			0.88	(5.11)[b]	1.14	(4.16)[b]
Prison	0.11	(0.04)	−0.14	(0.07)	−0.17	(0.11)
Probation	0.16	(0.10)	0.15	(0.08)	0.13	(0.07)
Requirements	0.41	(4.54)[b]	0.31	(2.42)	0.30	(2.19)
Surveillance	0.30	(1.75)	0.15	(0.36)	0.22	(0.74)
Knowledge	0.27	(4.00)[b]	0.25	(3.45)[a]	0.22	(2.46)
SSAC[e]					−0.61	(1.06)
USSAC[f]					0.12	(0.04)
Slope	−2.42	(10.23)	−2.14	(7.88)	−2.11	(7.27)
Mean of dependent variable (N)	0.30	(76)	0.30	(74)	0.30	(73)

[a]$p < 0.10$.
[b]$p < 0.05$.
[c]$p < 0.01$.
[d]$p < 0.001$.
[e]Report by parole/probation agent that offender was making satisfactory progress in substance abuse counseling.
[f]Report by parole/probation agent that offender was making unsatisfactory progress in substance abuse counseling.

Table 19.8 Log-Logistic Regression Models Examining Drug Involvement Classification and Treatment Progress for Offenders Being Jailed or Revoked During 12 Months of Community Supervision

	Dependent Variable: Jailed/Revoked					
Independent Variable	*Model 1[c] Beta (X^2)*		*Model 2[c] Beta (X^2)*		*Model 3[c] Beta (X^2)*	
LEGAL	−0.60	(3.03)[a]	−0.91	(5.48)[b]	−1.03	(5.94)[b]
TREAT			0.89	(4.24)[b]	0.20	(0.10)
Prison	0.07	(0.02)	−0.24	(0.17)	−0.50	(0.67)
Probation	−0.13	(0.05)	−0.09	(0.02)	−0.30	(0.26)
Requirements	0.05	(0.07)	−0.03	(0.02)	−0.11	(0.25)
Surveillance	0.52	(4.73)[b]	0.42	(2.54)	0.36	(1.54)
Knowledge	0.36	(6.05)[b]	0.38	(6.39)[b]	0.36	(5.23)[b]
SSAC[d]					0.45	(0.48)
USSAC[e]					1.85	(7.42)[c]
Slope	−2.05	(6.72)	−1.99	(5.72)	−1.62	(3.62)
Mean of dependent variable (N)	0.22	(55)	0.21	(52)	0.21	(51)

[a]$p < 0.10$.
[b]$p < 0.05$.
[c]$p < 0.01$.
[d]Report by parole/probation agent that offender was making satisfactory progress in substance abuse counseling.
[e]Report by parole/probation agent that offender was making unsatisfactory progress in substance abuse counseling.

DISCUSSION AND IMPLICATIONS

The focus of this article has been the examination of the SI program and the community performance of drug-involved offenders. As previously discussed, there is considerable diversity among SI programs in both goals and program elements. Thus, results from this study should be generalized to other SI programs with extreme caution. More definitive conclusions may be drawn when they are considered in relation to the findings of a multi-site study of SI (see MacKenzie, 1990).

The first issue addressed in this study was identification of different types of drug involvement. Over 50 percent of the offenders with legal drug histories were not identified by the division of probation and parole as being in need of treatment. Because of this difference, the distinction between these two classification schemes was deemed valid for further analyses.

Consistent with other research (MacKenzie, 1991), this study found that neither the prison parolee sample nor the probation sample were either significantly more or significantly less likely to fail than shock parolees (see Tables 19.4-19.8). Thus, there is no evidence to suggest that this SI program is particularly beneficial as a treatment modality in and of itself. In contrast, several very interesting findings were observed regarding the drug involvement of offenders in this study. These as well as several possible reasons for the lack of program impact are discussed below. In other research (e.g., Chaiken, 1989a, 1989b; Steer, 1980), substance abusers have been found to be resistant to treatment. Thus, it was expected that they might drop out of the shock program in greater numbers than nonusers. Particularly since the shock program appears to have "therapeutic integrity" (MacKenzie et al., 1989) and there is a generally high dropout rate, offenders with drug problems could reasonably be expected to be more likely to drop out. Data from this study did not support this expectation. Shock dropouts were in fact somewhat less likely than shock graduates to have a legal drug history or to report heavy drug use. It should be noted here that the classification for SI dropouts was assumed to be valid; it should be recalled that comparable information on drug use for the regular probation and parole samples was not available. Since the classification may not be completely valid, this conclusion must remain tentative.

Assuming that the classification is valid, however, the most likely explanation for this finding is that the treatment in this program, at least the drug treatment, is less intensive than that in other programs referred to in the literature. Even though treatment in this SI program appears to have "therapeutic integrity," intensive drug treatment programs specifically designed for substance abusers such as the SI programs in New York or Texas, may produce different results. These programs are currently being evaluated (see MacKenzie, 1990) and may provide more conclusive answers in this regard.

Although there is considerable diversity among SI programs, the Louisiana program appears to employ strategies that have been found in other research to benefit substance abusers (Cullen & Gendreau, 1989). For this reason it may be tempting to view SI as a potential treatment for drug or substance abusers. Indeed, there may be a tendency for policymakers to view boot camp as a treatment, that is, it may be seen as a program capable of instilling within drug offenders the discipline or whatever else they are presumed to lack that "caused" them to become involved with drugs. Such a notion simply is not supported by this research. White shock offenders, who did appear to be a somewhat more serious group of offenders, did not perform any worse than a comparable group of regular population parolees or a group of probationers, they also did not perform any better. There is thus no evidence to support the notion that boot camp in and of itself is adequate as a treatment modality.

A longer program (see Anglin & Hser, 1990) may be more successful, or one that incorporates intensive substance abuse treatment within the shock program may be more likely to produce a positive effect. For example, New York's shock program incorporates a therapeutic "Network" emphasizing community living and socialization skills and intensive drug treatment for all offenders. Furthermore, it is a mandatory six-month program.

In contrast, while the Louisiana SI program has some treatment components and drug programs such as AA and NA, it does not have drug treatment as such. One reason that SI in Louisiana does not have more sophisticated drug treatment components at this time is that it is strictly "low-budget," that is, the program budget is simply taken out of the normal prison operating budget.

Although the variables examined in this study were not particularly useful for explaining drug arrests, several interesting findings emerged in regard to drug screens, arrests of any type, and the likelihood of being jailed or revoked. First, it appeared that legal drug offenders were somewhat more likely to have a positive drug screen; however, once the effect of required treatment was controlled, they were no more likely than other in the analyses examining arrests of any type and the likelihood of being jailed or revoked. In both of these analyses legal drug offenders were in fact less likely to fail, particularly after the effect of required treatment was partialled out.

Thus, there were major differences in performance between offenders having only a legal drug history and offenders who were required to attend treatment. Indeed, it appears from these analyses that offenders arrested or convicted of a drug offense who were not also judged to need treatment actually were less likely to have any arrest or to be jailed or revoked during one year of community supervision. This finding suggests that targeting offenders for drug treatment programs based only on a legal drug history would not be the most efficient utilization of program resources.

One question this finding raises is what the requirement for treatment means in this context. As previously discussed, it was assumed that being required to obtain treatment was indicative of drug abuse. This explanation is plausible since it might be expected, consistent with the findings of this study, that drug abusers would have more difficulty in community supervision. Concomitantly, this interpretation also would suggest that legal drug offenders who were *not* currently drug abusers would be less likely than others to have any arrest or to be jailed or revoked.

A second interpretation of the effect of the requirement for treatment is that it may represent an element of arbitrariness in the administration of justice. Specifically, the requirement to obtain treatment may be imposed when a more restrictive sanction is seen as desirable or necessary. In support of this interpretation, it was found that both the shock and regular parolee samples were more likely to be required to attend treatment than probationers even though they were no more likely that probationers to have a legal drug history. Additionally,

it also may represent a harsher response to drug-involved offenders by the criminal justice system since legal drug offenders also were more likely to be required to attend treatment.

Depending on one's perspective, this also may be interpreted as some kind of a labeling effect. From this point of view, offenders identified as substance abusers may be treated as such, which "causes" their performance to be consistent with the label. Because of some of the problems with the traditional labeling perspective (see Wellford, 1975) and because subsequent research has shown that the primary influence of labeling is through informal labels, appears long preceding the application of formal labels by the criminal justice system (Wellford, 1987), we believe that the poorer performance of LDPSC-identified drug abusers probably would be explained better as a partial function of differential treatment. That is, although we attempted to control for such differences, it is possible that there are uncontrolled differences in the supervision level and program requirements for these offenders. In addition, we have too little information on these offenders to attempt to infer anything about what effect this label may have had on their performance.

A final issue raised by this research pertains to community treatment. In other research (Cullen & Gendreau, 1989; Gendreau & Ross, 1987) after-care for offenders and substance abusers has been considered crucial for success. At the same time it must be remembered that increasing after-care also means an increase in supervision, which research has shown may increase the probability of failure (e.g., Petersilia & Turner, 1990). In the present research drug abusers in treatment were more likely to have a positive drug screen and to have an arrest of any type. Although supervision level was controlled in this study, it is possible that this group's increased probability of failure may have been due in part to some aspect of supervision related to the requirement to attend treatment.

The analyses of the probability of being jailed or revoked suggest another explanation. Although the effect for drug abusers in treatment was significant, it appears that this effect may be explained by the effect of making unsatisfactory progress in treatment. In contrast, offenders making satisfactory progress in treatment were no more likely to fail than others. This suggests that it maybe beneficial for criminal justice officials to develop a mechanism for identifying a subset of offenders doing poorly in treatment and then providing additional support or whatever is needed to increase their likelihood of success.

It should be noted that these explanations assume that the offenders are in fact receiving treatment in the community. However, no information was available on the quality of this treatment, since it was not LDPSC-directed treatment but rather some community-based treatment program, such as Narcotics Anonymous. Since there was no information on the quality or exact content of this treatment, no definitive conclusions can be drawn regarding the poorer performance of these offenders.

A final alternative explanation may be that although community treatment and/or aftercare are important for reintegration into the community, successful reintegration may be possible only for offenders who have made a significant change in their behavior before returning to the community. This suggestion is supported by other research. For example, in Florida, Kim et al. (1990) found that drug offenders, or abusers, were unlikely to change their consumption behaviors simply by going to prison. Given offenders' lack of change, the result of utilizing community resources, for example, increasing supervision and requiring drug tests, can be expected to result in very high recidivism rates (see also Phillips, 1990). Thus, while increasing treatment and consequently supervision levels may be seen as an integral part of utilizing community resources, one likely outcome will be increased recidivism rates.

NOTES

1. See, for example, the Bureau of Justice Statistics (1988) finding that only 6.2 percent of the offender population was in treatment; similarly, Chaiken (1989) reported that 11 percent was in treatment.

2. Shock dropouts are reviewed for parole just as other inmates are; however, unless they are removed from the SI program for medical reasons, they are unlikely to be granted parole the first time they are reviewed. Dropping out of the program by choice or being removed for disciplinary reasons counts against them in the parole review process.

REFERENCES

Andrews, D. A., & Kiessling, J. J. (1980). Program structure and effective correctional practices: A summary of the CAVIL research. In R. R. Ross and P. Gendreau (Eds.), *Effective correctional treatment*. Toronto: Butterworths.

Anglin, M. D., & Hser, Y. (1990). Treatment of drug abuse. In M. Tonry and J. Q. Wilson (Eds.), *Drugs and crime Vol. 13*. Chicago: The University of Chicago Press.

Ball, J. C., Shafer, J. W., & Norco, D. N. (1983). The day-to-day criminality of heroin addicts in Baltimore: A study in the continuity of offense rates. *Drugs and Alcohol Dependence, 12*, 119-42.

Bandura, A. (1979). The social learning perspective: Mechanisms of aggression. In H. Toch (Ed.), *Psychology of crime and justice*. New York: Holt, Rinehart, & Winston.

Chaiken, M. R. (1989a). *In-prison programs for drug involved offenders*. Washington, D.C.: National Institute of Justice, Issues and Practices.

Chaiken, M. R. (1989b). *Prison programs for drug-involved offenders*. Washington, D.C.: National Institute of Justice, Research in Action.

Cullen, F. T., & Gendreau, P. (1989). The effectiveness of correctional rehabilitation: Reconsidering the "nothing works" debate. In L. Goodstein and D. L. MacKenzie (Eds.), *The American prison: Issues in research and policy*. New York: Plenum Press.

Gendreau, P., & Ross, R. (1987). Revivification of rehabilitation: Evidence from the 1980's. *Justice Quarterly, 4*, 349-408.

Greene, W. H. (1990). *Econometric analysis*. New York: MacMillan Publishing Company.

Kim, L., Benson, B. L., Rasmussen, D. W., & Zuehlke, T. W. (1990). *An economic analysis of recidivism among drug offenders*. Unpublished paper. Florida State University. Tallahassee, FL.

Lipton, D., Martinson, R., & Wilks, J. (1975). *The effectiveness of correctional treatment: A survey of treatment evaluation studies*. New York: Praeger.

Louisiana Department of Public Safety and Corrections. (1987). *IMPACT: Purposes, policies and procedures*. Unpublished manuscript. Baton Rouge, LA: Louisiana state government.

MacKenzie, D. L. (1990). Boot camp prisons: Components, evaluations, and empirical issues. *Federal Probation, 54*(3), 44-52.

MacKenzie, D. L. (1991). The parole performance of offenders released from shock incarceration (Boot Camp Prisons): A survival time analysis. *The Journal of Quantitative Criminology 7*(3), 225-237.

MacKenzie, D. L., Gould, L. A., Riechers, L. M., & Shaw, J. W. (1989). Shock incarceration in Louisiana: Retribution or rehabilitation? *JOCS, 14*, 25-40.

MacKenzie, D. L., & Shaw, J. W. (1990). Inmate adjustment and change during shock incarceration: The impact of correctional bout camp programs. *Justice Quarterly, 7*, 125-50.

MacKenzie, D. L., & Gowdy, V. (1990). *An evaluation of shock incarceration in Louisiana.* Unpublished manuscript. Final report to the National Institute of Justice. Washington, D.C.: National Institute of Justice.

McGlothlin, W. H., Anglin, M., & Wilson, B. D. (1977). *An evaluation of the California Civil Addict Program.* Rockville, MD: National Institute on Drug Abuse.

Neter, J., Wasserman, W., & Kutner, M. H. (1989). *Applied linear regression models. 2nd ed.* Homewood, IL: Irwin, Inc.

Parent, D. (1989). *Shock incarceration: An overview of existing programs.* National Institute of Justice report. Washington, D.C.: National Institute of Justice.

Petersilia, J., & Turner, S. (1990). Comparing intensive and regular supervision for high-risk probationers: Early results from an experiment in California. *Crime and Delinquency, 36*, 87-111.

Phillips, L. (1990). *The political economy of drug enforcement.* Paper presented at the Annual Western Economic Association Meeting, San Diego.

Rasmussen, D. W., & Benson, B. L. (1990). *Drug offenders in Florida.* Unpublished summary of an economic analysis of recidivism among drug offenders in Florida. Policy Sciences Program. Florida State University. Tallahassee, FL.

SAS Institute Inc. (1986). *SUGI supplemental library user's guide, version 5 edition.* Cary, NC: SAS Institute Inc.

Schmidt, P., & Witte, A. (1988). *Predicting recidivism using survival models.* New York: Springer-Verlag.

Sechrest, L., White, S. O., & Brown, E. D. (1979). *The rehabilitation of criminal offenders: Problems and prospects.* Washington, D.C.: National Academy of Sciences.

Simpson, D. D. (1979). The relation of time spent in drug abuse treatment to posttreatment outcome. *American Journal of Psychiatry, 136,* 1449-53.

Steer, R. A. (1980). Psychosocial correlates of retention in methadone maintenance treatment. *International Journal of Addictions, 15,* 1003-09.

U.S. Department of Justice. Bureau of Justice Statistics. (1988). *Drug use and crime.* Washington, D.C.: U.S. Department of Justice.

U.S. Department of Justice, National Institute of Justice. (1990). *Searching for answers: Research and evaluation on drugs and crime.* A report to the President, the Attorney General, and the Congress. Washington, D.C.: National Institute of Justice.

U.S. Department of Justice, National Institute of Justice Drug Use Forecasting. (1990). *Drugs and crime 1989.* Washington, D.C.: National Institute of Justice. Research in Action.

Wellford, C. (1987). Delinquency prevention and labeling. In J. Q. Wilson & G. C. Loury (Eds.), *From children to citizens, vol. 3: Families, schools, and delinquency prevention* (pp. 257-67). New York: Springer-Verlag.

Wellford, C. (1975). Labeling theory and criminology: An assessment. *Social Problems, 22,* 332-45.

Wexler, H. K., Lipton, D. S., & Johnson, B. D. (1988). *A criminal justice strategy for treating cocaine-heroin abusing offenders in custody.* Washington, D.C.: National Institute of Justice, Issues and Practices.

Wish, E. D., & Johnson, B. D. (1986). The impact of substance abuse on criminal careers. In A. Blumstein, J. Cohen, J. A. Roth, & C. A. Visher (Eds.), *Criminal careers and "career criminals."* Washington, D.C.: National Academy Press.

Part VIII

SYSTEM-LEVEL IMPACTS

20

The Impact of Shock Incarceration Programs on Prison Crowding

Doris Layton MacKenzie

Alex Piquero

From 1980 to 1990, state and federal prison populations rose 134% to a record 771,243 inmates. By 1990, prisons were operating between 18% and 29% in excess of capacity (Greenfeld 1992). Faced with this crisis in prison crowding, states searched for ways to alleviate the pressure on prisons. Intermediate sanctions were viewed by many as a viable method of addressing the problem. Although originally designed and supported as a method of helping offenders become law-abiding citizens, many intermediate sanctions are currently being promoted and developed with the express purpose of reducing prison crowding (Palumbo, Clifford, and Snyder-Joy 1992). As such, they are expected to provide alternatives to incarceration and lead to a reduction in the number of offenders in prison.

However, in many situations, the goal of reducing prison crowding goes unrealized because intermediate sanctions that were designed as alternatives to incarceration have actually been used for offenders who would otherwise have received a lesser, not a more punitive sentence (Austin and Krisberg 1981; Morris and Tonry 1990). In fact, in a study of community correctional programs, Hylton (1980) found that instead of reducing prison populations, as they were designed to do, the programs actually tripled the proportion of persons under state control. In other words, these programs not only strengthened the net, they also created new nets in the form of community corrections to control more offenders.

In another study, Palumbo, Clifford, and Snyder-Joy (1992) examined the effect of a home arrest program in Arizona. Not only was the program not cost-effective, but there were actually increased rates of technical violations for those in the house arrest program compared to those

Reprinted with permission of *Crime and Delinquency,* from MacKenzie, D. L. & Piquero, A. (1994). *Crime & Delinquency, 40*(2), 222–249. This article was originally presented as a paper at the Annual Meeting of ASC, October 1993, Phoenix, Arizona. This investigation was supported in part by grant #90-DD-CX-0061 from the National Institute of Justice, Office of Justice Programs, U.S. Department of Justice to the University of Maryland. Points of view in this article are those of the authors and do not necessarily represent the official position of the U.S. Department of Justice.

supervised on regular parole. Furthermore, the house arrest program resulted in placing inmates in house arrest who would have otherwise been on regular probation, thereby widening the net of control. Similar net widening has also been found in juvenile arbitration procedures (Ezell 1989), in the Japanese juvenile justice system (Yokoyama 1986, 1989), and in a study of electronic monitoring in British Columbia, Canada (Mainprize 1992).

Not everyone considers net widening to be a disadvantage of intermediate sanctions; some argue for deterrence, just deserts, and more punishment. In their opinion, the only way we can keep our streets safe is by increasing social control, and this means increasing the number of prison beds. Conservative legislators often support intermediate sanctions in the belief that they will both reduce costs and, at the same time, provide greater control over offenders who might be given probation. From this perspective, any reduction in prison crowding will occur because offenders will be deterred from committing new criminal activities and, therefore, the crime rate will be reduced.

In contrast, those who advocate increased diversion, decriminalization, due process, and decarceration to shrink the net argue that the United States has the highest national incarceration rate and, furthermore, that we can no longer afford to build prisons and keep prisoners locked up for lengthy periods of time. In their opinion, most offenders will eventually be returned to the street and the prison is not the best way to change offenders so that they will not return to criminal activities when they are released. Intermediate sanctions provide a reasonable alternative to incarceration for those who would otherwise be imprisoned.

In their recent book, Morris and Tonry (1990) argued that a reasonable system of sanctions may increase control over some offenders and decrease it over others. Judges are frequently forced to choose between nominal supervision in the community versus a traditional prison sentence. In many cases, offenders are given the benefit of the doubt and receive probation. However, if an intermediate punishment is entered into the equation, judges tend to sentence to the intermediate punishment those offenders formerly treated more leniently rather than those who would otherwise receive a

prison sentence. From a judge's perspective, there is often a need for more restrictive punishments than probation for more serious probationers. Thus, although some individuals involved in developing intermediate sanctions may have expected these programs to reduce prison crowding, reducing crowding may not be the highest priority for all decision makers. Rather, the goals of different decision makers may actually conflict.

Although many studies have found that intermediate sanctions may increase the net of control, there is evidence that some of them have the desired effect of reducing prison populations. For example, in a study of community corrections in Colorado counties, Covey and Menard (1984) found that offenders in the diversion program more closely resembled incarcerated offenders than they did those placed on probation. They concluded that, although this was not true of all counties, in many, the diversion program did appear to reduce prison commitment rates.

After a similar study examining the impact of community corrections programs in four Kansas counties, Jones (1990) concluded that without them, the prison system in Kansas would be facing far worse problems than its present crowding crisis. However, he did find differences among the four counties studied. Using a time series analysis of monthly prison admissions of program-eligible offenders in each county, he found that in two of them, the community corrections programs had indeed drawn participants from the prison-bound population; in the other two counties they had not. He emphasized that net widening is not an inevitable by-product of community-based alternative programs and under some circumstances, programs designed as alternatives to incarceration can achieve their goals.

Boot Camp Prisons

One intermediate sanction, which has become increasingly popular in the past decade, is boot camp prisons. The number and size of these prisons for adult felons have been rapidly escalating. Since boot camps first began in Georgia and Oklahoma in 1983, 29 states and the

Federal Bureau of Prisons have opened 46 boot camps. The original camps were small in size, but by 1993 there were over 7,500 prison beds in adult correctional systems devoted to boot camp programs.

There are many reasons for the rapid growth of boot camp prisons. Politicians and policy-makers, fearful of a "Willie Horton problem," can appear to be tough on crime by supporting boot camps (MacKenzie and Parent 1991). They, as well as the public, seem to think that boot camps address the lack of discipline and self-control, which they believe are characteristic of young, nonviolent offenders. Correction officials, in contrast, emphasize the importance of these programs in rehabilitating offenders, reducing recidivism, and providing drug education (MacKenzie and Souryal 1991).

Almost everyone expects the boot camps to reduce prison crowding. They differ, however, in how they expect this reduction to occur. Some believe that crowding will be reduced by lowering recidivism rates because fewer offenders will be arrested, convicted, and returned to prison. Thus fewer prisoners will enter prison and the need for prison beds will be reduced.

However, there are different opinions about the mechanisms that initiate these changes in individual offenders. Some argue that recidivism will be reduced because offenders will be deterred from committing new crimes; other argue that the programs will rehabilitate offenders so they will not return to criminal activities once they have been released. In both of these situations, offenders are expected to change as a result of the programs and, therefore, they are expected to have lower rates of recidivism.

Another way boot camp prisons may affect prison crowding is by reducing the time offenders spend in prison. An offender who receives a 5-year sentence to a traditional prison might be eligible for parole after serving one third of the sentence and, with additional time off for good behavior, might be paroled from prison after serving 2 years. In contrast, an offender who completes a boot camp program may be eligible for parole after serving a much shorter time. For instance, an offender with the same 5-year sentence might complete a 3-month boot camp program and be eligible for release after serving only 3 months. In the former case, a prison bed would be needed for 24 months, whereas the boot camp bed would be needed for only 3 months—a difference of 21 months. The boot camp may, in such cases, represent a method for some offenders to earn their way out of prison earlier than they would otherwise be released.

To have an impact on prison crowding, there must be a sufficient number of eligible inmates who successfully complete the program in a shorter time than they would have served in prison. Many shock programs have rigid eligibility criteria that will severely restrict the type of offender who will be considered acceptable for the program. Furthermore, if the program is lengthy or if there is a long wait between entering prison and entry to the program, the net reduction in days served may be minimal. There is evidence from previous studies that offenders with shorter sentences will not volunteer or will drop out of a shock program (MacKenzie, Shaw, and Gowdy 1993). They seem to use a rational decision-making model by weighing the choice of doing "tough time" in the boot camp versus easier but longer time in a traditional prison.

Along with a reduction in recidivism rates and shortening of time in prison, there are other factors that will influence the potential of boot camps to have an impact on prison crowding. One factor that is vitally important is whether offenders are drawn from those who under other circumstances would be incarcerated. If they are not, and the incarceration net is widened by selecting offenders who would otherwise have been on probation or in some other program (e.g., diversion), then the boot camp would increase the number of offenders in prison.

The present study examined five boot camp prisons and explored their potential for reducing prison crowding in the state correctional system. Five states, Florida, Georgia, Louisiana, New York, and South Carolina, participated in an evaluation (MacKenzie 1990). The study had three major components: (a) a process evaluation, (b) a study of offender changes, and (c) an examination of the potential impact of the programs on prison crowding, the focus of this article. The process evaluation included a description of the development and implementation of the boot camp prisons in each site. Interviews were conducted with participants, staff, and administrators, and written

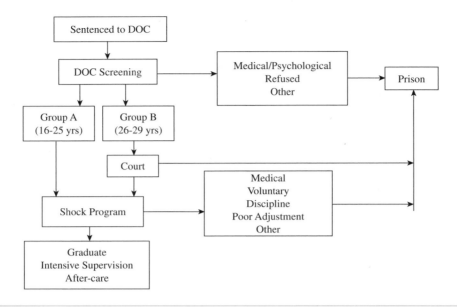

Figure 20.1   Flowchart Showing Entry and Exit Decision Making for the New York Boot Camp
Prison, 1990

reports, policies and procedures, and program documentation were examined. The goals of each program were identified in this process. Consistent with the development of other intermediate sanctions (Morris and Tonry 1990), the two major goals of all five boot camp prisons were (a) changing offenders, and (b) reducing prison crowding (MacKenzie and Souryal 1993). The latter, however, was not a primary goal of many of the individuals interviewed. Many of those working directly with inmates in the shock program emphasized its importance in having an impact on the lives of individual offenders and were not as concerned about reducing prison crowding. However, in almost all of the states, prison crowding had provided a major impetus for developing the boot camp prison.

THE FIVE BOOT CAMP PROGRAMS

Offenders incarcerated in each of the five boot camp prisons were separated from general population inmates in a military-like atmosphere emphasizing strict rules and discipline and were required to participate in drill and physical training. Beyond this common core, there were many differences among programs.[1] Some

emphasized treatment, such as education, counseling, or vocational training during the time offenders are incarcerated. For example, inmates in Louisiana and New York boot camp prisons spent 3.5 hours and more than 5 hours per day, respectively, in treatment and education programs. In contrast, inmates in Georgia spent a very short period of time per day in rehabilitative type activities.

Different Program Models

Of particular importance to this study were the differences among sites in entry and exit decision making. To examine differences among programs, we constructed flow charts for each site to describe the process of selection, rejection, dismissal, and completion for each shock program.

A comparison of two flow charts, New York and Georgia, highlights some of the major differences in decision-making processes. In New York, the offenders were sentenced to a term of imprisonment under the supervision of the department of corrections. The department screened the offenders; those who were evaluated as eligible and suitable for the shock incarceration program were given the opportunity to volunteer (Figure 20.1). If they successfully

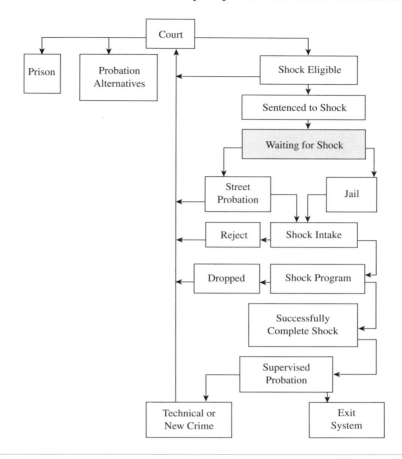

Figure 20.2   Flowchart Showing Entry and Exit Decision Making for the Georgia Boot Camp Prison, 1989

completed the program, they served 180 days in prison. If they left for any reason, they were required to return to prison and to serve until they were paroled. The only change in this procedure is that there are now some additional restrictions for offenders who are between 26 and 29 years of age.[2]

As can be seen in the flow chart in Figure 20.2, the decision-making process was very different in Georgia. The chief probation officer determined whether the offender was eligible for the program. A contact was made with the shock staff for verbal confirmation of acceptance to the program and if the answer was "yes," the probation chief certified to the court that the offender had been accepted into the program. The court could then sentence the offender to the program as a condition of probation. The court retained responsibility over the offender if

there were any changes in status (whether they were rejected by the department of corrections (DOC), dismissed from the program, or their probation was revoked).

When the flow charts from the five shock programs were compared, large differences among programs in the process of entry and exit decision making became evident. There were two basic variants in the selection procedure. In the first, the sentencing judge placed the offender in the program and maintained decision-making authority over him or her until release from the program. At the other extreme, the DOC had complete control over offenders who entered the program. Those who were dismissed before completing the program in this model were sent to prison.

Differences in entry decision-making can easily affect the impact of the shock program on the larger correctional system. As Morris and Tonry (1990) argued: when the court has placement control, the shock program may be more likely to be used as an alternative to probation. If, on the other hand, the DOC has control over who enters the program, there is a higher probability that offenders entering the program would have otherwise spent time in prison.

When we examined the process evaluations of the five sites, we identified at least three variations in placement decision making:

- Judge places in shock and maintains full control over offenders: Georgia, South Carolina.
- DOC selects for shock, judge approves: New York (ages 26–29), Florida.
- DOC has full control over who enters and judge has little or no control: New York (ages 16–25), Louisiana.

Judges had full control over sentencing offenders to shock in both Georgia and South Carolina. In South Carolina, as in Georgia, the judge sentenced offenders to the shock program and offenders remained under the jurisdiction of the court for 90 days. After at least 75 but no more than 90 days, the sentencing judge had the option to either place a shock inmate on probation or convert the offender to the general prison population. Completion of the shock program, therefore, did not ensure release to probation. Offenders who were not placed on probation prior to the 91st day were automatically converted to general population status. Preliminary data from the program indicated that approximately 6% of the offenders who completed the program were converted to the general prison population.

A major issue in South Carolina and Georgia is whether judges used the program as an alternative to probation. If this is the case, they may have sentenced offenders to the program who would have otherwise simply received probation. This is not an unreasonable use of the program because in many cases a judge may believe an offender needs a more restrictive sanction than probation, but something less than a long term of incarceration. At the same time, this practice clashes with the stated goal of reducing crowding.

In the remaining types of entry, the DOC selected offenders and the judge had varying levels of influence over placement. In these states, the possibility of net widening should be less of a concern. In Florida, the DOC selected offenders for the shock program, although the judge must have approved the selection. Similarly, offenders aged 26–29 in New York, who the DOC selected as candidates for the program, must also have had the judge's approval before actually entering. Decisions regarding entry to shock incarceration were the responsibility of the DOC in Louisiana and New York (ages 16–25), although the judge must have recommended it for offenders in Louisiana. In both states, offenders who were not admitted to shock were sent to a traditional prison.

States that place prison-bound offenders in shock incarceration may face other problems in seeking to reduce prison crowding. Most sites have fairly restrictive criteria for inmates who are permitted to enter the program. In such situations, one danger may be that the number of offenders considered appropriate may be less than the number of beds. Rather than increasing the number of probation-type offenders entering the program, the problem here would be one of too few offenders entering. In other words, the number of participants might be insufficient to fill the allocated beds or to have an impact on crowding.

Characteristics of Offender Participants: Eligibility and Suitability Criteria

To have an impact on crowding, a sufficient number of offenders must enter the shock program. Prior to entry, offenders are evaluated for "appropriateness" for shock. All states have legal mandates that restrict participation to certain classes of offenders. Most states also have additional criteria—which we call suitability criteria—that are consistently used to make decisions regarding qualifications for entry into the shock program. The reasons for the development of suitability criteria vary. For example, in Louisiana, offenders over the age of 39 were considered unsuitable, due to the medical evaluation teams' recommendation that if individuals 40 or older were going to participate in the rigorous physical activity required by the program, additional medical tests would be necessary. Considering the small number of legally eligible offenders over 40, the DOC decided that the cost of such tests would be prohibitive.

Another suitability criterion adopted in Louisiana was a restriction on the entry of offenders with a history of sex offenses. The sex offender prohibition arose early during the operation of the shock program when an offender who had done well in it was denied parole by the board because he had been convicted of a sex offense. The DOC felt strongly that all offenders who successfully completed the program should be released, but the parole board refused to release certain offenders. To avert future problems such as this one, the department in conjunction with the parole board developed a list of "types" of offenders who might be accepted for the program, but not necessarily be paroled; those judged unsuitable were not admitted.

Although the suitability criteria differed among states, all states had some criteria that were consistently used to limit entry to the program. Most programs were designed for youthful offenders. Indeed, Georgia and New York had legislative mandates that limited the age of participants. South Carolina restricted the age further to a maximum of age 24. Florida had no legislative maximum; however, the department set a maximum age of 25 as one of its suitability criteria. Like Florida, Louisiana had no legislative maximum; however, the DOC set a maximum age of 39 as one of its suitability criteria.

In addition to the age requirement, three states had a legislative mandate that offenders not have any mental or physical impairment that would prevent them from participating in a rigorous shock program (e.g., Georgia, Florida, South Carolina). In Louisiana and New York, the DOC has added this requirement to its list of suitability criteria. Also related to the health of offenders, Georgia and South Carolina specify that offenders must be free of any contagious or communicable diseases.

The second basic characteristic of offenders entering the shock programs is that, as compared to prison-bound offenders, in general they tended to be lower-risk offenders. This is ensured by various legislative restrictions on sentence length, types of sentence, types of offenses, and criminal histories of offenders. When considering criminal history, Florida and

Georgia require that the offender be convicted of a first felony and Florida specifies no previous incarceration; others, such as Louisiana, permit an offender convicted of a second felony to enter if there has been no previous incarceration in a state prison.

Georgia and South Carolina do not statutorily restrict offenders who previously have been incarcerated, but in these states the DOC imposes the condition that the offender have no previous incarcerations as a suitability criterion. In some states, the DOC is even more restrictive regarding criminal history. For example, Louisiana and New York require that offenders have no history of any serious sex offense, and Louisiana and New York will not permit an offender who has a history of assaultive or violent behavior to enter the program. New York requires that offenders have not been convicted of any abscond or escape offense, and the Florida DOC requires that offenders be classified as either medium or minimum security.

In addition to restrictions on criminal history, some states have restrictions on current offense. Most states make the assumption that eligible offenders will be convicted of nonviolent offenses, but New York and South Carolina make this explicit. In contrast, Florida only stipulates that offenders not be convicted of a capital or life felony crime.

A final restriction on offender eligibility is on type and length of sentence. Although there is some variation in the legislative technicalities of these requirements, this is probably due more to variation in sentencing across states rather than to types of offenders eligible. New York requires only that offenders be sentenced to an indeterminate term of imprisonment; however, offenders must be parole eligible within 3 years. More restrictive in its guidelines, South Carolina requires that offenders be convicted of an offense that carries at least a 5-year prison sentence. In Louisiana, offenders must be sentenced to 7 years or less and they must be parole eligible. Similarly, offenders must be sentenced to 6 years or less in Florida and also be parole eligible. As noted above, Florida permits some offenders convicted of violent offenses to enter the program; however, the restriction on sentence length and security classification would limit the seriousness of eligible offenders. At the

Table 20.1 Program Characteristics and Capacity for Five State Shock Programs Showing Graduation and Dismissal Rates for a 1-Year Period

	Placement Authority				
	Florida: DOC	Georgia: Judge	Louisiana: DOC	New York: DOC	South Carolina: Judge
Voluntary					
Entrance	no	yes	yes	yes	no
Exit	no	no	yes	yes	no
Capacity (beds)	100	250	120	500/1,500	120
Total exits	329.5[a]	932	298	953 (1988)/	470
(date)		(1989)	(1987)	2,993 (1990)	(1989)
Graduated					
n	159.7	849[b]	169	743	395
Percentage	48.5	91.1	56.7	68.7/ 1,907 63.7	84.0
Time in days	100.5	89	125.7	180	84.2
Dismissed, percentage	51.5	9.0	43.3	31.1/36.3	16.0
Reasons for dismissal, percentage					
Discipline	39.9	3.3	7.4	16.8/7.3	8.3
Medical	8.6	5.7	3.7	1.3/1.3	7.6
Voluntary	—	—	27.5	7.9/12.3	—
Other	3.1	—	4.7	5.1/15.3	—

Note: DOC = department of corrections. Values are given for 2 years for New York, 1988 and 1990, when the capacity had greatly increased. If the values did not differ, only one value is given.
[a]This value was calculated as the average from 10/87 to 1/91.
[b]These estimates were based on percentages from actual data for 1984 to 1989.

other extreme, offenders in Georgia must be sentenced to 1 to 5 years of probation, with shock incarceration being a special condition of their probated sentence.

If the program is considered to be an early release from prison (important if the program is expected to reduce crowding), the legal eligibility criteria were most likely developed to limit the severity of the current offense and the past criminal history of offenders who would be eligible for the program and hence early release. The dilemma is that a sufficient pool of offenders who are judged eligible and suitable must be available to enter the program.

Thus, in the majority of states, eligible offenders generally must be young, physically and mentally healthy, and serving short sentences. They cannot have had a very serious past history of crime; in all sites a previous incarceration disqualified an offender from entry. Such

severe restrictions on entrants may limit the pool of eligible offenders, and this may be a particular problem in states that select participants from prison-bound offenders. The problem is that there may be too few offenders evaluated as appropriate (eligible and suitable) for entry and, therefore, the number of participants may be insufficient to have an impact on crowding.

Program Characteristics, Capacities, and Completion Rates

As shown in Table 20.1, these five state programs differ in program capacity, program length, percentage of entrants dismissed prior to graduation, voluntary entry and exit, and the placement authority.[3] In Georgia and South Carolina, the judge has the responsibility for entry decisions, and offenders who are evaluated as unsuitable or who drop out of the program are returned to the court for resentencing. In contrast, in Florida, Louisiana, and New York, offenders are first sentenced to prison and are then selected for program participation by the DOC. If inmates in these states are dismissed from the program or if they voluntarily drop out, they serve the remainder of their sentence in prison. Programs also differ in whether offenders volunteer to participate or whether they can drop out voluntarily. In two states (Florida and South Carolina) offenders do not volunteer to enter and they cannot voluntarily leave. On the other hand, in Louisiana and New York, offenders volunteer to enter and can voluntarily leave. The Georgia program permits voluntary entrance but offenders cannot leave voluntarily.

New York had by far the largest capacity (500), and by 1991 this capacity had been increased to 1,500. Georgia's capacity was much smaller (250); however, approximately the same number of offenders completed the Georgia program in a 1-year period, 932 versus 953 in New York. This shows the influence of both length of time offenders spend in the program and the number of participants who do not complete. Offenders in the Georgia program spend an average of only 89 days in the program and only 9% were dismissed prior to completing the program. In New York these numbers are very different. New York has the largest number of offenders in shock, but the program has the longest duration (180 days). In addition, a substantial number of the entrants do not complete the program (31%).

In the two states (Georgia and South Carolina) where the judge has the most authority over placement in the programs, the largest number of entrants complete shock (8.9% and 16% dismissal rates, respectively). In the other three states, the DOC has control and the non-completion rates are much higher (ranging from 31.3% to 51.5%).

A relatively high percentage of noncompleters in the two states where judges have authority over offenders are dismissed from shock for medical reasons. In Florida, New York, and Louisiana, the sites where the DOC has authority over decisions after offenders are dismissed from shock, offenders leave either voluntarily or for disciplinary reasons. Offenders in the

Florida program cannot leave voluntarily, so the majority of those who leave do so for disciplinary reasons. In New York and Louisiana, offenders can voluntarily exit, but surprisingly, the rates of disciplinary dismissals are high in New York, whereas voluntary exit is high in Louisiana.

Thus the biggest differences in dismissal rates are between the sites where the judge has authority over the offender after dismissal and the sites where the DOC has authority. The DOC-authority sites have much higher dismissal rates. Furthermore, in the DOC-authority sites, offenders leave for reasons that are more under their own control (poor behavior or volunteering out) whereas judge-authority dismissals are more often for medical reasons.

METHODOLOGY

The model used to estimate bed space needs was based on one developed by MacKenzie and Parent (1991) to estimate the impact of the Louisiana boot camp program on the prison beds needed to accommodate the inmates entering prison. The model estimates the total person-months of confinement saved by determining the difference between the average prison term and the average shock incarceration duration, and multiplying that difference times the program capacity (or the actual number admitted in a year). The initial months saved are then discounted by (a) the probability that the persons would not have been confined (they would have been on probation) and (b) the time served by those who drop out, "wash out," or who are revoked. The model calculates the impact of the program on prison beds and on person-months of confinement.

The variables used in these analyses were program capacity, annual shock capacity, probabilities of washing out and dropping out, probability of imprisonment for washouts, probability of imprisonment for voluntary dropouts, revocation rates for shock graduates, probability of revocation for probationers, average term of imprisonment for shock-eligible offenders, average shock duration, duration of imprisonment for shock dropouts, duration of imprisonment for shock washouts, duration of

Table 20.2 Summary of Variables Used in Bed Space Model for Five State Boot Camp Prisons

	Florida	Georgia	Louisiana	New York[a]	South Carolina
Capacity					
Beds available	100	250	120	500/1,500	120
Total annual capacity (beds/year)	363.6	1,000	360	1,000/3,000	480
Actual yearly completions	329.5	932	298	953/2,993	470
Probability					
Offender would be imprisoned					
Offender would be on probation					
Imprisonment for dropout	0	0	1	1	0
Imprisonment for washout	1	.37	1	1	1
Voluntary dropout	0	0	.28	.08/.12	0
Nonvoluntary removal (washout)	.52	.09	.16	.23/.24	.16
Revocation shock graduate	.16	.27	.17	.16/.09	.24
Revocation probationer	.29	.16	.10	.15/.14	.31
Durations of imprisonment					
Shock duration (months)	3.3	3.0	4.0	6.0	3.0
Shock dropout (months)	0	0	13.7	18.1	0
Shock washout (months)	9.5	2.6	14.5	20.4	12.0
Shock-eligible prisoners (months)	8.5	9.6	20.5	17.9	12.4
Shock graduates revoked (months)	13.4	13.4	10.7	20.6	13.2
Shock-eligible probationer (months)	14.5	22.6	12.0	18.6	10.4

[a]Values for 2 years are given for New York, 1988 followed by 1990, when the capacity has been increased.

imprisonment for shock graduates who were revoked, duration of imprisonment for shock-eligible offenders who were revoked, on probation (see appendix for definitions of data). Data were obtained from official records and from the results of studies examining each program.[4] Shown in Table 20.2 are the data for each boot camp program.

ESTIMATING BED SPACE NEEDS

No data were available on the probability that these offenders would be in prison versus probation.[5] Therefore, we employed different models to examine the impact of the shock program on prison crowding if 0%, 25%, 50%, 75%, or 100% of the shock entrants were taken from prison-bound entrants (Table 20.3). The other variables were the best available estimates of probabilities and durations. By varying the estimates, we could examine the potential these programs had for influencing the need for prison beds.

The bed space model examined the net change in prison beds needed per year as a result of a shock incarceration program.[6] We calculated the person-months of confinement saved by the program and then reduced this by the person-months lost because of the dropouts, the washouts, and the revocations. The resulting estimate of the person-months of confinement was then changed to the number of beds saved (or lost) in a 1-year period as a result of the boot camp program.

For example, Florida's boot camp program had an annual capacity of 363.63. If 50% of these offenders would have been prison bound (and, conversely, the remaining 50% would have been probationers), the program would have saved approximately 336 person-months of confinement. However, the program lost 1,396 person-months of confinement due to washouts and revocations (there were no dropouts in Florida) for a net loss in person-months (336 minus 1,396 or −1,067 person-months). This translates to the need for an additional 88 prison beds per year (−1,067 person-months/12 months) because of the boot camp prison.

RESULTS

It was clearly evident from the process evaluation of these boot camp prisons that a major goal of all of them was to reduce prison crowding. The bed space analysis examined the effect on need for prison beds depending on whether the entrants to the boot camp prisons were chosen from those who would otherwise be prison-bound offenders or probation bounded. Five different variants of the model were examined to inspect how these changed the beds needed. The first model (standard model) examined the changes in bed space when the total annual capacity was used for annual capacity in the model. The second model changed the value for the annual capacity to the number of actual completions in the year (see Table 20.2). Model 3 examined the effect on bed space by reducing the recidivism rate by 50%. The fourth model reduced the washout rate by 50%, and the fifth model included a term in the calculations to account for additional beds saved due to the parolee return to prison rates.

As expected, as the percentage of prison-bound offenders in the boot camp declined (and conversely probationers increased), the need for prison beds increased. The larger the percentage of the offenders who would otherwise have been

in prison, the larger the impact on beds needed, or conversely saved (Table 20.3). Figure 20.3 shows the change in estimated bed space savings for four states using the standard model. As the probability that these offenders would have been imprisoned increased to 100%, instead of needing additional beds (indicated by "−" in Table 20.3) there were beds saved in all systems except in Florida. Even when all of the offenders would have been prison bound, the Florida system would need an additional 24 beds to accommodate the boot camp program.

What is evident from these models is that the predominant factor driving the need for beds is whether the program is used for prisoners or probationers. Widening the net to include a large percentage of probationers means an increased need for prison beds. However, the design and operation of the specific program also had a significant impact on the number of beds needed. A comparatively long program like New York (6 months), which devoted a large number of beds to boot camp offenders, could have had a major impact on prison crowding. Furthermore, changing the parameters in the model also created considerable differences in the estimated need for prison beds in New York (Figure 20.4). For example, if all entrants are prisoners (e.g., probability of imprisonment = 100%), reducing the washout rate led to an increased savings of 478 beds (1,515 compared to 1,037 at the current washout rate).

The third model we examined for all five states changed the recidivism rates for the shock graduates. This analysis addressed the issue of the short-term impact on prison beds if the recidivism rates of those who successfully completed the shock program were cut in half. Recidivism rates in Georgia (27%), and South Carolina (24%) were high, and reduction of them did increase the bed space savings (or reduced the loss). This was particularly noticeable in Georgia where the estimate was that 404 beds (a difference of 137 beds) would be saved by the program if all of those admitted to the program were prison bound and the recidivism rate was cut in half.

The results from the model reducing the washouts was similar to the results from the recidivism model. When the washout rates were cut in half, the states with the highest washout

Table 20.3   Results of Five Different Models Used to Estimate Beds Saved (+) or Needed (−) by Five State Prison Systems as a Result of the Boot Camp Prison Showing Differences as a Function of the Probability That the Offenders Would Have Been Prison Bound if the Boot Camp Prison Had Not Existed

Models	Probability of Imprisonment				
	0%	25%	50%	75%	100%
Standard model					
Florida	−153	−121	−88	−56	−24
Georgia	−230	−106	18	143	267
Louisiana	−277	−133	12	156	300
New York	−2,807	−1,846	−885	76	1,037
South Carolina	−174	−84	7	97	188
Actual completions					
Florida	−139	−109	−80	−51	−22
Georgia	−214	−99	17	133	249
Louisiana	−229	−110	10	129	249
New York	−2,801	−1,842	−883	75	1,034
South Carolina	−171	−82	7	95	184
Reduced recidivism					
Florida	−137	−105	−73	−40	−8
Georgia	−93	31	156	280	404
Louisiana	−261	−117	28	172	316
New York	−2,653	−1,692	−731	230	1,191
South Carolina	−121	−30	60	151	241
Reduced washouts					
Florida	−95	−63	−31	1	34
Georgia	−240	−116	8	133	257
Louisiana	−257	−112	32	177	321
New York	−2,329	−1,368	−407	554	1,515
South Carolina	−146	−56	35	125	216
Saving prison revocation (parole)					
Florida	−153	−89	−25	39	103
Georgia	−230	−30	169	369	568
Louisiana	−277	−123	30	184	338
New York	−2,807	−1,689	−570	549	1,668
South Carolina	−174	−52	71	194	317

Note: Calculations for New York are based on 1990 data from Table 20.2.

rates saved the most beds. This made a difference of 478 beds in New York (1,515 compared to 1,037).

A fifth model was developed to reflect the impact of the program if the savings from parolees were incorporated into the model. The original model developed by MacKenzie and Parent (1991) did not include time estimates for parolees. In a review of the current article, Aziz and Korotkin (personal communication 1993) argued that the recidivism rates and duration of imprisonment for shock-eligible parolees

should be added to the person-months of confinement saved by the program. Model 5 gives the bed space loss or savings when we added the person-months of confinement saved because prison parolees who are revoked will be returned to prison to serve time (see Table 20.3).

This model could prove to be controversial because it assumes that if the capacity (annual capacity) for shock was used for prisoners, these prisoners would also be released at some point and some proportion of them would be revoked. Thus, in the model, the time they

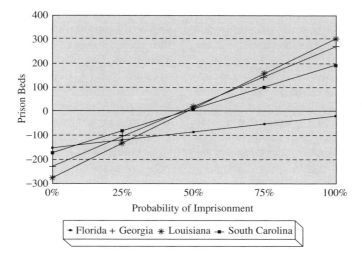

Figure 20.3   Estimates of Bed Space Needs and Savings for Four States Showing Changes as a Function of the Probability That Entrants Would Have Been Imprisoned if the Boot Camp Programs Did Not Exist

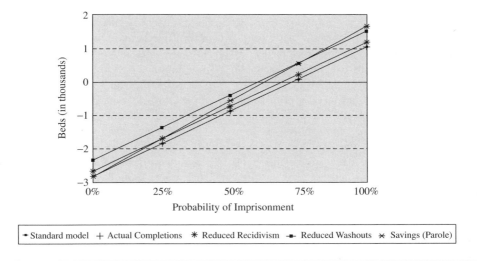

Figure 20.4   Estimates of Five Different Bed Space Models for New York Showing the Changes That Occur as a Function of Changes in the Probability of Imprisonment and Program Characteristics

spend in prison after revocation (the duration) is added to the time saved by the shock program because these offenders would now be shock offenders and not prison parolees. Because the prisoners who are shock eligible would spend between 8.4 and 20.5 months in prison (Table 20.2), any impact on prison beds would not occur until much later.

As shown in Table 20.3, adding this savings to the model created a major difference in the estimated bed space. If the programs targeted prison-bound offenders, all of them would result in saving beds. The number of beds saved would be substantial in New York, and in Florida, this model predicted a bed savings if 75% to 100% of the offenders would have been prison bound.

Another important consideration in improving the model is to include the time shock offenders have to wait prior to entering the shock program. Many programs admit participants in platoons or squads. If there are stringent eligibility requirements, offenders may have to wait several months in prison or jail before being admitted to the boot camp.[7] This time was not included in the early release calculations. To examine the impact of a 2-month waiting period on the demand for bed space, we added 2 months to the shock durations in the model and recalculated the bed space for the different probabilities of imprisonment. At 75% probability of imprisonment, this model estimated that the states would save 21 beds (Florida), 202 beds (Georgia), 124 beds (Louisiana), 49 beds (New York), and 114 beds (South Carolina), a fairly substantial reduction from the original estimates in the model (see Table 20.3).

DISCUSSION

After reviewing the decision making (see flow charts) and examining the program characteristics, we conclude that there is every reason to believe that the models that most appropriately represented the situation in Florida, Louisiana, and New York were those that are based on 75% to 100% of the shock entrants being prison bound. In all three of these states, the boot camp entrants had been sentenced to prison. Furthermore, those who were judged to be ineligible or unsuitable or who leave the program after entry must complete their sentence in a traditional prison. Although there may have been some who plea bargained or who were sent to prison by the judge because there was a boot camp, in the vast majority of cases we believe that they would have been prison bound had the boot camp not existed. If this assumption is correct, then the most appropriate estimates from the models for these states are the columns representing 75% to 100% probability of imprisonment.

At 100% probability of imprisonment, the different Louisiana models varied from a low of 249 to a high 338; at 75% probability of imprisonment, these values varied from 129 to 184. If most of the offenders had been in prison and the size of the program stayed the same, changes in the characteristics of the program in the models would not have a major impact on the prison system. Thus, if Louisiana wants to have an impact on prison crowding, it will be important to insure that the participants are selected from those who would otherwise be in prison.

These results are very different for the New York program. First of all, the size of the program means that it could have a significant impact on the prison system. If all of the participants were prison bound, 1,037 to 1,668 beds could be saved by the shock program. However, when only 75% of the participants would be prisoners, only 76 to 549 beds would be saved. Thus even small changes in the percentage of offenders who are prison bound could have a major impact on the prison system. However, the bed savings also depends on other characteristics of the program. If all of the inmates would have been prison bound, as few as 1,037 beds would be saved by the program if the actual completion rates are used to estimate bed space savings. Changes in actual completion or recidivism rates would have a minimal effect on bed space. A much larger impact comes from the model that reduces the number of washouts.

Florida presents a very different picture from the other states. As noted, after examining the program we believe that a large share of these participants would have been prison bound if the program did not exist. Therefore, we focused on the estimates of beds needed or saved if 75% or 100% of the offenders were prisoners. As shown in Table 20.3, three of the models predict that the program will result in an overall need for prison beds, although the need will be small (ranging from a need for 8 to 56 additional beds). The results seem to be driven by the high washout rate and the small difference between the time served in shock and the time served in prison by those who were shock eligible but did not go to shock.[8] When the washout rate in Florida was reduced, there were bed savings, although this was only 34 beds. However, in the new model adding in the savings due to parolee revocations and their time in prison, 230 beds were saved. It may be reasonable to use this model to estimate bed space savings in Florida because the shock-eligible prisoners spent a relatively short period of time in prison. In any case, even if all of the offenders were prison bound, the shock program would have had a minimum effect on prison beds given the overall size of the Florida prison population and therefore, the program has not accomplished the goal of reducing prison crowding. The Florida example demonstrates how important it is to design an intermediate sanction with the program goals clearly recognized. Furthermore, even a program that targets prison-bound offenders may have trouble reducing prison crowding if other aspects of the program are not carefully planned.

After reviewing the decision-making process, we concluded that many of the offenders in boot camps in Georgia and South Carolina would have been given probation if the boot camp had not existed. It this is true, the boot camps in these two states would have increased the demand for prison beds.

Incarcerating offenders is expensive. Per day costs for incarcerating offenders in the boot camp programs vary greatly among states. In reports describing the programs, South Carolina, New York, and Georgia reported per day costs of $34.22, $68.50, and $44.58, respectively. There may be many hidden costs to boot camps that are not reflected in the per diem costs and these estimates do not include capital outlay costs. However, these can be used as rough estimates to convert the bed space estimates to costs. Using the 75% probability of imprisonment as a conservative estimate, the predicted savings from the new model (model 5) and the average per diem cost of incarcerating an offender ($49.10), Florida, Louisiana and New York would save an estimated $698,939, $3,297,556, and $9,838.904, respectively, per year because of the boot camp prisons. On the other hand, Georgia and South Carolina, at the time of this study, were probably taking many offenders who otherwise would have been on probation. If the same model and the same cost estimates are used, but the probability of imprisonment is reduced to 25% (i.e., 75% would have been on probation), the model estimates that programs in Georgia and South Carolina

would cost the states $537,645 and $931,918, respectively, per year.

Boot camp prisons have attracted the attention of correctional professionals and politicians. Many people believe that one benefit of these programs will be a reduction in prison crowding. Although an intermediate sanction like boot camp may increase the net of correctional control, this is not necessarily always the case. The analyses completed in this article demonstrate how important program design is if the goal of an intermediate sanction is to reduce the prison population. The programs have the potential for reducing prison crowding; however, they also have the potential for substantially increasing the number of offenders in prison. The major factor that will make the difference will be the degree to which the participants would otherwise have been imprisoned. The larger the program, the more important this will be because even if 50% of the offenders were prison bound, the program could result in the need for a considerable number of additional beds. If the goal of a boot camp prison is to reduce prison crowding, a jurisdiction designing a boot camp prison must ensure that offenders participating are those who would otherwise be sent to prison.

There are other factors that will influence the number of beds needed by the prison system. Reducing recidivism rates and lowering the dropout and washout rates will also result in bed savings. Even what appears to be a small change in the prison situation, such as increasing the waiting time between entry to prison and administrating to the boot camp, can have a substantial impact on the need for prison beds. However, these will not overcome the influence of net widening. There is no support for the position that boot camp prisons will significantly impact prison crowding by reducing recidivism rates unless they are combined with a program that shortens the prison term of offenders who would otherwise be in prison.

Although many people argue that intermediate sanctions automatically widen the net of control, we argue that widening the net is not an automatic effect of all intermediate sanctions. Determining the impact of such sanctions is an empirical question that can be answered using appropriate data. The model proposed in this article can be used to determine the potential of an intermediate sanction for reducing or increasing the need for prison beds.

APPENDIX

Program capacity of each shock program was based on the number of beds available at the time of the data collection for the study (see Table 20.1).

Annual shock capacity represents the number of offenders who could complete the program in a 1-year period considering the number of beds available.

Probabilities of washout and dropout. The probabilities for nonvoluntary removal or washout (disciplinary, psychological, medical, or other) and voluntary removal or dropouts (inmate voluntarily drops), were based on 1-year dropout and washout rates. New York and Louisiana were the only two states that allowed offenders to drop out of the program voluntarily. The probability of dropping out was set to 0 for the programs that did not allow offenders to drop out.

Probability of imprisonments for washouts. In Florida, New York, and Louisiana, offenders were under supervision of the DOC and those who were dismissed were sent to prison to serve the remainder of their sentence; therefore the probability was set to 1.

In Georgia and South Carolina, offenders were returned to the court and the court decided on the sentence. We had data from a small sample of cases in Georgia indicating that 36.8% of the dismissals were sent to prison and therefore the probability of imprisonment for dropouts in Georgia was set at .368. These 36.8% had been dismissed from the programs for disciplinary reasons. The remaining 63.2% were dismissed for medical reasons and were given probation.

Data indicating the time served in prison for those who washed out of the South Carolina program and interviews with program staff suggested that almost all of those who washed out were sent to prison. Therefore, the probability of imprisonments for washouts in South Carolina

was set to 1. This may overestimate the number sent to prison. However, the impact on the bed space model would be minimal because the washout rate was low (approximately 16%).

Probability of imprisonment for voluntary dropouts. In Florida, Georgia, and South Carolina, inmates were not allowed to voluntarily drop out of the shock program; therefore, the probability of imprisonment for a dropout was set at 0. Conversely, in the two states that allow inmates to voluntarily drop out (New York and Louisiana) the probability of imprisonment for a shock dropout was set to 1 because, in both of these states, inmates who drop out of shock must finish the remainder of their sentence in prison.

Revocation rates for shock graduates from Florida, Georgia, and South Carolina represented estimates from survival analyses examining the performance of offenders during 1 year of community supervision (Souryal and MacKenzie 1993). Revocation rates for New York (New York State Department of Correctional Services 1993) and Louisiana (MacKenzie and Parent 1991) were taken from previously completed work. Revocation rates for shock graduates varied between 9% for New York (in 1990) and 27% for Georgia.

Probabilities of revocation for probationers were taken from data estimating recidivism rates for samples of probationers who would have been eligible for the shock program but were instead given a sentence of probation. These are either estimates from survival analyses (Souryal and MacKenzie 1993) or they were taken from the same agency reports or publication as the revocation rates for the shock graduates (referenced above).

Average terms of imprisonment for shock eligible offenders were calculated for a sample of offenders within each state who had been eligible for the boot camp program but had served time in traditional prisons.

Average shock durations in months were obtained from each site for a sample of offenders. Average shock durations varied from state to state, usually between 3 and 6 months. Note that this does not include possible waiting time in prison before being admitted to the boot camp program.

Durations of imprisonment for shock dropouts were calculated to be a number other than 0 only for Louisiana and New York, which were the two states that allowed offenders to drop out. The durations were obtained from previously reported data (MacKenzie and Parent 1991; New York State Department of Correctional Services 1990). For the other sites, the probability of a voluntary dropout was set to 0 and, therefore, the duration of imprisonment for a shock dropout was set at 0 because this would not be used in the calculations of the model.

Durations of imprisonment for shock washouts were calculated from small samples of offenders who were released from prison after serving time in traditional prisons following their dismissal from the shock program. Only a limited number of cases were identified for the duration of imprisonment for the Georgia shock washouts and shock-eligible probationers, and thus these numbers should be interpreted with caution. In Georgia the average number of months served by shock washouts was less than the shock program because 63.2% were placed on probation after the dismissal and, therefore, served less time than they would have in the shock program.

Durations of imprisonment for shock graduates who were revoked were obtained from the samples of shock graduates who had been revoked after being released from the shock program. This was the average time they spent in prison after being revoked. In Florida, Georgia, and South Carolina, the durations of imprisonment for the shock graduates and shock-eligible probationers who were revoked were truncated because some of the offenders were still in prison at the time of data collection. Therefore, this estimate is shorter than would otherwise be the case. The majority of the shock-eligible probationers in Georgia had absconded while on probation, and therefore the number of offenders who were imprisoned was quite small.

Durations of imprisonment for shock-eligible offenders who were revoked on probation were

calculated in the same manner as was the duration for the shock graduates who were revoked.

NOTES

1. For a more complete description of the programs, see MacKenzie and Souryal 1993. The data for this study were collected in 1990, and program descriptions are based on the characteristics of the programs at the time of data collection. Since that time, there have been substantial changes in many of the programs. For instance, Georgia has made substantial changes in all aspects of its program (Flowers, Carr, and Ruback 1991). South Carolina changed from being the responsibility of the department of probation to being the responsibility of the department of corrections. The express purpose of this change was to maximize the shock program's ability to reduce prison crowding by insuring that the offenders participating in the program were prison bound.

2. In 1988 New York permitted offenders up to but not including 26 years of age to enter the program. This was amended in 1989 when inmates age 26 through 29 were admitted to the program with some additional restrictions. By 1992, the age limit was again increased (to 35 years) and the additional requirements for older inmates were eliminated.

3. The capacity of New York's program was greatly increased in 1990 and therefore the values shown in the table include both the 1988 and 1990 values.

4. The numbers and probabilities for Louisiana were taken from the previously published report that was used as a model for this study (see MacKenzie and Parent 1991).

5. In a survey, researchers in New York (New York State Department of Correctional Services 1991) asked judges if they had changed their sentencing practices as a result of the shock program. Only 5% responded that they had sentenced nonviolent felons to prison rather than jail or probation because of the shock program. Another 5% said that they gave longer sentences to insure that offenders would not be eligible for shock, and 14% said they gave shorter sentences to assure that offenders would be eligible for the shock program. This suggests that only a small percentage of the judges are using the program as an option for offenders who would otherwise be on probation.

6. A detailed description of the formula for calculating bed space estimates is given in MacKenzie and Parent (1991).

7. In examining their early boot camp, New York researchers found that inmates had served an average

of 57 days in prison or jail before being admitted to the boot camp. Additionally, during interviews with program officials and inmates in many states, mention was made of a long waiting period between the time of entering prison (or volunteering for the boot camp) and admittance to the program.

8. The amount of time the boot camp participants served was not that much different than the time they would have to spend in a traditional prison. This small difference in time may also account, in part, for the high washout rate in Florida.

REFERENCES

Austin, James and Barry Krisberg. 1981. "Wider, Stronger and Different Nets." *Journal of Research in Crime and Delinquency* 18:165–96.

Covey, Herbert and Scott Menard. 1984. "Community Corrections Diversions in Colorado." *Journal of Criminal Justice* 12:1–10.

Ezell, Mark. 1989. "Juvenile Arbitration: Net-Widening and Other Unintended Consequences." *Journal of Research in Crime and Delinquency* 26:358–77.

Flowers, G. T., T. S. Carr, and R. B. Ruback. 1991. *Special Alternative Incarceration Evaluation.* Atlanta: Georgia Department of Corrections. Unpublished manuscript.

Greenfeld, Larry A. 1992. *Prisons and Prisoners in the United States.* Washington, DC: U.S. Department of Justice, Bureau of Justice Statistics, NCJ-137002.

Hylton, J. H. 1980. *Community Corrections and Social Control: A Canadian Perspective.* Regina, Canada: University of Regina.

Jones, Peter. 1990. "Community Corrections in Kansas: Extending Community-Based Corrections or Widening the Net?" *Journal of Research in Crime and Deliquency* 27:79–101.

MacKenzie, Doris L. 1990. "Boot Camp Prisons: Components, Evaluations, and Empirical Issues." *Federal Probation* 54:44–52.

MacKenzie, Doris L. and Dale Parent. 1991. "Shock Incarceration and Prison Crowding in Louisiana." *Journal of Criminal Justice* 19:225–37.

MacKenzie, Doris L., James W. Shaw, and Voncile B. Gowdy. 1993. *An Evaluation of Shock Incarceration in Louisiana.* Washington, DC: U.S. Department of Justice, National Institute of Justice.

MacKenzie, Doris L. and Claire Souryal. 1991. "Boot Camp Survey: Rehabilitation, Recidivism Reduction Out Rank As Main Goals." *Corrections Today*, October, pp. 90–96.

———. 1993, September. *Multi-Site Study of Shock Incarceration: Process Evaluation.* Unpublished report to the National Institute of Justice.

Mainprize, Stephen. 1992. "Electronic Monitoring in Corrections: Assessing Cost Effectiveness and the Potential for Widening the Net of Social Control." *Canadian Journal of Criminology*, April, pp. 161–80.

Morris, Norval and Michael Tonry. 1990. *Between Prison and Probation: Intermediate Punishments in a Rational Sentencing System.* New York: Oxford University Press.

New York State Department of Correctional Services and New York State Division of Parole. 1990. *The Second Annual Report to the Legislature: Shock Incarceration in New York State.* Unpublished report by the Division of Program Planning, Research and Evaluation and the Office of Policy Analysis and Information.

———. 1991. *The Third Annual Report to the Legislature: Shock Incarceration in New York State.* Unpublished report by the Division of Program Planning, Research and Evaluation and the Office of Policy Analysis and Information.

———. 1993. *The Fifth Annual Report to the Legislature: Shock Incarceration in New York State.* Unpublished report by the Division of Program Planning, Research and Evaluation and the Office of Policy Analysis and Information.

Palumbo, D., M. Clifford, and Zoann Snyder-Joy. 1992. "From Net Widening to Intermediate Sanctions: The Transformation of Alternatives to Incarceration From Benevolence to Malevolence." Pp. 229–44 in *Smart Sentencing: The Emergence of Intermediate Sanctions*, edited by J. Byrne, A. Lurigio, and J. Petersilia. Newbury Park, CA: Sage.

Souryal, C. and Doris MacKenzie. 1993. "Shock Incarceration and Recidivism: An Examination of Boot Camp Programs in Four States." In *Intermediate Sanctions: Sentencing in the 90s*, edited by J. O. Smykla and W. L. Selke. Cincinnati, OH: Anderson.

Yokoyama, Minoru. 1986. "The Juvenile Justice System in Japan." In *Youth Crime, Social Control and Prevention*, edited by M. Brusten, J. Graham, N. Herringer, and P. Malinowski. Federal Republic of Germany: Centaurus-Verlags-Gesellschaft Pfeffenweiler.

———. 1989. "Net-Widening of the Juvenile Justice System in Japan." *Criminal Justice Review* 14:43–53.

Part IX

BOOT CAMPS IN THE FUTURE

21

WHERE DO WE GO FROM HERE?

Boot Camps in the Future

DORIS LAYTON MACKENZIE

GAYLENE STYVE ARMSTRONG

INTRODUCTION

The rebirth of correctional boot camps in the late 1980s, in an accepting political climate, sparked extensive discussions and debates ranging from the economic feasibility of boot camp to its appropriateness for various correctional populations. In view of the resurgence, policymakers asked a number of questions regarding the long-term viability of boot camps, and researchers explored these areas through a variety of empirical research studies. Early studies focused on the fundamental questions related to participant recidivism rates, cost-effectiveness, net widening, and impact on crowding (MacKenzie, 1991; MacKenzie & Parent, 1991; MacKenzie & Piquero, 1994; MacKenzie & Shaw, 1993). Stemming from a rudimentary understanding of the strengths and weaknesses of boot camp programs based on early research, more recent studies have considered the variation between programs, examined inmate perceptions of their environment and experiences, and examined intermediate psychological outcomes (Gover, MacKenzie, & Styve, 1999; MacKenzie, Wilson, Armstrong, & Gover, 2001; Styve, Gover, MacKenzie, & Mitchell, 2000).

Yet a number of questions remain unanswered, in part because of the extensive development and evolution of boot camp programs over the course of the past two decades.

In this chapter, we will briefly synthesize the general research trends before discussing two resulting issues that researchers and policymakers should consider when planning for the future of boot camp programs. We will discuss the need for an updated accounting of the effects of new-generation boot camps on offender recidivism rates. Finally, we will discuss the concerns related to the potential physical dangers presented to boot camp inmates (including inmate deaths), which some opponents to boot camps suggest are innately posed by the boot camp's programmatic structure. These concerns have been called to the attention of the public through the media and other public realms as the result of recent incidents that have occurred in some camps.

TRENDS OF EMPIRICAL RESEARCH ON BOOT CAMPS

Initially, the viability of boot camps as an alternative sanction was questioned. Some argued that because boot camps are residential facilities, they are much like prisons. From this perspective, the camps are not in line with the conception of an alternative sanction, which was described by Morris and Tonry (1990) as a form of punishment that can be placed on a continuum of severity between incarceration and probation. However, MacKenzie and Shaw (1993) argued that boot camps were not identical to a traditional prison term. They suggested that the camps are frequently used as an early-release option for less serious offenders, and as such, they could be considered intermediate sanctions. Many jurisdictions accepted this interpretation and considered boot camps as one of numerous intermediate sanctions available to offenders.

The earliest studies on the impact and effectiveness of boot camps began by examining individual sites, and soon moved toward more sophisticated multisite designs, some of which implemented randomization. We presented much of the empirical evidence resulting from the early research in the preceding chapters of this book. Although these studies provided some answers, they also raised a number of questions. The current philosophy and programmatic content of boot camps is the result of many successive generations of programs. Modern boot camps are only vaguely reminiscent of the programs reintroduced in the 1980s. This recent transformation of boot camp program content and philosophies has led to questions about the applicability of earlier research results to the current-day, or new-generation, boot camps.

Correctional researchers and decision makers in the political sphere have maintained an interest in the viability of the boot camps since the 1980s, along with continued public interest, which remains fueled by the media. As the programs have become more refined over the years, so has the research focusing on boot camps. Research questions seek to examine more than the surface-level worth of boot camp programs to also include more specific changes in intermediate outcomes such as antisocial attitudes (MacKenzie & Souryal, 1995), and effects on special populations such as boot camps for women (MacKenzie & Donaldson, 1996) or drug offenders (Shaw & MacKenzie, 1992). Given that more recent, larger-scale studies revealed that the variation in boot camp program content is immense, concerns regarding the generalizability of these early results became warranted, especially when researchers attempt to make statements about the impact of programs based on single-site studies. As MacKenzie and Rosay (1996) argued, the problem is that the programs differ dramatically in goals and components. Thus, knowledge about the effectiveness of one program may be dependent upon very atypical aspects of the program or even a charismatic leader, and not necessarily related to boot camp-type characteristics of the program. Thus, although early studies on boot camps were able to inform us about boot camps at a more basic level, programmatic evolution calls for more comprehensive, and more recent, empirical research on the topic.

BEGINNINGS OF COMPREHENSIVE STUDIES ON BOOT CAMPS

The uncertainty about the impact of variation within boot camp programs in the United States on outcomes prompted Doris MacKenzie, now at the University of Maryland, and her colleagues to begin a multisite study of adult boot camps. As presented in earlier chapters, findings from this large-scale research project demonstrated no significant differences in recidivism between offenders who were sent to boot camps and offenders who either served a longer period of time in prison or served their sentence on probation. The boot camps studied differed greatly in the components of the program (e.g., drug treatment, therapy, education), aspects that might be expected to influence outcomes. Yet no differences were found in recidivism. The finding of no differences in recidivism when camps were compared to other sentences within the same jurisdiction suggests, overall, that the boot camp atmosphere did not have an impact on recidivism.

However, the camps could be used to "signal" which inmates would do better after release. As MacKenzie (1997) noted in a recent summary of boot camp evidence, "In programs where a substantial number of offenders were dismissed from the boot camp prior to completion, the recidivism rates for those who completed the program were significantly lower than rates for those who were dismissed" (p. 9-27). This does not mean that the boot camp changed some offenders, because the inmates who succeeded in the camps most likely differed from those who failed prior to entering the camps. Thus, the boot camp only separated these two groups into those who would complete and those who would not. Additionally, those who completed had lower recidivism rates than those who were dismissed from the boot camp. Therefore, the completion of the boot camp signaled which inmates would have lower recidivism rates in the future.

Despite these results, the unique environment created by boot camps as compared to the majority of correctional programs was undeniable. As MacKenzie noted in Chapter 1 of this book, the activity and interest levels of the participants in these camps gave the impression that the camps were having some type of influence on the offenders. MacKenzie and colleagues began to probe further in measuring the actual differences in the environments that existed between boot camps and other types of programs. In 1996, MacKenzie and colleagues began another large-scale study of boot camps, this time comparing the environmental characteristics of a national sample of juvenile boot camps with more traditional juvenile correctional programs. MacKenzie and colleagues surveyed the residents within the residential facilities, as well as the staff employed within the programs and facility administrators. They found the conditions of confinement in the two environments to be perceived as distinct by both juvenile residents and facility staff (Mitchell, MacKenzie, Gover, & Styve, 2001; Styve et al., 2000). Although there was significant variation within the boot camp programs and the traditional programs, the researchers did find some consistencies across program type with respect to the environmental conditions. Interestingly, and contrary to the arguments of many opponents to the boot camp programs, the environments of the boot camps were not perceived to be negative and threatening, as opponents often argued. Instead, both the juveniles and staff reported the boot camp environment to be significantly more supportive, and safer, than traditional juvenile correctional facilities. However, one group did appear to have more problems in the boot camps; juveniles who had been abused in the past seemed to report more difficulties in the boot camps compared to their experiences in traditional facilities (MacKenzie et al., 2001).

The confrontational nature of the boot camps may be particularly difficult for them.

Although facilities that operated under a boot camp structure were different from other traditional programs, researchers observed that these programs had undergone significant metamorphosis as compared to boot camp programs in existence during the previous decades. Consequently, much of the earlier research related to recidivism outcomes (e.g., MacKenzie, Brame, McDowall, & Souryal, 1995) appeared to be dated, and the need for updated recidivism research was apparent.

RECIDIVISM IN NEW-GENERATION BOOT CAMPS: THE MARYLAND EXPERIMENT

As illustrated in earlier chapters, a substantial body of prior literature indicates that offenders who are sentenced to boot camp programs do not have significantly different rates of recidivism when compared to offenders serving traditional sentences (e.g., probation or prison). However, boot camps have experienced a significant transformation from their original design into the new generation of boot camps in the 21st century. These new-generation camps devote much more time in the daily schedule to treatment and education within the military environment. Consequently, people have questioned the validity of drawing conclusions based on the earlier research about the impact of boot camps on recidivism rates. Initial evidence suggests that the new generation of boot camps may be more effective in reducing rates of recidivism as compared to both previous boot camp programs and traditional correctional facilities. However, at this point, no study of adult programs has been completed using an experimental design to evaluate either the earlier or new-generation models of boot camp programs. Some of the studies of juvenile boot camps did use random assignment. However, these studies began when the camps were first opened. These camps had implementation difficulties, and, thus, results may be different for camps that have been in operation for a number of years. Researchers have not yet thoroughly addressed whether combining treatment with the military environment of boot camps yields lower recidivism rates than alternative correctional programs that emphasize treatment (e.g., prison treatment program) within a more traditional correctional environment.

In response to this void in the boot camp literature, researchers at the University of Maryland began a study in 2002 that randomly assigns adult inmates to either an adult boot camp in Maryland that is a well-established program with a strong treatment emphasis, or to an alternative correctional facility that also emphasizes therapeutic programming but without a military component (MacKenzie, 2001). The boot camp has been operating for more than 10 years and has a strong treatment emphasis. The research builds on prior literature, taking a two-pronged approach to assess the effectiveness of the boot camp program. First, researchers will assess the long-term impact of the boot camp program on participants' recidivism rates and compare those recidivism rates to inmates randomly assigned to the alternative correctional facility. Second, using pre- and posttest surveys, researchers will assess boot camp participants' initial levels of and changes in antisocial attitudes and values, and compare these measures to inmates assigned to the alternative correctional facility.

This study is a true randomized experiment. Each month, one group of inmates (a platoon) is deemed eligible for entry into the boot camp program. Eligibility for the experiment and, consequently, entry into the boot camp program is based on three criteria. First, the inmate must be a nonviolent offender. Second, the inmate must be sentenced for the first time to long-term adult incarceration, which means that they must not have had any prior jail stays of 60 days or more. Finally, the inmate must agree to a contract, which dictates participation in academic education, drug education/treatment, and life skills training. Although each inmate must first meet these criteria, ultimately, the final eligibility decision rests with the Parole Commission.

Once an inmate is deemed acceptable as per the criteria and Parole Commission, each inmate is then offered the opportunity to *voluntarily* participate in the boot camp program. If inmates agree to participate in the program, their sentence is reduced to a 6-month sentence from its original length. For the average offender, participation in the boot camp translates into a sentence reduction of about 18 to 24 months. Furthermore, if the

inmate agrees to participate in the program, he or she is required to sign a Mutual Agreement Programming (MAP) contract that summarizes the above-stated information.

After inmates sign their MAP contracts, researchers randomly assign inmates, using simple random assignment procedures, to the boot camp or the designated comparison facility. Before the inmate is informed of the facility to which he or she has been assigned, researchers ask the inmate to complete a 45-minute survey that assesses antisocial attitudes, cognitions, and behaviors. Six months after this intake process, researchers administer a similar survey to these same inmates before they graduate and are released into the community. By comparing the pre- and posttest surveys, researchers will be able to assess differences in change (or lack thereof) in antisocial attitudes/cognitions for inmates in the boot camp and the comparison facility. Additionally, researchers will conduct criminal record checks 12 months after inmates have been released into the community. To determine the impact of the boot camp on the recidivism rates of offenders, the rates of the boot camp participants will be compared to the recidivism rates of the control group.

Maryland's Toulson Boot Camp program, established in August 1990, is the boot camp involved in the experimental study. Toulson Boot Camp uses a military model with the typical components (see Chapter 2), but it also incorporates drug education, life skills training, and academic education. The program lasts 6 months and is divided into three different phases, each of which spans a 2-month period. The daily schedule and activities of the boot camp participants vary depending upon their phase in the program. Participants are in Phase I when they enter the camp. This phase emphasizes discipline and self-control in a highly structured daily schedule that focuses on military drill, physical training, academic education, and other therapeutic programs (e.g., Life Skills, Addiction Education/ Treatment). During the subsequent phases, Phases II and III, the daily activities have less emphasis on drill, physical training, and education, and more emphasis on work projects (e.g., carpentry, road crew).

Inmates who are not randomized into the Toulson Boot Camp program are admitted to the

Table 21.1   Characteristics of Participants Randomized into the Maryland Boot Camp Study

Characteristic N = 40	TBC (%) N = 39	MTC (%) N = 39
Race		
Black	97	95
White/other	3	5
Mean age	23	23
Education level		
High school dropout	72	82
Graduate/more than HS	28	18
Marital status		
Married	0	10
Single	57	51
Employment status (at arrest)		
Full/part-time	67	61
Unemployed/irregular	33	39
Primary conviction charge		
Property	5	5
Drug	92	90
Violent	3	5
Mean length of current sentence (mos.)	44.3	42.4
Mean number of prior arrests	6.0	5.5
Mean number of prior convictions	1.7	1.4
Mean number of SR prior arrests	8.1	8.1
Mean age at first arrest	16	16
Prior incarceration	23	28
Under influence at time of arrest		
Total (drugs, alcohol, or both)	38	49
Drugs only	15	18
Alcohol only	15	8
Both drugs and alcohol	8	23
Prior drug/alcohol arrest	97	97
Drug use 12 mos. prior imprisonment		
Cocaine	5	8
Marijuana	72	65
Prior treatment	26	26
Currently dependent on drug/alcohol	11	21
Currently need treatment	24	18

Metropolitan Treatment Center (MTC). The MTC is a more traditional prison facility that offers less structure than the boot camp. In this study, inmates assigned to MTC are prioritized for the therapeutic programming offered at MTC. The therapeutic programming focuses on academic education, addiction education/treatment, and life skills training similar to the therapeutic programming offered in the Toulson Boot Camp.

As of November 2002, 79 participants had been randomly assigned to either the Toulson Boot Camp ($n = 40$) or the Metropolitan

Treatment Center ($n = 39$). As indicated in Table 21.1, the typical participant is an African American male, approximately 23 years old, who is a high school dropout, single, employed more than part time and convicted of a drug charge. In the upcoming year, the researchers at the University of Maryland will assess preliminary data using self-report surveys of changes in antisocial attitudes and cognitions. Researchers will compare survey data completed during intake with the data from the survey the inmates will complete during an exit interview. Additionally, researchers will be extracting data from the participants' official criminal records once they have been released and have resided in the community for 12 months. Given the experimental nature of this study, we expect reliable and valid results regarding changes in antisocial attitudes and cognitions as a result of the boot camp or traditional correctional facility. Furthermore, the information obtained through the follow-up on the officially documented criminal activities of the participants will be a worthy contribution to answering questions about the viability of the new-generation boot camps as an alternative sanction.

INMATE DEATHS IN CORRECTIONAL CUSTODY: DO BOOT CAMPS POSE A HIGHER DANGER TO INMATES?

Some people believe that the boot camps should be eliminated because the military atmosphere of the camps poses an inherent danger to inmates regardless of what the empirical evidence has demonstrated. From this perspective, the strict discipline and harsh standards imposed by boot camp staff are some of the primary goals of boot camps. They believe the camps focus on punishment of the inmates, and they find this especially problematic for juvenile delinquents in the camps. However, research has found the opposite to be true. Based on their survey of all existing juvenile boot camp programs, MacKenzie and Rosay (1996) found that rehabilitation and lowering recidivism were important goals, and punishment was not. Furthermore, juvenile perceptions of danger in the camps are not significantly different from the levels perceived by juveniles in traditional facilities (Styve et al., 2000).

Although punishment is not an important goal of boot camps, and, on average, inmates do not believe the camps pose an elevated risk to them, some of the traditional activities, such as the exercise components that include lengthy runs, have been hazardous, resulting in a number of boot camp inmate deaths in the past few years. These deaths have occurred despite the medical checkups inmates receive during the intake and assessment process (Gover et al., 1999). Recent deaths in boot camps led one journalist to write:

My reading of the evidence suggests that the camps' clientele are nothing more than grist for a very profitable mill. The old-style reform school, but with "training" substituted for flogging, and phony "tough love" jargon substituted for the blunt (but more honest) cruelties of the original model, is enjoying a heady revival these days. It's a sellers market and business is booming. There's just one minor nuisance: the deaths. (Riak, 2003)

Furthermore, when sociologist R. Dean Wright of Drake University was asked to comment on the death of a boot camp inmate, he stated, "It's a situation that lends itself to abusive conditions. Any time you have someone use lock and key, the person who has the lock and key has the power to abuse, and they often do" (Blackwood, 2001).

Two recent incidents have called the boot camp methods into question. These incidents have been the unfortunate deaths of two juveniles in two different boot camps in the United States. Both deaths occurred while the youth were exercising. The first incident involved Gina Score, a young girl who was placed into a South Dakota boot camp program. According to a report in the *New York Times,* "Gina Score was placed in the camp in July 1999 after stealing a bike, skipping school and shoplifting. Two days into the program, the 5-foot-4, 226-pound girl joined other girls on a 2.7-mile required run" ("Boot Camp Death Prompts Changes," 2000). According to the publicized state investigator's report, Score collapsed during the run, frothing at the mouth; lost control of her bladder; progressively lost her ability to communicate; and eventually became completely unresponsive. The staff at the boot camp did not allow other residents to assist her, commenting that they should not make things "easy" or "comfortable" for her. Boot camp staff left Score where she fell for 3¼ hours before transporting her to the hospital. Upon her arrival at the hospital, Score's body temperature registered 108 degrees (the upper limit of the thermometer). Doctors were not able to revive her at any point and, consequently, pronounced her dead 1 hour after she was admitted into the hospital.

Shortly after Gina Score's death, counsel for the Children's Rights Division, Human Rights Watch, Michael Bochenek, submitted a letter to South Dakota Governor William Janklow detailing the above events and requesting immediate action be taken to alter South Dakota's juvenile sentencing guidelines and discipline practices. In the letter, Bochenek alleged that Rights Groups, parents of youths in this South Dakota facility, and the juveniles themselves have "charged that guards shackle youth in spread-eagled fashion after cutting their clothes off (practice known as 'four pointing'), chain youth inside their cells ('bumpering'), and place children in isolation twenty-three hours a day for extended periods of time" (letter available at www.nospank.net/hrw2.tm). The letter goes on to describe physical abuses of authority, including other inappropriate actions such as male guards supervising the strip searches of female juvenile delinquents, as well as "grossly inadequate mental health care, glaring deficiencies in education and other substandard conditions of confinement." According to the *New York Times,* Republican South Dakota Governor Janklow, who himself was a product of the Marines and thus very familiar with the boot camp regimen, "blamed 'rogue employees' for Score's death and other problems" ("Boot Camp Death Prompts Changes," 2000). Because of the incident, two staff members were charged but later acquitted on child abuse charges in the death and other alleged problems at the camp, including making girls run in shackles until their ankles bled.

In a 1998 incident, 16-year-old Nicholas Contreraz died at the privately operated Arizona Boys Ranch boot camp. According to an interview of fellow Boys Ranch resident Geoffrey Lewis by the Pinal County Sheriff's office:

> Lewis stated, Nick Contreraz was performing physical training (push-ups) in the amphitheatre. Mr. Lewis indicated due to Nick's lack of effort and aggressive behavior, he was being physically assisted. Mr. Lewis stated it had been forty minutes since the last hydration. So the staff took Nick to get water from his canteen. Mr. Lewis stated when staff was giving Nicholas water he did not respond. Mr. Lewis stated he had been playing like he was passing out several times during the day. Mr. Lewis stated the staff checked Nicholas' pulse and breathing and found nothing. Mr. Lewis and staff immediately administered CPR and called for assistance. Mr. Lewis stated CPR continued

until Nicholas was taken with medical assistance team. (police report available for viewing at http://www.nospank.net/azranch.htm)

According to a subsequent police report by attending Officer LeBlanc,

> The charging nurse Sue, from Northwest hospital contacted me to let me know that Mr. Contreraz had died and there were signs of abuse on the body. I asked what these were and she said he had abrasions from head to toe. He had bruising on his flanks, he had a rigid stomach and he had blood in his stomach. (police report available for viewing at http://www.nospank.net/azranch.htm)

An autopsy revealed that the boy died of complications from a lung infection that were exacerbated by physical activities at the Arizona Boys Ranch. Another autopsy by a forensic pathologist showed that the boy had been "manhandled," causing bruising, abrasions, scratches, and minor puncture wounds to the head and body. A 37-page Pinal County, Arizona Sheriff's report released on April 17, 1998, stated that some staff members thought that Contreraz was faking his breathing problems, even though he repeatedly coughed and vomited in the days before he died (Prison Privatisation Report International, 1998). As a result of the incident on April 26, 1998, two staff members were fired, four were suspended, and the program director was replaced. All 17 staff members employed at the Boys Ranch at the time were placed on Arizona's Child Abuser Directory, which is a confidential list used to screen people for foster care and other children's services. Prosecutors eventually dropped all charges initially filed against six boot camp staff members.

Critical incidents in boot camps, such as the Gina Score and Nicholas Contreraz cases, are not specific to programs designed for juvenile delinquents. Similar events have occurred in privately operated boot camps in which parents are able to voluntarily send their disruptive teen for a few weeks of boot camp training. These camps are outside of the criminal justice system realm. The programs are designed with the same military emphasis as the juvenile correctional boot camps, but they tend to focus more on the militaristic components than therapeutic treatment, reflective of earlier "Scared Straight" programs. Often, these privately operated boot camps are not accredited and are subject to little or no regulation.

These privately operated boot camp programs have also experienced tragic deaths of their residents. In 2001, a 14-year-old boy, Anthony Haynes, died in an Arizona desert boot camp after collapsing in the 111-degree heat. Haynes was sent to the camp by his mother after he slashed her tires and was caught shoplifting. Newspaper reports about the camp after Haynes's death reported that the daily regimen included forced marches; wearing black uniforms in triple-digit temperatures; in-your-face discipline; and a daily diet limited to an apple, a carrot, and a bowl of beans. According to reports based on a search warrant affidavit filed in July 2001, "On the day Haynes died, he reportedly was hallucinating and refusing water before camp supervisors took him to a nearby motel and left him in a tub with the shower running. They returned to find the boy face down in the water and that he had vomited mud," which boot camp staff had forced him to eat earlier in the day (Markham, 2002, p. 14).

Charles Long II, the head of the Arizona boot camp program, was subsequently arrested on charges of second-degree murder, aggravated assault, and eight counts of child abuse. A second staff member, Raymond Burr Anderson, was also arrested on child abuse charges for allegedly spanking, stomping, beating, and whipping more than 14 children. The case is set for a trial on November 18, 2003.

When disasters such as these cases occur in boot camp programs, opponents of the programs point to the risks of the boot camps, including the structure and the potential for abuse of authority by untrained or undertrained staff. Regarding Gina Score's death in South Dakota, Jerry Wells, director of the Koch Crime Institute, pointed to the staff as the cause of the death, suggesting the camp had "untrained staff." Wells stated, "The surprise to me was that it was a surprise, because it was a recipe for disaster" ("Boot Camp Death Prompts Changes," 2000). Because of these types of incidents, it is often no surprise that when people learn about boot camp programs, they experience a type of negative

"gut reaction" that forms the basis of their opinions about the programs. Media presentations of these incidents have helped to develop emotive responses to programs, such that it would seem boot camp programs are a dangerous alternative sanction. However, before final judgments are made, fatal incidents such as these must be placed into the context of all injuries and deaths, including suicides, that occur in other juvenile and adult correctional facilities across the country. What are the actual rates of deaths and/or severe injuries in boot camps as compared to other facilities? To truly determine the extent of the dangerousness of boot camps, we need to consider injuries and deaths in all types of correctional facilities, including traditional programs. The frequency of deaths in the boot camps must be compared to the frequency of deaths in traditional institutions.

Inmate deaths in correctional custody result from a variety of causes. Suicide is the most frequent cause of death in U.S. jails. In 2000, a rate of 90 to 230 deaths per 100,000 inmates was documented as a suicide in jail or prison, which is 16 times the rate for the general population (Bureau of Justice Statistics, 2002). Most of the people who commit suicide in jail have been arrested for nonviolent crimes. Ninety percent of suicides in jails occur as the result of hanging, and 50% of suicide victims in jail or prison are intoxicated with drugs or alcohol at the time of their death. The number of inmate deaths is such a concern that beginning in 2000, the Bureau of Justice Statistics began the Deaths in Custody survey. The survey collects a quarterly count of inmate deaths in each of the nation's 1,394 state prisons and 3,095 local jails. It includes the following background data on each deceased inmate: gender; age; race/ethnicity; legal status; offense types; length of stay in custody; the date, time, location, and cause of each death; and data on medical treatment provided for fatal illnesses/diseases.

These high rates of inmate deaths (including suicides) are not specific to the United States. A recent study, published in the *Canadian Medical Association Journal,* found that 283 men died in custody—137 in federal institutions, 88 in provincial prisons, and 58 in police cells—between 1990 and 1999 in Canada (Wobeser, Datema, Bechard, & Ford, 2002). This translates to a death rate among inmates of 420.1 per 100,000 in federal institutions and 211.5 per 100,000 in provincial institutions—much higher than the country's rate of 187.5 deaths per 100,000 Canadian men aged 24 to 49 in 1996. Wobeser et al. found that suicide (including that from strangulation and drug overdose) was, at 34%, the most common cause of death. Cardiovascular problems (including from drug use) at 22% and illicit drug use at 17% were the second and third most frequent causes. Six percent of deaths were homicides, and another 6% died from cancer. Other causes included death from diseases such as HIV/AIDS, hepatitis, and respiratory problems. In an interview regarding these results, Ford commented, "Most troublesome is the high suicide rate, which suggests a failure of the system. Fatal overdoses, as an example, were 20 to 50 times more common among the prison population than among the general male population" ("Inmates Have Much Higher Death Rate," n.d.).

How do the death rates in correctional boot camps compare to the rates in traditional prisons and juvenile facilities? We do not know. We were unable to locate the data we would need to make this comparison. Certainly, if the death and injury rates in boot camps are much higher than in traditional facilities, those data would support the critics' arguments against boot camps. From their perspective, the camps are a problem and should be closed down. On the other hand, if the death and injury rates are similar or lower in the boot camps, then different conclusions could be drawn about the camps.

The deaths we discussed in this chapter are tragic. Are they due to the boot camp model—a model that is inherently abusive? Or, are these deaths a result of poorly trained or abusive staff members? We do not know the answer to these questions. Certainly, the research we have done does not demonstrate that the boot camps we have studied always fare worse than other facilities when we ask inmates and staff about their experiences. Nor do recidivism rates or attitude changes suggest that the boot camp results in more criminal attitudes and behavior.

Our results may not apply to the camps where the deaths occurred. The boot camps that have permitted us to conduct research in their facilities may be much better managed and operated than boot camps that would not want the scrutiny of researchers. We have to have cooperation from administrators if we are going to conduct research in a facility. Poorly managed boot camps with untrained staff might hesitate to permit researchers to enter their facilities to conduct research.

The majority of the administrators we have interviewed are well aware that boot camp staff require close oversight. This is particularly true of new staff members who are being initiated into the program. According to administrators, some people who volunteer for work in boot camps have problems related to power. They want to have power over others and to demonstrate that they have this power. This presents a problem for the other staff and inmates because such power-hungry individuals are continually trying to show their control over others. They are not necessary focused on how to help inmates change in positive ways.

In comparison to traditional correctional facilities, we might expect more injuries in boot camps because inmates are required to participate in rigorous physical activity. Certainly, this physical activity carries with it the danger of some injuries even if staff are well trained to appropriately recognize problems. However, many inmates in the camps are proud of their physical development and general health that results from appropriate physical training. We have talked to some inmates who were overweight at the start of boot camps and reported that they lost weight, and others who were underweight and reported that they gained weight. Many have told us that they became much more physically fit. We have to ask what the alternative to this physical exercise might be. Which is better for these young people—to have a daily exercise program, or to sit watching TV during a large part of the day? Certainly, the staff must be trained appropriately if they are going to oversee the physical training. Age, weight, and many other characteristics must be considered in order to develop an individually appropriate training schedule.

Some jurisdictions apparently thought that they could begin one of the boot camps on their own, without the necessary training for staff, drill instructors, administrators, and medical personnel. From this perspective, the boot camps are dangerous. Rigorous physical activity and summary punishments carry some inherent danger in situations where correctional employees are not appropriately trained. But without the necessary data available on the rate of injuries and deaths in boot camps as compared to other types of programs, we must hesitate to draw any conclusions regarding these aspects of the program and instead encourage researchers and policymakers to pursue this area with vigor.

In conclusion, we have presented a great deal of policy-relevant research in this book. For jurisdictions considering opening or, conversely, closing boot camps, we believe that such research should be used to help decide whether correctional boot camps will meet the desired goals. For students and researchers, the book presents an example of a research program designed to look at various goals of the boot camps and to develop methods for examining whether the camps meet the stated goals. As happened in the past, we anticipate that interest in boot camps will ebb and flow over time; it is our hope that if this happens, this book will be valuable for future developers of boot camp-type correctional programs.

REFERENCES

Blackwood, A. (2001, July 6). *Death spotlights youth boot camps.* Retrieved March 23, 2003, from http://www.nospank.net/n-i06.htm.

Boot camp death prompts changes. (2000, December 10). *New York Times.* Retrieved March 23, 2003, from http://www.nospank.net/n-i06.htm.

Bureau of Justice Statistics. (2002). *HIV in prisons, 2000* (Bulletin NCJ 196023). Washington, DC: U.S. Department of Justice.

Gover, A., MacKenzie, D. L., & Styve, G. (1999). Boot camps and traditional facilities for juveniles: A comparison of the participants, daily activities, and environments. *Journal of Criminal Justice, 28*(1), 53-68.

Inmates have much higher death rate than general male population: Study by Marlene Habib. (n.d.). Retrieved November 11, 2002, from http://mediresource.sympatico.ca/health_news_detail.asp.

MacKenzie, D. L. (1991). The parole performance of offenders released from shock incarceration: A survival time analysis. *Journal of Quantitative Criminology, 7*(3), 213-236.

MacKenzie, D. L. (1997). Criminal justice and crime prevention. In L. W. Sherman, D. C. Gottfredson, D. L. MacKenzie, J. Eck, P. Reuter, & S. Bushway (Eds.), *Preventing crime: What works, what doesn't and what's promising.* Washington, DC: U.S. Department of Justice, Office of Justice Programs.

MacKenzie, D. L. (2001). *Experimental study of Maryland's boot camp program.* Grant proposal submitted to Maryland's Governor's Office of Crime Control and Prevention.

MacKenzie, D. L., Brame, R., McDowall, D., & Souryal, C. (1995). Boot camp prisons and recidivism in eight states. *Criminology, 33*(3), 401-430.

MacKenzie, D. L., & Donaldson, H. (1996). Boot camp prisons for women offenders. *Criminal Justice Review, 21*(1), 21-43.

MacKenzie, D. L., & Parent, D. G. (1991). Shock incarceration and prison crowding in Louisiana. *Journal of Criminal Justice, 19*(3), 225-237.

MacKenzie, D. L., & Piquero, A. (1994). The impact of shock incarceration on prison crowding. *Crime & Delinquency, 40*(2), 222-249.

MacKenzie, D. L., & Rosay, A. (1996). Juvenile boot camps in the United States. In *Boot camps: What works for whom? A practitioner's guide.* Lanham, MD: American Correctional Association.

MacKenzie, D. L., & Shaw, J. (1993). The impact of shock incarceration on technical violations and new criminal activities. *Justice Quarterly, 10*(3), 463-487.

MacKenzie, D. L., & Souryal, C. (1995). Inmate attitude change during incarceration: A comparison of boot camp with traditional prison. *Justice Quarterly, 12*(2), 325-354.

MacKenzie, D. L., Wilson, D., Armstrong, G. S., & Gover, A. R. (2001). The impact of boot camps and traditional institutions on juvenile residents: Perception, adjustment and change. *Journal of Research in Crime and Delinquency, 38*(3), 279-313.

Markham, C. (2002, February 20). Charges filed against boot camp leaders. *West Valley View* (Arizona), p. 14.

Mitchell, O., MacKenzie, D. L., Gover, A. R., & Styve, G. J. (2001). The influence of personal background on perceptions of juvenile correctional environments. *Journal of Criminal Justice, 29,* 67-76.

Morris, N., & Tonry, M. (1990). *Between prison and probation: Intermediate punishments in a rational sentencing system.* Oxford, UK: Oxford University Press.

Prison Privatisation Report International. (1998). *Arizona boot camp scandal* (Rep. No. 20). London: Prison Reform Trust.

Riak, J. (2003). *Deadly restraint.* Retrieved on June 9, 2003, from www.nospank.net/camps.htm.

Shaw, J., & MacKenzie, D. L. (1992). The one-year community supervision performance of drug offenders and Louisiana DOC identified substance abusers graduating from shock incarceration. *Journal of Criminal Justice, 20,* 501-516.

Styve, G. J., Gover, A. R., MacKenzie, D. L., & Mitchell, O. (2000). Perceived conditions of confinement: A national evaluation of boot camps and traditional facilities. *Law and Human Behavior, 24*(3), 297-308.

Wobeser, W. L., Datema, J., Bechard, B., & Ford, P. (2002). Causes of death among people in custody in Ontario, 1990-1999. *Canadian Medical Association Journal, 167,* 1109-1113.

INDEX

Note: Page numbers in *italic* type refer to tables.

ABOUT THE EDITORS

Doris Layton MacKenzie, Ph.D., is Professor in the Department of Criminology and Criminal Justice at the University of Maryland and Director of the Evaluation Research Group. Previously, she was a faculty member at Louisiana State University, where she was honored as a "Researcher of Distinction," and was awarded a Visiting Scientist position at the National Institute of Justice. As Visiting Scientist, she provided expertise to federal, state and local jurisdictions on correctional boot camps, correctional policy, intermediate sanctions, research methodology, experimental design, statistical analyses, and evaluation techniques.

As an expert in criminal justice, Dr. MacKenzie has consulted for state and local jurisdictions and has testified before U.S. Senate and House Committees. She has an extensive publication record on such topics as examining what works to reduce crime in the community, inmate adjustment to prison, the impact of intermediate sanctions on recidivism, long-term offenders, methods of predicting prison populations, self-report criminal activities of probationers, and boot camp prisons. She directed funded research projects on the topics of "Multi-Site Study of Correctional Boot Camps," "Descriptive Study of Female Boot Camps," "Probationer Compliance With Conditions of Supervision" and "The National Study of Juvenile Correctional Institutions" and "What Works in Corrections." She is past chair of the American Society of Criminology's Division on Corrections and Sentencing. She earned her doctorate from Pennsylvania State University.

Gaylene Styve Armstrong, Ph.D., is Assistant Professor in the Department of Criminal Justice and Criminology at Arizona State University West. Her research has focused on corrections, juvenile delinquency, and applied statistical modeling. She was principal investigator on a grant funded by the National Institute of Justice that examined the effects of privatization on environmental quality in juvenile correctional facilities. This research on privatization resulted in a book titled *Private vs. Public Operation of Juvenile Correctional Facilities*. Some of her other recent research can also be found in *Crime and Delinquency, Justice Quarterly,* and *Journal of Research on Crime and Delinquency*. She was nominated for the Carnegie Foundation's U.S. Professor of the Year Award for her excellence in teaching. She obtained her doctorate in criminology and criminal justice from the University of Maryland.